Zoroastrian Scholasticism in Late Antiquity

EDINBURGH STUDIES IN ANCIENT PERSIA

SERIES EDITOR
Lloyd Llewellyn-Jones, Cardiff University

EDITORIAL ADVISORY BOARD
Touraj Daryaee, Andrew Erskine, Thomas Harrison, Irene Madreiter,
Keith Rutter, Jan Stronk

TITLES AVAILABLE IN THE SERIES

Courts and Elites in the Hellenistic Empires: The Near East After the Achaemenids, c. 330 to 30 BCE
Rolf Strootman

Greek Perspectives on the Achaemenid Empire: Persia through the Looking Glass
Janett Morgan

Semiramis' Legacy: The History of Persia According to Diodorus of Sicily
Jan P. Stronk

ReOrienting the Sasanians: East Iran in Late Antiquity
Khodadad Rezakhani

Sasanian Persia: Between Rome and the Steppes of Eurasia
Edited by Eberhard W. Sauer

Plutarch and the Persica
Eran Almagor

Archaeology of Empire in Achaemenid Egypt
Henry P. Colburn

Zoroastrian Scholasticism in Late Antiquity: The Pahlavi Version of the Yasna Haptaŋhāiti
Arash Zeini

FORTHCOMING TITLES

Achaemenid Kingship, Alexander the Great and the Early Seleucids: Ideologies of Empire
Stephen Harrison

Socioeconomic Transformation in the Sasanian Empire: Late Antique Central Zagros
Hossein Habibi

The Bactrian Mirage: Iranian and Greek Interaction in Western Central Asia
Michael Iliakis

Visit the Edinburgh Studies in Ancient Persia website at
edinburghuniversitypress.com/series/esap

Zoroastrian Scholasticism in Late Antiquity

The Pahlavi version of the *Yasna Haptaŋhāiti*

Arash Zeini

EDINBURGH
University Press

Edinburgh University Press is one of the leading university presses in the UK. We publish academic books and journals in our selected subject areas across the humanities and social sciences, combining cutting-edge scholarship with high editorial and production values to produce academic works of lasting importance. For more information visit our website: edinburghuniversitypress.com

© Arash Zeini, 2020, 2022

Edinburgh University Press Ltd
The Tun – Holyrood Road,
12(2f) Jackson's Entry,
Edinburgh EH8 8PJ

First published in hardback by Edinburgh University Press 2020

Typeset in 11/13pt Junicode
by Servis Filmsetting Ltd, Stockport, Cheshire

A CIP record for this book is available from the British Library

ISBN 978 1 4744 4288 6 (hardback)
ISBN 978 1 4744 4289 3 (paperback)
ISBN 978 1 4744 4290 9 (webready PDF)
ISBN 978 1 4744 4291 6 (epub)

The right of Arash Zeini to be identified as the author of this work has been asserted in accordance with the Copyright, Designs and Patents Act 1988, and the Copyright and Related Rights Regulations 2003 (SI No. 2498).

Contents

List of Figures	xiii
List of Tables	xiv
Acknowledgements	xv
Series Editor's Preface	xvii
Preface	xix
Conventions	xxiv
Abbreviations	xxvi

Part I Introduction

1.	Introduction	3
	1.1 The *Yasna Haptaŋhāiti*	3
	1.2 The Pahlavi text	7
	1.3 Why a new edition of the PYH?	8
	1.4 The present edition	9
	1.4.1 *Emendatio*	10
	1.4.2 Base text	11
	1.4.3 Numbering the stanzas of Y 35	13
	1.4.4 Glosses	14
	1.4.5 The otiose stroke	18
	1.5 Manuscripts	19
	1.5.1 Pt4	19
	1.5.2 Mf4	20
	1.5.3 F2	21
	1.5.4 R413	21
	1.5.5 T6	22
	1.5.6 E7	23
	1.5.7 J2	24
	1.5.8 K5	25
	1.5.9 M1	25
	1.6 Manuscript filiation	26
2.	The *Zand*	28
	2.1 Early research	29

	2.2	Marginalisation of texts	31
	2.3	Perceptions of the *Zand* in Iranian studies	34

3. Scholasticism — 40
   - 3.1 Strong sense of tradition — 44
   - 3.2 Concern with language — 48
   - 3.3 Proliferativity — 51
   - 3.4 Completeness and compactness — 55
   - 3.5 Epistemological accessibility of the world — 55
   - 3.6 Systematicity — 57
   - 3.7 Self-reflexivity — 59
   - 3.8 Summary — 60

4. Fire in Zoroastrianism — 63
   - 4.1 The Older Avesta — 64
     - 4.1.1 The *Gāθās* — 65
     - 4.1.2 The YH — 69
     - 4.1.3 Summary — 70
   - 4.2 The Younger Avesta — 73
     - 4.2.1 Summary — 74
   - 4.3 Pahlavi literature — 76
     - 4.3.1 The *Gāθic* fire in the *Zand* — 77
     - 4.3.2 PY 17.11 — 79
     - 4.3.3 *Bundahišn* — 81
     - 4.3.4 *Pahlavi Rivāyat* accompanying the *Dādestān ī Dēnīg* — 82
     - 4.3.5 *Wizīdagīhā ī Zādspram* — 83
     - 4.3.6 *Dēnkard* — 85
     - 4.3.7 Summary — 90
   - 4.4 Correlative systems — 91
   - 4.5 Summary — 94

5. Precis: *yasn ī haft hād* — 98
   - 5.1 PY 35 — 98
     - 5.1.1 *humatān hūxtān huwarštān* — 98
     - 5.1.2 The *dēn* — 100
     - 5.1.3 PY 35.1 — 103
   - 5.2 PY 36 — 104
     - 5.2.1 The three steps — 105
   - 5.3 PY 37 — 109
   - 5.4 PY 38 — 110
   - 5.5 PY 39 — 110
   - 5.6 PY 40 — 111
     - 5.6.1 A commitment to the *dēn* — 112
   - 5.7 PY 41 — 114
     - 5.7.1 PY 41.4 — 115
     - 5.7.2 PY 41.6: *ān ī ōy* 'that which is his' — 115
     - 5.7.3 *hamē tā ō wisp* 'always until all' — 118

Part II Text and translation

6. PY 35 — 125
   - 6.1 PY 35.0 — 125
   - 6.2 PY 35.1 — 127
   - 6.3 PY 35.2 — 128
   - 6.4 PY 35.3 — 129
   - 6.5 PY 35.4 — 130
   - 6.6 PY 35.5 — 131
   - 6.7 PY 35.6 — 132
   - 6.8 PY 35.7 — 133
   - 6.9 PY 35.8 — 134
   - 6.10 PY 35.9 — 135
7. PY 36 — 136
   - 7.1 PY 36.1 — 136
   - 7.2 PY 36.2 — 138
   - 7.3 PY 36.3 — 139
   - 7.4 PY 36.4 — 140
   - 7.5 PY 36.5 — 141
   - 7.6 PY 36.6 — 142
8. PY 37 — 143
   - 8.1 PY 37.1 — 143
   - 8.2 PY 37.2 — 144
   - 8.3 PY 37.3 — 145
   - 8.4 PY 37.4 — 146
   - 8.5 PY 37.5 — 147
9. PY 38 — 148
   - 9.1 PY 38.1 — 148
   - 9.2 PY 38.2 — 149
   - 9.3 PY 38.3 — 150
   - 9.4 PY 38.4 — 151
   - 9.5 PY 38.5 — 152
10. PY 39 — 154
    - 10.1 PY 39.1 — 154
    - 10.2 PY 39.2 — 156
    - 10.3 PY 39.3 — 157
    - 10.4 PY 39.4 — 158
    - 10.5 PY 39.5 — 159
11. PY 40 — 160
    - 11.1 PY 40.1 — 160
    - 11.2 PY 40.2 — 162
    - 11.3 PY 40.3 — 163
    - 11.4 PY 40.4 — 164
12. PY 41 — 165
    - 12.1 PY 41.1 — 165

12.2	PY 41.2	166
12.3	PY 41.3	167
12.4	PY 41.4	168
12.5	PY 41.5	169
12.6	PY 41.6	170

Part III Miscellaneous observations

13. **PY 35** — 173
    - 13.1 PY 35.0 — 173
        - 13.1.1 *yazom* — 173
        - 13.1.2 *kē radīh pad frārōnīh* — 175
        - 13.1.3 *budabāgān* — 181
        - 13.1.4 *kē-iz* — 184
        - 13.1.5 *pad ārzōg* — 184
        - 13.1.6 *mazdēsnān* — 185
    - 13.2 PY 35.1 — 187
        - 13.2.1 *dahišn* — 187
        - 13.2.2 𐭡𐭥𐭬 *bom* — 188
        - 13.2.3 *abar griftār* — 188
        - 13.2.4 *ō xwēš kardan* — 189
        - 13.2.5 *mard ō mard* — 190
    - 13.3 PY 35.2 — 194
        - 13.3.1 *hād* — 194
    - 13.4 PY 35.3 — 195
        - 13.4.1 PY 35.3a — 195
    - 13.5 PY 35.4 — 197
    - 13.6 PY 35.5 — 198
        - 13.6.1 PY 35.5a — 198
        - 13.6.2 PY 35.5c — 198
    - 13.7 PY 35.6 — 199
        - 13.7.1 Text division — 199
        - 13.7.2 PY 35.6a — 199
        - 13.7.3 *ašmā* — 199
    - 13.8 PY 35.7 — 201
        - 13.8.1 *wālunīh* — 201
    - 13.9 PY 35.8 — 202
14. **PY 36** — 204
    - 14.1 PY 36.1 — 204
        - 14.1.1 *pad warzišn* — 204
    - 14.2 PY 36.2 — 205
        - 14.2.1 *kār* — 205
    - 14.3 PY 36.3 — 208
        - 14.3.1 The fire of the exegetes — 208
    - 14.4 PY 36.5 — 210

		14.4.1 *abāmēne*	210
		14.4.2 ⟨hlwstʾ⟩	212
	14.5	PY 36.6	213
		14.5.1 PY 36.6	213
		14.5.2 *sraēštąm* 'nēk'	214
		14.5.3 *niwēyēnišn dahom*	215
15.	PY 37		217
	15.1	PY 37.1	217
		15.1.1 Y 5	217
		15.1.2 *iϑā*	218
		15.1.3 *āṯ* 'ēdōn'	226
		15.1.4 *iϑā āṯ* 'ēdar ēdōn'	227
		15.1.5 The creations	232
		15.1.6 *bun ud bar*	234
		15.1.7 (P)Y 37.1b	239
	15.2	PY 37.2	241
		15.2.1 *ōy kē … aziš*	241
	15.3	PY 37.3	244
		15.3.1 *tan ud ǰān*	244
		15.3.2 *narān*	244
	15.4	PY 37.4	247
		15.4.1 *amahraspandān*	247
16.	PY 38		249
	16.1	PY 38.1	249
		16.1.1 *mādagān*	249
		16.1.2 *az ahlāyīh abāgīh*	250
	16.2	PY 38.2	251
		16.2.1 *īžā-*	251
		16.2.2 *yaošti-*	251
		16.2.3 *fərašti-*	251
		16.2.4 *ārmaiti-*	251
	16.3	PY 38.3	252
		16.3.1 PY 38.3	252
		16.3.2 The waters	253
		16.3.3 *hudahagīh*	256
		16.3.4 *hušnāyišnagīh*	256
	16.4	PY 38.4	258
		16.4.1 **dadag*	258
		16.4.2 *wehdahāg*	258
	16.5	PY 38.5	260
		16.5.1 PY 67.6–8	260
		16.5.2 *xōn*	260
17.	PY 39		263
	17.1	PY 39.1	263
		17.1.1 *ǰān*	263

		17.1.2	*amāgān*	264
		17.1.3	*ā-š dād*	264
	17.2	PY 39.2		266
		17.2.1	PY 39.2	266
		17.2.2	*daitīkān-iz*	266
		17.2.3	*wānīdār ... windišn ... weh mard*	267
	17.3	PY 39.3		270
		17.3.1	*āt̰ iϑā* 'ān ēdōn'	270
		17.3.2	*weh nar ān ī weh mādag*	270
	17.4	PY 39.4		272
	17.5	PY 39.5		273
		17.5.1	Recitation instructions	273
18.	PY 40			274
	18.1	PY 40.1		274
		18.1.1	*mehīh*	274
		18.1.2	*man*	274
		18.1.3	PY 40.1b	275
		18.1.4	*manīgān*	275
	18.2	PY 40.3		276
		18.2.1	*ān hērbed*	276
		18.2.2	*amāgān*	276
	18.3	PY 40.4		277
		18.3.1	*išt*	277
19.	PY 41			279
	19.1	PY 41.2		279
	19.2	PY 41.5		281
		19.2.1	*bēnd*	281
		19.2.2	Recitation instructions	281

Part IV Epilogue

20.	Reflections on the *Zand*	285
	20.1 WBW translation	286
	20.2 Simplified morphology	291
	20.3 Translation techniques	291
	20.4 Auxiliary science	293
	20.5 Transmission	294
	20.6 Concluding thoughts	300

Appendices

A	Transliteration and apparatus		305
	A.1	PY 5	305
		A.1.1 PY 5.1	305
		A.1.2 PY 5.2	306

	A.1.3	PY 5.3	307
	A.1.4	PY 5.4	308
	A.1.5	PY 5.5	309
	A.1.6	PY 5.6	310
A.2	PY 35		311
	A.2.1	PY 35.0	311
	A.2.2	PY 35.1	313
	A.2.3	PY 35.2	314
	A.2.4	PY 35.3	315
	A.2.5	PY 35.4	317
	A.2.6	PY 35.5	318
	A.2.7	PY 35.6	320
	A.2.8	PY 35.7	321
	A.2.9	PY 35.8	322
	A.2.10	PY 35.9	323
A.3	PY 36		324
	A.3.1	PY 36.1	324
	A.3.2	PY 36.2	325
	A.3.3	PY 36.3	326
	A.3.4	PY 36.4	327
	A.3.5	PY 36.5	328
	A.3.6	PY 36.6	329
A.4	PY 37		331
	A.4.1	PY 37.1	331
	A.4.2	PY 37.2	332
	A.4.3	PY 37.3	333
	A.4.4	PY 37.4	334
	A.4.5	PY 37.5	335
A.5	PY 38		336
	A.5.1	PY 38.1	336
	A.5.2	PY 38.2	337
	A.5.3	PY 38.3	338
	A.5.4	PY 38.4	340
	A.5.5	PY 38.5	341
A.6	PY 39		344
	A.6.1	PY 39.1	344
	A.6.2	PY 39.2	345
	A.6.3	PY 39.3	346
	A.6.4	PY 39.4	347
	A.6.5	PY 39.5	349
A.7	PY 40		351
	A.7.1	PY 40.1	351
	A.7.2	PY 40.2	353
	A.7.3	PY 40.3	354
	A.7.4	PY 40.4	355

	A.8	PY 41		356
		A.8.1	PY 41.1	356
		A.8.2	PY 41.2	357
		A.8.3	PY 41.3	358
		A.8.4	PY 41.4	360
		A.8.5	PY 41.5	361
		A.8.6	PY 41.6	362

B Y 9.1 — 364

    B.1 *miθrō ziiāṯ zaraθuštrəm* — 364

        B.1.1 Distribution — 365

C Fire in the Older Avesta — 368

D *iθā* — 371

E MSS Concordance — 374

Bibliography — 375

Index of passages quoted — 396

List of Figures

1.1	The start of the YH in Pt4	7
1.2	Geldner's genealogy of the exegetical *Yasna*	12
1.3	Dividing device in PY 10.20	17
1.4	(P)Y 41.2b–c in Pt4	24
13.1	*mazdēsnān*	185
15.1	Stanza marks in Pt4	242
15.2	Stanza marks	243
16.1	Y 38.3 in F2	252
16.2	Marginal note in PY 38.4	258
17.1	*daitīkān-iz*	267
B.1	Y 9.1c	367

List of Tables

1.1	Manuscript dates	19
4.1	The five fires in the Y, PY and Bd	82
4.2	The five fires	84
13.1	Distribution of *yaštan*	174
13.2	Coordination	184
15.1	*iϑā* in MP texts	218
15.2	*iϑā* in context	219
15.3	*iϑā* in Y 33.1	222
15.4	*iϑā* in Y 45.3	223
15.5	*iϑā* in Y 53.6	225
15.6	*āt̰* and *āat̰* in the YH	227
15.7	*iϑā* in the *Gāϑās*	228
15.8	*nar* and *nārīg*	245
16.1	*mādag*	250
16.2	PY 38.2	250
16.3	The waters in the Bd and the PYH	255

Acknowledgements

I am delighted to express my gratitude to a number of individuals whose support has been crucial to the realisation of this project, which goes back to my doctoral research at the School of Oriental and African Studies, University of London. First and foremost, I must thank Almut Hintze, at whose suggestion I began working on the Pahlavi version of the *Yasna Haptaŋhāiti*. I am deeply indebted to Nicholas Sims-Williams for his generous counsel. François de Blois, the quiet man of Iranian Studies, offered insightful comments on early drafts and played an instrumental role in discovering the joy of academic curiosity. Alan Williams and Judith Josephson contributed much to this work with their constructive feedback and criticism.

I have greatly appreciated many illuminating discussions with Oktor Skjærvø. He generously shares with me and the scholarly community a vast array of his unpublished material, which I have used extensively throughout my work. Maria Macuch also trusted me with unpublished material that proved very useful. Dan Sheffield and Yuhan Vevaina deserve special thanks for responding to various calls for help. I owe thanks to Miguel Ángel Andrés-Toledo, Adam Benkato, Shervin Farridnejad, Juanjo Ferrer, Götz König, Maria Kritikou, Céline Redard, Kianoosh Rezania, Shai Secunda, Dan Shapira, Ursula Sims-Williams, Samuel Thrope, Mihaela Timuş and the late Carsten Bettermann. I am glad Leon Goldman put his fear of technology aside on a daily basis to call me. It is always good to talk. To Alberto Cantera I am grateful for his friendship and the quality of questioning everything. Jan Espelta, an old friend, with whom I first watched *Die Reise des Löwen*, I owe thanks for good old times. Thank you for introducing me to *Howard Anthony Trott*, a lovely man and father. I wonder what became of him. I thank Claudius Naumann, from *Freie Universität Berlin*, for kindly providing me with his Pahlavi font.

I am grateful to the Arts and Humanities Research Council, the Ouseley Memorial Fund and the Soudavar Foundation, whose funding helped support my research. The images of the manuscripts used in this book are from the

Avestan Digital Archive, Freie Universität Berlin, and published with their permission.

It is my pleasure to express my gratitude towards the amazing staff of the Edinburgh University Press for their relentless assistance throughout the publication process.

I dedicate this book to my sons, Hourmazd and Siavash, my best friends, and a source of constant joy and much trouble too. I owe them more than they can imagine and am certain Robert Walser would have been envious of our walks.

Series Editor's Preface

Edinburgh Studies in Ancient Persia focuses on the world of ancient Persia (pre-Islamic Iran) and its reception. Academic interest with and fascination in ancient Persia have burgeoned in recent decades and research on Persian history and culture is now routinely filtered into studies of the Greek and Roman worlds; Biblical scholarship too is now more keenly aware of Persian-period history than ever before; while, most importantly, the study of the history, cultures, languages and societies of ancient Iran is now a well-established discipline in its own right.

Persia was, after all, at the centre of ancient world civilisations. This series explores that centrality throughout several successive 'Persian empires': the Achaemenid dynasty (founded c. 550 BCE) saw Persia rise to its highest level of political and cultural influence, as the Great Kings of Iran fought for, and maintained, an empire which stretched from India to Libya and from Macedonia to Ethiopia. The art and architecture of the period both reflect the diversity of the empire and proclaim a single centrally constructed theme: a harmonious world-order brought about by a benevolent and beneficent king. Following the conquests of Alexander the Great, the Persian Empire fragmented but maintained some of its infrastructures and ideologies in the new kingdoms established by Alexander's successors, in particular the Seleucid dynasts who occupied the territories of western Iran, Mesopotamia, the Levant and Asia Minor. But even as Greek influence extended into the former territories of the Achaemenid realm, at the heart of Iran a family of nobles, the Parthian dynasty, rose to threaten the growing imperial power of Rome. Finally, the mighty Sasanian dynasty ruled Iran and much of the Middle East from the third century CE onwards, proving to be a powerful foe to Late Imperial Rome and Byzantium. The rise of Islam, a new religion in Arabia, brought a sudden end to the Sasanian dynasty in the mid-600s CE.

These successive Persian dynasties left their record in the historical, linguistic and archaeological materials of the ancient world, and Edinburgh

Studies in Ancient Persia has been conceived to give scholars working in these fields the opportunity to publish original research and explore new methodologies in interpreting the antique past of Iran. This series will see scholars working with bona fide Persian and other Near Eastern materials, giving access to Iranian self-perceptions and the internal workings of Persian society, placed alongside scholars assessing the perceptions of the Persianate world from the outside (predominantly through Greek and Roman authors and artefacts). The series will also explore the reception of ancient Persia (in historiography, the arts and politics) in subsequent periods, both within and outwith Iran itself.

Edinburgh Studies in Ancient Persia represents something of a watershed in better appreciation and understanding not only of the rich and complex cultural heritage of Persia, but also of the lasting significance of the Achaemenids, Parthians and Sasanians and the impact that their remarkable civilisations have had on wider Persian, Middle Eastern and world history. Written by established and up-and-coming specialists in the field, this series provides an important synergy of the latest scholarly ideas about this formative ancient world civilisation.

Lloyd Llewellyn-Jones

Preface

The present volume contains at its core an edition of the Middle Persian (MP) translation of the Avestan ritual text *Yasna Haptaŋhāiti* (YH) or Middle Persian *Yasn ī haft hād* 'Yasna in Seven Chapters'. The Avetsan texts and their Middle Persian translations, known as *Zand*, bear no author attribution, and no absolute dates are available for either group of texts. The linguistic difficulties associated with the *Zand* have somewhat lead to its marginalisation in the study of Zoroastrianism. Contrary to previous work on various *Zand* texts, the present study attempts, to the extent possible, to understand the exegesis of the *Yasna Haptaŋhāiti* as a text in its own right by extending the investigation to a wider range of MP texts and assuming a religio-cultural perspective in the approach to the *Zand*. For that reason, the examination of the translation technique employed in the Pahlavi translations of the Avestan *Yasna Haptaŋhāiti* is not the focus of the study.

In the decade since Stausberg (2008) observed that research on Zoroastrianism had witnessed considerable innovation, we have seen substantial progress in the study of Zoroastrian rituals,[1] and major projects are now under way to produce new editions of Avestan rituals and texts. When a small, less visible discipline progresses rapidly and innovates seismically, it is perhaps advisable to introduce the primary sources briefly and remark on some issues concerning terminology before advancing the discussion.

THE *AVESTA*

The sacred texts of the Zoroastrians are collectively referred to as the *Avesta*, a heterogeneous collection of texts dating to the first and second millennia before the common era. On linguistic grounds, the *Avesta* is commonly

---

[1] See Cantera's (2016a) assessment of work done by Jean Kellens.

divided into Old (OAv.) and Young Avestan (YAv.) compositions.² The text of the *Yasna* ritual contains the 17 *hāiti* of the five *Gāθās* (compositions commonly attributed to the figure of Zaraθuštra), the seven *hāiti* of the *Yasna Haptaŋhāiti* (YH), the *yaθā ahū vairiiō* and *airiiaman išiia* prayers. These texts together constitute the OAv. corpus. Some scholars date the Older *Avesta* into the middle of the second millennium BCE on the basis of the archaic character of its language.³ The YAv. passages are believed to have been composed at a later date. Although the *Avesta* is often regarded as a book today, particularly by the practitioners of the religion, it must have existed only in form of an 'oral scripture' in the first stages of its transmission.⁴

PRAYERS

Scholars commonly refer to the following four Avestan compositions as prayers or sacred formulae: *yaθā ahū vairiiō*, *ašǝm vohū*, *yeŋhē hātąm* and the *airiiaman išiia*. Cantera (2014a), for instance, prefers prayer, while Vevaina (2012) uses both. In fact, these compositions are perhaps neither prayers nor sacred formulae in a strict Christian or Buddhist sense. Rather, they are movable components within the Zoroastrian textual and ritual tradition. For convenience, I have retained the term prayer to refer to these four compositions.

ZARAΘUŠTRA

The question of Zaraθuštra's historicity still seems to be of some interest among scholars, the most recent trend having been started by Kellens and Skjærvø.⁵ Gershevitch (1993: 12) identified the 'authorship of the Gathas' as the very first of the 'four cardinal points of the Gathic horizon' that serve as a compass for every scholar of the *Gāθās*. He criticises Kellens and Pirart (1988) in an unusually sharp tone, assuring us that the 'disruption by Kellens and Pirart, in 1988, of the consensus on it, *can* only be short-lived'. We cannot give a satisfactory and factual answer to the question of Zaraθuštra's historicity. However, if we consider the suggestion of his non-historicity on a methodological level we can disregard Zaraθuštra's role as the author in our approach to the *Gāθās* and the *Avesta*.

---

² For a detailed discussion of chronology, dialects and geography of OIr. languages, see Skjærvø (1995b). Kellens (1989) and Schmitt (2000: 25) express similar views.
³ See, for instance, Boyce (1992: 45), Boyce (2001: xiii) and Skjærvø (2005–6: 29). See also Sims-Williams (1998) and Hintze (2009a).
⁴ On *Avesta* as sacred scripture, see Shaked (2003).
⁵ Among others, see Kellens (2006) and Skjærvø (2005–6) in a study on orality.

Preface

The present volume contains at its core an edition of the Middle Persian (MP) translation of the Avestan ritual text *Yasna Haptaŋhāiti* (YH) or Middle Persian *Yasn ī haft hād* 'Yasna in Seven Chapters'. The Avetsan texts and their Middle Persian translations, known as *Zand*, bear no author attribution, and no absolute dates are available for either group of texts. The linguistic difficulties associated with the *Zand* have somewhat lead to its marginalisation in the study of Zoroastrianism. Contrary to previous work on various *Zand* texts, the present study attempts, to the extent possible, to understand the exegesis of the *Yasna Haptaŋhāiti* as a text in its own right by extending the investigation to a wider range of MP texts and assuming a religio-cultural perspective in the approach to the *Zand*. For that reason, the examination of the translation technique employed in the Pahlavi translations of the Avestan *Yasna Haptaŋhāiti* is not the focus of the study.

In the decade since Stausberg (2008) observed that research on Zoroastrianism had witnessed considerable innovation, we have seen substantial progress in the study of Zoroastrian rituals,[1] and major projects are now under way to produce new editions of Avestan rituals and texts. When a small, less visible discipline progresses rapidly and innovates seismically, it is perhaps advisable to introduce the primary sources briefly and remark on some issues concerning terminology before advancing the discussion.

THE *AVESTA*

The sacred texts of the Zoroastrians are collectively referred to as the *Avesta*, a heterogeneous collection of texts dating to the first and second millennia before the common era. On linguistic grounds, the *Avesta* is commonly

---

[1] See Cantera's (2016a) assessment of work done by Jean Kellens.

divided into Old (OAv.) and Young Avestan (YAv.) compositions.[2] The text of the *Yasna* ritual contains the 17 *hāiti* of the five *Gāθās* (compositions commonly attributed to the figure of Zaraθuštra), the seven *hāiti* of the *Yasna Haptaŋhāiti* (YH), the *yaθā ahū vairiiō* and *airiiaman išiia* prayers. These texts together constitute the OAv. corpus. Some scholars date the Older *Avesta* into the middle of the second millennium BCE on the basis of the archaic character of its language.[3] The YAv. passages are believed to have been composed at a later date. Although the *Avesta* is often regarded as a book today, particularly by the practitioners of the religion, it must have existed only in form of an 'oral scripture' in the first stages of its transmission.[4]

PRAYERS

Scholars commonly refer to the following four Avestan compositions as prayers or sacred formulae: *yaθā ahū vairiiō*, *aṣ̌ǝm vohū*, *yeŋ́hē hātąm* and the *airiiaman išiia*. Cantera (2014a), for instance, prefers prayer, while Vevaina (2012) uses both. In fact, these compositions are perhaps neither prayers nor sacred formulae in a strict Christian or Buddhist sense. Rather, they are movable components within the Zoroastrian textual and ritual tradition. For convenience, I have retained the term prayer to refer to these four compositions.

ZARAΘUŠTRA

The question of Zaraθuštra's historicity still seems to be of some interest among scholars, the most recent trend having been started by Kellens and Skjærvø.[5] Gershevitch (1993: 12) identified the 'authorship of the Gathas' as the very first of the 'four cardinal points of the Gathic horizon' that serve as a compass for every scholar of the *Gāθās*. He criticises Kellens and Pirart (1988) in an unusually sharp tone, assuring us that the 'disruption by Kellens and Pirart, in 1988, of the consensus on it, *can* only be short-lived'. We cannot give a satisfactory and factual answer to the question of Zaraθuštra's historicity. However, if we consider the suggestion of his non-historicity on a methodological level we can disregard Zaraθuštra's role as the author in our approach to the *Gāθās* and the *Avesta*.

---

[2] For a detailed discussion of chronology, dialects and geography of OIr. languages, see Skjærvø (1995b). Kellens (1989) and Schmitt (2000: 25) express similar views.
[3] See, for instance, Boyce (1992: 45), Boyce (2001: xiii) and Skjærvø (2005–6: 29). See also Sims-Williams (1998) and Hintze (2009a).
[4] On *Avesta* as sacred scripture, see Shaked (2003).
[5] Among others, see Kellens (2006) and Skjærvø (2005–6) in a study on orality.

The rejection of the author's intention as a paradigm of literary interpretation is shared by several schools of literary criticism such as *explication de texte*, *New Criticism* and *post-structuralism*. The strongest critique of the concept of the author's originality and intention came from the *New Critics*, who termed the expression 'intentional fallacy' for any methodological approach that uses the historical author's intention or biography for the interpretation of texts (Nünning 2004: 293). *Intentional fallacy* questions 'the assumption that a text is identical with its author's intentions' (Schmitz 2007: 92). Considering a literary work as an 'organic unit', the school of *New Criticism* declares the highlighting of the 'harmonious tension' between the various parts of a text as the task of the interpreter without recourse to any extra-textual material, hence the paradigm of 'close reading' (Schmitz 2007: 91). The dictum of only one possible meaning tied to the author's intention was rejected by prominent philosophers and literary critics such as Derrida, Foucault and Culler (Nünning 2004: 292). The post-structuralists later declared the 'death of the author', a term coined by the French literary critic Roland Barthes (Nünning 2004: 662), and further refined the concept proposed by the *New Critics* by replacing the author's dominant role with that of the recipient.[6] I believe that a paradigm shift in this direction may not be without benefit for our discipline and wonder whether we shall pronounce the death of the author in Iranian studies without getting involved in the question of Zaraϑuštra's historicity.

THE *ZAND*

Zand is the Zoroastrian term for the Middle Persian or Pahlavi versions of Avestan texts. These translations have come down to us in the bilingual Avestan-Pahlavi manuscripts, where the Avestan source text is divided in small textual units resembling a phrase. The Pahlavi translation of each unit follows immediately after the source text. Thus, despite the enigmatic character often ascribed to the *Zand*, its relationship to the source language and text is characterised by immediacy and proximity as preserved in the manuscripts.

The canonisation, textualisation and translation of the extant *Avesta* presumably took place during the late Sasanian era. Although the Zoroastrian MP texts often mention the *Zand*, they are silent on dates, authorship and the process of translation itself. Even after accounting for different linguistic

---

[6] I applied Barthes's 'Death of the author' to the discussion of Zaraϑuštra's historicity in a presentation at a conference held in Cambridge in 2008, independently taking up this branch of literary criticism at the same time as Dr Vevaina, who has drawn upon literary theories when approaching Zoroastrian interpretive literature (see Vevaina 2007, 2010b).

layers within the corpus of the *Zand*, its precise dating remains elusive. This is all the more surprising, as translating a sacred corpus into a vernacular is a significant undertaking in any religious tradition. The vernacularisation lends authority to the target language and will inevitably have implications for issues such as religious authority and text production.

THE *ZAND* AND LATE ANTIQUITY

In recent years, historians have variously argued for incorporating Sasanian history into studies of late antiquity. Already Brown (1971), dealt with 'Persia' in his work, while Morony (2008) explicitly argued for the inclusion of Sasanian Iran in these studies. The topic has been discussed in some detail, most recently by Humphries (2017), and there is little that I wish to add to the debate. Even a brief look at the work of scholars such as Daryaee (2008) or Canepa (2009) shows that the history of the Sasanians is now firmly included in scholarship on late antiquity. The inclusion of Zoroastrianism and the Sasanians by Nicholson (2018) is another recent example of this positive development.

I acknowledge that a meaningful periodisation of pre-Islamic Iranian history is not an easy task. The limited source material does not provide us with sufficient information on religious or ritual affiliations during the Achaemenid, Seleucid and Parthian eras. We do not know which exact role the royal families or empires might have played in the transmission of the *Avesta*. Beginning with the Sasanian era, however, we have in the Middle Persian corpus an undisputed witness of an explicit reception of the *Avesta* as an antique text, thus qualifying the *Zand* as a late antique product, which continues and re-examines the religio-cultural legacy of late antiquity.

By viewing the *Zand* as an extension and cultural transformation of antique Iranian religious, ritual or textual traditions, my approach to the use of late antiquity is guided and inspired by views put forward by Brown and particularly Stroumsa (2012). This volume does not intend to argue for continuity or disruption in an Iranian religious tradition, but seeks to illuminate the mechanisms of cultural transformation which underlie the priestly re-evaluation of past traditions.

NOTES ON TRANSLATING THE *ZAND*

The style and language of the *Zand* are significantly more obscure compared to non-translation Pahlavi texts. In my translation of the PYH, I have sought to reflect the flavour of the *Zand* and preserve its tone as closely as possible by relying on a literal translation. My approach has several implications for my translations. Firstly, I have left Avestan quotations in the *Zand* untranslated, again, to approximate the translators' approach. This is particularly conspicuous in the case of PYH 38.3 and 5, where the *Zand* leaves the names of the waters untranslated. Secondly, I have considered each section of the *Zand*, which follows and corresponds to an Av. cola, as a self-contained unit of meaning. A different approach was taken by Mills (1905a) in his translation of the PYH. He divides the text according to modern stanza boundaries and operates freely with the various syntactic units within each stanza or paragraph. This method enables the modern translator to produce a literary translation of the *Zand*, but ignores the compositional structure of the text. The paragraphs are constructs that do not reflect the reality of the manuscripts. My translation is built upon the assumption that each line of *Zand* must have been conceived as a small independent unit of meaning, presumably dictated by the perceived structure of the scripture. After all, the scholastics chose this particular set-up for the *Zand* and not larger stanzaic divisions although they could have been aware of such boundaries.[7]

---

[7] For a relevant discussion of translation approaches, see Garzilli (1996).

Conventions

The primary focus of this volume is the Pahlavi translation of the *Yasna Haptaŋhāiti* (YH), which in this edition is based on the manuscript Pt4 (see Section 1.4.2). For the convenience of the reader and to facilitate comparison, I reproduce the Avestan text of the same manuscript. The translation of the Avetsan is by Hintze (2007a). I have used the following symbols in the apparatus:

+	Corrected spelling errors
ᵃᵇᶜdef	Superscript words or characters
~~abc~~	Sequence struck out or deleted in the MSS
•	Sequence of illegible characters
[ABC]	Indicates hypothetical reading
\<lbr\>	Line break

In cases where a word occurs more than once on the same line, a small index number in the critical apparatus denotes the order of the words. YH refers to the Av. version of the text, PYH to its *Zand*, while (P)YH is used in instances where the text as a whole is intended. Lowercase letters after stanza numbers such as PYH 37.1b indicate the cola divisions of the stanza in the bilingual manuscripts. The collated text of PY 5 is given in Appendix A.1. Avestan quotations that appear within Pahlavi passages are not italicised in order to set them apart from Pahlavi.

Whenever possible, the transliteration and transcription of the MP passages follow MacKenzie (1967, 1990).[1] In the following instances, however, I follow recent trends rather than MacKenzie:

- ⟨'⟩ vs. ⟨A⟩ for ᴗ in heterograms
- ⟨ʿ⟩ vs. ⟨O⟩ for ׀ in heterograms

---

[1] On the state of transliteration and transcription in MP, see Sundermann (1989: 145–7).

- ⟨H⟩ vs. ⟨E⟩ for 𐭤 in heterograms
- ⟨Ḥ⟩ vs. ⟨H⟩ for 𐭇 in heterograms
- ⟨K⟩ for 𐭪 in 'YK as well as KN
- ⟨pt'⟩ for ⟨PWN⟩
- ⟨mynwd⟩ *mēnōy* rather than ⟨mynwk⟩ *mēnōg*
- ⟨gytyy̱⟩ *gētīy* rather than ⟨gytyk⟩ *gētīg*²

It has not always been possible to replicate the peculiarities of the scribes' handwriting in the apparatus. For instance, at times the connection ⟨g/d/y-⟩ + ⟨-m⟩ resembles ⟨'m⟩. The second tooth, however, is just a rounding up of the ⟨g/d/y⟩ before it turns down to connect to ⟨-m⟩. This mannerism of the scribes' handwriting is impossible to replicate with the fonts. I have ignored spelling variants between 𐭀 and 𐭁 such as in 𐭀𐭌𐭍𐭉𐭀 and 𐭁𐭌𐭍𐭉𐭀.³

When quoting passages from other editions, I have removed punctuation signs from the original text, but have retained any additional editorial marks used by the editors. In cases where a new and up-to-date edition has not been available, or where the exact context has been important, I have used a single manuscript's reading rather than an edition. However, as there are a number of significant text-critical differences between the Iranian and Indian manuscripts of the *Bundahišn*, transcribing individual MSS would result in substantially different texts for the passages. Therefore, I follow Pakzad's (2005) edition, as variants are duly noted in its critical apparatus. All translations are mine unless otherwise noted.

The names of scribes and priestly redactors are given as they occur in catalogues or other reference material.

I refer to a number of additional manuscripts that are available from the *Avestan Digital Archive* (ADA). These are peripheral to my edition and have not been listed in the bibliography. Prof. Cantera has shown that Geldner's numbering of the *Wisperad* is in need of revision. However, since Cantera's new numbering scheme has not been officially published, I use Geldner's system. Cantera's preliminary results are accessible via the ADA website.

---

² In transcribing *mēnōy* and *gētīy*, I follow Skjærvø (1995a: 269). See also Skjærvø (2008a) and recently Skjærvø (2009b: 481, fn. 12).
³ See, for instance, PYH 35.9 in Pt4 and E7.

Abbreviations

LANGUAGES

IE	Indo-European
IIr.	Indo-Iranian
InsMP	Inscriptional Middle Persian
InsPa.	Inscriptional Parthian
MMP	Manichaean Middle Persian
MIr.	Middle Iranian
MP	Middle Persian
OAv.	Old(er) Avestan
OIr.	Old Iranian
OP	Old Persian
Pa.	Parthian
Pz.	Pāzand
Skt.	Sanskrit
Ved.	Vedic
YAv.	Young(er) Avestan
ZMP	Zoroastrian Middle Persian

TEXTS

AWN	*Ardā Wirāz nāmag*
Bd	*Bundahišn*
ČHP	*Čīdag handarz ī pōryōtkēšān*
Dd	*Dādestān ī Dēnīg*
Dk	*Dēnkard*
G	*Gāh*
FīŌ	*Frahang ī ōīm*
Herb	*Hērbedestān*
MHD	*Mādayān ī Hazār Dādestān*

MX	*Mēnōy ī Xrad*
N	*Nērangestān*
Ny	*Niyāyišn*
PRDd	*Pahlavi Rivāyat* accompanying the *Dādestān ī Dēnīg*
PG	Pahlavi *Gāθā*
Purs	*Pursišnīhā*
PV	Pahlavi version
SktY	Sanskrit *Yasna*
S	*Sīrōzag*
SW	*Srōš Wāǰ*
Suppl.ŠnŠ	Supplementary texts to the *Šāyest nē Šāyest*
SYtSŠ	*Srōš Yašt Sar Šab*
ŠnŠ	*Šāyest nē Šāyest*
ŠGW	*Škand Gumānīg Wizār*
(P)Wd	(Pahlavi) *Wīdēwdād*
(P)Wr	(Pahlavi) *Wisperad*
WZ	*Wizīdagīhā ī Zādspram*
(P)XA	(Pahlavi) *Xorde Avesta*
(P)XN	(Pahlavi) *Xwaršēd Niyāyišn*
(P)Y	(Pahlavi) *Yasna*
(P)YH	(Pahlavi) *Yasna Haptaŋhāiti*
(P)Yt	(Pahlavi) *Yašt*
ZFJ	*Zand ī Fragard ī Juddēwdād*
ZGK	*Zand ī Gōmēz Kardan*
ZWY	*Zand ī Wahman Yasn*

OTHER ABBREVIATIONS

abl.	ablative
acc.	accusative
ADA	Avestan Digital Archive (https://ada.geschkult.fu-berlin.de/)
aor.	aorist
CA	critical apparatus
dem.	demonstrative
du.	dual
f.	feminine
fn.	footnote
fol.	folio(s)
gen.	genitive
ind.	indicative
indef.	indefinite

in marg.	*in margine*
instr.	instrumental
ipt.	imperative
InPY	Indian Pahlavi *Yasna*
InYS	Indian *Yasna sāde*
IrPY	Iranian Pahlavi *Yasna*
IrYS	Iranian *Yasna sāde*
m.	masculine
MS	manuscript
MSS	manuscripts
nom.	nominative
ntr.	neutral
opt.	optative
pl.	plural
pres.	present
pron.	pronoun
sec.m.	*secunda manu*
sg.	singular
STr.	Sanskrit translation
subj.	subjunctive
subscr.	*subscriptum*
superl.	superlative
superscr.	*superscriptum*
Trc.	Transcription
Trl.	Transliteration
WBW	word-by-word
ZDMG	Zeitschrift der Deutschen Morgenländischen Gesellschaft

For Hourmazd & Siavash

Part I

Introduction

1. *Introduction*

> Was diese Stücke so schwierig macht, ist das Vage ihres Inhaltes. Sie bewegen sich immer in Gefühlen der allgemeinsten Art und es ist unendlich schwierig einen leitenden Gedanken zu entdecken, der durch ein ganzes Capitel geht.
>
> Spiegel (1859: viii) on *Zand*.

1.1 THE *YASNA HAPTAŊHĀITI*

The *Yasna Haptaŋhāiti* (YH) is a ritual text arranged in seven *hāiti* ('chapter' or 'division') and composed in a language identical in grammar and phonology to the Old Avestan of the *Gāθās* (Narten 1986: 20).[1] It is embedded in the text of the *Yasna* (Y) ritual, beginning with Y 35 and ending with Y 41.[2] As the *Yasna* is commonly divided into 72 *hāiti*, the *Yasna Haptaŋhāiti* is thus positioned right at the centre of one of Zoroastrians' most significant daily rituals. In an attempt to define the ritual properties of the text with familiar terms, Narten (1986), Boyce (1992) and Hintze (2002, 2009a) suggest that the YH was the liturgical kernel text of the *Yasna* ritual.

Although the question as to whether the figure of Zaraθuštra represents the *Gāθic* poet, a generic poet sacrificer or the founder of the religion may seem anachronistic today, it has shaped previous scholarship. Narten (1986: 35–7), for instance, considers the attribution of the YH to Zaraθuštra, a view shared by Boyce (1992, 1997b, 2001) and Hintze (2007a). Schwartz, however, regards the YH as slightly younger than the *Gāθās* and disagrees

---

[1] Av. *hāiti* is a technical term denoting the divisions of the *Yasna*. Etymologically, it refers to 'binding', but in practice corresponds more closely to what we would call chapter in a text such as the *Yasna*.

[2] On the extent of the YH and its compositional structure, see Narten (1986: 17–20) and Hintze (2007a: 6–20), respectively. Recently, Cantera (2012) has argued that the YH was originally a monolithic composition in one *hāiti*, a suggestion taken up in part by Pirart (2013). For my views on the extent of the YH, see Zeini (Forthcoming).

with the supposition of Zaraϑuštra's authorship.[3] Kellens and Pirart (1988: 36–9) consider the YH to resemble the *Gāϑās* in language and estimated date of composition, but dispute Zaraϑuštra's authorship as well. Unlike Schwartz, they propose a competing 'l'école haptahâtique', which supposedly did not recognise Zaraϑuštra as its religious leader (Kellens and Pirart 1988: 39). Humbach (1991: 7) does not address the authorship of the YH and merely notes that it originates 'from the period of the early Mazdayasnian church'. Despite disagreements over such details, a consensus exists on the proximity of the YH to the *Gāϑās*. The priestly tradition has preserved Zaraϑuštra as the name of the *Gāϑic* poet, and while various YAv. passages suggest that the YH was recognised as a sacred text (Narten 1986: 17), we are unaware of any traditional attribution of the YH to Zaraϑuštra.

Fire plays a central role in Zoroastrianism, dominating the ritual performed by the priests in fire temples or in private by the laity, a practice for which Zoroastrians have come to be known as fire worshippers. The predominance of the fire is also a main feature of the YH, pointing perhaps to the old age of the text and the fire's significance for the Avestan rituals and sacrifices. The invocation and subsequent identification of the ritual fire as the fire of *Ahura Mazdā* in Y 36.1–3, right at the centre of the *Yasna* ritual, represent the earliest textual references to the fire in a ritual context. The ritual continues and concludes with various requests among which one in Y 40.2 for the fellowship with *Ahura Mazdā*, and one in Y 41.2 for his good rule stand out. The sacrificers seem to underline their belonging to a community ruled by *Ahura Mazdā*. Likewise, in the *Zand* the fire is the agent that will grant the requested reward to the participants of the ritual. Here, however, the reward is designated as Ohrmazd's religion (*dēn*). In return, the participants of the ritual vow to spread the *dēn*. The commitment to the *dēn* and its dissemination are central themes in the *Zand* of the YH, and as such the text is crucial to understanding the religion's reception and development in late antiquity, as we seem to witness a shift from ritual practice to perhaps a more organised form of religion and religiosity. Such a transformation or reinterpretation of the ritual and its practices are not surprising in the face of the millennia that lie between the Avestan compositions and the *Zand* as a product of Sasanian world-view.

The Av. YH has received considerable attention, the first scholarly publication on this text dating back to a study by Baunack (1888). Although largely outdated, Baunack offers a balance between philological commentary and a close reading of the text, examining its various aspects as well as the religion as a whole. Geldner (1896–1904: 31) describes the YH briefly,

---

[3] Personal communication.

characterising the text as 'ein ganz eigenartiges Textstück' with a language temporally comparable to that of the *Gāθās*, but simpler content. He observes that Zaraθuštra's name is not mentioned, but generally views the text as a continuation of *Gāθic* thoughts. In a dedicated study, Wesendonk (1931) endeavours to provide a close reading of the text from a religious studies vantage point, offering a number of insightful observations, which in part anticipate many results of later scholarship.[4] Among others, Wesendonk (1931: 3) correctly assumes that the language of the YH is OAv., and discusses the significance of the fire in the YH (Wesendonk 1931: Sec. IX) and its identification with *spəṇta- mainiiu-* (Wesendonk 1933: 113). In both studies, Wesendonk treats the YH as a text marking an intermediate stage in the development of the Zoroastrian religion (Wesendonk 1931: 5, 31). He attributes the text to a priestly circle, presumed to have been active immediately after the founder's own time. In Wesendonk's view, they reinterpreted the content of the *Gāθās* in the YH, thus establishing a Zoroastrian priestly tradition (Wesendonk 1931: 4–9). To that end, he partly foresees Kellens and Pirart's (1988: 36–9) suggestion of a competing YH-school rivalling the *Gāθic* community. Nevertheless, Wesendonk's research is largely outdated by today's standards. From a methodological point of view, three main arguments can be made against his approach. First, his research has very strong historicising tendencies: he attempts to locate the YH geographically and associate it with names mentioned in the *Avesta* such as the legendary *Saēna* from the *Frawardīn Yašt* (Yt 13). Second, at times he advocates a very literal interpretation of the text. In a discussion of the waters as *Ahura Mazdā*'s spouses (Sec. XI), he traces the roots of the Zoroastrian next-of-kin marriage (*xwēdōdah*) to the YH. He then links the image of *Ahura Mazdā* surrounded by his wives to the idea of the ideal ruler, suggesting that the Medean and Achaemenid kings followed this practice advocated in the YH (Sec. XII). Such readings promote a simplistic and literal view of religious texts. On the one hand, we do not have a definitive answer to the question of the Achaemenids' religiosity. Their knowledge of a text such as the YH cannot be taken for granted. No doubt, MP texts repeatedly refer to *xwēdōdah*. Yet, in the *Zand* of the YH we find no references to this practice. Thus, it may be safe to suggest that at a minimum the exegetes did not associate passages of the YH with *xwēdōdah*. Third, Wesendonk operates strongly on the assumption of Zaraθuštra's authorial intention, for example, by attributing to the YH distortions of the original dogmas:

---

[4] In a later publication on the Iranian religious world view, Wesendonk (1933) discusses the YH in one rather small chapter, which is largely based on his earlier work.

> Ein neuer Geist macht sich in dem Yasna haptaŋhāti- geltend. Wenn dadurch auch der Kern des eigentlichen Dogmas abgeändert und entstellt wird, so ist der Yasna haptaŋhāti- unternommene Versuch, von einem veränderten Standpunkt aus die Gedankenwelt Zarathuštra's umzudeuten, doch für die Weiterbildung der mazdaistischen Religion äußerst wichtig geworden. (Wesendonk 1931: 5)

The text was then overlooked for nearly a century, the neglect possibly arising out of the unequivocal judgements of scholars such as Bartholomae (1904: 1272), who, opposing Baunack's views, suggested that the YH was a prosaic composition and certainly not as old as the *Gāϑās*:

> Im übrigen muss gegenüber BN.s [i.e. Baunack's] Ausführungen Stud. I. 447 ff. betont werden, 1) dass der *Yasna Hapt.* von Haus aus prosaisch abgefasst, und 2) dass er ganz sicher nicht so alt, geschweige denn älter als die fünf *Gāθā* ist.

No further research was carried out on the text until the publication of Narten's critical edition in 1986, which rekindled academic interest in the text. Her assertion that its language is OAv. (Narten 1986: 20, 28) resulted in the text's inclusion in later editions of the OAv. corpus published by Kellens and Pirart (1988), Humbach (1991) and West (2010). Narten's study of the text's poetic features stands out. She describes the language of the YH as artful prose, close to poetry ('kunstvoll gestaltete, dichtungsnahe Prosa') (Narten 1986: 21). In her overview of the language and style of the YH, Narten (1986: 21–3) lists 15 different stylistic figures, the use of which she illustrates by citing 42 instances from the YH.

Kellens and Pirart (1988: 36–9) consider the YH's language to be prose and generally close to OAv. They explain the lexical differences between the two groups of OAv. texts by attributing the YH to a different ideological school of thought, namely 'l'école haptahâtique'.

In his seminal work, Watkins (1995: 232) agrees with Narten on the poetic nature of the YH's language and categorises the the text as a 'non-metrical rhythmic/syntactic' form of 'liturgy', rooted in the IE poetic language (Watkins 1995: 276).

Most recently, Hintze (2007a) has published an edition of the YH in English. In agreement with Watkins, Hintze (2007a: 2–5, 21) argues that the YH is an example of IE 'liturgical poetry'. She points out poetic similarities and metrical differences between the *Gāϑās* and the YH, considering both texts to be poetry. In her view, the *Gāϑās* are 'governed by the *rhythm of syllables*' and the YH by 'the *rhythm of words*' (Hintze 2007a: 5). Hintze (2007a: 6–20) expands her analysis to include the compositional structure of the text. Her investigation of this rather neglected aspect offers further support for the notion of the YH as IE liturgical poetry.

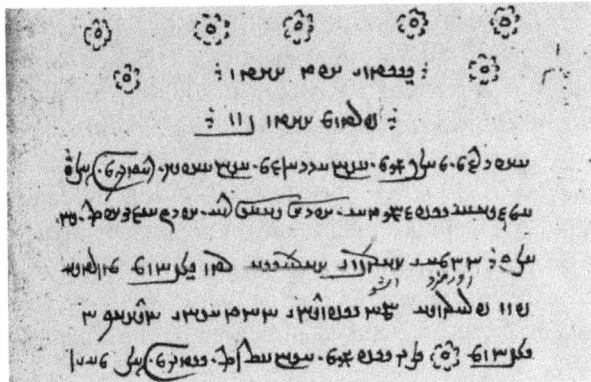

Figure 1.1 The start of the YH in Pt4

In Iran, Mirfaxrāi (2003) published a Persian translation of the Avestan text accompanied by a commentary. She confines herself to Geldner's edition of the text, while her commentary is mostly a summary of other views.

1.2 THE PAHLAVI TEXT

The text of the PY is transmitted in the bilingual Pahlavi *Yasna* MSS, where the Pahlavi version immediately follows the Avestan text to which it relates. Although the individual *hāiti* of the *Yasna* are often marked in the MSS, either by some blank space between two sections (e.g. F2 T6, J2 M1) or by some graphical ornaments (e.g. G97 B3 L17 S1), the words *Yasna Haptaŋhāiti* do not occur at the start of the text as a title, but in the *Yasna* for the first time in a formula at the end of the YH's final stanza in 41.6: *yasnəm sūrəm haptaŋhāitīm ašāuuanəm ašahe ratūm yazamaide* 'We sacrifice to the strong ritual, the *haptaŋhāiti*, the orderly *ratu* of *aša*'.[5] With the exception of the manuscript T6, a title is only attested in Pahlavi at the start of the text in the manuscripts of the IrPY: *yasn ī haft hād* 'The ritual in seven chapters' (Pt4 F2 E7)[6] or *yašt ī haft hād bun* 'The beginning of the ritual in seven chapters' (Mf4 R413).

Passages of the (P)YH occur widely across the Zoroastrian literature. They are repeated or referred to in the manuscripts of the *Avesta* at the *hāiti*, stanza and phrase levels. Examples include (P)Y 5, which occurs early on in the *Yasna* and causes the abbreviation of (P)Y 37 in some

---

[5] Further references to the text are found in Y 57.22, 71.12, Wr 2.7, 16.4, 17.1, 21.0, *Gāh* 1.5, N 28, 47 and 63.

[6] These MSS have ⟨yst'⟩ for *yasn*. For a brief note on the confusion between final ⟨-sn'⟩ and ⟨-st'⟩, see Cantera (2004: 15, fn. 64).

MSS; (P)Y 58.8 which is identical to Y 36.6 and (P)Y 68.23 which incorporates Y 36.6b. (P)Wr 16.4 mentions the YH as a text, while Wd 10.8 and N 17.2 refer to PY 35.4.[7] In addition, we find discussions and frequent references to passages of the YH in the Pahlavi literature. Most prominently, Dk 9.12.1–32 (*Sūdgar Nask*), 9.35.1–26 (*Warštmānsr Nask*) and Dk 9.57.1–30 (*Bag Nask*) contain commentaries on the YH.[8] Y 5 (= Y 37) is alluded to in a number of passages discussing religious matters (see Section 15.1.2). More recently, *The Council of Iranian Mobeds* has proposed a *Norūz* prayer, entitled اوستای سال نو 'Avesta of the New Year', which consists of Y 37.1, 39.2 and 39.3 followed by the *Hamāzur* prayer.[9]

1.3 WHY A NEW EDITION OF THE PYH?

In contrast to its Avestan version, the Pahlavi YH (PYH), and for that matter the Pahlavi *Yasna* (PY) as a whole, have received little attention, and a complete English edition of neither is available to date. Spiegel (1858) was one of the first to reproduce the text of both the PY and Pahlavi *Wisperad* (PWr). His edition of the PY, which naturally contains the PYH (Spiegel 1858: 151–60), gives the text in original script and is based on a single MS, namely K5 (Spiegel 1858: 4). Although he makes extensive use of the *Zand* in his approach to Avestan, both his translation, Spiegel (1859), and commentary, Spiegel (1868), only reflect upon the Av. *Yasna*.

Mills (1905b)[10] offers the only critical edition of the PYH prior to Dhabhar (1949). His article contains a collated and transliterated version of the text, while a translation was published later (see Mills 1905a). He considers PY 42 an appendix to YH and prints it at the end of the text. Mills made a significant contribution to the study of the PYH by attempting a complete edition of the PY as a text in its own right. However, despite his erudite scholarship and familiarity with the texts, his editions are now outdated. His transcription of the text, for instance, has been superseded by a more complete understanding of the heterograms, which are no longer treated as Aramaic loanwords in MP. While Mills supplies some footnotes, his edition lacks a critical apparatus. Thus, despite the title's claim that the text has been 'edited with all MSS. collated' (Mills 1905b: 105), the constituted text cannot

---

[7] I discuss a number of such cases throughout the present volume. See, for instance, Section 13.5. Most recently, Hintze (2013b) has analysed the quotations of the YH in the Younger *Avesta*. She shows the extent of textual stratification within the *Avesta* and demonstrates how deeply the Younger *Avesta* is rooted in the compositional traditions of the Older *Avesta*.

[8] See Section 4.3.6.

[9] The text is available from www.anjomanemobedan.com. As Dastur Kamran Jamshidi informs me, this prayer was arranged four or five years ago (personal communication from 25 March 2013).

[10] This article is not listed in the bibliography of Mills compiled by Gropp (1991).

be verified against a critical apparatus with variant readings. Furthermore, his translation paradigm is no longer acceptable today, and the collated text and translation are not otherwise accompanied by a commentary.

Dhabhar's (1949) critical edition of the PY remains the principal edition of the PYH. His edition is accompanied by a glossary, but it lacks a translation and commentary. Dhabhar constitutes the text based on four MSS. Today, however, we have more MSS at our disposal, which improve our understanding of the text's written transmission. Furthermore, Dhabhar suppresses the differences between eteo- and heterographic spellings across manuscripts. For example, Pt4 Mf4 F2 R413 T6 E7, J2 have ⟨'w'⟩ in PYH 35.1c, but Dhabhar favours ⟨'L'⟩ (K5 M1) without noting the variant ⟨'w'⟩ in his apparatus. He applies the same principle to the spelling of verbal forms, most prominently to ⟨YDBḤWN-m⟩, ⟨ycm⟩ and ⟨ycwm⟩.[11]

A recent edition of the Pahlavi version of the OAv. corpus by Malandra and Ichaporia (2010) is chiefly a transcription of Dhabhar's (1949) text and lacks a critical apparatus, translation and commentary. However, this edition contains a significantly improved glossary and offers references to the wider Pahlavi literature in footnotes. The publication includes Ichaporia's translation of PY 28 in an appendix.

A complete edition of the PY is therefore a desideratum, to which the present study hopes to make a small contribution by revisiting the text of the PYH.

1.4 THE PRESENT EDITION

A major task of a critical edition, particularly that of an ancient text, is the *constitutio textus*, the constitution or reconstruction of a presumably lost original on the basis of established editorial principles (Nünning 2004: 651).[12] The reconstructed text can be that of a lost original composition or a lost ancestor of a group of manuscripts. Eclecticism seems to be the favoured methodology for compiling critical editions in Iranian studies,[13] where the production of a grammatically intact text seems to be the predominant goal.[14]

In the present edition, no attempts have been made to critically reconstruct one version of the text based on variant readings. Much like a diplomatic or a non-eclectic edition, the text of the present edition is based on one manuscript, namely Pt4, while the apparatus records variants as in a

---

[11] I suspect that the quality of Dhabhar's collated text suffered from the disastrous fire of 1945 in the *Fort Printing Press*, which destroyed parts of his work (Dhabhar 1949: III).
[12] For a critique of this approach, see McGann (1992).
[13] See, for instance, Geldner (1886–96), Gershevitch (1967), Insler (1975), Narten (1986), Kellens and Pirart (1988, 1990, 1991), Panaino (1990, 1995a), Humbach (1991) and Hintze (2007a).
[14] For an assessment of the eclectic method in textual criticism of the New Testament, see Epp (1976).

variorum edition. On occasion, I point out discrepancies and mistakes in the manuscripts of one or both families in the commentaries, but these have had no bearing on establishing a text. I have only emended the text of Pt4 in cases of obvious spelling mistakes.

Despite the preference given to Pt4, I will briefly discuss *emendatio*, a commonly required step in the process of compiling critical editions, in light of my own work.

1.4.1 *Emendatio*

The problematic notion of an original author and text has long been acknowledged in the Classics,[15] and prompts a legitimate question: if the original text is a construct, then what indeed is the object and goal of any emendation? The question is even more pronounced in the case of the *Zand*, for which both the authorship and date of composition are unknown. Our lack of understanding about the oral transmission of the text and its transition to a literary form further complicate the task of *emendatio*. Would a text constituted on the basis of philological principles reflect an archetype or a representation of the text in a certain point in time? Or does the newly established text reflect the ancestor of a group of MSS? In light of the above questions, we must ask whether stratified texts can at all be revised to a presumed lost original.

On one hand, no consensus exists as to what the original text of the *Avesta* and its PV could have been. The idea of an Arsacid archetype, proposed by Andreas (1904), has long been rejected in Iranian studies (see Henning 1941). Hoffmann and Narten (1989) remain faithful to the idea of an archetype, but shift its date to the Sasanian era, mainly on account of their dating of the invention of the Av. script to this era.[16] Kellens (1998) rejects this dating in accord with Blois (1990) and questions the paradigm of a Sasanian archetype proposed by Hoffmann and Narten (1989). He pays particular attention to the relationship between the transmitted *Avesta* and the one detailed in the *Dēnkard*, suggesting that the extant MSS continue the tradition of a ritual *Avesta* but not the one described in the *Dēnkard*. The issue of an original composition and that of the archetype is further complicated by the texts' assumed history of oral transmission and inevitable disturbances, a fact also

---

[15] See the Foreword in McGann (1992: xiv): 'At the close of the eighteenth century, F. A. Wolf's *Prolegomena ad Homerum* (1795) acknowledged that the search for the author and intention of *The Iliad* could recover nothing but fragments without a single unifying authority, just as J. G. Eichhorn's *Introduction to the Old Testament* (1780–83) had shown that the contradictory, historically diverse strata of the Hebrew Bible could not be resolvable into a consistent text.'

[16] The reconstruction of a Sasanian archetype as an editorial goal was already suggested by Spiegel (1882: 588).

acknowledged by Hoffmann and Narten (1989: 21). As regards the Avestan text, nearly two millennia separate any original composition from a Sasanian or post-Sasanian archetype and a few centuries the archetype from the earliest MSS. As Spiegel (1882: 586) rightly observes, the text must have undergone significant changes during the centuries. The issue is not less complicated in the case of the *Zand*. If we posit an early Sasanian date for the oldest sections of the *Zand*, we must still account for several centuries of oral transmission before the texts were committed to writing. And there still remains the gap between the start of the written transmission and the oldest MSS.

On the other hand, the Pahlavi version of the IrPY contained in Pt4 Mf4 F2 R413 T6 E7 seems to show a larger degree of variation in content compared to the Avestan text.[17] This is not surprising, as the aim of any exegesis is to continuously interpret the sacred corpus, which it also attempts to codify and preserve in an *authentic* state.[18] The Sanskrit, NP and Gujarati versions of the *Yasna* are testimonies to this ongoing process of interpretation. The differences between the Pahlavi versions of the *Yasna*, however, have important implications for the study of the MSS and the aims of an edition. Firstly, it is no longer enough to examine the filiation of the MSS only on the basis of the Av. text. Manuscripts may appear to belong to the class of the IrPY, for example by including the preface of Hōšang Sīyāwaxš's codex, while the manuscript's *Zand* may have been subject to rigorous revisions of a later date (see Section 1.5.6). Secondly, a proposed original text cannot be reconstructed by taking into account editorial interventions that might have been made later. Admittedly, revisions found in more modern manuscripts could theoretically represent corrections based on older MSS. However, the provenance of such revisions is presently not determined. Even if it were, emendations of the PY would still be difficult to justify if the divergences represented texts transmitted in different schools or traditions. The reconstruction of an Ur-text or the archetypal ancestor of a group of MSS cannot be upheld indiscriminately.

1.4.2 Base text

Due to their age, the MSS of the InPY (K5 J2) may seem a better choice for the base text. However, I have given preference to the rather late IrPY manuscript Pt4 for its perceived accuracy, the higher number of IrPY manuscripts available to me and Pt4's provenance, which through the colophon can be traced back beyond 1020 CE (see Cantera and Vaan 2005: 40).

---

[17] See Section 1.5.
[18] An example of this continuous process of interpretation has recently been highlighted by Cantera and Andrés Toledo (2008).

Although in Geldner's (1886–96: xxxiv) proposed stemma, manuscripts of both classes go back to one scribe, namely Māhpanāh (ca. 1200 CE), seemingly suggesting an equally reliable provenance for both classes, I am critical of his methodology of reconstructing the written transmission of these MSS.

Geldner's genealogy of the exegetical *Yasna* rests on the assumption that all bilingual MSS of the *Yasna* can ultimately be traced back to the MS of Farnbag (ca. 1110), who, according to Geldner's interpretation of Hōšang Sīyāwaxš's preface, combined the Pahlavi and Avestan texts of the *Yasna* for the first time. Geldner then proposes a date of ca. 1200 CE for the common ancestor of the Ir- and InPY due to their shared readings and suggests that the SY branched off some time earlier, that is, after Farnbag (ca. 1110). There are, however, a number of problems with Geldner's proposed genealogy and the graphical representation of his stemma can be deceptive as the connections between some of the MSS are far less clear than indicated (see Figure 1.2).

The genealogy known to us through Hōšang Sīyāwaxš's preface, which forms the basis for Geldner's reconstruction, is that of the IrPY. As for the InPY, Mihrabān is 'silent as to his source' for J2, and only K5 can be traced back to a lost manuscript dated ca. 1270 CE (Geldner 1886–96: xxiv). Thus on the face of it, the IrPY and the InPY do not intersect with a shared scribe named in any colophon and could represent two different

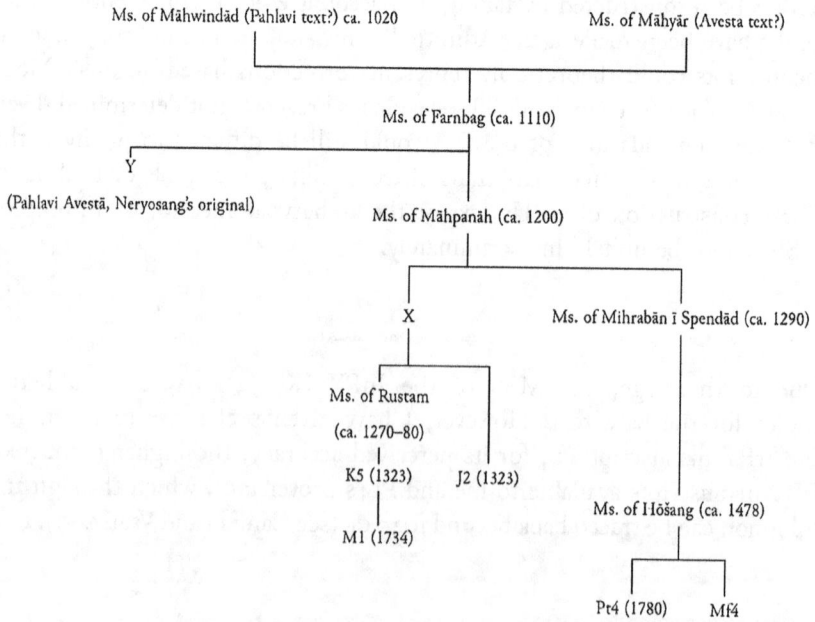

Figure 1.2 Geldner's genealogy of the exegetical *Yasna*

Introduction 13

lines of transmission. Moreover, Hōšang Sīyāwaxš's preface does not indicate that the two texts were then combined for the first time.[19] As such, other combined copies may have existed, which could have been the predecessors of the various classes of the bilingual *Yasna* MSS. In the current state of our knowledge, the idea of a single source for the Ir- and InPY is a conjecture on Geldner's part no matter how many shared and divergent readings between the various families one might adduce.[20] And so would be any suggestion that separate lines of transmission existed. In this context, I would like to draw attention to a remark by Mills (1893: vi), who in a summary of *Yasna* MSS speaks of a manuscript that only contains the Pahlavi text of the *Yasna*:

> There are others containing the Zend text of the Yasna interspersed with that of other books, and there is one manuscript known containing the Pahlavi translation only, without the Zend text.

Although the identity and whereabouts of this manuscript are presently unknown, its re-emergence would necessitate a re-evaluation of the single source theory. We know of a similar MS for the *Wīdēwdād*, the *Zand ī Fragard ī Juddēwdād* (ZFJ), which preserves a different tradition than the *Zand* of the PWd.[21]

The idea that all MSS of the 'Zendavesta' represent the same text regardless of their origin and age, was already expressed by Westergaard (1852–54: I 15) and later also confirmed by Spiegel (1882: 589). This might have been the background to Geldner's approach to the MSS of the two classes. However, the text of the PYH does not converge across the manuscripts. The younger MSS show a greater variation in the *Zand*, so that we can consider manuscripts' age a differentiating factor. Whatever socio-cultural circumstances of the nineteenth century triggered the revision of some MSS in India, we have to acknowledge the results in our editions. The MSS collated in the present study suggest a grouping as IrPY (Pt4 Mf4), revised IrPY (F2 R413 T6 E7) and InPY (K5 J2 M1).

1.4.3 Numbering the stanzas of Y 35

Narten (1986: 17) argues that the YH starts at the second strophe of Y 35.[22] Consequently, in her summary of the YH's structure she assigns nine stanzas to Y 35 (Narten 1986: 18). Narten's discussion takes into account

---

[19] For a discussion of this preface and the difficulties involved in its interpretation, see Cantera and Vaan (2005: 40), who suggest a slightly modified genealogy for the IrPY.
[20] Cantera and Vaan (2005) do not question the one source theory.
[21] On ZFJ, see König (2010).
[22] For the various discussions of the extent of the YH, see Narten (1986: 17) with references. For my own discussion of the topic, see Zeini (Forthcoming).

linguistic and textual evidence. She shows that the Zoroastrian tradition considered the second stanza to be the beginning strophe of the *hāiti*. Narten, however, leaves out two important Pahlavi passages which would have further supported her point. Firstly, Y 35 is described as having nine stanzas in Suppl.ŠnŠ 13:[23]

> **Suppl.ŠnŠ 13.16** *yasn bun kardag nō wačast u-š bun humatanām u-š sar humatanām*
> The beginning section of the *Yasna* has nine stanzas. Its beginning is *humatanām* and its end is *humatanām*.

Secondly, in the IrPY manuscripts the concluding instructions at the end of Y 35 assign nine strophes to this *hāiti*: *nō wičast sē gāh* 'nine stanzas, three verse lines' (see Sections 6.10).

I have modified the numbering of the stanzas in Y 35 in order to acknowledge the tradition's view. In my edition, the *hāiti* starts with 35.0 and ends with 35.9.

1.4.4 Glosses

With the exception of Spiegel's (1858) edition of the PY, it has been customary to identify and mark so-called glosses and comments in modern editions of the *Zand* by way of brackets or other formatting devices. While the origin of this practice is difficult to identify, it has often been hinted at. The predominant view seems to be that glosses represent a separate layer of text, which must be marked. Mills (1887: xxxviii), for example, proposes that in cases where MP glosses do not correspond to the *Gāϑic* text, they should be 'set apart as from a later hand':[24]

> Then, again, a question of the utmost importance meets us in estimating the glosses, which are often, but not always, from a later hand. [...]; but a final translation should be made more strictly in the light of the Gâthic, so far as it affords on its side positive indications, and the glosses, where they do not correspond, should be set apart as from a later hand.

Although less concerned with identifying different strata in the text, Bang (1890: 365) too suggests that the correspondence between Avestan and its PV should be the guideline for identifying glosses: 'Ueberhaupt ist mit kleinen Ausnahmen alles, wofür sich kein Aequivalent im Grundtext bietet, in die Glossen zu verweisen.'[25] Malandra and Ichaporia (2010: 1) prefer a different terminology, calling the translation 'Gloss' and the so-called glosses

---

[23] I discuss this passage in more detail in Zeini (Forthcoming).
[24] See also Mills (1894: XV).
[25] Applying this method, Bang's identification of the glosses agrees with Dhabhar (1949), with the exception of two differences in PY 28.2a and PY 28.2c.

'Comment', but also presume later additions, which must have found their way into the main text of the *Zand*:

> One is a near word for word gloss (Gloss, PhlGl) of the Avestan; the other consists of fairly brief comments (Comment). Clearly the gloss is the basic text, to which comments were appended. These comments have every appearance of being marginal or interlinear notes which the owner of a manuscript may have scribbled as he read the Gloss.

The problem of terminology aside, the issue at hand is not whether the *Zand* contains any additional material. In fact, as a commentarial tradition the *Zand* will by definition go beyond the source text.[26] And, I do not dispute the value of a secure and reliable identification of the various strata of the *Zand*.[27] The question is to what extent these additional words represent a secondary layer by a later hand.[28] Do linguistic features justify a categorisation of certain sections as later additions? If Malandra and Ichaporia (2010: 1) were right that the *Comments* are marginal and interlinear notes, when were they incorporated into the main text, and for what reason?

To start with, it is questionable whether a correspondence between the words of the two texts is a reliable measure for identifying the various strata of the text. In PY 35.3a, for example, we have *ān ī gōspandān dahišn āb* for *gauuōi* ⁺*ad-āiš*. In previous editions, *āb* 'water' is set in brackets.[29] Although the Av. phrase does not mention water, there is no linguistic or palaeographic indication that *āb* was added later to the PV. For example, no linguistic features identify *āb* as a later form. At the same time, it is perceivable that *āb* was part of the traditional interpretation of this passage, as *āb* explains what is to be given to the cattle. If *āb* is not a later addition but an integral part of the passage's *Zand*, it should be treated as such, given that in the MSS such words are never separated from the main text by the use of any devices.[30]

Even in cases where older and younger grammatical forms have been presumed to have been preserved side by side, the evidence of the extant MSS seems to support a rather inclusive approach without any graphical distinction between such sections. Klingenschmitt (2000: 192), for instance, adduces words from PWd 4.1 (in L4) as an example of stratification,

---

[26] The style of the Zoroastrian exegetical literature and particles that introduce comments have been the subject of a dedicated study by Skjærvø (2010c).

[27] A necessary step towards this goal is the dating of the sages mentioned in the *Zand*. For a recent attempt, see Secunda (2012) with references.

[28] In a presentation in 2009 at the University of Salamanca, I hypothesised that the *Zand* consists of two broad strata. Comments with a more literary structure, I argued, represent the older, orally transmitted, literary version of the text, while I considered those sections following the Av. word order to be of a younger age, most likely composed when the texts were committed to writing.

[29] See Mills (1905b: 106), Dhabhar (1949: 167) and Malandra and Ichaporia (2010: 47).

[30] See also Cantera (2004: 240, 244), who observes that glosses and comments are not marked in the MSS.

suggesting that an older form '⟨kwnd⟩ *kund*' and the younger form '⟨kwnyt⟩ *kunēd*' 'he does' were preserved in translation and commentary, respectively. Although Klingenschmitt does not discuss the issue of brackets, it is noteworthy that L4 does not graphically or otherwise distinguish any strata in the text.[31]

By artificially separating important components of the text, we disturb the natural flow of the language and present a distorted picture of the scribal tradition, which did not utilise dividing or marking devices. A comparison of Mills's (1905b: 111) and Dhabhar's (1949: 173) rendering of PY 39.3a should illustrate this point:

(P)Y 39.3a ... *vaŋhuščā īṯ vaŋᵛhīščā īṯ*
Mills : ... *weh* [*nar*] *ud ān ī weh* [*mādag*] (*ud*) *any amahraspandān*
Dhabhar: ... *weh nar ud ān ī weh mādag any amahraspandān*

Although both texts are similar, the brackets in Mills's interpretation suggest that both Av. forms were translated as *weh* 'good', and that presumably secondary additions clarified the gender by way of apposition. This, however, is an assumption not supported by any textual evidence. Nothing in the text indicates that *nar* and *mādag* were added later. To the contrary, the fact that *ān ī* precedes *weh mādag* suggests that *mādag* was an integral part of the translation, unless we assume that *ān ī* was added to the *Zand* at the time *mādag* was added as a gloss to *weh*. The latter assumption, however, would be as hypothetical as the first. In Mills's rendering, the *original* translation appears to disregard the intricacies of Avestan, whereas Dhabhar presents us a nuanced translation, where the translator understood the grammatical gender of the original.

The marking of glosses, as proposed by Mills and Bang, has less to do with the *Zand*'s stratified nature, but is a remnant of a practice of the nineteenth century, reflecting the time's understanding of the originality of text and authorship: 'a gloss, if it proved to have been written by the same person who composed the text, would be decisive in determining the rendering' (Mills 1887: xxxviii). As such, identifying glosses was not limited to the *Zand* and was shared by scholars of Av. philology as well. In his examination of the YH, Baunack (1888: 404) asserts that the text is attributable to one author despite the many *added fragments* ('eingefügten ... Bruchstücken') which he believes able to identify:

---

[31] I shall point out that while I found ⁂ *kund* in L4, I was unable to verify Klingenschmitt's reading of ⟨kwnyt⟩. A few lines after ⟨kwnd⟩, ⁂ (⟨ḤDWN-yt⟩ *gīrēd* occurs twice. However, his transliteration of *kunēd* as ⟨kwnyt⟩ suggests that he did not read ⁂ as *kunēd*, as the transliteration should then have been ⟨ᴮYDWN-yt⟩. As for ⟨kwnd⟩, it can of course also be an erroneous spelling for an intended *kunēnd*, which seems to fit the context better. While T44 agrees with L4, B1 has ⁂, supporting *kunēnd*. See also F10 where we find ⁂. For more examples of ⟨kwnd⟩ and a discussion, see also Klingenschmitt (2000: 210–11).

Ein Hauptergebnis meiner Interpretation des *Y. h.* ist, dass derselbe seinem Inhalte nach ein einziges, wohlgefügtes Ganze bildet (abgesehen von einigen angehängten oder eingefügten, leicht erkennbaren Bruchstücken), dass er demgemäss von einem einzigen Verfasser concipiert und ausgeführt sein muss.

Thus, Baunack dedicates an entire section to a detailed examination of so-called additions ('Zusätze') to the Av. YH, called glosses (Baunack 1888: 401–13). In his view they appear before or after the word they explain: 'Die Glosse steht vor oder hinter dem zu erklärenden Worte oder doch in der Nähe desselben' (Baunack 1888: 405). The list of identified glosses is long and cannot be summarised here in full. Among the more curious cases is his postulate that the simple name '*ahura*' or '*mazdā*' is often glossed in the YH to yield the complete double name *ahura mazdā* (Baunack 1888: 408). Therefore, he declares '[*ahura*]' a gloss to *mazdā* in Y 35.3, 9 and 38.1, setting '*ahura*' in brackets to mark it as a gloss. In Y 36.6, Baunack (1888: 406) declares *imā raocā̊* 'these lights here', now viewed as an integral part of the stanza, an added gloss to the following *barəzištəm *barəzəmanąm* 'highest of heights'. Baunack's ultimate goal was to restore the YH's assumed metrical form by identifying additions in the text (Baunack 1888: 401), a number of which he declares worthless (Baunack 1888: 409ff.).

Most importantly, segmenting the text of the *Zand* into an actual translation and additional layers of comments imposes an artificial distinction that ignores the reality of the MSS, where we find no punctuational marks that persistently distinguish between the various layers. Only very rarely is a section of the PV set apart from the rest by some sort of decorative ornaments. In Pt4, for instance, two such ornaments can be found in PY 10.20 (see Figure 1.3). However, such marks are rather rare and often not consistently set in the MSS.[32]

Beside fragmenting the text of the *Zand*, the brackets used in editions also represent an anachronism, by applying a translation paradigm to a text

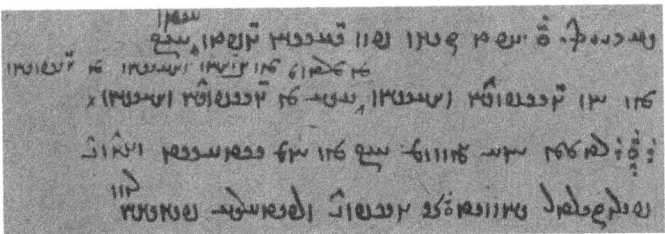

Figure 1.3 Dividing device in PY 10.20

[32] The ornamental flower dividing ⟨LTMH⟩ from the previous Pahlavi section in PY 10.20 is surprisingly found in the InPY K5 J2 M1 T55b, but not in the IrPY F2 T6.

that most likely did not recognise such an approach. In scholarly translations words that are not present in the original are often given in parentheses, but the *Zand* as it is transmitted in the MSS is rather inclusive. Therefore, I have avoided the use of brackets in the rendering of the PYH while I do recognise that the *Zand* frequently contains text that does not match the Av. version in a one-to-one manner.

1.4.5   The otiose stroke

The Pahlavi letter ı leaves much room for interpretation and uncertainty by representing ⟨w, n, r⟩, ⟨ʿ⟩ in heterograms and the otiose stroke ⟨'⟩ in word final position. Nyberg (1964: ix) observes that the otiose stroke is set after phonetically spelt words ending in ⟨b, c, k, n, w, r, p, t⟩. This rule, however, is applied in the MSS with a wide margin of variation, be it across the MSS or within individual manuscripts. Pt4, for instance, seems to have the tendency of omitting the otiose stroke after a final ⟨-n⟩ in PY 35.0, but not so in PY 35.1. Pt4 has ⟨gwspnd'n⟩ as well as ⟨dhšn'⟩ in PY 35.3a, but also ⟨gwspnd'n'⟩ in PY 35.6b. See also ⟨'DYN'⟩ in PY 35.2a but ⟨'DYN⟩ in PY 35.4a, and ⟨wyh mynšn' whwmn⟩ in PY 37.5. In Pt4 we often find the otiose stroke after a final ⟨-t'⟩ and ⟨-k'⟩,[33] however, without this rule being consistently applied. For instance, Pt4 omits the otiose stroke after ⟨hpt⟩ in ⟨yst' Y hpt h't'⟩ in PY 35.0, but sets it in ⟨k'mk'⟩ and ⟨nywk'⟩ in PY 35.2. The otiose stroke is also missing in the many instances of ⟨LK⟩. In J2, by contrast, the spelling ⟨LK'⟩ is more common (PY 35.9, 39.4 or 40.1).

Any rule concerning the otiose stroke seems to have been observed more regularly after certain words, rather than in each instance of a final ⟨b, c, k, n, w, r, p, t⟩. For instance, as Nyberg rightly states, the stroke is not set after the adverbs *abāz*, *čiyōn* and *frāz*. Out of seven occurrences of ⟨cygwn⟩ in the PYH, we only find the stroke set once in PY 35.5 in E7. Similarly, the stroke is almost always set in ⟨'ytwn'⟩, the exception being the manuscript F2 (PY 39.4 and 40.2) and some instances in R413 where we find ⟨'ytwn⟩. In PY 35.3 we seem to witness a tendency for Pt4 to set the otiose stroke after a final ⟨-n⟩ if ⟨-š-⟩ occurs in the word. See also PY 37.5, where Pt4 Mf4, K5 read ⟨wyh mynšn' whwmn⟩ in contrast to J2 (⟨whwmn'⟩).[34] While in all instances the variation is too large, we can see that the otiose stroke is rarely set against the rule observed by Nyberg. I assume the rules concerning the otiose stroke were not strictly active by the time these MSS were copied. I have thus refrained from standardising the use of the otiose stroke in my edition and

---

[33] See the many examples in PY 35.0.
[34] Concerning the otiose stroke and the *ezāfe*, see PY 37.4 and 5 for the wide margin of variation across both families of MSS.

reflect its application as found in Pt4. This has of course implications for my interpretation of the text, as the otiose stroke will at times be read as the conjunction *ud* 'and'. This is a major problem in editions of Middle Persian texts to which even the eclectic approach will not contribute a definitive solution.

1.5 MANUSCRIPTS

For his edition, Dhabhar (1949: 1) collated four manuscripts: KS Mf4, K5 J2.[35] KS and Mf4 reproduce the preface of Hōšang Sīyāwaxš's codex and are thus thought to be independent copies of the same ancestor (Geldner 1886–96: xxv; Dhabhar 1949: 7). Geldner (1886–96: xxiv) considers K5 and J2 to be closely related. KS and Mf4 represent the Iranian (IrPY), and K5 and J2 the Indian (InPY) class of PY manuscripts. In the present study, the former group has been extended by a fresh collation of Pt4 F2 R413 T6 E7, and the latter by M1. Both classes and the MSS Pt4 Mf4, K5 J2 M1 have been extensively discussed by Geldner (1886–96: i–liv) and Dhabhar (1949: 1–15).[36] The commonly accepted dates for these MSS are shown in Table 1.1.[37]

Table 1.1 Manuscript dates

InPY	1323	K5 J2
	1734	M1
IrPY	1780	Pt4 Mf4
	1813	F2
	1835	R413
	1842	T6
	1865	E7

1.5.1 Pt4

567 pages, 13 ⅜ × 8 ⅛ in., 21 lines to the page. According to Dastur Sanjana's family tradition, Pt4, an IrPY, was copied 1779–80 CE in Nawsari by Dastur Kavasji Sohrabji, and is considered to be 'one of the most important Yasna codexes' (Geldner 1886–96: xiii). This dating has commonly been accepted.[38]

---

[35] KS, which was not accessible to me, is an 'exact counterpart' of Pt4 (Dhabhar 1949: 6), bearing siglum T54 in Dhabhar's (1923: 128) catalogue.
[36] For a useful overview of Geldner's *Prolegomena*, see Hoffmann (1984). See also Hintze (2007a: 22–7) and Cantera (2011).
[37] For the dates of Pt4 and Mf4, see Section 1.5.1.
[38] For a discussion of Pt4, Mf4 and their colophons, see Cantera and Vaan (2005) with references.

A facsimile of Pt4 is kept at the Bodleian Library, known as *MS. Zend d.2*. The whereabouts of the original manuscript are presently unknown.[39]

Pt4 features occasional interlinear and marginal glosses in New Persian, however, less so in the YH. The handwriting of the NP glosses is not as ornate and beautiful as that of Mf4. Pt4 tends to prefer the personal ending ⟨-wm⟩ for the 1sg. and pl. For example, in PY 35.3b in ⟨mynwmc⟩, ⟨wrcwmc⟩ and generally in ⟨ycwm⟩ (see Section 13.1.1). The manuscript also makes use of the rather rare ꜣ to mark ⟨l⟩, such as in PY 35.1a ⟨'hlwb'⟩, ⟨'hl'dyh⟩ and ⟨p'hlwm⟩ in PY 5.4a, PYH35.3c and PY 37.4a.

The facsimile of Pt4 was prepared for Dastur Sanjana, who had gifted the MS to the Bodleian Library. However, the facsimile did not satisfy the Dastur who asked Pt4 to be returned to him in exchange for the facsimile, which is now kept at the Bodleian Library. The brief history of the facsimile has been preserved on the inner side of the cover:

> This volume was executed for the person mentioned on the opposite page in return for his gift. He did not regard the conditions prescribed by him as having been fulfilled, and his gift was returned to him on June 7, 1893, with the stipulation that he should return either it or the facsimile. He returned the facsimile, which reached the library Nov. 19, 1894.
>
> In scores of places the photograph failed to catch marginal letters or parts of them, either because they were on the edge of the page or because the volume was too tightly bound. These omissions I supplied (it took me some day or two): the scale of them is not likely to be identical with that of the photographs – but otherwise I think they will be found faithful to the minutest particular. E.W.B.N.

The opposite page reads:

> Platinotype facsimile of MS. Zend c.3 in the Bodleian Library, Oxford. being the copy of the yasna with Pahlavi translation presented by Prof. Dastur Darab Peshotan Sanjana, B. A., J. P.

1.5.2 Mf4

721 pages, 11 × 7 ⅛ in., 17 lines to the page. Published in facsimile by Jamaspasa and Nawabi (1976a), Mf4 is undated but considered to be 'somewhat younger than Pt4', to which it is closely related (Geldner 1886–96: xi).[40] Mf4 too features Hōšang Siyāwaxš's preface and is written in clear handwriting with marginal and interlinear notes of various length in NP. A number of the marginalia are cut off in the facsimile. In the YH the highest concentration of these notes can be found in Y 36 and Y 37. A long marginal note in New Persian stands out in Y 42.

---

[39] I consulted the facsimile of Pt4 on 2 February 2009 at the Bodleian Library and have subsequently indexed and published it (see Zeini 2012).

[40] For (P)Y 5, see vol. 19 (Jamaspasa and Nawabi 1976a).

1.5.3 F2

395 pages, 9.25 × 11.75 in., 15 lines to the page. An IrPY in two volumes copied by Dastur Sohrabji Kavasji Sohrabji Meherji Rana, F2 dates to Samvat 1870 (1813 CE) (Dhabhar 1923: 1).[41] It features a comprehensive interlinear NP version of the Avestan and MP text. Kept at the *First Dastur Meherji Rana Library*, this is a different MS from the F2 described by Geldner (1886–96: iii). The latter is an Iranian *Xorde Avesta*.

The filiation of F2 has so far not been determined. As my apparatus shows, F2 frequently agrees with the readings of the IrPY, but due to the limited data collected here this is not a reliable measure on its own. Two other features of F2, however, clearly point towards a close relationship with the IrPY. Firstly, F2 agrees with the IrPY MSS R413 T6 in abbreviating PY 35.1, 35.4 and PY 37, the latter also abbreviated by E7. Secondly, and more significantly, at the end of each *hāiti* F2 records the number of stanzas and lines of the *hāiti*, a feature of the IrPY not shared by K5 J2 M1.

In order to substantiate Geldner's view that the Iranian MSS surpass the Indian ones in correctness, Dhabhar (1949: 11) lists 25 exemplary differences between Mf4 KS and K5 J2. Compared to these, F2 reveals only one clear agreement with the InPY: ⟨...⟩ in PY 46.6c. In PY 19.6, F2 has ⟨...⟩ in favour of InPY ⟨...⟩ as opposed to IrPY ⟨...⟩. Likewise, in PY 42.2 it departs from IrPY ⟨...⟩, reading ⟨...⟩ in dependence from InPY ⟨...⟩. F2 offers a possibly independent reading ⟨...⟩ in PY 11.4 as opposed to IrPY ⟨...⟩ and InPY ⟨...⟩. In the remaining 21 cases F2 agrees with Dhabhar's examples from the IrPY. Of these, five are not exactly identical with the readings of Mf4 KS, but clearly descend from them. A similar view also emerges from a comparison of F2 with data provided by Geldner (1886–96: xxviii–xxix) for Avestan. Of 36 exemplary disagreements between Pt4 Mf4 and K5 J2, F2 agrees 28 times with the IrPY and only 8 times with the InPY.

1.5.4 R413

919 pages, 31.5 × 20.7 cm, 13 lines to the page. A facsimile of this manuscript was published in two volumes by Jamaspasa and Nawabi (1976e).[42] According to its colophon, R413 was completed in A.Y. 1204 (1835 CE) by Burjor Pahlan Peshotan Ratanji Sohrab Peshotan Limji Meherji.[43] Jamaspasa suggests that R413 is a copy of Mf4 and that it reproduces Hōšang Sīyāwaxš's preface. This preface, however, seems to be missing in the facsimile volume.

---

[41] The manuscript has been indexed and published by Circassia and Kangarani (2011).

[42] (P)Y 5 appears in vol. 17, and the (P)YH in vol. 18.

[43] In his introductory notes to the facsimile, Jamaspasa refers to pp. 917–19 for the colophon (see Jamaspasa and Nawabi 1976e). But in the facsimile the colophon appears on pp. 913–15.

Contrary to Jamaspasa, I believe this manuscript to be either a direct copy from F2, or to share its ancestor, as a number of its readings and peculiarities agree with F2. Among these the irregular division of the Avestan text in both MSS in PY 38.3 stand out (see Section 16.3.1). The *Zand* of line (a) is missing both in F2 and R413. While this section is given in the margins of F2, it is missing in R413 entirely. This indicates that rather than being copied from Mf4, R413 must have been copied from F2 before the missing text was added in the margins of F2. R413 follows F2 also in a number of other readings in PY 38.3: ⟨'p'ryk⟩ vs. ⟨'p'rykc⟩ of the other MSS, ⟨šwsl⟩ vs. ⟨Y šwsl⟩, *huuapaŋhā̊* and a missing ⟨BYN⟩ in PY 38.3c. Similarly, both F2 and R413 share a number of significant readings and omissions in PY 38.5. For example, in line (a) parts of the *Zand* are missing both in F2 and R413.[44] In line (b), both MSS omit ⟨'dwn' Y 'wlwl⟩, and prefer ⟨whšyt⟩ to ⟨whšyhyt⟩. In the same line, there are also a number of less significant agreements between the two manuscripts, such as in ⟨ZK Y⟩ versus ⟨ZK⟩ and in an omitted ⟨Y⟩. Furthermore, in PY 41.3a and PY 5.2b R413 follows F2 in writing ⟨ycBḤWN-⟩ rather than ⟨YDBḤWN-⟩. In PY 5.5b, F2 has as opposed to the expected . Following F2, it seems, R413 has . Obviously, the incorrect spelling of ⟨hwrdt⟩ was noticed and corrected, possibly sec.m., while no correction was made to ⟨'mwrdt⟩.

R413 also shows frequent signs of editorial interventions. For instance, in PY 35.3c, where *kū-š hērbedestān kard ēstēd ud kē an-ašnawāg* is missing, and the Avestan is divided into four sections rather than three: **(c)** *surunuuatascā asurunuuatascā kē-iz ašnawāg kū-š nē kard ēstēd ā-š ēdōn kunišn kū-š bīm nēst* **(d)** *xšaiiaṇtascā axšaiiaṇtascā kē-iz pādixšā kē-iz a-pādixšā*. R413 also shows signs of scribal carelessness. In PY 35.3 ⟨MY'⟩ is followed by ⟨W w'stl⟩ but then struck out. See also PY 35.6b-c for some more divergences. Similar errors and differences are found in other *hāiti* of the YH as well.

1.5.5 T6

296 folios, 11.9 × 9.5 in., 13 lines to the page. T6 is an IrPY with extensive NP interlinear glosses and occasional marginal notes in NP.[45] Kept at the *First Dastur Meherji Rana Library*, it has been described by Dhabhar (1923: 109).[46] T6 has two colophons. The first (fol. 5v–8v) is in MP and reproduces that of Hōšang Siyāwaxš's codex. As already observed by Dhabhar (1923: 109), it is not copied from Pt4 but most likely from Mf4. On fol. 8v, for instance,

---

[44] F2 reproduces the missing text in the margins.
[45] The abbreviated Y 37, the stanzas 39.4–5, 41.5–6 and the formulae at the end of the YH do not have any NP glosses.
[46] T6 has been indexed and published by Andrés-Toledo (2010).

T6 reads *ud rēš ud škēn ō ruwān nē be rasēd ō tan* which is missing in Pt4 but present in Mf4. More importantly, this first colophon (fol. 8v) contains a postscriptum, dating the original MS, presumably Mf4, to A.Y. 1149 (1780 CE).[47] The scribe, who copied the original manuscript in Nawsari, India, is identified as Dastur Kavus son of Dastur Sohrab son of Dastur Rostam son of Dastur Manak son of Mehrnush descendant of Mahyar Rana.

The second colophon, located at the end of the MS (fol. 295v), is in NP and identifies the scribe of T6 as Mowbed Sohrab son of Dastur Faramarz son of Dastur Sohrab son of Dastur Rostam from the line of Dasturan Dastur Mahyar Rana. The date of completion is written out as 1011 (1642 CE), but given as 1211 (1842 CE) in numerals above the word ⁀ 'year' without any correction marks. The correct date, however, must be A.Y. 1211, for this MS cannot be older than the MS it was copied from, which is dated 1780 CE. Dhabhar (1923: 109) accepts 1211 as the correct date.

1.5.6 E7

870 pages, 14.9 × 9.2 in., 10 lines to the page, featuring wide vertical space between the lines, perhaps intended for interlinear glosses which are not present. An IrPY in two volumes, Dhabhar (1923: 65) describes E7 as a copy of Hōšang Sīyāwaxš's codex without dating the MS. Jamaspasa considers it a copy of Mf4 and describes the paper as bearing the watermark 'Charles and Thomas – London 1865' (Jamaspasa and Nawabi 1976b).[48] Neither author mentions a colophon, but E7 reproduces Hōšang Sīyāwaxš's preface with divergences that make a direct connection with Pt4 or Mf4 rather difficult. Overall, E7 offers readings that are close to Pt4. In PY 39.4a, for instance, E7 agrees with Pt4 Mf4, K5 M1 on ⟨MND'M⟩, while F2 R413 T6 prefer ⟨MND'M Y LK⟩. In PY 39.4b, where Pt4 has ⟨Z̶K̶ 'w'⟩, E7 is the only MS that incorporates Pt4's struck out ⟨ZK⟩ in the main text. All other MSS have ⟨'w'⟩. In Pt4, Y 41.2c was left out by the scribe who added it as a subscript insertion immediately following line (b) (Figure 1.4). As a result the *Zand* of line (b–c) occur together and are not separated by the Av. text. E7 takes this scheme up and divides this stanza into (a) and (b–c).

Compared to R413, E7 seems to be a more precise manuscript and stands out among the MSS of the present study for its many divergences from the text of the PY. Some of these differences may be due in part to the relative modernity of E7, where variants could have been consolidated into an alternative reading. Such may be the case in PY 35.2a. Of all the collated

---

[47] See also Dhabhar (1949: 6).
[48] The watermark is not visible in the facsimile edition, but I have taken this date as a *terminus post quem* for E7. The manuscript may of course be of a later date.

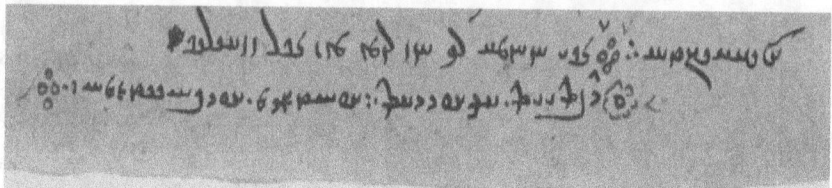

Figure 1.4 (P)Y 41.2b–c in Pt4

MSS, E7 is the only manuscript that includes the expected ⟨'whrmzd⟩ within the text itself: ⟨'whrmzd⟩ Pt4 (superscr.) F2 (in marg. sec.m.) T6 (in marg.) E7; deest Mf4 R413, K5 J2 M1. Likewise the variants ⟨mynwmc⟩ and ⟨MND'M-c⟩ in PY 35.2b consolidate in E7 to ⟨ZNH MND'M-c mynwmc⟩: ⟨mynwmc⟩ Pt4; ⟨mynmc⟩ Mf4, J2; ⟨MND'M-c⟩ F2; ⟨mynmc⟩ R413, K5 M1; ⟨MND'M⟩ T6 (mynym superscr.); ⟨MND'M-c mynwmc⟩ E7.

E7 also introduces variants which are not found elsewhere. In PY 35.2c, E7 reads ⟨YḤBWN-'nd ZK Y L YḤBWN-yt⟩ in contrast to ⟨YḤBWN-'nd⟩ and ⟨YḤBWN-yt⟩ in the other MSS.[49] A final comment in PY 36.6c appears only in E7 and T6 as part of the text in complete form (see Section 14.5.1). More significantly, E7 includes interpretations, which are known from the NP glosses and commentaries present in MSS such as F2 and T6. In PY 35.3a, F2 and T6 gloss Av. *adāiš* with داون آب و خورشن 'giving of water and fodder' and داون آب وعلف 'giving of water and grain', respectively. Likewise, ⟨MY'⟩ is glossed آب و خورشن in F2 and آب وعلف in T6. E7 incorporates this late interpretation in the *Zand* of PY 35.3a: *āb ud xwarišn*. Another instance is the final word in PY 35.3c ܡܘܟܫܢ, which I have read *hammōxtišn*.[50] This addition is not found in any of the other MSS, but allusions to *teaching* are found in the NP glosses in F2 and T6, particularly F2 where *axšaiiaṇtascā* and *a-pādixšā* are glossed از نالایقی آموزنده ست 'it is instructive due to unworthiness'. Such variations could suggest that E7 may belong to a tradition such as the exegetical movement proposed by Cantera and Andrés Toledo (2008).

1.5.7 J2

385/389 folios, 10 ¾ × 8 ¾ in., 15 lines to the page. J2 belongs to the class of the InPY and was copied by Mihraban Kaikhusrow and dated day Vohuman, month Fravardin, A.Y. 692 (26 January, 1323 CE) (Geldner 1886–96: iv). No genealogical information is mentioned in J2's colophon. Kept at the Bodleian

---

[49] E7 does not attest a corresponding phrase in Avestan.
[50] The expected form is *hammōzišn* 'teaching, learning'.

Library, J2 is the oldest extant PY manuscript and was published as facsimile by Mills (1893).[51]

1.5.8 K5

327 folios, 10 ¾ × 8 ¾ in., 17 lines to the page. An InPY, K5 was copied in Cambay by Herbad Mihraban Kaikhusrow Mihraban Spendad Mihraban Marzban Bahram in Samvat 1379 (17 November, 1323 CE) (Geldner 1886–96: vi). According to the colophon, K5 is a copy of a now lost manuscript by the scribe's great great uncle, dated by Geldner (1886–96: xxiv) to about 1270 CE. K5 was first published in Copenhagen and later reprinted by Nawabi (1978).[52] Due to its better state of preservation compared to J2, I have given K5 precedence in my apparatus.

1.5.9 M1

This InPY is kept at the *Königliche Hof- und Staatsbibliothek*, Munich (Geldner 1886–96: x).[53] According to the colophon, it was copied in A.Y. 1103 (fol. 766r), 1734 CE, by Mowbed Kavus son of Dastur Fereydun (son of) Dastur Bahman Bahram Faramarz (fol. 765v) in Surat, India (fol. 766v). M1 is a transcript and a very exact copy of K5. As the apparatus of the present edition shows, only rarely does M1 disagree with K5. Two strong agreements, for instance, are found in PY 5.6 (Appendix A.1.6). In PY 5.6a, K5 and M1 have ⟨QDM 'w' 'LH⟩ as opposed to just ⟨QDM⟩. And in PY 5.6b these two MSS have ⟨cyk'mc-D cyk'mc-HD L'WHL *ati* cyk'mc-HD⟩, while other MSS only have ⟨cyk'mc (H)D cyk'mc-HD⟩. A minor disagreement appears in PY 37.5a where M1 has ⟨ycm⟩ versus ⟨YDBHWN-m⟩ in K5. The only significant difference between K5 and M1 within the YH is in the division of the MP translation in PY 39.3. In contrast to the other MSS (Section 10.3), M1 has:

(a) *āt iϑā yazamaidē vaŋhūšcā īt vaŋᵛhīšcā īt* ∵ *ān ī ēdar ēdōn yazom weh nar ud weh mādag*
(b) *spəntāŋg aməšāŋg yauuaējiiō yauuaēsuuō* ∵ *ān ī amahraspandān kē abzōnīg hēnd ud amarg hamē zīndag ud hamē sūd*

---

[51] My collation is based on the facsimile, but I also consulted the original in February 2009 at the Bodleian Library. An online version of J2 has been published by Ferrer (2012). J2 is not in a good state of preservation. When no other variants were to be noted, I have silently suppressed the damaged readings in J2, if enough was legible to guess or assume the word.
[52] (P)Y 5 is in vol. 56, and the (P)YH in vol. 43.
[53] M1 has been indexed and published by Ferrer (2010).

(c) yōi vaŋhə̄uš ā manaŋhō š́iieiṇtī yā̊scā ⁺uitī ∵ kē pad wahman mānend pad frārōnīh ud kē-iz ēdōn wahman ā-š yazom

1.6 MANUSCRIPT FILIATION

For more than a century, manuscripts of the *Avesta* have been largely studied in the context of the Avestan text transmitted therein, most prominently by Geldner (1886–96) in his *Prolegomena*, but also by Humbach (1973), Hoffmann (1969) and Hoffmann and Narten (1989). The resulting lack of data for the Pahlavi version of the *Yasna* makes a broader examination of its written transmission difficult. Kellens (1998) highlights the shortcomings of Geldner's *Prolegomena*, but does not examine the Pahlavi or Sanskrit text of the bilingual MSS. Cantera, building on Kellens (1998), has further scrutinised Geldner's (1886–96) edition in a series of articles, lectures and material published on his website.[54] Yet, despite advances made in this area, Geldner's proposed filiation for Pt4 Mf4 as IrPY, and K5 J2 M1 as InPY seems to remain valid (see Cantera 2011).[55] Likewise, I have accepted Geldner's general scheme as a guideline for this study.[56]

Manuscripts designated as IrPY in the present edition, Pt4 Mf4 F2 R413 T6 E7, share two distinct characteristics: the inclusion of Hōšang Siyāwaxš's preface and the recording of the number of stanzas and lines at the end of each *hāiti*, a feature not found in the MSS of the InPY, K5 J2 M1.

Within the class of the IrPY two subgroups can be distinguished. Broadly speaking, Pt4 and Mf4 form one group, their close relationship having already been observed by Geldner (1886–96: xi). The more recent manuscripts form a second group, for they exhibit variations that do not appear in Pt4 and Mf4. These differences, however, are not consistent among all the MSS of the second group, as can be seen in the case of E7 (Section 1.5.6). It is also noteworthy that of all the manuscripts only F2 and T6 consistently provide NP interlinear glosses for both the Avestan and the MP text. Considering the vertical space between the lines in these manuscripts, it is safe to assume that they were added at around the same time as the MSS were copied.

Beside the main characteristics of the two classes mentioned above, the MSS of the IrPY and InPY reveal a number of other differences. Ignoring a wide range of spelling errors, the IrPY always prefers ⟨YMRRWN-⟩ while

---

[54] See http://ada.usal.es.

[55] Dhabhar (1949: 1–8) examines the Pahlavi content of the bilingual MSS, but he too relies on Geldner's categories of Ir vs. InPY.

[56] It would be premature to discuss manuscript filiation based on data collected in this study, which is by definition limited to the PV of the YH. Distinguishing features of a manuscript may not be distributed evenly among all *hāiti* of one manuscript. In one MS we may find a concentration of errors within the text of the YH, but not in its other *hāiti*.

the InPY persistently reads ⟨YMLLWN-⟩ (PY 35.2b, 35.8a, 36.6a and 40.1a). In PY 35.7b the IrPY reads ⟨kt'l⟩ in contrast to ⟨kt'lc-HD⟩ of the InPY. In PY 41.2b, the MSS of the InPY have *huxwadāy* for Av. *huxšaϑrastū*, while all MSS of the IrPY have *ohrmazd*. But the differences are not always consistent across the classes (see Section 13.2.4). An illustrative example is PY 35.8a, where we find ⟨gwbšnyh⟩ Pt4 Mf4 E7; ⟨gwbšnyh Y⟩ F2 R413, J2; ⟨gwbšnyh L⟩ T6 and ⟨gwbšn' Y⟩ K5 M1. The best reading is ⟨gwbšnyh⟩ of Pt4 Mf4 E7 without the *ezāfe*, which allows us to render the following *Ohrmazd* as vocative in agreement with the Av. original. Although the IrPY provides the better reading, the variants cross families.

The flexibility of the scribes is best demonstrated by the variations in dividing Y 35.6.[57] In Y 35.6a all MSS agree in the wording and length of the Pahlavi section, *ān ī ohrmazd yazišn ud niyāyišn ēdōn az ān ī ašmā pahlom menom*, which corresponds to *ahurahiiā zī aṯ vō mazdā̊ yasnəmcā vahməmcā vahištəm aməhmaidī*. The Av. text, however, is divided differently across the manuscripts. Pt4 E7, K5 J2 M1 have *ahurahiiā zī aṯ vō mazdā̊ yasnəmcā*, while Mf4 F2 have *ahurahiiā zī aṯ vō mazdā̊ yasnəmcā vahməmcā*. However, the *Zand* also translates *vahištəm aməhmaidī* ' *pahlom menom*'. This discrepancy is addressed in R413 T6, where Y 35.6a reads **(a)** *ahurahiiā zī aṯ vō mazdā̊ yasnəmcā vahməmcā vahištəm aməhmaidī*, synchronising the Avestan text with its PV. Thus, two late MSS correct an error, which was only partially addressed in Mf4 F2.

To sum up, K5 and J2 are copied by the same scribe in the same year (1323) and are thus of an older date compared to the so-called Iranian MSS. M1, a considerably younger manuscript (1734), is a very careful copy of K5. The situation of the IrPY is more complicated. Based on the variant readings collected in this study, I propose the following filiation for the manuscripts of this family:

- Pt4 (1780)
  - E7 (1865)
- Mf4 (1780)
  - F2 (1813) R413 (1835) T6 (1842)

---

[57] Here, I ignore the variant readings of individual words and give the Av. text of this stanza in normalised form after Hintze (2007a: 86).

2. *The Zand*

Man sollte doch endlich einmal aufhören, das alte, seit 1630 bestehende Vorurtheil zu wiederholen, als ob die Parsen von ihren heiligen Schriften nichts mehr verständen. ... [W]arum vollends unter den Sâsâniden die érânischen Priester ihre Religionsbücher nicht verstanden haben sollen, ist gar nicht einzusehen, damals, als die theologische Gelehrsamkeit viel galt und eine beträchtliche Anzahl von Priestern die Pflicht und die Mittel hatten, eingehenden Studien obzuliegen.

Spiegel (1882: 588)

The term *zand* 'commentary, explanation' (MacKenzie 1990: 98), refers to the Pahlavi version (PV) or translation of the *Avesta*, which is for most part found in the bilingual manuscripts.[1] Its perceived proximity to the *Avesta* is best reflected in the oft-repeated term *abestāg ud zand* '*Avesta* and *Zand*'—a fixed expression in the MP literature that led early scholars into erroneously using *Zand* as the name of the Avestan language (Haug 1878: 67ff.).

The frequent references to *dēn* or *abestāg* in MP literature, in phrases such as *čiyōn az dēn/abestāg paydāg* 'as it is revealed in the *dēn/abestāg*', highlight the canonical scripture's importance to the composers of the texts and may allow for the categorisation of a vast amount of the MP literature as ongoing, albeit second order interpretations of the *Avesta*.[2] Commentaries on the *Avesta* are found, for example, in Book 9 of the *Dēnkard*. The Zoroastrian interpretive tradition, however, is not limited to the MP material. The Sanskrit translations (STr.), commonly ascribed to *Neryosang*, Gujarati and

---

[1] For a detailed discussion of the meaning of *zand* and its scholarly reception, see Cantera (2004: 1–13).
[2] *dēn* is commonly held to be a reference to the Zoroastrian religion. Tavadia (1956: 36) seems to use *dēn* and *abestāg* interchangeably: 'Die Quelle, *dēn* oder *apastāk*, war ursprünglich nur in einer alten, toten Sprache, der Awestasprache, vorhanden.'

New Persian commentaries and translations of the *Avesta* represent other strands of this tradition. In particular, the Av. interpretation of the *yaϑā ahū vairiiō*, *aṣ̌əm vohū* and *yeŋ́hē hātąm* texts, often referred to as prayers, in Y 19–21 indicates that the exegesis of the *Avesta* was extant already in Old Iranian times.

2.1 EARLY RESEARCH

Lawrence H. Mills was one of the first to embark on a critical edition of the complete PY.[3] In his edition of the five *Gāϑās*, Mills (1892, 1894) included the Pahlavi, Sanskrit and New Persian translations of the Avestan text, and offered both a commentary and dictionary.[4] He went on to publish other chapters of the PY in a series of articles in various journals between 1890 and 1914.[5] The collated text of PY 1 was published in Mills (1903), its translation in Mills (1904) and subsequently as a monograph in 1910. This edition included the Avestan, Pahlavi, Sanskrit and New Persian texts in transliteration, as well as translation. Mills (1906) also published the collated PY 1 in Pahlavi script with variant readings, but without transliteration and translation.[6] He continued to edit 51 of the 72 chapters of the *Yasna*, including the *Gāϑās*.[7] It seems, however, that he was unable to continue the publication of the *Yasna* in dedicated monographs. While some of the titles of his various articles suggest that the Pahlavi text of the *Yasna* is collated from manuscripts, an opening footnote at times alerts the reader to the omission of the variant readings due to space limitation (see Mills 1903).

As regards the *Zand* in general, Parsi priests and scholars made valuable contributions to its study early on. Among these, the works of Dhalla (1908, 1918), Unvala (1924) and Dhabhar (1927, 1949, 1963) stand out for their high scholarly standard.

Asli (1918) offers a brief and general overview of the *Zand*, examining a few exemplary passages. Although he claims to maintain a balanced view, his introductory presentation of Iranian history is one-sided and reflects the impact of the academic debate between the *Traditionalist* and *Vedic* schools on Parsi scholarship in India.[8] Asli views the PV as indispensable

---

[3] For a particularly useful overview on previous research, see Josephson (1997) with references.
[4] I was unable to find any reliable bibliographical information on vol. 3, which was supposedly published in 1902.
[5] For a bibliography of Mills's work on the PY, see Gropp (1991: 79).
[6] This work is not listed in Gropp's bibliography of Mills.
[7] These numbers are based on Gropp's (1991) bibliography with the addition of articles not listed by him.
[8] The *Traditionalists* believed that the *Zand* was a helpful tool in the interpretation of the *Avesta*, while the *Vedic* school emphasised the value of the comparative linguistic method. Cantera (2004: 44–65) discusses this debate in some detail.

to a better understanding of the *Avesta* and attributes 'errors' in the *Zand* to the 'incompleteness of the Pahlavi grammar' and the many glosses to the 'linguistic difficulty' in dealing with the poetic character and language of the *Avesta* (Asli 1918: 113, 114).

The significance of the *Zand* for a continuous interpretive tradition within Zoroastrian priestly scholarship is best signified by Punegar (1943). Explaining a selection of Avestan words from Y 38.5, he interprets the waters described therein as a metaphor for bodily hormones. This interpretation of the Avestan stanza is clearly based on the passage's *Zand* (see Section 16.3.2).

Kanga (1975) published the Pahlavi commentary on the *aṣ̌əm vohū* prayer in transcription, translation and original. He also published the *Zand* of the *Spəṇtā Mainiiu Gāϑā* with a transcription, translation and a reproduction of the text based on Dhabhar's (1949) edition (see Kanga 1976). He uses a slightly outdated method to transcribe the Pahlavi passages and his edition of the texts is not accompanied by a commentary or manuscript readings.

Recent linguistic research on the *Zand* includes the work of Klingenschmitt (1969, 1971, 1972, 1978). With the critical application of philological methods to the MP version of single passages, he directs attention to the value of these texts for research on the *Avesta* and argues that these translations can effectively aid in the interpretation of difficult passages. Klingenschmitt, however, does not offer an edition of any text.

Three of the shorter Avestan-Pahlavi bilingual texts, *Vaeϑā Nask*, *Pursišnīhā* and *Ērbedestān*, were edited and published by Humbach and Jamaspasa (1969), Humbach and Jamaspasa (1971)[9] and Humbach and Elfenbein (1990), respectively. Examining the Avestan and Pahlavi versions of Y 30.3–4 and Y 45.2, Humbach (1996) stresses the importance of the study of the *Zand* for a better understanding of the development of the Zoroastrian religion through the Sasanian era. He considers the *Zand* to be a 'word-to-word translation' of the *Avesta*, believing that the simplified morphology and the rigid word order of the MP language hindered the production of a reliable translation (Humbach 1996: 259). The *Hērbedestān* (vol. 1) and *Nērangestān* (vols 2–4) have also been edited by Kotwal and Kreyenbroek (1992, 1995, 2003, 2009).

The *Niyāyišn* and the *Srōš Yašt* are the subject of two essentially lexicographic studies by Taraf (1981) and Dehghan (1982). The significance of both works lies in the inclusion of the texts' Pahlavi and Sanskrit translations. Pointing out the importance of historical-comparative linguistics, Taraf suggests that these translations could serve as a secondary aid in approaching Avestan. The Avestan, Pahlavi and Sanskrit texts, however, are not critically

---

[9] For a review of this study, see MacKenzie (1972).

constituted by means of manuscript consultation. Both Taraf and Dehghan follow Geldner (1886–96) for Avestan, Dhabhar (1927) for Pahlavi, and Bharucha (1906) for the Sanskrit passages. The German translation of the Avestan passages in both studies is based, with minor modifications, on Wolff (1910). Taraf notes that her translations of the Pahlavi and Sanskrit passages are literal. Dehghan does not translate the Pahlavi and Sanskrit passages and uses established dictionary definitions in his glossaries. In both studies the philological commentary is followed by three tri-lingual glossaries.[10] The earliest date Taraf and Dehghan agree upon for the compilation of the Pahlavi translations is the late Sasanian era, possibly even post-Sasanian, in Dehghan's view. Both authors consider MP's simplified morphology a handicap to translating the highly inflected Avestan and suggest that various Pahlavi translations are erroneous due to misunderstandings or false etymologies.

Unlike Dehghan, Kreyenbroek (1985) does not confine himself to Y 57 but also examines Y 56–57, Yt 11, including their *Zand*, as well as passages in the wider Pahlavi literature dealing with *Sraoša*. While no critical manuscript readings or glossaries are provided, Kreyenbroek offers three rich commentary sections with his translation, including variant readings when required. In other chapters Kreyenbroek outlines the development of the figure of *Sraoša* in Av. and MP literature.[11] As Malandra (1987) points out, a closer study of the relationship between the *Avesta* and the *Zand* must have been outside the scope of Kreyenbroek's work.

Josephson (2003) has selectively discussed the PV of the *Gāϑās*. Among recent Parsi scholars, Ichaporia (2003) has paid attention to the PY. Recent reviews of the STr. of the *Yasna* include studies by Degener (1991) and Humbach (2003).

2.2 MARGINALISATION OF TEXTS

As Crosby (2005) highlights, the choice of source material that is translated in the course of scholarly engagement with a religion significantly impacts the faith's academic representation and reception. She asserts that the neglect of a large body of scripture undermines academic research and teaching. Discussing Theravada-Buddhism, she argues that nineteenth-century romanticism and the Victorian preference for a religion that was both ethical and rational-scientific played a crucial role in determining which Buddhist texts would be translated by European scholars. Texts that did not mirror

---

[10] Dehghan follows Hoffmann in transcribing the Avestan text, but oddly follows Bartholomae (1904) in the glossary.
[11] For a review of Kreyenbroek's study, see Sundermann (1987) and Malandra (1987).

scholars' expectations were ignored and dismissed as later developments or even corruptions.¹² A similar development is evident in the study of Zoroastrianism and its textual sources.

The first European scholarly work on Zoroastrianism is held to be Thomas Hyde's *Historia religionis veterum persarum eorumque magorum*, published in 1700.¹³ The significance of Hyde's work lies in his attempt to use primary source material, in this case the *Sad Dar*, and to evaluate Arabic sources on Zoroastrianism as opposed to Greek reports (Stroumsa 2002: 219).¹⁴ Although Hyde's turning to the faith's source material constituted a break from past traditions, the freshness of his approach soon faded for two chief reasons. Firstly, he remained traditional by embedding Zoroastrianism within the Abrahamic tradition.¹⁵ Secondly, Anquetil-Duperron's (1771) *Zend-Avesta* superseded Hyde's work by introducing the *Avesta* to Europe.¹⁶ As we know today, Anquetil-Duperron did not directly translate from Avestan, but used the *Zand* for translating the *Avesta* with the aid of his Parsi teachers (Cantera 2004: 38). Thus, although the study of the *Zand* marked the beginning of the scholarship on Zoroastrianism, in the coming centuries scholars paid marginal attention to this corpus of texts.

Various factors have contributed to the neglect of groups of texts in Iranian studies. A romantic notion of Zaraϑuštra as the founder of the religion and the assumption of an authorial intention may have been among the factors that facilitated the disregard of particular texts.¹⁷ In Iranian studies, scholars considered, among others, the PV of the *Avesta* to be farther removed from the assumed founder's original composition. The YAv. sections of the *Avesta* shared a similar fate. In some scholars' views, these texts represented a corrupt version of an originally lofty message which was no longer understood. While it is justified to distinguish and characterise stratified texts on philological grounds, their neglect based on an assumed authorial intention deprives religious studies of texts pertaining to a faith's development.¹⁸

The YH is a good example of a text that was neglected for decades, despite early recognition of the similarity between its language and that of the *Gāϑās*.

---

¹² Bronkhorst (2011) makes a similar observation, which I discuss at the end of Section 2.3.
¹³ See Cantera (2004: 35) and Stausberg (2008: 562). For an appraisal of Hyde's work, see Stroumsa (2002).
¹⁴ According to Stroumsa (2002: 226–7), Hyde invented the term *dualismus* to translate *thanawiyya* from Arabic.
¹⁵ See Stroumsa (2002: 230) and Stausberg (2008: 562).
¹⁶ For more on this, see Stroumsa (2002: 216, 219) and Cantera (2004: 36–9).
¹⁷ For a history of the European reception of Zaraϑuštra, see Stausberg (1998).
¹⁸ The rejection of the author's intention as a paradigm of literary interpretation is shared by schools of literary criticism such as *explication de texte*, *New Criticism* and *post-structuralism* (Nünning 2004: 36). Roland Barthes, for instance, rejects the idea of texts being an 'expression of an intention' (Schmitz 2007: 126) and instead focuses on the reader who will invent the intention of the text as he reads and interprets it.

However, since its content was not ascribed to the *Gāθic* community or dated to that time, it was deemed inferior (see Haug 1862: 161). Thus, in his *Brief Survey of Zend Literature*, Haug (1862: 219) states:

> Next to the Gâthas in rank stands the 'Yasna of Seven Chapters' [...]. From reasons pointed out above, we cannot regard it as a genuine work of Zarathushtra Spitama himself. It appears to be the work of one of the earliest successors of the prophet, called in ancient times *Zarathushtra* or *Zarathushtrôtema* [...], who, deviating somewhat from the high and pure monotheistic principle of Spitama, made some concessions to the adherents of the ante-Zoroastrian religion by addressing prayers to other beings than Ahuramazda.

Haug (1862) rejects the YH in his revolutionary attribution of the *Gāθās* to Zaraθuštra. Other scholars seem to have followed his judgement. The fascination with Zaraθuštra as a prophet and author is apparent in most of the scholarly writings of the nineteenth and at times even the twentieth centuries. Ragozin's (1889) assessment of the *Yasna Haptaŋhāiti* is a particularly illustrative example.[19] Ragozin portrays the founder figures of religions as exceptional humans ahead of their time with pure and lofty messages, which are subsequently reinterpreted and altered beyond recognition for the sake of their followers' 'average minds' (Ragozin 1889: 109). Quoting Mills (1887: 281), Ragozin (1889: 109–10) uses the YH to describe the process of decline with regard to the original author's message:

> 11. 'With the "Yasna of Seven Chapters,"' remarks the same scholar, 'which ranks next in antiquity to the Gâthas, we already pass into an atmosphere distinct from them. The dialect still lingers, but the spirit is changed.' The fact is that all history shows how impossible it is for any religion or doctrine to maintain itself on the level of absolute loftiness and purity on which it was placed by the founder or reformer. *He* is one man in a nation, above and ahead of his time, his race, nay, mankind in general; so are, in a lesser, [sic] degree, his immediate followers, his first disciples. But the mass of those who learn from him and them – the herd – is composed of average minds, which, after the first enthusiasm has cooled and the novelty has worn off, feel but ill at ease on an altitude that makes too great demands on their spiritual powers. [...] Then begins the work of adaptation; the new religion is half unconsciously fitted to the old; there is a gradual revival of ancient ideas, ancient poetry, ancient forms and usages – and scarce a lifetime has elapsed after the reformer has passed away, when his work is changed beyond recognition, and the doctrine and practice of those who still call themselves his followers, have become a medley of what he taught and the very things against which he rose in protest. Still, *on the whole*, there is real progress: the new spirit remains, the standard has been raised, and a new step taken towards the ideal – a step which can never be retraced.
> 12. Of this process of adaptation the collection of prayers in Gathic dialect, set apart in the body of the Yasna-liturgy under the name of 'Yasna of Seven Chapters,' offers a striking illustration, though it is of course impossible to surmise how long an interval

---

[19] For another such example, see the Introduction in Mills (1887).

separates them from those older Gathas which may be said to embody the Zoroastrian Revelation. Set forms of invocation and a regular working ritual, presupposing a strictly organized class of priests, have gathered round the substance which alone engrossed the prophet; his abstract speculations have become greatly materialized, and the allegorical forms of speech in which he but sparingly indulged have crystallized into personifications solid enough to start a new myth-development.

The Pahlavi versions of the *Avesta* are another example of neglected texts in Iranian studies. Philological predilections of the nineteenth and twentieth centuries were certainly among the most important factors that led to the disregard of the *Zand* as an academic subject, for its study was abandoned soon after its usefulness in promoting a better understanding of the *Avesta* was questioned. As outlined by Josephson (1997: 12–13) and Cantera (2004: Ch. 2), the debate between the *Vedic* and the *Traditional* schools regarding the *Zand*'s value to the study of the *Avesta* determined its fate on a philological level.[20] Moreover, MP is linguistically less relevant to the study of the older layers of Indo-European languages and attracts less attention from Indo-Europeanists than Old Persian or Avestan (Klingenschmitt 2000: 196).

The scholars' preferential treatment of the *Gāθās* as original compositions was also variously taken up by the Zoroastrian community. Such a view is reflected, for instance, in the preference for a 'return to the *Gāθās*' which is more prominent among Iranian Zoroastrians and converts. These groups often reject the authority of ritual texts such as the *Wīdēwdād* and its Pahlavi version, which have come to be regarded as inferior texts and obstacles to the process of religious innovation.

Thus, despite its enormous significance as an exegetical tradition, the *Zand* has come to play a peripheral role in the study of Zoroastrianism and is often regarded as a complementary discipline to Avestan studies. The value of the *Zand*, however, does not lie in its linguistic contribution to the understanding of the *Avesta*, but in its mere existence as a specimen of an interpretive tradition. Without a closer examination of its content and its relationship with the wider Pahlavi literature, our understanding of Zoroastrianism in late antiquity will be incomplete.

2.3 PERCEPTIONS OF THE *ZAND* IN IRANIAN STUDIES

Spiegel (1860) offers one of the earliest descriptions of the *Zand*,[21] strongly arguing throughout that the *Zand* be viewed as an auxiliary tool in the

---

[20] The course of events in the twentieth century that led to further neglect of the *Zand* by philologists has been discussed by Josephson (1997: 13–17).

[21] See also his grammar of MP, Spiegel (1856), where he variously discusses passages from the Pahlavi translations.

study of the *Avesta*, while acknowledging that the translations also had their limitations. He was likely one of the first to depict the Pahlavi renderings as slavish ('knechtisch') and word-by-word (WBW) translations (Spiegel 1860: 26ff.). Despite his efforts to integrate the Pahlavi translations into *Avesta* studies, he accords almost no relevance to the *Zand* for investigations of Zoroastrian hermeneutics (Spiegel 1860: 67).

In his balanced evaluation of the *Zand*, *Zur Beurtheilung der traditionellen Uebersetzung des Avesta*, Hübschmann (1872) too views the *Zand* as relevant for the study of the *Avesta*. He remains neutral in the debate between the *Traditional* and *Vedic* schools, suggesting that while explaining the *Avesta*, the *Zand* should be compared with the *Avesta* itself and Sanskrit (Hübschmann 1872: 640):

> Die Wahrheit wird, auch hier, in der Mitte der Gegensätze liegen, und die Methode wird die richtige sein, die der Tradition einen im Ganzen nicht geringen Werth beilegt, und wenn sie von ihr bei der Erklärung des Avesta ausgeht, vor Allem das Avesta selbst und dann besonders das lexicalisch und grammatisch so wichtige Sanskrit als Hauptcorrective der Tradition benutzt.

Hübschmann (1872: 642–3) is widely known for another statement which has been taken up by many scholars. He posits that the Pahlavi *Wīdēwdād* (PWd) offers the most fruitful material for the study of the *Avesta*, though less so the PY, and argues the Pahlavi *Gāθās* are virtually of no relevance:

> Die Ausbeute wird freilich eine verschiedene sein: reich für den Vendidad, befriedigend für den jüngern Jasna, aber dürftig für die Gathas, deren Verständniss, dem allerdings grosse Schwierigkeiten entgegenstehen, gewiss früh schon verloren ging, woher es denn kam, dass die Uebersetzer, vom Sinn nicht geleitet und der Grammatik unkundig, eine bis auf Einzelnheiten unbrauchbare Uebersetzung lieferten, der gegenüber Roths Urtheil viel treffender als Spiegels ist.

Along with Spiegel (1860), it is Haug's (1878: 338) following description of the *Zand* that has had a lasting influence on its scholarship:[22]

> The Pahlavi versions of the Avesta throw but little light upon the obscure passages in the original text, which are generally rendered by a slavishly literal translation, or even transliteration, with some faint attempt at explanation, more or less unfortunate in its result. The chief value of these versions consists in the longer commentaries which are often interpolated, especially in the Vendidad. They also indicate how the original Avesta was understood in the later Sasanian times, and how it is understood by the present Dasturs, who rely almost entirely upon the Pahlavi version.

Although Haug recognises the value of the glosses or commentaries, it is striking how little agency he awards to the translators themselves. His

---

[22] Haug, it seems, published different revised editions of his book. An earlier edition, namely Haug (1862), possibly the first edition, does not contain this passage.

judgement of the *Zand* as being a 'slavishly literal translation' has been accepted by most scholars. Following Haug, Taraf (1981), Dehghan (1982), Humbach (1996), Kreyenbroek (1996, 1999), Ichaporia (2003), Cantera (2004: 240), Macuch (2009b) and Malandra and Ichaporia (2010) all agree that the *Zand* represents a word-by-word translation.[23] These scholars also consider the simplified morphology of MP and its rigid word order an impediment to translating the *Avesta*.

In an assessment of the Pahlavi *Gāθās* (PG) Bang (1890) offers a surprisingly fresh overview of the *Zand* and its relationship with Avestan. Within the philological debates of the nineteenth century, Bang's position as a *Traditionalist* emerges from his admittedly mild polemic against the *Vedic* school. He accounts for the limitations of the *Zand* but emphasises its historical importance as a didactic tool for the Zoroastrian priesthood. He asserts that if carefully approached, the *Zand* could still function as intended, namely as a tool to be used in conjunction with the *Avesta* to aid in better understanding its language. He further suggests consulting the Sanskrit translations for help with difficult passages. As a proof of concept he examines Y 28.1–4.

West (1896–1904: 84) describes the *Zand* of each *book* of the *Avesta* separately and notes that the PY comprises 39,000 words. He goes on to state:

> It contains no long commentaries and very few short ones; but in other respects the word-for-word Pahlavi translation is arranged in the same way, with interspersed glosses, as that of the Vendidad.

Agreeing partly with Haug (1878), Tavadia (1956: 39) describes the *Zand* as consisting of a slavish WBW translation and comments engaging with these translations. Tavadia also agrees with Hübschmann's (1872) assessment with regard to the quality of the *Zand*:

> Diese bestehen 1. aus einer sklavischen Wort-für-Wort-Wiedergabe des Awestatextes, 2. aus erklärenden, d. h. entweder dem Satz zustimmenden oder ihn ablehnenden Bemerkungen und 3. aus kürzeren oder längeren Kommentaren als Ergänzungen zum Gegenstand der einzelnen Abschnitte.

Klíma (1959) offers a particularly negative account of the *Zand*, describing it as a mere guess-work and proposing that Avestan was no longer understood by the translators. He finds that the translations together with the comments are largely unintelligible:

> Sie sind in die awestischen Handschriften so eingegliedert, daß nach einem awestischen Abschnitt (*lemma*) eine fast immer buchstäbliche, aber eben deshalb häufig

---

[23] Degener (2000) seems to share this view as well.

ungenaue und unklare Übersetzung folgt. Deshalb erklären die Übersetzer oft manche Ausdrücke durch zusätzliche *Glossen*, die aber manchmal den Sinn überhaupt nicht beleuchten. Bisweilen ist die Übersetzung zu frei. Viele Wörter wurden nicht mehr richtig verstanden. Ein großer Anstoß für die Übersetzer bestand darin, daß sie sich in der awestischen Wortbiegung und Syntax nicht genügend auskannten und daß sie den Satzsinn lediglich zu erraten versuchten. (Klíma 1959: 35)

Kreyenbroek (1996: 225) suggests that the *Zand* embodies an attempt to preserve through translation a substantial text in a sacred language only 'half-understood'. He goes on to state:

> As is well known this was achieved by a process of word-for-word translation, which nearly always used the same Middle Persian word for an Avestan one – or indeed for clusters of sounds which seemed similar to it [...] – and showed a certain disregard for the syntactical differences between the two languages. (Kreyenbroek 1996: 225)

In an article on exegesis in the Zoroastrian tradition, Kreyenbroek (1999) describes the *Zand* as a mechanical translation in which the nuances of the original were lost:

> [...], the finer shades of meaning of the original must have been lost quite early – a situation which paved the way for the adoption of a system of translation, only conceivable in a non-written tradition, whereby each Avestan word [...] was rendered by one Middle Persian term. The original Avestan word-order was usually preserved in spite of the wide differences between the two natural languages in this respect.

Recent descriptions of the *Zand* are included in the work of Tafazzoli (1997), Macuch (2009b) and Malandra and Ichaporia (2010), who agree in essence with what I have discussed so far. It appears that most scholars concur in their assessment of the *Zand* as an attempt to translate Avestan by means of a WBW rendering of the original, without considering the different syntax of the two languages.

Shaked's (1996) close reading of the Pahlavi text of Y 28 shifts away from such judgements and represents a fresh approach to the *Zand*. He regards the *Zand* as an interpretive approach to the *Avesta* and concludes that most of the translations are legitimate even if compared with modern philological paradigms:

> Most of the translations occurring in the Zand are perfectly correct, or at least as acceptable philologically as our own. [...] It is a work of interpretation, and it uses various techniques for reading the Gāthās in the light of the most important questions of Zoroastrian outlook and theology. This is an approach to scriptures employed in various civilizations. (Shaked 1996: 649–50)

A century after Mills's pioneering work on the PY, Josephson (1997), focusing on the *Zand* of the *Hōm Yašt*, offers the first modern, critical edition of the PV of an Avestan text.²⁴ In her examination, Josephson (1997: 18) attempts a fresh interpretation of the *Zand* by going 'beyond the statement that the Phl. translation is a word for word rendering of the original' and makes the Pahlavi translation techniques the subject of a study for the first time.²⁵ She offers an overview discussing the grammatical relationship between the source and target languages (pp. 120–52). Josephson concludes with a set of balanced observations on various aspects of the PV of the *Hōm Yašt* (pp. 153–65). She argues that the exegetes had a far more profound understanding of the source language than is commonly assumed. A shortcoming of her work, however, is the elimination of the Pahlavi comments from the text of the Pahlavi *Hōm Yašt*. Her study is not only a corrective to previous scholarship, but has helped in revitalising the study of the *Zand* as a discipline in its own right. It opened the way for further examinations, best represented by Cantera's philological analyses of issues such as chronology, dating, composition and transmission, as well as translation techniques of the Pahlavi *Wīdēwdād*. In a study of a select number of words, Josephson (1999) went on to examin the translators' methodology in determining the meaning of Avestan words (see Section 20.1). This remains the only work dedicated to the study of semantics in relation to the *Zand*.

Based on the study of grammatical forms found in the PWd, Cantera (1999a) argues for an older age of the language of the PWd as opposed to the so-called Book Pahlavi. He also discusses the relationship between the PY and PWd by examining the Pahlavi translations of OAv. quotations in the PWd (see Cantera 2006). The most comprehensive modern work on the *Zand* in general has been carried out by Cantera (2004).²⁶ In detailed surveys he deals with issues such as the meaning of the term *zand*, the history of Avestan studies with regard to the PWd, the transmission of the *Avesta* and issues of dating and the technique of the Pahlavi translations.²⁷

It emerges from the above outline that a large portion of the previous research has been focused on the translation techniques or the linguistic study of the *Zand*. Even Cantera's (2004) investigation of the texts' composition and transmission remains faithful to the linguistic methodology.²⁸ While the judgement of the scholars as to the *Zand*'s quality of translation may vary in detail, they mostly investigate the quality of the *Zand* or its significance for

---

[24] Beside Mills, who dedicated several articles to the PV of this text, an early attempt to compile a critical edition under consideration of both the Sanskrit and the *Zand* was undertaken by Unvala (1924).
[25] For a review of this study, see Cereti (1998), Cantera (1999b) and Degener (2000).
[26] For reviews of this work, see Mayrhofer (2005), Vaan (2007), Skjærvø (2008a) and Zeini (2008). For a brief discussion of some aspects of his work, see Section 20.1 and 20.5.
[27] Cantera's edition of the Pahlavi *Wīdēwdād* has not been published, though his dissertation is available from his website (see Cantera 1998).
[28] See Sections 20.1 and 20.5.

the study of the *Avesta*. Such assessments are particularly problematic, as the exegetes did not approach the *Avesta* with the same linguistic paradigms and knowledge as the modern scholar.

More than a century and a half after Spiegel (1860: 67) denied the relevance of the *Zand* for the study of Zoroastrian hermeneutics, the matter still awaits elucidation and almost no attempts have been made to relate the body of texts commonly referred to as *Zand* to the wider context of other MP texts and the *Avesta*. We have to ask ourselves how relevant the *Zand* was for the Zoroastrian priests of late antiquity in dealing with issues of their time. To answer these questions, I will look at the context in which the *Zand* and the PYH stand rather than the linguistic quality of the translations. In doing so, I follow the paradigm of the *invisible interpreter*, promoted by the indologist Bronkhorst (2011). He argues against measuring ancient texts and foreign cultures with the gauge of modern scholarship. In a brief discussion of *Yāska's Nirukta* and the grammar of *Pāṇini*, he states that modern scholarship has mostly illuminated those aspects of these works that resonate with the scholars' own questions, neglecting to study these witnesses as texts in their own right (Bronkhorst 2011: 36). In his view, such approaches 'domesticate' ancient or other cultures by pretending, for instance, that *Pāṇini* was a philologist in the modern sense (Bronkhorst 2011: 37). According to Bronkhorst, the same applies to Indian philosophy or ancient history. To minimise domestication or its opposite, namely cultural relativism, he makes a rather simple recommendation: 'The general rule should however be clear: the more contextual information we provide, the less we domesticate the foreign culture by adapting it to our own' (Bronkhorst 2011: 42). Thus the aim of the invisible interpreter is not objectivity of research. Rather, the invisible researcher will attempt to present ancient works in their own context as much as possible.

As such, the quality of the MP translations and the process of translation are not the main concerns of the present study. In Chapter 3, I argue that a vast number of MP texts, including the *Zand*, take a scholastic approach to the *Avesta*. To do so, I utilise Cabezón's (1994, 1998) framework of a decontextualised scholasticism. In my translation of the PYH I seek to mirror the complex and difficult language of the *Zand*, rather than superimposing a literary translation on a text which was never meant to be a literary rendering of the *Avesta*. My commentaries reflect on context whenever possible. In Section 13.2.5, for instance, I suggest that even difficult translations such as *mard ō mard* are firmly embedded in a long-standing tradition of exegesis. I have also attempted a preliminary investigation of the legal relevance of some of the translations (Sections 15.1.6 and 15.1.7).

3. Scholasticism

> When nothing could be composed any more in the ancient language, of which even the learned priests had only an imperfect understanding, the Avesta could still undergo change and adaptation by using the instrument of *Zand*.
>
> Shaked (2003: 73)

Any expression of thought, be it religious or otherwise, inadvertently provokes the act of interpretation or exegesis. Religious traditions in particular interpret their sacred literature so as to sustain the contemporary relevance of their scriptures. Such commentaries are often produced by generations of exegetes, resulting in stratified texts. Different religious traditions have dealt differently with the transmission of the source texts and their exegesis, partly under the influence of external factors or technological innovations. Printing, for instance, substantially changed the face of the talmudic manuscript page. While the manuscripts only carried the text of the Talmud, already the earliest printed Talmud, dated 1483, included two different commentaries in the margins (Fram 2005: 91). In subsequent decades the page of the Talmud became more complex and accommodated different strata of commentaries and references.

Zoroastrian priests sought to make Avestan texts comprehensible to their contemporaries by adding Middle Persian translations and sporadic comments to the source texts. That the *Zand* was considered comprehensible and more widely understood emerges from the accounts of the *Avesta*'s transmission in *Dēnkard* and from a passage in ZWY (see Section 3.7). Although the *Zand* could have been initially transmitted orally, it has come down to us in bilingual manuscripts of Avetsan texts, where they are at times accompanied by interlinear translations or commentaries in the margins of the manuscripts in a third language such as Persian.

Western scholars acknowledged the *Zand*'s worked up and stratified nature early on, which may have contributed to its recognition as exegetical literature:[1]

> [W]e should especially claim for the renderings that they are a mass of overworked material, which, of course, rather heightens than lowers their value to the close expert, for the more numerous are the strata of consecutive treatments, the keener becomes our hope of the gems of antiquity. (Mills 1900: 290)

Exegesis, however, is not limited to canonical religious literature and covers a wider spectrum of phenomena. Interpreting the meaning of his name, the Rastafari *Howard Anthony Trott* offers a particularly illustrative example of religious exegesis that is not motivated by scripture:[2]

> I cyaah even tell yuh of my name because tru di carryin aweh into captivity wi get some different kind ah name weh nevah really originally belong to us. These are name given to our parents in slavery now, yuh know wha i mean? So wi don't know if 'Howard' mean hard life, how hard; 'Anthony': how hard and stony; 'Trott': i trod. Trod mean run or walk, trod. So hear weh i name: how hard, how hard, how hard and stony i trod!

In order to locate himself within the wider Rastafari world-view, Howard associates his name with Rasta vocabulary through similarities in sound. Scholars have often pointed out assonance and homophony as the cause for etymological translations in the *Zand* as well.[3] Thus, irrespective of motives and object of interpretation, exegetical traditions seem to share some aspects of methodology. However, the question of exegetical methodology has largely been ignored in Iranian studies. Shaked's and Josephson's (1999) works are noteworthy exceptions. Shaked (1996), for instance, examines the PV of Y 28 as an exegetical text in its own right, also comparing it with exegesis in Jewish and Islamic traditions (see Chapter 2). In a later publication, Shaked (2003: 73) offers an innovative view on the function and importance of the *Zand* for the Zoroastrian tradition:

> When nothing could be composed any more in the ancient language, of which even the learned priests had only an imperfect understanding, the Avesta could still undergo change and adaptation by using the instrument of *Zand*.

In recent years, Vevaina (2010a, 2012) has pioneered the study of Zoroastrian exegesis, particularly by examining MP texts such as the *Dēnkard*. Seeking to illuminate Zoroastrian exegetical principles, Vevaina (2010a: 118) describes the *Dēnkard*'s 'schematizing' of the 21 *nasks* of the *Dēnkard Avesta* in light

---

[1] See also the Introduction in Mills (1910).
[2] The quote is from Howard's opening voice over in 'Die Reise des Löwen', a 1992 documentary directed by Fritz Baumann.
[3] See, for instance, Klingenschmitt (1969: 993).

of the *yaϑā ahū vairiiō* as an 'epistemo-hermeneutical' project.[4] By assuming a new perspective grounded in theories of scholasticism, I hope to further contribute to the debate on exegesis in Zoroastrianism, and elucidate a better understanding of the religious and cultural milieu from which these texts emerged.

A widely noted feature of scholasticism is its tendency to harmonise inconsistencies found in textual material. Within medieval scholasticism, and more generally philosophy of the Middle Ages, this tendency is the result of the philosophers' attempts to reconcile Christian theology and doctrine with the newly rediscovered 'intellectual heritage of antiquity' (Kenny and Pinborg 1982: 11).[5] Cabezón (1998) observes similar efforts in other religious cultures.

On the surface, the Medieval scholastic methodology closely resembles the manner of commentary we find in the *Zand*: *scholium*, denoting a note on a passage, often in the margins; *gloss*, a short paraphrase of a passage, frequently found above the line and *literal commentaries*, which follow the phrasing of the original text as closely as possible and introduce paraphrases, i.e. glosses, with *quasi diceret* 'as if he were to say'.[6] But these general similarities, however apparent they may be, do not suffice to qualify the *Zand* as scholastic. Inspired by ancient Greek philosophy, particularly logic, medieval scholasticism has its origins in Christianity.[7] Bowker (1997: 866), for instance, defines it as a 'Christian intellectual movement'. Thus, like many other terms in the study of religions, *scholasticism* foremost describes a specific phenomenon linked to Christianity. As a deeply Christian philosophical and theological methodology, scholasticism as a term cannot be casually borrowed to analyse other traditions and must be adapted to the new context. Historically, European medieval scholasticism emerged out of monasticism, a practice that never developed in Zoroastrianism. Though medieval scholasticism is grounded in a specific historical and religio-cultural context, if recast carefully it can offer a useful framework for studying other cultures.

Cabezón (1994, 1998) has been a persuasive advocate for the application of scholasticism as a cross-cultural category in the study of religions. He argues that a process of 'abstraction and decontextualization' is required before the term can be used comparatively (Cabezón 1994: 11), a process already started

---

[4] Vevaina (2010a) anticipates many results of my investigation into scholasticism and correlative structures. However, his work is based on different theoretical models. For a brief discussion of Vevaina's work, see also Section 3.8.

[5] According to Pieper (1978: 24–40), already Boethius suggested that reason should be connected with faith, thereby defining one of the hallmarks of medieval philosophy. On medieval philosophers' tendencies to harmonise, see also Kenny and Pinborg (1982: 18, 30).

[6] Ebbesen (1982: 102) gives a brief overview of the devices at the disposal of both late ancient and medieval scholiasts.

[7] On the links between medieval scholasticism and its antecedents, see Marenbon (2010).

by the French philosopher Paul Masson-Oursel in his essay *La scholastique* from 1920 (Cabezón 1994: 13). Valuable contributions have been made by Henderson (1991) in a by now classic study of the Chinese commentarial traditions. Cabezón (1994) himself showcased the process of abstraction in his examination of Tibetan Buddhism, establishing eight characteristics for scholasticism as a cross-cultural category. He conveniently summarises those in a later publication (Cabezón 1998: 4–6):

1. Strong sense of tradition
2. Concern with language
3. Proliferativity or textual inclusivity
4. Completeness and compactness
5. Epistemological accessibility of the world
6. Systematicity
7. Rationalism
8. Self-reflexivity

Scholasticism is often associated with canons and commentaries, leading to definitions limited to one specific trait of scholasticism, namely its 'preoccupation with the exegesis of canonical texts' (see Cabezón 1994: 212).[8] On that account, the *Zand*'s proximity to the *Avesta*, of which it offers an exegesis, makes the *Zand* a strong candidate for the title scholasticism. Cabezón's definition of scholasticism, however, goes beyond this one feature. In his view, preoccupation with exegesis is a consequence of a strong *sense of tradition* and just one of the eight characteristics of scholasticism. By examining select passages in light of seven of the categories, I shall show how far the *Zand* and other MP texts qualify as scholastic literature.[9]

Despite strong links between religious exegesis and scholasticism, the secondary literature on Zoroastrianism does not consider the *Zand* within such a framework. Mills (1900: 288) was perhaps one of the first to recognise the scholastic qualities of the *Zand*, when he referred to the Pahlavi commentators as 'scholiast'. When the terms *scholasticism* and *scholastic* are invoked at all in Iranian studies, it is primarily in a general sense, conveying a notion of commentary, and no attempts have been made to qualify the texts as scholastic literature.[10]

---

[8] Cabezón's observation relates to points made by Henderson (1991), but see also Henderson (1998: 163).

[9] I have not included *rationalism* in this study, as it needs further investigation reserved for an upcoming article.

[10] For example, in the four chapters on *Persian philosophy* in the *Companion encyclopedia of Asian philosophy* (Carr and Mahalingam 1997) we only find 'Magian scholastics' (Boyce 1997a: 1) and 'scholasticism' (Williams 1997: 21) in two side remarks. Skjærvø (2010c) has used the term 'scholastic literature' in the title of an article where he investigates several particles frequently found in the *Zand*. More recently, Secunda (2012) has used the term 'scholastic generations' in his dating of the Sasanian sages.

While the *Zand* is the primary focus of this study, it cannot be its only subject, for the *Zand*'s closeness to the *Avesta* defines its scope and context. The *Zand* foremost offers a rendering of the Av. texts; most of the additional comments in the *Zand* are concerned with an interpretation of that rendering. Valuable as the *Zand* is as a primary witness to Zoroastrian exegesis, by definition it lacks general religious discourse. Since the vast majority of the extant MP texts are religious literature, it will be in these works where we must search for further context that will facilitate the appraisal of the Zoroastrian tradition as a whole. This is not to say that each MP work will be evaluated as if it were scholastic in nature. Rather, the wider MP literature will be consulted for a better understanding of the *Zand*'s likely historical context. In doing so, the assumption is made that the MP literature as a whole contains earlier ideas while the texts' composition or redaction might be of a later date, in-so-far as they are datable.[11]

3.1 STRONG SENSE OF TRADITION

Tradition refers to identity as defined by a sense of belonging to a religious community and sharing its history, but can also extend to include priestly schools and lineages (Cabezón 1998: 4). As Cabezón rightly observes, a strong identification with a tradition will often result in a commitment to its preservation. As such, the very existence of the *Zand* demonstrates the exegetes' commitment to preserving the textual sources of their religious tradition, namely the *Avesta*.

A commitment to one's own tradition manifests itself in phrases that invoke the authority of the *Avesta* or the *dēn*. These abound in MP texts: *pad weh dēn ōwōn paydāg* 'It is evident in this manner in the good religion' (Bd 1.1), *az abestāg paydāg* 'It is evident from the *Avesta*' (PRDd 17d12, Purs 6). Such phrases serve multiple purposes. They underline the cited statement's authority and authenticity, but also serve to show that the priestly engagement with matters of religion is based on a traditionally accepted wisdom, namely the *dēn* or the *Avesta*.

We also note a preoccupation with priestly schools and lineages in passages where the opinions of exegetes are recorded. These are more commonly found in the *Zand* of various Avestan passages. Although the primary sources do not mention any distinct priestly schools by name, rough contours of affiliations are visible in the texts.[12] A more explicit testimony to the

---

[11] Shaked (1994: 6) takes a similar approach to dates and content of MP literature. For a history of MP literature, see Boyce (1968a) and Macuch (2009b).
[12] For the most recent discussion of named priests and their dates, see Secunda (2012) with references.

Zoroastrian sense of lineage is found in Bd 35A, a chapter dedicated to the genealogy of priests (*dūdag ī mowbedān*).[13]

In a discussion of the transmission and perception of religious tradition within ninth-century Pahlavi literature, Bailey (1943: 149–76) highlights the term *paywand* 'connection' as an epitome of Zoroastrian religious tradition. Bailey (1943: 149) substantiates his view by the STr. of MX 26.12, where *paywand* is translated *āmnāya*, 'sacred tradition, sacred texts handed down by repetition' in the dictionary of Monier-Williams (1899: 147). Bailey also cites Iranian loanwords in Armenian to the same effect. In his view, *paywand* and the verb *paywastan* 'join, connect' (from **pati* + **band* 'to bind'), which he translates 'transmit, hand down' (Bailey 1943: 149), signify the perceived continuity of the religious tradition on the part of the Zoroastrian priests.[14] Thus, when the transmission of the *Avesta* and its *Zand* are discussed in Dk 8.6.1, it is the verb *paywastan* that denotes transmission (see Bailey 1943: 167): ⟨Pahl.⟩ *zand ō amā rāy nē paywast* 'The *Zand* of ⟨Pahl.⟩ has not been handed down to us', or literally 'the *Zand* of ⟨Pahl.⟩ did not connect to us'.[15]

A similar notion of uninterrupted connection and transmission is also conveyed by the MP term *pōryōtkēš* '(one) of the first teachers of the Mazdean religion', which is often translated 'ancient sages'.[16] MP *pōryōtkēš* derives from Av. *paoiriiō.ṯkaēša-* 'primordial teaching' and thus continues a Zoroastrian literary convention, whereby authority and tradition are maintained by reference to ancient sages. In Dk 6, for instance, their authority is invoked in order to assert the importance of the traditional interpretation, which is ascribed to these sages:

Dk 6.C26[17] *ēn-iz ēdōn kū zand kār ud dādestān juttar nē gōwišn ud kunišn ud rāyēnišn čiyōn ān ī pōryōtkēšān [guft ud] kard ud čāšt ud ul āwurd čē-š ahlomōγīh pad-iš ō gēhān āyēd kē zand kār ud dādestān juttar čāšēd ud gōwēd ud kunēd čiyōn ān ī pōryōtkēšān guft ud kard ud *čāšt ud ul āwurd*

This too is thus: One should not speak, do or arrange the business of Zand differently from what the original orthodox [spoke,] did, taught and brought forth. For heresy comes to the world by one who teaches, speaks or does the business of Zand differently from what the orthodox spoke, did, taught and brought forth.

---

[13] For the text, see Pakzad (2005: 407–9). It is noteworthy that the priestly genealogies in Gujarati continue this tradition.

[14] Central to his view is again MX 26.12, where he translates *ham paywand* 'precisely the whole tradition'. This translation, however, is questionable. See the translation of *ham-paywandīh* as 'kinship' by Shaked (1979: 336), which seems more likely. But this has no implication on Bailey's overall reasoning, particularly as his translation of the verb *paywastan* is appropriate.

[15] For the passage, see Madan (1911: 681) and Sanjana (1916: 11). Cantera (2004: 14) reads ⟨Pahl.⟩ as *waxtar* and posits a derivation from Av. **vaxəδar-* as opposed to Av. *vaxəδra-* 'prayer'.

[16] See, for instance, Zaehner (1975: 20) and Shaked (1979: 353).

[17] Text and translation after Shaked (1979: 154–5).

The authors of such counsels represent themselves as the legitimate heirs of ancient sages, whose tradition they continue and protect. And in this way, a direct line of priestly transmission is established that links the traditional interpretation, namely the *Zand*, to the beginnings of the Zoroastrian community. As such we witness the construction of a priestly tradition that traces its own origins back to Zardušt in the *Zand* of the *Yasna* and the *Yasna Haptaŋhāiti* too.

Within the PYH, the 1sg. possessive pronoun *manīgān* 'mine, my people, my followers' occurs twice, translating the Av. hapax legomenon *mauuaiϑīm* 'worthy of someone like me':[18]

PY 40.1c *kē mizd ō manīgān frāz dahē ān ō dēnīgān abāyed dād ohrmazd*
PY 41.5c *ē mizd ī ō manīgān frāz dahē ān ī ō dēnīgān abāyed dādan ohrmazd*

The above passages do not specify which group of people *manīgān* denotes. However, *manīgān* occurs a number of times in the PY, variously translating dat. 1sg.pers.pron. *maibiiācā* 'me' in PY 28.7b, 28.8b, 49.8c; dat. 1sg.pers.pron. *maibiiō* in PY 31.4c, 48.8b; dat. 1pl.pers.pron. *ahmaibiiācā* 'us' in PY 28.6c,[19] and finally the adj. *mauuaitē* in PY 46.7a.[20] In all of these passages, the exegesis explicitly links *manīgān* with disciples (*hāwištān*). In PY 31.4 and 46.7, for instance, *manīgān* is explained as *hāwištān ī man* 'my disciples'. That the association between *manīgān* and *hāwištān* extends to PY 40.1, emerges from PY 7.24c, a paraphrase of PY 40.1c:

PY 7.24c *kē mizd ō manīgān frāz dahē ān ī ō dēnīgān*[21] *ohrmazd ān ī ō*[22] *manīgān hāwištān ī man abāyēd dād ē*[23] *ō-iz man dah*

Which prize will you give to my people? That which must be given to the religious ones, O *Ohrmazd*, that which is for my people, (namely) my disciples, may you give (it) also to me.

A brief analysis of the remaining passages will allow us to view PY 40 in a larger context. In PY 48.8 the poet wonders about the right reverence which will enable his disciples to receive the prize from *Ohrmazd*: *kadār ēd ī tō tarsagāhīh kē az tō manīgān ohrmazd kū hāwištān ī man ā-šān mizd padiš rasēd* 'Which is this your reverence by which my people, that is my disciples, will

---

[18] On *mauuaiϑīm*, see Hintze (2007a: 289ff.) with references. For a brief note on *manīgān*, see Skjærvø (2010a: 208).
[19] *ahmaibiiā* is also attested in PY 40.3 where it is translated *ō amā*.
[20] *mauuaitē* also occurs in PY 44.1, translated as *amāwandīh* 'strength'.
[21] سنوسیدم Pt4.
[22] سلدوم Pt4.
[23] ام Pt4.

receive the prize from you, O *Ohrmazd*?'. And in PY 28.7, it is the post of high-priesthood that the poet wishes for his disciples:

PY 28.7b[24] *u-m dahē tō spandarmad ān ī az wištāsp xwāhišn mowbedān mowbedīh ud manīgān-iz hāwištān ī man ā-šān mowbedān mowbedīh dah*

And give to me, you *Spandarmad*, that which is to be asked of *Wištāsp*, (namely) high-priesthood, and also to my people, (namely) my disciples, give them high-priesthood.

We also find mention of disciples of disciples, reminiscent of PY 35.1 and the debate in *Pursišnīhā* 18 (Section 13.2.5). The most relevant reference of this kind is in PY 28:

PY 28.8b[25] *ohrmazd ā-m pad xwāhišn windēnē mard ī frašōštar kū-m frašōštar pad hāwištīh be dahē ud manīgān-iz frašōštar ā-š hāwištīh dah*

O *Ohrmazd*, you cause me to find through desire the man who is *Frašōštar*, that is, you give me *Frašōštar* as a disciple, and also my people, (that is), give *Frašōštar* disciples.[26]

We can thus establish that *manīgān* refers to the poet's disciples and that the poet wishes high-priesthood and disciples for his disciples. The concern for the well-being of disciples and priestly succession is best expressed in PY 28.8c:

PY 28.8c *ō-iz awēšān ēg rād hē hamē tā ōy*[27] *wisp pad wahman kū frašōštar ud hāwištān ī frašōštar tā tan pasēn hamē nēkīh padiš kun*

Through *Wahman* you are then generous to them too, always until all; that is, always exercise goodness for *Frašōštar* and the disciples of *Frašōštar* until the future body.

It is significant that goodness is requested for the disciples of *Frašōštar* until the end of the tangible existence (*hamē tā ō wisp* and *tā tan pasēn*). It therefore seems plausible to suggest that the text refers to successive Zoroastrian priests and disciples who will follow *Frašōštar*. If so, the text considers every Zoroastrian priest to be a descendant of *Frašōštar*, who was a disciple of Zardušt, the founder of the religion. In this way, the exegetes construct their own heritage and priestly tradition which they trace back to Zardušt, his favourite disciple *Frašōštar* and king *Wištāsp*. As Cabezón mentions, a strong sense of tradition is one of the predominant features of a scholastic tradition. In this case, the *Zand* functions as a tool by which the

---

[24] Text after Pt4. See also the translation by Shaked (1996: 653).
[25] Shaked (1996: 653) translates this line differently.
[26] In PY 49.8 too, *manīgān-iz* is glossed *hāwištān ī frašōštar*.
[27] Pt4 has *ōy*, but we expect *ō* in this expression, which is further discussed in Section 5.7.3.

exegetes define their own ancestry in the closest possible proximity of the scripture, which underlines the authority of their claim.

And it is certainly not mere chance that in a small collection of counsels ascribed to ancient teachers of the religion, *čīdag handarz ī pōryōtkēšān* 'selected counsels of ancient sages', the knowledge of one's own religious belonging and genealogy is recommended to those who reach the age of 15:

> ČHP[28] *pōryōtkēšān ī fradom dānišnān pad paydāgīh ī az dēn bē guft estēd kū harw mardōm ka ō dād ī 15 sālag rasēd ēg-iš ēn and tis bē dānistan abāyēd kū kē hēm ud kē xwēš hēm ud az kū mad hēm ud abāz ō kū šawēm ud az kadām paywand ud *tōhmag hēm u-m čē xwēškārīh ī gētīy ud čē mizd ī mēnōy ud az mēnōy mad hēm ayāb pad gētīy būd hēm ohrmazd xwēš hēm ayāb ahreman [. . .] u-m dēn kadām*

> The ancient sages of primordial knowledge have said in accord with the religion that everyone who reaches the age of 15 must then know these things: 'Who am I and to whom do I belong? And where have I come from and where will I go to? And from which family and lineage am I, and what is my duty in the *gētīy* and what the reward of *mēnōy*? And did I come from *mēnōy* or was I (already) in the *gētīy*? Do I belong to *Ohrmazd* or *Ahreman*? [. . .] And what is my religion?'

The detailed answers, omitted here for reasons of space, identify the individual as a supporter of *Ohrmazd*. In Dk 6.D9 we find a shorter and more distilled version of the above passage, this time ascribed not to the ancient sages (*pōryōtkēšān*), but to a particular one, namely *Ādurbād*:

> Dk 6.D9[29] *ham ādurbād rāy gōwēnd kū-š guft kū harw kas bē abāyēd dānistan kū az kū āmad hēm ud čim ēdar hēm ud abāz ō kū šawēm ud man pad bahr ī xwēš dānēm *kū az ohrmazd ī xwadāy āmad hēm ud a-pādixšāy kardan ī druz rāy ēdar hēm ud abāz ō ohrmazd šawēm*

> They say concerning the same Ādurbād that he said: Every person ought to know: 'Where have I come from? For what purpose am I here? Where do I return?' I, for my part, know that I came from Ohrmazd the Lord, that I am here so as to make the demons powerless, and that I shall return to Ohrmazd.

Here too, one's religious tradition, purpose and identity are clearly defined.

3.2 CONCERN WITH LANGUAGE

Scholastic engagement with language can take place on three levels: language as scripture, which is the source for scholastic speculation; language as the medium of expression; and language itself as the object of examination (Cabezón 1994: 193–4). He also points out that such concern for language

---

[28] Text after Jamasp-Asana (1897: 41).
[29] Text and translation after Shaked (1979: 184–5).

might express itself in form of preoccupation with proper social or ritual behaviour (Cabezón 1998: 5).

The significance of good speech (*hūxt*) is often pointed out in MP literature in connection with good thoughts (*humat*) and good deeds (*huwaršt*). But to what extent does the literature engage with language as defined by Cabezón? The *Zand* as transmitted in the multilingual MSS of the *Avesta* is an indisputable witness to the engagement of the Zoroastrian priests with language as scripture. In these manuscripts, the Avestan source text is divided in small units of text, which are followed by a rendering in one of the target languages, be it Pahlavi, Sanskrit, New Persian or Gujarati. In all target languages the close rendering of the Av. units is at times followed by a paraphrase or an explanatory note. The division of the Av. sections into cola, which are rendered into a target language and then further explained, shows the extent of the exegetes' concern with language as scripture, the meaning transmitted thereby and the precision of the translation. In PY 35.1a, for example, we find a rather difficult translation of Av. *humatanąm hūxtanąm huuarštanąm iiadacā aniiadacā* 'Of good thoughts, good words, good deeds both here and elsewhere' into Pahlavi: *humatān hūxtān huwarštān ka ēdar dahišn u-š pad-iz ī ān ī any dahišn* 'Of good thoughts, good words (and) good deeds, when (in) this creation, and also in that which is the other creation, that is, goodness comes from it here and also there'.[30] The relationship between Av. *iiadacā aniiadacā* and its corresponding PTr. *ka ēdar dahišn u-š pad-iz ī ān ī any dahišn* is obscure at best. However, the intended meaning of the clause is clarified by the following *kū-š ēdar ud ānōh-iz nēkīh aziš* 'that is, goodness comes from it here and also there'. Although the hermeneutics behind such comments may ultimately remain unclear, they bring us one step closer to the intended meaning of the preceding translation. In such passages, which abound in the *Zand*, we witness the exegetes at work. First an attempt is made to render the Av. section into a literal Pahlavi, which often, but not always, follows the word order of the source. If the result is unsatisfactory or difficult to understand, the exegetes add an explanation, which might represent the traditional and transmitted interpretation of the passage. One may conclude that the translation is kept literal on purpose, suggesting that the *Zand* was partly intended as a didactic tool. The comments are then added, we could argue, to preserve meaning where necessary. Cantera (2004: 244–53) observes that in some cases disagreements between commentators are recorded in the comments. In his view, these are due to differing interpretations of the Av. grammar by the exegetes.

---

[30] For a commentary on this passage, see Section 13.2.1.

Moreover, except for the Pahlavi *Zand*, which directly relates to the Avestan source, all other target languages also engage with Pahlavi to some extent. It has often been pointed out, for instance, that the Sanskrit translation is based on the Pahlavi version of the *Yasna*, while traces of an engagement with Avestan are also attested. Some MSS, such as F2 and T6, offer an interlinear rendering in Persian of both the Av. and the Pahlavi versions of the text. It is noteworthy that the Persian translations of the Av. and Pahlavi texts are different and not identical on a WBW level. Finally, in one manuscript, KM7, we find the *Yasna* in a combination of Avestan, Pahlavi and Sanksrit.[31]

An example of language as a medium of expression and philosophical speculation is perhaps found in the *Sūdgar Nask* of Dk 9. This *nask*'s commentaries on the *Avesta* are challenging in that their connection with the source text is rather elusive.[32] These commentaries qualify as examples of the second type of engagement with language, as they are far removed from the original text although explicitly linked to specific *hāitis*. While this *nask*'s content does not showcase philosophical speculation on part of the translators, it shows more generally how language functions as a medium of expression in close connection with scripture.

In the wider MP literature we also find reflections upon language. The MP word *uzwān*, or its metathesized form *zuwān*, denote both language and tongue. Of the tongue and the onslaught of the evil, Ohrmazd states:

> PRDd 3.2[33] *ohrmazd guft kū ēd rāy *čē andar tan ī mardōmān handām ī uzwān arzōmandtar ā ān be ō uzwān pēš rasēd*
>
> *Ohrmazd* said: 'Because in the human body the organ of the tongue (is) the most valuable, then it first comes to the tongue'.

According to Williams (1990: II 122), the significance of the tongue must lie in its ability to utter the holy word (*mānsarspand*), which is variously defined as 'pure praise of the *yazads*' (*abēzag stāyišn ī yazadān* in Bd 26.100).[34] The holy word itself, Williams states, 'is the most effective weapon against Ahriman, and the most efficacious means of healing'. Such notions also emerge from Dk 3.364, a section dedicated to the significance of speech and the tongue or language:

---

[31] KM7 was recently discovered in Iran by Prof. Cantera. Not much is known about this manuscript, except that it is kept at Iran's *National Library*.
[32] For more on the *Sūdgar Nask*, see Section 4.3 with references to Vevaina's work.
[33] Text and translation after Williams (1990: II 7).
[34] See also Dd 39.6: *abēzag stāyišnīh gōwišn yazadān*.

Dk 3.364.1[35] *abar sūd ī az gōwāgīh ō xwēš kardan ud zyān ī aziš az xwēš spōxtan az nigēz ī weh-dēn hād uzwān dād estēd pad abzārīh ī mardōm ō xwēšēnīdan ī padiš wazurg sūd ī az gōwāgīh ud nixwārag ī uzwān ō gōwāgīh kām*

From the exposition of the good religion on the benefits of speech which one ought to make one's own, and the harm that emanates from it which one ought to keep away from oneself: The tongue has been created as a means for the people by which they ought to appropriate the great benefits of speech and the haste of the tongue for the desire of speech.

It seems, the tongue or language are viewed as a tool by which humans can reap the benefits of the right speech. An almost modern definition of speech is finally offered in Dd 39.11, where two functions are attributed to the mouth: speaking (*guftan*) and eating (*xwardan*). While the text shifts away from the tongue as an organ, it defines the purpose of speech more explicitly as communication:

Dd 39.12[36] *čē guftārīh ān ī andarīg xwēšišn ō bērōn-iz *āgāhīh paywandēnēd pad xwardārīh ān ī bērōnīg xwarišn ō andarōn freh zīwišn ī gyān rasēd*

For, speech joins the internal possession with the outside for knowledge, (and) through eating the external food reaches the inside for prolonging life.

Although rudimentary and not further expounded upon, the above passage clearly shows that reflections upon speech and language were not unknown to the Zoroastrian tradition.

3.3 PROLIFERATIVITY

Scholiasts tend to be textually and analytically inclusive, an important characteristic in scholastic traditions that leads to rapid textual growth (Cabezón 1998: 5). Thus, according to Cabezón, the scholastic canon is more likely to include than exclude inconsistent texts. As such, elaborate analysis of scripture (analytical proliferativity) as well as commentary not only serve to reconcile inconsistencies, but also lead to the development of a conceptualised understanding of the underlying tradition (Apple 2009: 18). Most significantly, due to these tendencies scholastic proliferativity becomes a contributing factor in the construction of networks of correspondences or correlative structures, which I discuss in greater detail in Chapter 4.

A number of MP texts display a tendency towards analytical proliferativity. Questions of ritual, for instance, are discussed in some detail in *Nērangestān* with recourse to passages from the *Avesta*. The very detailed responses in the

---

[35] For the text, see Madan (1911: 348) and Dresden (1966: 565). For a translation of the whole section, see Sanjana (1897: 429).
[36] Text and translation (with modifications) after Jaafari-Dehaghi (1998: 166–7).

Dādestān ī Dēnīg are another example of analytical proliferativity, along with the *Zand ī Fragard ī Juddēwdād*, where issues of doctrine are discussed with utmost care, partly by recording the diverging opinions of the priests. Textual inclusivity is perhaps best represented by the *Dēnkard*, where seemingly unrelated texts are compiled (see Chapter 4).

We witness the productive nature of Zoroastrian exegesis also in the *Zand*, most prominently in the long commentaries of the PWd. Although in a different context, Shaked (2003: 73) offers an apt description of the *Zand*'s proliferativity:

> When nothing could be composed any more in the ancient language, of which even the learned priests had only an imperfect understanding, the Avesta could still undergo change and adaptation by using the instrument of *Zand*.

Regardless of how well the priests understood Avestan, for which we have little direct evidence, it is true that the *Zand* became a tool by which the ancient texts could be expanded and perhaps extended to contemporary issues. A particularly illustrative example of such proliferativity is found in Y 9.1, when Zaraϑuštra meets *Haoma*. In this stanza, the exegetes seem to construct new Av. sentences which they incorporate in the commentary on Y 9.1. The Av. version of the passage is not further problematic:

Y 9.1 (a) *hāuuanīm ā ratūm ā haomō upāit zaraϑuštrəm*
(b) *ātrəm pairi yaoždaϑəntəm gāϑāsca srāuuaiiaṇtəm*
(c) *ā dim pərəsaṯ zaraϑuštrō kō narə ahī*
(d) *yim azəm vīspahe aŋhə̄uš astuuatō sraēštəm dādarəsa x^vahe gaiiehe x^vanuuatō aməṣ̌ahe*

(a) At the time of *Hāwan*, *Haoma* approached Zaraϑuštra.
(b) He [Zaraϑuštra] was purifying the fire and reciting the *Gāϑās*.
(c) Zaraϑuštra asked him: 'Who, O man, are you?
(d) (You), who (are) the most beautiful I have seen of the entire corporeal existence, (and) of your own splendid immortal life'.

This stanza's *Zand*, omitted in Josephson's (1997) edition, extends the content of the Av. version by a comment on Zaraϑuštra's question about *Haoma*'s identity:

PY 9.1 (a) *pad hāwan radīh pad hāwan gāh hōm pēš raft ō zardušt*   1
(b) *pad ātaxš-gāh pērāmōn yōjdahrēnišnīh ka-š ātaxš-gāh kāmist šustan gāhān*   2
srāyišnīh ka-š ān ašemwohū sē guft kē frawarānē ō pēš   3
(c) *u-š az ōy pursīd zardušt kū kē mard hē hād nē pad yašt ī fradom bawēd az*   4
pēš paydāg u-š dānist ēn kū hōm ōh rasēd kē mad būd ā-š pursīdan abāyist miϑrō   5
upāit zardušt ān paydāg kū-š šnāxt ēd rāy ān zamān abāg yazadān wēš būd ēstād   6
u-š yazad āšnāgtar bawēd hēnd u-š ēn fragard warm bawēd u-š abāyist rāy abāg   7
hōm ul guft ∵ ast kē ēdōn gōwēd hād ∵ ohrmazd guft ēstād kū harw dō ōh rasēnd   8
ud ka hōm mad bawēd ā-š madan šnāsēd zarduxšt miϑrō ziiāṯ zaraϑuštrəm   9

(d) *kē man az harwisp axw ī astōmand ā-m nēktar dīd hē čē-t ān ī xwēš gyān nēk kard ēstēd ud amarg bād ā-š tan pad frārōnīh amarg kard ēstēd nē ēdōn čiyōn awēšān kē gōšt ī jam jūd u-šān andar tan amarg kard ēstād tā bē az tan harw kas-ēw amarg ∵ amərəza gaiiehe stūna*

1 *pēš*] ~~abar~~ (*pēš* in marg.)
2–3 *ka-š ... srāyišnīh*] in marg.
5 *miϑrō*] 𐭬𐭩𐭲𐭥𐭫; (in marg.: خورشیدی); subscr. below 𐭬𐭩𐭲𐭥𐭫: روی
6 *upāit*] 𐭥𐭯𐭠𐭩𐭲 𐭠𐭯𐭮
9 *zarduxšt*] sec.m. in marg.
9 *miϑrō ziiāṯ zaraϑuštrəm*] sec.m. in marg.
11 *tan*] in marg.
11 *amarg*] *ā amarg*
11 *nē*] *rāy* del., *nē* in marg.
13 *amərəza*] مرگ بی subscr.
13 *gaiiehe*] جان را subscr.
13 *stūna*] از ستیز subscr.

(a) At the morning time, at the *hāwan gāh*, *Hōm* approached Zardušt.
(b) He [Zardušt] was purifying around the fire-stand, when he wished to wash the fire-stand (while) reciting the *Gāϑās*, when he said that *ašemwohū* three times, which (comes) before the *frawarānē*.
(c) And Zardušt asked him: 'Who are you, O man?' That he is not at the first prayer, is evident from the previous. And he knew that *Hōm* may come. He had to ask him, who had arrived, (for) *Mihr* approached Zardušt (too). It is evident, that he [Zardušt] recognised him [*Hōm*], for at that time he had been with the *Yazadān* more and he knew the *Yazad* [*Hōm*] better and he knew this section by heart. And what was necessary, he bespoke with *Hōm*. There is one who says so: 'That is, *Ohrmazd* may have said that both [*Hōm* and *Mihr*] may come. And when *Hōm* has come, he [Zardušt] will recognise him coming. *Mihr* knew Zardušt.
(d) (You), who I view as more beautiful than all the corporeal existence, because your own soul was made beautiful and immortal. That is, his body is made immortal by means of goodness and not thus like those who chew *Jam*'s flesh. And in body they may have been made immortal, until except of body everyone was immortal.

Zardušt is performing a ritual, when he is approached by *Hōm*. When asked about his identity, *Hōm* replies in PY 9.2: *hōm hom zardušt hōm ī ahlaw ī dūrōš* 'I am *Hōm*, O Zardušt, the righteous, death-averting *Hōm*'. The ensuing conversation between the deity and Zardušt in (P)Y 9 suggests that this is their first encounter. For the commentators, however, the question arises as to why the founder of the religion had not recognised *Hōm*, a deity whose plant plays a central role in the *Yasna* ritual.[37] The issue is clarified in a comment in PY 9.1c. The exegetes assert that Zardušt knew that *Hōm* would come (*u-š dānist ēn kū hōm ōh rasēd*), but that he had to ask as he was also expecting *Mihr*. An encounter between Zardušt and *Mihr*, however, is

---

[37] For the *haoma*- ritual and the deity, see Boyce (2003) with references.

otherwise unknown. Thus, following the stanza's *haomō upāit zaraϑuštrəm* (Y 9.1a), the commentators construct a new and otherwise unattested Av. clause, which they adduce as evidence that Zardušt was also approached by *Mihr*: *miϑrō upāit zardušt* 'Miϑra approached Zardušt'.[38] To further support this, an anonymous exegete is quoted to the effect that *Ohrmazd* may have announced to Zardušt that he may be approached by both deities. Moreover, the exegetes assure us that Zarduš had already recognised *Hōm*, for Zarduš had spent enough time with the deities (*ān paydāg kū-š šnāxt ēd rāy ān zamān abāg yazadān wēš būd ēstād*). The extant sources, however, know nothing of a meeting between Zaraϑuštra and *Miϑra*. To make this meeting more plausible, another Av. clause is constructed: *miϑrō ziiāt̰ zaraϑuštrəm* 'Miϑra knew Zaraϑuštra'.[39] Another layer of commentary is added by later exegetes, when ⟨MP⟩ is glossed خوبروی 'beautiful', thus reading the MP as if it stood for خوبروی 'beautiful'. This novel reading is then taken up in various NP interlinear glosses and marginalia in the MSS F2 and T6.[40]

The above passage is a fitting example of scholastic proliferativity as defined by Cabezón. The source text is not only translated, but analysed carefully, whereby perceived curiosities are explained in detail and substantiated by commentaries and new compositions. If these are inconsistent with the scripture (Zarduš meeting *Mihr*), then further commentaries are added, which are in turn substantiated by evidence (*miϑrō ziiāt̰ zaraϑuštrəm*). It seems secondary that the new evidence is not consistent with the rest of the scripture. These newly introduced inconsistencies can trigger other commentaries by later generations or other exegetical schools, in part paving the way for the emergence of complex networks of correspondences.

Late commentaries in NP make the *Zand* and the Av. versions themselves the subject of further analysis, thus continuing the exegetical tradition of the Pahlavi *Zand*.[41] Considering the late dating of the manuscripts F2 and T6, we can conclude that scholastic proliferativity was not limited to one era or exegetical tradition within the Zoroastrian priestly and scribal schools. In the case at hand, this scholastic feature is visible in the approach to scripture across eras and languages.

---

[38] The reading *miϑrō upāit* was first suggested by Skjærvø (2009c: 706).
[39] My translation of *ziiāt̰* as 'knew' reflects the exegetes' understanding of the verb's meaning. For further notes, see Appendix B.
[40] In various MSS *miϑrō* is translated or glossed نو 'appearance'.
[41] F2 and T6 both have extensive marginal comments on *Jam*'s flesh.

3.4 COMPLETENESS AND COMPACTNESS

Cabezón (1994: 79) defines completeness as the viewpoint that 'nothing essential is left out' in scripture and that 'it contains nothing unessential' (compactness), later adding that completeness and compactness relate to soteriological and doctrinal matters (Cabezón 1998: 5). However, to what end would priests consider their religious tradition incomplete with respect to salvation and doctrine? Most religions tend to offer a complete solution to questions and problems they identify with regards to mankind's position in life. It is perhaps more fitting to follow Henderson (1998: 164) in broadening the concept of completeness to include the more general concepts of 'knowledge or truth'. In the Zoroastrian tradition, the comprehensiveness ascribed to the scripture seems to be linked with the category of the *epistemological accessibility of the world*, the assumption that the world is intelligible through knowledge (Cabezón 1998: 5).

3.5 EPISTEMOLOGICAL ACCESSIBILITY OF THE WORLD

What are the Zoroastrian views on the accessibility of the world? In an often cited passage from Dk 4 on the transmission of the *Avesta*, a larger section is dedicated to what Shaked (2003: 71) deems 'a religious manifesto' of King Xōsraw I (532–70 CE).[42] For our question the following excerpt is relevant:

> Dk 4.25[43] awēšān kē gētīyān ō šnāxtan ī dādār ud abdīh mēnōyān čiyōnīh ī dahišn az dādār fradom ayāftan nē šāyistan ayāb hamāg ayāftan šāyistan guft pad[44] kam dānišn waranīg awēšān kē paydāgīh ī az dēn ēdōnīh ud pad-iz hangōšidag ast ī šnāxtan šāyistan guft pad uskārgar ud ān kē rōšn nimūdan pad dānāgīh dēn-āgāhīh dāštan ud az ān čiyōn harw dānāgīh bun dēn ham pad nērōg ī mēnōyīg ud ham pad paydāgīhēnīdārīh gētīyīg ān ī kas dānāgīhā guft ka-iz-iš az kadām abestāg paydāgīh hammis[45] nē dāšt ēg-iz pad paydāgīh ī az dēn hangārd kē xwēškārīh pad hamōg[46] frāz ō yazadān-zādagān burd

> Those who say that the ones of the *gētīy* cannot know, in the first place, the creator, the marvels of the *mēnōy* ones and the nature of the creation by the creator, or that they can obtain all (that knowledge), are of little knowledge and greedy. Those who say that one can know the revelation, which is from the *dēn*, in the correct manner and also through likeness, are thinkers. And that one, who throws light on (the matter) through knowledge, possesses religious knowledge. And since the root of all knowledge is the *dēn*, both by the *mēnōy*

---

[42] This passage has been discussed in some detail by Shaked (2003) and Cantera (2004: Ch. 3).
[43] For the text, see Madan (1911: 414–15) and Dresden (1966: 509).
[44] Manuscript B has ⟨pt' pt'⟩.
[45] Manuscript B reads ⟨...⟩.
[46] Manuscript B reads ⟨...⟩.

power and by the *gētīy* manifestation, that one said wisely: even when it does not stem from a particular revelation from the *Avesta*, even then it should be considered as manifest from the *dēn*, (when) someone takes the duties in likeness (with the scripture) to the children of gods.

To begin with, those who deny or claim that insight into the creation is possible, are both degraded as people of little knowledge. But the text goes on to suggest that knowledge of religious revelation is possible, differentiating between at least two types of insight. Firstly, those who understand the religious revelation (*paydāgīh ī az dēn*), are labelled thinkers. Secondly, those who can demonstrate and throw light on it, presumably the revelation, through knowledge, are given the title of having religious knowledge, which seems to stand higher in the hierarchy of knowledge. Finally, in Dk 4.25 the *dēn* is called the root of all knowledge (*harw dānāgīh bun dēn*). Considering that in a preceding section *Xōsraw* requests of Zoroastrian priests visions of the *mēnōy* and its corporeal counterpart, the *gētīy*, it seems that knowledge of the creation is possible as well, assuming it is deduced by way of religious knowledge:

Dk 4.22[47] *u-mān ohrmazd mowbed ān*[48] *xwānd xwānēm kē mēnōy-wēnišnīh andar amāh paydāgīhist u-mān frāx-čārīh mēnōy-wēnišnīh gētīy handāzag nimāyišnīhā-iz harw 2 ēwēnag spurrīg az-išān xwāst xwāhēm*

And we call those (people) *mowbed*s of *Ohrmazd*, who reveal to us the vision of the *mēnōy*. And we will request of them the vision of the *mēnōy* abundantly and that also the (right) measure of *gētīy* (vision) to be shown to us, both in complete manner.

If the creation is intelligible through knowledge, and the root of all knowledge is the religion, then the religious tradition or scripture must contain knowledge required for the understanding of the world. It is, therefore, not surprising that scientific knowledge is recognised as having been part of the scripture:

Dk 4.19[49] *šābuhr ī šāhān šāh ī ardaxšīrān nibēgīhā-iz ī az dēn bē abar bizišhīh ud star-gōwišnīh ud čandišn ud zamān gyāg gōhr jahišn bawišn wināhišn jadag ērīh ud gōwāgīh ud abārīg kirrōgīh ud abzār andar hindūgān hrōm abārīg-iz zamīgīhā pargandag būd abāz ō ham āwurd ud abāg abestāg abāz handāxt*

Šābuhr, the king of kings, son of *Ardaxšīr*, collected again also the writings, which were external to the religion, concerning medicine, astronomy, movement, time, space, essence, fortune, becoming, destruction, form, good conduct and

---

[47] For the text, see Madan (1911: 413) and Dresden (1966: 510).
[48] Manuscript B reads ⟨ZK ZK⟩.
[49] For the text, see Madan (1911: 412–13) and Dresden (1966: 511). For a detailed discussion of this passage, see Bailey (1943: 81ff.).

rhetoric and other arts and skills. These were dispersed in India, Rome and other lands, and he made them reckon again with the *Avesta*.

While insight gained by religious knowledge seems to be the preferred mode of insight (Dk 4.25), scientific knowledge is not excluded from the *dēn* and was explicitly collected and marked as that which is not religious (*az dēn bē*). Therefore, we can conclude that religious knowledge or the *dēn* contained scientific knowledge and insight into the universe. The inclusive character of the Zoroastrian tradition is also explicitly highlighted in the opening statement of Dk 5:

> Dk 5.1[50] *pērōzgarīh ī dādār ohrmazd xwarrah ī wisp-dānāgīh axwīg dēn mazdēsn*
>
> The victory of the creator *Ohrmazd*, the glory of the Mazda-worshipping religion, that contains all knowledge relating to existence.

Consistent with the account of *Šābuhr*'s collection of the dispersed knowledge, in the above passage the *dēn* is described as encompassing all knowledge that relates to the existence (*wisp-dānāgīh axwīg*). A similar notion also emerges from Dk 8:

> Dk 8.1.6[51] *ud čim ī sē-bazišnīh[52] ī dēn-*ōšmurišn[53] nigēz ast ī wisp dānišn kār ud ēwēnag ī ham dēn dānišn ud kunišn ēd ī sē ī nibišt*
>
> And (of) the meaning of the tripartite counting of the *dēn*, the exposition is that (it) encompasses all knowledge and actions, and the manner of both the knowledge and actions of the *dēn* is this of the three which is written.

Thus, detailed accounts of the creation and the world in the *Bundahišn*, *Wizīdagīhā ī Zādspram* and other MP texts are only a logical consequence of the Zoroastrian views concerning the relationship between religious tradition and knowledge. The list of arts and skills collected by *Šābuhr* also shows the Zoroastrian tendency to view the tradition as complete and that scripture could grow to include material that dealt with non-religious matters (proliferativity). In fact, Cabezón views the categories *completeness* and *epistemological accessibility* as related to *proliferativity*.

3.6 SYSTEMATICITY

Scholastics are driven by a concern for 'order in exposition' (Cabezón 1998: 5), whereby their writings often reflect the orderliness that underlies the world.

---

[50] For the text, see Madan (1911: 55) and Dresden (1966: 494).
[51] For the text, see Madan (1911: 677) and Dresden (1966: 305). For a slightly different translation, see Vevaina (2007: 72).
[52] Manuscript B reads ⟨bwcšnyh⟩.
[53] Manuscript B has ⟨MYTWN-šn'⟩ instead of ⟨MNYTWN-šn'⟩.

Attention to structured writing is evident in a number of MP texts. The admonition literature, *handarz*, employs rhetoric devices to that end. Parallelism is one such device often encountered:

> **Dk 6.283**[54] *u-šān ēn-iz ōwōn dāšt kū was [mardōm kē harw] ahlāyīh ī-š ast az was-xwāstagīh ud was mardōm kē harw druwandīh ī-š ast driyōšīh rāy*
>
> They held this too in this manner: Many are the people whose every righteousness is from the abundance of wealth, and many are the people whose every wickedness is due to poverty.

In colophon B of the manuscript MK, *frārōnīh* and *ahlāyīh* are assigned to *gētīy* and *mēnōy*, respectively:

> **Col. B** *gētīy ēdōn čiyōn tan kāmag andar frārōnīh ud mēnōy ēdōn čiyōn ruwān kāmag andar ahlāyīh*
>
> Thus, like the body, *gētīy* has its purpose in goodness, and like the soul, *mēnōy* has its purpose in righteousness.

In Dk 6.C49–C72, parallelism extends from one paragraph to the other, while other admonitions systematically explore cause and effect. The structural parallelism of these *handarz* is not only due to the systematic approach of the exegetes, but also reflects the parallels between the worlds of *mēnōy* and *gētīy* as well as between good and bad creation.

However, the Zoroastrian tradition takes systematicity one step further by applying the paradigm to the scripture itself. This feature is most prominent in the *Dēnkard*'s description of the *Avesta*:

> **Dk 8.1.5**[55] **ōšmurišn*[56] *ī dēn mazdēsn bazišn sē gāhān ī ast abartar mēnōy-dānišnīh mēnōy-kārīh ud dād ī ast abērtar*[57] *gētīy-dānišnīh ud gētīy-kārīh ud hādamānsarīg ī ast abērtar āgāhīh ud kār ī abar ān ī mayān ēd dō*
>
> The counting of the Mazda-worshipping religion is in three parts: *gāhān* ('Gāθās'), which consists of the higher *mēnōy* knowledge and *mēnōy* actions, and *dād* ('Law'), which mostly consists of *gētīy* knowledge and *gētīy* actions and *hādamānsarīg* ('Ritual formulae'), which mostly consists of knowledge and action about that, which lies between the (previous) two (parts).

The systematic division of the *Avesta* into three parts is further related to the compositional structure of the *yaθā ahū vairiiō* prayer:[58]

---

[54] Text after Shaked (1979: 110–11). I have 'normalised' Shaked's Pahlavi transcription.
[55] For the text, see Madan (1911: 677) and Dresden (1966: 305).
[56] Manuscript B has ⟨MYTW-šn'⟩.
[57] Manuscript B reads ࡃ. Cantera (2004: 14) transcribes it as *azērdar* 'lower'. His translation, however, does not fit the context. Vevaina (2007: 69) prefers *abartar*, which requires an unnecessary emendation. I read ࡃ as *abērtar*, which is well attested and fits the context better.
[58] See Vevaina (2007: 68ff.) for a detailed analysis of the *ahunawar* and its relationship with the *Avesta*. For some reason he does not discuss Dk 8.1.7–8.

Dk 8.1.7–8[59] *ōh-iz ahunawar ī dēn-*ōšmurišn*[60] *bun sē gāh ān ī fradom gāhānīgīh ud ān ī didīgar hādamānsarīgīh ān ī sidīgar dādīg abartar ud mahist aziš hād hēnd bazišn bahr 21 ī xwānīhēnd nask*

Likewise, the *ahunawar*, which is the foundation for the counting of the *dēn*, has 3 verse lines (*gāh*)[61]: the first one concerns the *gāhān*, and the second concerns the *hādamānsar*, and the third one the *dād*. Highest and greatest, of its parts there have been 21 sections, which are called *nasks*.

In Dk 8.1.9–11 each part is then assigned seven *nasks*, which together make up the 21 *nasks* of the elusive Sasanian *Avesta*. The text then goes on to describe the individual parts and sections and their relationship in greater detail.

A structured view of the scripture is also apparent in Suppl.ŠnŠ 13, a section beginning with the words *čim ī gāhān ēn* 'The meaning of the *Gāθās* is this'. In this chapter, the extent and content of the OAv. texts are defined according to numerological criteria.[62]

3.7 SELF-REFLEXIVITY

Cabezón (1994: 22) understands self-reflexivity as the scholastics' deliberate attention to their own undertaking, because it 'had to be justified to others, defended against rival theories of philosophical speculation, and in this way established on firm footing'. While systematic philosophical speculation is not a proliferative feature of antique and late antique Zoroastrian literature, establishing authoritative versions of religious scripture, that is, of the *Avesta* and its *Zand*, through debates and recording of various views is a topic that is often referred to in Zoroastrian texts.

A number of Middle Persian texts contain reports of religious councils in which the redaction of an authoritative version of the *Avesta* was fiercely debated.[63] According to these texts the aim of the councils was to gather the *Avesta* dispersed by Alexander to establish one authoritative version from the competing schools. Most likely, the development of the Avestan script was the result of such councils, with the ultimate goal of committing both corpora to writing.[64]

I have suggested elsewhere that accounts such as the report of the transmission of the *Avesta* in Dk 4 should be viewed as 'legitimate literary

---

[59] For the text, see Madan (1911: 677-88) and Dresden (1966: 305).
[60] Manuscript B has ⟨MYTW-šn'⟩.
[61] Here *gāh* refers to verse lines, as in the concluding statements at the end of OAv. chapters of the *Yasna* in the multilingual MSS. See, for instance, Section 6.10.
[62] I discuss Suppl.ŠnŠ 13 in more detail in Chapter 4. See also Zeini (Forthcoming).
[63] Cantera (2004: 106–24) has most recently discussed these accounts and their academic reception in great detail.
[64] On dating the Av. script, see Hoffmann and Narten (1989) and Blois (1990).

witnesses reflecting the exegetes' scholastic desire for the formation, systematic arrangement and continuous interpretation of scripture during late antiquity' (Zeini 2018: 160). As such, these accounts, which are not limited to Dk 4, epitomise the Zoroastrian tradition's own reflection on the process of establishing an authoritative set of scripture and thus meet the slightly modified requirements of self-reflexivity, Cabezón's eighth scholastic category.

3.8 SUMMARY

During late antiquity Zoroastrianism witnessed the emergence and development of different religious cultures which interacted with one another within a relatively small geographical confine. The religious exchange that took place between Rabbinic Jews and Zoroastrians under Sasanian rule (224–651 CE), for example, has greatly interested scholars in both fields in recent years.[65] However, scholars of Zoroastrianism seem less inclined to produce comparative studies or explore their object of study from within theoretical frameworks. Studies by Yuhan Vevaina and Rezania (2010, 2015) stand out.

Vevaina's examination of the schematic view of the 21 *nask*s of the *Dēnkard Avesta*, although based on different theoretical paradigms, anticipates much of my research into scholasticism (see Vevaina 2010a). In a recent article with the programmatic sub-title *Towards a mapping of the hermeneutic contours of Zoroastrianism*, Vevaina (2012) seeks to illuminate the exegetical principles of the *Dēnkard* and other MP texts by employing methodologies from Jewish studies. Kugel's (1981) *omnisignificance*, which Vevaina first discussed in his dissertation, builds the backdrop to his reading of the texts:

> For the basic assumption underlying all of rabbinic exegesis is that the slightest details of the biblical text have a meaning that is both comprehensible and significant. Nothing in the Bible, in other words, ought to be explained as the product of chance, or, for that matter, as an emphatic or rhetorical form, or anything similar, nor ought its reasons to be assigned to the realm of Divine unknowables. Every detail is put there to teach something new and important, and it is capable of being discovered by careful analysis. (Kugel 1981: 104)

The relevance of *omnisignificance* lies in the assertion that exegesis is motivated by features of a 'base-text' (Vevaina 2012: 470). Preoccupation with scripture as a base-text is one of the core principles that motivates scholastics. However, while Kugel's *omnisignificance* incorporates many

---

[65] For these comparative studies, see the work done by Bakhos and Shayegan (2010), Yaakov Elman, Kiperwasser, Kiel (2016), Mokhtarian (2015) and Secunda (2009, 2013).

aspects of Cabezón's scholasticism, it rests on a single assumption based on the study of rabbinic exegesis. By contrast, Cabezón's framework operates with an abstract set of categories which do not lean on a single assumption of omnisignificance associated with a particular text. As such, it is hoped, this framework will allow a more refined textual analysis when applied to any tradition.

The eight characteristics proposed by Cabezón (1998: 6) are intended as 'a heuristic, as a starting point' rather than a rigid definition of scholasticism. In fact, the application of scholasticism as a cross-cultural category to various traditions has shown that the eight features can occur in various constellations and with different intensities across cultures (Cabezón 1998: 246). Much like Cabezón's heuristic, the above analysis is a first attempt to examine MP literature from within a theoretical framework and highlight scholastic traits of select passages from across MP literature.

The application of a theoretical model is not an end in itself and must contribute to a better understanding of the subject matter. Cabezón's framework achieves this in more than one way. While previous scholarship on the *Zand* has mainly been driven by philological and linguistic considerations, my analysis refocuses our attention on the study of the priestly exegesis of the *Avesta*. Rather than conceiving of the MP translations of the *Avesta* as a problematic translation project at a time when knowledge of Avestan was unsatisfactory, we can approach the *Zand* as an hermeneutic undertaking, which found further reflections in the non-translation Pahlavi literature.[66] As Cabezón (1994: 74) rightly observes, 'hermeneutics is the *theory* of scriptural interpretation', while 'exegesis is its *practice*'. Moreover, the implications of Cabezón's work are visible in the development of further theoretical models such as that of correlative structures. The examination of perceptions of the fire in Zoroastrianism in Chapter 4 shows that such models have utility in the study of Zoroastrian exegesis by providing further cultural context that elucidates the mechanisms by which manuscript traditions evolve. Finally, the shared language and terminology of the scholastic model may open up new opportunities for cross-cultural, comparative studies with other traditions that share all or some of the features of Zoroastrian exegesis. It is hoped that the above examination, preliminary as it is at this point, will provide more context and insights into the principles governing the structure and composition of the *Zand*, enabling us to further refine our understanding of this much neglected tradition.

However, in order to achieve a more nuanced study of Zoroastrian scholasticism a range of issues must be addressed. Foremost, we must engage with Cabezón's proposed framework on a theoretical level. Clooney (1998: 183), for instance, raises an important question by suggesting that

---

[66] For an example, see my commentary on *mard ō mard* in Sections 13.2.5 and 15.1.6.

the extent to which a tradition is scholastic needs to be more clearly defined. In other words, we need to ask how many categories or texts need to be examined before qualifying a tradition as scholastic. Can the discourse of late antique Zoroastrianism be scholastic as a whole or will the appellation apply to a group of texts? Clooney (1998: 187) also suggests a distinction between *intellectualist* and *performative* scholasticisms, linking them to a preference for 'comprehensive understanding' and 'formation in right thinking and acting', respectively. The informed reader will notice that both types would appropriately describe different MP texts. Moreover, some of the categories proposed by Cabezón, such as *completeness and compactness*, require clarification as to what their exact definition entails and how these refined categories would relate to Zoroastrianism. I have excluded *rationalism* from the above discussion, as it needs further investigation as to its relevance for Sasanian and post-Sasanian Zoroastrianism.

The elusive character of the *Zand* makes its translation and evaluation a very difficult task. Therefore, large portions of the *Zand* remain unedited. Likewise, the *Dēnkard*, despite its close relationship with the *Avesta* and the *Zand*, remains largely unpublished. Zoroastrian studies have thus been deprived of a treasure-trove of exegetical texts, which are crucial for a better understanding of the religion's development. The notoriously difficult and uncertain dating of most MP texts poses another challenge to any systematic discussion of the material. The common assumption that a large group of the texts date to the early Islamic era but contain Sasanian, or possibly older, material leads to an inclusive view, which may not reflect the historical reality of the texts and their content. Although a certain affinity between the *Zand* and the *Dēnkard* cannot be denied, it is by no means permissible to treat them as texts belonging to the same era. As such, the selection of texts discussed in this chapter serves as a starting point, giving an overview which could be refined in subsequent examinations. Bilingual texts where MP passages relate to non-canonical Av. texts, such as the *Hērbedestān* and *Nērangestān*, could be considered as candidates for performative scholasticism. The *Pursišnīhā*, although not strictly a bilingual text, deserves further attention, as it frequently quotes Av. passages along with their *Zand* to substantiate the answers to the questions, which give this little work its name.[67] The *Dēnkard* relates to the *Avesta* in more than one way. Its detailed description of the supposed Sasanian *Avesta* on one hand (Book 8) and its threefold analysis of the content of the *Avesta* on the other (Book 9), make the *Dēnkard* a candidate for further studies in *proliferativity* and *systematicity*.

---

[67] I have discussed those passages of the *Pursišnīhā* that relate to the (P)YH as part of the commentary.

4. *Fire in Zoroastrianism*

> Any text is the absorption and transformation of another.
>
> Kristeva (1980)

Most observers, modern or ancient, would state that fire plays a pivotal role in Zoroastrianism. It appears to dominate the ritual performed by the priests in fire temples (*ātaškade* in Persian) or in private by the Zoroastrian laity, a practice for which Zoroastrians have come to be known as *fire worshippers*. Priestly and academic scholarship traces the roots of the fire's centrality back to prehistoric times, viewing it as a continuation of common Indo-European and Indo-Iranian traditions.[1] Boyce (1987), for instance, suggests that the cult of the fire predates Zoroastrianism and likely originates in IE traditions. In her view, it is the ever-burning hearth fire which is often regarded as the predecessor of the Zoroastrian fire.[2] Mobad Azargushasb (1971) considers fire to be a universally revered element, respected in various cultures across ethnic boundaries. Dastur Kaikhusroo Jamaspasa (2003) describes the fire in terms reminiscent of (P)Y 36.6: 'Fire also brought a bit of the heavens down to earth as it resembled the sun in the sky.'[3]

Within the extant corpus of Avestan texts, Y 36 contains one of the earliest references to the fire in the context of an Avestan ritual. With Y 36 marking the middle of the 72 *hāiti* of the *Yasna*, the fire occupies a central position in

---

[1] See Shahmardan (1967), Azargushasb (1971), Boyce (1977, 1996), Jamaspasa (2003) and West (2007).

[2] The above views are the result of Boyce's idea of a *conservative continuity* in Zoroastrianism, which was first expressed and extended to the fire in Boyce (1968b, 1975). For a comprehensive discussion of the concept of the ever-burning fire and and assessment of Boyce's scholarship on the subject, see König (2015).

[3] Most likely, Jamaspasa's description is influenced by the results of modern scholarship. For another modern priestly interpretation of the fire and the YH's role in the *Yasna* ritual, see Kotwal and Boyd (1991: 13, 112ff.). For an assessment of the *Yasna* ritual in MP literature, see Shaked (2004).

the ritual and emerges as one of the principal concepts of Zoroastrianism. The *hāiti* also marks the start of a departure from a single fire towards multiples with highly complex connections encountered in later texts. The tendency to build layered and complex networks of ideas has long been recognised in manuscript traditions (see Section 4.4). In the following, I shall trace the development of the fire in Zoroastrian textual traditions from the Older *Avesta* through to the MP texts, examining to what extent a scholastic view of the scripture could have influenced the unfolding of the fire's position within later forms of Zoroastrianism.

However, before I proceed with the actual study, some preliminary remarks on the term 'fire' are in order. The word for fire is *ātar-* in OAv., YAv. as well as OP; *ātaxš* and *ādur* in Middle Persian and Parthian, and *ʾtr* in Sogdian. It is cited four times in the Bactrian documents as a loanword from MP *ādur*.[4] In New Persian it is known as *ātaš* and *āδar*.

Fire is associated with the *aməša- spənta-* 'life-giving immortal' or 'bounteous immortal' *aša-* 'order' or *aša- vahišta-* 'best order',[5] which, according to Boyce (1990, 1996), links the fire with the concept of order.[6] In the Zoroastrian calendar, day nine is dedicated to *ātar-*, but not a *Yašt*. Furthermore, *aša- vahišta-* and *ātar-* are associated with the mid-day or second *gāh*, namely *rapihwin* or Av. *rapiϑβina-* (Narten 1982: 122).[7]

4.1 THE OLDER AVESTA

In the OAv. corpus *ātar-* 'fire' is attested 12 times, of which four occur in Y 36.[8] By contrast, *xšaϑra-* 'rule', another important notion in Zoroastrianism, occurs over 70 times in the OAv. corpus and is the subject of an entire *Gāϑā*, *Vohuxšaϑrā Gāϑā* (Y 51), thereby statistically outranking the concept of the fire in Zoroastrianism in the Older *Avesta*.

Some of the attributes associated with the fire in the OAv. are most explicitly mentioned in Y 34.4, in a stanza that reads like a definition of the fire:[9]

---

[4] As αδορο it depicts the name of a month in document da. It is mentioned once as αδοραστο, a word of uncertain meaning in document m and twice in document bh as part of a patronymic or family name αδοροφαρνιγανο (Sims-Williams 2007).

[5] Scholars' preferences differ widely in translating the pivotal term *aša-*. Hintze (2007a) prefers 'truth' while noting 'rightness' and 'order', the latter preferred by Skjærvø (2003). For an insightful discussion of the term's scholarly reception and meaning, see now König (2018: 118–26).

[6] For the various aspects associated with the fire, see also Boyce (1986, 1987).

[7] See also Dk 9.9.8. Narten (1982) critically evaluates the relationship between *aša- vahišta-* and *ātar-*.

[8] The evidence is as follows: Y 31.3, 31.19, 34.4, Y 36.1–3 (twice in 36.3), Y 43.4, 43.9, 46.7, 47.6 and 51.9. I have only considered *ātar-*. Semantically close concepts such as *sūca-* 'radiance' or *suxra-* 'red' have been ignored. For my translation of all eight *Gāϑic* stanzas, see Appendix C.

[9] If not otherwise mentioned, all OAv. texts are after Humbach (1991). Translations are mine.

Y 34.4 at̰ tōi ātrə̄m ahurā   aojōŋhuuaṇtəm ašā usə̄mahī
asīštīm ə̄mauuaṇtəm   stōi rapaṇtē ciϑrā.auuaŋhəm
at̰ mazdā daibišiiaṇtē   zastāištāiš dərəštā.aēnaŋhəm

Thus, O *Ahura*, we wish your strong fire, the swiftest (and) most powerful, to be
    a brilliant support to the supporting one in accordance with *aša*,
but, O Wise One, a visible harm to the hostile one by means of its hands.

Most significantly, the fire is clearly perceived as belonging to *Ahura Mazdā* (*at̰ tōi ātrə̄m ahurā* 'Thus, O *Ahura*, your fire').[10] It is further described as strong, swift, powerful and a brilliant support to *Ahura Mazdā*'s supporters, delivering visible harm to opponents. In an attempt to further grasp the OAv. notion of the fire, I have divided the relevant stanzas into several groups.

4.1.1 The *Gāϑās*

4.1.1.1 *aša-*

As already observed by Narten (1982: 106, 121–3), in the Older *Avesta* fire is strongly associated with *aša-*. With the exception of Y 51.9, *aša-* occurs in seven out of eight OAv. attestations of *ātar-*: Y 31.3, 31.19, 34.4, 43.4, 43.9, 46.7 and 47.6. The two terms are most explicitly linked in Y 43.4: *āϑrō ašā.aojaŋhō* 'the fire, strong through *aša*'. Scholars translate Y 34.4, *ātrə̄m ... aojōŋhuuaṇtəm ašā*, similarly, presumably in light of Y 43.4, implying that the fire is strong through *aša-*.[11] Tempting as this interpretation might be, the evidence points towards a more complex relationship between the two terms. No doubt, in Y 43.4 it is clearly stated that the fire's strength is through *aša-*. This statement, however, is reversed in Y 46.7, where it is the fire that strengthens *aša-*: *aniiə̄m ϑβahmāt̰ āϑrascā manaŋhascā   yaiiā̊ šiiaoϑanāiš   ašə̄m ϑraoštā ahurā* 'whom other than your fire and thought, through whose actions one nourishes *aša*, O *Ahura*?'. If the relationship between *ātar-* and *aša-* is in part defined by a mutual strengthening, there is no binding argument for translating *ātrə̄m ... aojōŋhuuaṇtəm ašā* in Y 34.4 as 'the fire, strong through *aša*'. It is more likely that *aojōŋhuuaṇtəm*, an adjective in acc.s.m., describes the acc.sg.m. noun *ātrə̄m*. If this is the case, then it is support and visible harm that are granted by means of or in accordance with *aša-* in Y 34.4 (see Section 4.1). This view is not problematic if we consider *aša-* an underlying principle governing the intangible and the material world. A similar notion is echoed in Y 31.3: *yąm*

---

[10] See also Bartholomae (1904: 315): 'im **gAw.**, persönlich und göttlich gedacht, meist als dem *MazdāhAh*. angehörig'.
[11] See Insler (1975: 55), Narten (1982: 106), Humbach (1959: 106, 1991: 140), Humbach and Faiss (2010: 100), Kellens and Pirart (1988: 126) and most recently West (2010: 87).

dā̊ mainiiū ā𝜃rācā   ašācā cōiš rānōibiiā xšnūtəm 'The satisfaction, which you created with (your) spirit and assigned to both parties by means of the fire and aša.'[12]

In the other stanzas the two terms also stand in close proximity. So, for instance, in Y 43.9, when the poet expresses the wish to serve the fire, implying that thereby one will revere aša-: at ā 𝜃βahmāi   ā𝜃rē rātąm nəmaŋhō   ašahiiā mā   yauuaṯ isāi maniiāi 'Your fire. I will consider the gift of reverence for aša as much as I may be able.' In Y 31.19 and 47.6 we find the fire and aša- in the same stanza as well (see Section 4.1.1.2).

Thus, while the proximity of ātar- and aša- in the above stanzas suggests a strong conceptual association between them, I do not see a one-directional link between the fire's strength and aša-, particularly not, as it is also stated that aša- can gain strength through the fire (Y 46.7). Rather, the fire seems to be an agent that delivers judgement that has been drawn up in accordance with aša-.

4.1.1.2 Distributor

In a number of stanzas the fire is depicted as *Ahura Mazdā*'s agent, distributing reward and punishment, respectively, to those supportive of and hostile to *Ahura Mazdā*. In Y 31.3, for instance, we see the fire together with aša- as the distributor of satisfaction (see Section 4.1.1.1). This is also the case in Y 31.19: 𝜃βā ā𝜃rā suxrā mazdā   vaŋhāu vīdātā rąnaiiā̊ 'at (the time of) the good distribution to both parties by means of your red fire, O Wise one'.[13] In Y 34.4, *Ahura Mazdā*'s fire is requested to dispense support and visible harm by means of its hands. We encounter this concept once more in Y 43.4, where *Ahura Mazdā*'s rewards are said to be assigned to the deceitful and truthful one through his fire's heat.[14] In Y 47.6 the poet requests distribution in accordance with aša- by means of the fire:

Y 47.6 tā dā̊ spəṇtā   mainiiū mazdā ahurā
ā𝜃rā vaŋhāu   vīdāitīm rānōibiiā
ārmatōiš   dəbązaŋhā ašaxiiācā
hā zī pouruš   išəṇtō vāurāite

---

[12] This translation agrees with Insler (1975: 37). Narten (1982: 106) and Humbach (1991: 126) interpret the enclitic conjunction -cā as coordinating the spirit and the fire, assigning the distribution to aša. Grammatically, all interpretations of the three instrumentals and the conjunctions are acceptable. However, I find it semantically difficult to involve the fire in the creation of satisfaction and prefer to coordinate ā𝜃rācā   ašācā. Moreover, this reading of the stanza agrees with the role of the fire as a distributor of satisfaction (see Section 4.1.1.2).

[13] To make sense of this line, I operate with the difficult assumption that the loc.sg.m./n. vaŋhāu 'good' refers to loc.sg. vīdātā 'distribution' from the f. vīdāiti-. For alternative translations, see Insler (1975) and Humbach (1991).

[14] aši- is to be understood as the share given to each person according to his/her actions. Bartholomae (1904: 241) states: 'ašay- f. "was einem auf Grund seiner Leistung – in gutem und schlimmem Sinn – zukommt; Anteil, Los, Verdienst, Lohn, Belohnung"; bes. beim letzten Gericht'. See also Hintze (2007a: 332): aši- 'bestowal, reward'.

By means of that bounteous spirit (and) the fire, O Wise Lord, you shall give the
 distribution at the good to both parties
in accordance with the solidity of right-mindedness and *aṣ̌a*.
For, that shall retain the many who approach.

And finally, in Y 51.9 the fire is once more depicted as the distributor of satisfaction:

Y 51.9 *yąm xšnūtəm rānōibiiā dā̊   θβā āθrā suxrā mazdā
aiiaŋhā xšustā aibī   ahuuāhū daxštəm dāuuōi
rāšaiieŋhē drəguuaṇtəm   sauuaiiō aṣ̌auuanəm*

Which satisfaction you shall give to both parties by means of your glowing fire, O
 Wise One!
With the molten metal, a sign shall be given among the beings,
to cause harm to the deceitful ones (and) to revitalise the truthful ones.

4.1.1.3   *rāna-*

OAv. *rāna-* 'fighter, fighting parties' occurs in Y 31.3, 31.19, 43.12, 47.6 and 51.9 (see Humbach 1991: II 60).[15] With the exception of Y 43.12, in all the other stanzas in which OAv. *rāna-* occurs, *ātar-* is cited as well. Thus, a very strong link is established between the fire and *rāna-* in the *Gāθās*: Y 31.3, 31.19, 47.6 and 51.9.

These stanzas focus on the distribution of rewards to two fighting parties, and hence only represent a variation of the theme of the fire as the distributor of rewards (see Section 4.1.1.2). Within the four stanzas where *ātar-* and *rāna-* occur together a type of thematic parallelism or a mini ring composition stands out. The first and final stanzas of this group belong together by a resemblance of the stanzas' first line:

Y 31.3 *yąm dā̊ mainiiū āθrācā   aṣ̌ācā cōiš rānōibiiā xšnūtəm*
The satisfaction, which you created with (your) spirit and assigned to both parties
 by means of the fire and *aṣ̌a*

Y 51.9 *yąm xšnūtəm rānōibiiā dā̊   θβā āθrā suxrā mazdā*
Which satisfaction you shall give to both parties by means of your glowing fire, O
 Wise One!

---

[15] Bartholomae (1904: 1523) translates *rāna-* 'Streiter, Kämpfer', a translation which he confirms by PY *pahikārdārān* 'fighters, dispute parties'. He posits that OAv. *rāna-* renders *rə̄na-* 'meeting, fight, dispute' in YAv., distinguishing it from YAv. *rāna-* 'thigh' ('der äusserste Teil des Oberschenkels; Oberschenkel überhaupt') (Bartholomae 1904: 1523, 1527). Insler (1975) prefers 'faction' for OAv. *rāna-*, while Kellens and Pirart (1990: 311) merely note: 'de sense et d'étymologie inconnus'. Vaan (2003: 474) agrees with Bartholomae. Humbach (1991: II 60), however, disagrees, preferring 'scales, balance': 'The word cannot be separated from YAv. *rāna-* du. 'thigh', but it cannot have exactly the same meaning'. Like Bartholomae, Humbach's interpretation of *rāna-* as 'scales, balance' is based on a comment in the PY.

Y 31.19 and 47.6 form the middle group by a reference to the difficult expression of 'distribution at the good':

31.19 *ϑβā āϑrā suxrā mazdā   vaŋhāu vīdātā rąnaiiå*
at (the time of) the good distribution to both parties by means of your red fire, O Wise one.

47.6 *tā då spəṇtā   mainiiū mazdā ahurā
āϑrā vaŋhāu   vīdāitīm rānōibiiā*

By means of that bounteous spirit, O Wise Lord, (and) the fire you shall give the distribution at the good to both parties

4.1.1.4 Protection

Anxiety for protection is another theme repeated throughout the *Gāϑās* and twice in the stanzas relevant to our discussion: Y 34.4 and 46.7. This anxiety prompts the *Gāϑic* poet to ascertain *Ahura Mazdā*'s support in Y 34.5:

*kaṯ və xšaϑrəm kā ištiš   šiiaoϑanāi mazdā yaϑā vā bahmī
ašā vohū manaŋhā   ϑrāiiōidiiāi drigūm yūšmākəm
parō vå vīspāiš parō.vaoxəmā   daēuuāišcā xrafstrāiš mašiiāišcā*

What (is) your power, what (is your) command, O Wise One, (which may protect me) for (my) actions as well as when I sleep?
Protect (me), your poor dependent, with *aša* (and) good thought.
We have declared you superior to all evil beasts, Daēvic as well as human.

Y 46.7 reiterates the question of Y 34.5, but also reveals that the *Gāϑic* poet has received a partial reply to his enquiry:

Y 46.7 *kəmnā mazdā   mauuaitē pāiiūm dadå
hiiaṯ mā drəguuå   dīdarəšatā aēnaŋhē
aniiəm ϑβahmāṯ   āϑrascā manaŋhascā
yaiiå šiiaoϑanāiš   ašəm ϑraoštā ahurā
tąm mōi dąstuuąm   daēnaiiāi frāuuaocā*

Whom, O Wise One, have you appointed as a protector for one like me,
when the deceitful one looks to harm me?
(Whom), O *Ahura*, other than your fire and thought,
through whose actions one nourishes *aša*?
Proclaim that message to my religious view.

This stanza explicitly reinforces the notion of the fire as a protector of *Ahura Mazdā*'s supporters, an idea expressed more mildly in Y 34.4.[16] Thus, in

---

[16] We encounter a similar motif in the *Yašts*, where *ātar-* is a helper of the *aməša- spəṇta-* (Narten 1982: 123). It is particularly relevant that in Yt 13.77 the fire joins *vohu- manah-* to protect the creation of *aša- vahišta-* against the attack of *aŋra- mainiiu-*. Narten suggests that Yt 13.77 could have been based on Y 46.7. See also Boyce (1996: 273), who suggests that Y 46.7 'came to be used as a protective *mąthra* or *bāj* when a shield was needed against evil'.

addition to the adjectives mentioned in Y 34.4, the fire appears to occupy a clearly defined role as a guardian appointed by *Ahura Mazdā* to protect his followers.

4.1.2   The YH

As already mentioned, *ātar-* occurs four times within the *Yasna Haptaŋhāiti*: Y 36.1, 36.2 and 36.3 (x2). Y 36.1 identifies the fire as *Ahura Mazdā*'s bounteous or generous spirit (*mainiiu- spəṇta-*) and as harm for the ones consigned to harm by *Ahura Mazdā*. Thus, Y 36.1 shares with Y 34.4 the association of the fire with injury and harm for the deceitful ones. It is with this fire that the sacrificers approach *Ahura Mazdā*. But in Y 36.2, this fire, *ātarə mazdå ahurahiiā* 'Fire of *Ahura Mazdā*', is in turn requested to come close. Y 36.3 brings the preceding two stanzas together as if this third stanza were a conclusion, by reasserting that this fire is *Ahura Mazdā*'s fire (36.2) and his most generous spirit (36.1). It is at this point that the sacrificers seem to take another step towards the fire. Thus, we see a tripartite structure associated with the ritual of the fire reflected in these three stanzas and three ritual steps before the actual *Yasna* ritual can continue. Y 36.4 and 5 take up the numerical motif once more by recounting tripartite constellations of what is good.

From a compositional point of view, Y 36 constitutes the central chapter of the *Yasna* text. With four of twelve OAv. citations of *ātar-* present in Y 36, there is no doubt that the fire occupies a central position in the YH and consequently in the *Yasna* ritual. It is thus likely that the YH played a crucial role in furthering the development and systematisation of the fire in the YAv. texts. The relevant passage is Y 36.3b, *ahiiā spə̄ništō ahī   hiiaṯ vā tōi nāmanąm vāzištəm*, rendered as *abzōnīg ast xwad tā ka ōy ī tō nām čiyōn ī wāzišt* in PY 36.3b. Narten (1986) and Kellens and Pirart (1988) disagree as to whether *mainiiuš spə̄ništō* or *vāzišta-* is the name of the fire.[17] Irrespective of this debate, however, I believe that the usage of *nāman-* 'name' in connection with *vāzišta-* 'most invigorating' could have served as a template for assigning names to fires, such as is the case in Y 17.11.

Avestan *nāman-* occurs four times in the OAv. corpus: Y 36.3, 37.3, 38.4 and Y 51.22. However, it only occurs in Y 36.3 with *ātar-*. Whether we take *vāzišta-* or *spəṇta- mainiiu-* as the name of the fire, Y 36.3 remains the only OAv. stanza to explicitly suggest *Ahura Mazdā*'s fire may have had a name. It would be presumptuous to assume that the YAv. concept of multiple fires

---

[17] Hintze (2007a, b) summarises the debate. For a general discussion of *vāzišta-*, see also Insler (1996).

is based on Y 36.3, but we can be certain that in the present corpus evidence of names being assigned to the fire appears in Y 36.3.

It is worth pointing out that no plural form of *ātar-* ever appears in the Older *Avesta* (see Hoffmann and Forssman 1996: 152). It is only in later YAv. compositions that we encounter a plural form of *ātar-* (see Section 4.2). Thus, I argue that the concept of multiple fires did not exist within the religious world view of the OAv. poets. If such a concept existed, it was not endorsed by the composing poets. The early *Gāθic* community encountered in the Older *Avesta* recognised only one fire, which was understood to be *Ahura Mazdā*'s fire. It further emerges from Y 36 that the ritual fire was understood as representing *Ahura Mazdā*'s fire in the context of the ritual. Whether this fire is *Ahura Mazdā*'s son is not specified in the Older *Avesta*. We can thus conclude that while we do not witness a highly systematised concept in the OAv. corpus, Y 36.3 may have provided a template for the YAv. compositions.

4.1.3 Summary

The OAv. material does not reveal a highly systematised notion of the fire. We encounter a single fire, belonging to *Ahura Mazdā*, which is strongly associated with *aša-*.[18] The fire's responsibility for the distribution of rewards or harm is motivated by its close association with *aša-*. This idea is further reinforced by the later association of *ātar-* with *aša- vahišta-*.

Scholars have stressed the role of the *Gāθic* fire in eschatology. Bartholomae (1904: 316) distinguishes between a ritual fire ('Opferfeuer') in Y 43.9 and an eschatological ordeal fire ('Ordalfeuer') in Y 31.3, 31.19, 47.6 and 51.9. Likewise, Insler (1975) sees a reference to final judgement in Y 31.3, 31.19, 43.4. In Humbach's (1991: II 60) interpretation of *rāna-* as 'scales, balance' the link between fire and the distribution of rewards according to scales or balance gains an eschatological meaning as well. In these instances it is the distribution of reward and punishment that motivates this interpretation and the assertion of a link with individual or universal eschatology. And in most cases, universal eschatology is the preferred arena for the fire's activity. Boyce (1987), for instance, states:

> Zoroaster developed this cultural inheritance yet further when he apprehended fire as the creation of Aša Vahišta (q.v.), and when he saw fire as the instrument of God's judgement at the Last Day. Then a fiery flood of molten metal will cover the earth, and men will undergo thereby a last judicial ordeal [. . .] The cult of fire thus became for the prophet one of profound moral and spiritual significance.

---

[18] Narten (1982: 106) points out that this fire does not depict the natural phenomenon. As *Ahura Mazdā*'s fire it is most likely the essence or idea of the fire.

However, as Shaked (1998) rightly points out, very little can be gleaned from the *Gāθās* about the notion of eschatology in *Gāθic* Zoroastrianism. The association of fire with universal eschatology is a hypothetical one. In fact, the *Gāθic* poet's concerns for a protector and supporter seem to point to the material world (see fn. 16). If so, punishment and reward may refer to judgement in this world rather than judgement at the end of the material world. The molten metal mentioned in Y 51.9, for example, can be interpreted as referring to events in this world as well: 'With the molten metal, a sign shall be given among the beings, to cause harm to the deceitful ones (and) to revitalise the truthful ones.' If the molten metal was to serve as a sign to people, perhaps as a warning sign, the judgement day would be an inappropriate time. We have to consider the possibility that the molten metal here refers to the judiciary heat ordeal rather than to an eschatological event. Unfortunately, the sketchy *Gāθic* evidence does not facilitate the reconstruction of a complete and clear picture.

Zoroastrian eschatology is most conspicuous in the MP literature, and the Pahlavi *Yasna*'s tendency to interpret Avestan passages in light of eschatology has long been noted (see Shaked 1996; Josephson 2003; Vevaina 2007). The final comment in PY 36.2c, for instance, interprets the ritual context and the request as a preparation for eschatological events: *pad ān ī meh kār be rasēd pad passāxt ī pad tan ī pasēn* 'Arrive at the great event, at the trial of the final body.' At the same time, PY 36.1c appears to pertain to disrespect for the fire in the material world. Many of Boyce's assertions rest on her idea of conservative continuity in Zoroastrianism, an assumption which allowed her to fill the many gaps that we encounter in the intellectual history of Zoroastrianism. However, the connection between many *Gāθic* passages and ideas expressed in the MP literature, including the various *Zand*, remain at best unclear.

In her study of the YH, Narten (1986: 156) classifies Y 36.3 as a consecration formula for the fire. Assuming two fires that are different in essence, Narten conjectures that it is at this point of the *Yasna* ceremony that the ritual fire is identified with *Ahura Mazdā*'s heavenly fire (Narten 1986: 26).[19] Cantera (2012: 219) also states that a consecration of the fire takes place in Y 36, and Hintze (2007a: 6), following Narten, suggests that in Y 36.2 the heavenly fire is requested to 'merge with the ritual fire'. She notes that the two fires have already merged by Y 36.3, where the ritual fire is once more addressed as *Ahura Mazdā*'s heavenly fire and as his most bounteous spirit.[20] However, the assumption of two essentially different fires and their merging during

---

[19] Based on such observations, Narten (1986: 34) goes on to suggest that the YH is a liturgical text. For a brief discussion of the consecration formula in the PYH, see Section 14.3.1.

[20] For an overview of Narten and Hintze's views on the YH's ritual significance and the role of the fire therein, see Narten (1986: 25–8), Hintze (2004, 2007a: 6–20 and 2007b).

the ritual is not convincing. The OAv. texts do not distinguish between a heavenly and a worldly or ritual fire, rather, they speak of *Ahura Mazdā*'s fire. In the case of the YH too, the community seems to be sacrificing in front or the presence of the fire that they perceive as the deity's fire (36.1). If a consecration were taking place in the YH, which I doubt is the case, the alternative scenario could be that from Y 36.3 onward the deity is present in the ritual fire without the need of two essentially different fires merging. Hintze (2007a: 6) does suggest that the deity is present in the fire in Y 36.3, but still presupposes that this presence is the result of the fusion of two fires. Narten and Hintze thus surmise that the fire of *Ahura Mazdā* is a heavenly fire, which merges with the earthly fire for the purpose of the ritual. To substantiate their view, they point to the far-deictic pronoun *huuō* 'that one there' (Y 36.2) supposedly pointing towards the abode of the deity. But they neglect the fact that the fire addressed in Y 36.2 with *huuō* is the same fire as in Y 36.1 and 3. The YH does not indicate a change in the essence of the fire from Y 36.1 to 36.3, such as Hintze (2007a: 6) states:

> The second chapter, Y 36, begins with the affirmation that the worshippers approach Ahura Mazdā and his most bounteous spirit in 'community' (*vərəzə̄na-*) with the ritual fire (36.1). This is followed in stanza two by an invitation to Ahura Mazdā's heavenly fire to come down and merge with the ritual fire. Such a fusion of the heavenly and earthly fires must take place between the recitation of stanzas two and three, because the latter explicitly identifies the ritual fire with both Ahura Mazdā's heavenly fire and his most bounteous spirit.

The significance of the deixis associated with *huuō* is motivated by context. In Y 36.1 and its *Zand*, the sacrificers address and approach the deity: *ahiiā. ϑβā. āϑrō. vərəzə̄nā. paouruiiē. pairijasāmaidē mazdā. ahurā* 'With the community of this fire at first we approach you, O *Ahura Mazdā*' and *ϑβā ϑβā mainiiū spə̄ništā* 'you with your most generous spirit'. In Y 36.2 and 3, however, the community addresses the fire, thus using *huuō* 'you there'. The sacrifice is taking place in front of one type of fire which is burning in the ritual space. My interpretation also takes into account the fact that the following *yə̄ ā axtiš ahmāi yə̄m axtōiiōi dåŋhē* 'which is truly harm for the one whom you assign to harm' in Y 36.1b–c can only denote the fire that we already know from the *Gāϑās*. I do not see any evidence for a heavenly fire of *Ahura Mazdā* which is different than the ritual fire.[21]

---

[21] It must have been this single ritual fire, *Ahura Mazdā*'s fire, which morphed into the concept of an ever-burning fire through centuries of scholastic engagement and building of various networks of correspondences (Section 4.4). This includes the development and correlation of *Wahrām* fires, which *Zādspram* discusses in his anthology (Section 4.3.5).

4.2 THE YOUNGER AVESTA

The association of the fire with *Ahura Mazdā* is developed further in the YAv. sections of the *Yasna* text, while references to *ātar-* increase concurrently.²² Right at the beginning of the *Yasna*, in Y 0.2, the fire is introduced as *Ahura Mazdā*'s son:

Y 0.2 āϑrō ahurahe mazdå puϑrahe
tauua ātarš puϑra ahurahe mazdå

Of the fire, of the son of *Ahura Mazdā*,
your fire, the son of *Ahura Mazdā*

This set phrase, declaring the fire as *Ahura Mazdā*'s son, marks a development from the OAv. to YAv. *Yasna*, and is constantly repeated throughout the text.²³ This change, however, is not restricted to the *Yasna*. In a remarkable sequence in the *Zamyād Yašt* (Yt 19.46), when the fire is sent by the *spəṇtō mańiiuš* 'Bounteous Spirit' to seize the *Glory*, the fire is introduced as *ātrəmca ahurahe mazdå puϑrəm* 'and the fire, the son of *Ahura Mazdā*' (see Hintze 1994: 241). In the consecutive stanzas, Yt 19.47–49, the text speaks again of *Ahura Mazdā*'s fire: *ātarš mazdå ahurahe* 'the fire of *Ahura Mazdā*'. This suggests that it is the *Gāϑic* fire of *Ahura Mazdā* which is designated as *Ahura Mazdā*'s son in the YAv. texts. Similarly, in the *Wīdēwdād* the fire's designation is *ahurahe mazdå puϑrəm* 'the son of *Ahura Mazdā*'.²⁴

Y 0.11 repeats the phrase of Y 0.2, but adds *maṯ vīspaēibiiō ātərəbiiō* 'with all the fires', occurring 12 times in the YAv. *Yasna*, once in *Niyāyišn* (Ny) 5.6 and once in *Sīrōzag* (S) 1.9, which contains Ny 5.6. Since no plural form of *ātar-* is attested in OAv. (see Section 4.1.3), we may view the instr.pl. *ātərəbiiō* as one of the earliest attested allusions to the existence of multiple fires in the *Avesta*. Thus, a group of fires emerge in the YAv. *Yasna* that seem to accompany *Ahura Mazdā*'s single fire, which in turn has developed into *Ahura Mazdā*'s son. It is likely that the fires invoked in Y 0.11 are the five fires mentioned in Y 17.11, repeated again in Y 59.11:²⁵

Y 17.11 ϑβąm. ātrəm. ahurahe. mazdå. puϑrəm. yazo
ātrəm. bərəzisauuaŋhəm.²⁶ yazo
ātrəm. vohu.friiānəm.²⁷ yazo

---

²² Although in part outdated, Wesendonk (1931: 25–30) offers probably one of the earliest and for the time most comprehensive surveys of the fire in the *Avesta*, anticipating much of the later scholarship on the fire, the YH and much of what I discuss in this section.
²³ Variations of *āϑrō ahurahe mazdå puϑrahe* and *ātarš puϑra ahurahe mazdå* occur 18 and 11 times in the YAv. *Yasna*, respectively. The former 17 and the latter five times before Y 28 and respectively once in Y 66.11 and six times after Y 53. See Bartholomae (1904: 312–16) for attestations of *ātar-*.
²⁴ See, for instance, V 5.2, 8.14–15 and 22, 15.45 and 48.
²⁵ Text after Pt4, translation with modifications after Hintze (2007b: 122).
²⁶ See Bartholomae (1904: 961).
²⁷ See Bartholomae (1904: 1433).

ātrəm. uruuāzištəm.²⁸ yazō
ātrəm. vāzištəm.²⁹ yazō
ātrəm. spə̄ništəm.³⁰ yazō
xšaϑrəm. nafəδrəm. nairiiosaŋhəm. yazatəm. yazō
ātrəm. vīspanąm. nmānanąm. nmānō.paitīm. mazdaδātą̊°m. ahurahe. mazdå. puϑrəm. ašauuanəm. ašahe. ratūm. yazō maṱ. vīspaēibiiō. ātərəibiiō

We sacrifice to you, the fire, son of *Ahura Mazdā*.
We sacrifice to the fire of high strength.
We sacrifice to the fire who loves what is good.
We sacrifice to the most joyful fire.
We sacrifice to the most invigorating fire.
We sacrifice to the most bounteous fire.
We sacrifice to Nairyōsaŋha, the grandson of rule, worthy of sacrifice.
We sacrifice to the fire, the master of all houses, set in place by Mazdā, to the son
    of *Ahura Mazdā*, the orderly one, the *ratu* of order,
together with all fires.

Of the five fires mentioned in this passage, three are known as adjectives from Y 36.2–3 (Hintze 2007b: 122): *ātrəm uruuāzištəm* = *uruuāzištō*, *ātrəm vāzištəm* = *vāzištəm* and *ātrəm spə̄ništəm* = *spə̄ništō*. Narten (1986: 157, fn. 84) suggests that the three names in Y 17.11 derive from Y 36. The origin of the two other names that occur in Y 17.11 but not in the YH remain unexplained: *ātrəm bərəzisauuaŋhəm* and *ātrəm vohu.friiānəm*. These two names are not otherwise linked in a semantically close relationship with the fire in the Older *Avesta*. Their absence in the YH may be attributable to a number of factors such as the ritual context of the liturgical text, though such claims are difficult to verify. Beside the names cited in Y 17.11, other epithets of the fire are known as well: *nəmišta-* 'most venerating' in Y 36.2 and *spənjayri-* 'spurting prosperity' in Wd 19.40 (Hintze 2007a: 141).³¹

4.2.1 Summary

According to Knipe (1972), a similar development from one fire toward a pentad also takes place in Hinduism. He speculates that the five-fold Iranian fires and their locations are most likely inherited from Indo-Iranian traditions (Knipe 1972: 40, fn. 27). No doubt he is right that the fire's presence in the heavens, human bodies, plants, clouds and on earth reflects the penetrating presence and the cosmic importance that was assigned to it by Zoroastrians as well as the Vedic society. Other resemblances that he alludes to, such as

---

²⁸ See Bartholomae (1904: 1545).
²⁹ See Bartholomae (1904: 1417).
³⁰ See Bartholomae (1904: 1618).
³¹ As Hintze (2007b) has argued, Avestan *spənjayri-* is an epithet of the fire *vāzišta-* and not the name of a demon in Wd 19.40.

the dwellings of the fires, seems to invite a comparative approach. However, Knipe's comparison between the two traditions is somewhat misguided, as the locations assigned to the Iranian fires are only known through the much later Pahlavi literature. These texts may reflect old ideas, but the considerable difference in the age of the Indian and Iranian texts makes the suggestion of common Indo-Iranian roots somewhat difficult.

It is not clear whether the son of *Ahura Mazdā* is a separate fire in the Younger *Avesta*, making a total of six fires, or whether this fire embodies fire in general.[32] While the pentadic or six-fold structure presented in Y 17.11 signals the development of a more complex system, the text itself does not reveal more information on the nature or function of these fires. Considering the extant Zoroastrian corpus, it seems likely that Y 36.3, rather than supplying the names, served as a template for assigning names to fires by associating *ātar-* and *vāzišta-* with *nāman-* (see Section 4.1.3). Two other adjectives in Y 36, *uruuāzištō* and *spəništō*, were later reinterpreted as names as well. Although the exact process by which this (re)interpretation took place cannot be retraced with any amount of certainty, it is not an isolated instance. We know other OAv. concepts that have similarly been adopted into the Younger *Avesta*. For example, the YAv. expression *ahurānī- ahurahe*, mainly attested in the text of the *āb zōhr* 'The water ritual' (Y 62.11 to Y 70), is a reinterpretation of OAv. *ahurāniš ahurahiiā* in Y 38.3 (see Hintze 2007a: 232–5).[33] A similar process of adoption has been argued for OAv. *yazamaidē* 'we sacrifice to', which does not occur in the *Gāθās* but 17 times in the YH (Hintze 2007a: 159). The expected YAv. form is **yazamaiδe*, with an intervocalic *-δ-* and a short final *-e*. However, due to the retention of the OAv. intervocalic *-d-* in YAv. *yazamaide*, Narten (1986: 168) and Hintze (2007a: 159) view the YAv. form as a loan word from OAv. and propose that the YH may have served as a template for the frequent *yazamaide* formulae in the Younger *Avesta*.

The surviving texts and manuscripts thus seem to support the conclusion that the YH and perhaps other OAv. sections had some influence on the composition and development of the technical terminology of the Younger *Avesta*. More broadly, in the relationship between the two layers of the *Yasna*, parts of the Younger *Avesta* constitute an exegesis of the Older *Avesta* in agreement with the scholastic categories outlined in the previous chapter. In the above examples, the elaborations of the Younger *Avesta* on the fires display

---

[32] A five-fold structure is also visible in the number of the *aməša- spənta-* and the *Niyāyišn* (Boyce 1996: 212, 271). The number of the *Gāθās* and the *gāh* are five as well.

[33] The relationship between the two expressions has been debated and cannot be established beyond doubt. Hintze (2007a: 232–5), who summarises the debate in detail, offers the most convincing arguments for a relationship between Y 38.3 and Y 68.

a tendency toward scholastic scholastic proliferativity (see Section 3.3). Moreover, the exegetes' preference for the Older *Avesta* as scripture is evident in the exegesis of the OAv. prayers *yaϑā ahū vairiiō*, *ašəm vohū* and *yeŋ́hē hātąm*, which has survived in the YAv. *Bagān Yašt*, Y 19–21. These three chapters preserve one of the earliest examples of canonical commentary in Zoroastrianism. A presumably later insertion of a formula in archaic YAv. (Humbach 1991: 116), suggests an early veneration of the *Gāϑās* as form of deified scripture:

> *nəmō və̄ gāϑā̊ ašaonīš*
>
> Homage to you, O orderly *Gāϑās*.

Each of the five *Gāϑās* is preceded with this introductory formula (Y 28.0, 43.0, 47.0, 51.0 and 53.0). The archaic form of the language, the personification of the *Gāϑās* and the direct address highlight the high status ascribed to the *Gāϑās* early on. Additionally, Y 28, is preceded by a verse that suggests that the *Gāϑās* were possibly considered ritual offering to the *aməšā spəṇtā*:

> *yānīm manō yānīm vacō yānīm šiiaoϑnəm ašaonō zaraϑuštrahe*
> *fərā aməšā spəṇtā gāϑā̊ gə̄uruuāin*
> *nəmō və̄ gāϑā̊ ašaonīš*
>
> Boon granting is the thought, boon granting is the word, boon granting is the action of orderly Zaraϑuštra.
> May the bounteous immortals accept the *Gāϑās*.
> Homage to you, O orderly *Gāϑās*.

4.3 PAHLAVI LITERATURE

MP texts frequently define the *Avesta*, or more generally the *dēn*, as the source of their knowledge: *čiyōn az dēn/abestāg paydāg* 'as it is manifest in the *dēn/abestāg*' or *gōwēd pad dēn* 'it says in the *dēn*'.[34] Yet, due to the historical lacunae in the transmission of the extant corpus we are unable to fully comprehend the developments of ideas from the Av. to MP literature. It remains unclear whether the more complex structures of the later tradition such as the YAv. fires, are YAv. innovations or continuations from older times resurfacing in later texts. Be that as it may, the exegesis of the *Gāϑās*, which started in the Younger *Avesta*, is more pronounced in the MP literature. Here we find scholastic interpretations of *Gāϑic* concepts and complex systems reminiscent of correlative structures known from other cultures.

---

[34] It is customary to translate *gōwēd* in this context as 'there is one who says'. I prefer 'it says' and 'it is said'.

4.3.1 The *Gāϑic* fire in the *Zand*

Surprisingly, the *Gāϑic* fire is not part of a more complex and elaborate structure in the *Zand* either. Translated *ātaxš*, in six out of eight stanzas it appears in the context of *judgement*: PY 31.3, 31.19, 34.4, 43.4, 47.6 and 51.9. This judgement is presumably the ordeal (*war*) as pointed out in PY 31.3, 34.4, 43.4 and 47.6. In five of the six stanzas, PY 31.3a, 31.19c, 43.4c–d, 47.6b and 51.9a, it is said of the fire that it reveals those who are saved and those who are condemned (*kū bōxt ud ēraxt paydāg kard*):

> PY 31.3a[35] *ka-t dād pad mēnōyīgīh ātaxš ī ašwahišt u-t čāšt ō pahikārdārān šnāxtārīh kū-t bōxt ud ēraxt paydāg kard*
>
> PY 31.19c *ēd ī tō ātaxš ī suxr ī ohrmazd wizārišn be dahēd ō pad pahikārdārān kū bōxt ud ēraxt paydāg be kunēd*
>
> PY 43.4c–d *kē dahēd rāst ud druwandān ud ahlawān-iz kū bōxt ud ēraxt paydāg kunēd ∵ ēd ī tō ātaxš ī garm ka-š ān kē pad ahlāyīh ōz kū-š war sālār ān ī nēk*
>
> PY 47.6b *ātaxš wizārišn be dahēd ō *pahikārdārān*[36] *kū bōxt ud ēraxt paydāg kunēd*
>
> PY 51.9a *kē šnāyīdārīh ō pahikārdārān dahēd kū bōxt ud ēraxt paydāg kunēd dahēd ēd ī tō ātaxš ī suxr ohrmazd*

PY 31.19 and 47.6b refer to the judgement most explicitly: *(ātaxš) wizārišn be dahēd ō pahikārdārān kū bōxt ud ēraxt paydāg (be) kunēd* 'The fire declares the decision to the disputants, that is, it reveals the saved and the condemned ones.' PY 34.4a belongs with the above group. It does not mention *bōxt ud ēraxt*, but in a comment refers to the fire as the ordeal-master (*war sālār*):

> PY 34.4a *ēdōn ēd ī tō ātaxš ī ōzōmand ohrmazd ā-š pad ōy kē ahlāyīh hunsandīh kū-š hunsandīh pad ān zamān war sālār ān kē kār ud kirbag kard ēstēd*

Thus, this your strong fire, O *Ohrmazd*, is then content on account of righteousness, that is, its contentment is at that time (when)[37] it is the ordeal-master.[38] That one who has performed actions and meritorious deeds.[39]

---

[35] Texts after Pt4.
[36] Pt4 has *pahikārdārišn*.
[37] While Pt4 omits *ka*, it is attested in T6, J2 M1.
[38] Commonly, the *war sālār* is thought of as a person who oversees or conducts the ordeal (see Macuch 1993: 108). Here the term is used in a figurative sense.
[39] The syntactic position and relationship of *ān kē kār ud kirbag kard ēstēd* is not very clear. My translation takes into account the repetition of this stanza in Pahlavi Ny 5.17, where we find an additional comment: *kū hunsandīh pad ān zamān ka war sālār ān kē kār kerbag kerd ēstēd kū hunsandīh ān zamān bawēd ka andar mardōm ahlāyīh ud kerbag ēstēd* '..., that is, contentment will be achieved at that time when righteousness and meritorious deeds exist among people'.

A similar notion emerges from a passage in Dk 9 on the *spəṇtā.mainiiu gāθā*:

> **Dk 9.40.12**[40] *ud ēn-iz kū ātaxš wizārišn be dahēd ō *pahikārdārān*[41] *kū bōxt ud ēraxt paydāg*[42] *kunēd ka-š ān kē stabr bowandag menišnīh ud ahlāyīh-iz padiš war sālār ud ān was ka nigerēnd ā-šān wurrōyēd druwandān ān ī nērang ī war*
>
> And this too, that the fire declares the decision to the disputants, that is, it reveals the saved and the condemned ones, when he is that one who embodies strong right-mindedness and also righteousness, (namely) the ordeal-master. And it is enough when they observe, then the formula of the ordeal chooses them as deceitful.

These passages clarify that *kū bōxt ud ēraxt paydāg kunēd* refers to the declaration of the judgement, as it explains *ātaxš wizārišn be dahēd* 'the fire declares the decision'. The interpretation of the fire as a judge and ordeal-master resonates with PRDd 18d14, the seventh complaint of the fire to *Ohrmazd*:

> **PRDd 18d14**[43] *haftom ān ka pad war ī passāxt ka-m bōxt ud ēraxt paydāg be kard jud-dādestān hēnd kū-š nē-iz pad čim dādestān kard*
>
> Seventh (is) that, when at the ordeal of the test, when the saved and the damned are declared by me, they will disagree, saying: 'Truly, he has not acted with reason and justice'.

The above passage suggests that it is the fire that makes and reveals the judgement and not *Ohrmazd*. In fact, in PRdD 18d21 the fire agrees to be created in the material world only after *Ohrmazd* has promised to make it the gatekeeper at the entry to *wahišt*:

> **PRDd 18d21**[44] *pas-iz ātaxš pad tan be ō gētīg dād andar nē estād tā-š ohrmazd pušt abāg be kard u-š pad dar ī wahišt pādixšāy be kard u-š wazr-ē frāz awiš dād u-š framūd kū harw kē-š tō aziš nē hušnūd hē pad ēn warz be ō dušox abganēd* **18d22** *u-š pas pad dādan ō gētīg ham-dādestān būd*
>
> Even then the fire did not agree to being created bodily in the material world, until Ohrmazd provided him with a safeguard, and made him the lord at the gate of Heaven. And he brought forth a mace for him, and he ordered him, saying: 'Everyone with whom you are not pleased, cast down into Hell with this mace. And then he agreed to his being created in the material world.'

Thus, in the *Zand* the *Gāθic* fire is considered a judge in the ordeal. The fire's complaint in PRdD 18d14, where *war ī passāxt* 'the ordeal of the test' is mentioned, and *Ohrmazd*'s subsequent concession to make the fire the

---

[40] Text after Dresden (1966: 161).
[41] B has *pahikārān*.
[42] Barely readable.
[43] Text and translation after Williams (1990: I 99, II 37).
[44] Text and translation after Williams (1990: I 101, II 38).

gatekeeper of *wahišt*, suggest that it is the eschatological ordeal where the fire will act as a judge.

In the two other remaining *Gāθic* stanzas the fire is once venerated and another time described as a protector:

PY 43.9d *ēdōn ō ēd ī tō ātaxš rād hom pad niyāyišn* 'Thus, I am generous to this your fire through prayer.'

PY 46.7c *anī az ašmā ātaxš ud wahman čē ašmāh rāy dānom kū-m pānagīh kunēd* 'Other than you, O fire and *Wahman*, for I know of you that you protect me.'

The *Zand* of both passages take up the themes of the respective *Gāθic* verses.

4.3.2   PY 17.11

In contrast to the *Zand*'s approach to the *Gāθic* fire, PY 17.11 is more verbose and reveals the *Zand*'s proliferative tendency. The simple list of the Av. stanza (see Section 4.2) is here enriched by further information on the fires:

PY 17.11[45] *tō ātaxš ī ohrmazd pus andar yazišn yazom ∴ ātaxš ī buland sūd yazom wahrām pad ēwkardagīh ∴ ātaxš ī weh franāftār yazom ān andar tan ī mardomān ∴ ātaxš ī frāx zīwišn yazom ān andar urwar ∴ ātaxš wāzišt yazom ān dēw spenjruš zanēd ∴ ātaxš ī abzōnīg yazom ān andar garōdmān pēš ī ohrmazd pad mēnōyīh ēstēd ∴ xwadāy ī nāf nēryōsang dād yazom ∴ ātaxš harwispēn mān mānbēd ohrmazd-dād ī ohrmazd pus ī ahlaw ī ahlāyīh rad yazam abāg harwispēn ātaxšān ∴*

We worship you, the fire of *Ohrmazd*, son (of *Ohrmazd*) in the worship ∴ We worship the fire of high profits, victorious through union ∴ We worship the fire that is the propagator of good. That one resides in the body of mankind ∴ We worship the fire of prosperous life. That one resides in plants ∴ We worship the fire *Wazišt*. That one slays the demon *Spenjruš* ∴ We worship the fire that is bountiful. That one stands in front of *Ohrmazd* in *garōdmān* in *mēnōyīh* ∴ We worship the lord of the family, the just *Nēryōsang* ∴ We worship the fire, the master of all houses, created by *Ohrmazd*, the son of *Ohrmazd*, the righteous authority of righteousness, with all the fires ∴

Of the three adjectives used in Y 36 and repeated in Y 17.11, *vāzištəm* is the only one not translated in PY 36.3b and PY 17.11.[46] In PY 36.3b *wāzišt* is not further described and is only referred to as a name, *abzōnīg ast xwad tā ka ōy ī tō nām čiyōn wāzišt*, underlining its Middle Persian perception as such.

---

[45] Text after Dhabhar (1949: 93–4).
[46] Bartholomae (1904), Nyberg (1974) and MacKenzie (1990) do not furnish further information on the meaning of MP *wāzišt*. Hintze (2007a: 361) suggests 'most enlivening, most invigorating, most energizing' for *vāzišta-*. Bartholomae (1904: 1417) translates it as 'der am besten vorwärts bringt, der förderlichste, nützlichste'. Kellens and Pirart (1988: 135) prefer 'très convoyeur' and 'le plus convoyeur' (Kellens and Pirart 1990: 303), with a commentary in Kellens and Pirart (1991: 138). Considering the translations offered by Bartholomae and Kellens and Pirart, it is possible that MP *wāzišt* derives from ¹*wāzīdan, wāz-* 'move, carry away; fly' (see MacKenzie 1990: 89). Nyberg (1974: 207) considers *wāzīdan* a causative of *wazīdan, waz-* 'move, blow (of wind)'. Finally, see Hintze (2007a: 133–44) for a commentary on *nāmanąm vāzištəm*.

It is PY 17.11 that identifies *wāzišt* as the slayer of a demon: *ān dēw spenjruš zanēd*.⁴⁷ A peculiarity of the fire *wāzišt* is its connection with water. Hintze (2007b: 119) states that 'it belongs, together with the star Tištar, to a group of beneficent beings producing rain'.⁴⁸

In PY 17.11, *ātrəm uruuāzištəm* is translated *ātaxš ī frāx zīwišn* 'fire of prosperous life', while in PY 36.2 Av. *uruuāzištō* is translated *urwāhmanīh* 'joy'. Most likely, the translators of PY 36.2 did not perceive *uruuāzištō* as a name, in which case they would have chosen a name such as *urwāzišt*; a development which indeed occurred later, as evident in Bd 18 (see Table 4.1). Thus, the comments in PY 36.2 and PY 17.11 remain very close to the original. The comment on *ātaxš ī frāx zīwišn* in PY 17.11 identifies it as the fire residing in plants: *ān andar urwar*. Williams (1990 II: 158) suggests that the assonance between Avestan *uruuāzištəm* and MP *urwar* motivated this comment. This is while a cognate of Avestan *uruuāzištəm* 'most joyful', a superl.acc.sg. from the verb *uruuāz* 'to be joyful' (Hintze 2007a: 357), is attested in MP as *urwāz-* 'rejoice' (see MacKenzie 1990: 85). If so, the *Zand*'s comment would be based on a linguistically incorrect interpretation of Avestan *uruuāzišta-* 'most joyful'. However, the translation in PY 36.2, *urwāhmanīh* 'joy', shows that the correct meaning of this word was known. Thus, the identification of this fire's location as in plants, *ān andar urwar*, must have other reasons.

Avestan *spə̄ništa-* 'most bounteous' is rendered as *abzōnīg* in both passages, with a comment in PY 17.11 characterising it as the fire burning before *Ahura Mazdā*: *ān andar garōdmān pēš ī ohrmazd pad mēnōyīh ēstēd*. This is indeed the first reference to an intangible (*mēnōy*) fire that resides with *Ohrmazd* in *Garōdmān*, and as such a break with the OAv. evidence – both in the *Gāθās* and in the *Yasna Haptaŋhāiti* – and the *Zand* of Y 36.1, where the ritual fire is described as θβā mainiiū spə̄ništā 'with your most generous spirit' and translated *pad ēd ī tō mēnōy ī abzōnīg* 'with this your bountiful spirit'.

The seeming inconsistencies between PY 17.11 and PY 36.2–3 in translating the names of the fires must be attributed to differences in the original. Adjectives in Av. Y 36 are translated as such, but when the same adjectives move closer to names at a later stage (Y 17.11), the Pahlavi translation reflects this development. Thus, in both passages the PY faithfully translates the Avestan original.

Although PY 17.11 constitutes a more evolved concept of the fire, the additional information is limited to the dwelling of the individual fires,

---

⁴⁷ According to Hintze (2007b: 130) Wd 19.40, *ātrəm vāzištəm frāiiazaēša daēum.janəm spəṇjayrīm* 'You shall worship the most invigorating fire the one that slays the demon, the one that spurts prosperity', shows that the demon slaying fire is not a MP invention.
⁴⁸ Connecting *apąm napāt-* with various other IE myths, West (2007: 270) suggests a connection between the fire and water in IE poetry. While the value of the waters in Zoroastrianism is indisputable (Boyce 1996: 155–6), it is unclear how the association between *wāzišt* and water may have developed.

and the text does not specify their exact number. The uninitiated reader is inclined to include *ātaxš ī ohrmazd pus* as one of the fires, making it a total of six fires, while other MP texts clearly speak of five fires (see below).

4.3.3 Bundahišn

In a chapter on the nature of the fire, Bd 18 continues the commentarial tradition of Y 17.11, starting with a list of the five-fold fires:

> Bd 18.1[49] *abar čiyōnīh ī ātaxš gōwēd pad dēn kū panj ēwēnag ātaxš brēhēnīd ēstēd čiyōn ātaxš ī burzišwang ātaxš ī hufryān ud ātaxš ī urwāzišt ud ātaxš ī wāzišt ud ātaxš ī speništ*
>
> On the nature of the fire, it says in the *dēn* that five types of fire are fashioned, namely the fire *Burzišwang*, the fire *Hufryān*, the fire *Urwāzišt*, the fire *Wāzišt* and the fire *Speništ*.

Bd 18.2, much like PY 17.11, assigns each fire a dwelling, and Bd 18.3 additionally identifies the fires' nutritive habits without naming the individual fires discussed. The type of nutrition is limited to *āb* 'water' and *xwarišn* 'food' and corresponds with the residence and type of the fire. *ātaxš ī urwāzišt*, for example, is described as follows: *ud ēk āb xwarēd ud xwarišn nē xwarēd čiyōn ān ī andar urwarān kē-š pad āb zīwēd ud waxšēd* 'And one consumes water and does not eat food as it is that one which is in the plants, which live and grow by means of water.'[50] The text continues with a mythological account of the three *ātaxš ī wahrām* 'the victorious fire': *ādur ī farrōbāg ud gušnasp ud burzēnmihr*.[51]

Remarkably, the names of the fires in Bd 18 differ from those listed in PY 17.11 (see Table 4.1).[52] As already noted by Bartholomae (1904: 961), the order of the fires is identical in the two texts, but the comments on *ātaxš ī burzišwang* and *ātaxš ī speništ* are reversed in Bd 18:[53]

> **PY 17.11** *ātaxš ī buland sūd yazom wahrām pad ēwkardagīh ... ātaxš ī abzōnīg yazom ān andar garōdmān pēš ī ohrmazd pad mēnōyīh ēstēd*
>
> **Bd 18**[54] *ātaxš ī burzišwang ātaxš ī pēš ī ohrmazd xwadāy waxšēd ... ātaxš ī speništ ān ī andar gēhān pad kār dāšt ēstēd ud ātaxš-iz wahrām*

---

[49] Text after Pakzad (2005: 228).
[50] Text after Pakzad (2005: 229).
[51] For another short account on the three *ātaxš ī wahrām* and their history, see Mazdapur (1999: 250–2).
[52] The MSS note the names differently.
[53] See also Williams (1990 II: 157ff).
[54] The passage about *burzišwang* is only attested in K20 and M51, and Pakzad (2005: 228, fn. 2) does not include it in his constituted text.

Table 4.1 The five fires in the Y, PY and Bd

Y 17.11	PY 17.11	Bd 18
ātrəm bərəzisauuaŋhəm	ātaxš ī buland sūd	ātaxš ī burzišwang
ātrəm vohu.friiānəm	ātaxš ī weh franāftār	ātaxš ī hufryān
ātrəm uruuāzištəm	ātaxš ī frāx zīwišn	ātaxš ī urwāzišt
ātrəm vāzištəm	ātaxš wāzišt	ātaxš ī wāzišt
ātrəm spəništəm	ātaxš ī abzōnīg	ātaxš ī speništ

With the exception of the comments on *ātaxš wāzišt*, which reflect a variation in the name of the demon between PY 17.11 and Bd 18.2, the other comments are in agreement with one another.[55]

4.3.4 *Pahlavi Rivāyat* accompanying the *Dādestān ī Dēnīg*

A similar account of five fires is provided in PRDd 18. While PY 17.11 and Bd 18 do not explicitly identify the fires' creator and origin, PRDd 18d1 relates the origin of the fire to *Ohrmazd* and the endless light (*asar-rōšnīh*):[56]

> **PRDd 18d1**[57] *gyāg-ē paydāg kū ātaxš ēdōn arzōmand ohrmazd ān ī ātaxš tan ud gyān az wārom ud menišn ī xwēš be brēhēnīd u-š brāh ud xwarrah az rōšnīh ī asar-rōšnīh be brēhēnīd u-š panj be kard*
>
> (In) one place (it is) revealed that the fire (is) so valuable, Ohrmazd created the body and soul of Fire from his own mind and thought, and he created its radiance and glory from the light of the Endless Light. And he made five (fires).

PRDd 18d2 briefly describes the properties of the five fires without giving their names. The text then continues to impart various other accounts such as a complaint of the fire in an assembly with the *Amahraspandān*,[58] on establishing *ātaxš ī wahrām* and its merits, and a dialogue between *Ohrmazd*, Zardušt, *ruwān ī Kersāsp* and *ātaxš*.[59]

The complaining *ātaxš* in PRDd 18d3–22 is not further identified. Presumably, this fire is the son of *Ohrmazd*, who features in the conversation between *Ohrmazd*, Zarduš and *ruwān ī kersāsp* in PRDd 18f1–36. The other sections of this chapter are dedicated to the victorious fire (*ātaxš ī wahrām*).

---

[55] See Hintze (2007b) on the variations of the name noted as *dēw spenjruš* in PY 17.11.
[56] In Bd 3 the creation of the fire as an element is attributed to *Ohrmazd* without mention of the five fires.
[57] Text and translation after Williams (1990: I 97 and II 36).
[58] The complaints are reminiscent of the commentary in *Sūdgar Nask* (Dk 9.11). See Sections 4.3.1 and 4.3.6.
[59] See Williams (1990: vol. II) for his commentary, which contains much insightful information. For a synopsis of *Kersāsp*'s story, see also Dk 9.15.

4.3.5 Wizīdagīhā ī Zādspram

In contrast to *Dēnkard* and the *Bundahišn*, which are undated compilations commonly assigned to the ninth century, the *Wizīdagīhā ī Zādspram* (WZ) has a known author and can therefore be securely dated to the ninth century.[60]

In WZ, the creation story and the order of the five-fold fires change:

WZ 3.77[61] čiyōn haftom ō ātaxš mad ān-iš pad ham ātaxš <padīrag kōxšīd ān ātaxš> ō ēwēnagān †panj <baxt> ī xwānīhēd abzōnīg weh-franaftār urwāzišt wāzišt <ud> †buland-sūd

Seventh, as he [*Ahreman*] came to the fire, he [*Ohrmazd*] fought against it with the fire as well. That fire was divided into five types, which are called *abzōnīg*, *weh-franaftār*, *urwāzišt*, *wāzišt* and *buland-sūd*.

Here the fires are created in the battle against *Ahreman's* onslaught, a detail missing in PRDd 18. In the subsequent sections, WZ 3.78–82, which I paraphrase here, Zādspram elaborates on the five fires: the *abzōnīg* fire (WZ 3.78) was created in *Garōdmān* and is represented by the earthly fire. Its bountifulness (*abzōnīgīh*) is explained as its ability to increase all species to their own nature. The fire *weh-franaftār* (WZ 3.79) dwells in people and cattle. It helps with the digestion of food, heats the body and brightens the eyes. Created in their seed, *urwāzišt* lives in plants (WZ 3.80). Its duties are to bore the earth, to heat and warm up water, thereby making the plants' blossoms delightful, beautiful and fragrant. It ripens the fruits and garnishes them with many tastes. The fire *wāzišt* (WZ 3.81) moves about in clouds and smites the atmospheric gloom and darkness. It makes the coarseness of the atmosphere thin and light-natured and melts hail. In order to make the clouds full of drops and warm, it moderately warms up the water which the clouds hold. *buland-sūd* is the fire in the sky (WZ 3.82). It is the glory whose abode is in the *Wahrām* fire like a house lord in the house. Its bountiful strength comes from the glow of the fire, the burning of the fragrance, the purity of place, the praise of the *Yazadān* and the performance of good deeds.

In agreement with (P)Y 17.11, all Pahlavi accounts mention *buland sūd* or *burzišwang* first and *abzōnīg* or *speništ* last (see Table 4.2). In Bd 18 these two fires appear in the same order as in (P)Y 17.11, but the comments are reversed. Curiously, in WZ the order of these two fires is reversed along with the respective comments.[62] It is also noteworthy that the *wāzišt* fire's opposition

---

[60] On Zādspram himself, see Sohn (1996: 28–34).

[61] Text after Gignoux and Tafazzoli (1993: 54), who have emended the passage as it is wanting in the MSS. See their critical notes and also Anklesaria (1964: 40).

[62] The different order of the fires in Zādspram's anthology is conspicuous and reminds us of Bd 18, where the comments on *ātaxš ī burzišwang* and *ātaxš ī speništ* are misplaced. Although Zādspram does not include the comments from the *Bundahišn* in his anthology, it is possible that he changed the position

Table 4.2 The five fires

Y 17.11	PY 17.11	Bd 18	PRDd 18d2	WZ 3.77
bərəzisauuaŋhəm vohu.friiānəm	buland sūd weh franāftār	burzišwang hufryān	andar garōdmān andar tan ī mardōmān	abzōnīg weh franāftār
uruuāzištəm	frāx zīwišn	urwāzišt	dēw ī spanjagr padiš zanēd	urwāzišt
vāzištəm	wāzišt	wāzišt	andar āb ud urwar	wāzišt
spəništəm	abzōnīg	speništ	be ō gētīg kāmist dād	buland sūd

to a demon is not mentioned in WZ 3.81, while Zādspram's familiarity with the myth is evident from WZ 3.17:

> **WZ 3.17**[63] *andar ān abr ud wārān būd* *tazišn <ud> pahikafišn ī Tištar ud Ātaxš ī Wāzišt pad hamēstārīh ī Apōš ud Sponjagr
>
> In those clouds and rain there was the chase and fight of *Tištar* and the fire *Wāzišt* in opposition to *Apōš* and *Sponjagr*.

The interpretive tradition culminates when Zādspram expands the fire's role to the physiological realm.[64] While similar accounts appear in other texts, such as the *Bundahišn*, Zādspram's detailed attention to the fire's role in the anatomy of humans seems to be an innovation. Fire serves two purposes in Zādspram's anthology. Firstly, he uses fire metaphorically to describe *gyān* 'soul, ghost',[65] as in the following passage:

---

of the two fires to correct the misplacement he found in Bd 18. This is not further surprising, as the *Bundahišn* may have been the intellectual background to the physiology found in WZ Sohn (see 1996: XV). Likewise, Zādspram may have relied on the PY for his elaboration on the *Ahunwar* prayer (see Gropp 1991). We might, however, ask why Zādspram would rely on the *Bundahišn* for the description of the fires and not the PY? From a methodological vantage point, the search for Zādspram's source might be a futile one. In a religious tradition with a predominant oral transmission and large gaps in the written transmission, it is difficult to pinpoint the source for Zādspram's version. No doubt a prominent priest such as Zādspram was familiar with the various Zoroastrian myths and might have consciously chosen this particular order for the fires. None of the texts discussed so far indicate that the fires had to adhere to the order found in (P)Y 17.11. Just as the wording of all the passages discussed above differ in their literary expression and content, the order in which the fires were discussed might have been subject to individual preferences as well. As we have seen, the texts do not show a unified and monolithically transmitted religious tradition, but attest variation in whether they use names for the fires and in the choice of names.

[63] Text after Gignoux and Tafazzoli (1993: 42).

[64] For discussions of Zādspram's view of human physiology, see Bailey (1943: 104ff.) and Sohn (1996: 1–39).

[65] Sohn (1996: 153) translates *gyān* as 'life, life-fire' ('Leben, Lebensfeuer'), while Gignoux and Tafazzoli (1993: 402) simply prefer 'life' ('vie'). Sohn's translation is probably based on *gyānīg ātaxš* 'Lebensfeuer', attested only once in WZ 29.6 with an uncertain reading (Sohn 1996: 52, 100; Gignoux and Tafazzoli 1993: 96, 259, 356). Gignoux and Tafazzoli (1993: 97) translate it as 'le feu vital'. Sohn's 'Lebensfeuer', however, by and large seems to be confirmed by the usage of *gyān* in the text.

WZ 29.3[66] *ud gyān kē tan zīndag dārēd be ō ātaxš ī andar gumbad abar gāh nišānēnd (4) … ham-gōnag *gyān gōhar rōšnīh ud garmīh u-š maništ andar dil čiyōn ātaxš abar ādur-gāh ud xōn andar rahagān *tāxtag hamāg tan garm dārēd brāh payrōg abar barēd pad dō rōzan ī abar sar ī xwad hēnd čašmān be abganēd wēnāgīh ī čašmān ud hu-bōyāgīh ī wēnīgān ud āšnawāgīh ī gōšān ud mizagdārīh ī dahān ud pahrmāhāgīh ī tanān ud jumbāgīh ī *ēwēnag az ham čihr*

And the soul, which keeps the body alive, (is like) the fire that they enthrone in the fire-temple. (4) … Likewise, the substance of the soul is light and warmth. Its abode is in the heart like the fire on the fire altar. And blood flows through the veins, keeping the body warm. It carries up the brilliance and light and throws them through the two windows that are in its own head, (namely) the eyes. The sight of the eyes and the smelling sense of the nose and the hearing of the ears and the taste sense of the mouth and the touch sense of the body and the motion are of the same essence.

Zādspram first describes how fire lights and warms up a fire temple and how this light is visible through its windows. The soul has a similar function in that it sits in the middle of the body and provides it with light and warmth, which it carries to the eyes, the windows of the body.

Secondly, he views the fire as an essential building block of the human body (WZ 30.23–32). Here, WZ 30.31 is particularly illustrative:

WZ 30.31[67] *ud ēn *sē ātaxš ān ī andar sar āsrōn čihrag u-š ādur Farrōbāg ayār-tar ān ī andar dil artēštār čihrag u-š ādur Gušnasp ayār-tar ud ān ī andar kumīg wāstaryōš čihrag u-š ādur Burzēnmihr ayār-tar*

And (of) these three fires, the one in the head is of the essence of the priests and has the *Farrōbāg* fire as its helper; the one in the heart is of the essence of the warrior and has the *Gušnasp* fire as its helper, and the one in the stomach is of the essence of the husbandmen and has the *Burzēnmihr* fire as its helper.

Zādspram creates a network of correspondences by relating three fires to three locations in the human body, then linking these to social classes and victorious fires.[68]

4.3.6 *Dēnkard*

Book 9 of the *Dēnkard* maintains a very close tie to the scripture by containing three commentaries on the *Avesta*: *Sūdgar Nask*, *Warštmānsr Nask* and *Bag Nask*. Within these three *nasks*, Dk 9.12.1–32 (*Sūdgar*), 9.35.1–26 (*Warštmānsr*) and 9.57.1–30 (*Bag*) relate to the (P)YH. The

---

[66] Text after Sohn (1996: 51, 53). See also Gignoux and Tafazzoli (1993: 94, 95).
[67] Text after Sohn (1996: 71).
[68] As I have pointed out at the end of Section 4.1.3, I believe that the concept of the ever-burning fire in Zoroastrianism, and more generally in Iranian culture must be the result of the above scholastic development.

extensive commentaries of the *Sūdgar Nask* are most challenging, resembling a free interpretation without reflecting immediately recognisable content of the original text.[69] By contrast, the exegetical style of the *Warštmānsr* and the *Bag Nask* generally conforms to the original and is less obscure.

The introductory statements to Dk 9.11 and 9.12 suggest that the commentary on the YH is organised by an internal logic of a narrative and ordered sequentially. The narrative starts in Dk 9.11 on Y 34:

> Dk 9.11.1[70] *dahom fragard yāšyōsn abar garzišn ī ātaxšān mēnōy ō ohrmazd az mardōmān haft dar*
>
> The tenth *fragard*, the *Yā.šiiaoϑanā*, is about the complaint of the Spirit of the Fires to Ohrmazd about the seven types of people.

In the succeeding section, a summary of the YH, the gods attend to the complaints put forward in the previous section:

> Dk 9.12.1[71] *yāzdahom fragard esn abar hanjaman ī mēnōyān yazdān garzišn ī ātaxš rāy*
>
> The eleventh *fragard*, the *Yasna (Haptaŋhāiti)*, is about the assembly of the gods of the world of thought because of the complaint of the fire.

The spirit of the fires complains about a number of issues (Dk 9.11), leading to an assembly of the deities of the intangible world (Dk 9.12). Dk 9.11 resembles the laments of the fire in PRDd 18d8–15, which takes place in an assembly of the *Amahraspandān* (see Section 4.3.4). While the texts are substantially different in their formulations, both Dk 9.11 and PRDd 18d8–15 correspond in the order and type of the complaints. A noteworthy difference between the two texts is that a single fire laments in PRDd 18d, whereas here it is the spirit of the fires that complains. The actual content of Dk 9.12, however, is difficult, if not impossible, to link to the text of the (P)YH by any textual references. The following paragraph serves as an example:

> Dk 9.12.3[72] *guftan ī ātaxš kū agar nē ān ēwēnag-ēw az ān kū ēdōn čiyōn-am xwāhišn kard kū ēdōn az*[73] *rošnēnēm*[74] *ohrmazd āgāh hē*[75] *andar dāmān kū ēdōn nē šāyēm dād*[76] *ēg man ohrmazd stān ēg man ānōh bē dah pad mayān ērān-wēz*
>
> The saying of the fire that: '(If)[77] not (in) that one manner, for (it is) thus how I pleaded that I shall light up, O *Ohrmazd*, you know that you shall not establish

---

[69] For an analysis of the *Sūdgar Nask*, see Vevaina (2007).
[70] For the complete text and translation, see Vevaina (2007: 251–5).
[71] For the complete text and translation, see Vevaina (2007: 256–66).
[72] Text after Dresden (1966: 243).
[73] B has ⟨'NH⟩.
[74] B has ⟨lwšn•ynm⟩.
[75] B has ⟨ḤWH'-yy̆⟩.
[76] B has a gap and then ⟨t'⟩.
[77] DH D10a J5 have *agar* here, missing in B K43b.

me in this manner among the creations. Then, take hold of me, O *Ohrmazd*, then establish me there, in the middle of *Ērān-wēz*.'[78]

The fire that is then placed in *Ērān-wēz*, is the *Wahrām* fire. By contrast, the *Warštmānsr Nask* generally hews to the original, featuring quotations from the *Zand* of Y 36:

> Dk 9.35[79] (10) *ud ēn-iz*[80] *kū an ham mēnōy ī abzōnīg kē fradom ud hamē bawam ud nē pad tis bē frēftom* (11) *abar dād ī ohrmazd ātaxš ō srāyišn ud ayārīh ud pānugīh ī mardomān ud yaštan ud ayārēnīdan ī mardōm ud mēnōy ī ātaxš ō ōy kē-š* urwāhmanīh ud ō ōy kē-š[81] *niyāyišn kunēd niyāyišn kardan* (12) *ud ān ī meh kār ī ast passāxt ī pad tan ī pasēn kē*[82] *padiš dām abēzag bawēd pad ātaxš bawēd xwāst abāyist ī mardom az yazadān āyift rāy* (13) *ēn-iz kū če ēdōn tō zardušt šnāyēnīdārtom kū-mān weš pad rāmišn tuwān kardan hu-madārīhatar hēm kū-mān weh tuwān madan ka az amā xwāhē zardušt kē amahraspand hēm* (14) *ud abar nimūdan ī ohrmazd ō zarduxšt dāmān pad tan ī pasēn.*

> (10) And this, too, that I am the bountiful spirit who (was) at first and always will be, and I am not deceived by anything. (11) About *Ohrmazd*'s creation of the fire for shelter, help and protection of mankind, and mankind's worship and help; and (about) the spirit of the fire (being) for him, whose joy it is, and for him who praises it for the sake of praising (it). (12) And that great event, that is the ordeal at the (time of) the final body, by which the creation becomes pure, happens through the fire; (and) about the necessity of seeking the boon from the *Yazadān* by mankind. (13) This, too, is said that since you, O Zardušt, are thus most pleasing, that is, you can soothe us the most, we are better-comers, that is, we can approach better, when you want it from us, O Zardušt, we who are the Bounteous Immortals. (14) And about *Ohrmazd* showing to Zardušt the creations in the final body.

The third of the commentaries, the *Bag Nask*, takes a similar approach to the YH as the *Warštmānsr Nask*:

> Dk 9.57[83] (12) *ud ēn-iz kū-š pahrēz ud tarsagāhīh ī ātaxš kard bawēd kē ō ātaxš rād abar tis be dahēd ud pahrēz ud tarsagāhīh ī ātaxš kunēd ud ōy padiš ham mizd bawēd* (13) *ud ēn-iz kū kē pad urwāhmanīh dēn ī ohrmazd čāšēd ā-š pahrēz ud tarsagāhīh ī ātaxš čiyōn az dēn paydāg kard bawēd ēd-iz rāy čē-š ān-iz hammōxt pad kunišn ī az ān hammōzišn ham bawēd* (14) *ud ēn-iz kū niyāyišn ī niyāyišn niyābagān wizārd bawēd kē wahman dōšēd* (15) *ud ēn-iz kū-š ātaxš pad ān ī meh kār ī ast passāxt ī pad tan ī pasēn zōrēnīd bawēd kē ātaxš pad ātaxš nāmīh xwānēd ēd-iz rāy čē-š nām abar čiyōnīh ī stāyišnīg nihād estēd ud ka-š pad ān nām xwānd ēg-iš stūd ud zōrēnīd bawēd*

---

[78] The essence of the fire's statement is: 'If I cannot be established in the manner that I requested, that is up in the sky, then, O *Ohrmazd*, you shall establish me right in the middle of *Ērān-wēz*.' For an alternative translation, see Vevaina (2007: 263).
[79] Text after Dresden (1966: 172).
[80] B has ⟨WZNH wc⟩.
[81] ⟨'wlw'hmn'yh W 'L 'LH MNW-š⟩.
[82] B has ⟨MN⟩.
[83] Text after Dresden (1966: 213). I have ignored minor spelling irregularities.

(12) And this too, that care and reverence are performed for the fire by him who generously gives things to the fire and performs care and reverence for the fire. And he too receives the reward. (13) And this too, that he who teaches the *dēn* of *Ohrmazd* with joy, he has performed care and reverence for the fire, as it is manifest from the *dēn*, also because that which he teaches equals the action which is from that teaching. (14) And this too, that the praise of those who deserve praise is fulfilled (by him) who loves *Wahman*. (15) And this too, that the fire is strengthened at that great event which is the trial of the final body by him who calls the fire with the name of the fire, also because its name rests upon the praiseworthy nature and when it is called by that name, then it is praised and strengthened.

Here too, a number of direct quotations from the PYH bind commentary to the source: *pahrēz* (36.1), *tarsagāhīh* (36.4), *urwāhmanīh* (36.2), *ān ī meh kār ī ast passāxt ī pad tan ī pasēn* (36.2). Dk 9.57.15 stands out, as it explains why the name of the fire matters: addressing the fire by its name (36.3) at the *frašgird* (36.2), strengthens it.

The comparison of the three *nask*s seems to suggest that the exegetes could have taken a levelled interpretive approach to the *Avesta*. Curiously, it is the second commentary, the *Warštmānsr Nask*, that is closest to the original, resembling 'a literal textual commentary' (Vevaina 2007: 11), while the *Sūdgar Nask* is somewhat distanced from the original text. The *Bag Nask* seems to occupy the middle ground, by being more interpretive than the *Warštmānsr* but still more literal than the *Sūdgar Nask*. One question is how Dk 9.12 and 9.35, the two extremes, relate to each other and ultimately to the YH. Despite apparent differences between the two *nask*s and a lack of obvious references to the YH in Dk 9.12, I argue that both sections maintain a strong link to the YH, particularly Y 36.

In the footnotes of his edition, Vevaina (2007) draws attention to a number of references from Dk 9 to other Zoroastrian texts, highlighting the *Dēnkard*'s intertextual reading of the Zoroastrian canon. Although not discussed by Vevaina, Dk 9.12 contains a number of references to the fire, one of which I shall briefly discuss here:

Dk 9.12.5[84] *u-š ēdōn pad gōwišn guft kū ēdōn tō kē man ātaxš hē *rōyišnēnē-š*[85] *pad harwisp mān kū rasē ud harwisp wis harwisp zand harwisp deh ēdōn tō burzānd āb ud urwar ud kē-iz ahlawān frawahr ka tō bē pad abespārišnīh*[86] *zōhr frāz barēnd mardōm ka ō tō ēsm frāz barēnd ī bušk ud pad rōšn ēdōn guft kū ēn ādur gušnasp*

And thus at (the time of) the speech, he said: 'In this manner, you, who are my fire, shall grow in every dwelling, where you arrive, and (in) every village, every district, (and in) all lands. And they shall thus honour you, the waters, the

---

[84] Text after Dresden (1966: 242–3).
[85] B has ⟨lwdšn'ndyh⟩ or ⟨lwdšn'ndyš⟩. DH reads ⟨lwdšndnyš⟩.
[86] B has ⟨ʾnᴾskʾlšnyh⟩.

plants and also the *Frawahr*s of the righteous ones, when people carry forth offerings to entrust to you, when they carry forth for you firewood, which is dry and (inspected) by light'. And he thus said: 'This is the *Gušnasp* fire'.

Ohrmazd's address to the fire, *tō kē man ātaxš hē* 'you, who are my fire', is reminiscent of the various Av. expressions where the fire is associated with *Ahura Mazdā*, foremost in Y 34.4: *aṯ tōi ātrə̄m ahurā*. Dk 9.35 corroborates this interpretation, when it invokes the fire as a support for people, *abar dād ī ohrmazd ātaxš ō srāyišn ud ayārīh ud pānagīh ī mardomān*, establishing links to Y 34.4 and 46.7.[87] Thus, both the *Sūdgar* and the *Warštmānsr Nask* allude to Y 34 in their commentaries on the YH. The reason for these allusions lies in the fact that the commentators of the *Dēnkard* associated Y 34 with the fire. This is not surprising, for, as I suggest in Section 4.1, Y 34.4 'reads like a definition of the fire'. The discussion of the fire's complaints in Dk 9.12 suggests that the point of reference to the YH is the fire too. The fire being the common denominator between Y 34 and the YH, the narrative of the fire's lamentation is covered by the commentaries of the *Sūdgar Nask* on Y 34 and the YH.[88] It is noteworthy that the above section alludes to Y 37 by mentioning the water, plants and the *Frawahr*s of the righteous ones. These allusions and cross-references to the YH and the *Gāθās* firmly link the commentaries of the *Sūdgar* and the *Warštmānsr Nask* with the scripture.

However, Dk 9.12.5 operates within a larger exegetical context and goes beyond the scripture by invoking other MP passages:

PRDd 18d20[89] *u-š be ō ātaxš guft kū pad mardomān nēkīh kunē andar hamāg mān ud andar hamāg wis ud andar hamāg zand ud andar hamāg deh ud awēšān tō burzēnd kē āb kē urwar ud kē ahlawān frawahr ka zōhr be ō tō barēnd ud ka ēsm frāz ō tō dārēnd hušk ī pad rōšnīh nigerīd*

And he said to Fire: 'Do good among men, in all dwellings and in all villages and in all districts and in all lands; and they will honour you, (those) who (are) the water, the plants and the *fravašis* of the righteous ones, when they [*i.e.* men] bring to you the offering, and when they present to you wood, dry, which has been inspected in the light.'

One passage reads as a paraphrase of the other. Dk 9.11 and 12 do not only represent an enlarged and elaborate version of the fire's complaints found in PRDd 18, but also create an intricately constructed 'mosaic of quotations'.[90]

---

[87] See Section 4.1 and the sub-section *Protection* therein.
[88] As I have indicated above, Dk 9.12 is part of a larger narrative which starts in Dk 9.11, binding these two sections together. Particularly so, as the narrative of the fire's lamentation does not extend beyond these two sections. Dk 9.10 is about sins such as anal sex, while 9.13 is about the praise of Zardušt.
[89] Text and translation after Williams (1990: I 101 and II 38).
[90] Julia Kristeva suggests that each text is the result of an intersection of other texts. This view is best described by her famous statement that 'any text is constructed as a mosaic of quotations; any text is the absorption and transformation of another' (Kristeva 1980: 66).

According to Dk 9.12, the YH 'is about the assembly of the gods of the world of thought because of the complaint of the fire'. This content summary, however, does not agree with the text of the (P)YH. The link between Dk 9.12 and the YH is the fire. It is important to note that the commentators are not reducing the content of the YH to that of PY 36. In the *Zand* of the YH, it is the fire that is knowledgeable in the *dēn* (PY 36.3) and it is the fire that will grant the reward which is the *dēn* (see Section 5.1.2). As such, the fire dominates the ritual and is the text's main protagonist. It is in this light that the YH functions as a pretext for gathering disparate narratives about the fire. Dk 9.12 also illustrates how the wider exegetical literature relied on the canonical *Zand*. It seems fair to suggest that while the content of Dk 9.12 may seem challenging at first, its commentary is informed by a close reading of the *Zand*. Moreover, Dk 9.12 shows how freely the exegetes interpreted and approached their scripture. Both the *Warštmānsr* and the *Sūdgar Nask* contain a host of disparate texts being linked to the scripture. These sections are fitting examples of the scholastic proliferativity of late antique Zoroastrianism.[91]

4.3.7 Summary

Fire as a literary motif seems to have been subject to interpretation and reinterpretation in the Pahlavi literature. The notion that one fire resides within the human body was already expressed in PY 17.11: *ātaxš ī weh franāftār ān andar tan ī mardomān*. In a general statement, Bd 1a.3 declares that the seed of mankind and cattle is essentially made of fire:

> **Bd 1a.3**[92] *čiyōn gōwēd pad dēn kū fradom dām hamāg ābē(w) sreškē(w) būd kū hamāg az āb būd jud tōhm ī mardōmān ud gōspandān čē ān tōhm ātaxš tōhm*
>
> As it says in the religion: (At) first, the creation was all a water drop, that is, everything was from water, except the seed of mankind and cattle, for that seed was (of) the essence of fire.

Accordingly, in Bd 18.2 the description of *ātaxš ī hufryān*, which is the same as PY 17.11's *weh franāftār*, expands to include cattle as well: *ān ī andar tan ī mardōmān ud gōspandān* 'that which is in the body of mankind and cattle'.[93] Likewise, when elaborating on the nature of semen, Zādspram relates male sperm to fire (Sohn 1996: 14).

It is exceedingly difficult to establish a chronological relationship between the *Avesta*, the *Zand* and MP texts. While the passages discussed in this

---

[91] A fully qualified statement about the *Sūdgar Nask* requires further research, as Dk 9.12 also contains material that goes beyond the fire. It is not immediately recognisable how these passages relate to the YH.
[92] Text after Pakzad (2005: 26).
[93] See Pakzad (2005: 228) for the text.

chapter show that the fire's scanty properties grow in scope and quality, it remains uncertain to what extent this development represents an evolutionary progress.

4.4 CORRELATIVE SYSTEMS

According to Farmer, Henderson and Witzel (2000), exegetical engagement with heavily layered and at times inconsistent textual material led in most pre-modern religious traditions to the development of *correlative systems*, defined as 'a general propensity to organize natural, political/social, and cosmological data in highly ordered arrays or systems of correspondence' (Farmer et al. 2000: 49). As Farmer et al. note, the term *correlative thinking* was first coined by Sinologists specialising in pre-modern China, but similar systems have also been known in other cultures, such as Hinduism, where they are referred to as *bandhu* 'relation, bond, connection'.[94] The authors assert 'that the deepest roots of correlative thought lay in neurobiological processes' (Farmer et al. 2000: 49), and that later textual traditions developed these thoughts into high-correlative systems (Farmer et al. 2000: 56), which in turn are defined as 'multileveled reflecting cosmologies, nested hierarchies, [and] abstract systems of correspondences' (Farmer et al. 2000: 48). According to the authors, correlative systems emerged in most civilisations and thus provide the basis for 'a potent cross-cultural framework for premodern studies in general' (Farmer et al. 2000: 48). In this model, correlative as well as high-correlative tendencies or systems are viewed as by-products of continuous exegesis. By operating on textual material, exegetes cause an ever-growing set of correspondences, which in time evolve into (high-)correlative structures. The framework developed by Farmer et al. (2000) builds upon and extends Cabezón's cross-cultural scholasticism, particularly the paradigm of proliferativity (see Section 3.3). In light of the above, the reception and representation of the fire within Zoroastrian religious literature seems to reflect diachronic changes towards an increasingly more correlative system, which was presumably brought about by a long-standing tradition of exegesis.

The long history of exegesis in Zoroastrianism has variously been pointed out.[95] Vevaina (2007: 96), for example, suggests that the origins of the Iranian 'practice of canonical commentary' may reach as far back as the YAv. period. His conclusion that an exegetical tradition may have originated in the

---

[94] Drawing parallels between the Indian and Iranian traditions, Vevaina (2010a) discusses *bandhus* in some detail. Although Vevaina does not explicitly discuss correlative structures, he takes a similar approach to the development of complex networks of correspondences.
[95] For my own brief discussion, see Section 4.2.1.

immediate vicinity to the OAv. texts seems also to be supported by the inner- and inter-textual references between the Older and the Younger *Avesta*, as pointed out by Hintze (2002). The traditional text order of the *Yasna* would then reflect not only an original order of the text, as suggested by Hintze, but also how exegesis shaped the *Avesta* itself early on. This particular strand of Zoroastrian exegesis culminates in the correspondences established between the *yaϑā ahū vairiiō* prayer and the Sasanian *Avesta*, which has been studied in much detail by Vevaina (2007). Thus, it is safe to assume a continuous exegetical tradition, operating on the scripture and various canonical texts from their earliest attestation through to late MP texts.

As Farmer et al. (2000) point out, philologists have often examined material that reflects correlative thinking, but little attention has been paid to these structures beyond the study of pre-modern China.[96] The presence of corresponding structures have long been acknowledged in Zoroastrianism as well. Gignoux (2004b), for instance, in his discussion of micro- and macrocosm theory in Iranian pre-Islamic thought draws attention to various sets of correspondences. Among others, he outlines the parallels that are drawn in Bd 28.4 between seven constituent parts of the human body and their cosmic counterparts. Human skin is likened to the sky, flesh to earth, bones to mountains, veins to rivers, blood to water, the belly to the ocean and hair to plants. In his comparative study, Gignoux discusses the topic in light of the doctrine of micro- and macrocosm and humorism, proposing a non-Iranian origin for the theory.[97] More recently, Vevaina (2007: 80–98) has convincingly compared *dēn-ōšmurišnīh* with the concept of *bandhus* in the *Upaniṣad*. However, scholars of Zoroastrianism have not discussed networks of correspondences as by-products of exegesis in a manuscript tradition, employing an overarching framework such as correlative structures.

In his discussion of the micro- and macrocosm doctrine, Gignoux (2004b) points out a number of textual mistakes, which he attributes to scribes and copyists. In his view, these disturb the logic of the correspondences. In particular, he regards the above-mentioned *aškamb* 'belly' in Bd 28.4 as an editorial mistake, without suggesting a new reading. The underlying assumption for his approach is that an original doctrine disseminated to Iran via religious contact, possibly through Syriac sources, and that the logic of the doctrine must have been lost in later stages. Religious contact cannot be excluded as an influence in the dissemination of ideas or the development of complex networks of correspondences. In fact, Farmer et al. (2000: 69) acknowledge that 'syncretic fusions' significantly contributed to

---

[96] See Farmer et al. (2000: 49–54) for an assessment of the state of affairs in Indology.

[97] Gignoux has discussed the subject in a number of articles arguing for a Greco-gnostic origin of the theory, particularly in Gignoux (1994). See Gignoux (2004b) for further references.

the stratification of texts. However, proposing editorial mistakes to eliminate purported inconsistencies may be presumptuous. For, as already pointed out, the presence of these correspondences in MP literature can also be, at least in part, the result of exegetical processes working on older material. Two important arguments can be made against Gignoux's interpretation of Bd 28. First, in Pakzad's (2005) edition of the *Bundahišn* there are no indications that *aškamb* 'belly' is a problematic reading from a text-critical point of view. Second, in Bd 28.4 the seven parts of the body are not explicitly referred to as such, but appear in a long list enumerating other correspondences between the human body and cosmic objects. In contrast to Gignoux's approach, it seems more productive to embrace the content of the texts rather than assuming editorial mistakes when the content does not match hypothetical or superimposed patterns. Even if the micro- and macrocosm doctrine was imported from Greco-gnostic circles at some unspecified stage, there is no reason why it should have not been adapted to its Zoroastrian context. Texts such as Bd 28 are better understood as representing correlative structures, acknowledging the exegetical processes behind such results, rather than operating with the unsupported assumption of mistakes in the texts. As Gignoux himself rightly and importantly observes, such explicit correspondences are not found in the *Gāθās* or the Younger *Avesta*, but only in the MP literature. Without fully excluding religious contact as a factor in the emergence of ideas or correspondences, here the pattern of growth agrees well with the observations of Farmer et al. (2000). We must realise the potential of exegetical manuscript traditions in producing correlative structures and complex networks of correspondences. One consequence of this view is to acknowledge contradictions as a result of the layering process within textual traditions (Farmer et al. 2000: 69). While according to Farmer et al. (2000: 66) 'the levels of internal contradiction' can be subject to regional variation, they are likely to be found in most exegetical traditions. As noted before, scholastic proliferativity is one cause of stratification, by which contradictions can enter into religious traditions.

As Farmer et al. (2000: 50) observe, most correlative and high-correlative structures rest on or are associated with bipartite concepts which later evolve into more complex networks. Examples of such binary oppositions are *brahman* : *ātman*, heaven : earth or limited : unlimited. Similar dichotomies also exist in the oldest layers of Zoroastrian texts: corporeal : spiritual, bounteous spirit : evil spirit and endless light : limited light.[98] In the networks which later develop out of these rather simple dichotomies, beings of divine

---

[98] We also know concepts such as limited time : limitless time from later Pahlavi sources. But it is difficult to ascertain to what extent they were already known in the OAv. texts.

origin are often linked with other, at times less divine, beings. Such complex networks are also present in Zoroastrianism. *Bundahišn* 26 and 28, for instance, lay out a complex network of links between the *amahraspandān* 'bounteous immortals', the *yazadān* 'divinities', their corresponding divine or cosmic *ham-kārs* 'collaborators' and earthly creations as well as their *ahrimanic* 'evil' counterparts. These expand over the bipartite concept of *mēnōy: gētīy* and are also reflected in the Zoroastrian calendar.[99]

4.5 SUMMARY

Reviewing textual evidence of the fire from the earliest references through to some of the prominent examples in the MP literature, it becomes evident that the fire's properties grow through commentarial reinterpretation from the *Gāθās* through to WZ 3.78–82, finally culminating in an elaborate and intricately worded description of human physiology (WZ 30).

In the *Gāθās*, the fire is presented as belonging to *Ahura Mazdā* and is associated with *aša-*, *rāna-* and distribution of rewards. We witness the first step of a development, when *Ahura Mazdā*'s fire morphs into *Ahura Mazdā*'s son. As such, this fire strongly features in the *Yasna*, but also in other YAv. texts (see Section 4.2). This seemingly minute progress is remarkably accompanied by a shift to a more formulaic and ritualistic form of language, for instance, in the *Yasna* and *Wisperad*. In the first *Wisperad* chapter to follow the YH after Y 42 we read:

> **Wr 16.1**[100] *ātrəmca iδa ahurahe mazdå puθrəm yazamaide*
> *ātarš.ciθrəsca yazatō yazamaide*
> *ātarš.ciθrəsca rašnušca yazamaide*
> *ašāunąmca frauuašaiiō yazamaide*
> *sraošəmca yim vərəθrājanəm yazamaide*
> *narəmca yim ašauuanəm yazamaide*
> *vīspąmca yąm ašaonō stīm yazamaide*
>
> And here we sacrifice to the fire, son of *Ahura Mazdā*,
> and we sacrifice to the *Yazatas* of the seed of the fire,
> and we sacrifice to *Rašnu* of the seed of the fire,
> and we sacrifice to the *Frauuašis* of the orderly ones,
> and we sacrifice to victorious *Sraoša*,
> and we sacrifice to the orderly man,
> and we sacrifice to the entire existence of the orderly ones.

Other YAv. passages such as Y 17.11 or Y 62.2 also make use of a more formulaic language. While we may expect a formalised form of expression in

---

[99] Gignoux (2004b) also mentions a number of correspondences.
[100] Text after Geldner (1886–96: II 24). In Cantera's (2016b) revised numbering of the *Wisperad*, Geldner's Wr 16.1 has been renumbered to Wr 21.2.

the context of a ritual text, the change signals a development towards a fixed form of scripture even if an orally transmitted one. And the fire becomes the subject of a number of other YAv. compositions, such as the *Ātaš Niyāyišn*, the *Wīdēwdād* and the *Zamyād Yašt*.

The mention of five fires in Y 17.11 marks the next important stage in the development of the fire. *Ahura Mazdā*'s fire first emerges as his son and is then accompanied by a pentad of fires. Although not further specified, the adjectives or names of the fires imply associated functions, which are only laid out in the passage's *Zand*. Here starts a development, which is then continued in the MP texts, finally featuring the fire in a rather complex network of correspondences. I am inclined to attribute this process of growth, which starts with a single fire, to Zoroastrian exegesis, continuously operating on the *Avesta* and other canonical texts.

The fire's development, however, does not come to an abrupt halt in the Zoroastrian MP literature. To the contrary, Zādspram's fire seems to have evolved into a literary motif in the shape of the *fire within* in Persian poetry. An explicit reference to an eternal fire within is found in a *ghazal* by Hāfez (fourteenth century):

از آن به دیر مغانم عزیز میدارند   که آتشی که نمیرد همیشه در دل ماست

They cherish me in the cloister of the Magi
For the undying fire is always in our heart

The lack of known authorship and the uncertain dating of the textual material are two of the biggest challenges in historical research on Zoroastrianism. The most accurate parameters in determining the chronology of the Av. compositions are of linguistic nature, based on which the Av. corpus has been divided into OAv. and YAv. sections. These uncertainties apply to the Av. compositions as well as the much later Pahlavi literature. In particular, the lack of dates affects the academic representation of the history and chronology of religious thought. Thus, research on history of ideas, a challenging undertaking in the best of circumstances, faces exceptional obstructions in the study of Zoroastrianism. The overarching theoretical framework discussed above is particularly interesting in Zoroastrian studies as it assumes a gradual rate of growth for textual material in commentarial traditions. In an ideal situation, much like a laboratory experiment, the degree by which correlative tendencies are present in a particular text could be indicative of the text's position within a relative chronology of texts.[101]

---

[101] In fact, Farmer and his collaborators are working on a computer simulation program which, it is hoped, can fill in historical gaps in the development of commentarial traditions. While the authors

More importantly, the paradigm of textual growth as a result of exegesis, as demonstrated by the example of the fire's progression, calls for caution in the comparison of Avestan material with MP texts. Ideas and myths encountered in the *Avesta* can grow into complex structures over time, without having been known in their complexity in Avestan times.

As mentioned in the previous section, the fire is not the only example of correlative growth in Zoroastrianism. MP and other Zoroastrian texts preserve many examples of complex networks, where macro- and microcosmic structures are interlinked. One such example is the prominent Zoroastrian concept of *dēn*.[102] Often associated with 'perception' or 'vision' on account of its derivation from the verb *dī* 'to see', Av. *daēnā-*, attested in Old as well as YAv. compositions, makes an extraordinary development towards an ever-increasing complexity which culminates in a parable in the *Škand Gumānīg Wizār*, comparing the *dēn* with a tree:

> ŠGW 1.11[103] The Religion of omniscience (is) like a mighty tree (12) with one trunk, two great boughs, three branches, four off-branches, and five roots.

The text goes on to interrelate each of the constituent parts of the tree with religious concepts and social classes, which are described and interrelated in further detail:[104] Of the above parts of the tree the trunk is the 'mean', the two boughs are 'action and abstention', and the three branches represent the triad *humat hūxt huwaršt*. The four 'off-branches' stand for social classes: – priesthood, warriors, husbandmen and artisans – while the five roots symbolise the *mānbed* 'master of the house', *wisbed* 'village headman', *zandbed* 'headman of a district', *dehbed* 'country headman' and *Zaraϑuštrōtom*, or the highest religious authority. Of human beings, the text continues, the head corresponds to the priesthood, the hands to the warrior, the belly to the husbandmen and the feet finally to the artisans. Each social class is then linked with a 'virtue'. The concept of the *dēn* thus grows to reflect the entire society and its various aspects such as tilling the earth. In this late text, the *dēn* takes its place at the core of human life, governing and connecting its various faculties. And it is perhaps in this light that one should read Dk 5.1 where all knowledge is attributed to the *dēn*:[105]

---

have already published theoretical discussions of the subject matter and a software prototype has been developed, it remains to be seen to what extent this undertaking will be successful.

[102] For a brief discussion of the *dēn* in general and in the PYH, see Section 5.1.2.
[103] Translation after Zaehner (1975: 86). This parable is also discussed by Shaki (1994).
[104] The following paraphrase is based on Zaehner (1975: 86ff.).
[105] Shaki (1994) quotes a number of other *Dēnkard* passages where it is said that the *dēn* encompasses all knowledge in the form of innate wisdom (*āsn xrad*). I have checked two of these passages and hesitate to agree with Shaki's translations without further investigation.

Dk 5.1[106] *pērōzgarīh ī dādār ohrmazd xwarrah ī wisp-dānāgīh axwīg dēn mazdēsn*

The victory of the creator *Ohrmazd*, the glory of the Mazda-worshipping religion, that contains all knowledge relating to existence.

Finally, I shall mention that while the framework of correlative structures has received wide-spread attention in the study of religions, Bronkhorst (2008) has recently questioned its cross-cultural applicability in Indology. He acknowledges the presence of (high-)correlative systems in India, but does not believe these emerged in the way proposed by Farmer et al. (2000), that is, as by-products of continuous exegesis (Bronkhorst 2008: 19). I hope to have demonstrated the presence of correlative as well as high-correlative systems in the Iranian tradition, and their dependency on the exegetical tradition.

---

[106] For the text, see Madan (1911: 55) and Dresden (1966: 494).

5. *Precis: yasn ī haft hād*

Scholars recognised shared features and differences between the YH and the *Gāθās* early on and have variously attempted to describe them. Wesendonk (1931: 5), for instance, explains the variances by attributing the YH to a priestly school active after Zaraθuštra's time. He also suggests that abstract ideas present in the older *Avesta* developed into concrete form in the YH:

> Hatte aber Zarathuštra sich einen unpersönlichen und rein geistigen Gottesbegriff vorgestellt, so wird er im siebenteiligen Yasna konkretisiert. (Wesendonk 1931: 31)

Narten (1986: 28–37) explains the differences between the two groups of OAv. texts by way of the different literary genres the texts belong to, while Kellens and Pirart (1988: 36–9), much like Wesendonk, explain the differences by attributing the YH to a 'l'école haptahâtique'. Be that as it may, as a text in its own right the Pahlavi version of the YH represents a novel interpretation of the Avestan version.

5.1 PY 35

The central themes of PY 35, the introductory chapter of the YH, are the triad *humat hūxt huwaršt* and the *dēn*, concepts that are closely related to the notion of the reward (*ān ī ōy*) and the dissemination of the *dēn*.

5.1.1 *humatān hūxtān huwarštān*

The formulaic expression *humat(ān) hūxt(ān) huwaršt(ān)* 'good thoughts, good words, good deeds' is widely attested in the PY as well as the Pahlavi literature.[1] Dk 9.35, the interpretation of the YH, describes the triad's significance:

> **Dk 9.35.1**[2] *12om fragard yasn abar paydāgīh ī humat hūxt ud huwaršt az dēn mehmānīh ī dēn pad humat hūxt ud huwaršt kē humat hūxt ud kē huwaršt xwēšēnēd ā-š ahlawīh ud ān ī ahlawān mizd xwēšēnīd bawēd*
>
> The 12th section, the *yasn*, is on the manifestation of good thoughts, good words and good deeds from the *dēn*. The presence of the *dēn* is through good thoughts, good words and good deeds. Whoever makes good thoughts, good words and good deeds his own, he appropriates righteousness and the reward of the righteous ones.

The performance of good thoughts, good words and good deeds is thus the condition for the presence (*mehmānīh*) of the *dēn*,[3] and leads to the reward designated for the righteous ones. A section of Dk 8.20 reads like a paraphrase of the final section of the above passage:

> **Dk 8.20.63**[4] *abar kū frārōnīh*[5] *ī menišn gōwišn kunišn ī mardōm hamāg az frārōnīh ī spenāg mēnōy ud mardōm xwad ō xwēš kunēnd u-šān pad ān rāh mizd rasēd*
>
> About the goodness of people's thoughts, speech and deeds which are all from the goodness of the Good Spirit. And (if) people themselves appropriate (it) they will receive the reward on account of that path.

The text suggests that in order to receive the reward a commitment has to be made to appropriate (*ō xwēš kardan*) the triad. By associating good thoughts, good words and good deeds with the *dēn* and the reward, Dk 9.35.1 and 8.20.63 anticipate PY 40.2 and the final stanza of the YH, PY 41.6, where the requested reward is the *dēn* (see Section 5.7.2). The *Dēnkard*'s linking of the YH's first with its final strophe shows that a strong logical structure was associated with the text. Since the request for the reward depends on the realisation of good thoughts, good words and good deeds, the commitment to the triad constitutes the very first stanza of the YH. Only thus can the ritual begin, which will end with the request. It is not a coincidence then that Y 35.1 is repeated at the end of the YH. On one hand, it completes the cycle of the composition, on the other, it reaffirms the sacrificers commitment to

---

[1] On the Av. formula and the YH, see Narten (1986: 86–8) with references. A definition of the triad is found in *ayādgār ī wuzurgmihr* 11–22 (see Orian 1992). For another definition, see *wisp humat bun* where we also find echoes of PY 35.1 (see Dhabhar 1927: 25, Dhabhar 1963: 43). For my discussion of the triad's role in the PYH, see Section 5.2.1.

[2] Text after Dresden (1966: 653).

[3] On the presence of *dēn*, see Shaked's (1979: 12–13) interpretation of Dk 6.27: *u-šān ēn-iz ōwōn dāšt kū ahlāyīh ud dēn mehmānīh ēd* †*hu-dārišn ud hu-bahrīh* (?) *ud hunsandīh* 'They held this too: Righteousness and making religion dwell (in oneself) consist in this: holding well, having a good share, and being content.'

[4] Text after Dresden (1966: 290).

[5] B reads ⟨pl'lwn'yh⟩.

the *dēn* by underlining their willingness to adhere to good thoughts, good words and good deeds.

5.1.2 The *dēn*

A significant feature of the PYH, in contrast to the Avestan version, is the exegetes' emphasis on the *dēn*. In the Av. YH, the word *daēnā-*, variously translated as 'belief, vision' or 'vision soul', occurs five times: Y 35.0, 37.5, 39.2, 40.1 and 41.5.[6] In the PYH, by contrast, we encounter the word *dēn* 14 times: PY 35.0 (2x), 35.2, 35.5, 35.6, 35.7, 35.8, 36.1, 36.3, 37.5, 39.2, 40.1, 40.4, 41.4.[7] Seven of these occurrences are within chapter 35 of the PYH.

The increased presence of the word, particularly in PY 35, is due to a number of references to the *dēn* that do not translate a word in the original. As I have pointed out in Section 5.1.1, already the *Dēnkard* highlights the connection between the (P)YH, the triad *humatān hūxtān huwarštān* and the *dēn*:

> **Dk 9.35.1** *120m fragard yasn abar paydāgīh ī humat hūxt ud huwaršt az dēn mehmānīh ī dēn pad humat hūxt ud huwaršt kē humat hūxt ud kē huwaršt xwēšēnēd ā-š ahlawīh ud ān ī ahlawān mizd xwēšēnīd bawēd*
>
> The 12th section, the *yasn*, is on the manifestation of good thoughts, good words and good deeds (as evident) from the *dēn*. The presence of the *dēn* is through good thoughts, good words and good deeds. Whoever makes good thoughts, good words and good deeds his own, he appropriates righteousness and the reward of the righteous ones.

The PYH is perceived as being about the manifestation of the triad, which in turn is necessary for the presence of the *dēn*.[8]

As I suggest in Section 13.2.5, already the expression *mard ō mard* in PY 35.1 seems to contain a coded reference to the *dēn* and its dissemination through teaching. But it is in PY 35.2a where we find the first explicit mention of *dēn* that does not translate an Av. word. The sacrificers side with *aṣ̌a-* and choose because of it (Y 35.2a) to think, speak and perform (Y 35.2b) those actions that are best for both existences (Y 35.2c). This choice to think, speak and perform the best actions reflects a commitment to good thoughts, good words and good deeds. Therefore, in the *Zand* of Y 35.2a the commentators emphasise that their desire for *ahlāyīh* (*aṣ̌a-*) is nothing else than a desire for *dēn*:

---

[6] For a discussion of *daēnā-* and its etymology, see Hintze (2007a: 58–60), Hintze (2013a) and Cantera (2013: 97) with references. For an interpretation of *daēnā-* from the vantage of epistemology, see König (2018: III).

[7] The term *dēnīgān* 'the religious ones' appears in PY 40.1 and 41.5.

[8] The prominent position given to the triad in the Av. YH has been discussed by Hintze (2007a: 8–9).

Y 35.2 (a) *tat̰ at̰* ⁺*varəmaidī ahurā mazdā aṣ̌ā srīrā*
(b) *hiiat̰ ī mainimadicā vaocōimācā* ⁺*varəzimācā*
(c) *yā hātąm* ⁺*š́iiaoϑənanąm vahištā x́iiāt̰ ubōibiiā ahubiiā*

PY 35.2 (a) *ō ēn ēdōn ēg kāmag dahom ohrmazd kē ahlāyīh nēk dēn*
(b) *ēdōn ēn menom-iz ud gōwom-iz ud warzom-iz*
(c) *kū-m az hastān mardōmān pad kunišn pahlom bād andar har dō axwān kū mizd dahānd*

(a) O Ohrmazd, in this way, I then desire this, which is good righteousness, (namely) religion.
(b) Thus, I think, speak and also practise this,
(c) (so) that among the existing people, I shall receive through actions the best in both existences, that is, they shall give reward.

The exegetes seem to argue as follows: good thoughts, good speech and good deeds are the condition for the presence of the *dēn*. If one adheres to the former for the sake of *aṣ̌a-*, then *aṣ̌a-* or *ahlāyīh* must be the same as the *dēn*. The *Zand* passage, thus, establishes an expected relationship between *humatān hūxtān huwarštān* and the *dēn*, but more importantly, suggests a connection between *aṣ̌a-*, *ahlāyīh* and the *dēn*. Moreover, the translators seem to make a conscious effort to explicate any references to the *dēn* with the aim to remove any uncertainty in the passages they perceive as ambiguous.

The next such reference is found in PY 35.5b. In the preceding line, PY 35.5a, knowledge of *wehīh* 'goodness' is related to males and females. Like *ahlāyīh*, *wehīh* is then defined as *dēn*, which the males and females are to disseminate, teach and practise (PY 35.5b).

The notion that the Y 35 is a declaration of the sacrificers' commitment to the *dēn* is most explicitly expressed in the following stanza:

Y 35.6c *tat̰ at̰ vō vərəziiāmahī fracā vātōiiāmahī yā.tō isāmaidē*

It is precisely this that we shall practise for you and make (it) known as much as we can.

PY 35.6c *ēdōn ān ī ašmā warzom dēn ud frāz-iz āgāhēnom ō kasān ān and čand pad tuwān xwāstār hom*

Thus, I practise that which is yours, the *dēn*, and I also make it known to others, I am willing (to do it) as much as is in (my) power.

The Av. and the MP versions agree in lines (a–b) that it is best to praise and worship the deity and to care for the cattle. Consequently, in line (c) the original asserts a dedication to those actions (*tat̰ at̰ vō vərəziiāmahī*). In the *Zand* of line (c), however, the commitment shifts to the *dēn*, *ān ī ašmā warzom dēn* 'I practise that which is yours, the *dēn*', and its proclamation:

ud frāz-iz āgāhēnom ō kasān 'And I also make (it) known to others.'⁹ The NP glosses in F2 and T6 continue the Pahlavi interpretation of this stanza.

In Y 35.6c, *tat̰ at̰ vō vərəziiāi.mahī* is glossed وآن ایدون دین شمارا اعتیار کنم 'And thus, I chose your religion.'¹⁰ T6 reads وآنا ایدون دین شمارا اعتیار کنم من نفس خود یعنی به ذات خود 'And thus I chose your religion, (my) own mind, this is, for (my) own nature', and goes on to translate *vātō.aiiā.mahī. yātō. ašā.maide* as بدهم خبر دین رادر میان خلق و دیگر مردمانرا از فرمان دین آگاه کنم 'I proclaim the religion amongst the people and inform other people of the instructions of the religion.'

In PY 35.7a, it is said that one should maintain the *dēn* through guardians and community. And in PY 35.8a, the sacrificers once more assert the proclamation of the *dēn*:

> PY 35.8a *ēn ēdōn saxwan gōwišnīh ohrmazd dēn ī ohrmazd pad ahlāyīh menīdārīh ī weh frāz gōwom pad frārōn menišnīh*
>
> This word, spoken in this manner, O *Ohrmazd*, (namely) the religion of *Ohrmazd*, I will proclaim by good consideration of righteousness, (namely) by good thought(s).

To summarise, *ahlāyīh* and *wehīh* are both defined as *dēn* (PY 35.2 and 5), and *dēn* as belonging to *Ohrmazd* (PY 35.6). At the same time we witness a strong desire to proclaim, practise and teach the religion to others (PY 35.7 and 8). But what is the context for this desire and what role does it play in the ritual?

The sole purpose of a ritual seems to be the request for a prize or reward. As I have argued in Section 5.7.2, in the PYH the prize is that which belongs to *Ohrmazd* (*ān ī ōy*), namely the *dēn*. Therefore, the ritual starts with the sacrificers' confirmation of their knowledge of *Ohrmazd*'s *dēn* and their strong commitment to its practice and dissemination (PY 35). In the second chapter of the text, PY 36, the fire is invoked as being knowledgeable in the *dēn* of *Ohrmazd* (PY 36.3). Thus, its presence is necessary for the ritual. At this stage the ritual has been initiated, and an invocation starts in praise of *Ohrmazd*, the waters and other creations (PY 37–39). In the two final chapters, PY 40 and 41, the prize is then finally defined as *Ohrmazd*'s *dēn* and requested of the fire. In this light, the statement in Dk 9.35.1, *mehmānīh ī dēn*

---

⁹ For a discussion of 'yours' and its referent, see Section 13.7.3. For the proclamation of the *dēn*, see Section 5.6.1.

¹⁰ The 1pl.subj.pres.act. *vərəziiāmahī* is divided in two parts. The first part, *vərəziiāi*, corresponds to the 1sg. verb اعتیار کنم 'I chose', while the second part, *mahī*, is glossed as من 'I'.

pad humat hūxt huwaršt 'The presence of the *dēn* is through good thoughts, good words and good deeds', seems to refer to the ritual significance of the (P)YH. The sacrificers' repeated commitment throughout the (P)YH to *humat hūxt huwaršt* prepares the grounds for the presence (*mehmānīh*) of the *dēn* in the ritual, that is, through the presence of the fire. No doubt, the acceptance of *Ohrmazd*'s *dēn* as a reward goes beyond the ritual and has implications for one's life. These effects are alluded to in Dk 6.27: *u-šān ēn-iz ōwōn dāšt kū ahlāyīh ud dēn mehmānīh ēd ⁺hu-dārišn ud hu-bahrīh (?) ud hunsandīh* 'They held this too: The presence of righteousness and *dēn* are this: holding well, having a good share, and being content.'[11]

The complexity of the term *dēn* has long been recognised.[12] This highly multivalent word is attested as *daēnā-* in Avestan, as *dēn* in MP and MMP and as *dīn* (دين) in NP. Although *dīn* mostly denotes 'religion' in NP, the term has been associated with various meanings and religious concepts throughout its history. Shaki (1994) suggests that the term has represented concepts such as 'spiritual attributes', 'vision', perhaps 'conscience' and thus 'religion'. It has also been noted that the *dēn*, appearing in the form of a female human, guides the soul of the deceased in the after-world. More recently, Vevaina (2010a: 118) has suggested that the MP term *dēn* signifies 'the entire religious tradition of Zoroastrianism as represented by its corpus of sacred texts, both in Avestan (*abestāg*) and in Pahlavi (*Zand*)' in contexts involving Zoroastrian scripture. His interpretation is based on his reading of passages from the *Dēnkard* relating to the *Ahunwar* prayer and the 21 *nasks* of the *Dēnkard Avesta*. This totality of scripture signified by *dēn*, as suggested by Vevaina, might have given rise to the semantically very close notion of 'religion' in NP. The examination above and in Section 5.6.1 suggest that in the PYH *dēn* refers to the Mazda-worshipping religion or the *dēn ī weh ī mazdēsnān* 'the good religion of Mazda-worshippers', as it is called in PY 35.0c. Although the PYH's usage of the term lacks the complexity of the *Dēnkard*'s commentaries on the *Ahunwar* prayer, this *dēn* or religion is ultimately the sum of the religious instruction that the Zoroastrian tradition has handed down through priestly teaching, another prominent element in the PYH, which was also taken up by the commentaries in the *Pursišnīhā*.

5.1.3 PY 35.1

In contrast to other paragraphs of Suppl.ŠnŠ 13, which include the number of stanzas and often a brief summary of the content, at times accompanied

---

[11] Text after Shaked (1979: 12–13).
[12] For a general discussion of *dēn*, see Shaki (1994). Zaehner (1975: 80–96) offers a brief introduction and translated excerpts from Pahlavi texts on 'the good religion'.

by a numerological interpretation, Suppl.ŠnŠ 13.16 only delineates the extent of Y 35 (see Zeini Forthcoming).

In Suppl.ŠnŠ 13.16, where nine stanzas are attributed to Y 35, Y 35.1 is regarded as the YH's beginning strophe (see Kotwal 1969: 46):[13]

> Suppl.ŠnŠ 13.16[14] *yasn bun kardag 9 wačadast u-š bun* humatanąm *u-š sar* humatanąm
>
> The beginning section of the *Yasna* has nine stanzas. Its beginning is *humatanąm* and its end is *humatanąm*.

Dk 9.35 (*Warštmānsr Nask*) starts the description of the YH with Y 35.1, indicating that it too regards this stanza as the first strophe of the YH. PY 35.1 is repeated at the end of the YH; constitutes (P)Y 68.20; makes up the first paragraph of *zand ī gomēz kardan* (see Dhabhar 1927: 2) and is mentioned in Wd 10.4 as one of the stanzas that are recited twice.

The *Zand* of Y 35.1 and Y 68.20 differ, although the differences are minimal and most likely due to errors in copying:

> PY 68.20[15] (a) *humatān hūxtān <u>ud</u> huwarštān <u>kē</u> ēdar-<u>iz</u> dahišn u-š pad-iz* ī̶ *ān ī any dahišn kū-š ēdar ud ānōh-iz nēkīh aziš*
> (b) *ān ī warzīd tā nūn ud ān-iz ī warzīhēd az nūn frāz*
> (c) *hom abar griftār kū ō xwēš kunom ān ī mard ō mard be abespārdār kirbag ī̶ pad dād rāh čiyōn weh hom kū čiyōn pahlom ō xwēš kunom-<u>iz</u>*

In the examined MSS, Y 35.1b ends with the Av. verbal form *mahī* 'we are', whose MP translation, *hom* 'I am', occurs at the beginning of PY 35.1c followed by *abar griftār* 'appropriator'.

5.2 PY 36

It has variously been pointed out that the context of Y 36 is dominated by the fire and its consecration (36.3).[16] It has also been argued that Y 36 might have served as a template in assigning names to other fires (Section 4.1.2). Suppl.ŠnŠ 13 shows another aspect of priestly exegesis associated with (P)Y 36. In a brief description of this OAv. chapter we read:

> Suppl.ŠnŠ 13.17[17] *ahyā θwā āϑrō 6 wačadast az ān 6 war ī garm ī pad* hūspāram *pad čaϑrayāim āϑrayąm kard ēstēd*
> *ahyā θwā āϑrō* has six strophes. The six heat ordeals which are in the *hūspāram* were established from that [Y 36] according to the *čaϑrayāim āϑrayąm*.

---

[13] The number of the stanzas stated in the concluding enumeration at the end of PY 35.9 is also nine.
[14] Text after Kotwal (1969: 46–7).
[15] Text after Pt4. I underline words that do not occur in PY 35.1, and strike out text that is missing in PY 68.20.
[16] For more on PY 36 and the fire, see Chapter 4. For a brief discussion of PY 36.1, see Section 20.1.
[17] Text after Kotwal (1969: 46–7).

According to the above passage, the six heat ordeals, which are not further specified here, correspond to the number of stanzas of Y 36. It would certainly be premature to assume based on this passage that in ancient times Zoroastrians used fire itself in ordeals. However, it seems evident that through its heat the fire was associated with this type of ordeal.[18]

5.2.1   The three steps

PY 36.6 offers a challenging interpretation of the Av. original:

PY 36.6 (a) *nēk ēd ī tō kirb u-t ān az kirbān niwēyēnišn dahom ohrmazd kū andar gēhān ōh gōwom kū kirb ēd ī tō nēktar*
(b) *ēn ruwān ō ān rōšnīh ī bālist az ān ī pad čašm paydāg bālēnānd*
(c) *ānōh kū xwaršēd guft kū-m ruwān ō xwaršēd pāyag rasād*

(a) Beautiful is this your form. And of all forms I attribute that one to you, O Ohrmazd, that is, in (this) world I say it in this way: (of) form(s), this which is yours is more beautiful.
(b) May they exalt this soul to that light which is the highest of that which is visible to the eye.
(c) There, which is called the sun, that is, my soul shall reach the sun station.

The various stations, *star* 'start', *māh* 'moon' and *xwaršēd pāyag* 'sun station', occur throughout the PY and the wider Pahlavi literature, but the soul (*ruwān*) and the sun station (*xwaršēd pāyag*) might seem unmotivated here by the context of (P)Y 36.6c.[19] As we shall see, these references are triggered by the exegetes' interpretation of PY 36 and the ritual.

In a number of MP passages it is suggested that the three stations are reached by three steps, which correlate to *humat hūxt huwaršt*:[20]

MX 6.1[21] *šašom purišn pursīd dānāg ō mēnōy ī xrad* (2) *kū wahišt čiyōn ud čand* ...
(8) *mēnōy ī xrad passox kard* (9) *kū wahišt fradom az star pāyag tā māh pāyag*
(10) *ud didīgar az māh pāyag tā xwaršēd pāyag* (11) *ud sidīgar az xwaršēd pāyag tā garōdmān kū dādār Ohrmazd abar nišīnēd* (12) *ud wahišt ī fradom humat ud didīgar hūxt ud sidīgar huwaršt*

(1) Sixth question: The sage asked of the spirit of wisdom: (2) 'How is heaven and how many are there?' ... (8) The spirit of wisdom replied: (9) 'The first heaven is from the star station to the moon station, (10) and the second is from the moon station to the sun station, (11) and the third is from the sun station to

---

[18] As Kotwal (1969: 103, fn. 28) points out, the meaning of *čaϑrayāim āϑrayąm* remains unclear.
[19] For a discussion of the various stations and heavens, see Panaino (1995b), and on the cosmography of Yt 12 including the heavens, Goldman (2015). On the steps taken to the various stations and their correlation with *humat*, *hūxt* and *huwaršt*, see AWN 7 in Shaked (2004: 341).
[20] The triad and the stations occur throughout MP texts. Here, I discuss passages most relevant to the present context.
[21] Text after Anklesaria (1913: 39).

paradise [*garōdmān*], where *Ohrmazd* is enthroned. (12) And the first heaven is *humat*, and the second is *hūxt*, and the third is *huwaršt*.

Although the above passage does not mention three steps, the relationship between the stations and the triad is unmistakeable. In PRDd 23, a chapter on the fate of the soul, we read that it reaches the stations with each step it takes with *humat*, *hūxt* and *huwaršt*:

PRDd 23.13[22] *ruwān fradom gām ī frāz nihēd ān gyāg kū star pad humat bē nihēd didīgar gām ān gyāg kū māh pad hūxt bē nihēd sidīgar gām ān gyāg kū xwaršēd pad huwaršt bē nihēd ud čahārom gām andar garōdmān ī rōšn bē nihēd*

By the first step which the soul takes, it reaches that place where the stars are, through good thought. It takes the second step through good speech into that place where the moon is. It takes the third step through good deed into that place where the sun is, and it takes the fourth step into paradise, which is light.

Here, *humat*, *hūxt* and *huwaršt* represent the steps taken by the soul, but they also dwell in the respective station.[23] Thus, the soul can be elevated to the stations, as suggested in PY 36.6c where it is hoped that the soul will reach the sun station. Finally, AWN 9 seems to allude to PY 36.6 when the sun or *huwaršt* station is called highest of heights:

AWN 9[24] *ka sidīgar gām frāz niham pad huwaršt ānōh kū huwaršt pad mehmānīh ō ānōh rasīdom *rōšnīh ī bālistān bālist xwānēnd*

When I take the third step through good deed, there where good deed is present, there I reached the light which they call the highest of heights.

These passages from the non-translation MP literature attest to the notion of the soul moving through the various stations by taking steps with *humat*, *hūxt* and *huwaršt*. They also confirm that the sun station was perceived as being light and the highest height. It is precisely this notion that informs the exegetes' interpretation of Y 36.6.

The triad *humat hūxt huwaršt* is praised at the very start of the *Yasna Haptaŋhāiti*, namely in the first stanza of the text (PY 35.1a). Its practice is further alluded to in PY 35.2b (*ēdōn ēn menom-iz ud gōwom-iz ud warzom-iz*).

---

[22] Text after Williams (1990: I 119). My translation and understanding of the unusual syntactic position of *pad humat* is motivated by a passage in AWN 7: *ud pas naxust gām frāz niham ō star pāyag pad humat ān gyāg kū humat pad mehmānīh* 'And then I take the first step into the star station through good thought, that place where good thought is present' (text after Vahman 1986: 99). For an alternative translation, see Williams (1990: II 48).

[23] As has been variously observed, passages such as PRDd 23.13 speak of four steps. Moreover, as Vahman (1986: 234) points out some MP texts extend the concept of the heavens and stations to correlate them with the number of the *Amahraspandān*. The triad is thus another illustrative example for the development of correlative structures in Zoroastrianism (see Chapter 4). Noteworthy is PRDd 65, a detailed discussion of the individual stations in the context of a rather complex network of references. For a discussion of this final chapter of the PRDd, see Williams (1990: II 268).

[24] Text after Vahman (1986: 101).

PY 36 seems to take up the motif by explicit textual references, but perhaps also by ritual action.[25] In PY 36.4a–b we find an implicit reference to good thought, good speech and good deed: *weh menišn … kunišn ud gōwišn*. But in the next stanza, PY 36.5b, the triad is explicitly mentioned: *pad harwisp humat ō tō ud pad harwisp hūxt ō tō ud pad harwisp huwaršt be rasom* 'I arrive before you with all good thoughts, and with all good words and with all good deeds.' The sacrificers approach the fire (*ō tō be rasom*) with the triad, perhaps taking three symbolic steps, each representing *humat*, *hūxt* and *huwaršt*. Therefore, in PY 36.6 the sacrificers express the wish for their soul to reach the sun station. Thus, the soul and the request for its exaltation to the highest light, the sun station, are not triggered only by the presence of *rōšnīh ī bālist* 'highest light', for Av. *imā raocā̊ barəzištəm*, and *xwaršēd* 'sun', for *huuarə̄*, in PY 36.6, but also by the internal logic and the narrative structure of PY 36, which is firmly rooted in the apparently widespread notions of the three steps required to reach the sun station. Finally, PY 36.6 seems to anticipate the soul's journey after death towards the sun station and ultimately to *Ohrmazd* himself.

That the three steps played a role in the ritual, is corroborated by the *Dēnkard*'s interpretation of Y 50.1–11:

> Dk 9.43.7[26] *ud abar čim ī gām sē az zōt gāh abestāg gōwišnīhā frāz raft ī zōt pas az yašt pad ātaxš sar pad parwāzišn ō āb zōhr barišnīh ul uzīdan ī amahrspandān hamē hanjaman ī hampursagīh zarduxšt sar pad sē gām az zamīg ō xwaršēd pāyag pad humat hūxt huwaršt*
>
> And about the purpose of the three steps taken by the *Zōt* from the seat of the *Zōt* while reciting the *Avesta* after the end of the fire ritual, for the flight which is carried for the *āb zōhr*, for the going up of the *Amahraspandān*, always at the end of the assembly of Zardušt's consultation by three steps from the earth to the sun station by *humat*, *hūxt* and *huwaršt*.

As Vevaina (2010c) points out, in 'the modern *Yasna* ritual, these three steps are taken during the recitation of *Yasna* 64.3-4 = *Yasna* 50.7-8 (the *Ātaš niyāyišn*) before the beginning of *Yasna* 65 (the *Ābān niyāyišn*)'. Vevaina goes on to state that '*Yasna* 50.8 contains the statement "with the steps (*pada-*) that are renowned as those of the milk libation (*ižā-*)," which evidently prompted the exegesis'. However, considering the link between the three steps and the *Ātaš Niyāyišn*, I am inclined to suggest, contra Vevaina, that these three steps are not a a reflection of the milk libation, but most likely a ritual reference to PY 36.6. That the steps are taken during the *Ātaš*

---

[25] Already Narten (1986: 86ff.) points out that the triad occurs in Y 36 as well. Hintze (2007a: 9) adds further evidence for parallels in the compositional structure of Y 35 and 36.
[26] Text after Dresden (1966: 156).

Niyāyišn is not a coincidence. One might hypothesise that the three steps might have been part of ritual actions of the *Yasna Haptaŋhāiti*.

In an extensive analysis of the Zoroastrian intercalation ceremonies transmitted in Avestan, Cantera (2013) examines how the ritual might be reflective of the soul's journey after death.[27] Cantera (2013: 119) suggests, mostly without recourse to the *Zand*, that the *Staota Yesniia* bring the sacrifcer's soul to paradise 'after the offering of the sacrificial meat to the Fire during the Yasna Haptaŋhāiti'. Cantera (2013: 120) goes on to observe:

> In the following paragraph (Vyt4.6 [29]), a difficult text, the *haṇdāiti* of the Staota Yesniia is compared to a victorious horse that brings the sacrificer to the finish. In this context, the Vahištōišti Gāθā represents the union of the sacrificer's soul with its Vision (s. Kellens 1995: 38 ff.) and the Airiiaman Išiia the final eschatological reward (s. FrW4.1): the access to Paradise. This reading of the Staota Yesniia might explain why in V21 (which follows the recitation of the Ariiman [sic] Išiia) the vocatives (V21.5, 8, 13) are directed to the sun, the moon and the stars, the three levels leading up to Paradise from the Bridge of Cinuuaṯ.

Cantera (2013: 117) also argues, that in the ritual the sacrificer's soul accompanies the soul of the sacrificial animal on a journey to the other world into the presence of *Ahura Mazdā*. Thus, he attributes, contra Panaino (2004), the ritual inactivity of the *zaotar* from Y 36 to 58 to a state of temporary death or immobilisation in which the priest's body remains. It is precisely this journey and this moment in the ritual that PY 36.6 refers to. The soul is here exalted to the final station on its way to *garō nmāna-*. Thus a link is established between the wordly triad of human actions, *humat hūxt huwaršt* and the celestial stations of the stars, the moon and the sun. In the continuation of the ritual, beyond Y 36, the soul then continues its journey towards the highest level and its ultimate goal, into the presence of *Ahura Mazdā* in *garō nmāna-*.

It is instructive to take another look at Dk 9.35, the interpretation of the YH, where the relationship between triad and the *dēn* is described:

> **Dk 9.35.1**[28] *120m fragard yasn abar paydāgīh ī humat hūxt ud huwaršt az dēn mehmānīh ī dēn pad humat hūxt ud huwaršt kē humat hūxt ud kē huwaršt xwēšēnēd ā-š ahlawīh ud ān ī ahlawān mizd xwēšēnīd bawēd*

> The 12th section, the *yasn*, is on the manifestation of good thoughts, good words and good deeds from the *dēn*. The presence of the *dēn* is through good thoughts, good words and good deeds. Whoever makes good thoughts, good words and good deeds his own, he appropriates righteousness and the reward of the righteous ones.

---

[27] Various aspects of Cantera's article have recently been discussed in some detail by König (2018).
[28] Text after Dresden (1966: 653).

Good thoughts, good words and good deeds are here not mere moral prescriptions for the followers of the religion, but a reference to a significant moment in the ritual in Y 36.6: They describe a crucial moment in the soul's journey into the presence of *Ahura Mazdā*, that is, the last celestial station before the soul can meet *Ahura Mazdā* for a consultation (*frašna*) in *garō nmāna*, and thus a bridge, as it were, between the tangible world and the heavenly realm of the deity. This must be the reason why the triad *humat hūxt huwaršt* is the condition for the presence (*mehmānīh*) of the *dēn*, as it enables the sacrificer or his soul to travel to its ultimate goal in turn enabling, *apud* Cantera (2013), the moment of the consultation and vision.

5.3 PY 37

The central section of the YH starts with (P)Y 37 extending to (P)Y 39 (Hintze 2007a: 9). These three chapters contain a number of praise formulae in honour of *Ohrmazd*'s creations. In Suppl.ŠnŠ 13, this chapter is characterised as follows:

Suppl.ŠnŠ 13.18[29] *iϑā āat̰* yazamaide *ǰ wačadast stāyišn ud spās az ōhrmazd pad dādan ī wēh dahišnān*

The *iϑā āat̰ yazamaide* has five strophes, (offering) praise and gratitude to *Ohrmazd* on account of creating the good creations.

Modern priestly scholarship propagates a similar view:

Y.37 (= Y.5) includes, besides the grace said before meals [...], sincere expressions of thanksgiving for the guardian spirits (*fravashis*) of holy men and women, for the excellent and most bountiful Best Righteousness, and for all creations of Ahura Mazda. (Kotwal and Boyd 1991: 112)

Being identical to Y 5, Y 37 is abbreviated in the exegetical manuscripts of the nineteenth century: F2 R413 T6 E7. The four MSS follow different patterns in abbreviating the chapter:

F2 *iϑā. āat̰. yaz ahurəm. mazdą̇m.* ʿD *vaŋuhīmcā. ārmaitīm. yeŋhe. hātą̇m.* ʿD LʿYŠH
R413 *iϑā. āt̰. yaz.* ʿD *vaŋuhīmcā. ārmaitīm. yeŋhe. hātą̇m.* ʿD LʿYŠH
T6 *iϑā. āat̰. yazamaide vaŋuhīmcā. ārmaitīm. yeŋhe. hātą̇m.*
E7 Line (a) o ʿD LʿYŠH BRʾ KRYTWN-m *yeŋhe. hātą̇m.*[30]

The MSS of the Skt. *Yasna* display similar variations when abbreviating the chapter. Manuscript T7, a SktY manuscript kept at the *First Dastur Meherji Rana Library* (see Dhabhar 1923: 110), uses Pahlavi terminology

---

[29] Text after Kotwal (1969: 46–7).
[30] E7 gives the Av. text and the *Zand* of line (a) before abbreviating the chapter.

for the abbreviation: *iδā. āaṯ. y ahurəm. mazdąm.* 'D LʿYŠH *yeńhe. hātąm.*
It is perhaps significant that three (M G18b G27) out of the four (2101)
Iranian *Wisperad sāde* manuscripts available from the ADA website do not
abbreviate this chapter, but overall no shared patterns are recognisable among
the different families of manuscripts.

5.4 PY 38

(P)Y 38 is dedicated to praises for the earth, the females, the waters
and the good names. Suppl.ŠnŠ 13, however, connects this stanza with
Wīdēwdād 3, emphasising one aspect of PY 38, namely the praise for the
earth. Suppl.ŠnŠ 13 mentions the fire, but not the waters:

> **Suppl.ŠnŠ 13.19**[31] imąm āaṯ ząm *5 wačadast az ān 5 āsānīh ud 5 anāsānīh ī zamīg ī pad wandīdād pad sidīgar fragard paydāg be kard ēstēd kū zamīg fradom āsānīh az ān zamīg ka-š mard ī ahlaw abar frāz rawēd didīgar ka-š mān ī wehān ud ātaxšān abar kunēd sidīgar ka-š jōrdā abar kārēnd ud nasā pahrēz kunēd tasom ka-š harw stōr abar zāyēnd panjom ka-š harw stōr abar mēzēnd u-š fradom anāsānīh az ān ī arzūr grīwag dar ī dōšox didīgar ka-š rist abar *nigānēnēnd sidīgar ka-š hazzān abar kunēd tasom az ān ka-š sūrāg ī xrafstarān panjom ka-š mard pad wardagīh abar be barēd ī ahlaw*

> The *imąm āaṯ ząm* has five strophes. The five comforts and the five discomforts of the earth, which are in the third chapter of the *Wandīdād*, are manifest from those (five strophes of the *imąm āaṯ ząm*): The first comfort of the earth is from that land when a righteous man walks forth upon it. The second (comfort) is when he builds the dwelling of the good ones and the fires upon it. The third one is when they sow corn upon (the earth), and he protects it from dead matter. The fourth is when all cattle are born upon (the earth), fifth when all cattle urinate upon it. And its first discomfort is from the *Arzūr* hill, the gate of hell. The second (discomfort) is when they bury the dead upon (the earth). The third is when he builds graves upon it. Its fourth (discomfort) is from that when there are burrows of obnoxious creatures. The fifth is when one takes captive on (this earth) a righteous man.

5.5 PY 39

In the final chapter of the middle section of the YH, the praise formulae
are dedicated to the souls of the various parts of the creation: the cattle and
its creator, harmless animals and the good people. Praises and sacrifice are
also offered to the *Amahraspandān* and *Ohrmazd*. In the concluding stanza,
PY 39.5, the sacrificers reaffirm their dedication to *Ohrmazd*.

---

[31] Text after Kotwal (1969: 46–7).

Surprisingly, Suppl.ŠnŠ 13 describes this chapter in rather simple terms with a reference to (P)Y 37:

Suppl.ŠnŠ 13.20[32] *iϑā 5 wačadast čiyōn ān-iz ī pēš*

iϑā has five strophes, like that one which was before.

5.6 PY 40

Suppl.ŠnŠ 13 describes this chapter as follows:

Suppl.ŠnŠ 13.21[33] *āhū aṯ paitī 4 wačadast abar arzōmandīh ī āb zamīg urwar ud gōspand rāy*

āhū aṯ paitī has four strophes on the value which is on account of water, the earth, the plants and cattle.

In a numerological speculation, the four strophes of (P)Y 40 are related to water, earth, plants and the cattle, although none of these are mentioned in the Avestan or Pahlavi version of the chapter.

The final two chapters of the YH, Y 40 and 41, continue the ritual that started in (P)Y 36, but was interrupted by the invocations in (P)Y 37–39. In the Pahlavi version of the YH, the fire joins in the ritual in (P)Y 36, as it is knowledgeable in the *dēn*, the sacrificers' requested reward (Section 5.1.2). It is perhaps not a coincidence that the resumption of the ritual and the end of the invocations are marked by two explicit references to (P)Y 36. The first reference is from the penultimate stanza of (P)Y 39 and comes after the last of the praise formulae, repeating a clause from PY 36.5:

(P)Y 36.5a *nəmaxiiāmahī išūidīiāmahī ϑβā mazda ahura*
niyāyišnēnē u-m abāmēnē tō ohrmazd kū-m abām pad tō bawād

(P)Y 39.4c *aϑā nəmaxiiāmahī aϑā išuidiiāmahī ϑβā mazdā ahurā*
u-m ēdōn niyāyišnēnē u-m ēdōn abāmēnē tō ohrmazd kū-m abām pad tō bawād

The second reference is from the final stanza of (P)Y 39, (P)Y 39.5b. Here, *ϑβā pairijasāmaidē 'ō tō be rasom'* is reminiscent of *ϑβā ... pairijasāmaidē 'ō tō ... be rasom'* in (P)Y 36.5b, where the sacrificers symbolically or ritually approach the fire (Section 5.2.1). With these references to (P)Y 36 the ritual action continues where it was halted by the invocations, and the concluding section of the text, (P)Y 40 and 41, is initiated.

---

[32] Text after Kotwal (1969: 47).
[33] Text after Kotwal (1969: 47).

5.6.1 A commitment to the *dēn*

In her commentary to *aϑā x^vaētuš* 'likewise families', Narten (1986: 281–5) suggests that the request for fellowship in Y 40.4 could refer to proselytism. Hintze (2007a: 303) follows this interpretation and adduces further evidence in support of the existence of proselytism in the early days of Zoroastrianism in an interpretation of the Av. sections of Herb 5 (see Hintze 2009b). However, as Macuch's (2009a) edition of the *Zand* to the same text shows, the commentators, presumably Sasanian sages, do not share the same sense of disseminating the religion with the Av. original. Although Narten's analysis of Y 40.3–4 has no bearing on the passage's Pahlavi version, or for that matter on the PYH in general, it is worth noting that the *Zand*, not only of the YH, is explicit about the proclamation of the religion to others.

A similar notion emerges, for instance, from PY 12.8:

> **PY 12.8**[34] *mazdēsn-om kū mard weh-mard-om ud mazdēsnīh ī zardušt franāmom kū andarg ī wattarān gōwom*
> *stāyom xwad ud franāmom kū andar gēhān rawāg bē kunom*
> *stāyom humat ī pad menišn ud stāyom hūxt ī pad gōwišn ud stāyom huwaršt ī pad kunišn ...*
>
> I am a Mazda-worshipper, that is, I am a good man and I profess to Zardušt's Mazda-worshipping (religion), that is, I speak (of it) amongst the evil ones.
> Indeed, I praise and proclaim (it), that is, I propagate (it) in the world.
> I praise the good thought that is in thought and I praise the good speech that is in speech and I praise the good deed that is in action ...

As I argued in Section 5.1.2, the *dēn* occupies a prominent place in the *Zand* of the YH. The ritual is dedicated to the request for the *dēn* and already in PY 35 the text displays a strong commitment to proclaiming and promulgating the *dēn*. Much like the *frauuarānē* (Y 12–13), often referred to as the Zoroastrian profession of faith, where the sacrificers are said to choose the Mazda-worshipping religion, in PYH the performers of the sacrifice pledge to practise that which is the very essence of the religion they choose, namely *humat hūxt huwaršt*.[35]

And as already pointed out, this notion of commitment and proclamation survives in the NP glosses in the MSS F2 and T6 (Y 35.6c) and re-emerges in PY 40. In a marginal note on PY 40.3, T6 preserves another reference to the idea of the religion being disseminated by the priesthood:

یعنی آنجان، هیربدان یعنی اوستادی کنندگان پاک و استوار کردن پاک و استوکه مراد اشوی دارندگان مرادبه ای هورمزد که کار دین رواج پذیرد

---

[34] Text after Pt4.

[35] Cantera (2015) has recently challenged the view that the *frauuarānē* is a profession of faith, suggesting that the formula allows the officiating priest to present his own ritual choice (Cantera 2015: 94).

This means: give me, O *Ohrmazd*, such *hērbeds*, that is, pure and righteous teachers and pure and righteous disciples who are the desire of the keepers of righteousness, so that the works of the religion can be accepted widely.

And in F2 in a marginal note on this stanza Zarduśt requests disciples from *Ohrmazd*:

زراتشت گوید هورمزد راکه مرا شاکردان اشو بدی

Zarātošt says to *Hourmazd*: 'Give me righteous disciples!'

Both marginal notes are inspired by this stanza's interpretation of the Av. version:

> **PY 40.3** (a) You give me thus that which belongs to men, O *Ohrmazd*, disciples of men, teacher-priests, righteous ones who desire righteousness. Those teacher-priests,
> (b) who shall guide them [*hāwištān*], shall then be my fellows for that long coming and increase, (namely) the final body, through that which is strong, through action.
> (c) You give us that one who provides us peace.

While the original speaks of 'order, order desiring men, non-violent herdsmen',[36] the *Zand* requests disciples and teachers (*hāwištān ī mardān hērbedān*) who will guide the community. In PY 40.1, *manīgān* alluded to the request for disciples. So PY 40.3 makes this reference explicit and continues the theme of discipleship (see Section 3.1). In this way, both stanzas belong together and seem to link to PY 28, where the request for disciples is one of the central themes. At first glance, the association of the PYH with passages referring to mytho-epic figures, *Wištāsp* and *Frašōštar*, may seem random. However, the shared vocabulary of Y 28 and PY 40 suggests a thematic connection between these two chapters. The stanzas of chapter 40 not only allude to teachers and disciples (PY 40.1 and 3), but also mention *tan ī pasēn* (PY 40.2 and 3), another oft repeated expression in PY 28. Most significantly, PY 40.2 shares with PY 28.8 the idea of prevalence until the end of the *gētīy*, expressed by the rather rare expression *hamē tā ō wisp tā tan ī pasēn*. It is hardly a coincidence that the *Zand* of PY 40 connects these stanzas with teachers, disciples and the spread of the religion. The exegetes promoted the idea that the founder of the religion required disciples who would help to disseminate the religion. Most likely, they related this notion to the concerns of their own time, perhaps in an effort to underline their own continuous relevance as maintainers of the

---

[36] The translation of *ašāunō ašacinaŋhō* 'order, order desiring men' as *ahlaw ī ahlāyīh kāmag* is not further surprising, but the translation of *aidiiuš vāstriiāŋg* is unclear. It most closely corresponds to *ī ka-šān hāzānd* in the stanza's MP translation.

religion. They certainly viewed the priesthood as leaders, if not as sovereigns with worldly powers:

> **PY 49.8d** *hamē tā ō wisp framānbed hānd kū frašōštar ud hāwištān ī frašōštar tā tan ī pasēn hamē pādixšāyīh dah*
>
> They shall be commanders always until all; that is, grant to *Frašōštar* and the disciples of *Frašōštar* continuous authority until the future body.

In conclusion, if we read PY 28 and PY 40 together, it emerges that the idea of disseminating the religion was not limited to Av. texts,[37] but that the concept of publicly proclaiming a religious affiliation was known in the *Zand* and prevailed in the NP glosses. Embedded in an eschatological context and framework (PY 49.8d), the promulgation of the *dēn* defined the role of the priests in a much larger context than just studying and teaching the religion. By receiving the *dēn* in the ritual, and relating themselves to the primordial sages of old, an association they wish to maintain until the end of time, Zoroastrian priests transcend themselves and assume, as it were, a cosmic responsibility.

5.7 PY 41

The final chapter of the YH is dedicated to the request for the reward (41.5 and 6) and starts with praises of *Ohrmazd* and *Ašwahišt* (41.1). It is stated that the reward will bring about *Ohrmazd*'s good rule over men and women (41.2). Therefore, the sacrificers pledge obedience to *Ohrmazd*, hoping to receive body and soul from him (41.3). The reward, the *dēn*, is then desired for providing peace until the event of the final body (41.4).[38] The sacrificers further condition the distribution of the reward by *Ohrmazd* upon the accomplishment of praises and formulas (41.5). It becomes evident that those who master and accept the praise of the deity and the relevant words and formulas belong to the community (*manīgān*) of the *dēn* (*dēnīgān*). The *Yasna Haptaŋhāiti* closes with a final emphasis on the receipt of the reward, the *dēn*, for both existences so that the community of the *dēn* may achieve the guardianship and righteousness of *Ohrmazd* until *frašgird*.

---

[37] Hintze (2009b) gives an overview of Av. passages where the dissemination of the religion is a theme.
[38] On PY 41 and the reward, see Section 5.7.2.

The Suppl.ŠnŠ provides a very brief description of Y 41:[39]

Suppl.ŠnŠ 13.22[40] *stūtō ġarō*[41] *šaš wačast humatanąm dō jār huxšatrōtemāi*[42] *sē jār būdan ī pusarān ī zarduxšt rāy*

stūtō garō has six stanzas, *humatanąm* (is to be recited) two times (and) *huxšatrōtemāi* three times on account of the existence of *Zarduxšt*'s sons.

5.7.1 PY 41.4

In PY 36.2 the fire is explicitly invited to join the ritual for the sake of the great affair (*ān ī meh kār*), which is explained as the trial of the final body (*passāxt ī pad tan ī pasēn*). It appears that the fire propagates the *dēn*, in which it is knowledgeable, to prepare the world for the *frašgird*.[43] The notion of preparing the world for the final events by propagating the religion also emerges from PY 41.4, where we find similar themes: the sacrificers gain worth by the retribution of the reward (*mizd pādāšn*), which is the *dēn*. The stanza further corroborates on this thought by linking strength (*amāwand*) to what belongs to *Ohrmazd* (*xwāstār pad ēd ī tō*), namely his religion (*dēn ī tō*), and his future arrival (*dagr rasišnīh*),[44] which will last until the final body (*tan ī pasēn*).[45] The notion of *tan ī pasēn* thus links PY 36.2 to 40.2 and 41.4, underlining, as it were, the narrative structure of the PYH, which evolves around universal eschatology in which the fire plays a significant role as the transmitter of religious knowledge. The eschatological context in which the ritual is placed, suggests that the exegetes viewed the ritual as a preparation for the final body, or perhaps as an enactment of *frašgird* itself.

5.7.2 PY 41.6: *ān ī ōy* 'that which is his'

Y 40.2 and 41.6 are commonly thought to represent a request for reward, addressed to *Ahura Mazdā*.[46] It is also assumed that fellowship (*haxəmā*) and union (*sarəm*), achieved by means of the prize (*yā*), are sought with

---

[39] For a discussion of the extent of Y 41 and its reception in the Suppl.ŠnŠ, see Zeini (Forthcoming).
[40] I quote the Suppl.ŠnŠ according to F35, published by Jamaspasa and Nawabi (1976c: 143–7). Kotwal (1969: 10) collated it only indirectly. I have preserved the MS's rendering of Av. words.
[41] Kotwal (1969: 47) has *stūtō garō vahmǝ̄ng*.
[42] '*huxšatrōtemāi*' refers to Y 35.5 and is written ⟨Av.⟩. The number of the repetitions for Y 35.5 agrees with the number stated in Wd 10.7–8 and the instructions at the end of Y 35.5.
[43] On proclaiming and committing to the *dēn*, see Section 5.1.2 and 5.6.1.
[44] MacKenzie (1990) gives 'long' as the only meaning for *dagr*, while noting its relationship with New Persian *dēr*. The latter, however, can also mean 'late, a long time'. In the present context, *dagr* conveys 'a long time' in the sense of 'future' which emerges from its association with *tan ī pasēn*.
[45] See also Dk 7.8.50 where these themes reoccur.
[46] See Hintze (2007a: 7–8), Narten (1986), Humbach (1991) and Kellens and Pirart (1988). See also Spiegel (1859: 141).

Ahura Mazdā and *aṣ̌a-*.⁴⁷ This view is largely based on Narten's (1986: 297–302) morphological and syntactic analysis of *ahiiā* 'of that',⁴⁸ a gen.sg. of the neutral-deictic dem.pron. *a-* 'that', which has been interpreted as 'referring back to *mīždəm*' in Y 40.1c and 41.5c (Hintze 2007a: 293).⁴⁹ However, the Av. text does not define what the sacrificers expect as reward. In the *Zand* of these stanzas, *ān ī ōy* alludes to an unidentified object, possibly the reward, belonging to a third person, while *ān ō amā dahē* directs the request to an elusive entity, leaving it uncertain as to how the exegetes interpreted these stanzas of the YH.

The phrase *ān ī ōy* corresponds to *ahiiā*. While in the PY *ōy, ō* and *ān* can correspond to *huuō*, it is not necessary that here *ōy* translates *huuō*, a nom.sg.m. of the far-deictic dem.pron. *auua-* 'that there'. Rather, *ī ōy* defines *ān* more closely, while *huuō* is perhaps implied by the 2sg.opt. *dahē* or left untranslated. Unlike the Av. *ahiiā* which agrees with the preceding *mīždəm* (Y 40.1c and 41.5c) in gender, at least if one agrees with Narten, the simplified inflection of MP conceals *ān*'s referent. However, in PY 28.1 the exegetes too connect *ahiiā* with reward, translating it *ān mizd ī ōy ī ohrmazd xwēš* 'that reward of his, which is *Ohrmazd*'s own':

Y 28.1 *ahiiā yāsā nəmaŋhā ustānazastō rafəδrahiiā*

With homage (and) with hands stretched up, I ask for (this) from that: for the support

PY 28.1 *ān mizd ī ōy ī ohrmazd xwēš xwāhem pad niyāyišn ka ǰādag-gōwīh ī yazadān ud wehān kunem ustān-dast menišnīg pad rāmišn ī xwēš*

I desire that reward, which is *Ohrmazd*'s own, in (my) prayers when on behalf of others I thoughtfully, with my hands stretched up (and) in my own peace praise the gods and the good ones.

NP interlinear glosses in F2 reflect a similar understanding in (P)Y 40.2 and 41.6 when both *ahiiā huuō* and *ān ī ōy* are glossed مز 'reward'. Moreover, in PY 40.2 T6 explicitly links the reward to *Ohrmazd* by incorporating the *Zand*'s interpretation of *ahiiā* from PY 28.1, glossing *ahiiā huuō* with آن مزدتوای هورمزدکه از آن خویش است⁵⁰ 'That reward of yours, O *Ohrmazd*, which is your own' and *ān ī ōy* with که آن مزدتوای هورمزدکه از آن خوداست.⁵¹ In PY 45.3, too, we find *ān ī ōy* directly

---

⁴⁷ See Narten (1986: 28, 146) and Hintze (2007a: 7–8), but also Humbach (1991) and Kellens and Pirart (1988).

⁴⁸ Humbach (1991: I 149–50) and Hintze (2007a: 292–3, 321–3) follow her. Kellens and Pirart (1991: 153) exclude Y 41.6 from the YH (Kellens and Pirart 1988: 140), interpret *ahiiā* differently, but supply 'récompense' in Y 40.2 as well (Kellens and Pirart 1988: 139; Kellens and Pirart 1991: 149).

⁴⁹ Likewise, Spiegel (1868: 316).

⁵⁰ The MS reads مر.

⁵¹ T6 has no NP glosses to (P)Y 41.6.

linked with *Ohrmazd*: *ēdōn frāz gōwom andar axwān ān ī ōy ohrmazd xwēš* 'Thus, I proclaim in the existences that, which belongs to him, is *Ohrmazd*'s own.' Thus, a longstanding tradition linked *ahiiā* and *ān ī ōy* to the reward, which was thought to belong to *Ohrmazd*.[52] However, the questions remain as to what the reward is and to whom the request is addressed.

In PY 36.3 we find a comparable phrase, *ān ī ohrmazd*, where that, which belongs to *Ohrmazd* is construed as the *dēn*:

> PY 36.3a *ātaxš pad ān ī ohrmazd āgāh ast pad dēn ī ohrmazd*
>
> The fire is knowledgeable in that, which belongs to *Ohrmazd*, in the *dēn* of *Ohrmazd*.

Likewise, PY 41.4 reads: *pad ēd ī tō pad dēn ī tō* 'for this which is yours, for your religion'.[53] Therefore, *ān ī ōy* appears to signify *dēn ī ohrmazd*, a notion which also emerges from Dk 7.8.50:

> Dk 7.8.50 *be amāwandīh pērōzgarīh banded ō ān ī ōy dēn ī ohrmazd ud pad ān amāwandīh ud pērōzgarīh hamē az ān franāmīd bawēnd ka awēšān rasēnd kē pus ī zarduxšt hēnd kē kunēnd frašgird andar axwān a-zarmān a-marg ud a-sōhišn ud a-pōhišn dagr hamē tā ō wisp*
>
> He will tie strength (and) victory to that which is his, (namely) *Ohrmazd*'s religion. And by that strength and victory they will continuously profess to it [*dēn*], when those arrive, who are the sons of *Zarduxšt*, who will bring about the *frašgird* in the existences, ageless, immortal and unfeeling and incorruptible, continuing at length[54] until all.

If *ān ī ōy* refers to *Ohrmazd*'s *dēn*, then the addressee of the request must be the fire. It is in this light that in PY 36.3 the fire is described as knowledgeable in the *dēn* of *Ohrmazd*. Consequently, by receiving *Ohrmazd*'s *dēn*, in PY 40.2 and 41.6 the sacrificers request brotherhood (*ham-brādagīh*) and guardianship (*sālārīh*) from the fire rather than *Ohrmazd*.

This perception of the fire challenges the established view by shifting agency from the deity to the fire, and allows for a number of interpretations. Firstly, it is the fire that distributes *Ohrmazd*'s *dēn* as the reward. Accordingly, the fire's brotherhood and leadership is sought by the sacrificers.[55] To achieve their goal, the sacrificers approach the fire in two stages. In the

---

[52] The exegetes' above interpretation of *ahiiā* does not blindly extend to all of the OAv. attestations of the pronoun. They appear to have had a nuanced knowledge of Av., even if its implied semantics involved complex syntactic relationships.

[53] For a similar equation between *ān ī ohrmazd* and *dēn ī ohrmazd*, see PY 7.24, 28.4b, 45.4e, 51.19c and 54.1f. See also PY 45.8, 48.3, 49.1: *rāstīh ī ohrmazd dēn ī ohrmazd* 'the rectitude of *Ohrmazd*, the *dēn* of *Ohrmazd*'.

[54] Beside its literal meaning, *dagr* evokes here and elsewhere the idea of length of time that continues until *frašgird*, that is, future. See also PY 41.4: *pad dagr rasišnīh pad tan ī pasēn*.

[55] The fire thus acts as an intermediary between the sacrificers and the deity. A similar interpretation of the fire in the context of the YH is offered by Kellens (2000: 108–9).

first, in PY 40.2, they ask for *Ohrmazd*'s *dēn* in order to enter into the fire's brotherhood, which is explained as cooperation with the fire (*ham-kardārīh*). Presumably, only after their commitment to align their actions with the fire, can the sacrificers ask for the *dēn* in an attempt to obtain the fire's leadership in the second stage. Secondly, it appears that the fire propagates the *dēn*, in which it is knowledgeable, thereby preparing the world for the *frašgird*.[56] Finally, with PY 41.6 the concluding stanza of the YH connects with PY 36.1, the start of the actual ritual.[57] If the sacrificers approached the fire at the beginning with care and propitiation, in part due to its ability to harm those who inflict harm upon it (PY 36.1), they now seek the fire's brotherhood and leadership after having received *Ohrmazd*'s *dēn*. This anticipates the heat ordeal in which the fire will not harm the orderly ones, who are thus defined by the PYH as those who have received the *dēn* as the reward.

At first glance, the priestly exegesis of Y 40.2 and 41.6 seems to differ from its Western academic interpretation. Scholars widely agree that in Y 40.2 and 41.6 the OAv. dem.pron. *huuō* designates *Ahura Mazdā*.[58] This view attributes a far-deictic and vocative function to the pronoun. However, the deixis of the pronoun seems far less clear. Humbach (1991: I 107), for instance, points out that *huuō* assumes near-, far- and neutral-deictic functions in the OAv. corpus (also Hintze 2007a: 120). Therefore, the pronoun's deixis is not an argument for establishing its referent, which in Y 40.2 and 41.6 can contextually be either *Ahura Mazdā* or the fire. Moreover, the only other occurrence of *huuō* in the YH (Y 36.2) has unanimously been interpreted as referring to the fire. In my view, in Y 40.2 and 41.6 the poet builds on this precedent to invoke the fire once more, only this time for the sake of the request. In this way, the poet avoids any ambiguity as regards the addressee and links the ritual invitation (Y 36.2) to the request for the reward (Y 40.2 and 41.6). Both passages represent crucial moments of the ritual: firstly, the invitation for the fire to join the ritual fire, marking the beginning of the ritual; secondly, the request for the prize, which is the ritual's sole purpose and conclusion.

5.7.3 *hamē tā ō wisp* 'always until all'

The expression *hamē tā ō wisp* occurs three times in the PYH (40.2, 41.2 and 41.6). It is further attested in PY 7.25 (≈ 41.6), 28.8, 46.11, 49.8, 53.1, 53.4

---

[56] On this, see PY 40.3.
[57] The PYH thrives on a number of intricate cross-references.
[58] See Narten (1986: 145–7), Humbach (1991: I 107) and Hintze (2007a: 119–23) with references. See also West (2011: 46–8), who posits an emphatic function in partial agreement with Spiegel (1868: 316): '*Hvô* muss man entweder auf Ahura beziehen oder als verstärkenden Zusatz zu *né*'.

and Dk 7.8.50. The expression's literal, 'always until for all', and intended meanings seem rather obscure. The preposition ō may tempt a translation as 'always (and) for all', but tā makes this interpretation difficult.[59] In all of its attestations, hamē tā ō wisp corresponds to āiiu- vīspa- 'for all time'.[60] Undoubtedly, wisp expresses Av. vīspa- 'all', but it is not obvious how in this construction hamē 'always' corresponds to āiiu- 'lifetime'.[61]

In Dk 7.8.50, where hamē tā ō wisp concludes the paragraph, West (1897: 105) translates the phrase 'including all'. Mills (1905a: 73, 74, 76) translates the phrase literally as 'forever until all' (PY 40.2) and 'for ever until all' (PY 41.2 and 41.6). In PY 28.8, Shaked (1996: 653) renders hamē tā ō wisp as 'always ... to ... all'. While the referent of the expression remains unclear in West's translation, Shaked takes it as a reference to Frašōštar and his disciples. Both editors thus assume a statement of inclusion, presumably referring to persons mentioned in the respective paragraph.

Within the PYH, the intended meaning of hamē tā ō wisp is made explicit in its first occurrence in PY 40.2 by the immediately following phrase tā tan ī pasēn 'until the future body'.[62] Although this addition is missing in PY 41.6, the parallelism of the two stanzas suggests that the same meaning would apply here as well:

Y 40.2 *tauuacā haxəmā ašaxiiācā vīspāi yauuē*

ō ēd ī tō ham-brādagīh ham-kardārīh ī ahlāyīh-iz hamē tā ō wisp tā tan ī pasēn

Y 41.6 *tauuacā sarəm ašaxiiācā vīspāi yauuē*

ō ēd ī tō sālārīh ud ahlāyīh hamē tā ō wisp

The connection between hamē tā ō wisp and tā tan ī pasēn is perhaps less explicit in some of the following passages but still strongly evident:

PY 28.8c *ō-iz awēšān ēg rād hē hamē tā ō wisp pad wahman kū frašōštar ud hāwištān ī frašōštar tā tan ī pasēn hamē*[63] *nēkīh padiš kun*

Through *Wahman* you are then generous to them too, always until all; that is, always exercise goodness for *Frašōštar* and the disciples of *Frašōštar* until the future body.

PY 46.11e *u-šān hamē tā ō wisp tā ō tan ī pasēn andar druzōdmān astišn ast*

And they exist always until all, until the future body, in the House of Deceit.

---

[59] For a brief discussion and translation of *tā ō*, see Skjærvø (2009b: 489) and Weber (2009: 541), respectively.
[60] In the YH, OAv. *yauuē* is a dat.sg. of *āiiu-* ntr. 'life, lifetime' (Hintze 2007a: 333). In connection with *vīspa-*, Bartholomae (1904: 1264) translates *āiiu-* 'für die ganze Dauer, für alle Zeit'. On *yauuōi* versus *yauuē* < *-ōi*, see Humbach (1991: I 61 and II 26).
[61] Rather than translating *vīspāi yauuē* (Y 28.8, PY 40.2, 41.2, 41.6 and Y 46.11), the *Zand* seems to follow the word order of *yauuōi vīspāi* (Y 49.8, 53.1 and 4), which contains the expected OAv. *yauuōi*.
[62] On *tan ī pasēn* and resurrection, see Hutter (2009).
[63] Dhabhar (1949: 127) has *hamāg*, which Shaked (1996: 651) retains. Pt4, however, reads *hamē*.

PY 49.8d *hamē tā ō wisp framānbed hānd kū frašōštar ud hāwištān ī frašōštar tā tan ī pasēn hamē pādixšāyīh dah*

They shall be commanders always until all; that is, grant to *Frašōštar* and the disciples of *Frašōštar* continuous authority until the future body.

PY 53.1c *az ahlāyīh abāgīh ohrmazd ā-m hamē tā ō wisp hu-axwēnād kū-m tā tan ī pasēn hamē nēw-dilīh dahād*

In accordance with righteousness, *Ohrmazd* will continuously (grant) me a good existence until all; that is, he will continuously grant me bravery until the future body.

The unmistakable association between *hamē tā ō wisp* and *tā tan ī pasēn* leaves no doubt that the commentators placed the expression in an eschatological context.[64] In my opinion this interpretation extends to PY 41.2 and PY 53.4 as well, despite the fact that in these two stanzas *hamē tā ō wisp* does not occur in conjunction with *tan ī pasēn*:

PY 53.4d *ohrmazd dahišn pad dēn ī weh hamē tā ō wisp ān ēstād ī pad dēn ī weh rāy*

Ohrmazd creates through the good religion, always until all; it shall endure, which is through the good religion.

A similar notion emerges from the passage in Dk 7, which establishes a further link between *hamē tā ō wisp* and *frašgird*:

Dk 7.8.50 *be amāwandīh pērōzgarīh banded ō ān ī ōy dēn ī ohrmazd ud pad ān amāwandīh ud pērōzgarīh hamē az ān franāmīd bawēnd ka awēšān rasēnd kē pus ī zarduxšt hēnd kē kunēnd frašgird andar axwān a-zarmān a-marg ud a-sōhišn ud a-pōhišn dagr hamē tā ō wisp*

He will tie strength (and) victory to that which is his, (namely) *Ohrmazd*'s religion. And by that strength and victory they will continuously profess to it [*dēn*], when those arrive, who are the sons of *Zarduxšt*, who will bring about the *frašgird* in the existences, ageless, immortal and unfeeling and incorruptible, continuing at length until all.

In the examined passages, *hamē tā ō wisp* delineates a well-defined time span, namely the lifetime of this existence, as it ends at the event of *tan ī pasēn*. Therefore, in this context *hamē* cannot denote the condition of endlessness or eternity.[65] In a discussion of *uba- ahu-* 'both existences', Narten (1986: 292, fn. 23, 293) prefers a non-eschatological interpretation of *vīspāi yauuē* in favour of an individual lifetime ('individuelle Lebensdauer').[66] The *Zand*'s

---

[64] For the *Zand*'s tendency to interpret Av. passages in light of eschatology, see Shaked (1996), Josephson (2003) and Vevaina (2007).

[65] It remains to be examined whether *hamē* ⟨hm'y⟩ can be translated 'eternal' in such contexts. See, for instance, Shaked (1971: 96) in Dk 3.193.2: *zamān xwad hamē* 'Time by itself is eternal'.

[66] For an alternative interpretation of *vīspa- āiiu-*, see Rezania (2010: 38–42). On *uba- ahu-*, see also Swennen (2016).

addition of *tan ī pasēn*, however, strongly links *hamē tā ō wisp* with universal eschatology, pointing to *frašgird* and thus eliminating the possibility of an individual lifetime and eschatology in the PY. The phrase *hamē tā ō wisp* then conveys the meaning 'always and for all time remaining until *frašgird*'. A fitting translation might thus be 'until the end of this existence'. However, in light of the *Zand*'s literal wording, I have preferred a rather literal translation.

Part II

Text and translation

6. PY 35

6.1 PY 35.0

(a) ahurəm. mazdąm. ašauuanəm. ašahe. ratūm. ẏazo aməšā. spəṇtā. huxšaϑrā. huδåŋhō. yazo
(b) vīspąm. ašaonō. stīm. ẏazo mainiiēuuīmcā. gaēiϑiiąmcā
(c) bərəjā. vaŋhəuš. ašahe. bərəjā. daēnaiiå. vaŋhuiiå. māzdaiiasnōiš.

We worship the Wise Lord, the truthful model of truth.
We worship the Bounteous Immortals of good rule, the beneficent ones.
We worship the entire spiritual and material
existence of the truthful one
with esteem for good Truth,
with esteem for the good Mazdā-worshipping belief.

yasn ī haft hād

fradom hād bun
(a) ohrmazd ī ahlaw ī ahlāyīh rad yazom kē radīh pad frārōnīh amahraspandān ī huxwadāyān ī hudahāgān yazom
(b) harwisp ān ī ahlawān stī yazom kē mēnōy ud kē-iz gētīy
(c) pad ārzōg ī ō ān ī weh ahlāyīh abāyist ī ō kār ud kirbag rāy ud ārzōg ī dēn ī weh ī mazdēsnān abāyist ī ō dēn rāy

Beginning of the first chapter

(a) I worship righteous *Ohrmazd*, the authority of righteousness, who (exercises) authority through goodness. I worship the *Amahraspandān*, who are good rulers, who are the beneficent ones.

(b) I worship the entire existence of the righteous ones, which is both *mēnōy* and also *gētīy*,

(c) with desire which is necessary for good righteousness, which is for works and good deeds, and desire which is necessary for the good religion of Mazda-worshippers, which is for the religion.

6.2 PY 35.1

(a) *humataną̇m. hūxtaną̇m. huuarəštanąm. iiadacā. aniiadacā*
(b) *vərəziiamananą̇mcā. vāuuarəzananą̇mcā. mahī*
(c) *aibījarətārō. naēnēstārō. yaϑinā. vōhunąm. mahī*

Of good thoughts, good words, good deeds both here and elsewhere
being done and having been done
we are welcomers,
not revilers of such good (things) are we.

(a) *humatān hūxtān huwarštān ka ēdar dahišn u-š pad-iz ī ān ī any dahišn kū-š ēdar ud ānōh-iz nēkīh aziš*
(b) *ān ī warzīd tā nūn ud ān-iz ī warzīhēd az nūn frāz*
(c) *hom abar griftār kū ō xwēš kunom ān ī mard ō mard be abespārdār kirbag pad dād rāh čiyōn weh hom kū čiyōn pahlom ō xwēš kunom*

wičast bišāmrūdīg gōwišn

(a) Of good thoughts, good words (and) good deeds, when (in) this creation, and also in that which is the other creation, that is, goodness comes from it here and also there,
(b) (of) those which have been performed till now, and also (of) those which will be performed from now on,
(c) I am an appropriator, that is, I make my own that which a man consigns to a man, (namely) the justly (performed) good deeds, as I am good, that is, I make (it) my own, as it is best.

Strophe to be recited twice.

6.3 PY 35.2

(a) *tat̰. at̰. vairimaidī. ahura. mazdā. ašā. srīrā*
(b) *hiiat̰. ī. mainimadicā. vaocōmācā. varəzimācā*
(c) *yā. hātą̇m. š́iiaoϑənaną̇m. vahištā. x́iiāt̰. ubōibiiā. ahubiiā*

O Wise Lord, because of beauteous truth
we have certainly chosen this:
that we may think, speak and perform those
existing actions which may be best
for both existences.

(a) *ō ēn ēdōn ēg kāmag dahom ohrmazd kē ahlāyīh nēk dēn*
(b) *ēdōn ēn menom-iz ud gōwom-iz ud warzom-iz*
(c) *kū-m az hastān mardōmān pad kunišn pahlom hād andar har dō axwān kū mizd dahānd*

(a) O *Ohrmazd*, in this way, I then desire this, which is good righteousness, (namely) religion.
(b) Thus, I think, speak and also practise this,
(c) (so) that among the existing people, I shall receive through actions the best in both existences, that is, they shall give reward.

6.4 PY 35.3

(a) *gauuōi. adāiš. tāiš. šiiaoϑanāiš. yāiš. vahištāiš. fraēšiiāmahī*
(b) *rāmācā. vāstrəmcā. dazdiiāi*
(c) *surunuuatascā. asurunuuatascā. xšaiiaṇtascā. axšaiiaṇtascā*

For the benefit of the cow by (doing) these,
(namely) these best actions,
we urge
those who listen and those who do not,
those who rule and those who do not
to provide peace and pasture.

(a) *ān ī gōspandān dahišn āb ud ān ī awēšān kunišn pahast awēšān mardōm ī andar ēn gēhān kār pahlom framāyišn*
(b) *u-šān rāmišn-iz ud wāstar-iz dahišn gōspandān rāmišn ud abē-bīmīh*
(c) *kē-iz āšnawāg kū-š hērbedestān kard ēstēd ud kē-iz an-āšnawāg kū-š nē kard ēstēd ā-š ēdōn kunišn kū-š bīm nēst ud kē-iz pādixšā ud kē-iz abādixšā*

(a) That which is to be given to the cattle, is water, and that which is to be made for them, is shelter. The people that are in this world are to be ordered (to perform) the best deed for them.
(b) And they are to be given peace as well as pasture; peace and the condition of fearlessness for the cattle.
(c) He who is a listener, that is, he has attended the priestly school, as well as he who is not a listener, that is, he who has not attended (it), his actions have to be in such a manner, that (the cattle) does not fear, and also he who is a ruler as well as he who is not a ruler.

6.5 PY 35.4

(a) huxšaϑrōtəmāi. bāat̰. xšaϑrəm. ahmat̰. hiiat̰. aibī
(b) dadəmahicā.¹ cīšmahicā. huuąnmahicā
(c) hiiat̰. mazdāi. ahurāi. ašāicā. vahištāi

As far as we are concerned,
we offer, assign and impart
the rule to the one whose rule is indeed the very best,
namely the Wise Lord,
and to the best Truth.

(a) ō pad ōy ī huxwadāytom ēg xwadāyīh az ān ka-m abar kū-m nēkīh aziš
(b) dahom xwad ud čāšom ō kasān kū be dahēd ud ān-iz ī kunom kū dārišn be kunom
(c) ō kē ohrmazd ud ašwahišt-iz

wičast srišāmrūdīg gōwišn

(a) Sovereignty, then, belongs to him, who is the best-ruling one, for he is above me, that is, my goodness is from him.
(b) I offer myself and teach others to offer (themselves) and I also perform it, that is, I maintain it.
(c) To him, who is *Ohrmazd* and also to *Ašwahišt*.

Strophe to be recited thrice.

---

¹ Pt4 corrects daδəmahicā to dadəmahicā with a superscript d written above -δ-.

6.6 PY 35.5

(a) *yaϑā. āat̰. utā. nā. vā. nāirī. vā. vaēdā. haiϑīm*
(b) *aϑā. hat̰. vōhū. tat̰.ɔ̄ədū vərəziiō.tū.cā. it̰. ahmāi. fracā. vātōiiō.tū. it̰*
(c) *aēibiiō. yō. īt̰. aϑā. vərəziiąn. ẏaϑā. īt̰. astī*

Just as now a man or a woman
knows what is real,
so (do they know) what is really good.
Therefore let them now also put it into practice
and let them make it known to those
who shall practise it in the way
that it really is.

(a) *ēdōn ān ī har dō nar ud nārīg āgāh bawēnd āškārag*
(b) *ēdōn ān ast wehīh dēn ud ān-iz āgāhīhā dahēnd ō kasān kū be čāšēnd ud warzēnd-iz any frāz ān ō ōy any āgāhēnēnd*
(c) *awēšān-iz ī any hērbed ēdōn ast čiyōn ān warzēnd kū ān ī hāwišt kunēd ā-š abar ōh šawēd ud ān ī hāwišt az kasān abar šawēd ā-š abar nē šawēd*

(a) In this way, it is evident that which both a male (being) and a woman know.
(b) Thus, that is goodness, (namely) religion, and that too they disseminate to others, that is, they teach and they also practise (it) for others, (that is), they make (it) known to others.
(c) Also those who thus have other teachers, practise it like that, that is, that which the disciple performs, he [the teacher] receives it in the usual way, and that which the disciple receives from others, that he [the teacher] does not receive.

6.7 PY 35.6

(a) *ahurahiiā. zī. aṯ. və̄. mazdå. yasnəmcā*
(b) *vahməmcā. vahištəm. aməhmaidī. gə̄ušcā. vāstrəm*
(c) *taṯ. aṯ. vō. vərəziiāmahī. fracā. vā.tə̄iiāmahī. yā.tō isā.maidē*

For we recognised
that the worship and praise
of the Wise Lord alone
and pasture of the cow is best for you.
It is precisely this that we shall practise for you
and make (it) known
as much as we can.

(a) *ān ī ohrmazd yazišn ud niyāyišn ēdōn az ān ī ašmā pahlom menom*
(b) *ud ān-iz ī gōspandān kār kū az kār ī gētīy pahrēz ī gōspandān pahlom menom*
(c) *ēdōn ān ī ašmā warzom dēn ud frāz-iz āgāhēnom ō kasān ān and čand pad tuwān xwāstār hom*

(a) Of that which is yours I thus consider the worship and praise of *Ohrmazd* to be best,
(b) and that too which is the care for the cattle, that is, of the worldly work I consider the care for the cattle (to be) best.
(c) Thus, I practise that which is yours, (namely) the religion, and I also make it known to others, I am willing (to do it) as much as is in (my) power.

6.8 PY 35.7

(a) *aṣ̌ahiiā. āat̰. sairī. aṣ̌ahiiā. vərəzə̄nē*
(b) *kahmāicīt̰. hātą̇m. jījišą̇m. vahištą̇m. ādā. ubōibiiā ∴ ahubiiā*

I now tell every (human) being
that in union with Truth,
(and) in the community of Truth
the desire to gain (one's living) is best
for both existences.

(a) *kē pad ahlāyīh ēdōn sālārīh u-š ahlāyīh wālunīh kū dēn pad sālār ud wālun dārēd*
(b) *kadār az hastān mardōmān kē zīwišnōmandīh ēdōn čiyōn guft pahlom dahišn pad har dō axwān*

wičast bišāmrūdīg gōwišn

(a) He, who is righteous thus (exercises) guardianship, and his is the community of righteousness, that is, he looks after the religion through guardians and community.
(b) Whoever of the existing people, whose livelihood is in this manner, as it is said, they shall be given the best in both existences.

Strophe to be recited twice.

6.9 PY 35.8

(a) imā. āat̰. uxδā. vacā̊. ahurā. mazdā. ašəm. maniiā. vahehiiā. frauuaocāmā
(b) ϑβąm. at̰. aēšąm. paitiiāstārəmcā. fradaxštārəmcā. dadəmaidē

These words now,
O Wise Lord,
we proclaim as solemn utterances,
with very good concentration on Truth.
We designate
you only as their
listener and teacher.

(a) *ēn ēdōn saxwan gōwišnīh ohrmazd dēn ī ohrmazd pad ahlāyīh menīdārīh ī weh frāz gōwom pad frārōn menišnīh*
(b) *ud tō ēg az awēšān padīrišn ēstišnīh ud frāz daxšagīh dahom kū az amahraspandān tis ī tō wēš padīrom ud pad daxšag be kunom-iz*

(a) I will proclaim this word, spoken in this manner, O *Ohrmazd*, (namely) the religion of *Ohrmazd*, by good consideration of righteousness, (namely) by good thought(s).
(b) And to you, then, I dedicate from them the permanence of acceptance and widespread indication, that is, I accept your affairs more (readily) from the *Amahraspandān* and I also practise (your affairs) by indication.

6.10 PY 35.9

(a) *ašā.aṯ.cā hacā. vaŋhəušcā. manaŋhō. vaŋhəušcā. xšaθrāṯ*
(b) *staotāiš. θβāṯ. ahurā. staotōibiiō. aibī. uxδā. θβāṯ. uxδōibiiō. yasnā. θβāṯ. yasnōibiiō*

On account of truth,
of good thought
and of good rule,
through these (verses), O Lord, praise now (follows on) from praise,
solemn utterance now from solemn utterance,
worship now from worship.

(a) *az ahlāyīh abāgīh az ašwahišt hammis ud ān-iz ī weh-menišn wahman ud ān-iz weh-xwadāyīh xšahrewar*
(b) *stāyišn ī tō ohrmazd ham az stāyišnān abar ud saxwan ī tō ohrmazd ham az saxwanān abar ud yazišn ī tō ham az yazišnān abar*

yeṅhē. hātąm ∵ yazišnīgīhā bišāmrūdīg gōwišn ∵ nō wičast sē gāh

(a) With the assistance of righteousness, together with *Ašwahišt*, and also that of good thought, (namely) *Wahman*, and also that of good rule, (namely) *Xšahrewar*.
(b) Your praise too, O *Ohrmazd*, is above praises and your speech too, O *Ohrmazd*, is above speeches and your worship too is above worships.

yeṅhē. hātąm. In the manner of worship, to be recited twice. Nine stanzas, three verse lines.

7. PY 36

7.1 PY 36.1

(a) *ahiiā. ϑβā. āϑrō. vərəzə̄nā. paouruiiē. pairijasāmaiδē. mazdā. ahurā ∵ ϑβā.*
(b) ~~ϑβā.~~ *ϑβā. mainiiū. spə̄ništā. yō. ā. axtiš*
(c) *ahmāi. yə̄m. axtōiiōi. dā̊ŋhē*

Together with the community of this fire here,
we approach you, O Wise Lord, at the beginning,
(we approach) you together with your most bounteous spirit
who indeed (is) harm for the one
whom you consign to harm.

yasn dudīgar bād
(a) *ēdōn ō ēd ī tō ātaxš pad warzišn fradom be rasom ohrmazd pad pahrēz ud šnāyēnīdārīh*
(b) *pad ēd ī tō gāhān pad ēd ī tō mēnōy ī abzōnīg čiyōn az dēn paydāg*
(c) *kē ō ōy xīndagīh kū pad abar ātaxš anāgīh kunēd ān-iz ō ōy xīndagīh dahēd kū ān-iz pad ōy anāgīh kunēd*

Yasn, the second chapter
(a) Thus, at first I arrive before this your fire by practising, O *Ohrmazd*, with care and propitiation.
(b) With these your *Gāϑās* with this your bountiful spirit, as is manifest from the religion.

(c) He who (gives) illness to it, that is, he inflicts harm upon the fire, that one too gives him illness, that is, that one too inflicts harm upon him.

7.2 PY 36.2

(a) *uruuāzištō. huuō. nā. ẏā.tāiiā. paitī.jamiiā̊. ātarə. mazdā̊. ahurahiiā*
(b) *uruuāzištahiiā. uruuāziiā. nąmištahiiā. nəmaŋhā. nå*
(c) *mazištā̊. ẏā̊ŋhąm. paitī.jamiiā̊*

You there, the most joyful one,
may you come close to us for the sake of the request,
O fire of the Wise Lord!
May you come close to us,
with the joy of the most joyful one,
with the veneration of the most venerating one,
for the greatest of the appeals.

(a) *pad urwāhmanīh ō ōy mard pad tuwān be rasēd ātaxš ī ohrmazd kū frēb gīrēd*
(b) *pad urwāhmanīh ō ōy kē-š urwāhmanīh aziš ud pad niyāyišnōmandīh ō ōy ī niyāyišnōmand mard*
(c) *pad ān ī meh kār be rasēd pad passāxt ī pad tan ī pasēn*

(a) With joy for that man, arrive with strength, O fire of *Ohrmazd*, so that you restrain deceit.
(b) With joy for him, from whom is joy and with praiseworthiness for him who is the praiseworthy man.
(c) Arrive at the great event, at the trial of the final body.

7.3 PY 36.3

(a) ātarš. *vōi.* mazdā̊. ahurahiiā. ahī. mainiiuš. vōi

(b) ahiiā. spə̄ništō. ahī. hiiaṯ. vā. tōi. nāmąnm. vāzištəm

(c) ātarə. mazdā̊. ahurahiiā. tā. θβā. pairijasāmaidē

You are truly the fire of the Wise Lord.
You are truly his most bounteous spirit.
We approach you,
O fire of the Wise Lord,
(while uttering) what is indeed the most invigorating of your names.

(a) ātaxš pad ān ī ohrmazd āgāh ast pad dēn ī ohrmazd ud pad mēnōyīgīh āgāh ast ān-iš ast ka-š pad wahrāmīh be nišānēnd

(b) abzōnīg ast xwad tā ka ōy ī tō nām čiyōn ī wāzišt

(c) ō ātaxš ī ohrmazd ī tō pad ān ī harw dō be rasom kū-š hixr ī mēnōy ud gētīy aziš abāz dārom

(a) The fire is knowledgeable in that which belongs to *Ohrmazd*, in the religion of *Ohrmazd*, and is knowledgeable in the *mēnōy*. It has that (knowledge) when they establish it as *Wahrām* fire.

(b) Bountiful it is indeed, as long as your name is like *Wāzišt*.

(c) I arrive before the fire of *Ohrmazd*, that is you, in both, that is, I hold back from it the filth of the spiritual and material world.

7.4 PY 36.4

(a) *vōhū. ϑβā. manaŋhā. vohū. ϑβā. ašā*
(b) *vaŋhuiiā. ϑβā. cistōiš. ∴ šiiaoϑnāišcā. vacəbīšcā. pairijasāmaidē*

We approach you
with good thought,
(we approach) you with good truth,
(we approach) you with deeds and words
of good insight.

(a) *pad ān ī weh menišn ō tō ān ī weh tarsagāhīh ō tō*
(b) *pad ān ī weh frazānagīh ō tō pad-iz kunišn ud gōwišn be rasom*

(a) I arrive before you with good thoughts, with good reverence,
(b) with good wisdom, as well as with actions and speech.

7.5 PY 36.5

(a) *nəmaxiiāmahī. išūidiiāmahī. θβā. mazdā. ahurā*
(b) *vīspāiš. θβā. humatāiš. vīspāiš. θβā. hūxtāiš. vīspāiš. θhuuarštā.iš. pairijasāmaid•e*

We pay homage, we bring refreshment
to you, O Wise Lord
We approach you
with all good thoughts,
with all good words,
with all good deeds.

(a) *niyāyišnēnē u-m abāmēnē tō ohrmazd kū-m abām pad tō bawād*
(b) *pad harwisp humat ō tō ud pad harwisp hūxt ō tō ud pad harwisp huwaršt be rasom*

(a) You cause me to worship and you place me in debt, O *Ohrmazd*, that is, my debt will be to you.
(b) I arrive before you with all good thoughts, and with all good words and with all good deeds.

7.6 PY 36.6

(a) *sraēštąm. aṯ. tōi. ∴ kəhrpə̄m. kəhrpąm. ∴ āuuaēδaiiāmahī. mazdā. ahurā*
(b) *imā. raocå. barəzištəm. barəzimanąm*
(c) *auuaṯ. yāaṯ. huuarə̄. auuācī*

We now declare, O Wise Lord,
that this light here
has been the most beautiful manifestation of your manifestations,
ever since yonder highest of heights
was called the sun.

(a) *nēk ēd ī tō kirb u-t ān az kirbān niwēyēnišn dahom ohrmazd kū andar gēhān ōh gōwom kū kirb ēd ī tō nēktar*
(b) *ēn ruwān ō ān rōšnīh ī bālist az ān ī pad čašm paydāg bālēnēnd*
(c) *ānōh kū xwaršēd guft kū-m ruwān ō xwaršēd pāyag rasād*

yeŋhē. hātąm ∴ yazišnīgīhā ēvāmrūdīg gōwišn ∴ šaš wičast sē gāh

(a) Beautiful is this your form. And of all forms I attribute that one to you, O *Ohrmazd*, that is, in (this) world I say it in this way: (of) form(s), this which is yours is more beautiful.
(b) They exalt this soul to that light which is the highest of those which are visible by the eye.
(c) There, which is called the sun, that is, my soul shall reach the sun station.

yeŋhē. hātąm. In the manner of worship, to be recited once. Six stanzas, three verse lines.

8. *PY 37*

8.1 PY 37.1

(a) *iϑā. āat̰. yazamaide. ahurəm. mazdąm. yō. gąm.cā. aṣ̌əmcā. dāt̰*
(b) *apascā. dāt̰. uruuarās̊cā. vaŋhīš*
(c) *raocās̊cā. dāt̰. būmīmcā. vīspācā. vohū*

In this way we now worship the Wise Lord,
who has created the cow and truth,
(who) has created the waters and the good plants,
(who) has created light and the earth
and all that is good.

yasn sidīgar bād
(a) *ēdar ēdōn yazom ohrmazd kē gōspand ud ahlāyīh-iz dād*
(b) *u-š āb-iz dād ud urwar-iz ī weh*
(c) *u-š rōšnīh dād ud būm-iz ud harwisp-iz ābādīh bun ud bar*

Third chapter of the *Yasna*
(a) Here, I thus worship *Ohrmazd*, who created cattle and righteousness too.
(b) And he also created water and also the good plant.
(c) And he created light and also the earth and all prosperity too, (namely) root and fruit.

8.2 PY 37.2

(a) *ahiiā. xšaθrācā. mazōnācā. huuapaŋhāiščā*
(b) *tə̄m. at̰. yasnanąm. puruuatātā̊. yazo*
(c) *yōi. gə̄uš. hacā. š́iieiṇtī*

by his rule, greatness and skills.
We worship him with the most excellent worship (of those)
who are on the side of the cow.

(a) *ōy kē xwadāyīh ud mehīh padiš u-š hu-pānagīh aziš*
(b) *ān ēdōn az yaštārān ī andar ēn gēhān pad pēš-rawišnīh yazom pad pēšōbāyīh*
(c) *kē pad gōspandōmandīh mānēnd awēšān yaštār*

(a) He who owns sovereignty and greatness and offers his good-protection.
(b) On account of (their) prominence, on account of (their) leadership, I thus worship those among the worshippers of this world,
(c) who stand on the side of the cattle, (namely) their worshippers.

8.3 PY 37.3

(a) *tə̄m. at̰. āhūriiā. nāmə̄nī. mazdåuuarā. spəṇtōtə̄mā yazō*
(b) *tə̄m. ahmākāiš. azdəbīšcā. uštānāiscā. yazō*
(c) *tə̄m. aṣ̌āunąm. frauuaṣ̌īš. narąmcā. nāirinąmcā. yazō*

We worship him in the form of his lordly names,
(which are) welcome to the Wise one (and which are) the most bounteous ones.
We worship him with our limbs and lives.
We worship him in the form of the choices of the truthful ones,
both men and women.

(a) *ān ēdōn kē xwadāy nām ud pad dānāgīh dōšīd ēstēd abzōnīgīh yazom*
(b) *ōy kē amāgān tan ud ǰān zīwišn aziš yazom*
(c) *ōy kē ahlawān frawahr narān ud nārīgān yazom*[1] *aziš yazom*

(a) I thus worship that one whose name is the lord and is liked on account of (his) knowledge, (namely) bountifulness.
(b) I worship him from whom is the life-force of our body and life.
(c) I worship him from whom is the *Frawahrs* of the righteous ones, both male (beings) and women.

---

[1] Although attested in Pt4 and Mf4, *yazom* is superfluous here.

8.4 PY 37.4

(a)[2] *ašəm. ẏat̰. vahištəm. ẏazo*
(b) *hiiat̰. sraēštəm. hiiat̰. spəṇtəm. aməšəm*
(c) *hiiat̰. raocōṇŋhuuat̰. hiiat̰. vīspā. vōhū*

We worship best Truth,
the most beautiful one,
the bounteous immortal,
that is full of light,
that provides all that is good.

(a) *ahlāyīh ēdōn ī pahlom yazom ašwahišt*
(b) *ī nēkīh ī abzōnīg ī amarg*
(c) *ī rōšn tan ī ōy ī kē harwisp ābādīh nēkīh aziš*

(a) In this way, I worship excellent righteousness, (namely) *Ašwahišt*,
(b) which is goodness, bountiful, immortal,
(c) with a luminous body, which is the one from whom is all prosperity (and) goodness.

---

[2] Pt4 has this line in the margins.

8.5 PY 37.5

(a) *vohucā. manō. yazō vohucā. xšaϑrəm*
(b) *vaŋhīmcā. daēnąm. vaŋhīmcā. fsəratūm. vaŋhīmcā. ārmaitīm*

And we worship good Thought,
and good Rule,
and good Belief,
and good Joy,
and good Right-mindedness.

(a) *ān-iz ī weh menišn wahman yazom ud ān-iz ī weh xwadāyīh xšahrwar*
(b) *ān-iz ī weh dēn ud ān-iz ī weh sālārīh hordād ud amurdād ud ān-iz ī weh dōys^ar bowandag-menišnīh spandarmad*

yeńhē. hātąm ·: yazišnīgīhā ēvāmrūdīg gōwišn ·: panǰ wičast abāg iϑā i sē gāh

(a) I also worship the good thought, *Wahman*, and also the good rule, *Xšahrwar*,
(b) also the good religion and also the good guardianship, *Hordād* and *Amurdād*, and also the good-eyed right-mindedness, *Spandarmad*.

yeńhē. hātąm. In the manner of worship, to be recited once. Five stanzas with *iϑā i*, three verse lines.

9. PY 38

9.1 PY 38.1

(a) *imąm. āat̰. zą̇m. gənābīš. haϑrā. yazo*
(b) *yā̊. nā̊. baraitī. yā̊scā. tōi. gənā̊. ahurā. mazdā*
(c) *ašāt̰. hacā. vairiiā. tā̊. ẏazo* ∴

Now we worship this earth here
together with the noblewomen.
(We worship the earth) that bears us
and we worship
these noblewomen of yours, O Wise Lord,
who are excellent on account of Truth:

yasn čahārom hād
(a) *ēn zamīg abāg mādagān ēdōn yazom*
(b) *kē amā burdār kē-iz tō mādag ohrmazd kū tō xwēš*
(c) *az ahlāyīh abāgīh az ašwahišt hammis pad kāmag awēšān yazom*

Yasn, the fourth chapter
(a) In this way, I worship this earth with the females,
(b) (the earth) which bears us, also those who are your females, O *Ohrmazd*, that is, (they are) your own.
(c) According to wish, I worship them with the assistance of righteousness, together with *Ašwahišt*.

9.2 PY 38.2

(a) īžā̊. yaoištaiiō. fraštaiiō. ārmaitaiiō
(b) vaŋhīm. ābīš. ašīm. vaŋhīm. īšīm
(c) vaŋhīm. āzūitīm. vaŋhīm. frasastīm. vaŋhīm. pārəṇdəm. yazo

(noblewomen like) Invigoration, Vitalization, Perfection, Right-mindedness.
Together with them we worship good Reward,
good Strengthening,
good Libation,
good Glory
(and) good Abundance.

(a) ka pad abzōn āyōzānd ud pursišn bowandag menišnīh kū ān tis pursānd ašmā abzōn bawād ud man bowandag menišnīh bawād
(b) ān ī weh tarsagāhīh pad awēšān ā-m dahēd ud ān ī weh xwāhišn xwāstag
(c) ud ān ī weh abzōn ud ān ī weh frāz wābarīgānīh ud ān ī weh pārand yazom

(a) When they strive for increase and ask right-mindedness, that is, that thing (that) they shall ask of you shall be plentiful, and right-mindedness shall be mine.
(b) May you, through them, give me the good reverence, and the good desire, (namely) wealth.
(c) I worship good increase and good trustworthiness and the good *Pārand*.

9.3 PY 38.3

(a) *apō. aṯ. yazō maēkaintīšcā. həbauuaintīšcā. frauuazaŋhō*
(b) *ahurānīš. ahurahiiā. hauuapaŋhā̊. hupərəθβā̊scā. vā̊*
(c) *hauuōγžaθå̄scā. hušnāθrå̄scā. ubōibiiā. ahubiiā. cagəmā*

We worship
the tasty and sap-providing waters,
the lordly ones who move swiftly
by the Lord's skill.
(We worship) you, who are easy to cross,
smoothly flowing
and with good places for bathing,
(you who are) a gift for both existences.

(a) *āb ēdōn yazom ī* maikiint *pašsing ī pad urwar abar ēstēd miznē ud ān-iz ī* hēbuuainti *garān tazišn ān-iz ī* frauuāzi *ī wārānīg*
(b) *ud ān* ahurānīš *armēšt ud čāhīg ud abārīg-iz āb ī anāmčištīg ud ān ī* ahurahiiā *ī šuhr ud ān ī* hauuapaŋhāi *mēšag huwidaragīh ašmā ā-mān dahēd kū-mān nam andar tan rawāg bawād*
(c) *hudahagīh ars ud hušnāyišnagīh kū-mān xwēy az tan be āyād ud ān ī andar dō axwān kāmag rōγn*

(a) In this way, I worship the waters, which are *maikiint* the drop (of water) that stands on top of the plants, (namely) dew, and also that which is *hēbuuainti* the heavy flowing one, also that which is *frauuāzi*, which is the rainy one,
(b) and the *ahurānīš*, the stagnating (waters), and the ones in the wells and the other unspecified waters, and that which is *ahurahiiā*, which is the semen, and that which is *hauuapaŋhāi*, (namely) urine. Give us your good-passage, so that moisture may flow in our bodies.
(c) (I worship) beneficence, (namely) tears, and good-gratitude, so that sweat may leave our bodies, and (I worship) that which is desired in both existences, (namely) butter.

9.4 PY 38.4

(a) *ūitī. yā. vō. vaŋhīš. ahurō. mazdā̊. nāmą̇m. dadāt̰*
(b) *vaŋhudā̊. hiiat̰ vā̊. dadāt̰. tāiš. vā. yazo*
(c) *tāiš. friiąn.mahī. tāiš. nəmax̌iiāmahī. tāiš. išūidiiāmahī*

Thus, with these names which
the Wise Lord assigned to you, O good ones,
when he was making you into providers of good (things),
with these (names) we worship you,
with these (names) we please (you),
with these (names) we pay homage (to you),
with these (names) we bring (you) refreshment.

(a) *ēdōn ašmā kē weh hēd ā-tān ohrmazd nām dād ī wehdahāg*
(b) *ud kē-š ō ašmā dād pad awēšān ašmā yazom*
(c) *u-m pad awēšān franāmād u-m pad awēšān niyāyišnēnād u-m pad awēšān abāmēnād*

(a) Thus, you who are good, *Ohrmazd* gave you names, namely 'providers of good (things)'.
(b) And with those (names), which he gave you, I worship you.
(c) And he shall lead me with those, and he shall make me venerate with those and he shall make me indebted with those.

9.5 PY 38.5

(a) *apascā. vå. azīšcā. vå. mātarą̊šcā. vå. agəniiå. drigudāiiaŋhō*
(b) *vīspō.paitīš. āuuaocāmā. vahištå. sraēštå. auuā. vō̌. vaŋhīš. rātōiš*
(c) *darəgōbāzāuš. nåšū. paitī. viiādå. paitī. sə̄ṇdå. mātarō. jītaiiō*

We call upon you as the waters,
(we call upon) you as milch cows,
(we call upon) you as mother-cows,
O prize cows,
who care for the destitute, provide drink for everyone,
O best, most beautiful ones!
Enjoying far-reaching achievements
because of your generosity, O good ones,
I want to facilitate
your pleasant distributions,
O living mothers!

(a) *āb ī ašmā ān ī azīš ašmā xayūg ud ān ī mātrə̄š ašmā āb ī andar hambawišnīh ī narān ud mādagān tōhm ud ān ī agəniiå xōn ud ān ī driyōš dāyagānēnīdār āb andar pusyān*

(b) *ud ān ī vīspō.pit ān guft āb ī pad urwarān ēwan ī urwar padiš waxšīhēd ud ān ī pahlom ud nēktar āb ī tantōhmag ī az urwar ēdōn ō ašmā kē weh hēd rād hom*

(c) *kē pad dagrand bāzāyīh nayēd ān gēhān tan pad jud dahišnīh ud jud gōwišnīh mātarō.jītaiiō šīr*

yeńhē. hātąm ∴ yazišnīgīhā ēvāmrūdīg gōwišn ∴ panj wičast sē gāh

(a) Your waters, *azīš*, your saliva, and *mātrə̄š*, your water which is in the union of the male and female semen, and *agəniiå*, blood, and that one which nurses the needy, the water in the womb,

(b) and *vīspō.pit*, that one is said to be the water that is in the plants, the trunk of the plants grows by it, and that one which is the best and most beautiful, the water of the seed of the body which is from the plants. In this way, I am generous to you, who are good.

(c) He, who leads the material body by possessing long arms, by separate creation and separate speech, *mātarō.jītaiiō*, (namely) milk.

yeṅhē. hātąm. In the manner of worship, to be recited once. Five stanzas, three verse lines.

10. *PY 39*

10.1 PY 39.1

(a) *iϑā. āat̰. yazō gə̄uš. uruuānəmcā. tašā.nəmcā*
(b) *ahmākə̄ṇg. āat̰. urunō. pasukanąmcā. yōi. nā̊. fijišəṇtī*
(c) *yaēibiiascā. tōi. ā. yaēcā. aēibiiō. ā. aŋhən* ∴

In this way we now worship
the cow's soul and (her) maker.
Now we worship our own souls
as well as those of the domestic animals
which desire to gain our support,
(the animals) for which people here indeed (shall be available)
and which indeed shall be available for people here,

yasn panǰom hād
(a) *ēdar ēdōn yazom kē ān ī gōspandān ruwān tan ǰān dād ohrmazd*
(b) *ud ān ī amāgān ruwān ud paswīkān-iz kē amā zīwišn xwāstār hēnd nēkīh ā-š dād*
(c) *awēšān-iz ī tō ān ī artēštār awēšān kē hēnd wāstaryōš ā-š dād*

Yasn, the fifth chapter
(a) Here, in this way I worship (the one) who created the cattle's soul, body (and) life, (namely) *Ohrmazd*.
(b) And our souls as well as (that of) the domestic animals, which seek livelihood from us, (namely) beneficence, for he created (them).

(c) Also those who are yours, (namely) the warrior, (and) those who are husbandmen, for he created (them).

10.2 PY 39.2

(a) *daitikanąmcā. aidiiūnąm. hiiat̰. urunō. yazo*
(b) *aṣ̌āunąm. āat̰. urunō. yazo kudō.zātanąmcīt̰. narąmcā. nāirinąmcā*
(c) *yaēṣ̌ąm. vahehīš. daēnå. vanaiṇtī. vā. və̄ŋhən. vā. vaonarə. vā*

and (we worship) the soul
of the wild animals,
insofar as they are harmless.
Now we worship the souls of the truthful ones,
men and women,
wherever they may have been born,
whose very good beliefs
prevail, will prevail or have prevailed.

(a) *daitīkān-iz ī ayārān kē ruwān ā-šān yazom*
(b) *ān ī ahlawān ruwān ēdōn yazom kū zādagān-iz narān ud nārīgān-iz*
(c) *kē awēšān weh dēn hēnd pad ēwkardagīh wānīdār hēnd artēštār ud windišn wanghān hēnd wāstaryōš ud weh mard hēnd āsrōn*

(a) Also the wild animals that are helpers, whose souls I worship.
(b) In this way I worship the souls of the righteous ones, wherever (they were) born, male (beings) as well as women,
(c) who are collectively of the good religion, (who) are conquerors, (namely) warriors, (who) are earners, (namely) husbandmen and (those who) are good men, (namely) priests.

10.3 PY 39.3

(a) *āat̰. iδā. yazō vaŋhušcā. īt̰. vaŋhīšcā. īt̰*
(b) *spəṇtāŋg. aməšāŋg. yauuaējiiō. yauuaēsuuō*
(c) *yōi. vaŋhə̄uš. ā. manaŋhō. š́iieṇtī. yā̊sca. uitī*

Finally in this way we worship
the good bounteous immortals,
both male and female,
who live forever, who thrive forever,
(the male ones) who are on the side of good thought
and (the female ones) who (are) as well.

(a) *ān ēdōn yazom weh nar ān ī weh mādag any amahraspandān*
(b) *kē abzōnīg hēnd ud amarg ud hamē zīndag ud hamē sūd*
(c) *kē pad wahman mānēnd pad frārōnīh ud kē-iz ēdōn wahman ā-š yazom*

(a) Thus I worship the good male (and) the good female, (namely) the other *Amahraspandān*,
(b) who are bountiful and immortal, always alive and always advantageous,
(c) who dwell with *Wahman* in goodness and who are thus also (like) *Wahman*, I worship him.

10.4 PY 39.4

(a) *yaϑā. tū. ī. ahura. mazdā. mə̄nghācā. vaocascā. dåscā. varəšcā. yā. vohū*
(b) *aϑā. tōi. dadəmahī. aϑā. cīšmahī. aϑā. ϑβā. āiš. ẏazo*
(c) *aϑā. nəmax̌iiāmahī. aϑā. išūidiiāmahī. ϑβā. mazdā. ahurā*

As indeed, O Wise Lord,
you think, speak, create and practise
these (things) which (are) good,
so we offer (them) to you,
so we assign (them to you),
so by them we worship you,
so we pay homage,
so we bring refreshment
to you, O Wise Lord.

(a) *čiyōn tō pad ān ī har dō tis ī mēnōy ud gētīy ohrmazd menišn hē kū tis ī tō ōh menišn ud gōwišn hē kū tis ōh gōwišn ud dahišn hē ud warzišn hē ī kū weh warzom*
(b) *ēdōn ō tō dahom xwad ud ēdōn čāšom ō kasān kū be dahēd ud ēdōn tō pad āyišn ud šawišn ka andar gēhān ōh āyom ud ōh šawom ōh yazom*
(c) *u-m ēdōn niyāyišnēnē u-m ēdōn abāmēnē tō ohrmazd kū-m abām pad tō bawād*

wičast bišāmrūdīg gōwišn

(a) One has to think about your affairs, O *Ohrmazd*, in the way that you think about the affairs of both *mēnōy* and *gētīy*, and speak the affair in the way that you speak (it). And you create, and you practise that which is good, (so) do I practise (it).
(b) Thus, I offer myself to you, and in this way I teach others to offer (themselves), and thus by coming and going I worship you in this way, (namely) when I come and go in this way in the world.
(c) And in this way you cause me to venerate (you) and you make me indebted to you, O *Ohrmazd*, that is, may my debt be to you.

Strophe to be recited twice.

10.5 PY 39.5

(a) *vaŋhə̄uš. x̌aētə̄uš. x̌aētātā*
(b) *vaŋhə̄uš. aṣ̌ahiiā. ꜽβā. pairijasāmaide*
(c) *vaŋhuiiā̊. fsəratuuō. vaŋhuiiā̊. ārmaitōiš*

We approach you in the relationship of a good relative
to good Truth,
to good Joy,
to good Right-mindedness.

(a) *pad weh xwēšīh ka tō xwēš hom xwēšrawišnīh hom ka pad xwēšīh ī ašmā ēstom*
(b) *pad ān ī weh tarsagāhīh ō tō be rasom*
(c) *pad ān ī weh sālārīh ka sālārīh pad frārōnīh kunom ud pad ān ī weh bowandag menišnīh ka tis bowandag menišnīhā kunom*

yeṅhē. hātąm ∴ yazišnīgīhā bišāmrūdīg gōwišn ∴ panǰ wičast sē gāh

(a) Through good ownership, (that is), when I am yours I belong (to you), (namely) when I am in your ownership.
(b) I approach you with good respect,
(c) with good guardianship, when I practise guardianship through goodness, and with right-mindedness, when I do things with the right mind setting.

yeṅhē. hātąm. In the manner of worship, to be recited twice. Five stanzas, three verse lines.

11. *PY 40*

11.1 PY 40.1

(a) *āhū. at̰. paitī. adā.hū. mazdā. ahurā. mazdąmcā. būiricā. kərəšuuā.*[1]
(b) *kərəšuuā.*[2] *rāitī. tōi. xrapaitī. ahmat̰. hiiat̰. aibī*
(c) *hiiat̰. mīždəm.*[3] *mauuaiϑəm. fradadāϑā. daēnābiiō. mazdā. ahurā* ∴

Here especially during these offerings,
O Wise Lord,
exercise your wisdom and wealth!
Through your generosity there shall take shape
— as far as we are concerned —
the prize which you have allocated to someone like me
for the sake of our beliefs, O Wise Lord:

yasn šašom bād
(a) *ka-tān andar ān axwān ēdōn abar dahānd ohrmazd mehīh ud bowandagīh pad kardārīh man kū ān tis kunēnd ud gōwānd ī-tān mehīh ud bowandagīh paydāgtar bawād*
(b) *rād hom ō ēd ī tō xrad pānagīh ō dēn ī tō az ān ka-m abar kū-m nēkīh az ān*
(c) *kē mizd ō manīgān frāz dahē ān ō dēnīgān abāyed dād ohrmazd*

---

[1] Added superscriptum at the end of the cola in Pt4.
[2] Pt4 deletes by an overline stroke.
[3] Pt4 reads *mīžəm*.

Yasn, the sixth chapter

(a) When in those existences they thus bestow upon you, O *Ohrmazd*, greatness and completeness by means of actions, that is, they practise and speak that thing, (so) that your greatness and completeness shall be more manifest.

(b) I am generous towards this wisdom of yours (and offer) protection for your religion, for it is higher than me, that is, my goodness is from that.

(c) Which prize will you give to my people? That (prize) must be given to the religious ones, O *Ohrmazd*.

11.2 PY 40.2

(a) *ahiiā. huuō. nō. dāidī. ahmāicā. ahuiiē. manaxˇiiāicā*
(b) *tat̰. ahiiā. yā. tat̰. upājamiiāmā*
(c) *tauuacā. haxəmā. aṣ̌axˇiiācā. vīspā. yaouuē* ∵

You there, give us from this (prize)
for both this and the spiritual life,
(give us) this from this (prize)
by which we shall attain the following:
fellowship with you and Truth
for all time!

(a) *ān ī ōy ān ō amā dahē pad-iz ēn axwān pad-iz mēnōyān*
(b) *kū ēdōn pad ān ēdōn abar rasēm*
(c) *ō ēd ī tō ham-brādagīh ham-kardārīh ahlāyīh-iz hamē tā ō wisp tā tan ī pasēn*

(a) That which is his, give us that in these existences, also in the *mēnōy* (existences),
(b) (so) that thus by means of that we thus attain
(c) this your fellowship, cooperation and also righteousness always until all, until the future body.

11.3   PY 40.3

(a) *dāidī. at̰. nərə̨š́. mazdā. ahurā. aṣ̌āunō. aša.cinaŋhō*
(b) *aidiiūiš. vāstriiə̄ng. darəgāi. īžiiāi. bəzuuaitē. haxmainē*
(c) *ahmaibiiā. ahmārafənaŋhō* ∴

Grant, indeed, O Wise Lord,
truthful, truth-desiring men,
non-violent herdsmen,
for long-lasting, invigorating, firm fellowship,
(grant) to us
(men) who are supported by us,

(a) *dahē-m ēdōn ān ī mardān ohrmazd hāwištān ī mardān hērbedān ahlaw ī ahlāyīh kāmag ān hērbed*
(b) *ī ka-šān hāzānd ā-m ō ān ī dagr rasišn ud abzōn tan ī pasēn pad ān ī stabr pad kār hambrādag bawānd*
(c) *ō amā ān ī amāgān rāmēnīdār dahē*

(a) You give me thus that which belongs to men, O *Ohrmazd*, disciples of men, teacher-priests, righteous ones who desire righteousness. Those teacher-priests,
(b) who shall guide them [*hāwištān*], shall then be my fellows for that future arrival and the increase, (namely) the final body, through that which is strong, through action.
(c) You give us that one who provides us peace.

11.4 PY 40.4

(a) *aϑā. xaētuš. aϑā. vərəzə̄nā. aϑā. haxə̄mą̇m. x̌iiāt̰.*[4]
(b) *x̌iiāt̰.*[5] *ẏāiš hišcišmaidī. aϑā. vō. utā. x̌iiāmā. mazdā. ahurā. ašauuanō. ərəšiiā. ištə̄m. rāitī*

likewise (grant us) families,
likewise communities!
May thus be the fellowships
with which we shall associate ourselves.
May we thus also be yours, O Wise Lord,
being truthful and inspired
because of your granting what we desired.

(a) *ēdōn xwēš ud ēdōn wālun ēdōn hambrādag ā-m hād kū-m dahād*
(b) *ka-šān hāzānd ēdōn pad ān ī ašmā dēn ēdōn hād ohrmazd ahlaw ud rāst hād pad išt rād hād pad xwāstag hāzānd*

yeṅhē. hātą̇m ∴ yazišnīgīhā ēvāmrūdīg gōwišn ∴ čahār wičast ī sē gāh

(a) In this way, I shall have my own, in this way (I shall have) the community, in this way (I shall have) the fellows, that is, he shall grant (them) to me.
(b) When they shall thus guide them with that religion of yours, so shall it be, O *Ohrmazd*. It shall be righteous and right. It shall be generous through *išt*, (namely) through wealth. They shall guide.

yeṅhē. hātą̇m. In the manner of worship, to be recited once. Four stanzas, three verse lines.

---

[4] Added superscriptum at the end of the cola in Pt4.
[5] Pt4 deletes by an overline stroke.

12. *PY 41*

12.1 PY 41.1

(a) *stūtō. garō. vahmə̄ṇg. ahurāi. mazdāi. aṣ̌āicā. vahištā*
(b) *dadəmahicā. cīšmahicā. ācā. āuuaēδaiiamahī* ∴

We offer, assign and dedicate
praises, hymns and prayers
to the Wise Lord
and to the best Truth.

yasn haftom bād
(a) *stāyišn ud gīrišn ud niyāyišn ō ohrmazd ud ašwahišt-iz*
(b) *dahom xwad ud čāšom ō kasān ud ān-iz niwēyom pad guft*

Yasn, the seventh chapter
(a) Praises, acceptance and prayers to *Ohrmazd* and also *Ašwahišt*.
(b) I myself offer and teach others and I also announce it by speech.

12.2 PY 41.2

(a) *vōhū. xšaϑrəm. tōi. mazdā. ahurā. apaēmā. vīspāi. yaouuē*
(b) *huxšaϑra.stū. nō. nā. vā. nāirī. vā. xšaētā*
(c) *ubōiiō. aŋhuuō. hātąm. hudāstəmā* ∴

May we obtain, O Wise one,
your good rule
for all time!
May a good ruler,
a man or a woman,
rule over us
in both existences,
O most beneficent of those who exist!

(a) *ān ī weh xwadāyīh tō ohrmazd be ayābēnd hamē tā ō wisp*
(b) *ān ī ohrmazd tō ō amā kē nar ud nārīg hēm ā-t pādixšāyēnēd*
(c) *andar har dō axwān hastān hudahāgtom*

(a) They will obtain, O *Ohrmazd*, your good rule, always until for all.
(b) That which belongs to *Ohrmazd*, will make you rule over us, who are male (beings) and women,
(c) in both existences, O most beneficent of the existing ones.

12.3 PY 41.3

(a) humāīm. ɪβā. īžīm. yazatəm. asaŋhācim.¹ dadəmaide
(b) aϑā. tū. nə̄. gaiiascā. astəṇtā̊scā. x̌iiā̊
(c) ubōiiō. aŋhuuō. hātąm.² huδāstəmā

We regard you as the good-powered, invigorating
venerable one, whose companion is Truth.
May you then thus be for us life and corporality
in both existences,
O most beneficent of those who exist!

(a) ka hu-framānīh ī tō kū framān ī tō barānd ud abzōn kū tis ī tō abzāyēnd
    u-t yazišn az ahlāyīh abāgīh dahānd kū-t az ašwahišt hammis ōh yazānd
(b) ēdōn az tō amā tan ud ǰān bād kū-mān apagaiiehe ma bawād
(c) andar har dō axwān hastān hudahāgtom ōy dahē

wīcast bišāmrūdīg gōwišn

(a) When (they place themselves in) your good rule, that is, they shall obey you, and growth, that is, they increase your affairs, and (when) they worship you with the assistance of righteousness, that is, they shall worship you together with *Ašwahišt* in the usual way,
(b) in that way, our body and life shall be from you, that is, we shall not be lifeless.
(c) In both existences, O most beneficent of the existing ones. You give (it) to him.

---

¹ We would expect *ašaŋhācim*.
² Pt4 has *h•ātąm*.

12.4 PY 41.4

(a) *hanaēmācā. zəmācā. mazdā. ahurā*
(b) *ϑβahmī. rafnahī. darəgaiiå̄ aēšācā. ϑβā. ə̄mauuaṇtascā. buiiamā*
(c) *rafōšcā. tū. nō̄. darəgəmcā. uštąm. hātąm. hudāstəmā* ∴

May we earn and obtain, O Wise Lord,
your lifelong
support!
May we become vigorous and strong through you
and may you support us
for a long time and according to (our) wish,
O most beneficent of those who exist!

(a) *arzānīgēnē-m pad mizd pādāšn u-m zēnāwandēnē ohrmazd*
(b) *tō pad rāmēnīdārīh pad dagr rasišnīh pad tan ī pasēn xwāstār hom pad ēd ī tō pad dēn ī tō ud amāwand bawānd*
(c) *rāmēnīdārīh tō ō amā pad dagr rasišnīh ī andar hastān hudahāgtom ā-mān dahē*

(a) Make me worthy through the retribution of the reward and make me vigilant, O Ohrmazd.
(b) I desire you for providing peace, for the future arrival, (namely) for the final body, for this which is yours, for your religion. And they shall be strong.
(c) May you provide us with peace for the future arrival among the most beneficent of the existing ones.

12.5 PY 41.5

(a) ϑβōi.³ staotarascā. mą̇ϑranascā. ahurā. mazdā
(b) aogəmadaēcā. usmahicā. vīsāmadaēcā
(c) hiiat̰. mīždəm. mauuaēϑəm. fradadāϑā. daēnābiiō. mazdā. ahurā

We declare ourselves, aspire and volunteer
to be your praisers and poets, O Wise Lord.
The prize which you have allocated to someone like me
for the sake of our beliefs, O Wise Lord:

(a) ka ō ēd ī tō stāyīdārīh ud māns*ᵃ*rīgīh ohrmazd
(b) abar rasānd ud hunsand hēnd ud padīrānd kū be padīrānd ud hunsandīhā ōh kunānd
(c) ē mizd ī ō manīgān frāz dahē ān ī ō dēnīgān abāyed dādan ohrmazd

wičast bišāmrūdīg gōwišn

(a–b) When they attain this your praise and the words, O *Ohrmazd*, they are content and shall accept, that is, they shall accept and act contently.
(c) May you give my people the reward, that which must be given to the religious ones, O *Ohrmazd*.

---

³ Pt4 reads MN ϑβōi.

12.6 PY 41.6

(a) *ahiiā. huuō. nə̄. dāidī. ahmāicā. ahuiiē. manaxˇiiāicā*
(b) *tat̰. ahiiā. yātat̰. upājamiiāmā*
(c) *tauuacā. sarəm. ašaxˇiiācā. vīspāi. yaoē*

You there, give us from this (prize)
for both this and the spiritual life,
(give us) this from this (prize)
by which we shall attain the following:
union with you and Truth
for all time!

(a) *ān ī ōy ān ō amā dahē pad-iz ēn axwān pad-iz mēnōyān*
(b) *kū ēdōn pad ān ēdōn abar rasēm*
(c) *ō ēd ī tō sālārīh ud ahlāyīh-iz hamē tā ō wisp*

yeŋhē. hātąm ∴ yazišnīgīh ēvāmrūdīg gōwišn ∴ humatanąm ∴ bišāmrūdīg gōwišn ∴ yaϑā. ahū. vairiiō ∴ časrušāmrūdīg gōwišn ∴ ašəm. vōhū ∴ srišāmrūdīg gōwišn ∴ yasnəm. sūrəm. haptaŋhāitīm. ašauuanəm. ašahe. ratūm. yazo ∴ pad yasn ī abzār ī haft hād ī ahlaw ī ahlāyīh rad yazom

yeŋhē hātąm ∴ yazišnīgīhā ēvāmrūdīg gōwišn ∴ šaš wičast sē gāh

(a) That which is his, may you give us, in these as well as in the *mēnōy* existences,
(b) (so) that thus by means of that, we may in this way attain
(c) this guardianship of yours as well as righteousness always until all.

yeŋhē hātąm is to be recited once in the manner of worship. *humatanąm* is to be recited two times. *yaϑā ahū vairiiō* is to be recited four times. *ašəm vōhū* is to be recited three times. We sacrifice to the strong *Yasna Haptaŋhāiti*, the orderly *ratu* of *aša*. We worship through the powerful Worship of Seven Sections, which is righteous (and) the authority of righteousness.

yeŋhē hātąm, in the manner of worship, to be recited once. Six stanzas, three verse lines.

Part III

Miscellaneous observations

13. *PY 35*

13.1 PY 35.0

13.1.1 *yazom*

In the PYH, Av. *yazamaidē*, a 1pl.ind.pres.mid. from the thematic stem *yaza-* of the root *yaz* 'to worship' (Hintze 2007a: 156–62) or 'to sacrifice', is translated with the verb *yaštan, yaz-* 'to worship'. The verb is usually spelt ⟨YDBḤWN-⟩ in the MSS, although the phonetic spelling ⟨yc-⟩ is also found.[1] While ⟨YDBḤWN-⟩ consistently takes the phonetic complement ⟨-m⟩, ⟨yc-⟩ varies in its endings between ⟨-m⟩ and ⟨-wm⟩ (see Table 13.1). Considering that *yazamaidē* is a 1pl., the question is whether ⟨YDBḤWN-m⟩, ⟨ycm⟩ and ⟨ycwm⟩ represent the sg. or pl. of the first person.[2] In the PYH, Mills (1905b: 105) reads *'yežbexūnam'* and *'yažōm'* and interprets both forms as 1sg.: 'I sacrifice' (Mills 1905a: 55). Dhabhar (1963: 4, fn. 4) suggests MP *'om* (1st.sg.)' for Av. 1pl. *mahī* in PY 35.1. Andrés-Toledo (2009) and Skjærvø (2010d) prefer the 1sg. *yazam*, while Malandra and Ichaporia (2010: 181) posit a 1pl. in *yazom*.

In ZMP the phonetic complement ⟨-m⟩ is usually vocalised as *-am* and interpreted as the ending of the 1sg.pres. (Skjærvø 2010a: 217–19).[3] However, as MMP has ⟨-wm⟩ for the 1pl.ind. (Sundermann 1989: 149, fn. 86; Skjærvø 2010a: 217), and most likely reflects an older stage of MP (Sundermann 1989:

---

[1] Using heterographic and eteographic spellings indiscriminately is an accepted scribal convention. Pt4, for instance, has ⟨YDBḤWN-m⟩ in PY 35.0a and ⟨ycwm⟩ in PY 35.0b. The spelling ⟨ycwm⟩ is not confined to the PYH. In J2, for instance, we find it in Y 6.13c, 6.13f, 6.15c, 6.17a.

[2] The above forms, be they sg. or pl., correctly reflect the mood and tense of *yazamaidē*. The translation of the middle voice as active is due to the simplified verbal inflection of MP (Sundermann 1989: 148; Josephson 1997: 138).

[3] For discussions of MP's verbal system, see Salemann (1895–1901: 312), Tedesco (1923: 302), Henning (1933, 1958), Sundermann (1989: 149) and Weber (2007: 947).

Table 13.1 Distribution of *yaštan*

	⟨YDBḤWN-m⟩	⟨ycm⟩	⟨ycwm⟩
Pt4	35.0a (2x), 37.2b, 37.3a–c, 37.4a	37.1a	35.0b, 37.5a
Mf4	35.0a, 37.2b, 37.3a–c, 37.4a, 37.5a	35.0a, 35.0b, 37.1a	
K5	35.0a (2x), 37.3a–c, 37.5a	37.2b, 37.4a	35.0b, 37.1a
J2	35.0a, 37.1a, 37.2b, 37.3a–c, 37.5a	35.0b, 37.4a	35.0a

149), we may be inclined to view ⟨ycwm⟩ of the PY MSS as preserving an old 1pl. Moreover, a similar distribution can be observed in both InsMP and InsPa, where the phonetic verbal complements attached to heterograms differ from those attached to phonetically written verbs. Heterograms take ⟨-m⟩ for the 1pl., while eteograms have ⟨-wmy⟩ (InsMP) and ⟨-ywm⟩ (InsPa) (Skjærvø 1983: 137, 138).[4] Therefore, it may be tempting to interpret the alternation in these MSS between ⟨-m⟩ for ⟨YDBḤWN-⟩ and ⟨-wm⟩ for ⟨yc-⟩ as a remnant of an old orthographic rule otherwise only known from the inscriptions.

However, as the endings for the 1sg. and pl. are largely indistinguishable in ZMP (see Sundermann 1989: 149), there is no evidence that a postulated *yazom* could represent an older stage of the language in these MSS and thus the 1pl. Indeed, in the MSS ⟨-m⟩ and ⟨-wm⟩ can correspond to Av. verbs in 1sg. as well as 1pl. For instance, OAv. 1sg.subj. *yazāi* 'I want to worship', attested three times in the *Gāθās*, shows a similar variation in its *Zand*: PY 33.4 ⟨ycšn ḤWH-wm⟩ (Pt4 Mf4), ⟨ycšn ḤWH-m⟩ (F2, K5 J2 M1), ⟨ycšn ḤWH-d⟩ (T6); PY 50.4 ⟨YDBḤWN-m⟩ (Pt4 Mf4 F2 T6, K5 J2 M1) and PY 51.22 ⟨YDBḤWN-m⟩ (Pt4 Mf4 F2 T6), ⟨ycwm⟩ (K5 M1), ⟨ycm⟩ (J2).[5] Furthermore, enclitic pronouns found elsewhere in the PYH do not support the interpretation of the verbal ending ⟨-m⟩ as 1pl. Thus, *kū-m* in *menom-iz ud gōwom-iz ud warzom-iz kū-m* (PY 35.2b–c), and *arzānīgēnē-m ... u-m zēnāwandēnē* in PY 41.4a–c, where the pronoun in sg. contrasts with *amā* and *ā-mān dahē*.[6] More importantly, in the Sanskrit YH *yazamaidĕ* is translated *ārādhaye*, a 1sg.ind.pres.mid. from *ārādh* 'to honour, worship' (Monier-Williams 1899: 150).[7] The preference for the middle voice could

---

[4] See also Skjærvø (1986: 430): '(cf. the Middle Persian 1st plural in -om, inscriptions -wmy, Manichean -wm)'.

[5] On ⟨ḤWH-wm⟩, see Section 13.2.2.

[6] The above reading is based on Pt4, but see my apparatus for the variations across the MSS. An 'instability in the use of numbers' was also noticed by Utas (1976: 95) in a similar investigation of verbs in 1sg. and pl. in the *Ayādgār ī Zarērān*.

[7] See Spiegel (1861: 158–70), Bharucha (1910: 80–6) and also Taraf (1981: 114): 'Für Aw. yazamaide 1.Pl. hat Pü. yazēm 1.Pl./Sg. und Sü. ārādhaye 1.Sg.' My own preliminary survey confirms that across the *Yasna ārādh* translates *yaz*.

suggest that in this instance the SY was translated from Avestan rather than MP, where the voice is lost. Irrespective of the middle voice shared between *yazamaidē* and *ārādhaye*, which might be a coincidence, here we have indisputable evidence that at least one strain of the priestly tradition at some point (re)interpreted *yazamaidē* or its MP translation as representing a 1sg.

While we might safely assume that the grammatical number of *yazamaidē* was known to the exegetes, there is hardly any reason why the priestly tradition could not have preferred a singular regardless of the plural of the original. For instance, the social context in which the *Zand* came to be, could have prompted a shift in number to emphasise the role of the officiating priest rather than the community of sacrificers. Or the 1sg. could have been used in an attempt to harmonise the PYH with the singular found in the *Gāϑās*. Be that as it may, it is unlikely that the Pahlavi *Yasna*, as transmitted in the MSS, represents one particular stage of the MP language. Like any other stratified corpus, the *Zand* preserves linguistic features that belong to different stages of the language. The simplified inflection of MP, however, makes the identification of such phenomena difficult. Therefore, it remains to be seen whether in the PY a form such as ⟨ycwm⟩, which occurs both in the earliest MSS such as J2 as well as in the much younger Pt4, represents an older stage of the language in which *yazom* would have been a 1pl.

13.1.2 *kē radīh pad frārōnīh*

The YAv. opening formula of the YH, *ahurəm mazdąm ašauuanəm ašahe ratūm yazamaide*, and its kernel, *ašauuanəm ašahe ratūm*, occur numerous times in the YAv. *Yasna*.[8] But it is only in the *Zand* of Y 35.0 that the PV is extended by *kē radīh pad frārōnīh*. If righteous (*ahlaw*) Ohrmazd is the highest instance in matters of righteousness (*ahlāyīh rad*) and *frārōnīh* means 'righteousness, honesty' (MacKenzie 1990: 32), then the question arises as to how the clause in question relates to the preceding statement. What is the difference between *ahlāyīh* and *frārōnīh* which frequently occur together in the PY?[9]

Dhabhar (1949: 77) suggests a multitude of meanings for *frārōnīh*: 'righteousness, honesty, integrity, excellence, piety, virtue, propriety, rectitude, regularity, uprightness, good conduct'. Nyberg (1974: 76) translates it

---

[8] For the former, see Y 16.1, 17.1, 59.1, 63.3, 71.2 and 4. The formula also opens many chapters of the Wr.

[9] For *ahlaw*, see Gignoux (1984), and for *mard ī ahlaw*, see König (2005).

'honesty, righteousness, probity'.[10] Williams (1990: II 252) notes the semantic proximity accorded to *ahlāyīh* and *frārōnīh* by scholars and emphasises *abārōnīh* 'sinfulness' as the opposite of *frārōnīh* 'honesty' (Williams 1990: I 301). Shaked (1996: 652–3) translates *frārōnīh* 'righteousness' and *pad frārōnīh* 'in doing good things', while Skjærvø (2010a: 261) posits 'morally good' and 'goodness' for *frārōn* and *frārōnīh*, respectively.

As Skjærvø (2010a: 262) rightly notes, the suffix *-īh* is commonly used in exegetical passages to quote a preceding word. If the commentators intended as much here, we would expect the enclitic possessive pronoun *-š* after *kē*: **kē-š radīh pad frārōnīh* 'whose *radīh* is through goodness'.[11] Moreover, such instances seem to be followed by *ēd* 'is this'. In PY 35.0a, however, the manuscripts do not transmit *kē-š*, *radīh-š* or *ēd*.

In non-translation Pahlavi literature, the semantics of *frārōn* and *frārōnīh* (*frārōn/-īh*) seem to be appropriately captured by 'good conduct', 'honesty' and 'morally good'. See, for example, the following moral instructions:[12]

> MX 1[13] (42) *tuxšāg ud paymānīg bāš* (43) *ud az frārōn-tuxšāgīh ī xwēš xwar*
>
> Be diligent and moderate and eat from your own good endeavour.
>
> (46) *az xwāstag ī kasān ma appar* (47) *kū-t frārōn-tuxšāgīh ī xwēš wany nē bawēd*
>
> Do not steal from the property of others, so that your own good endeavour may not be lost.

However, even in such instances the actual meaning of *good* and *honest* remains unclear. Does *frārōnīh* vaguely encompass commonly accepted rights and wrongs such as being diligent and moderate, and how is it anchored in the Zoroastrian code of conduct?

In the PY, the attestations of *frārōn/-īh* are countless. The pair predominantly occurs in the so-called commentarial parts of the *Zand*, and thus does not directly correspond to an Av. word, but is often triggered by or collocated with, among others, *frazānag/-īh* (PY 30.9, 44.10, 47.2=18.3 etc.), *humānišnīh* (PY 1.6, 3.8, 30.10 etc.), *hudānāg* (PY 1.1) and *ahlāyīh*. At times, the use of *frārōn/-īh* appears to be motivated by a preceding *weh* or *hu-*, a phenomenon which explains the correlation with *humānišnīh* and *hudānāg*. Some other examples include:

---

[10] Nyberg (1974: 76) derives *frārōn* from 'OIr **frārda-van-* < **fra-arda-*'. However, the development of the cluster *-davan-* to *-ōn* is doubtful. Quoting Horn (1893: 276), Dhabhar (1949: 77) also mentions '*frā + rūn*'.

[11] See PY 4.8 quoted by Skjærvø (2010a: 262): *mihr … ī hazār-gōš … u-š hazār-gōšīh ēd* 'Mihr of thousand ears, and his having thousand ears, is this.' See also PY 9.2 where the possessive pronoun is attached to *dūrōšīh*: *hōm ī ahlaw ī dūrōš hād dūrōšīh-iš ēd* 'The righteous, death-destroying Hōm, his being death-destroying is this.'

[12] For other examples, see Dk 6.43, 53, 68, 82 and 83 in Shaked (1979).

[13] Text after Anklesaria (1913: 13).

PY 33.10c *weh-im waxšēnē menišn xwadāy kū-m frārōntar be kun*[14]

You cause my disposition to grow well, O Lord, that is, make me better.

PYt 1.15 *hudānāg nām hom kū frārōn-dānāg nām hom*

By name I am the well-knowing one, that is, by name I am the good-knowing one.

SYtSŠ 20[15] *xōb gōwišn kū ān ī frārōn gōwēd*

(Of) good speech, that is, he speaks that which is good.

On their own, these passages contribute little to our understanding of the semantic nuances associated with *ahlāyīh* and *frārōn/-īh* in the PY. What is the relationship between the two terms in those exegetical sections of the PY, where *frārōn/-īh* appears to explain *ahlāyīh*?

In PY 47.2, *Ohrmazd* is pictured as the father of *ahlāyīh*:

PY 47.2d *ān ī frazānag kū frazām ī tis pad frārōnīh dānēd ud ān pid ī ahlāyīh pad dānāgīh kū parwardārīh ī dāmān pad frārōnīh kunēd*

The wise one, that is, he knows the end of things through goodness, and that father of righteousness through knowledge, that is, he performs the nourishment of the creations by goodness.

Here, *Ohrmazd* is described as the origin of *ahlāyīh*, while his activity, namely the nourishment of the creations (*parwardārīh ī dāmān*), is qualified by *frārōnīh*. Similarly, in the following two passages *frārōnīh* occurs with *ahlāyīh* in proximity of verbs of action:

PY 8.1 *kū pad ahlāyīh ō amā bē rasād pad frārōnīh*

That he shall come to us through righteousness, (namely) by goodness.

PY 28.8a[16] *pad ahlāyīh pahlom ōh ham-dōšēnd pad frārōnīh*

They thus love each other through excellent righteousness, (namely) by goodness.

When in PY 45.2 *Ohrmazd* is distinguished from the evil spirit in a series of statements, it is *frārōnīh* that qualifies *Ohrmazd*'s wisdom, desire, speech and deeds:

---

[14] The above passage translates *vohū uxšiiā manaŋhā xšaϑrā*, continued *ašācā uštā tanūm* 'According to wish, grow through good thought, rule and order, in (your) body.' Since the *Zand* does not render the Av. instr. *manaŋhā xšaϑrā* by way of *pad*, I have translated *xwadāy* as vocative, taking account of its position in the clause. An alternative translation could be: 'You cause me to grow well, O Lord of thought.' In PY 68.23a *weh-im waxšēne menišn xwadāy* is followed by: *kū-m frārōntar be kunēd*.

[15] Text after Dhabhar (1927: 115).

[16] See also Shaked (1996: 651, 653).

PY 45.2c–d[17] *kū nē amā menišn man nē ān menom ī tō menē čē man ān ī frārōn menom ud tō ān ī abārōn menē ud nē hammōxtišn čē man ān ī frārōn hammōzom tō ān ī abārōn hammōzē nē xrad čē man xrad pad frārōnīh dārom tō pad abārōnīh*

nē kāmag čē man kāmag pad frārōnīh dārom ud tō pad abārōnīh nē saxwan čē man ān ī frārōn gōwom ud tō ān ī abārōn gōwē nē kunišn čē man kunišn frārōn ud tō abārōn

Not our disposition, I do not think that which you think, for I think that which is good and you think that which is wrong, and not teaching, for I teach that which is good (and) you teach that which is bad, not wisdom, for I maintain wisdom by goodness, (and) you maintain (it) by wrongfulness.

Not desire, for I maintain desire by goodness and you by wrongfulness, not speech, for I speak that which is good, and you speak that which is wrong, not deeds, for my deeds are good, and yours wrong.

Thus far, *ahlāyīh* appears to be a rather abstract concept of which *Ohrmazd* is the originator. By contrast, *frārōnīh* qualifies actions and attributes if they occur in close proximity of *ahlāyīh*. The commentators must have viewed a direct association between *ahlāyīh* and actions as impermissible. Therefore, they felt compelled to explain seemingly deviant collocations:

Y 47.1b *hacā ašāṯ š́iiaoϑanācā vacaŋhācā*

With action and speech in accordance with *aša*

PY 47.1b *az ān ī ahlāyīh kunišn gōwišn kunišn ī frārōn rāy ī-m ōh kard ud gōwišn ī frārōn rāy ī-m ōh guft*

Of the deed and speech of righteousness, on account of the good deed which I thus performed and on account of the good speech which I thus spoke.

In the Av. original *š́iiaoϑna-* 'action' and *vacah-* 'speech' are not linked with *aša-* as if they were action and speech of *aša*. Rather, they are to be performed in compliance with *aša-*. This nuance, however, seems to be lost in the PV of the passage: 'Of the deed and speech of righteousness'. The commentators are aware of this difference and therefore explain the PV by qualifying deed and speech through goodness (*kunišn/gōwišn ī frārōn*). Thus, the evidence suggests that a direct association between *ahlāyīh* and actions are untenable in the *Zand*.

The relationship between the two terms is made explicit in the *Zand* of the *ahunawar* prayer:[18]

---

[17] The combination of the obl. personal pronoun *man* with a verb in 1sg.pres. seems unusual for MP. Most likely the personal pronouns *man* and *tō* are used as a stylistic feature to underline the contrast between *Ohrmazd* and the evil spirit, rather than reflecting NP influence. PY 45.2 is paraphrased in PY 19.15.

[18] In an e-mail, dated 15 July 2009, Professor Skjærvø suggested to me that the relationship between *radīh* and *frārōnīh* is 'connected with the exegesis' on the *ahunawar* prayer.

PY 0.15[19] *čiyōn axw kāmag čiyōn ohrmazd kāmag*
ēdōn radīhā ēdōn frārōnīhā az ahlāyīh kār ud kirbag čēgām-iz-ēw kār ud kirbag ēdōn frārōnīhā kardan čiyōn ohrmazd kāmag kū-š[20] *ahlāyīh az hamāg abardom dād kū-š abāyist ōh ahlāyīh* [...]

As is the desire of the existence, as is *Ohrmazd*'s desire,
works and good deeds that (stem) from righteousness, are thus authoritative, they are thus good [*frārōnīhā*]; whatever works and good deeds, they are thus to be performed well [*frārōnīhā*], as is *Ohrmazd*'s desire; that is, he created righteousness as the highest of all, that is, it was necessary for him (that) righteousness was in this way. [...]

According to the above passage, those deeds are authoritative (*radīhā*) and good (*frārōnīhā*), which comply with *ahlāyīh* (*az ahlāyīh kār ud kirbag*). This is expressed by the preposition *az*, which functions as an abl. here, much like Av. *ašāt* 'in accordance with *aša-*'. However, the performance of the deed itself is described as good, expressed by the adverbial form of *frārōnīh* in close proximity of the verb: *frārōnīhā kardan*. Thus, the adjective *frārōn* and its derivatives, *frārōnīh* and *frārōnīhā*, are reserved for the description of actions and deeds that comply with the concept of *ahlāyīh*. Finally, resonating PY 47.2, in the *Zand* of the *ahunawar* prayer the exegetes expel all doubts about the supremacy of *ahlāyīh* as *Ohrmazd*'s highest creation: *kū-š ahlāyīh az hamāg abardom dād*.

As abstract as the distinction between the two terms may appear, it serves a practical purpose. It seems that MP *ahlāyīh* retains the semantic complexity of Av. *aša-*, conveying a meaning along the lines of 'order', or to borrow the words of Schlerath (1986: 200), as the coherence of the world order ('die Stimmigkeit der Weltordnung').[21] If we define *frārōnīh* as the manifestation of the concept of *ahlāyīh* through deeds and actions, then *frārōnīh* is a term of morality, indicating the compliance of a deed with the divine concept of *ahlāyīh*. Thus, as the realisation of *ahlāyīh*, *frārōnīh* is a powerful scale to measure religiously relevant deeds. The scale is justified by its use in the sacred corpus in close proximity to *Ohrmazd*, who in PY 45.2 is qualified as *frārōn* numerous times. And in his exegesis of the *ahunawar* prayer Zādspram (WZ 1.14) explicitly defines *frārōn* as that which is according to *Ohrmazd*'s

---

[19] The *ahunawar* prayer (PY 27.13) is repeated throughout the *Yasna*. I have chosen this stanza because of its extended commentary.
[20] This and the final clause are only attested in J2. Here, Dhabhar (1949: 4) reads *u-š*, but despite the tear in the MS the bottom tip of ⟨K⟩ is visible.
[21] While I leave *aša-* largely untranslated, I accept Skjærvø's (2003) general views on the concept of *aša-*. For a summary of the discussions pertaining to *aša-*, see Hintze (2007a: 53–8) and more recently König (2018: 115–50).

wish: *fradom kū har tis ān frārōn ī ohrmazd kām* 'Firstly: of all things, those are good, which are (according to) *Ohrmazd*'s desire'.[22]

Moreover, as Bowker (1997: 329) notes, exegesis seeks out 'legitimate meaning in the light of continuing and developing understanding'. Similarly, Macuch (2009a: 251–2) observes that the task of the Pahlavi commentators 'was not only to explain the archaic text to their contemporaries, but also to demonstrate its continuing relevance to their own age'. In PY 35.0a, *kē radīh pad frārōnīh* clarifies why righteous *Ohrmazd* is the authority of righteousness (*ohrmazd ī ahlaw ī ahlāyīh rad*). Not because he created it, but because he maintains his own divine concept of *ahlāyīh* by way of his compliant actions. His desire to maintain *ahlāyīh* is what qualifies him as a *rad*. I suspect that here the qualification of *Ohrmazd* through *kē radīh pad frārōnīh* also defines the requirement for the position of a priestly *rad* (*radīh*), namely compliance with *ahlāyīh*. *rad*s often served as judges under the Sasanians (Stausberg 2002: 257), making their association with ethical qualities plausible.[23]

The following passages further highlight how the commentarial tradition connected *frārōnīh* with matters of kingship and law as the applicable dimension of *ahlāyīh*:

> PY 20.3[24] *kē ō ahlāyīh xwadāyīh čāšēd kū pādaxšāyīh pad frārōnīh kunēd hād dādestānīh ay kū pad ahlāyīh xwadāyīh čāšēd kū pādaxšāyīh pad frārōnīh dārēd*
>
> He, who assigns lordship to righteousness, so that it reigns by goodness; that is, judgement is this, that he teaches lordship by righteousness, so that he maintains kingship through goodness.
>
> MX 0.39[25] *čē yazadān dēn rāstīh ud dād frārōnīh*
>
> For, the *dēn* of the *yazadān* is rectitude, and (their) law is goodness.

In order to reflect this difference between *ahlāyīh* and *frārōnīh*, I have adopted Skjærvø's (2010a: 261) definition of *frārōnīh*, regarding it as 'goodness' in terms of a deed's compliance with *ahlāyīh*. This interpretation of *frārōnīh*, if accepted, has implications for our translation of *ahlāyīh* as well. The term 'righteousness' implies an adherence to moral principles. The term *ahlāyīh*, however, seems to denote an abstract cosmic or universal set of rules.[26] Thus, 'order' might be a suitable translation for both *aṣa*- and *ahlāyīh*.

---

[22] Text after Anklesaria (1964: 4). See also Gignoux and Tafazzoli (1993: 32). For a discussion of Zādspram's commentary on the *ahunawar*, see Gropp (1991).

[23] For a discussion of the Zoroastrian priesthood, see Kreyenbroek (1987).

[24] I quote this passage after Pt4, as the MSS disagree about *ahlāyīh* and *frārōnīh* in the first instance after *ay*. All MSS render *ay* as ᛗ rather than ᛃ.

[25] I am grateful to Prof. Skjærvø for bringing this passage to my attention in an e-mail dated 15 July 2009.

[26] *ahlāyīh* may have applied to the domain of ethics as well. The problem is that 'righteousness' limits *ahlāyīh* to this domain only and suppresses the complexity of the original term.

The distinction between *ahlāyīh* as an abstract set of rules governing the intangible world and *frārōnīh* as the manifestation of *ahlāyīh* in the material world is attested at least in one passage. In colophon B of the manuscript MK, *frārōnīh* and *ahlāyīh* are assigned to *gētīy* and *mēnōy*, respectively. This division is not explicitly reflected in the passages discussed above, but is consistent with my interpretation:

Col. B *gētīy ēdōn čiyōn tan kāmag andar frārōnīh ud mēnōy ēdōn čiyōn ruwān kāmag andar ahlāyīh*

Thus, like the body, *gētīy* has its purpose in goodness, and *mēnōy*, like the soul, has its purpose in righteousness.

As a concluding thought, I would like to share the observation that the relationship between *ahlāyīh* and *frārōnīh* resembles that between *r̥ta* and *dharma* in the Vedic tradition. As Holdrege (2004: 216) remarks, '[w]hile *r̥ta* is used as the overarching term for the cosmic order, *dharma* is used to refer to the "upholding of *r̥ta*" (*r̥tasya dharman*) (R̥g Veda 9.7.1, 9.110.4)'. She goes on to quote Halbfass (1988: 315–16) that *dharma* is 'the continuous *maintaining* of the social and cosmic order and norm which is achieved by the Aryan through the performance of his Vedic rites and traditional duties' (emphasis in original). As we have seen above, *frārōnīh* often occurs with the verb *dāštan, dār-* 'to have, hold, keep, preserve' which is etymologically related to *dharma*.[27] Therefore, I would like to propose that the notion of maintaining cosmic order through *frārōnīh* may share its origin with the Vedic tradition.

13.1.3 *hudahāgān*

The compound adjective *hudahāgān*, here spelt ⟨Pahlavi⟩ (Pt4 Mf4 R413 T6 E7) and ⟨Pahlavi⟩ (F2, K5 J2 M1), corresponds to YAv. *huδā̊ŋhō* 'well providing'.[28] In the PYH we also find *hudahagīh*[29] (PY 38.3) and *hudahāgtom* (PY 41.2–4). Although the adjective is predominantly found in the *Zand*,[30] its attestation is not restricted to this corpus, and it occurs, albeit less frequently, in the wider Pahlavi literature as well.[31]

---

[27] Ved. *dharma* derives from the root *dhr̥* 'to keep, hold, uphold', and MP *dāštan*, Av. *dār-*, OP *dār-* derive from **dar* 'to hold, keep' < PIE **dʰer-* 'to hold'. For a full list of cognates and attestations, see Cheung (2007: 57–9).

[28] For *hud/šāh-*, see Narten (1982: 87) and Narten (1986: 285ff.) with references. For its attestation, see Bartholomae (1904: 1823, 1825), who posits the stems *hu-d/šā(y)-* and *hu-d/šāh-*.

[29] On this form, see Section 16.3.3.

[30] In the PY, for instance, *hudahag(ān)* appears numerous times, characterising *gōspand* (PY 3.1 etc.), the *amahraspandān* (PY 2.2 etc.) and once *hōm* (PY 9.16). See also Wr 7.4 where it occurs with *gāw*, Ny 1.8, S 1.22 and 2.22 with *wād* and finally with *zamīg* in S 1.28 and 2.28.

[31] See Bd 1a.4, Dd 64.23, Dk 7 and Suppl.ŠnŠ 15.9.

Bartholomae (1904: 1825) initially vocalised the variant spellings of this adjective as *hudāk* and *hudāhak*, viewing the latter as the older form: 'Mutterform von *hudāk*' (Bartholomae 1904: 1826, fn. 3). However, he later prefers *hudahāk* to *hudāhak*, while maintaining *hudāk* (Bartholomae 1906: 45). He argues that the sequence *-ahā-* was contracted to *-ā-*, thus deriving *hudāk* from *hudahāk*, in analogy to MMP ⟨gwny'g⟩ *gōnyāg* 'beautiful' which he derives from **gōnaδahāk* (Bartholomae 1906: 45). Nyberg (1974: 102) views it as a loan from Av., suggesting *hu-dāhak* 'bounteous'. MacKenzie (1990: 44), followed by Josephson (1997: 57–8), reads ⟨hwd'(h)k'⟩ and transcribes it as *hudā(ha)g* 'good, beneficent'.[32] Dhabhar (1949: 46, 47) prefers *hū-dahāk* 'well-yielding' and *hū-dahak* 'giving good, well-yielding, well-created, well-giving'. Elsewhere, we find *hudahāk* 'well-yielding' (Humbach and Jamaspasa 1971: I 52) and *hudahag* (Skjærvø 2010d).

In suggesting that the long vowel in *hudā(ha)g* reflects the vocalism of the Av. stem *hud/δāh-*, scholars posit a loan from Avestan without a plausible derivation in MP. It is not uncommon for a loan or learned word to retain the sound structure of the language of origin. However, the adjective need not be a loan, for the variants noted above can be transcribed more plausibly as *hudahāgān* (𐭧𐭥𐭣𐭠𐭧𐭪) and *hudahagān* (𐭧𐭥𐭣𐭧𐭪). In either case, the prefix *hu-* 'good-, well-' constitutes the first term of the compound, while the second term is built from the present stem *dah-* 'to give, create' to which the present participle suffix *-ag* or the agent noun suffix *-āg* are attached.[33] Accordingly, the spellings would be ⟨hwdhk'⟩ and ⟨hwdh'k'⟩. However, the notoriously multivalent Pahlavi script leaves room for the interpretation of the sequence -𐭧𐭪- in 𐭧𐭥𐭣𐭧𐭪. The viable candidates are *-āh-*, *-hā-* and *-ah-*. As laid out above, I have already ruled out *-āh-* in favour of *-hā-*, positing a compound with an agent noun as its second member: *hudahāgān*. But the reading *-ah-* remains a possibility, as an *'ālep* could have been added before the *ḥēṯ* to disambiguate 𐭧𐭥𐭣𐭧𐭪 to prevent a reading as **hudāgān*.[34] We find this type of disambiguation in ⟨b'hl⟩ *bahr* which is set apart from ⟨b'l⟩ *bār* by means of ⟨-'h-⟩. Other examples include ⟨d'hm⟩ *dahm* versus ⟨d'm⟩ *dām* and possibly ⟨g(')hl⟩ *gahl* versus ⟨g'l⟩ *gāl*.[35] Furthermore, the sequence ⟨-'h-⟩ represents *-ah-* in ⟨d'hlyc⟩ *dahlīz* and ⟨d'hwm⟩ *dahom*. Presumably, the prefix *hu-* and the context ruled out a confusion with 𐭣𐭧𐭪 *Dahāg*, a

---

[32] Josephson (1997: 58, fn. 36) suggests that '*hudāg*' is the 'usual translation' for Av. *hud/δā-*. As noted by her, in PY 9.16b it actually translates Av. *huδātō* 'well-created'. Thus the *Zand* adds: *weh hōm ī hudahag kū pad frārōnīh dād ēste* 'O good *Hōm*, the beneficent one, that is, you have been created through goodness.'

[33] For the suffixes, see MacKenzie (1990: 5–6) and Weber (2007: 952, 955–8). In contrast to Sundermann (1989: 150) who only describes the suffix *-ag* as forming present participles, Weber (2007: 958) adds *-āg* to this category as well. Skjærvø (2010a: 245) notes *-ag* as forming past verbal adjectives.

[34] See, for instance, PWd 21.1 where 𐭧𐭥𐭣𐭧𐭪 is transcribed *hudāk* in F10.

[35] For the meanings of the above words, see MacKenzie (1990).

legendary dragon king, and ⟨dhk'n'⟩ *dehgān* 'farmer'. It is therefore possible that ⟨hwdhk'n'⟩ *hudahagān* constitutes the older form, while ⟨hwdh'k'n'⟩ represents an orthographic disambiguation. However, in PY 35.0 a case can be made for a reading of ⟨hwdhk'n'⟩ as *hudahāgān*, as the syntax of the *ezāfe* suggests that here *hudahāg* was used as an agent noun.

In PY 35.0a, the *Zand* shows a peculiar use of *ī*: *amahraspandān ī huxwadāyān ī hudahāgān*.[36] Although *huxwadāyān* and *hudahāgān* correctly reflect the pl. number of the Av. attributive adjectives, *huxšaϑrā huδåŋhō*, their agreement in number with *amahraspandān* is against the rules of ZMP governing the *ezāfe*. In MP, the particle *ī* commonly links a noun with a following adjective. As Boyce (1964: 43) observes, in MMP the 'most rigid' rule concerning the *ezāfe* is 'that it cannot be used with adjectives in the plural form'. Similarly, Sundermann (1989: 156) suggests that the use of the connective particle *ī* and congruence are mutually exclusive. He points out, that in ZMP, the singular form of the adjective was generalised and that it is not required for the attributive adjective to agree with the qualified noun in number. This, he argues, is in contrast to MMP where congruence can replace the use of the particle *ī*. Thus, the expected alternatives could be *amahraspandān hudahagān* in compliance with MMP or *amahraspandān ī hudahag* in ZMP. Surprisingly, an alternative without the *ezāfe* is attested in PY 35.0a in the MSS F2 R413 T6, K5 M1.[37] Among these MSS, R413 T6 have the agent noun ⟨hwdh'k'n'⟩ rather than the adjective ⟨hwdhk'n'⟩, which we find in F2, K5 J2 M1. The second alternative is attested in PY 58.5 (see Dhabhar 1949: 250), where the sg. forms still translate the Av. pl. *huxšaϑrā huδåŋhō*. In PY 35.0a, J2 offers yet another alternative: *amahraspandān ud huxwadāyān ud hudahagān*. However, these variations notwithstanding, the use of the substantive *huxwadāyān* in the first part of the phrase in all the MSS supports a reading of the second term as a substantive. Therefore, rather than postulating an ungrammatical use of *ī* in the present passage, I interpret ⟨hwdhk'n'⟩, attested in Pt4 Mf4 R413 T6 E7, as the agent noun *hudahagān*. Similarly, in F2 we find both *huδåŋhō* and *hudahagān* glossed as نیکی‌دهند 'provider of goodness' and in T6 نیکی‌دهند and نیک‌دهند 'well-provider', respectively.

---

[36] In PY 3.3, *ābān ī wehān ī Ohrmazd-dād ud abārīg āb* 'the good waters created by *Ohrmazd* and other waters' corresponds to *apąm vaŋʰhīnąm mazdaδātanąm* 'of the good, Mazda-created waters'. Without recourse to Av. the correct translation of *ābān ī wehān* would be 'the waters of the good ones', while the expected form would be *ābān ī weh* 'the good waters'. In such cases, the *Zand* echoes the congruence of the Av. original.

[37] K5 M1 have *xwadāyān*.

Table 13.2 Coordination

	A Bcā	Acā Bcā
A *ud* B	35.4c	35.8b, 41.4a
A B-*iz*	35.6c, 38.1b	35.1b
A-*iz* B		35.5b
A *ud* B-*iz*	39.3c	35.0b, 35.1a, 37.1a
A-*iz ud* B		36.4b
A-*iz ud* B-*iz*	41.1a	35.3b, 37.1b
∅	41.4c	41.4b, 41.4c

13.1.4 *kē-iz*

The PY divides Y 35.0b into a main and a subordinate clause by rendering the adjectives *mainiiəuuīmcā gaēθiiąmcā* as *kē mēnōy ud kē-iz gētīy*. The second *kē* was most likely added to accommodate the enclitic -*iz*.[38] In the PY, the adverbial enclitic ⟨-(y)c⟩ -*iz* 'also, even' corresponds to the enclitic coordinating conjunction -*cā* 'and'. Av. -*cā̆* may be used in different types of coordination in Avestan.[39] However, no one-to-one correspondence seems to exist between the various Av. patterns and their respective MP versions. A coordination of a certain type in the Av. original can thus be rendered in a number of ways in MP as shown in Table 13.2.

13.1.5 *pad ārzōg*

Here, *pad ārzōg* 'with desire' translates *bərəjā*, an instr.sg.f. of the root noun *bərəj*- 'esteem, respect, honour' (Hintze 2007a: 335).[40] In all of its six attestations *bərəj*- governs the gen. or dat. of *aṧa*- 'order' or *daēnā*- 'belief' (Hintze 2007a: 50).[41] In PY 35.0c, the relationship between *aṧahe* and *bərəjā* is expressed by the syntagma *ī ō*, whereby the preposition *ō* marks *ahlāyīh* as the object of *ārzōg*. In the second part of the phrase *pad* is missing before *ārzōg*, but must have been viewed as implied, as it is added in the manuscripts F2 and T6.

---

[38] For the vocalisation of ⟨-c⟩, see Sims-Williams (1981: 173).

[39] For a categorised list of all occurrences of -*cā* in the YH, see Hintze (2007a: 336). For coordination in Av., see Skjærvø (2010b: 149).

[40] As Hintze (2007a: 51, fn. 5) points out, MP *ārzōg* derives from *ā-bərəj-u- and is thus etymologically related to Av. *bərəj*-.

[41] On an intriguing interpretation of the meaning of *daēnā*-, see Cantera (2013).

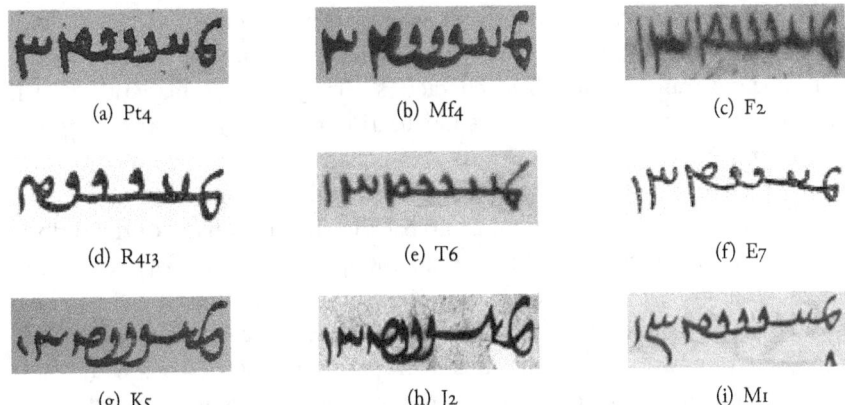

Figure 13.1 *mazdēsnān*

13.1.6 *mazdēsnān*

Figure 13.1 illustrates the PV of the Av. gen.sg. *māzdaiiasnōiš* 'Mazda-worshipping' in PY 35.0c.[42] All MSS agree in their spelling, except T6 and E7, which prefer a form resembling ⟨mhst'n'⟩.[43] I have interpreted the variants as ⟨mẓdyst'n'⟩ and ⟨mẓdst'n'⟩ for T6 and E7.

The Av. noun *mazdaiiasna-* 'Mazda-worshipper' and the adjective *māzdaiiasni-* 'Mazda-worshipping' as well as their expected MP counterparts have been discussed at some length.[44] One question in the rather complex discussion is whether ZMP only preserves *māzdēsn* a form derived from the lengthened grade, as advocated by MacKenzie (1990: 55),[45] Nyberg (1974: 130) and Panaino (1993, 2003). It has also been debated whether InsMP *mzdysn* could represent *mazdēsn* derived from the full grade (Huyse 1999a: II 2–4, 2006) and how it could have developed in ZMP. Panaino's arguments in favour of *māzdēsn* have been discussed and rejected by Skjærvø in Alram et al. (2007: 30–33) and partially by Huyse (1999b). As Skjærvø rightly observes, the adjective *māzdaiiasni-* is commonly 'rendered in Pahlavi by the plural form' (Alram et al. 2007: 32). He correctly interprets the term as *mazdēsnān* 'of the *mazdēsn*s, Mazdayasnians'. The spelling is reflected in the forms listed above in Figure 13.1.

---

[42] In R413 -*ān* is at the start of the next line.
[43] In T6 we find a NP interlinear gloss to this effect, مّاّزاّر, while *māzdaiiasnōiš* is glossed ذوّمّاّزاّر. On the spelling ⟨mhst'n'⟩ in this context, see Skjærvø's section in Alram, Blet-Lemarquand and Skjærvø (2007: 32).
[44] On the Av. terms, see Bartholomae (1904: 1160, 1169) and Benveniste (1970).
[45] In the main entry MacKenzie notes *māzdēsn* ⟨m'zd(y)sn'⟩ 'Mazda-worshipping, Mazdean' and records five different spellings in the Pahlavi key (col. 132–4).

As Skjærvø convincingly argues, ⟨mẕd-⟩ represents ⟨mẕd-⟩ *mazd-* (Alram et al. 2007: 33). We thus expect the remaining characters, ᛞ, to spell -*ēsn*. Skjærvø transliterates these characters ⟨-yyṣn'⟩. His explanation that it 'would represent an attempt at rationalization of a form that might appear disturbing (m'st' = *māst* 'sour milk')' is unconvincing. Beside ᛞ we also find the spelling ᛞ in the MSS (Figure 13.1), which I analyse as ⟨-yst⟩. The replacement of ⟨-n⟩ with ⟨-t⟩ must go back to the quick hand of the scribes, who would have connected ᚢ to ı with a loop: ᚢ → ᛞ (see Barr 1936: 396). In the younger MSS F2 T6 E7, M1 where ᚢ is substituted by ᛯ the final character is still interpreted as ⟨-t⟩. A similar tendency can be observed in ⟨yst'⟩ for *yasn* 'worship'. If the substitution of the cluster ⟨-sn-⟩ with ⟨-st-⟩ was an accepted scribal convention, then it might be justified to reflect the original spelling in the transliteration.

13.2   PY 35.1

13.2.1   *dahišn*

The subordinate clause *ka ēdar dahišn u-š pad-iz ī ān ī any dahišn* corresponds to the Av. hapax legomena *iiadacā aniiadacā* 'both here and elsewhere'.[46] Both Mills (1905a: 56) and Dhabhar (1963: 4) translate *dahišn* here as 'dispensation', while Hintze (2007a: 64) prefers 'performed'.

According to Dhabhar (1963: 4, fn. 3), here *dahišn* translates *-da-* in *iiadacā aniiadacā*, suggesting that the exegetes analysed *iiadacā aniiadacā* as a derivation from the root *dā* 'to give; to create'. Dhabhar's interpretation seems to be supported by PY 29.8 where we find *ēd man dahišn* ڪاسمبا[47] 'I announced this creation' for *aēm mōi idā vistō* 'This has been found by me here.' However, in PY 35.1 *dahišn* could be the exegetes' contextual interpretation of the Av. adverbs *iiadacā aniiadacā*, presumably regarding it as a reference to *gētīy*, here, and *mēnōy*, the other creation. That the meaning of the adverbs must have been known to the commentators emerges from PY 57.33, where *kē ēdar-iz ud ō ānōh-iz any-iz gyāg* 'which both here and there (and) also elsewhere' corresponds to YAv. *iδatca ainiδatca iδatca* 'here, elsewhere as well as here'. Likewise, in PY 68.21 *iδāt* seems to have been translated as '*ēdar*': *vaŋʰhīm iδāt ādąm vaŋʰhīm ašīm* 'Here, the good retribution, the good reward', *ān-iz weh dahišn ī ēdar ān-iz weh tarsagāhīh ī ānōh* 'Also that good distribution here (and) also that good reverence there.' The mention of *ānōh* 'there' in PY 68.21, which does not correspond to a word in the Av. original, suggests that a division between here and there was assumed, reminding us on PY 35.1a. That the same distinction between here and there was applied to PY 35.1a also emerges from the comment at the end of the line: *kū-š ēdar ud ānōh-iz nēkīh aziš*. Therefore, in PY 35.1 I have translated *dahišn* as 'creation'.

It is unlikely that in the above passage *dahišn* is a necessitative participle referring to *humatān hūxtān huwarštān*, as the triad usually occurs with the verb *warzīdan* 'work, act, practise'. Thus, for instance, in PY 35.1b, in AWN 101.17, *ud be warzēd humat ud hūxt ud huwaršt* 'And practise good thoughts, good words and good deeds' (see Jamaspji Asa and Haug 1872: 136), or in *wisp humat bun: har kas kē harwisp humatān ud hūxtān ud huwarštān warzēd* 'Whoever practises good thoughts, good words and good deeds' (see Dhabhar 1927: 25). Moreover, the adjective *any* 'other' in *ān ī any dahišn* suggests that *dahišn* is a noun rather than a necessitative participle.

---

[46] On the Av. adverbs, see Hintze (2007a: 61-3).
[47] The spelling of the verb's stem as ڪاسمبا in Pt4 F2 T6, J2 M1 is reminiscent of the verb *niwistan* 'to announce, consecrate'. Presumably, the intended verb is *windādan* 'to find, obtain'. The NP glosses in F2 T6 are derived from عاصل کرون 'to obtain'.

In light of the above evidence, I am inclined to reject Dhabhar's view of *dahišn*, and suggest that *ēdar ... ān ī any* correctly translate *iiadacā aniiadacā*, much like PY 57.33, and that *dahišn* further qualifies the meaning of here and there.

The reading of the first ᭨ in PY 35.1a as *aziš* by Mills (1905a: 56) and Dhabhar (1963: 4) is most likely motivated by *aziš* at the end of the same line. In this interpretation the 'dispensation' (*dahišn*) is caused by *humatān hūxtān huwarštān*. If this was the case, we would expect a second *aziš* after *ān ī any dahišn*, which is not attested. And a collocation of the triad with *dahišn* to this effect is not known to me.

13.2.2 ᭨ *hom*

The MSS Pt4 Mf4 E7 consistently attest the spelling ᭨ instead of ᭨. Nyberg (1964: 175) and Heston (1976: 178) interpret this form as ⟨HWH-wm⟩ and ⟨HWEwm⟩, respectively, and transcribe it as *hom*, considering it to be a 1sg.ind.pres.act. of the copula ⟨h-⟩ 'to be'. In Nyberg's view the 1pl.ind.pres.act. of ⟨h-⟩ is ᭨ ⟨HWH'-ym⟩ *hēm* in ZMP, possibly *hom* in Pz. and ⟨hwm⟩ in MMP. Although in the present context the interpretation of ᭨ as *hom* is justified, it need not be based on a posited phonetic complement ⟨-wm⟩, for the doubling of the letter I at the final position in an heterogram is also an orthographic convention of late MP (Utas 1984: 63). To that end, the I attached to ᭨ ⟨-H-⟩ could have been interpreted as a final I and thus doubled on occasion. This observation is supported by forms such as ᭨ ⟨HWH'-ym⟩ *hēm*, ᭨ ⟨HWH'-d⟩ *hēnd* or ᭨ ⟨HWH'-yt⟩ *hēd*.[48] In PY 39.4, the manuscripts Pt4 Mf4 E7 also preserve ᭨ ⟨HWH'-yy̆⟩. Another, more likely explanation is that I ⟨-w⟩ was here used to mark word boundaries. However, it cannot be excluded that the scribes added a phonetic ⟨-wm⟩ guided by the pronunciation of the verb as *hom*.

13.2.3 *abar griftār*

Here, *abar griftār* translates Av. *aibī.jarətārō*, a nom.pl.m. from the stem *aibī.jarətar-* 'welcomer'.[49] While Dhabhar (1949: 163) prefers 'seizer, appropriator', Malandra and Ichaporia (2010: 98) suggest '*praiser', assuming a 'confusion of the verbs *griftan*, *gīr-* "to hold" and *gīr-* (pres. stem only and assimilated graphically to *griftan*) "to praise".' However, I am unable to verify

---

[48] See Nyberg (1964: 175), PY 38.4a and PY 39.1b–c.
[49] See Narten (1986: 88–90) and Hintze (2007a: 63ff.) for a discussion of the poetics of the antonyms *aibī.jarətārō* and *naēnaēstārō* 'not revilers'.

the attestation of a verb *gīr- with the meaning 'to praise' in MP.[50] More likely, here *griftār* is intended as an actor noun derived from *griftan, gīr-* 'take, hold, restrain'.[51] Although *abar* 'up; on, over' translates *aibī*, it must have also been perceived as adding a reflexive notion to *griftār* with the meaning 'to take over for oneself, to appropriate'. This view is confirmed by the comment, which follows *abar griftār*: *kū ō xwēš kunom* 'that is, I make (it) my own'.

As I discuss in Section 13.2.5, by reading *naēnaēstārō* as *mard ō mard* the *Zand* offers a radically different interpretation of this stanza, which motivates a commentary in *Pursišnīhā* 18. Consequently, *abar griftār* does not stand in a poetic reference to a word meaning 'not revilers', as argued by Narten (1986) and Hintze (2007a) for the Avestan version, but forms part of a different discourse, where the appropriation of good thoughts, good words and good deeds and their assignment to others are the focus. Ultimately, however, both versions agree in their universally positive outlook towards the triad *humatān hūxtān huwarštān*.

13.2.4 *ō xwēš kardan*

In the phrase ⟨script⟩ ⟨script⟩, here read as ⟨'w' NPŠH 'BYDWN-mm⟩, the verb can be interpreted as ⟨'ḤDWN-m⟩ *gīrom* 'I take' as well as ⟨'BYDWN-m⟩ *kunom*. Due to the preceding ⟨glpt'l⟩,[52] one may prefer *griftan, gīr-* 'take, hold, restrain'. Although semantically both readings would yield similar results, I have opted for the idiomatic expression *ō xwēš kardan* 'to make one's own, appropriate', which is common in MP and appears to be synonymous with *xwēšēnīdan* 'make ones own'.[53]

Rather than ⟨-m⟩, in PY 35.1, 35.4 and 39.5 we find the verbal complement ⟨script⟩ ⟨-mm⟩ (Pt4 Mf4) and ⟨script⟩ ⟨-m̥⟩ (K5 J2 M1) attached to the heterogram ⟨'BYDWN-⟩. Already Spiegel (1858: 11) noticed ⟨-m̥⟩, but could not explain it:

> Die zwei andern Ligaturen dagegen sind eigenthümliche Formen, die nur in der Handschrift des Yaçna vorkommen, nämlich ⟨script⟩, die sich in der 1. pers. sing. und plur. des Verbums findet, es ist mir unmöglich zu sagen, wodurch sie sich von der gewöhnlichen Form unterscheidet.

Nyberg (1964: 135, 179) views ⟨script⟩ as a 1sg.pres.act. ⟨'BYDWN-wm⟩ *kunom*, but does not explain this diacritic.

---

[50] Perhaps they have forms derived from the root *garH 'to greet, call' in mind, also attested in Av. as *auui gər-* 'to praise' (see Cheung 2007: 107). MP ⟨gl'myk'⟩ *grāmīg* 'treasured, dear' derives from this root.
[51] MacKenzie (1990) suggests 'held, taken; captive' for *griftār*.
[52] Here, *abar griftār* corresponds to *aibī.jarətārō*.
[53] For *ō xwēš kardan*, see PY 62.6 (=Ny 5.12), Dk 6.D12, Dk 6.E35a in Shaked (1979), and for *xwēšēnīdan* Dk 9.35.1.

The use of the diacritic sign ⟨X̣⟩ is not limited to the above Pahlavi MSS. In TD2, we find a similar hook under ⟨y⟩ in the phonetic complement ⟨-yt⟩. However, the diacritic sign is only used if the phonetic complement ⟨-yt⟩ is attached to the verbal heterogram ⟨ʾBYDWN-⟩. Verbal forms such as ⟨ʿZLWN-yt⟩ are never written with this diacritic. Thus, we consistently find ꜟꜟꜟꜟ, but ꜟꜟꜟꜟ (see Humbach and Jamaspasa 1971: II 12–13). In PY 40.1a, the MSS K5 J2 M1 use a similar diacritic in ⟨ʾBYDWN-yṇd⟩. None of the other verbs in the same stanza, including ⟨YMLLWN-ʾnd⟩ (K5 M1) and ⟨YMLLWN-d⟩ (J2), use this particular or similar diacritics. Therefore, I am inclined to suggest that ⟨-mm⟩, ⟨-ṃ⟩ and ⟨-yṭ⟩ are an orthographic convention motivated by the verb ⟨ʾBYDWN-⟩, perhaps to disambiguate its reading and to avoid confusions with *griftan, gīr-*. This lends further support to my reading of ꜟꜟꜟꜟ ꜟꜟꜟꜟ ꜟꜟ as *ō xwēš kardan* rather than *ō xwēš griftan*.

13.2.5 *mard ō mard*

As Humbach and Jamaspasa (1971: I 31, fn. a) and Hintze (2007a: 64) point out, *ān ī mard ō mard be abespārdār* corresponds to the Av. hapax legomenon *naēnaēstārō*.[54] Hintze (2007a: 64) also comments that the 'translators recognized neither a negation nor a form from the root *nid* "to blame, revile"'. As *naēnaēstārō* is a hapax legomenon, it is nearly impossible to investigate the relationship between the original and its translation. It is unlikely that the exegetes would have equated *naēnaēstārō* with *abespārdār* based on perceived phonetic similarity. They could have interpreted *naēnaēstārō* as a derivation from the stem *nar-* 'man', therefore translating it as *mard ō mard*. These explanations, however, are unsatisfactory and do not contribute to a better understanding of the passage's *Zand*.

The expression *mard ō mard* also occurs in MHD 2.2 (Macuch 1993: 40) and in Dk 6E.15 (Shaked 1979: 191). In those passages *mard ō mard* is motivated by the respective context and does not relate to PY 35.1, thus offering no help with the interpretation of the expression here.

Despite the *Zand*'s seemingly obscure translation of *naēnaēstārō* 'not revilers', the phrase *ān ī mard ō mard be abespārdār* 'that which a man consigns to a man' seems to be grounded in a well established, priestly tradition which associated *naēnaēstārō* with entrusting something to another man. The issue is taken up in *Pursišnīhā* 18:

---

[54] On *naēnaēstārō* 'not revilers', see Hintze (2007a: 63–6) with references.

Pur 18[55] *mard-ēw hāwišt-ēw ast ān hāwišt kirbag ī pad dād rāh ī-š az weh-dēnān abar šawēd ān-iz ī hāwištān ōy hāwišt kunēd ān hērbed ī naxwistīn ān kirbagīhā abar šawēd ayāb nē*

ān kirbag ī pad dād rāh ī ōy hāwištān rasēd ō hērbed nē rasēd ān ī pad hammōzišn hāwišt ōh any hāwišt hammōxtan hērbed-iz ō bawēd ∵ aēibiiō yō i̯t aϑa vərəziiąn yaϑā i̯t astī[56] *∵ awēšān ī ān ī hērbed ēdōn čiyōn ān ī warzēnd kū ān ī hāwišt kunēd ā-š abar ōh šawēd ān ī hāwišt az kasān abar šawēd ā-š abar nē šawēd*[57] *∵ ahurā zī at̰ vū mazdā̊ yasnəmca vahməmca vahištəm*[58] *∵ ān ī ohrmazd yazišn niyāyišn az ān ī ašmāh pahlom*[59]

A man has a disciple. That disciple receives the (merits) of the justly (performed) good deeds from the adherents of the good religion. Does that first teacher receive the (merits) of the good deeds performed by the disciples of that disciple, or not?

The teacher does not receive the (merits) of the justly (performed) good deeds that his disciples receive. The teacher receives the (merits) of teaching a disciple to teach other disciples. Those who shall practise it in the way that it really is. Those who thus have that teacher, they practise it like that, that is, that which the disciple practises, he [the teacher] receives it in the usual manner, (and) that which the disciple receives from others, that he [the teacher] does not receive. For the worship and praise of the Wise Lord alone is best for you. Of that which is yours the worship and praise of *Ohrmazd* is best.

Humbach and Jamaspasa (1971: 31) translate *mard-ēw hāwišt-ēw ast* as 'Question: (There is) a man who is a disciple, ...'. In my view, this translation neglects two important points. Firstly, the literal meaning of the construction with *ast* is 'there is a disciple to a man', thus my translation as 'A man has a disciple'. Secondly, Humbach and Jamaspasa's translation ignores the essence of the question, which is about the relationship between a teacher and a disciple with regards to the merits that they accrue. Thus, the question requires two persons. And so the *hērbed ī naxwistīn* 'the first teacher', mentioned at the end of the question, logically refers to the first man who has a disciple. If this interpretation is accepted, I would like to suggest that *mard-ēw hāwišt-ēw ast* 'A man has a disciple' refers to the two men expressed in *mard ō mard*, and that Pur 18 discusses the details of entrusting something to another man: *ān ī mard ō mard be abespārdār*.

At some point the question seems to have emerged as to how far the merits of teaching and good deeds transfer. Would the first teacher receive the merits of the good deeds performed by his disciples' followers? This is the

---

[55] Text transliterated after TD2, reproduced in Humbach and Jamaspasa (1971: II 12–13). Translation is mine.
[56] This Av. quotation is from Y 35.5c.
[57] This line corresponds to PY 35.5c.
[58] This quotation is from Y 35.6a and the first two words of line b.
[59] This section corresponds to PY 35.6a.

question that Pur 18 seeks to elucidate. No doubt, authoritative answers to these questions are of the utmost importance to the priests, as the outcome directly affects their profession. The pronounced judgement is substantiated through references to the YH, which features in Pur 18 through quotations, particularly (P)Y 35.6, highlighting the authority and relevance ascribed to the *Zand* for discussions of priestly function. The comment, *kirbag pad dād rāh*, which follows *ān ī mard ō mard be abespārdār*, explicitly links PY 35.1c to Pur 18, where *kirbag ī pad dād rāh* is mentioned in the question. Pur 18 also quotes from (P)Y 35.5 and 6. According to Pur 18 the merits of the laity's justly (*pad dād rāh*) performed good deeds are accrued by the disciples, but do not transfer to the teacher. By contrast, the merits of teaching seem to transfer across. The *Dēnkard*'s exegesis of PY 35 in *Bag Nask* reinforces this interpretation:

> Dk 9.57.1[60] *hād hamāgīh ī warzīdan ān-iz ī warzīhēd kirbag xwēšēnīd bawēd ahlaw kē ō ahlawān čāšēd nēkīh*
>
> That is, the totality of the merits of performing (good thoughts, good words and good deeds), also of those which will be performed, are appropriated by the righteous one who teaches goodness to the righteous ones.

The collocation *warzīdan ān-iz ī warzīhēd* in the above passage is a direct reference to PY 35.1b (*ān ī warzīd tā nūn ud ān-iz ī warzīhēd az nūn frāz*), while the verb *xwēšēnīd* alludes to *kū ō xwēš kunom* in PY 35.1c. These cross-references underline once more the authoritative character of the *Zand* for the wider Pahlavi literature. If we accept that here *nēkīh* refers to *dēn*, then the above passage discusses the merits of teaching and disseminating the good religion. Thus, according to Dk 9.57 the merits of performing virtuous deeds are accrued by those who teach the religion to others. To that end, that which a man consigns to another man in PY 35.1c (*ān ī mard ō mard be abespārdār*) is most likely the religion, which is spread by way of teaching.

These passages offer a unique and rare insight into the layered scholastic approach of the priests. In this particular case, we can discern three levels of scriptural exegesis. The *Zand* construes the Av. passage in a certain light. The *Dēnkard* offers a rather abstract interpretation of the *Zand*. And finally, the *Pursišnīhā* discusses the matter in the form of explicitly formulated religious questions, supporting its own views by going back to the *Avesta*.

To conclude, Pur 18 and Dk 9.57.1 indicate that stanzas of the YH were relevant to discussions of religious and priestly matters. The exegesis of the YH also reveals a rather sophisticated knowledge of the *Avesta* on part of the scholastics. By addressing the question of merits that transfer between

---

[60] Text after Dresden (1966: 612).

disciple and teacher, PY 35.5c takes up an issue that was first raised in PY 35.1c (*ān ī mard ō mard be abespārdār*). As we have seen, the relevance of PY 35.1 for the question also emerges from its exegesis in Dk 9.57.1. The exposition in Pur 18 adds further support to the notion that the logic and encoded meaning of the *Zand* were known to the priests, as *Pursišnīhā* quotes (P)Y 35.1 as well as (P)Y 35.5 and 6. The translators did thus not treat the stanzas of the *Avesta* as isolated units, but seem to have associated an internal logic with the various strophes. The expositions of Pur 18 further show the fine grained distinctions made in the classification of religious merit. To my knowledge, it has not been previously recognised that instructing disciples helps accumulate more merits than instructing laity in the performance of good deeds.

13.3 PY 35.2

13.3.1 *hād*

In the YH inflected forms of the root present stem *ah-/h-* of the root *ah* 'to be' are attested in the moods ind., opt. and subj. (see Hintze 2007a: 328). The 1pl.ind. *mahī* (Y 35.1), 3sg.ind. *astī* (Y 35.5) and 2sg.ind. *ahī* (Y 36.3) are translated as 1sg.ind. *hom*, 3sg.ind. *ast* and *ast*, respectively. While the 3pl.subj.act. *aŋhən* (Y 39.1) corresponds to the 3pl.ind.act. *hēnd*, the opt. mood is translated as subj.: 3sg.opt. *x́iiāṯ* (Y 35.2 and 40.4) → *hād* (3sg.), 1pl.opt. *x́iiāmā* (Y 40.4) → *hād* (3sg.), 2sg.opt. *x́iiā̊* (Y 41.3) → *hād* (3sg.). These discrepancies in number and mood between Avestan and MP confirm the observations made by Josephson (1997: 143–5).

13.4 PY 35.3

13.4.1 PY 35.3a

As already observed by Cantera (2006: 63–4), Cantera and Andrés Toledo (2008: 110–11) and Andrés-Toledo (2009: 308–12), Y 35.3a and its *Zand* occur also in Y 71.25 and in Wd 11.6. The significant differences between the various MSS are pointed out by the authors and can be summarised as follows:

PY 35.3a in Pt4 *ān ī gōspandān dahišn āb ud ān ī awēšān kunišn pahast awēšān mardōm ī andar ēn gēhān kār pahlom framāyišn*

PY 71.25a in Pt4 *ān ī gōspandān dahišn āb ud wāstar ud ān ī awēšān kunišn pahast*[61] *awēšān pahlom framāyišn*

PWd 11.6[62] *ān ī gōspandān dahišn [āb ud wāstar] ān ī awēšān kunišn [pahast <ī> awēšān mardōmān] pahlom framāyišn [kū-šān gōspandān rāy pahlom kār ēn kard bawēd pahast-ē bē kunēnd u-š āb ud wāstar dahēnd]*

In addition to the above authors' remarks, I would like to add that the comment *āb ud wāstar* from PY 71.25 and PWd 11.6 also occurs in the revised IrPY manuscript R413 as ⟨MY' W w'stl⟩. However, I hesitate to ascribe this additional comment in R413 to an influence from PY 71.25 or PWd 11.6, as in E7 we find ⟨W MY' W hwlšn'⟩ which does not seem to be attested in any of the other MSS. Rather, collocations with *wāstar* seem to be common in the context of the desired protection for the cattle. In two passages of the *Warštmānsr Nask*, for instance, we read:

Dk 9.35.3[63] ... *kū ān ī gōspandān az mardōmān niyāzag āb wāstar ud abē-bīmīh ān ī mardōmān az gōspandān ast xwarišn-iz ud wastarag*

... (This too) that that which the cattle needs of the people are water, fodder and fearlessness. That which people require of the cattle are food and clothes.

Dk 9.40.7[64] *abar dād ī ō ayārīh mardōm gōspand ō ayārīh ī gōspand rāmišn wāstar-iz*

About the creation of the cattle for the assistance of the people (and) peace (and) fodder for the assistance of the cattle.

A similar notion is also reflected in PY 10.20:

---

[61] ‮ڡصد ں سعں‬ Pt4.
[62] Text after Andrés-Toledo (2009: 311).
[63] Text after Dresden (1966: 653). This passage is in fact an exegesis of the YH.
[64] Text after Dresden (1966: 664).

PY 10.20a[65] *kū kē ō gōspandān niyāyišn az mardōm*[66] *kū āb ud wāstar dahēnd*[67] *ā-š az gōspandān niyāyišn šīr ud waččag*[68] *dahēnd mardōm rāy*[69]

He who praises the cattle, (that is), of those people who give water and fodder, the cattle praises him, (that is), they give milk and cubs for the people.

As Josephson (1997: 106, fn. 80) rightly points out, a similar passage is also attested in PRDd 17d4. The evidence suggests that fodder often occurs in the context of what is to be given to the cattle. Therefore, the additions in R413 and E7 may just be due to the scribes' momentary confusion with other well-known passages, particularly so, as in the first case *wāstar* is struck out and in the second case it is replaced by *xwarišn*.

Further to the above observations, in Bd 4 we find another paraphrase of PY 35.3a illustrating the flexibility with which scribes or composers quote passages from the *Zand*:

Bd 4.21[70] *u-š guft gāw kū ān ī gōspandān dahišn awēšān kunišn kār pahlom framāyišn*

Here, the comments after *dahišn* and *kunišn* are missing, suggesting that the texts could be modified to a certain degree when the context required it.

---

[65] Text after Pt4. For an alternative text and translation, and a discussion of this passage, see Josephson (1997: 105ff.).
[66] *az mardōm* written in the margins, most likely by a second hand.
[67] Superscr., sec.m.
[68] Pt4 has ١٩٩١. Both Josephson (1997: 5) and Cantera (1998: 501) read *wazag* with the meaning 'calves'.
[69] *dahēnd mardōm rāy* superscr.
[70] Text after Pakzad (2005: 62).

13.5 PY 35.4

PY 35.4 constitutes the second paragraph of *Zand ī Gōmēz Kardan* (Dhabhar 1927, 1963), while a paraphrase also occurs in Wr 8.2 (Dhabhar 1949: 306) and in PY 39.4b.

This stanza is mentioned in Wd 10.8 and N 17.2 as one of the strophes that are recited thrice. As Kotwal and Kreyenbroek (1995: 99, fn. 329) point out, the stanzas correspond in both texts. N 18.3 states that negligence to recite one of these and a number of other stanzas, including the YH as a whole, invalidates the worship.

13.6 PY 35.5

13.6.1 PY 35.5a

FiŌ 222 contains a verbatim quote of Y 35.5a and its *Zand*:

FiŌ 222[71] yaϑā āṱ utā nā vā nāiri vā vaēdā haiϑīm *ēdōn ān <ī> har dō nar ud nāirīg <āgāh> bawēnd āškārag*

Just as now a man or a woman knows what is real. In this way, it is evident what both a male (being) and a woman know.

Klingenschmitt (1968: 80) offers some comments on Reichelt's erroneous reading of ⟨YḤWWN-d⟩ as *dānēnd*. It is worth mentioning that Jamaspji and Haug (1867: 12) also read '*dânand*'.

13.6.2 PY 35.5c

PY 35.5c is quoted in Pur 18 (Humbach and Jamaspasa 1971: I 30–1).[72] Although the variations between the two texts are not significant, there are differences between Pt4 and the quotation in TD2 (Pur 18):[73]

Pt4 *awēšān-iz ī any hērbed ēdōn ast čiyōn ān warzēnd kū ān ī hāwišt kunēd ā-š abar ōh šawēd ud ān ī hāwišt az kasān abar šawēd ā-š abar nē šawēd*

TD2 *awēšān ī ān ī hērbed ēdōn čiyōn ān ī warzēnd kū ān ī hāwišt kunēd ā-š abar ōh šawēd ān ī hāwišt az kasān abar šawēd ā-š abar nē šawēd*

---

[71] See Jamaspji and Haug (1867: 12) and Klingenschmitt (1968: 80).
[72] For my discussion of Pur 18, see Section 13.2.5.
[73] See my apparatus, Section 6.6, for other variants in the PY.

13.7 PY 35.6

13.7.1 Text division

At times the boundaries of the divided text do not fully correspond between the original and its translation. PY 35.6a–b is one such case:[74]

Y 35.6 (a) *ahurahiiā zī at̰ və̄ mazdā̊ yasnəmcā*
(b) *vahməmcā vahištəm amə̄hmaidī gə̄ušcā vāstrəm*

PY 35.6 (a) *ān ī ohrmazd yazišn ud niyāyišn ēdōn az ān ī ašmā pahlom menom*
(b) *ud ān-iz ī gōspandān kār kū az kār ī gētīy pahrēz ī gōspandān pahlom menom*

Here, PY 35.6a also includes the translation of the first three words of Y 35.6b: *vahməmcā vahištəm amə̄hmaidī*. As a result, PY 35.6b only translates *gə̄ušcā vāstrəm*, the two final words of Y 35.6b. This asymmetric correspondence between source and original, however, is not an isolated case. Other examples include PY 35.1b–c (Section 13.2) and 36.1b–c (Section 20.1). We can explain the above asymmetry in a number of ways. For instance, by correlating *ān ī ohrmazd* to *ahurahiiā … mazdā̊* and viewing *yazišn ud niyāyišn* as a so-called gloss. Thus, Avestan *ahurahiiā zī at̰ və̄ mazdā̊ yasnəmcā* would yield **ān ī ohrmazd** *yazišn ud niyāyišn* **ēdōn az ān ī ašmā pahlom menom** in the Zand. We would then need to assume that *yasnəmcā* was left untranslated, which is also problematic and not a better solution to the enigma of this stanza.

13.7.2 PY 35.6a

Beside PY 35.5c, Pur 18 also quotes PY 35.6a (Humbach and Jamaspasa 1971: I 30–1).[75] The differences between the readings of the passage in Pt4 and TD2 are as follows:[76]

Pt4 *ān ī ohrmazd yazišn ud niyāyišn ēdōn az ān ī ašmā pahlom menom*
TD2 *ān ī ohrmazd yazišn niyāyišn az ān ī ašmāh pahlom*

13.7.3 *ašmā*

In PY 35.6a and c, the 2pl.pers.pron. *ašmā* 'you' corresponds to the 2pl.pers.pron. *və̄* 'for you'. It has been debated as to who the referent of the Av. enclitic pronoun *və̄* 'you' is.[77] According to Bartholomae (1904: 1312), it is *Ahura Mazdā*, while Narten (1986: 116) argues that it refers to the

---

[74] I have discussed the manuscript variants concerning this passage in Section 1.6.
[75] For my discussion of Pur 18, see Section 13.2.5.
[76] See my apparatus, Section 6.6, for other variants in the PY.
[77] See Narten (1986: 116–19) and Hintze (2007a: 87–90) with references.

listeners, who are presumably present at the ritual. By analysing the parallel structures of Y 35.6 and 7 and 35.3 and 4, Hintze (2007a: 88–9) adduces further evidence in support of Narten's view. The Pahlavi version introduces its own complications.

In Pur 18, Humbach and Jamaspasa (1971: 31) translate a paraphrase of PY 35.6a, *ān ī ohrmazd yazišn niyāyišn az ān ī ašmā pahlom*, as 'Thereby the excellent worship and praise of you, Ōhrmazd', understanding *Ohrmazd* as a vocative to which *ašmā* refers. The interlinear NP gloss in F2 on PY 35.6a supports this interpretation, suggesting that *ašmā* refers to *Ohrmazd*: ای هورمزد ایزشن و نیایش ایدون از آن شماکنم و بالاتر اندیشم 'O *Hourmazd*, I thus dedicate worship and praise to you and think higher.' The NP gloss to the Av. version makes the same assumption: وای هورمزد چه ایدون شما ایزشن و نیایش کنم از دیگر ایزدان 'And, O *Hourmazd*, thus I worship and praise you (more) than other deities.'[78] Nonetheless, the translation offered by Humbach and Jamaspasa (1971) is problematic, as in the above clause *Ohrmazd* cannot function as a vocative in the construction *ān ī ohrmazd*, making the assumption unlikely that in PY 35.6a the pronoun *ašmā* refers to the deity's name. To my mind, it is also unlikely that the translators intended a comparison here: praising and worshipping *Ohrmazd* is better than praising you. Moreover, in PY 35.6c, the pronoun must refer to *Ohrmazd*, as *ān ī ašmā* 'that which is yours' is defined as *dēn*.[79]

Perhaps the key to understanding the difficulty of this passage lies in the assumption of a disturbance in the Pahlavi translation. As pointed out in Section 13.7.1, in this passage the manuscripts bear witness to difficulties faced by the scribes in syncing the translation with the Av. original which could have also affected the word order of PY 35.6a. From PY 35.6c we know that *tat̰ at̰ vō* is translated *ēdōn ān ī ašmā*. Considering the word order of the Av. original, *ahurahiiā zī at̰ vō mazdā̊ yasnəmcā vahməmcā vahištəm aməhmaidī*, we would expect a translation such as *ān ī ohrmazd ēdōn az ān ī ašmā yazišn ud niyāyišn pahlom menom*. Admittedly, even this view does not offer a solution to the semantic problems of this passage. From PY 44.1, *niyāyišn ān kē ēdōn niyāyišn ī ašmāh dēn* 'praise is that which is thus your praise, (namely) the *dēn*' or 'praise is that which is thus the praise of your *dēn*', we can glean an approximation of the intended meaning of this line.[80]

---

[78] T6 has different, more complex, NP glosses, but semantically agrees with F2.
[79] On the *dēn* as that which belongs to *Ohrmazd*, see Section 5.7.2.
[80] I am currently working on an article on the problem of *ašmā* in the *Zand*.

13.8 PY 35.7

13.8.1 *wālunīh*

In PY 35.7a, *wālunīh* translates Av. *vərəzə̄nē* 'community', while *wālun* occurs in a comment at the end of the line. In his dictionary, MacKenzie (1990: 86, 192) only lists ⟨w'ln'⟩, reading it ⟨w'ln'⟩ *wālan* 'settlement, community'. He has no entry for the abstract noun constructed with the *-īh* suffix. By contrast, Dhabhar (1949: 3, 168) reads '*vālūn*', '*vālūnīh*' and '*vālūnīk*', while agreeing with MacKenzie on the meaning of the word.[81]

The spelling ⟨w'ln'⟩ (Pt4 Mf4 R413 E7) is ambiguous, as it can be transliterated both as ⟨w'lwn⟩ and ⟨w'ln'⟩. However, K5 J2 M1 attest ⟨w'ln'⟩ supporting ⟨w'lwn'⟩, while F2 and T6 have ⟨w'lwnyh⟩. Most importantly, the manuscripts unanimously spell the abstract noun as ⟨w'lwnyh⟩ (Pt4 Mf4 F2 R413 T6 E7, K5 J2 M1), rather than ⟨w'lnyh⟩, suggesting *wālunīh* in agreement with Dhabhar's reading.[82] The word occurs once more in PY 40.4a, this time translating the acc.pl. *vərəzə̄nā* 'community'. Here, Pt4 Mf4 E7, K5 J2 M1 read ⟨w'lwn'⟩, R413 being the only MS to attest ⟨w'ln'⟩. Again, F2 and T6 prefer ⟨w'lwnyh⟩. In light of this evidence, I have transliterated this word as ⟨w'lwn'⟩ and ⟨w'lwn⟩ rather than ⟨w'ln'⟩, preferring a transcription as *wālun* as opposed to *wālan*.

---

[81] This word is not listed by Nyberg (1974) or Malandra and Ichaporia (2010). I was unable to find it in any other glossaries.

[82] R413 has ⟨w'lwn YHSNN-yt⟩, which is effectively a correction to ⟨w'lwnyh⟩.

13.9 PY 35.8

The authority attributed to the (P)YH in debates of religious questions comes to light in another passage from the *Pursišnīhā*, where PY 35.8 and 9 are quoted:

Pur 19[83] [333v] *ēn* ⁺*sraw*[84] *ēd kē pēš abēr pad hamāg yazišn naxwist xšnaoθra gōwēnd ud pas ašemwohū ud ān* ⁺*sraw ī wēš az ašemwohū* [334r] *abēr*[85] *gōwēnd kū xšnaoθra pad čē bōzišn ī az wehdēn bē gōwēnd*

ōy[86] *kē pēš abēr ī xšnaoθra gōwēnd az ēn abestāg bē gōwēnd* ∴ *imā āṯ uxδā vacā ahura mazdā ašəm maniiā vahiiā frāuuaocāmā*[87] ∴ *ēn ēdōn saxwan gōwišnīh ī ohrmazd dēn ī ohrmazd pad ahlāyīh menīdārīh ī weh frāz gōwom pad frārōn menišnīh* ∴ *θβąm aṯ aēšąm paitiiāstārəmcā fradaxštārəmcā dadəmaide*[88] ∴ *tō ēg ī az awēšān* ⁺*padīrišn ēstišnīh*[89] *frāz dahišnīh*[90] *dahom kū az amahraspandān tis ī tō wēš padīrom ud pad dahišn*[91] *wēš bē kunom ka ēdōn pas az ohrmazd wahman rāy naxwist pas az xšnaoθra ud ahlāyīh ast ašawahišt stāyēd nē wahman ī fradom ī ōh ohrmazd nazdīktom ēd rāy čē ēn-iz gōwēd ham ēn gyāg* ∴ *ašā* [334v] *ašā aṯcā hacā vaŋhōušcā manaŋhō vaŋhōušcā xšaθrāṯ*[92] ∴ *az ahlāyīh abāgīh az ašawahišt hammis ān-iz ī weh menišn ī wahman ān-iz ī weh xwadāyīh šahrewar ud pad stōd ēsnān pahlom yazišn ī ohrmazd ud didīgar kardag pahrēzišn ud* ⁺*šnāyēnīdārīh*[93] *ī ātaxš ud sidīgar kardag*[94] *ēdōn yazišn ī ohrmazd kē-š gōspand ahlāyīh-iz dād pad abdom kardag stāyišn srāyišn ud niyāyišn ō*[95] *ohrmazd ud pas ašawahišt gōwēd*

This word which they recite immediately before the beginning of all rituals is (called) *xšnaoθra*, followed by the *ašəm vohū*. And that word which they recite many (times) before the *ašəm vohū*, that is, the *xšnaoθra*, for which salvation from the good religion do they recite it?

Those who recite the *xšnaoθra* at the beginning, recite it based on this *Avesta*: These words now, O Wise Lord, we proclaim as solemn utterances, with very good concentration on Truth.[96] I will proclaim these words of *Ohrmazd*, spoken in this manner, (namely) the religion of *Ohrmazd*, by good consideration of righteousness, (namely) by good thought(s). We designate you only as their listener and teacher. And to you, then, I dedicate from them the permanence of acceptance and widespread indication, that is, I accept your

---

[83] Text transliterated after TD2, reproduced in Humbach and Jamaspasa (1971: II 13–15). Translation is mine. For an alternative translation, see Humbach and Jamaspasa (1971: 32–3).
[84] تلمر TD2.
[85] ابر ابیر TD2.
[86] Here, we would expect *awēšān*, as the verb is in plural.
[87] This quotation corresponds to Y 35.8a, while the following line is from the passage's *Zand*.
[88] Here, *Pursišnīhā* quotes from Y 35.8b and its *Zand*.
[89] اوپرڤیتشلو TD2. I have emended the word to reflect the text of PY 35.8b.
[90] PY 35.8b has *daxšagīh* here.
[91] PY 35.8b has *daxšag* here.
[92] This line quotes Y 35.9a followed by its *Zand*.
[93] سناسیهرس TD2. Most likely a mistake for *šnāyēnīdārīh*. See *pad pahrēz ud šnāyēnīdārīh* in PY 36.1a, to which this passage alludes.
[94] This is a reference to Y 37.
[95] TD2 has ١۲.
[96] The translations of the Av. quotations are by Hintze (2007a).

affairs more (readily) from the *Amahraspandān* and I also practise (your affairs) more by indication. When they thus praise *Ašwahišt* (and) not *Wahman*, (who) is the first after *Ohrmazd* and after *xšnaoϑra* and righteousness (and) who in this way is closer to *Ohrmazd*, the reason for this too is explained in the same place: On account of truth, of good thought and of good rule. With the assistance of righteousness, together with *Ašwahišt*, also that of good thought which is *Wahman*, (and) also that of good rule, (namely) *Xšahrewar*. And it is said that in the *Stōd Yasn* first (takes place) the worship of *Ohrmazd*, and in the second section care and propitiation of the fire, and (in) the third section thus the worship of *Ohrmazd* who created the cattle and righteousness, and in the last section praise, recitation and prayers for *Ohrmazd* and then *Ašwahišt*.

The answer in Pur 19 seems to ignore the question which is about the salvation that may result out of *xšnaoϑra*. Instead, the exposition links *xšnaoϑra* to PY 35.8 and its *Zand*. It suggests that the *xšnaoϑra* is important, as the words of the ritual are those of *Ohrmazd* (PY 35.8a), which are at the same time dedicated to the deity (PY 35.8b). Although it is not part of the question, the answer also explains the reason why *Ašwahišt* receives a preferential treatment compared to *Wahman*. The explanation is based on PY 35.9 where *Ašwahišt* is mentioned before *Wahman*. It is noteworthy that the text refers to the YH as *Stōd Yasn*.[97]

---

[97] On the *Stōd Yasn*, see Hintze (2009a: 30ff.).

14. *PY 36*

14.1 PY 36.1

14.1.1 *pad warzišn*

In PY 36.1a, *pad warzišn* translates *vərəzə̄nā*, an instr.sg. of *vərəzə̄na-* ntr. 'community'. The conventional explanation for this curious translation would be that here the exegetes interpreted *vərəzə̄nā* as a derivation from the verbal root *vərəz* 'to practise'. However, *pad warzišn* seems to be motivated by the exegetes' interpretation of (P)Y 36.

Derivations from both *vərəzə̄na-* and *vərəz* occur a number of times in the YH.[1] Two more forms derived from *vərəzə̄na-* are attested in (P)Y 35.7 and 40.4, where loc.sg. *vərəzə̄nē* and acc.pl. *vərəzə̄nā* are both correctly rendered as *wālunīh* and *wālun*, respectively.[2] All forms derived from the verbal root *vərəz* are correctly rendered with *warzīdan* 'practise'.

Although PY 36.1a could be an exception to the otherwise correct translations of *vərəzə̄na-*, here *pad warzišn* is most likely an elliptic reference to *humatān hūxtān huwarštān*. As I discuss in Section 5.1.2, the commitment to the triad is of paramount importance in the (P)YH. Moreover, I hope to have shown that PY 36.5 refers to the three steps that are taken by the soul to reach the star, moon and sun stations (see Section 5.2.1). As we know, the three steps and stations correspond to *humatān hūxtān huwarštān*. Considering that the triad always occurs with the verb *warzīdan* (see Section 13.2.1), and that in PY 36.5 the fire is approached (*be rasom*) with (*pad*) the triad, I would like to suggest that PY 36.1a anticipates the end of this chapter in its first stanza by an encoded reference to the practice (*warzišn*) of *humatān hūxtān huwarštān*.

---

[1] For the attestations, see Hintze (2007a: 360 and 361).
[2] On *wālun*, see Section 13.8.1.

14.2 PY 36.2

14.2.1 kār

In PY 36.2c, *kār* 'affair' translates *yā̊ŋhąm*, a gen.pl. of *yāh-* ntr. 'supplication'.[3] In her commentary on *yāh-*, Narten (1986: 149–55) dismisses Bartholomae's (1904: 1291) translation as 'Krise, Entscheidung, Wendepunkt', and in light of the eschatological expectation as 'Schlußwerk', in favour of 'request' ('Bitte'). She argues that Bartholomae's suggestion may have been motivated by the term's Pahlavi translation, *kār*, which she considers weak and an indication of the difficulties the Pahlavi commentators must have faced translating *yāh-*: '[...], deren Blässe aber wohl ein Zeichen dafür ist, daß die Bedeutungsbestimmung des Wortes schon den Pahlavi-Theologen Schwierigkeiten bereitete, [...]' (Narten 1986: 150). Her judgement must have derived from the sense of urgency ('Dringlichkeit') that she recognises in Y 36.2 (Narten 1986: 151), but does not view as reflected in *kār*.

Although I do not dispute Narten's philological analysis of *yāh-* in the context of the YH,[4] I would like to point out that the Pahlavi exegetes must have recognised the same sense of urgency in this stanza but interpreted it in light of their own religious world view.

The tendency of the Pahlavi exegetes to interpret the *Avesta* in an eschatological context has long been recognised (see Section 4.1.3). PY 36.2 is an example of such interpretation, achieved by means of a comment at the end of the passage: *pad ān ī meh kār be rasēd pad passāxt ī pad tan ī pasēn* 'Arrive at the great event, at the trial of the final body.' The eschatological meaning is achieved through the fixed expression *tan ī pasēn* which is common in the PY (Josephson 2003: 31). The expectation of this very important Zoroastrian event, *tan ī pasēn*, is on its own sufficient to reflect any sense of urgency. The fire of *Ohrmazd* is requested to approach and merge with the ritual fire in preparation for the *frašgird* 'the restoration'. I also argue that through its close association with *frazām* in expressions such as *frazām ī kār* 'the end of the affair', MP *kār* in itself is semantically associated with eschatology.[5] An example from *Ayādgār ī Wuzurg-Mihr* 42 should illustrate this link:

---

[3] For a discussion of *yā̊ŋhąm*, see Hintze (2007a: 128–31).
[4] Hintze (2007a: 130) agrees with Narten on a non-eschatological interpretation of Y 36.
[5] I have discussed the link between *frazānagīh* 'wisdom' and *frazām ī kār* 'the end of the affair(s)' in my review of Cantera (2004). The relevant passages that I discuss suggest that there is a link between *frazām ī kār* and eschatology. These are: *Sīrōzag* 1.24, *Ohrmazd Yašt* 1.7. Among other texts, *Mēnōy ī xrad* 12.7–10, contains a very similar story (Anklesaria 1913: 54–5).

AW 42[6] *ēn-iz paydāg kū gannāg mēnōy pad dāmān ī ohrmazd tis-ē-iz ēn garāntar kard ka-š kirbag mizd ud wināh pādifrāh pad menišn ī mardōmān pad frazām kār be nihuft*

This is revealed too: *Gannāg Mēnōy* inflicted something even graver (than) this onto the creation of *Ohrmazd*. He concealed from the thought of people the reward of the good deed and the punishment for the sin at the end of the affairs.

The expression *frazām ī kār* seems to refer to the end of the material world, to *frašgird*. Thus, the exegetes' choice of *kār* to refer to eschatological events is justified and reflects their close reading of the *Avesta*. That their interpretation differs from that of a modern non-Zoroastrian philologist need not signal a failure of comprehension on their part.

A similar notion also emerges from PY 58.7:

(P)Y 58.7a[7] *nəmasə tōi ātarə ahurahē mazdå̄ mazištāi yā̊ŋhąm paitī.jamiiå̄*
Homage to you, O fire of *Ahura Mazdā*! May you come close for the greatest of the appeals.

niyāyišn ō tō ātaxš ī ohrmazd ī kē pad ān ī mahist kār bē rasē pad passāxt ī tan ī pasēn

Praised be you, O fire of *Ohrmazd*, who may arrive at that greatest event, at the trial of the final body.

Both in PY 36.2 and PY 58.7 *kār* is described by the adjectives *meh* 'great' and *mahist* 'greatest', emphasising the importance of the event. Further support for the stability of such interpretation is adduced by (P)Y 40.2, which resembles Y 36.2 in that both stanzas begin with a direct address and request to the fire during the ritual:

Y 36.2 *uruuāzištō huuō nå̄*
You there, the most joyful one,

Y 40.2 *ahiiā huuō nə̄ dāidī*
You there, give us from this (prize)

While Kotwal and Boyd (1991), Narten (1986) and Hintze (2007a) point out that this stanza addresses *Ahura Mazdā*, it should be noted that this is achieved by means of addressing the ritual fire.[8] The resemblance of both stanzas was recognised by the exegetes as well, who close PY 40.2 with a similar comment: *tā tan ī pasēn* 'until the final body'. Both passages represent crucial moments in the ritual: firstly, the presence of the fire in the ritual, which marks its beginning; secondly, the request for the prize, which is the

---

[6] Text after Jamasp-Asana (1897: 90), translation is mine.
[7] Text after Pt4.
[8] The request for a prize directed to the fire highlights the agency accorded to the fire, and underscores its role as an intermediary between the worshippers and *Ahura Mazdā*. A similar interpretation of the fire in the context of the YH is offered by Kellens (2000: 108–9).

sole purpose of the ritual itself. By ending both passages with a reference to *tan ī pasēn* the commentators set the ritual in an eschatological context – perhaps as an enactment of the expected future body and the *frašgird*.

Quoting Dastur Kotwal, Hintze (2007a: 140) reminds us that the modern priestly interpretation supports this notion:

> Being an epiphany of the light of Ahura Mazda and the very principle of energy that animates the entire creation, including the bodies of humans and animals, trees and plants, lightning and royal lineage, this fire is metaphysically linked to the fire that will purify all impurities at the end-time of the resurrection, when all will be 'made wonderful' (*frashegird*). (Kotwal and Boyd 1991: 13–14)

14.3 PY 36.3

14.3.1 The fire of the exegetes

Narten (1986: 26, 156) argues that the fire is consecrated between Y 36.2 and 3, which she views as the high point of the ritual:

> Feuerkonsekration und Transsubstantiation sind Höhepunkt der Ritualhandlung und Voraussetzung für die von Kap. 37 an beginnenden Verehrungsgebete und Bitten, die den Hauptteil des YH ausmachen. (Narten 1986: 156)

She interprets the first two clauses of Y 36.3, *ātarš vōi ... ahī, mainiiuš vōi ... ahī*, as a direct address to a supposedly heavenly fire of *Ahura Mazdā* which has now merged with the ritual fire: *ātarš. vōi. mazdå. ahurahiiā. ahī.* 'You are indeed the fire of *Ahura Mazdā* '. Most scholars seem to follow this interpretation.[9] The *Zand* of Y 36.2–3 offers a slightly different view.

Two problems complicate the analysis of these two stanzas. The first involves the ambiguous verbal forms in PY 36.2. Twice repeated, *be rasēd* translates the 2sg.opt.act. *paitī.jamiiå* 'may you come close'. MP *rasēd* can denote a 3sg.ind.pres.act. or a 2pl.ipt. of *rasīdan* 'to arrive'. If we take *be rasēd* as a 3sg., in agreement with its Skt. translation, then the stanza describes the fire's arrival without extending an invitation to the fire to join the ritual.[10] However, irrespective of our reading of this verbal form, the fire seems to approach or be present in the ritual space. Secondly, in contrast to the Av. version, the first two lines of PY 36.3 do not address the fire. PY 36.3a describes it by way of a verbal form in 3sg., *ātaxš pad ān ī ohrmazd āgāh ast* 'The fire is knowledgeable in that, which belongs to *Ohrmazd* ', where it is also stated that the fire receives its knowledge of the *dēn*, when it is enthroned as a *Wahrām* fire, leaving it open whether two essentially different fires have merged: *ān-iš ast ka-š pad wahrāmīh be nišānēnd* 'It has that (knowledge) when they establish it as a *Wahrām* fire'. In PY 36.3b and c the fire is spoken of in second person and as *Ohrmazd*'s fire, which is then approached by the sacrificers in PY 36.3c: *ō ātaxš ī ohrmazd ī tō ... be rasom* 'I arrive before the fire of *Ohrmazd*, that is you.'

Thus, PY 36.3a–b diverge from the Av. version by describing the fire's properties rather than addressing it as a heavenly fire as argued by Narten. And

---

[9] Hintze (2007a: 132–3) agrees with Narten. The translations of this stanza by Humbach (1991: 145), Kellens and Pirart (1988: 135) and West (2010: 173) indicate a similar understanding.

[10] In Y 36.2a, the Skt. translation has a 3sg. as well: *upari prāpnoti* 'he attains, arrives' (*pra + āp*). But in Y 36.2c, we find an unusual form in *upari prāptari*, perhaps a loc. of an agent noun in *prāptr̥-*.

the *Zand* attributes greater agency to the fire in the ritual. In PY 36.3a the fire is depicted as knowledgeable in the *dēn* of *Ohrmazd*. Therefore, its presence is essential in a ritual, in which the sacrificers request of the fire this very *dēn* as the prize (see Section 5.1.2).

14.4 PY 36.5

14.4.1 *abāmēne*

The attestation of *išūidiiāmahī*, a 1pl.ind.act. from the denominative present stem *išūidiia-* 'to bring strengthening', is confined to the YH where it occurs in 36.5, 38.4 and 39.4.[11] In all three instances it is translated by forms derived from the denominative verb *abāmēnīdan* 'to owe, be indebted'.[12] In PY 36.5a and 39.4c (≈PY 13.5c) we find *abāmēnē*, while in PY 38.4 the subj. form *abāmēnād* is used. According to Narten (1986: 160), the denom. stem *išūidiia-* derives from the noun *išud-* 'strengthening' which is attested in Y 31.14, 34.15 and 65.9. In these stanzas *išud-* is rendered as *abām* 'loan, debt'. It emerges from the evidence that derivatives of *abām* regularly translate *išud-* and *išūidiia-*. The reasons for this rendering, however, are obscure.

It is unlikely that *u-m abāmēne* constitutes a comment or gloss to *niyāyišnēne*, in which case we could argue that *išūidiiāmahī* was left untranslated. The fact that *išud-* is consistently rendered as *abām*, suggests that forms of *abāmēnīdan* correspond to *išūidiiāmahī*.

As already observed by Narten (1986: 159), in the YH *išūidiiāmahī* always occurs in a formulaic manner with *nəmaxiiāmahī* 'we pay homage', which shares its roots with *nəmah-* 'homage, reverence'. It has variously been pointed out that *nəmah-* has a homonym with the meaning 'loan', attested in Wd 4.1.[13] Considering the formulaic proximity between *nəmaxiiāmahī* and *išūidiiāmahī* in the YH, it might be tempting to propose that the exegetes connected *nəmaxiiāmahī* with *nəmah-* 'loan', extending its meaning to *išūidiiāmahī*. This, however, raises the question as to why *nəmaxiiāmahī* was not translated accordingly?

In fact, following Bartholomae (1917: 9–10), Cantera (1998: 185, 500) prefers *nihišnōmand* and *nihišn* for Av. '*nəmaŋhənte*' and '*nəmō*' in (P)Wd 4.1. In Cantera's view, the correct translation for *nəmah-* 'loan' is *nihišn*, whose spelling was later corrupted due to confusion with *niyāyišn* in translations of *nəmah-* 'homage'. In the PYH similar uncertainties are evident in the spelling of words containing *niyāyišn-*. These are *niyāyišnōmand/īh* in PY 36.2b, *niyāyišnēne* in PY 36.5a and 39.4c and *niyāyišnēnād* in PY 38.4c. With the exception of PY 36.2b, the two other forms occur together with *abāmēnīdan*. In contrast, *niyāyišn*, which occurs in PY 35.6a and 41.1a, has no variant

---

[11] For a discussion of this verb, see Narten (1986: 159–63). For references to further discussions, see Hintze (2007a: 345).

[12] See also Dhabhar (1949: 10).

[13] See Geldner (1896–1904: 48), Bartholomae (1904: 1070), Josephson (1997: 106) and Cantera (1998: 500–1).

readings. Does this evidence suggest a confusion with another word, perhaps *nihišn*, or do the variants signal uncertainties in the spelling of the word?

According to Cantera (1998: 501), the reading ⟨n(y)hšn'⟩ *nihišn* is supported by one instance in L4, which he transliterates ⟨nhšs'wmnd⟩ (see Cantera 1998: 185).[14] However, considering the evidence of the PY and those of the other MSS, I would transliterate the word in L4 as ⟨nydšdšnmnd⟩, viewing it as a wrong spelling for ⟨nyd'dšnwmnd⟩. The attested variants in L4 as well as those in the manuscripts of the PY are in my view not necessarily meaningful alternatives, but erroneous spellings for what is a complex and confusing cluster in Pahlavi script: ⟨-yd'dš-⟩. Although the above-mentioned *niyāyišn* in PY 35.6a and 41.1a seems to suggest otherwise, the MSS highlight that the writing of this sequence of characters is prone to mistakes. But even if *nihišn* was the correct reading, it remains doubtful whether *nihišn* is a legal term connected with *nihādag* 'foundation' as suggested by Bartholomae (1917). No doubt, *nihādag* is a legal term, and it is derived from the same verb as *nihišn*, namely *nihādan*, *nih-* 'to put, place, establish'. However, while *nihādag* is well attested in the MHD, *nihišn* is not.[15] It occurs a number of times in the PRDd, but not within a legal context. Therefore, Williams (1990: I 322) rightly considers *nihišn* a necessitative participle, while MacKenzie (1990) has no entry for the word at all. To my knowledge the word is not attested in the PY. In addition to the above, NP glosses in F2 and T6 show that the scribes or the exegetes connected *nəmaxiiāmahi* and *niyāyišnēnē* with نیایش. This same observation extends to the NP glosses in the PWd manuscripts where both the Av. and MP words are variously glossed نیایش: F10, T44, B1, G34 and G10.[16] The only deviation occurs in M3 where in a marginal note on (P)Wd 4.1 we read مرد نازند 'a destitute man'. Therefore, *nihišn* as a translation for *nəmah-* 'loan', suggested by Bartholomae (1917) and taken up by Cantera (1998), is a problematic proposition and not further substantiated by evidence.

The rather obscure NP commentaries in the above MSS suggest that the traditional exegesis saw a connection between *niyāyišn* and *abām*, which is also evident in the extended MP commentary to Wd 4.1. A close reading of Wd 4.1 and an investigation of *nəmah-* 'loan' are required, before the connection between *nəmaxiiāmahi*, *išuidiiāmahī* and *abāmēnīdan* can be fully examined.

---

[14] In his apparatus, Cantera also mentions ⟨nhssn"wmnd⟩ in the MS IM.
[15] On *nihādag*, see Macuch (1993: 258). She has no entry for *nihišn* in her glossary.
[16] All MSS are available from ADA.

14.4.2 ⟨hlwst'⟩

As the apparatus of the present edition shows, the MSS attest both ⟨hlwst'⟩ and ⟨hlwsp'⟩ for *harwisp* 'all', whereby ⟨hlwst'⟩ seems to be the dominant form.[17] Observing the frequent occurrence of ⟨hlwst'⟩, Klingenschmitt (2000: 202) suggests that this form may be a remnant of a dialectal form which has survived in MP. He considers ⟨hlwst'⟩ a north-west form, continuing an older **haru̯a-* + **u̯isa-* as opposed to ⟨hlwsp'⟩ < **haru̯a-* + **u̯ispa-*.[18] While this might be the case, one cannot exclude the likelihood of ⟨hlwst'⟩ being a graphical variant of ⟨hlwsp'⟩. Writing quickly, the scribes could have connected the final ⟨-p⟩ in ܠܘܪܣܝ with the following ⟨-'⟩, resulting in ܠܘܪܣܝ.

---

[17] See PY 35.0b, 36.5b, 37.1c and 37.4c.

[18] He seems to view the final ⟨-t⟩ as an *unorganic* ('unorganisch') addition: *harwist* < **harwis* (Klingenschmitt 2000: 202, fn. 37).

14.5 PY 36.6

14.5.1 PY 36.6

The YAv. stanza Y 58.8 quotes Y 36.6, preserving the OAv. stanza's wording. The *Zand* of Y 58.8, however, differs from PY 36.6:

> **PY 58.8**[19] (a) *nēk ast ēd ī tō kirb u-tān kirbān niwēyišn dahom ohrmazd kū andar gēhān ōh gōwom kū kirb ēd ī tō nēktar*
> (b) *ēn ruwān ō ān ī rōšn bālistān bālist rasēnānd kū ān bē xwaršēd pāyag guft kū-mān ruwān bē ānōh rasād*

By merging lines (b) and (c) of the Av. version into one, PY 58.8 is divided into two parts as opposed to three in (P)Y 36.6. The stanzas feature also differences in the translation of the Av. text.

Y 36.6b is also repeated in PY 68.23 and Ny 1.5 (*Xwaršēd Niyāyišn*). While the Av. version is identical in all three stanzas, the *Zand* of PY 68.23 and Ny 1.5 differs from PY 36.6b:

> **Y 36.6b**[20] *imā raocå barəzištəm barəzimanąm*
> **PY 36.6b** *ēn ruwān ō ān rōšnīh ī bālist az ān ī pad čašm paydāg bālēnēnd*[21]
>
> **Y 68.23** *imā raocå barəzištəm barəzəmanąm*
> **PY 68.23** *ēn ruwān ō ān rōšnīh bālist bālēnānd kū-m ruwān be ō xwarxšēd pāyag rasād*
>
> **Ny 1.5**[22] *imā raocā barəzištəm barəzamanąm*
> **PNy 1.5** *ēn ruwān ō ān ī rōšnīh bālistān bālēnānd ∴ kū-m ruwān be ō xwaršēd pāyag rasād*

As the present edition's critical apparatus reveals (Section 7.6), the *Zand* of PY 36.6c was revised by the scribes to reflect what we find in PY 68.23 and PNy 1.5:

> **PY 36.6c** *ānōh kū xwaršēd guft kū-m ruwān ō xwaršēd pāyag rasād*

The comment *kū-m ruwān ō xwaršēd pāyag rasād* which occurs after PY 36.6b's quotation in PY 68.23 and PNy 1.5, is not attested in Mf4, K5 J2 M1. But it was added to Pt4 above the line by a second hand. It occurs with slightly different wording in F2 (in marg.) and T6. It is attested in fragmentary form in R413, while the complete comment is included as part of the text in E7.

---

[19] Text after Pt4, while suppressing minor spelling peculiarities.
[20] Text after Pt4.
[21] Here, the MSS of the IrPY read ⟨bʼlynynd⟩ *bālēnēnd* as opposed to the InPY, which attests ⟨bʼlynʼnd⟩ *bālēnānd*.
[22] Text after J1 (Jamaspasa and Nawabi 1976d: 21). For the text, see also Dhabhar (1927: 17).

14.5.2 *sraēštəm* 'nēk'

The OAv. superlative *sraēšta-* 'most beautiful' occurs three times in the YH: 36.6, 37.4 and 38.5.[23] In Y 36.6, *sraēštəm* agrees with the acc.sg.f. noun *kəhrpām* 'manifestation' and is translated *nēk* 'good, beautiful'. In PY 37.4 and Y 5.4, *sraēšta-* is translated *nēkīh* 'goodness' and *nēktar* 'better' in PY 38.5. Thus, although the superlative *nēktom* 'best, most beautiful' is well attested in the *Zand*,[24] in the PYH *sraēšta-* is not translated with this superlative.

The first clause is not problematic: *nēk ēd ī tō kirb* 'Beautiful is this your form'. However, the recourse to *nēk* as opposed to *nēktom* semantically distances the PTr. from its source. The commentators must have been aware of this issue and compensate for it by adding: *kirb ēd ī tō nēktar* '(of) form(s), this which is yours is more beautiful'. Contrary to the PTr., the commentary does not seem to emphasise a particular form of *Ohrmazd* (*ēd ī tō kirb*), but the fact that his form or essence is more beautiful. NP glosses in the MSS F2 and T6 reflect a similar view:

F2 *sraēštąm at̰ tōi kəhrpəm kəhrpąm āuuaēδaiia.mahī mazdā ahurā*

و نیک هست ایدون ذات و از ذات دیگر انزدان ازین دهم کنم خودای هورمزد ثارا

nēk ēd tō kirb u-t ān az kirbān niwēyēnišn dahem ohrmazd kū andar gēhān ōh gowem kū kirb ēd tō nēktar

و نیک این تو ذات و ذات تو نیک اوی از دگر ذات انزدان و زین دهم ای هورمزد و یعنی اندر دنیای اوی کویم و یعنی ذات این تو نیکتر ست

T6 *sraēštąm at̰ tōi kəhərpəm kəhərpąm āuuaēδiia.mahī mazdā ahurā*

و نیک تر است ایدون این ذات تو از ذات دیگر فرشتگان آن مبارک ذات و جوهر تر ا ون میدهم و یاد میکنم در این یزشن و یشت ای هورمزد

And thus, this essence of yours is more beautiful than the essence of the other angles. In this worship and prayer I praise and remember that blessed essence and nature of yours, O Ohrmazd.

nēk ō ēd tō kirb u-t ān az kirbān niwēyēnišn dahem ohrmazd kū andar gēhān ōh gowem kū kirb ēd tō nēktar

و نیک ست اوی این ذات تو یعنی مبارک ذات تو و جوهر تر از ذات دیگر فرشتگان یاد میکنم و میخواهم در این یزشن ای هورمزد یعنی در میان تمام دنیان به کویم که ذات تو بسیار نیکتر ست از دیگر فرشتگان

And beautiful is this essence of yours, that is, I remember and desire your blessed essence and your nature (more) than the essence of other angles in this worship, O Ohrmazd, that is, among all worldly beings I say that your essence is so much more beautiful than (that of) other angles.

Both MSS consistently avoid a superlative in NP as well. We only find the adjectives نیک and نیکتر. Moreover, according to these later commentaries, *Ohrmazd*'s form was thought to be better or more beautiful than those of

---

[23] *sraēšta-* is derived from *srīra-* 'beautiful, splendid', which is attested in Y 35.3 and translated as *nēk*. On the expression *sraēštąm ... kəhrpąm kəhrpąm*, see Hintze (2007a: 150ff.) with references.
[24] The formulaic expression *mahist pahlom nēktom* 'greatest, best (and) most beautiful', for instance, translates *mazištaca vahištaca sraēštaca* 'id.' in Y 1.1 and variations thereof across the *Yasna*.

other deities (اِیزَدان) or angels (فِرِشْتَگان), but not necessarily the most beautiful one.[25] These interpretations, however, are at odds with a passage from Dk 9, where it is clearly stated that *Ohrmazd*'s form is the most beautiful one:

Dk 9.57.18 *ud ēn-iz kū-š kirb ī ohrmazd pad nēktōmīh stāyīd bawēd kē xwēš ruwān ō xwaršēd pāyagīh bālistēnēd ēd-iz rāy čē ān kirb ast ī ohrmazd ud pad xwaršēd pāyagīh bālist ud nēktom bawēd.*

And this too, that he who praises *Ohrmazd*'s bodily form as the most beautiful one, he elevates his own soul to the sun station; for, that bodily form is of *Ohrmazd* and is the highest and most beautiful one in the sun station.

14.5.3 *niwēyenišn dahom*

OAv. *āuuaēdaiiamahī* 'we declare' occurs in Y 36.6 and 41.1.[26] In PY 36.6 the verb is translated *niwēyenišn dahom*, while in PY 41.1 it is rendered *niwēyom*.

Most MSS examined here, prefer ⟨nwykynšn'⟩ *niwēyenišn*, as opposed to ⟨nwykšn'⟩ *niwēyišn* (K5 J2 M1) which goes back to *niwistan, niwēy-* 'to announce, consecrate'.[27] The verbal noun *niwēyenišn* is derived from the present stem *niwēyen-* of *niwēyenīdan*, a secondary formation with the suffix *-ēn-īdan*, which is used to form causative and transitive denominative verbs in MP (MacKenzie 1990: 30; Sundermann 1989: 151; Weber 2007: 949).[28]

In the secondary literature the MP verb and its derivatives are translated with 'to invite' and 'to announce'. Mills (1905a: 63, 74) translates *niwēyenišn dahem* 'I will deliver an inviting-announcement' and *ān-iz niwēyem* in PY 41.1 'and that also do I here make known'.[29] In ŠnŠ 9.11, Tavadia (1930: 120) prefers 'are to be invited' for the necessitative participle '*niveδenīšn*'. Dhabhar (1949: 186) assumes the meanings 'invitation, announcement, dedication, consecration' for *niwēyenišn*, while MacKenzie (1990: 60) suggests 'announce, consecrate' for the verb *niwistan, niwēy-* and 'announcement' for *niwēy-išn(īh)*. In Dd 2.13, Jaafari-Dehaghi (1998: 46–7, 272) translates *niwēyenīd* 'announced'. Durkin-Meisterernst (2004: 248) posits 'invited' for the past

---

[25] In both MSS *kirb* is translated *zāt* 'essence, nature, substance' and *jōhar* 'id.'.

[26] For a discussion of *āuuaēdaiiamahī*, a 1pl.ind.act. from a causative present stem *vaēdaiia-* of the root *vid* with the preverb *ā*, see Hintze (2007a: 148ff.), who also points out the technical meaning of the Vedic parallel *vedáya-* in the ritual context.

[27] MacKenzie (1990: 60) also notes the spelling ⟨nwyd-⟩ which preserves the root *vid* with the preverb *ni-*. The spelling ⟨nwyk-⟩ must be a scribal convention that distorts the original ⟨nwyd-⟩. For verbs in Middle and New Iranian languages formed from *vid*, see Cheung (2007: 408ff.).

[28] MacKenzie (1990: 60) considers the infinitive *niwēyenīdan* doubtful. However, the evidence of *niwēyenīdār* in PY 43.13 and *niwēyenīdagīh* in Dk 9.9.5–10 suggests that this infinitive may have been known.

[29] While Mills (1905a: 63, fn. 4) prefers 'to invite' for the root *vid*, the comment at the end of PY 36.6a, *kū andar gēhān ōh gōwom*, motivates him to translate *niwēyenišn dādan* as 'to deliver an inviting-announcement': 'Good is this Thy body. And to that Thy (body) of (all) bodies will I, O A., deliver an inviting-announcement.'

participles *nwyst* and *nwystg* in Pa. And in Dk 9.9.5–10, Vevaina (2007: 246–8) opts for 'has been invited' for *niwēyēnīdagīh*.

According to Cheung (2007: 408), the meaning of *vaēdaiia-* is modified by the preverbs *ā-* ('to announce') and *ni-* ('to invite, dedicate').[30] While both combinations are attested in Young as well as OAv., in MP only the construction with **ni-*, ⟨nwyd-⟩, seems to have survived. Thus, in the *Zand* we find *niwēyēnem* for YAv. *niuuaēδaiiemi* (Y 1.1ff.) as well as *āuuaēδaiiamahī* (Y 4.1ff.). Therefore, the translation of the MP forms will depend on the context of the passage.

In light of the ritual's development during Y 36, that is, the heavenly fire joining the ritual, the idea of an invitation to the fire may seem tempting. However, the fire of *Ohrmazd* has already joined the ritual space in PY 36.2a. If we agree with MacKenzie's definition, *niwēyēnišn dādan* can be literally translated 'to give an announcement' or by extension 'to attribute', which I have preferred here.

---

[30] Differently Bartholomae (1904: 1317–18). See also Gershevitch (1967: 293) (*āuuaēδaiiamahī* 'we attribute') and Rix and Kümmel (2001: 666).

15. *PY 37*

15.1 PY 37.1

15.1.1 Y 5

(P)Y 5 being a copy of (P)Y 37, the two chapters are in principle identical. However, beside the expected variant readings in the text of the two chapters, a number of more significant differences stand out in the manuscripts.[1]

In the revised IrPY manuscript R413, for instance, (P)Y 5.2a and b form one cola. Another of the revised IrPY manuscripts, T6, has a very different scheme of cola division: Y 5.1a, 5.1b–c, whereby parts of PY 5.1c are missing; Y 5.2a–b, 5.2c–5.3a, 5.3b, 5.3c–5.4c and 5.5a–b. Among the InPY manuscripts, K5 M1 have Y 5.1a–b, 5.1c.

In all the manuscripts collated here, the repetition instructions and the stanza and line counts are missing at the end of (P)Y 5. These are usually found in the manuscripts of the IrPY and are reserved for the OAv. chapters. Even in those manuscripts that abbreviate (P)Y 37, namely F2 R413 T6 E7, the instructions only occur at the end of (P)Y 37.

The most significant difference between (P)Y 5 and (P)Y 37 lies in the fact that Pt4 Mf4 E7, K5 J2 M1 append the Av. *yeŋhē hātąm* and its *Zand* to the end of (P)Y 5. As Cereti (1995: 197) points out, already West (1880: 214, fn. 3) observed that two thirds of the stanzas of the *Yasna* close with the *yeŋhē hātąm* prayer.

---

[1] For a complete critical apparatus for PY 5, see Appendix A.1.

Table 15.1 *iθā* in MP texts

iθā āt̰ yazamaidē	Herb 16.3, N 10.49; PRDd 57, 58.29; Suppl.ŠnŠ 13.18; ZWY 5.2
iθā	Dd 78; N 10.50, 10.56; PRDd 58.28, 58.55; Suppl.ŠnŠ 13.20; ŠnŠ 3.35, 5.2, 5.7; Wd 16.7; ZFJ
iθā ī haiθiiā	Suppl.ŠnŠ 13.42
iθā ī	Suppl.ŠnŠ 13.51

15.1.2 *iθā*

The OAv. formula *iθā āt̰ yazamaidē* as well as its abbreviated form *iθā*, occur in a number of MP texts, evoking Y 5.1 or Y 37.1 (see Table 15.1).[2] The demonstrative adverb *iθā* is also attested in four *Gāθic* passages. Conflicting analyses of the function of *iθā* in both MP and OAv. texts necessitate a review of the material.

15.1.2.1 *iθā* in MP literature

iθā āt̰ yazamaidē and *iθā* are frequently quoted in MP passages discussing the *drōn* ceremony. They are found, for instance, in N 10, PRDd 57 and PRDd 58. N 10.49 stipulates that the ritual texts are to be recited standing up. The passage makes a concession for cases in which this might not be possible, but exempts the recitation of *iθā āt̰ yazamaidē* from that rule. N 10.50 discusses the ritual gaze during the performance of the *drōn* ceremony. N 10.56 explains the sequence of recitation for *iθā* and the *aṣ̌əm vohū* prayer, presumably in the context of *bāj ī nān*. PRDd 57 recounts the *Zand* of the Avestan passage beginning with *iθā āt̰ yazamaidē* and that of the *aṣ̌əm vohū* prayer. While PRDd 57 does not contain a heading, it is surrounded by chapters discussing the *drōn* ceremony. In PRDd 58 *iθā āt̰ yazamaidē* (58.29) and *iθā* (58.28, 55) occur once more in a chapter discussing the *drōn* ceremony that closely resembles N 10.[3]

Herb 16.3, ŠnŠ 5.2 and 5.7 mention *iθā āt̰ yazamaidē* and *iθā* in a discussion of the sin of *drāyān-jōyišnīh* 'chattering while eating'.

---

[2] For a slightly modified version of this section, see Zeini (2015). For a selection of the texts discussed here, see Appendix D.

[3] For the text of PRDd 58, see Williams (1990: I 206–7 and 210–11). On the correspondence between N 10 and PRDd 58, see Jamaspasa (1985: 334), Williams (1990: II 252–3) and Kotwal and Kreyenbroek (1995: 17, 59, fn. 128).

Table 15.2 *iϑā* in context

Context	*iϑā āt̰ yazamaidē*	*iϑā*
drōn	N 10.49; PRDd 57, 58.29	N 10.50, 10.56
		PRDd 58.28, 58.55
drōn and menstr.		ŠnŠ 3.35, Wd 16.7, ZFJ
drāyān-jōyišnīh	Herb 16.3	ŠnŠ 5.2, 5.7
bāj ī nān	ZWY 5.3	
OAv.	Suppl.ŠnŠ 13.18	Suppl.ŠnŠ 13.20

In the *Zand ī Wahman Yasn* the merit of reciting '*iϑā āt̰ yazamaidē u ašǝm vohū*' is compared with the merit of King *Wištāsp*'s performance of the *dwāzdah-hōmāst*.[4]

ŠnŠ 3.35, PWd 16.7 and ZFJ mention *iϑā* in the context of the *drōn* ceremony performed by a menstruating woman.

In a chapter on the *Gāϑās* (*čim ī gāhān*), Suppl.ŠnŠ 13.18 and 20 use *iϑā* to refer to Y 37 and 39, and in Suppl.ŠnŠ 13.42 and 51 *iϑā ī* refers to Y 53.6, quoting the *Gāϑic* passage's opening words.

Scholars arbitrarily view *iϑā* as a reference to Y 5 or Y 37. While the two chapters are identical from a textual point of view, they serve different ritual functions and should not be confused with one another. According to West (1882: 233, fn. 1), *iϑā* quotes Y 5.1 in Dd 78. By contrast, Bartholomae (1904: 366) views *iϑā* as a reference to Y 37. Although he mentions West in his discussion of PRDd 57, Williams (1990: II 251–2) considers *iϑā* to be a reference to Y 37.1, suggesting it is 'widely used as a grace before eating'. However, in the glossary he posits that in PRDd 58.28 *iϑā* 'refers to the entire section Y. 5', while taking *iϑā āt̰ yazamaidē* in PRDd 57 and 58.29 as quotations 'from Y. 5.1 = Y. 37.1' (Williams 1990: I 357).[5] Cereti (1995: 195) views *iϑā āt̰ yazamaidē* in ZWY 5.3 as a 'set formula which introduces and by which is evoked Y 37'. Kotwal and Kreyenbroek (1995: 77, fn. 213 and 79, fn. 224) consider N 10.50 and 56 to be references to Y 5.1, recited during the performance of the separate *drōn* ceremony, but do not comment on *iϑā* in

---

[4] The rationale behind the comparison with the *dwāzdah-hōmāst*, a purity ritual performed during menstruation, is not clear. The key to understanding this passage lies in its eschatological reference to the end of time, *andar ān ī škoft āwām* 'in those hard times', a time when the religion is in disarray and religious duties are not performed in the proper manner. Thus, the recitation of '*iϑā āt̰ yazamaidē u ašǝm vohū*' simply refers to the daily performance of the *bāj ī nān*, and the great merit ascribed to its observation is an encouragement for the laity to observe their daily rituals. For a similar reference to the performance of *dwāzdah-hōmāst* in *Sad dar ī Bundahišn*, see Jong (2005: 194): 'And a ritual performed in that time will give as much merit as when they order a *dwāzdah-hōmāst* to be celebrated in another time.' For the *dwāzdah-hōmāst* ceremony, see Williams (1990: II 140) and Stausberg (2004a: 341–2).

[5] *iϑā* in PRDd 58.55 is not listed in the glossary and Williams does not comment on this paragraph.

N 10.49. Likewise, Karanjia (2004: 407, fn. 20) identifies *iϑā āṯ yazamaidē* as 'Ch. 3 of the text of the Bāj-dharnā'.[6]

Y 5 renders Y 37 verbatim and precedes it in the *Yasna*, as a result of which the MSS often abbreviate Y 37. Y 3–8 build a textual block that constitutes the smaller *Yasna* ritual, known as *yašt ī keh* or *yašt ī drōn* (Boyce and Kotwal 1971a: 63–4).[7] In the *Yasna* ceremony proper, as well as in the *yašt ī drōn*, the ritual tasting (*čāšnī*) of the consecrated bread (*drōn*) takes place at Y 8, whereby the recitation of Y 5 constitutes its grace (*bāj*).[8] In this way, Y 5 anticipates the ritual tasting of the consecrated bread in Y 8 and may have served as a template for the laity's daily prayer preceding each meal, known as *bāj ī nān*. Thus constituting the *bāj*, Y 5 plays a central role in the *drōn* ceremony, be it as part of the *srōš drōn* in the *Yasna* proper, the separate *yašt ī drōn*, or the daily *bāj ī nān*.

As the evidence demonstrates, the majority of the MP passages quoting *iϑā āṯ yazamaidē* and *iϑā* discuss the *drōn* ceremony or *bāj ī nān*. Thus, the quotations refer to Y 5.1 in its ritual function and not to Y 37.1. The exceptions are the discussions of the content of Avestan passages in Suppl.ŠnŠ 13.18 referring to Y 37, 13.20 referring to Y 39 and Suppl.ŠnŠ 13.42 and 13.51 referring to Y 53.6.

15.1.2.2 *iϑā* in the Older Avesta

According to Geldner (1886–96), *iϑā* occurs four times in the *Gāϑās*: Y 33.1, 45.3, 47.4 and 53.6.[9] Beside the usual scribal errors, his apparatus contains *aϑā* 'so, thus, in that manner' as well as *yaϑā* 'as' as variant readings for *iϑā* in all of the above passages. At first sight, this uncertainty seems to be mirrored in the *Zand*: in the PG *iϑā* is consistently translated as *ēdōn* 'thus', whereas in the YH it is translated as *ēdar* 'here' (see Section 15.1.4). As Kellens and Pirart (1990: 101) implicitly challenge the authenticity of *iϑā* in the OAv., the question arises as to whether *ēdar* and *ēdōn* both translate the same adverb in the YH and the *Gāϑās*.

Kellens and Pirart (1990: 222) view OAv. *iϑā* as a near-deictic modal adverb that can assume a correlative (Y 33.1, 45.3) as well as a non-correlative (Y 37.1, 39.1, 39.3, Y 53.6) function. They attribute its presence in Y 33.1 to the orthoepic diaskeuasis, suggesting it represents an adverb with a neutral deixis (Kellens and Pirart 1990: 101). In their view, *iϑā* in Y 45.3 is motivated

---

[6] Ch. 3 refers to Y 5 of the *bāj* ceremony which consists of Y 3–8.
[7] On *drōn* and *bāj* ceremonies, see Boyce and Kotwal (1971a, b), Choksy (1995), Stausberg (2004a: 351) and more recently Karanjia (2004).
[8] According to Kotwal and Boyd (1991: 94, fn. 89), the *drōn* ceremony that is part of the *Yasna* ceremony (*srōš drōn*) takes place between Y 3 and 8, but only consists of Y 3, 4, 6 and 7.
[9] See also Bartholomae (1904: 365–6), who follows Geldner.

by the occurrence of inflected forms of *varəz* 'to perform' both in Y 33.1 (*varəšaitē*) and 45.3 (*varəšəntī*).¹⁰ In Y 47.4 Kellens and Pirart prefer *aϑā* based on manuscript evidence, while they assign a near-deictic value to *iϑā* in Y 53.6. Drawing attention to Y 39.4 ('*yaθā ... aθā θβā āiš yazamaidē*') they conclude that the original form in Y 37.1, 39.1 and 39.3 must have been *aϑā*. Finally, taking into account that in Y 39.3, Y 45.3 and 47.4 *iϑā* follows a word with a final -*t̰*, Kellens and Pirart (1990: 101) conclude that *iϑā* represents a graphic variation of *aϑā* used after the dental implosive. In sum, Kellens and Pirart regard *iϑā* in Y 33.1 as the result of a later development, while in the YH, Y 45.3 and 47.4, they view it as uncertain. They seem to consider Y 53.6 as containing a near-deictic *iϑā*.

It remains unclear whether Kellens and Pirart assign *iϑā* a genuine deixis, as they do in Y 53.6, or whether they simply view it as a graphic variant of *aϑā*. Furthermore, while their conclusion may explain *iϑā* in Y 39.3, *āt̰ iϑā yazamaidē*, it leaves open the question of *iϑā* in Y 37.1 and 39.1, where the adverb precedes a word with a final -*t̰*: *iϑā āt̰ yazamaidē*. Their conclusion also contradicts their own suggestion that in Y 45.3 *iϑā* is motivated by Y 33.1. Moreover, if in Y 47.4 *iϑā* is the result of the preceding *nōit̰*, their emendation of *iϑā* to *aϑā* would operate against the very same phonetic or scribal rule they propose: -*t̰ iϑā*.¹¹ They also ignore the fact that the majority of the MSS transmit *aϑā* in Y 47.4 and not *iϑā*.

According to Wackernagel (1930–57: III 512) Av. *iϑā̆* 'thus, likewise' is an adverbial derivation from the pronominal stem *i-* with the IIr. modal suffix *-thā* 'how'. Likewise, *aϑā̆* 'thus, so' derives from the pronominal stem *a-* (Hintze 2007a: 332).¹² Furthermore, Wackernagel (1930–57: III 509) assigns the sounds *i*, *u* and *a* near-, far- and neutral-deictic values, respectively. Although the semantic proximity of *iϑā* and *aϑā* may suggest that the adverbs are interchangeable, the deixis associated with the vocalism of the pronominal stems *i-* and *a-* indicates otherwise.¹³ In light of the complex attestation of both adverbs in the MSS, the question we are left with is whether the occurrence of *iϑā* in the OAv. is motivated by a genuine deixis and the context of a passage or whether it constitutes a purely graphic variation of *aϑā*, as suggested by Kellens and Pirart.

---

¹⁰ Insler (1975: 211) and Humbach (1991: II 92) point out the correlation *yaϑā ... iϑā* in Y 33.1 and *iϑā ... yaϑā* in Y 45.3 as well, implying that a link exists between the two stanzas. Schmidt (1985: 9), however, rejects the idea of a correlative use in both stanzas based on a comparison with Ved. *itthá*.

¹¹ For their emendation, see Kellens and Pirart (1988: 167).

¹² Similar formations include Ved. *yathā* 'as', *kathā* 'how', Old, YAv. and OP *yaϑā̆* 'as', Old and YAv. *kaϑā̆* 'how?' as well as YAv. *kuϑa* 'id.' (Wackernagel 1930–57: III 444). See Bartholomae (1904: 62–4) for *aϑā̆* 'so' and Bartholomae (1904: 171–2) for YAv. *auuaϑa* 'thus, in that way'. See also Bartholomae (1904: 473) for *kuϑa* 'where to?'.

¹³ Differently Hintze (2007a: 120).

Table 15.3 *iϑā* in Y 33.1

	Y-IndS	Y-P	V-IndS
iϑā	Bh5, B3	Pt4 Mf4, K5 J2	ML630, B2, T46, G42
aϑā		F2, T6	B4, FK1

Kellens and Pirart (1990) do not substantiate their suggestion that *iϑā* represents a neutral deixis in Y 33.1. It also remains unclear what role the orthoepic diaskeuasis would have played in introducing *iϑā* in Y 33.1, especially since it is not preceded by a dental implosive. This neglect is remarkable, as they build their arguments for Y 45.3 on parallels with Y 33.1. While the linguistic difficulties associated with this stanza make its context notoriously elusive,[14] here *iϑā* appears to possess a near-deictic value.

Y 33.1 ⁺*yaϑā* ⁺*āiš iϑā varəšaitē yā dātā aŋhə̄uš paouruiiehiiā*
ratuš šiiaoϑanā razištā drəguuataēcā hiiat̰cā ašāunē
yexiiācā hə̄məmiiāsaitē miϑahiiā yācā hōi ārəzuuā

As by those, which are the laws of the primeval existence, the judge shall perform in this manner
the most just actions for the deceitful as well as the orderly one
and for him (*hōi*) whose (judgement) is established by deceit as well as virtue.

In this interpretation, the near-deictic demonstrative adverb *iϑā* contrasts with the neutral-deictic demonstrative pronoun *āiš* 'those'. Thus, the laws of the primeval existence (*dātā aŋhə̄uš paouruiiehiiā*), referred to by *āiš*, are naturally farther away, whereas *iϑā* expresses the closeness of the realisation of the most just actions (*šiiaoϑanā razištā*) by the judge (*ratuš*) here in this existence.[15] The manuscript evidence (Table 15.3) confirms *iϑā* as well:

Despite its comparatively simpler structure, the context of Y 45.3 offers no obvious clues as to the deictic value of *iϑā*:

Y 45.3 *at̰ frauuaxšiiā aŋhə̄uš ahiiā paouruuīm*
yąm mōi vīduuå mazdå vaocat̰ ahurō
yōi īm və̄ nōit̰ iϑā mąϑrəm varəšəṇtī
yaϑā īm mə̄nāicā vaocacā
aēibiiō aŋhə̄uš auuōi aŋhat̰ apə̄məm

I shall speak of the primeval one of this existence,
which the knowing one, the Wise Lord, told me.
Those of you (who) will not perform this formula in this manner,
as I shall conceive and speak it,
for those woe shall be at the end of existence.

---

[14] Some of the problems include conflicting interpretations of *āiš*, *dātā* and *ratuš*. See Insler (1975: 211), Schmidt (1985: 9), Kellens and Pirart (1991: 97–8) and Humbach (1991: II 92). For a particularly readable translation, see Bartholomae (1905: 35). For *hə̄məmiiāsaitē*, see Hintze (2008).

[15] See the introductory summaries by Insler (1975: 211) and Humbach (1991: II 92) for the context of Y 33 and its reference to this existence, which encompasses the individual judgement after death.

Table 15.4 *iϑā* in Y 45.3

	Y-IndS	Y-P	V-IndS
iϑā	Bh5, B3	Pt4 Mf4, K5 J2; F2	ML630, G42
aϑā		T6	T46, B4, FK1

If *īm* is taken as a near-deictic pronoun qualifying *mąϑrəm*,[16] then *iϑā* may refer to the non-realisation of *this* formula (*īm ... mąϑrəm*) in *this* manner (*nōit̰ iϑā ... varəšəṇtī*), that is, in the manner that the *Gāϑic* poet is about to pronounce. It seems to me less likely that *yōi īm ... aŋhat̰ apə̄məm* represents a direct speech by *Ahura Mazdā*, as suggested by Insler (1975: 256) and Humbach (1991: I 164, II 166). But even in that interpretation the context necessitates *iϑā*: 'Those of you (who) will not perform *this* formula in *this* manner', presumably referring to *Ahura Mazdā*'s own instructions to Zaraϑuštra. Be that as it may, here too the manuscript evidence (Table 15.4) supports *iϑā*:

That different deixes were assigned to the two adverbs emerges partly from Y 47.4 and most clearly from 53.6. In Y 47.4, despite the attestation of *aϑā* in ten MSS, Geldner (1886–96: I 167) prefers *iϑā* based on a reading from J2 and K5. By contrast, Kellens and Pirart (1988: 167) rightly prefer *aϑā*.[17] However, it is the context of this passage that offers the strongest argument in favour of *aϑā*. In Y 47.4, the *Gāϑic* poet distinguishes the actions of the orderly ones from those of the deceitful ones. The necessary distance between the two groups is expressed by means of *aϑā* 'in *that* manner':

Y 47.4 *ahmāt̰ mainiiə̄uš, rārəšiieiṇtī*[18] *drəguuaṇtō*
mazdā spəṇtūt̰, nōit̰ ' aϑa aṣ̌āunō[19]

The deceitful ones defect from the bounteous spirit,
O Wise one, not in that manner the orderly ones.

Y 53.6 is the only *Gāϑic* stanza to use both adverbs in close proximity:[20]

Y 53.6 *iϑā ī haiϑiiā narō aϑā jə̄naiiō*

---

[16] Differently Insler (1975: 256), who assigns a 'temporal force' to *īm* in this passage, translating it as 'now'.

[17] See also Kellens and Pirart (1991: 216).

[18] Uncertainty surrounds the meaning of the 3pl.ind.pres.act. *rārəšiieiṇtī* from the root *rah* 'to leave, fall off'. Humbach (1991: II 193) and Hoffmann and Forssman (1996: 186) seem to assign a causative meaning to the reduplicated stem + **ia*. Differently, Bartholomae (1904: 1517) and Cheung (2007: 140).

[19] On translating *aṣ̌āunō* as a nom.pl.m., see Bartholomae (1904: 246) and Kellens and Pirart (1990, 1991: 211 and 216).

[20] Although in a correlative function, the adverbs' occurrence in Y 19.12 suggests that their distinct deixes survived in YAv. as well: *yaϑa frā iϑa āmraot̰ ... iϑa dim para cinasti ... yaϑa īm vīspaṇm mazištəm cinasti ... aϑa ahmāi dāmąn cinasti*.

Insler (1975: 113) does not comment on *iθā ... aθā* in Y 53.6. His translation implies an emphatic function for both adverbs: 'These things are exactly true, men; exactly, women.' By contrast, Humbach (1991: I 193, II 243), in line with Kellens and Pirart (1990: 101), assigns distinct deictic values to both adverbs: 'In this respect the (instructions are) true, O men, in that respect (they are true), O women.' Humbach (1991: II 243) interprets *ī* as a pronoun representing the noun *sāx^və̄nī* 'instructions' from Y 53.5 and speculates – to my mind unconvincingly – that the different deictic ranges in Y 53.6 denote a varying relevance of instructions for men (*iθā*) and women (*aθā*). By contrast, Bartholomae (1904: 363) explicitly rejects *ī* as a nom.pl.n. and views it as an emphatic particle. He subsequently translates this passage as: 'So ist es in der Tat, ihr Männer und Frauen!' (Bartholomae 1905: 116).[21] However, Bartholomae's translation ignores the fact that two different adverbs are used in this passage. In an alternative interpretation suggested in the commentary, Humbach (1991: II 243) rightly considers *ī* to be a particle: 'like this (are) the true men, like that (are) the (true) women'.[22]

Thus far scholars have ignored the fact that the first line of Y 53.6 concludes an ethical imperative expressed in the final line of Y 53.5:

Y 53.5 *ašā və̄ aniiō ainīm vīuuə̄ŋhatū tat̰ zī hōi hušə̄nəm aŋhat̰*
Y 53.6 *iθā ī haiθiiā narō aθā jə̄naiiō*

Y 53.5 Each of you shall surpass the other in (matters of) *aša*, for that will be of good gain for him.
Y 53.6 This way, indeed, are true men, such are (true) women.

It is unlikely that the deictic range of *iθā ... aθā* expresses a physical distance between men and women or between the *Gāθic* poet and the women, as suggested by Skjærvø (2008b). It rather underscores in a poetic manner the fact that two distinct groups are being addressed: men and women. Thus, contrary to Humbach (1991: II 243), the ethical imperative expressed in Y 53.5 is valid both for men and women.

As a comparison of any group of the MSS quickly reveals, the deictic values accorded to *iθā ... aθā* in the above discussion were largely lost in the scribal tradition (Table 15.5):

---

[21] *haiθiiā* forms part of the main clause expressing the emphasis, and *narō* and *jə̄naiiō* are taken to be voc.pl. in a subordinate clause.
[22] This reading views *narō* and *jə̄naiiō* as nom.pl. and *haiθiiā* as an adjective agreeing with *narō*. Earlier, Humbach (1959: I 159) had translated this stanza as: 'So sind sie, die lauteren Männer und Frauen'. However, in the commentary he suggests that *ī* represents *sāx^və̄nī* (Humbach 1959: II 96). For yet another interpretation of this stanza, see also Schwartz (2003: 2–3).

Table 15.5 *iϑā* in Y 53.6

	Y-IndS	Y-P	V-IndS
aϑā … aϑā		Pt4, Mf4, F2, T6	ML630, B4
iϑā … aϑā	Bh5, B3	K5	
iϑā … iϑā			B2, T46
aϑā … iϑā			FK1
yaϑā … aϑā			G42
iϑi … aϑā		J2	

With a majority reading of eleven MSS against three, *aϑā* is not controversial in the second position, while the attestation of the initial adverb as *iϑā* is rather poor. However, *iϑā* in the initial position is supported by Suppl.ŠnŠ 13.42 and 51 as they refer to Y 53.6 with *iϑā ī haiϑiiā* and *iϑā ī*.[23] Most likely the occurrence of both adverbs in close proximity caused confusion in the manuscript tradition.

As for the YH, Kellens and Pirart (1990: 101) are puzzled by *iϑā* in Y 37.1, 39.1 and 39.3, seemingly expecting *aϑā* based on Y 39.4.[24] As Narten (1986: 167) has shown, *iϑā* functions as a near-deictic demonstrative adverb in Y 37.1, 39.1 and 39.3 pointing 'to the actual circumstances of the unfolding liturgy' (Hintze 2007a: 156). The *variae lectiones* offered by Narten and Hintze support *iϑā* as well. In Y 39.4, by contrast, it is not the actuality of the liturgy that is emphasised. Rather, as Hintze (2007a: 279) rightly points out, the correlative relation between *yaϑā* and a series of *aϑā* mirrors the relationship between *Ahura Mazdā*'s actions and the worshippers' veneration. Furthermore, as evident from Table 15.1, MP literature made extensive use of *iϑā* to refer to Y 5.1, which is a verbatim copy of Y 37.1. We can thus conclude that the use of the adverb in both chapters is at least as old as the quotations in the MP literature. Moreover, Suppl.ŠnŠ 13.18 and 13.20 explicitly refer to Y 37 and 39, respectively, using *iϑā*. This once again confirms that at least at the time of the composition of the Suppl.ŠnŠ these passages of the YH were known to use *iϑā* rather than *aϑā*.

The evidence points to the conclusion that Y 39.3 cannot be viewed separately from Y 37.1 and 39.1. While *āt̰* is not attested in the *Gāϑās*, the particle occurs nine times in the second position in the YH (Hintze 2007a: 272), with Y 39.3 (*āt̰ iϑā*) as the only exception. With this in mind, one must agree with Hintze (2007a: 272) when she views Y 39.3 as having an 'inverted

---

[23] See Table 15.1 and Appendix D.
[24] The mechanical comparison between two passages with similar wordings is a methodological fallacy often committed in Old Iranian studies. See, for instance, Kellens and Pirart (1991: 271), where they suggest that *ī haiϑiiā* stands for '*ī haiϑiiā /maϑrā/*', citing Y 31.6 *haiϑīm maϑrəm* as supporting evidence.

word order' compared to the two other passages. Thus, if the word order of Y 37.1 and 39.1 (*iθā āt̰*) is genuine, the presence of *iθā* in Y 39.3 cannot be explained by way of the preceding *āt̰*.

Both context and manuscript tradition confirm *iθā* as a near-deictic demonstrative adverb in Y 33.1, 45.3, 53.6 and the YH. Moreover, the MSS consistently preserve a neutral-deictic *aθā* in Y 47.4. There seems to be no evidence for *iθā* as a graphic variant of *aθā* as suggested by Kellens and Pirart.

A direct link between *iθā* and its closest Ved. cognate, *itthā́*, is difficult to establish.[25] Functionally, however, a partial link may exist between OAv. *iθā* and Ved. *itthā́* when Grassmann (1873: 204) and Monier-Williams (1899: 165) assert that *itthā́* is commonly used in connection with words expressing devotion to the gods.

15.1.3 *āt̰* 'ēdōn'

The PYH prefers *ēdōn* 'thus, so' for *āt̰* as well as *āat̰* (see Table 15.6).[26] By contrast, the FīŌ translates *āt̰* as 'ytwn', *ēdōn* but suggests 'DYN', *ēg* 'then, thereupon' for *āat̰* (Klingenschmitt 1968: XIII, 117). In the *Zand* of YAv. passages we find agreement with the FīŌ when *āat̰* is translated as *ēg* and at times as *čē* 'for, because, since, as, that' (see Josephson 1997: 194).

Narten (1986: 257–9) and Hintze (2007a: 272–3) suggest that YAv. *āat̰* derives from OAv. *āt̰*, although the latter is not attested in the *Gāθās*.[28] Acknowledging a divergence in the syntactic positions of both forms, Narten (1986: 258) further asserts a semantic difference between OAv. *āt̰* and YAv. *āat̰*.[29]

Noting the different meanings proposed for *āt̰* and *āat̰* by FīŌ, Narten (1986: 258) rightly suggests that the compiler of the *Frahang* must have considered both forms to be different words. She concludes, therefore, that in the FīŌ *āt̰* refers to the YH, while *āat̰* must refer to YAv. passages. Thus, Narten's view about the semantic differences between the two Avestan forms

---

[25] Although *itthā́* is a closely related formation, an exact Ved. cognate is not attested for OAv. *iθā* (Wackernagel 1930–57: III 512). Wackernagel (1930–57: III 445) posits a nom./acc.sg.n. *id* as the stem for *itthā́* (*id-* + *-thā*) but suggests that the adverb may be of uncertain meaning. Elsewhere he regards it as an isolated adverb with the uncertain meaning 'so' (Wackernagel 1930–57: II.1 68), but also considers an alternative meaning 'here' for *itthā́* (Wackernagel 1930–57: II.1 287). On *itthā́*, see also Mayrhofer (1992–2001: I 190).

[26] For Av. *āt̰*, see Narten (1986: 257–9) and Hintze (2007a: 272–3), who discuss it in detail and establish its meaning as 'now'. Differently Bartholomae (1904: 325), Humbach (1991) and Kellens and Pirart (1990: 128).

[28] When Jackson (1892: 202) and Klingenschmitt (1968: 117) use 'GAv.' and '*Gāθās*' in connection with *āt̰*, they certainly refer to the passages in the YH rather than to the *Gāθās*.

[29] Being a YAv. form, *āat̰* is not attested in the *Gāθās*. For *āat̰* in the YH, see Hintze (2007a: 272, fn. 34 and 334) who in agreement with Narten (1986: 258) considers this form to be a later YAv. intrusion. For the meaning and various functions of *āat̰*, see also Bartholomae (1904: 303–7).

Table 15.6 *āt̰* and *āat̰* in the YH

YH	Avestan	MP
35.6	yaϑā²⁷ āt̰ utā nā vā nāirī vā	ēdōn ān ī har dō nar ud nārīg
35.6	⁺tat̰.ə̄-ād-ū	∅
35.8	aṣ̌ahiiā āat̰ sairī	pad ahlāyīh ēdōn sālārīh
35.9	imā āt̰ uxδā vacā̊	ēn ēdōn saxwan gōwišnīh
37.1	iϑā āt̰ yazamaidē	ēdar ēdōn yazom
38.1	imąm āat̰ ząm ... yazamaidē	ēn zamīg ... ēdōn yazom
39.1a	iϑā āt̰ yazamaidē	ēdar ēdōn yazom
39.1b	ahmākə̄ṇg āat̰ urunō	ān ī amāgān ∅ ruwān
39.2	aṣ̌āunąm āat̰ urunō yazamaidē	ān ī ahlawān ruwān ēdōn yazom
39.3	āt̰ iϑā yazamaidē	ān ēdōn yazom
Y 5.6	yeŋhē hātąm āat̰	kē az astān ēdōn

in Old and YAv. passages is in precise agreement with the evidence of the FīŌ. However, in contrast to the FīŌ, the PYH never translates *āat̰* as *ēg* or *čē*, but instead prefers *ēdōn* (Table 15.6), possibly equating YAv. *āat̰* with its OAv. form *āt̰* in the YH. The PYH's evidence thus represents a striking proximity between the *Zand*'s notion and Narten's analysis of YAv. *āat̰* as being derived from OAv. *āt̰*. Moreover, the use of *ēdōn* for *āat̰* (< *āt̰*) in the PYH constitutes a difference between the *Zand* of the PYH and the FīŌ. If MP translations, either oral or written, preceded the compilation of the FīŌ (Klingenschmitt 1968: V, VI), then its compiler certainly did not account for this divergence in the *Zand* of the YH.

15.1.4 *iϑā āt̰* 'ēdar ēdōn'

With Y 37 begins the middle section of the text (Y 37–39), which contains seventeen *yazamaidē* 'we worship' formulae at its core (Y 37.1–39.4).[30] The Avestan formula *iϑā āt̰ yazamaidē* 'ēdar ēdōn yazom' occurs in Y 37.1 (= Y 5.1) and Y 39.1. The formula is also attested in Y 39.3 with an inverted word order, *āt̰ iϑā yazamaidē* 'ān ēdōn yazom'.[31]

If we presuppose a one to one correspondence between the word order of the Avestan and the *Zand*, then in Y 37.1 and 39.1 *ēdar* 'here' translates *iϑā* 'thus, so, in this way', while *ēdōn* 'thus, so' translates *āt̰* 'now'. This view is also corroborated by the interlinear glosses of the PY manuscripts F2 and T6,

---

[30] For a comprehensive overview and analysis, see Hintze (2007a: 6, 9–18, 155) with references.
[31] The inverted word order has been discussed by Narten (1986: 259) and Hintze (2007a: 272–3). For *ān ēdōn yazom*, see Section 17.3.1.

Table 15.7 *iϑā* in the *Gāϑās*

	Avestan	MP
33.1	*iϑā varəšaitē*	*ēdōn warzišn*
45.3	*nōit̰ iϑā mą̇ϑrəm varəšəṇtī*	*mānsᵃr nē ēdōn warzēnd*
53.6	*iϑā ī*	*ēdōn čiyōn*

which in Y 5.1 translate both *iϑā* and *ēdar* as NP اینجا, *injā* 'here'.[32] And indeed, in the YH *āt̰* is consistently translated as *ēdōn*.[33] Surprisingly, however, the *Gāϑic* evidence suggests that OAv. *iϑā* was regularly translated as *ēdōn* as well (see Table 15.7).[34] In the following, I will investigate how the *Zand*'s *ēdar* relates to Av. *iϑā*.

While noting *ēdar* as a translation for *iϑā* in Y 37.1 and 39.1, Bartholomae (1904: 365–6) suggests that Old and YAv. *iϑā̆* are commonly translated as *ēdōn*. Likewise, in translating the rendition of the *Zand* of Y 5 in PRDd 57, Williams (1990: II 94) indicates in parentheses that *iϑā* is translated as *ēdōn* and not *ēdar*: 'Here thus (*iθā ēdōn*) we worship Ohrmazd'.[35]

Although YAv. *iϑa* is regularly translated as *ēdōn*,[36] Bartholomae (1904: 366) records three instances of *iϑa* with the meaning 'here', suggesting a correspondence with *yaϑa* 'where' (Bartholomae 1904: 366, fn. 4). If this is true, then YAv. *iϑa* 'here' could have inspired the PYH's *ēdar* for *iϑā*. Of the three passages noted by Bartholomae, only Wd 7.52 and N 83.2 (101) have a PTr., the third being Yt 17.60.

In Wd 7.52 *iϑa* is translated with *ēdōn*:

Wd 7.52[37] *ušta iϑa tē narə*
Thus (it is) good for you, O man!

kū nēk ēdōn tō mard
That is, thus (it is) good (for) you, O man!

---

[32] Both MSS abbreviate Y 37.

[33] See Section 15.1.3, Table 15.6.

[34] OAv. *iϑā* also occurs in Y 13.4, where it is translated as *ēdōn*: *iϑā mainiiū mamanāitē iϑā vaocātarə iϑā vāuuərəzātarə* 'ēdōn pad menišn menom ēdōn gōwom ud ēdōn warzom' (For the *Zand*, see Zeini 2012: 157). Y 13 being a YAv. chapter, Bartholomae (1904: 366, fn. 2) remarks that in this passage OAv. *iϑā* represents *iϑa* or *iϑa*. Hoffmann and Forssman (1996: 236 and 239) consider the 3du.ind.perf.mid. and active forms of the verbs to represent pseudo OAv. constructions. According to Bartholomae (1904: 1136–9) the PTr. of '*manyav-*' is *mēnōg, mēnōgīh* or *mēnōgīhā*. The only exception noted by him is *wattar menišn* 'evil thought' for '*akascā mainyuš*' in Y 32.5. He does not mention the above *menišn* for *mainiiū*, nom.du. of *mańiiu-* m.

[35] Williams (1990: II 252) does not discuss the issue in his commentary.

[36] The passages quoted by Bartholomae are: Y 10.17, 19.12 and 14, Wd 4.48, 15.45, N 28.3 (46), 29.3 (47), 32.3 (50) and 49.4 (67). In N 28.3 (46), contrary to Bartholomae (1904: 365), Kotwal and Kreyenbroek (2003: 64) prefer TD's reading as *aϑa* 'thus'. They note MS HJ's reading, *iϑa*, in the CA.

[37] For the *Zand* see MS L4, fol. 125v. In the Av. passage L4 has acc.sg. *narəm* instead of the voc.sg. *narə*.

A deviation from the modal meaning of the Av. adverb seems unnecessary in this passage.

N 83.2 (101), in contrast, employs the far-deictic demonstrative adverb *ānōh* 'there' in the MP translation of the Av. passage:

N 83.2[38] *auua iϑa barənti *yauuahe vā gauuanahe vā*

and sows either corn or gauuana there

abar ō ānōh ē barēd jordā [<pad dānag>] ayāb *gauuina [pad jaw-ē]

and brings there either corn [with grains] or sorghum [with a seed]

Elsewhere, Kotwal and Kreyenbroek (2003: 287) translate *iϑa* as 'thus'. In N 83.2, however, they prefer 'thus; here, there' (see Kotwal and Kreyenbroek 2009: 110), perhaps motivated by the use of *ānōh* 'there' in the passage's PTr. Kotwal and Kreyenbroek's translation is in agreement with Bartholomae (1904: 366), who translates the passage as: 'wenn man in der Erde drei Furchen zieht (und) sie bringen (sva. säen) *hier* Getreide hinein' (Bartholomae 1904: 937; italics added). However, the context suggests a modal aspect for the adverb:

N 83.1[39] *yō zəmō tišrō *karšā̊ frakāraiieiti*
He who draws three furrows on the earth.

ka pad zamīg 3 kiš <pad> kārēd
When one ploughs three furrows in the earth.

N 83.3 *yezi tišrō *tarō.zānuuō *haϑrāciš haṇdarəžaṇti ratufriš*
if they tie three (twigs) together which are more than knee-high, they satisfy the Ratus.

agar 3 tar-*šnūg pad ham āgenēn ō ham dārēd [kū rāst] radīhā
If one holds together jointly three (twigs that are) more than the height of a knee [that is, straight], one acts in an authorised manner.

According to Kotwal and Kreyenbroek (2009: 73, fn. 233), N 83.3 stipulates that 'one should hold a *barsom* when sowing'. If this is the case, then the *Nērangestān* discusses the manner of sowing rather than its location. A *barsom* is to be held if three furrows are dug before the sowing. Therefore, N 83.2 may be better translated as:

83.1 He who draws three furrows on the earth, (83.2) (and) in this way sows either corn or gauuana, ...

---

[38] Text and translation after Kotwal and Kreyenbroek (2009: 72).
[39] Text and translation after Kotwal and Kreyenbroek (2009: 72).

YAv. *iϑa* also occurs in Yt 17.60:

Yt 17.60[40] *āat̰ mraot̰ ahurō mazdå*
aši srīre dāmiδāite
mā auui asmanəm frašusa
mā auuiząm ni.uruuise
iϑa mē tūm hąm.caraŋᵛha[41]
aṇtarə.arəδəm nmānahe
srīrahe xšaϑrō.kərətahe

Then Ahura Mazdā said:
O beautiful Aši, created by the creator,
do not move forth to the sky,
do not turn down to the earth.
Thus, do stay
inside my beautiful house,
made for the ruler.

Admittedly, the immediate context of *iϑa* in Yt 17.60 does not rule out a local meaning for the adverb. In this interpretation, *Ahura Mazdā* could be understood as requesting *Aši* to stay *here*, as opposed to moving to the sky or the earth.[42] On the other hand, the correspondence between *Ahura Mazdā*'s response in Yt 17.60, *iϑa mē tūm hąm.caraŋᵛha*, to *Aši*'s question repeated three times in the stanzas 17.57–59, *kuϑa hīš azəm kərənauuāni* 'how shall I treat them', suggests that here *iϑa* has a modal meaning.[43] Moreover, as *iϑa* is not used as an adverb of location in Wd 7.52 or N 83.2 (101), without further evidential support the meaning 'here' would represent an *ad hoc* definition. Therefore, I prefer the modal aspect of *iϑa* in Yt 17.60 as well.

Regardless of the meaning of *iϑa*, if it is indeed translated as *ānōh* in N 83.2, then it would exemplify the use of an adverb of location in MP for *iϑa*. This, however, is an isolated case, and I hesitate to link the translation of *iϑa* as *ānōh* in N 83.2 with *ēdar* in the YH. Most likely, Bartholomae based the meaning 'here' for YAv. *iϑa* on *ānōh* in N 83.2. However, as the above examination shows, such a conclusion is not justified for Av. *iϑa*.

It also seems less likely that *iϑā* was rendered as *ēdar* in light of OAv. *idā*, YAv. ²*iδa* 'here, hither' (see Bartholomae 1904: 364–5). OAv. *idā* is not well attested. Contrary to Bartholomae, who suggests that in Y 29.8 *idā* is translated as *ēdōn*, it was most likely translated as *dahišn*: *aēm mōi idā vistō* 'ēd man dahišn ⁺windem'. Alternatively, it can be argued that it was left

---

[40] Avestan text after Geldner (1886–96: II 239).
[41] On translating *hąm.caraŋᵛha* as 'stay, dwell, reside', see Cheung (2009: 52).
[42] See Darmesteter (1884: 282), Bartholomae (1904: 450), Lommel (1927: 166), Hintze (2000: 314) and Cheung (2009: 52).
[43] See Pirart (2006: 227, fn. 731), who reconstructs *iϑa mē tūm hąm.caraŋᵛha* as *iϑā mai tuvam ham-carahva*, subsequently translating *iϑa* as 'ainsi' (Pirart 2006: 140).

untranslated. It is noteworthy that in Y 10.1 and 10.17, *iθā* has been translated as *ēdar* as well as *ēdōn*, respectively (see Josephson 1997: 194).

As the above examination illustrates, word order alone is not a qualifying criterion for establishing a one-to-one correspondence between Av. and MP words. The connection between the PTr. and the Avestan original can be rather loose at times. For instance, on occasion Av. adverbs are left untranslated in the *Zand*. For instance, in the oft repeated formula across Y 4, *āat̰ dīš āuuaēδaiiamahī* 'Now, we dedicate those', the PTr. omits *āat̰*: *awēšān niwēyēnem* 'I consecrate them'.[44] At times the *Zand* offers interpretive translations without the intention of establishing novel meanings for the corresponding Av. words. All in all, it appears that the translation of adverbs does not conform to strict rules. Thus, *ad hoc* as well as *ad sensum* translations must be considered in the study of the *Zand* while variant translations of the same adverb occur.

Since rendering *iθā* as *ēdar* is not otherwise attested, we must consider the possibility that in the two YH passages *ēdar ēdōn* are connected with the collocation *iθā āt̰* rather than *ēdar* being a literal translation of *iθā*. Moreover, the use of *ēdar* certainly helps to avoid a doubling of *ēdōn* in Y 37.1 and 39.1.

Considering the individual constituents of the formula, Narten (1986: 167, fn. 1, 168, 259) convincingly argues that *iθā āt̰ yazamaidē* as a whole refers to the present stage ('aktuelle Gegenwart') of the liturgy and the manner of its performance in the presence of the fire.[45] Thus, the Av. formula underscores temporal, modal as well as spatial aspects of the ritual worship.

While Y 35 can be regarded as the introductory section of *yasn ī haft hād*, Y 36 represents a crucial moment in the ritual. According to Narten (1986: 26), in the Avestan version it is the moment of the fire's transformation. In my view, in PY 36 it is the presence of the fire of *Ohrmazd* that is the prerequisite for the actual sacrifice and worship to begin in Y 37.[46] Thus the nature of the ritual space has changed in Y 36; it no longer accommodates a ritual fire but the fire of *Ohrmazd*, which in the Avestan version (Y 36.3) is identified as *Ahura Mazdā*'s most bounteous spirit: *mainiiuš vōi ahiiā spəništō ahī* 'You are truly his most bounteous spirit'.[47] By using an adverb of location, *ēdar*, the *Zand* shifts the emphasis from an actual point in time to the physical space of the ritual and the presence of the fire. The fire's transformation is thus reflected by a transformation of the ritual space as well.

---

[44] See also Table 15.6 for some other examples of such omissions.
[45] See also Hintze (2007a: 156).
[46] For this interpretation of Y 36, see Narten (1986: 26, 155–6) and Hintze (2007a: 132–3). See also Kellens (2000: 108–9).
[47] Text and translation after Hintze (2007a: 132).

Alternatively, *ēdar* could have been used with a temporal sense in mind, referring not so much to the physical space than to a particular moment in the liturgy: 'Here, *at this point in the ritual*, we thus worship', reminding the worshippers of the praise and worship formulae that are about to begin in the middle section of the YH. Be that as it may, the Av. formula and its MP translation, *ēdar ēdōn yazom* 'Here we thus worship', both underscore the actuality of the liturgy.

15.1.5 The creations

(P)Y 37.1 contains an abridged account of *Ohrmazd*'s creations: cattle, order, water, good plant, light and the earth. While *gąmcā*, *aṣ̌əmcā* and *būmīmcā* are in acc.sg., *apascā*, *uruuarā̊scā vaŋʰhīš* and *raocā̊scā* are accusative plurals. Thus, the Av. version recounts *Ahura Mazdā*'s creation of the material world in general terms such as the cattle, waters, lights etc. In the *Zand*, however, all six creations occur in the unmarked form (singular) which could signal a shift in the interpretation of the Av. passage.

In MP, the plural of inanimate objects can be expressed by the unmarked form of substantives.[48] Thus, *āb* could denote the singular as well as the plural. In PY 38.3a, for instance, *āb* could refer to the types of waters that are about to be worshipped. But it could equally refer to the element water, whose various forms are subsequently worshipped. However, considering that both *ābān* and *urwarān* are attested in the *Zand*, we may ask why a plural form was not used in Y 37.1.[49]

My preliminary survey shows that *apō* and *apascā* are consistently translated *āb*.[50] In Y 3.7 and 4.11, for instance, *apasca* is rendered *āb*, while the gen.pl. *apąm* is translated *ābān*.[51] The translators could have interpreted the acc.pl.f. *apō* and its *Sandhi* form *apascā* as a singular, thus preferring *āb* to *ābān*. Concurrent to this observation, however, we find *apąm* translated as *āb* as well as *ābān*, suggesting that the translations of these forms may not be entirely mechanical.

---

[48] Sundermann (1989: 155) notes that in ZMP the plural of inanimate objects was replaced by indeclinable collective forms: 'Allerdings wird die Entwicklung der Plur.-Flexion durch die Ausbreitung undeklinierter kollektiver Formen unter inanimata bezeichnenden Substantiven durchkreuzt.'

[49] For *ābān*, see among others PY 3.3, 42.1b and 56.2. *urwarān* is attested in PY 2.11, PY 38.5b and PWr 21.1. On the use of the plural *ābān* outside the *Yasna*, see, for instance, ZWY 7.19: *frāz raw ō ēn ērān dehān ī man ohrmazd dād ud <pad> ātaxš <ud> ābān frāz yaz hādōxt ud dwāzdah hōmāst* 'Go forth to these Iranian lands which I, *Ohrmazd*, created and celebrate the *hādōxt* and the *dwāzdah hōmāst* for the fire and the waters' (text after Cereti 1995: 143).

[50] *apascā* occurs throughout the *Yasna* in the formula *imā̊. apasca. zəmasca. uruuarā̊sca. yaz.* (Y 6.15) and in *apasca. mazdaδātaiiā̊* (Y 7.7). See, for instance, Y 5.1, 2.16, 3.7, 6.15, 71.20 and Wr 16.3. For *apō*, see Y 44.4 and 63.3.

[51] For *apąm* translated *ābān*, see also Y 70.6.

Skjærvø (2009a: 21) points out that in MP the plural is used to express plurality, while the singular can refer to 'a class of objects' (Skjærvø 2010a: 205).[52] The use of the singular and plural of *āb* in some passages seems reminiscent of the rule observed by Skjærvø:

(P)Y 3.3[53] (b) *xšnūmaine aiβiiō vaŋhūbiiō apąm vaŋhūnąm mazdaδātanąm*
(f) *xšnūmaine apąm mazdaδātanąm*

To please the good waters, (and for the satisfaction) of the good *Mazdā*-created waters.
To please the *Mazdā*-created waters.

(b) *pad šnāyēnīdārīh ī āb ī weh ud nāmčištīg ābān ī wehān*[54] *ī ohrmazd dād ud abārīg āb*
(f) *pad šnāyēnīdārīh ī āb ī ohrmazd dād*

In praise of the good and well-known water, (and) the waters of the good ones which are created by *Ohrmazd*, and the other waters.
In praise of the waters created by *Ohrmazd*.

The exegetes interpret the dat.pl. *aiβiiō* 'waters' as referring to a certain well-known water (*nāmčištīg*), thus preferring the unmarked MP form *āb*, which can technically denote a plural. In the second instance the plural form *ābān*, corresponding to gen.pl. *apąm*, emphasises the plurality of waters created by *Ohrmazd*, further explained as the other waters (*abārīg āb*).[55] The gen.pl. *apąm* occurs once more in line (f), this time corresponding to an unmarked *āb*. It is unclear whether this *āb* refers to the well-known water of line (b), or to waters in general. In either case the plurality of the object does not seem to be significant, hence the unmarked form. The use of the marked and unmarked form of *āb* in the above stanza could suggest that rather than blindly following the Av. version, the exegetes employed grammatical forms to convey nuances that they associated with the original. However, since the exchange of marked and unmarked forms takes place in translations of formulaic expressions, the application of these forms could have become crystallised at some point.

---

[52] He illustrates his point with this example: *pad āsmān stārag ud axtar ud abāxtar ast* 'there are stars, constellations, and planets in the sky' (Skjærvø 2009a: 21).

[53] Text after Pt4.

[54] Note the literal translation of *apąm vaŋʰhīnąm* 'of the good waters' as *ābān ī wehān* 'waters of the good ones'. In ZMP, in contrast to MMP, the attributive adjective is not required to agree with the qualified noun in number. And the use of the connective particle *ī* and congruence are mutually exclusive (Sundermann 1989: 156). The expected form is *ābān ī weh* 'good waters'.

[55] In *abārīg āb* the plural context is sufficiently clear through *abārīg* 'other', so that the unmarked form *āb* can be used unambiguously. However, see also Bd 10.5 where we find *abārīg ābān: az ān čiyōn ān āb pad garmīh ud xwēdīh ud yōjdahrīh freh az abārīg ābān* 'Since that water in heat, moisture and purity is more than other waters' (text after Pakzad 2005: 140).

Be that as it may, viewed in the context of the wider MP literature, the unmarked forms *āb*, *urwar* and *rōšnīh* could denote an actual singular referring to the prototypes of the creations. It has been noted that in the *Avesta* the list of the creations was not systematised.[56] We do not find a standardised account of the creation in the Pahlavi literature either. The type and order of the creations are subject to a wide margin of variability. Two examples should illustrate this point:

> **AWN 14.9**[57] *ka-šān mēnōy ī āb ud zamīg ud urwar ud gōspand pēš estād ud āfrīn kard ud stāyišn ud spās ud āzādīh gōwēnd*
>
> When the *mēnōy* of water and the earth and the plant and the cattle stood in front of them and praised them and spoke (words) of praise, thanks and gratitude.
>
> **Dk 3.123.44** *ud gētīy dahišnān hangirdīgīh hēnd šaš āsmān āb ud zamīg ud urwar ud gospand ud mardōm*
>
> And the totality of the *gētīy* creations are six: the sky, water, the earth, the plant, the cattle and people.

Although AWN 14.9 does not recount the act of creation, but an encounter in the afterlife, the context suggests that here individual spirits are praised rather than the *mēnōy* of all waters. As we know the material world was first created motionless with prototypes of each of the creations. Only after *Ahreman* attacked and destroyed the prototypes did the material creations diversify. Bd 1 recounts the creation of the *gētīy*:

> **Bd 1.53**[58] *az dām ī gētīy nazdist āsmān didīgar āb sidīgar zamīg čahārom urwar panjom gōspand šašom mardōm haftom xwad ohrmazd*
>
> Of the *gētīy* creation first the sky, second water, third the earth, fourth the plant, fifth the cow, sixth people (and) seventh *Ohrmazd* himself.

While the lists of the creations do not agree with each other in the above accounts, it emerges from the MP literature that the first material creations were elements or prototypes. This understanding of the *gētīy*'s creation process could have been the basis for the *Zand* of passages such as Y 37.1.

15.1.6 *bun ud bar*

The expression ⟨bwn W bl⟩, *bun ud bar* is attested in a number of *Zand* passages, but does not correspond to a phrase in the Av. original. While the meaning of the individual components, *bun* 'base, foundation, bottom' and *bar* 'fruit, produce, profit', are sufficiently clear, the priestly interpretation

---

[56] Avestan passages have been discussed by Narten (1986: 169–71) and Kreyenbroek (1993).
[57] Text after Vahman (1986: 111).
[58] Text after Pakzad (2005: 23).

of the expression as a whole and its meaning in the *Yasna* have not been explored in more detail.[59]

Mills (1905a: 64) and Williams (1990: II 252) translate the expression as 'root and fruit', while Panaino (2002: 26–7) renders it as 'base and fruit' in Yt 1.7. In a brief note on *bun ud bar*, Dhabhar (1963: 100–1) suggests among others 'capital and interest' and 'everything from beginning to end' as possible translations. More recently, Macuch has discussed the terms *bun* 'substance, capital, principal, base' and *bar* 'fruit, increase' in the context of the Sasanian judiciary system.[60]

In the *Zand*, the expression regularly occurs after *harwisp huzāyišnīh* 'all good birth'[61] and *harwisp ābādīh* 'all prosperity'.[62] In PY 31.10, the expression comes after *ēdōn ān ī harw 2*, while in *Patit ī Pašēmānīh* 1.1.2 *bun ud bar* is not seemingly motivated by a word we can identify.[63] On the one hand, the collocation *bun ud bar* seems to emphasise totality, which the exegetes must have associated with the preceding *harwisp* 'all' and *harw 2* 'both'.[64] On the other hand, the expression must have been motivated by the immediately preceding word, be it *huzāyišnīh* or *ābādīh*, denoting the two aspects that apply to each legal object in Sasanian law (see below).[65]

Macuch asserts that in Sasanian legal terminology every 'legal object' (*xwāstag*) was divided into capital or substance (*bun*) and its yield (*bar*) (Macuch 2015: 248). Sasanian jurists also distinguished between two fundamental types of rights to legal objects: *xwēšīh* 'ownership' and *dārišn* 'possession' (Macuch 2015: 248–9). *xwēšīh* entitles the owner to full control of an object, while *dārišn* denotes the possession of an object without including full entitlement and ownership. She argues that the distinction between *bun* 'substance' and *bar* 'income' in relation to *xwēšīh* and *dārišn* was fundamental

---

[59] Concurrently, but independently from this brief note, Buyaner (2014) carried out a study into the supposed Indo-European roots of a MP metonymic figure including *bun ud bar*. I leave the evaluation of Buyaner's suggestion to the esteemed reader. I discuss the figure of *bun ud bar* in greater detail in a forthcoming paper.

[60] See Macuch (1993: 695, 697), Macuch (2005: 381), Macuch (2007: 198), Macuch (2009a: 262, 271), Macuch (2009c: 96–7) and Macuch (2015).

[61] See PY 1.6, 3.8, 4.11, 7.8, 13.4, 14.2, PWd 3.3, *Srōš Wāj* 1 and G 4.6 (*Ēbsrūsrim Gāh*). In PY 3.8, J2 and F2 replace *bun ud bar* with a comment from PY 2.6 (For J2, see Dhabhar 1949: 22). The MSS also alternate between *huzāyišnīh* and *huzīwišnīh* 'good life' for Av. *hujiiātə̄e* 'good life' and *hujītaiiō* 'good life'. In PY 3.8, 4.11 and 7.8, Pt4 translates *hujiiātə̄e* as *huzāyišnīh*. F2 agrees with Pt4 with the exception of PY 7.8 where it has *huzīwišnīh*. Both MSS have *huzāyišnīh* for *hujītaiiō* in PY 13.4, but *huzīwišnīh* in PY 33.10. The expected translation is *huzīwišnīh* 'good life' rather than 'good birth'. See also Bartholomae (1904: 609, 1821–2) and Dhabhar (1949: 86, 88).

[62] See PY 5.1 (= 37.1), 8.5, 11.12, 12.9, Yt 1.7, *Zand ī Nān, Stāyišn Dēnīh* (= Y 12.8–9) and *Hōšbām*.

[63] For a recent edition of the *patit* texts, see Buyaner (2016).

[64] See also Dhabhar (1963: 101, fn. 3), who suggests 'everything from beginning to end' as one of the possible translations.

[65] Not every occurrence of *harwisp*, *ābādīh*, *huzāyišnīh* or a combination thereof is glossed *bun ud bar*. For *harwisp huzāyišnīh* without the gloss, see PY 2.6, 3.8, 6.5 and 12.1. See PY 19.2 and 4, 22.3 and 22, 24.3 and 8, 25.3, 37.4, 42.3 and 70.1 for *harwisp ābādīh*.

to the development of institutions such as *stūrīh* 'substitute succession' and *ruwānagān* 'pious foundation' (Macuch 2015: 251). This division allowed the legal system to differentiate between ownership or possession of an object's (*xwāstag*) substance or income. Moreover, as Macuch (2015: 249) observes, in legal texts the ownership is always expressed by the verbal compound *pad xwēšīh dāštan* 'to possess in ownership'. As we shall see, the *Zand* retains the precision of the legal terminology and reinterprets the above terms in a theological context, placing the relationship between the deity as the creator, the *gētīy* as a legal object and the humans' rights to the material creation in the context of a legal contract. The commentary in PY 12.9 is illuminating:

> PY 12.9c[66] *ō ohrmazd harwisp ābādīh čāšom kū bun ud bar hamāg pad xwēšīh ī ohrmazd dārom* ...
>
> I assign all prosperity to *Ohrmazd*, that is, I possess both capital and yield in *Ohrmazd*'s ownership.

In agreement with PY 37.1, all prosperity (*harwisp ābādīh*) is assigned to *Ohrmazd*. By using legal terminology, the following comment construes this assignment as a legal transaction: both aspects of a legal object, namely capital and yield, are unambiguously assigned to *Ohrmazd* (*xwēšīh ī ohrmazd*), while the sacrificers only retain the right of possession. *Ohrmazd* is the designated owner (*xwēšīh ī ohrmazd*), while the verb clearly refers to the sacrificer (*dārom*). Thus, *Ohrmazd* retains the full ownership of his creation, the legal object, while humans are entitled to its substance and yield as possessors. Such notions of ownership also emerge from other passages:

> Y 0.5c[67] *frāz pad menišn ud frāz pad gōwišn ud frāz pad kunišn ud frāz pad axw menišnīg ud frāz pad tan ud ān-iz ī xwēš jān kū tan pad xwēšīh ī ašmāh dārom pad xwēšīh ī ašmāh dāštan ēd kū agar-im tan ruwān rāy bē abāyēd dādan be dahom*
>
> (I offer) forth by thought, and (I offer) forth by speech, and (I offer) forth by deeds, and (I offer) forth by focusing on the existence, and (I offer) forth by (my) body and also that which is my life,[68] as I possess (my) body in your ownership; 'to possess in your ownership' means this: if I have to give up my body on account of the soul, I will give (it) up.

Here too, the body, a material creation, is declared the property of the deities.[69] Since humans are not fully entitled to the ownership of their own body, it can be *sacrificed* for the soul should the need arise. A comment after a paraphrase of PY 0.5 in the *Patit ī Pašēmānīh* further elaborates on this concept:

---

[66] Text after Pt4.
[67] Text after Pt4.
[68] Shaked (1994: 56) translates *jān* 'vital soul'.
[69] The stanza does not specify whose property the body is. *ašmā* could refer to *Ohrmazd*, the *Amahraspandān* or the *yazadān*, as in Pt 1.1.2 (see above).

Pt 1.1.2[70] *tan ǰān* ~~ud ham~~ **nām ruwān bun ud bar ī xwāstag ī-m ast pad xwēšīh ī yazadān dārom pad xwēšīh ī yazadān dāštan ēn bawēd kū agar tis-ēw az ān rasēd ka-m tan ī ruwān rāy be abāyēd dādan be dahom*

Body and life, (by) the name soul.[71] I possess the substance and yield of my properties in the ownership of the *yazadān*; 'to possess in the ownership of the *yazadān*' is this: if something happens, so that I have to give up my body on account of the soul, I will give (it) up.

The legal aspect of the passage's language intensifies when relating the ownership of *bun ud bar* to the deities. The substance and yield of the legal object (*xwāstag*) are described as possessions in the ownership of the deities. The explanation of the phrase *pad xwēšīh ī yazadān dāštan* 'to possess in the ownership of the deities', designates the body once more as that which should be sacrificed for the soul. Although not explicitly stated, it seems as if body and life (*ǰān*) are the substance and yield of the soul whose full ownership lies with the deities. This sense of belonging to *Ohrmazd* and other deities is reminiscent of a passage from the *čīdag handarz ī pōryōtkēšān*:

ČHP[72] *kē hēm ud kē xwēš hēm ... ohrmazd xwēš hēm ayāb ahreman yazadān xwēš hēm ayāb dēwān ... ohrmazd xwēš hēm nē ahreman yazadān xwēš hēm nē dēwān*

Who am I and to whom do I belong? ... Do I belong to *Ohrmazd* or *Ahreman*? Do I belong to the deities or the demons? ... I belong to *Ohrmazd* and not *Ahreman*, I belong to the deities and not the demons.

And the notion of giving up material life for the sake of the soul is also known in the wider MP literature. One of the answers to a question about good rule (*hupādixšāyīh*) in MX 14 asserts that a good ruler will always sacrifice the body and soul for the sake of the good religion:

MX 14.16[73] *hupādixšāyīh ān bawēd kē ... (21) ud dēn ī weh ī mazdēsnān rāy tan ud ān-iz ī xwēš ǰān be abespārēd*

(16) Good rule is that one, which ... (21) and (the good ruler) will sacrifice body and also his own life for the good Mazda-worshipping religion.

---

[70] Text after Dhabhar (1927: 55) with indicated modifications. Considering his notes on his translation (see Dhabhar 1963: 100–1, 124–5), I have emended his readings, hoping to approximate the text of the manuscripts. Buyaner (2016: 64), also Buyaner (2014: 13), reads here: *ud tan gyān ud nām ruwān <ud> bun bar ī xwāstag ī-m hast |d| pad xwēšīh ī yazadān dārēm pad xwēšīh ī yazadān dāštan ēd bawēd kū agar čiš az ān rasēd kū-m tan ruwān rāy be abāyēd dādan be dahēm*. Buyaner's reading of *nām* seems correct, and Dhabhar's above reading can be emended to *tan ǰān nām ruwān bun ud bar ī xwāstag* with the intended meaning 'Body and life, (by) the name soul ...'. However, in light of *tan ud ǰān kē nām ī ōy ruwān ast* (see Dhabhar 1927: 63 and Buyaner 2016: 95), I hesitate to accept Buyaner's (2014: 14–17) interpretation of *tan gyān ud nām ruwān*. If my interpretation is accepted, then Buyaner's (2014: 16) argument of a 'threefold parallel construction' *ud tan gyān ud nām ruwān <ud> bun bar ī xwāstag* may be untenable.
[71] My interpretation of this clause is based on Pt 2.1.2: *tan ud ǰān kē nām ī ōy ruwān ast* 'Body and life whose name is soul' (text after Dhabhar 1927: 63).
[72] Text after Jamasp-Asana (1897: 41).
[73] Text after Anklesaria (1913: 60–1).

In the summary of the YH in the *Bag Nask* we find a similar view of the dedication of the body and life to the deities:

Dk 9.57.28[74] *ud ēn-iz kū huframānīh ud abzōn ī ohrmazd kard bawēd kē tan ud ǰān ō yazadān dahēd ∴ u-š tan ǰān ō yazadān dād bawēd kē dōstīh ō dēn ī zardušt dahēd*

And this too, that who(ever) dedicates his body and life to the deities, practises good command and increases *Ohrmazd*. And who(ever) dedicates friendship to Zardušt's religion, he has given his body and life to the deities.

In the above passages, the relationship between *Ohrmazd*, his creation and humans is described in legal terms, as if the two parties were bound by a legal contract. Humans are not entitled to full ownership of their own body. Rather, they have an obligation towards the deity and the *mēnōy*, which they fulfil by accepting to give up their body and its life (*ǰān*) when necessary. As Shaked (1994: 69) notes, *ruwān* is considered divine in MP texts and one 'is encouraged to do things "for the sake of one's soul"', a phrase that denotes performing pious deeds'. The *Zand* seems to extend this concept beyond just pious deeds to a readiness to give up life for the sake of the soul.

It is noteworthy that the priestly perception of the expression's individual components, i.e. *bun* and *bar*, remain rather elusive in the *Yasna*. Thanks to Macuch's efforts we know their legal definition, but it is unclear which parts of the tangible and intangible creation are understood to be *bun* or *bar*. PY 34.3a suggests that there might be a relationship between *mizd* 'reward' and *bun ud bar*:

PY 34.3a[75] *ēdōn ō*[76] *tō mizd ohrmazd kū* ⟨b^{wn}l⟩[77] *pad xwēšīh ī tō dārom ud niyāyišn ō ašwahišt-iz dahom ǰādagōwīh kunom*

Thus, I (assign) the reward to you, O *Ohrmazd*, that is I posses b^{wn}l in your ownership, and I also praise *Ašwahišt*, I practise intercession.

This passage has been subject to editorial revisions and the intended meaning is difficult to grasp, as it is unclear whether *mizd* relates to *bun*, *bar* or *bun ud bar*. The revisions also obscure whether *mizd* is assigned to *Ohrmazd* as Pt4 and J2 suggest, or whether the passage is about the reward belonging to *Ohrmazd*. A number of MP texts, most prominently Dk 3.393 and Dk 9.50, explore these links further. An in-depth analysis of these passages, however, is beyond the scope of this brief note.

---

[74] Text after Dresden (1966: 212).
[75] Text after Pt4, with essential variants pointed out below.
[76] 'w' Pt4, J2; ZK Y F2 T6; 'L K5 M1.
[77] b^{wn}l Pt4; ^{bwn} bl F2; bwn W bl T6; bl K5 J2 M1.

15.1.7 (P)Y 37.1b

As we saw in Sections 13.2.5 and 13.9, *Pursišnīhā* employs verses from the (P)YH as authoritative sources in the interpretation of religious questions. I have also drawn attention to the interplay between legal terminology and theological speculation in the discussion of the expression *bun ud bar* (Section 15.1.6). In another instance, the *Pursišnīhā* shows that the relevance of the scripture was not confined to debates of religious nature, but extended to legal questions:

> Pur 53[78] *2 mard ēk abāg did pahikār ud harw 2 brād*[79] *hēnd ēk gōwēd kū g̶ō̶w̶ē̶d̶ k̶ū̶ pidar ī man wahmān xwāstag ōh*[80] *man dād frāz ōh dādwarān šawēnd ud handarz ī pidar pad dādwarān dārēnd ud pad handarz ōwōn gōwēd kū-m wahmān xwāstag ōh wahmān pusar dādan nūn-iz*[81] *ān pusar ōwōn gōwēd kū ān kē pidarān guft kū-m wahmān xwāstag ōh tō dād frāz gīr pad ān kē-š nām burd u-š dādan nē guft ēg-iš nē dād bid u-t nē dahom ∴ dādwar*[82] *wizīr čiyōn kunišn ∴*
> *dādwar harw 2 xwāstag ōh ōy abespārišn čē agar ōh-iz ēg-iš pad abdom dād nē guft ēg-iš pad mayān xwāstag ud xwāstag dād guft u-š xwēš ∴ apascā dāṯ uruuarāscā vaŋhīš ∴ u-š āb-iz dād urwar-iz ī weh ud nē*[83] *kū-š dād pad āb guft u-š urwar nē guft čē-š āb ud urwar harw 2 dād*

> Two men have a dispute with each other, and they are both brothers. One says: 'My father gave me such and such property'. They go forth to the judges and place the father's testament before the judges. In the testament it says so: 'I give such and such property to son so and so'. And now that (other) son says so: '(Concerning) that which father said: "I gave you property such and such, accept it!", he did not say to give (the property) to the one whose name was mentioned. So, he did not give it. And I do not give it to you'. What decision is the judge to make?
> The judge should give both properties to him, for even if at the end he did not say (that it should be) given, in between he had said that the property and the property (should be) given, and (it should be) his own. ∴ He has created the waters and the good plants.[84] ∴ And he also gave water (and) also the good plant. That 'he gave' is said of the water, and it is not said of the plant, although he gave both water and the plant.

The dense legal language of this case complicates its comprehension. The final statement of the exposition is central to our understanding of PY 37.1b's relevance to the case. Emending the text slightly (Humbach and Jamaspasa 1971: 76, fn. 3), Humbach and Jamaspasa translate the final sentence as 'i.e. he has not said of waters that "he created", and he has not said of the

---

[78] Text transliterated after TD2 (see Humbach and Jamaspasa 1971: II 50–1). Translation is mine.
[79] bl'c' TD2.
[80] So TD2, but read *ō*.
[81] nwnc' TD2.
[82] d'twbl' TD2.
[83] This *nē* seems to be superfluous.
[84] Here Pur 53 quotes Y 37.1b.

plants, because he created both waters and plants' (Humbach and Jamaspasa 1971: 77). This translation, if I understand it correctly, neglects the fact that in both versions of Y 37.1b quoted in Pur 53, it is said of the water that the deity created it, a fact acknowledged by Humbach and Jamaspasa's translation of the quotations. My own translation addresses this issue, but fails to elucidate the case further. The final statement of Pur 53 seems to suggest that the property was to be given to both sons, as although 'created' is not mentioned twice in PY 37.1b, it nonetheless applies to both water and the plant. Therefore, the argument seems to be, although the father did not mention 'to be given' twice, the property should be given to both brothers. This interpretation, however, is contradicted by the first clause of the reply: *dādwar harw 2 xwāstag ōh ōy abespārišn*. We would expect *awēšān* if the property was to be given to both brothers, or *dādwar harw 2 xwāstag abespārišn* 'The judge should give both (brothers) the property'. Humbach and Jamaspasa (1971: 76, fn. c) also draw attention to a case of land and water distribution mentioned in MHD 105.10:

> MHD 105.10[85] Und jener (Satz), der gesprochen wurde: „Wenn er (= der Testator) auf dem Land, (11) das er Farroḫ (vermacht hat), und mit dem Wasser, das er im Testament Mihrēn vermacht hat, eine Wassermühle errichtet hat, (dann) gelangt die Wassermühle durch das (12) Testament nicht (an Farroḫ und Mihrēn)".

Although parallels between the two passages are undeniable, the elliptic presentation of the case in Pur 53 prevents a direct comparison. Moreover, Humbach and Jamaspasa seem to believe that PY 37.1b is quoted due to the mention of water. However, as I discussed above, the reference to PY 37.1b is due to its stylistic construction rather than its content. The fact that the verb is used once, but applies to two objects links PY 37.1b to the case and not the mention of water. Despite the evasive logic behind the above judgement, Pur 53 shows that the (P)YH had legal authority in disputes.

---

[85] Translation after Macuch (1993: 647).

15.2 PY 37.2

15.2.1 *ōy kē ... aziš*

Although Y 5 and Y 37 are identical, in Geldner's (1886–96: 26) edition Y 5.1 concludes with *ahiiā xšaϑrācā mazə̄nācā hauuapaŋhāiscā 'ōy kē xwadāyīh ud mehīh padiš u-š hu-pānagīh aziš'*, while Y 37.1 ends with *raocåscā dāt̰ būmīmcā vīspācā vohū* (Geldner 1886–96: 132). Thus, in his edition *ahiiā xšaϑrācā* marks the beginning of Y 37.2. Similarly, Dhabhar (1949: 37) includes *ōy kē ... aziš* in Y 5.1.[86] Analysing the syntactic relationship between Y 37.1 and 2, Narten (1986: 172–3) considers *ahiiā xšaϑrācā* to be an adverbial complement to the previous relative clause. Therefore, she assigns *ahiiā xšaϑrācā* contextually to Y 37.1. Likewise, Hintze (2007a: 168) concurs with Geldner's editorial decision in Y 5.1. However, Westergaard (1852–54: 17, 69) assigns *ahiiā xšaϑrācā* in both cases to the second stanza.[87]

Contrary to the views expressed by modern scholars, both in Y 37.2 and Y 5.2 the priestly tradition seems to have considered *ahiiā xšaϑrācā* to be part of the second stanza. The *Zand* of Y 5.1 is quoted in PRDd 57, *zand ī nān* and in Bd 14.14.[88] In PRDd 57 the final *bun ud bar* is missing, while Y 5.1 is repeated verbatim in *zand ī nān*. The *Bundahišn* paraphrases the stanza in question:

> **Bd 14.14**[89] *u-šān nazdist gōwišn ēn guft kū ohrmazd dād āb ud zamīg ud urwar ud gōspand ud star ud māh ud xwaršēd ud harwisp ābādīh kē az ahlāyīh paydāgīh gōwēd bun ud bar*
>
> And they said these as the first words: Ohrmazd created water and the earth and plant and the cattle and the stars and the moon and the sun and all prosperity, which is from the manifestation of righteousness. One says root and fruit.

In all three instances the *Zand* of Y 5.1 ends with *harwisp ābādīh* 'all prosperity', suggesting that Y 5.1 (= Y 37.1) was considered to end with *vīspācā vohū*. Moreover, the instructions at the end of Y 37 and Y 5, *panj wičast abāg iϑā sē gāh*, suggest that the exegetes attributed three lines to each stanza of these chapters, thus ending Y 37.1 with *vīspācā vohū*. Therefore, the traditional exegesis must have attributed *ahiiā xšaϑrācā* to Y 37.2. This view is further corroborated by stanza divisions which are marked in Pt4 with an elongated *'ālep̄* above the stanza's first word (Figure15.1).[90]

---

[86] Dhabhar (1949: 170) abbreviates Y 37.
[87] Brockhaus (1850: 14) gives *ahiiā xšaϑrācā* in Y 5.2 and abbreviates Y 37.
[88] See Appendix D and Dhabhar (1927: 2) for PRDd 57 and *zand ī nān*, respectively.
[89] Text after Pakzad (2005: 183), translation is mine.
[90] In Pt4 these signs are only found in chapters or groups of stanzas perceived as OAv. To my knowledge these marks have not previously been studied, but in the majority of cases they match the modern stanza divisions. Most likely, they mark the strophe boundaries in agreement with the count given at the end

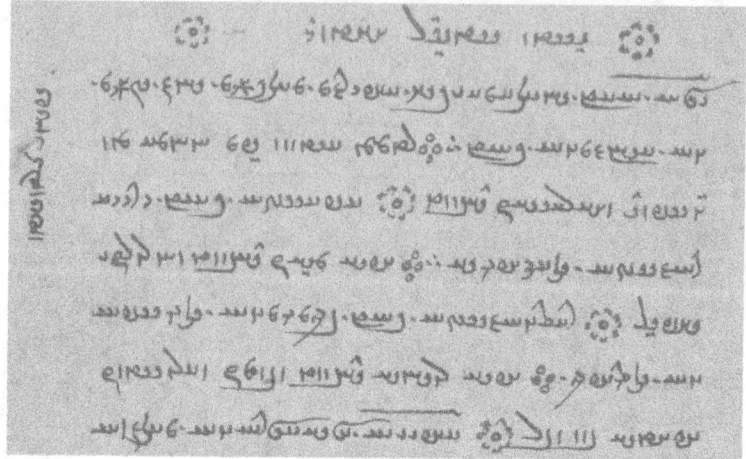

Figure 15.1 Stanza marks in Pt4

Contrary to Geldner's claim that strophes are not marked in the MSS (Geldner 1886–96: LII), stanza divisions are indicated in some of the manuscripts. Of the manuscripts available from the ADA website, the manuscripts Lb2 Bh5 G97 G26b (InYS), G27 2101 (IrWrS), 4010 4025 4040 4050 4060 4100 (IrWdS),[91] B4 (InWdS)[92] use decorative devices or other punctuations to separate stanzas. According to these MSS, Y 5.1 ends with *vīspācā vohū*.[93] The manuscripts Lb2 Bh5 G97 G26b, B4 do not generally use punctuation to mark stanzas, but use a decorative device in Y 5 after *vīspācā vohū* (Figure 15.2).

---

of each chapter. It is unknown whether these marks are a later addition by a second hand or not. An elongated *'āleṗ* is used in F2 T6 to relate marginal notes to specific words in the text.

[91] The ADA contains nine MSS of this family, of which six mark the boundaries.

[92] Of ten InWdS manuscripts available from ADA, B4 is the only MS to note the stanza boundary.

[93] In Y 37.1, the MSS B4 and FK1 abbreviate this stanza ending it with *vīspācā vohū*, again indicating a stanza boundary after these words. By contrast, G27b and G42 abbreviate Y 37 after *ahiiā xšaϑrācā*. ML630, B2, T46, Bh5, B3, F2 and T6 abbreviate Y 37 after *ahurəm mazdąm* or *yō gąmcā*.

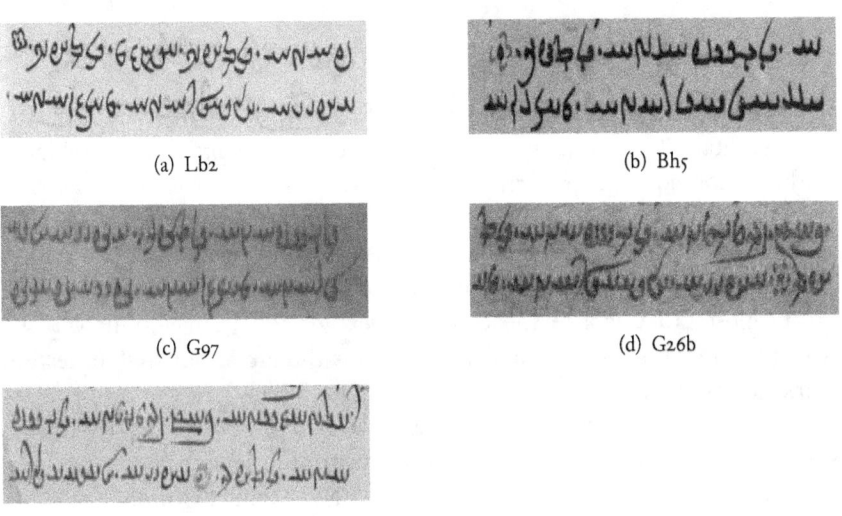

Figure 15.2 Stanza marks

15.3 PY 37.3

15.3.1 *tan ud ǰān*

In a discussion of the composition of man, Shaked (1994: 139–40) replaces the instrumental *uštānāišcā* in Y 37.3b with an acc.pl. '*uštānąnsca*' from Geldner's readings, consequently preferring *ōy kē amāgān tan ī ǰān zīwišn aziš yazom* to *ōy kē amāgān tan ud ǰān zīwišn aziš yazom*. In his view, the reading with *ud* assumes an elliptical construction in the Av. version, attempting a meaning such as 'by whom our body and soul derive their living' (Shaked 1994: 140). He proposes to translate the emended text of PY 37.3b as follows: 'We worship him who is (?) our body, of whom is the life of our soul' (question mark in original).

As discussed in Section 15.1.6, in the *legal contract* between the divine sphere and humans, the deities retain the ownership over the body (*tan*). As life (*ǰān*) is offered to the deities together with the body (Y 0.5c: *ud frāz pad tan ud ān-iz ī xwēš ǰān*), we may conclude that life is also held in possession and not in ownership. PY 37.3b alludes to this concept of possession without recourse to legal terminology: *ōy kē amāgān tan ud ǰān zīwišn aziš yazom* 'I worship him from whom is the life-force of our body and life.' Here, the text relates *tan ud ǰān* to the world of *mēnōy* from where they receive their life-force. A similar notion also emerges from PY 41.3b: *ēdōn az tō amā tan ud ǰān hād kū-mān apagaiiehe ma bawād* 'Our body and life shall thus be from you, that is, we shall not be lifeless.'

Although the deity's entitlement to the body or life are not discussed in this passage, both *tan* and *ǰān* depend on a divine sphere for their very existence, here expressed by *zīwišn* 'life-force' or 'livelihood'. It is perhaps through this dependency on the divine that humans only possess their body and life, a notion expressed by *pad xwēšīh ī ašmāh dāštan* 'to possess in your ownership'. Shaked's emendation and translation of PY 37.3b disturbs the line's allusion to the concept of ownership, but most importantly the unity of body and life.

15.3.2 *narān*

In PY 37.3c (= Y 5.3c), *narān ud nārīgān* 'males and women' translate the gen.pl. *narąmcā nāirinąmcā* 'men and women'. The collocation of *nar* and *nārīg* is not an isolated case within the PY, but is surprising, as it combines an adjective with a substantive. Within the PYH, *nar ud nārīg* and the plural *narān ud nārīgān* always correspond to the collocation of Av. *nar-* 'man' and *nāirī-* 'woman' (Table 15.8). While the variations of *nā vā nāirī vā* may rightly be translated as 'men and women', the *Zand*'s rendering is unusual, MP *nar* meaning 'male' rather than 'man'. The expected pairs in Pahlavi

Table 15.8 *nar* and *nārīg*

	Avestan	MP
35.5a	nā vā nāirī vā	nar ud nārīg
37.3c	narąmcā nāirinąmcā	narān ud nārīgān
39.2b	narąmcā nāirinąmcā	narān ud nārīgān-iz
41.2b	nā vā nāirī vā	nar ud nārīg

are *mardān* and *zanān*, as in Bd 5.3, Dk 7.3.38, PRDd 17b.1, and perhaps *mardān* and *nārīgān*, as in ZFJ on Wd 9.42 where we have *mard ī ahlaw ud nāirīg ī *ahlawēnī* 'the righteous man and the righteous woman'.[94] Another possibility could be *nar ud mādag* 'male and female', as in PY 39.3 and the wider MP literature. If not accompanied by *nāirī-*, Av. *nar-* seems to be translated *mard* 'man', which is the expected translation. In PY 39.2c, for instance, *vaonarə* is interpreted as a compound consisting of *vohu-* and *nar-* and translated *weh mard* 'good man'. Similarly, in PY 9.1c, *kō narə ahī* 'Who, O man, are you?' is translated *kē mard hē* 'Who, O man, are you?'. Moreover, according to FiŌ 69–71 ⟨GBR'⟩, *mard* is the designated translation for Av. *nar-*:

FiŌ 69–71[95] (69) *mard ka ēk* narš (70) *ka 2* nara (71) *ka 3* narō

(69) *mard* when it is one, *narš*, (70) when there are 2, *nara*, (71) (and) when there are 3, *narō*.

It emerges that while the meaning of the individual words was known, the translators preferred the MP cognates in translations of collocations involving *nar-* and *nāirī-*. It is noteworthy that MP *nārīg* is not common in non-translation MP texts and was perhaps mostly reserved for the *Zand*, where *nar ud nārīg* occur a number of times. To preserve something of the *Zand*'s style, I have translated *narān ud nārīgān* 'male (beings) and women'.

Although in FiŌ 69–71 *mard* is the suggested translation for Av. *nar-*, FiŌ 222, quoting (P)Y 35.5a, preserves the translation that we find in the manuscripts, namely *nar*. In a similar case, FiŌ 72 suggests *zan* as a translation for *nāirikā-*:

FiŌ 72[96] *NYŠH hmgwnk* nāirika nāirikaiiā̊ nāirikanąm

Woman likewise *nāirika nāirikaiiā̊ nāirikanąm*.

---

[94] I quote this passage from a transcription of the ZFJ kindly shared with me by Prof. Skjærvø.

[95] Text after Klingenschmitt (1968: 15). The Av. words *narš*, *nara* and *narō* are gen.sg., nom./acc.du. and nom.pl. of *nar-* m. 'man' (Klingenschmitt 1968: 15).

[96] Text after Klingenschmitt (1968: 15).

Although Av. *nāirikā-* 'woman' is a different word than *nāirī-*, the case is comparable to that of *nar-*.⁹⁷ As Klingenschmitt (1968: 15) notes, contrary to FiŌ 72 the *Zand* prefers to translate *nāirikā-* as *nārīg*. We must therefore agree with Klingenschmitt that the translation suggestions found in the FiŌ reflect the preferences of its compilers. It is unlikely that these are remnants of an alternative and lost *Zand*, as the Av. quotations in the FiŌ correspond to the translations of the extant *Zand*.

---

⁹⁷ *nāirikā-* derives from *nāirī-* via the suffix *-īka-* (Vaan 2003: 248), apparently without a noticeable change in the meaning.

15.4 PY 37.4

15.4.1 *amahraspandān*

MP *amahraspandān* corresponds to the Av. expression *aməša- spənta-*, a central concept in Zoroastrianism and well attested in YAv. texts.[98] The expression's OAv. attestation is confined to Y 37.4b and 39.3b where it occurs in the sequence *spənta- aməša-* as opposed to YAv. *aməša- spənta-*.[99] The so-called pseudo-OAv., plural *aməšā spəntā*, occurs only once in Y 35.0 where it is translated *amahraspandān*. In PY 35.8 and 39.3a, *amahraspandān* does not translate an Avestan word. Curiously, the OAv. sequence *spənta- aməša-* is not translated *amahraspandān* in the YH. For the acc.sg. *spəntəm aməšəm* in Y 37.4b we find *abzōnīg ī amarg* and for the acc.pl. *spəntəṇg aməšəṇg* in Y 39.3b *kē abzōnīg hēnd ud amarg*.

As Narten (1982: 76) and Hintze (2007a: 189) rightly observe, in the YH *spənta- aməša-* does not denote a group of deities with fixed members as in the Younger *Avesta*, but functions as a generic name referring to a group of divine beings. A similar understanding could have prompted the priests to translate the individual terms of the expression as *abzōnīg* 'bountiful' and *amarg* 'immortal', reserving the term *amahraspandān* as a proper name for YAv. *aməša- spənta-*, to which the components of the term *amahraspandān* correspond in sequence. It could also be argued that the reversed order in which the expression occurs motivated the alternative translation. At any rate, the reference to *amahraspandān* in PY 35.8b and 39.3a, where the name does not translate an Av. word, suggests that the priests presupposed the concept of *amahraspandān* for the Older *Avesta*.

The translation of the OAv. sequence *spənta- aməša-* as *abzōnīg* and *amarg* had implications for the *Zand* of YAv. passages. Inflected forms of YAv. *aməša- spənta-* are widely attested in the *Yasna*: *aməšā spəntā* (Y 0.5), *aməšanąm spəntanąm* (Y 0.8), the *Sandhi* form *aməšaēibiiasca spəntaēibiiō* (Y 4.2), *aməšaēibiiō spəntaēibiiō* (Y 4.4), *aməšąscā spəntą* (Y 13.3), *aməšəm spəntəm* (Y 13.8) and *aməšə̄ spəntə̄* (Y 15.1).[100] In all of these instances YAv. *aməša- spənta-* is translated *amahraspandān*, with the exception of Y 13.8 where we find *amarg ī abzōnīg* for *aməšəm spəntəm*. Such a form is further attested in Y 5.4 (=Y 37.4), 18.9, 27.15, 59.33, Wr 19.2, Yt 1.22 and Yt 3.1 and 2 where it is translated *amarg* and *abzōnīg*.[101] Although *aməšəm spəntəm*

---

[98] For a dedicated study of this concept, see Narten (1982).
[99] For detailed discussions of *spənta- aməša-* in the YH, see Narten (1986: 260ff.) and Hintze (2007a: 188 and 273ff.).
[100] This is not an exhaustive list of attestations, but represents the inflections we find in the *Yasna*.
[101] For Wr 19.2, see Dhabhar (1949: 319); for Yt 1.22, see Dhabhar (1927: 95) and for Yt 3.1 and 2 see Dhabhar (1927: 100–1).

reflects the expected YAv. sequence, it is the only form whose inflection (acc.sg.) agrees with the form attested in Y 37.4. The *Zand* of Y 37.4 must have been generalised and applied to the YAv. form as well. To my knowledge, the acc.pl. *spəṇtāṇg aməṣ̌āṇg* (Y 39.3) is not otherwise attested.

16. *PY 38*

16.1 PY 38.1

16.1.1 *mādagān*

As Hintze (2007a: 197) points out, scholars have debated the precise meaning of the Av. term *gənā-*.[1] The question is whether the female beings referred to by *gənā-* are human or associated with the realm of the divine. Drawing attention to a number of Vedic parallels, Hintze (2007a: 205) rightly concludes that in the YH the 'noblewomen' are the four entities who are mentioned in Y 38.2: *ižā-* 'libation', *yaošti-* 'vitalization', *fərašti-* 'perfection' and *ārmaiti-* 'right-mindedness'. In PY 38.1a and b, *mādagān* 'females' and *mādag* 'female' translate the instr.pl. *gənābīš* and the nom.pl. *gənā̊*, respectively.[2] The term *mādag* on its own, however, does not provide further information about the exegetes' interpretation of the passage and the term *gənā-*. The attestation of *mādag* in the PYH does not furnish further information either (Table 16.1).[3]

However, the *Zand* of Y 38.2 suggests that the priests did not associate the above-mentioned abstract concepts with females of divine origin. As Table 16.2 shows, the *Zand* pertaining to the four *gənā-* offers a very different view and context. For one thing, where we would perhaps expect a list of four names, the *Zand* constructs an obscure and difficult clause, where the hapax legomenon *yaoštaiiō*, for instance, features as an inflected verb (see Section 16.2.2).

---

[1] See Hintze (2007a: 196–209) for an extensive commentary on the topic with references. See also Narten (1986: 189–94).

[2] Both substantives are of the stem *gənā-* f. 'noblewoman, divine woman' (Hintze 2007a: 341).

[3] Both *mādag* and *mādagān* occur many times in the PY. The plural *mādagān*, for example, occurs repeatedly in the formulaic expression *burz ī xwadāy mādagān ī rōšn ī ābān nāf* in PY 1.5, 2.5, 3.7, 4.10 etc.

249

Table 16.1 *mādag*

	Avestan	MP
38.1a	gənābīš	mādagān
38.1b	gənā̊	mādag
38.5a	∅	narān ud mādagān
39.3a	vaŋhušcā īṯ vaŋᵛhīšcā īṯ	weh nar ān ī weh mādag

Table 16.2 PY 38.2

Avestan	Meaning	MP	Meaning
īžā̊	Invigoration	ka pad abzōn	When in increase
yaoštaiiō	Vitalization	āyōzānd	They strive
fəraštaiiō	Perfection	ud pursišn	And the question
ārmataiiō	Right-mindedness	bowandag menišnīh	Right-mindedness

16.1.2 *az ahlāyīh abāgīh*

The expression *az ahlāyīh abāgīh* 'with the assistance of righteousness' occurs in PY 35.9a, 38.1c and 41.3a, translating *aṣ̌aatcā hacā*, *aṣ̌āṯ hacā* and *aṣ̌aŋhācim*, respectively. The expression does not seem to be attested in the non-translation MP literature, while in the PY it is the standard translation for *aṣ̌āṯ*, the abl.sg. of *aṣ̌a-* ntr. governed by the adposition *hacā* 'from, in agreement with, on account of'.⁴ In all three occurrences in the PYH the expression is followed by the comment *az ašwahišt hammis* 'together with *Ašwahišt*', associating the rather abstract concept of *ahlāyīh* 'order' with *Ašwahišt*, the second of the *Amahraspandān* who is the guardian of the fire.

Evidently, the ablative case *aṣ̌āṯ* was not the only trigger for *az ahlāyīh abāgīh*, as in PY 33.10 and 44.15 the MP expression translates the instr.sg. *aṣ̌ā*. The adjective *aṣ̌aŋhāc-* 'who is in companionship with *aṣ̌a*', attested twice in the PY, is another exception to the above-mentioned rule. Although it is not composed of an abl. case with the adposition *hacā*,⁵ in PY 41.3 the acc.sg.m. *aṣ̌aŋhācim* is translated *az ahlāyīh abāgīh* and accompanied by the comment *az ašwahišt hammis*. Most likely, the exegetes analysed *aṣ̌aŋhācim* as a compound consisting of *aṣ̌a-* and the adposition *hacā*. Surprising as this translation may be, it is contextually correct. However, in its second attestation as *aṣ̌aŋhāxš*, in Y 56.3, the adjective was analysed differently, as it is translated *pad ahlāyīh* without the usual comment.

---

⁴ See, for instance, (P)Y 15.2, 28.2, 43.14, 44.17 and 45.4.
⁵ For a discussion of the adjective, see Narten (1986: 288ff.) with references.

16.2 PY 38.2

16.2.1 īžā-

A technical term of the ritual (Hintze 2007a: 211), *īžā-* is rendered as *ka pad abzōn*. As Hintze (2007a: 212) reminds us, in YAv. the term can have the meaning strength and prosperity. The MP translation in PY 38.2a, *abzōn* 'increase, growth', is semantically close to this meaning and translates *īžā-* also in PY 50.8 and 70.4.

16.2.2 yaošti-

A hapax legomenon, *yaošti-* 'vitalization' has variously been discussed.[6] Here, *yaoštaiiō* is translated as a 3pl.subj. *āyōzānd*. The context suggests that *āyōzānd* is an inflected form derived from the verb *²āyōzīdan, āyōz-* 'to trouble; strive'. The translators seem to have connected *yaoštaiiō* with forms derived from *yaoz-* 'to set in motion, undulate'.[7] For example, the 3sg.ind.pres.act. *yaozaiti* and the 3pl.ind.pres.act. *yaozəṇti* are both translated *āyōzēd* in PY 65.4.

It should be noted that forms derived from *yŭj-* 'to harness, yoke' (see Cheung 2007: 217) are also translated as *āyōz-* in the *Zand*. This, however, is the present stem of *āyōxtan/¹āyōzīdan, āyōz-* 'join, yoke' which can be difficult to distinguish from *²āyōzīdan, āyōz-*. Some examples include *yaojaṇtē 'āyōzēnd'* (Y 30.10), *yaogət̰ 'āyōzēd'* (Y 44.4), *yūjə̄n 'āyōzēnd'* (Y 46.11), *yūjə̄n 'āyōzēd'* (Y 49.9) and *yaojā 'āyōzam'* (Y 50.7). The inf. *yūxta* (Y 11.2) is rendered as *āyōxtār* 'joiner'.

16.2.3 fərašti-

Another hapax legomenon in the YH, *fəraštaiiō* 'perfection' is here analysed as a derivative from YAv. *frašna-* 'question' and translated *pursišn* 'question'.[8]

16.2.4 ārmaiti-

As expected, *ārmataiiō* is translated *bowandag menišnīh* 'right-mindedness'.

---

[6] For a summary of the discussions, see Hintze (2007a: 214–21).
[7] On the Av. verb, see Cheung (2007: 218).
[8] On *fərašti-*, see Hintze (2007a: 221ff.) with references. Most recently, Tremblay (2009) has discussed the term.

16.3 PY 38.3

16.3.1 PY 38.3

The manuscripts Pt4 Mf4 T6 E7, K5 J2 M1 divide this stanza into three cola, as is indicated in Section 9.3. In the revised IrPY manuscripts F2 and R413 lines (a) and (b) of the Av. text are not separated by the MP translation. In these MSS, the first Pahlavi section starts after *hupərəϑβåscā vå* at the end of line (b). Although blank space was left in F2, the *Zand* of line (a) is missing after the Av. section and appears in the margins, possibly written by a second hand. In R413 the *Zand* of line (a) is missing entirely.

It is perceivable that the *Zand* of line (a) was missing in the ancestral manuscript from which both MSS were copied. The scribe of F2 could have noticed this, leaving blank space for a later addition from another MS. The space, however, seems not to have been enough, so that the *Zand* of the passage was added in the margins. R413 was either copied from the same manuscript as F2, or from F2 prior to the addition of the *Zand* in the margins. Alternatively, we can posit that the different line division and the missing text in F2 is due to scribal error, and that R413 simply copied these from F2. At any rate, the agreements between F2 and R413 here and in PY 38.5 suggest that R413 was copied from F2 rather than Mf4, as suggested by Jamaspasa and Nawabi (1976e).

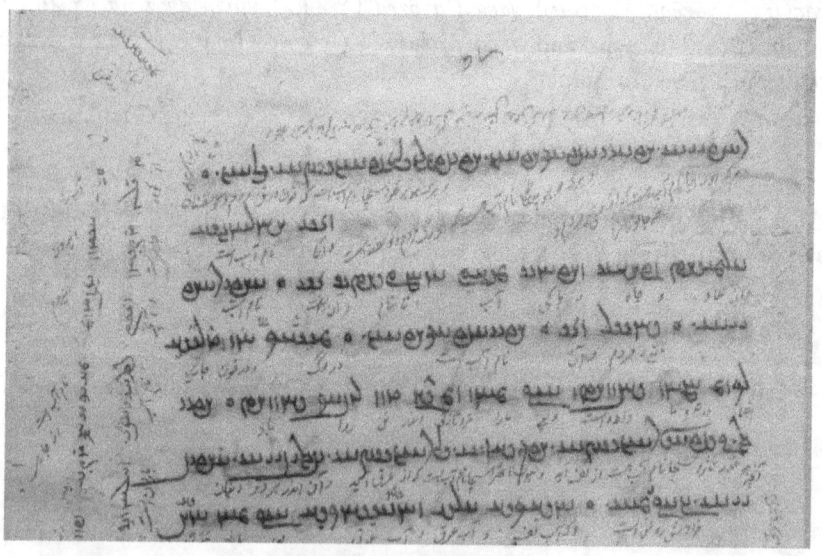

Figure 16.1 Y 38.3 in F2

(P)Y 38.3 also occurs in (P)Wd 11.5. For text-critical remarks on the transmission of this passage in the PWd, see Cantera (2006: 64) and Cantera and Andrés Toledo (2008: 111).

16.3.2 The waters

The Avestan root noun *ap-* f. 'water' occurs three times in the YH: 37.1, 38.3 and 38.5.[9] All three instances are acc.pl., *apō*, while in Y 37.1 and 38.5 the enclitic conjunction *-cā* causes the Sandhi form *apascā* (see Hoffmann and Forssman 1996: 136–7). In the PYH all three occurrences are translated *āb* 'water'.

The significance of water in Zoroastrian worship has variously been noted.[10] In the (P)YH, the identification of *āb* 'water' in PY 37.1 as *Ohrmazd*'s creation is a prelude to the actual praise of the waters in PY 38.3–5. Seven chapters of the *Yasna*, (P)Y 63–69, together constitute the actual water libation, commonly known as the *āb zōhr*.[11] Lines and verses from the (P)YH are often invoked within the *āb zōhr*, most notably from (P)Y 38.[12] Among other texts, Yt 5 and Ny 4 are dedicated to the deity *Arəduuī Sūrā Anāhitā*, the goddess of the waters. According to the latter, Ny 4.2, *Ohrmazd* ordered Zardušt to venerate the waters, denoted as *Ohrmazd*'s daughters:

Ny 4.2[13] *guft-iš ohrmazd ō spitāmān zarduxšt yaz*[14] *man duxt rāy ay spitāmān zarduxšt yaz āb ī ardwīsūr awinast hād awinastīh ēd kū pad awinastīh ān gyāg star pāyag ēstēd*

Ohrmazd said to *Spitāmān Zarduxšt*: worship my daughter, O *Spitāmān Zarduxšt*. Worship the waters of *Ardwīsūr*, the immaculate one. Being immaculate is this that by being immaculate she is stationed at that place, the star station.

As already noted by Bartholomae (1904: 1104) the enumeration of different types of waters in Bd 11b largely agrees with the *Zand* of Y 38.3:

---

[9] The word for water is widely attested in Old and Middle Iranian languages: as *ap-* in OP, as *ʾb* and *ʾb* in MMP and Pa., as *ʾp* in Sogdian and as αββο, -αβο in Bactrian.

[10] For related discussions, see Narten (1986: 26–7), Boyce (1996: 155–6) and Hintze (2007a: 7, 12–17). Water's religious significance for Sasanian architecture has been studied by Callieri (2006). Darrow (1988) discusses the 'dramatic relationship' between the fire and water in Zoroastrianism. See also Gignoux (2004a).

[11] The *āb zōhr* seems to be the canonical offering to the waters. On smaller and simpler offerings among Zoroastrians in Iran, see Boyce (1966: 111ff.), who offers an overview on the ritual of the waters.

[12] See, for instance, (P)Y 67.6–8 (≈ (P)Y 38.3–5), (P)Y 68.10 (≈ (P)Y 38.3). (P)Y 68.21 is particularly interesting as it consists of quotations from (P)Y 38.2–5. The *āb zōhr* also contains quotations from other *Yasna* passages.

[13] Text after Dhabhar (1923: 33).

[14] Dhabhar reads ⟨YDBḤWN-yh⟩.

Bd 11b.1[15] *pad dēn haftdah sardag āb gōwēd čiyōn ēk nam ī abar urwarān nišīnēd dudīgar ān ī garān tazišn ī ast rōdīhā sidīgar ān ī wārānīg āb čahārom ān ī čāhīg ān ī armēšt ud abārīg a-nāmčištīg panjom šuhr ī gōspandān ud mardōmān šašom gōmēz ī gōspandān ud mardōmān haftom xayūg ī gōspandān ud mardōmān haštom āb ī andar pōst ī gōspandān ud mardōmān nohom nam ud ars ī gōspandān ud mardōmān dahom xōn ī gōspandān ud mardōmān yāzdahom rōγn ān ī andar gōspandān ud mardōmān ud pad har(w) dō axwān kām dwāzdahom āb ī andar ham-bawišnīh ī gōspandān ud mardōmān sēzdahom xwēy*[16] *ī gōspandān ud mardōmān čahārdahom ān ī andar pusyān ī gōspandān ud mardōmān kē pus padiš parwarēnd pānzdahom ān ī azēr ī ēwan ī urwarān ī čiyōn guft kū har(w) ēwan-ē(w) āb-ē(w) srešk pad tah ātaxš čahār angust pēš šāzdahom ān ī andar urwarān gumēxt ēstēd kē āb ī tan-tōhmag gōwēd haftdahom šīr ī gōspandān ud mardōmān*

The *dēn* speaks of seventeen types of waters. The first is the moisture that sits on top of the plants. The second is that which flows heavily which are the rivers. The third one is the rainy water, (and) the fourth is that which is the well, the stagnating and the other unknown ones. The fifth is the semen of the cattle and the people, the sixth is the (consecrated) urine of the cattle and the people. The seventh is the saliva of the cattle and the people, the eighth the water under the skin of the cattle and the people, (and) the ninth the moisture and tears of the cattle and the people. The tenth is the blood of the cattle and the people, eleventh the butter which is in the cattle and the people and desired in both existences. The twelfth is the water which is in the union of the cattle and the people, (and) thirteenth the sweat of the cattle and the people. Fourteenth is that one which is in the womb of the cattle and the people, in which they nourish the embryo. Fifteenth is that which is under the trunk of the plants. As it is said, in every trunk there is some water, (which) will form drops at the bottom (if) fire is brought forward (to a distance) of four *angust*. Sixteenth is that which is mixed in the plants, which is called the water of the seed of the body. Seventeenth is the milk of the cattle and the people.

The above passage cites the *dēn* as the source of its knowledge: *pad dēn haftdah sardag āb gōwēd*. To that end, the list of the waters in Bd 11b.1 corresponds to information provided in PY 38.3 and 5, however, with a number of differences. Firstly, the order in which the fluids are mentioned differs between the two sources. Secondly, Bd 11b.1 does not give the Av. names associated with the various types of waters in PY 38.3 and 5. More importantly, there are a number of differences in the vocabulary and comments used in both texts. PY 38.3, for instance, uses the more general term *mēšag* 'urine' to describe *hauuapaŋhāi*, whereas Bd 11b.1 prefers the ritual term *gōmēz* 'urine' without mentioning the Av. name of this particular fluid. Table 16.3 summarises the differences between the two texts.[17]

---

[15] Text after Pakzad (2005: 158–9).

[16] Pakzad (2005: 159) reads *xwēd*. But as his apparatus indicates the intended word is *xwēy* 'sweat, perspiration', in agreement with PY 38.3c.

[17] I had to simplify the passages I quote in the table, but hope that some of the main differences are apparent.

Table 16.3 The waters in the Bd and the PYH

	Bd	PYH
1	nam ī abar urwarān	maikiiṇt: paššing, miznē
2	ān ī garān tazišn	hēbuuaiṇti: garān tazišn
3	ān ī wārānīg āb	frauuāzi: wārānīg
4	ān ī čāhīg	ahurānīš: armēšt ud čāhīg
5	šuhr	ahurahiiā: šuhr
6	gōmēz	hauuapaŋhāi: mēšag
7	xayūg	huwidaragīh: nam andar tan
8	āb ī andar pōst	hudahagīh: ars
9	nam ud ars	hušnāyišnagīh: xwēy
10	xōn	andar dō axwān kāmag: rōyn
11	rōyn	azīš: xayūg
12	āb ī andar hambawišnīh	mātrōš: āb ī andar hambawišnīh
13	xwēy	agəniiā̊: xōn
14	ān ī andar pusyān	driyōš dāyagānēnīdār: āb andar pusyān
15	ān ī azēr ī ēwan ī urwarān	vīspō.paitiš: āb ī pad urwarān ēwan
16	ān ī andar urwarān	pahlom ud nēktar: āb ī tantōhmag
17	šīr	mātarō.jītaiiō: šīr

Despite the differences between the two passages, the overall agreement between PY 38 and Bd 11b.1 indicates that the *Avesta*, or more precisely the PYH, was the source for the *doctrine* of the waters. The differences between the two texts are presumably significant, but not a unique case in the Zoroastrian tradition. The list of the five-fold fires is another illustrative example of variances in the literary transmission of motifs (Section 4.3.3).

It is also noteworthy that in PY 38 *āb* does not exclusively denote the element water, but refers to fluids in general.[18] However, it is unclear whether *āb* is used as a general term to refer to a number of fluids such as perspiration, saliva and milk, or whether the exegetes associated these fluids with the element of water. The passage is certainly reminiscent of the humorism theory, prompting Punegar (1943) to interpret the waters described here as bodily hormones. In contrast to humorism theory, however, the fluids described in PY 38 and Bd 11b.1 go beyond the human body extending to flora and fauna, as well as water as a natural phenomenon such as in rivers, rain and dew. It seems that along with the fire, water is seen as present in all creation. The notion that various forms of fluids are present in *Ohrmazd*'s

---

[18] The *Zand*'s interpretation of PY 38.3 and 5 is at stark variance with the Av. version. For more on this, see Section 16.5.2.

creation resonates well with Skjærvø's (2005: 74 and 82, n. 14) proposal to translate Av. *fraša-* as 'juicy' in OAv., suggesting that:[19]

> The expression has a double meaning: making the world here and now 'Juicy' through sacrifice both recreates the original state of the world and anticipates its end, when it will also be permanently 'Juicy', as the world returns to the state it was in when first established by Ahura Mazdā. (Skjærvø 2005: 74)

16.3.3 *hudahagīh*

In PY 38.3c, ہوس۫وہ, followed by *ars* 'tear (drop)', seems to correspond to the Av. hapax legomenon *huuōyžaθåscā*.[20] Mills (1905a: 110) reads ہوس۫وہ as *h-v-g-ž-akīh*, also weighing the possibility of *hū-ašk-īh*, presumably compelled by the following *ars*. Dhabhar (1949: 47) prefers *hvagjīkīh*, stating that it was 'a mere transcription' of *huuōyžaθåscā*, while Malandra and Ichaporia (2010: 50) transcribe *hudāgīh* 'beneficence'. All examined MSS attest ہوس۫وہ or ہوس۫وہ, which, in line with my interpretation of *hudahāgān* (see Section 13.1.3), I read as *hudahagīh* 'beneficence'.

In F2 ہوس۫وہ is glossed as spittle or saliva (وکه آب تف) while *ars* is glossed as sweat (وآب عرق). In T6 ہوس۫وہ is transcribed into NP as هوشکی جو and interpreted together with *ars* as saliva and tears, respectively: که آب دهن باشد وارس که اشک چشم باشد. A marginal note in T6 on *ars* defines it more closely as tear, the fluid which keeps the eyes fresh and is the source of eye sight: آرس بفتح اول و سکون ثانی بمعنی اشک چشم باشد و آب چشم هم هست که از آن چشم را تازگی هست و چشمه مینائی را نیز گفته اند.

16.3.4 *hušnāyišnagīh*

In the MSS, we find a number of difficult readings for the *Zand*'s interpretation of the Av. hapax legomenon *hušnāθråscā*.[21] While Mills (1905a: 110) prefers *hušnāyešnīh*, Dhabhar (1949: 48) reads *hušnāyasnikīh* 'good bathing or swimming'. Malandra and Ichaporia (2010: 50, 139) prefer *hušnāsēnagīh* 'good swimming, bathing', suggesting that it may have originally been connected with swimming, and that it may have later been confused with a derivation

---

[19] A similar notion survives in the NP expression آب زیر پوستش افتاد, literally meaning 'Water is flowing under her/his skin', suggesting that someone is looking healthy and well.
[20] On *huuōyžaθa-* 'smoothly flowing', see Narten (1986: 218–22) and Hintze (2007a: 236ff.) with further references.
[21] See the apparatus in Section 9.3.

from the verb *šnāxtan, šnās-* 'know, recognise'. In contrast to the previous readings, I have opted for *hušnāyišnagīh* 'good-gratitude'.

The attested variants fall into two broad groups. The manuscripts K5 M1 of the Indian branch have ⟨hwšn'ysnkyh⟩, preferred by Dhabhar,[22] while the MSS of the Iranian family read ⟨Pahlavi⟩ (Pt4 T6 E7) and ⟨hwšn'yšnkyh⟩ (Mf4 F2).[23] Although the ending ⟨Pahlavi⟩ (Pt4 T6 E7) indicates a ⟨g/d/y-yh⟩, we can posit a dwarfed ⟨-k-⟩ for Pt4 E7, a stylistic peculiarity which is not uncommon in the MSS. T6, however, has ⟨Pahlavi⟩ which eliminates the possibility of a dwarfed ⟨-k-⟩. However, the ending of this word is not generally problematic, and we can leave the question open. Important is that five of six MSS of the IrPY attest ⟨hwšn'yšn-⟩ which supports the word's reading as *hušnāyišnagīh*. F2 and T6 give the meaning of the word as آبِ عرق 'water of perspiration'. T6 transcribes the word into incomprehensible NP as هوشتایش and هوشتابانی, indicating uncertainties in the reading. The NP transcription found in Pt4 may be more accurate: هوستایشن 'good praise'. The many uncertainties in the spelling of the word complicate the interpretation of the passage. Pt4 F2, for instance, emend ⟨Pahlavi⟩ *xwēy* 'sweat' to ⟨Pahlavi⟩ *ōš* 'consciousness, intelligence; death; dawn', while T6 E7 combine the endings to ⟨Pahlavi⟩. Taking the manuscript evidence at face value, I would like to suggest that a type of magical thinking seems to be at play here: by offering good gratitude, it is expected that sweat will leave the bodies of the worshippers.

---

[22] The reading in J2 is illegible: ⟨hw'•nkyh⟩.
[23] R413 has ⟨Pahlavi⟩ which is presumably a spelling error.

16.4 PY 38.4

16.4.1 *dadag*

All examined MSS divide the text in the following manner:

(P)Y 38.4 (a) ⁺*uitī yā və̄ vaŋ"hīš ahurō mazdā̊* ⁺*nāmąm dadāt̰* (b) *vaŋhudā̊ hiiat̰ vā̊ dadāt̰ tāiš vā̊ yazamaidē*

(a) *ēdōn ašmā kē weh hēd ā-tān ohrmazd nām dād ī wehdahāg* (b) *ud kē-š ō ašmā dād pad awēšān ašmā yazom*

In line (a), the Av. text ends with *dadāt̰* 'he assigned', translated *dād* in the *Zand*, while the MP version ends with *ī wehdahāg*, translating *vaŋhudā̊* 'providing good (things)' which is the first word of line (b).[24] The variance between the original and translation, caused by the line division, is addressed in T6 with a superscript note above *kē-š*: ܣܘܝܕܘ.[25] Although the second word can be read *jadag* 'omen; form, property', diacritic marks in a marginal comment (Figure 16.2) suggest a reading as *dadag. Moreover, a NP note in the same marginal comment clarifies that an agent noun with the meaning 'giver' or 'creator' was intended: ودهنده یعنی بہترہندہ 'well-giver, meaning better-giver'.

Thus, we can assume that the ambiguous and otherwise unknown form ܣܘܝܕܘ was meant to be read as *dadag 'giver'. This marginal note in T6 is an instructive example of Zoroastrian scriptural exegesis of the late nineteenth century.

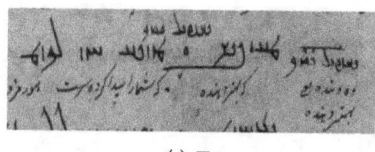

(a) T6

Figure 16.2 Marginal note in PY 38.4

16.4.2 *wehdahāg*

As Hintze (2007a: 241) points out, scholars have debated whether *vaŋhudā̊* '*wehdahāg*' qualifies *Ahura Mazdā* or the waters. She rightly draws attention to the double accusative in connection with *dā* 'to render', thus analysing the

---

[24] On the two occurrences of *dadāt̰* in PY 38.4, see Hintze (2007a: 240). For a discussion of *vaŋhudā̊*, see Hintze (2007a: 241).

[25] It is possible that this addition is by a second hand, as here the spelling of *weh* as ܣܘܝܕ differs from ܣܘܝܕ elsewhere in T6.

first part of line (b), *vaŋhudā̊ hiiat vå dadāt*, as 'when he (i.e. Ahura Mazdā) made you (i.e. the waters) into providers of good (things)'. The *Zand*'s analysis of the Av. construction is somewhat different. Separated from line (b) and connected to the preceding *dād* with the *ezāfe*, *wehdahāg* functions like an apposition to the preceding *nām* 'name': *ā-tān ohrmazd nām dād ī wehdahāg*. In line (b), *ud kē-š ō ašmā dād pad awēšān ašmā yazom*, the exegetes clarify the syntax of the sentence by marking its object, *ašmā*, with the preposition *ō*: 'he gave to you; he created for you'. This effectively rules out the waters, *ašmā*, as the direct object of the verb *dād*: 'he made/created you'. Even if we set the *Zand*'s line divisions differently and omit the conjunction *ud* against Pt4 Mf4 E7, J2 to define the clause as *ī wehdahāg kē-š ō ašmā dād*, *wehdahāg* would syntactically not qualify the waters, but *nām*.

16.5   PY 38.5

16.5.1   PY 67.6–8

(P)Y 38.3–5 are repeated in (P)Y67.6–8 as part of the *āb zōhr* ritual. Although the variant readings of the stanzas' repetition in the two chapters are not significant from a text-critical point of view, I reproduce the text as it occurs in the *āb zōhr*:

> PY 67.6[26] (a) *āb ēdōn yazom ī mākaiin̰t paššing ī ī pad urwar abar ēstēd miznē ud ān-iz ī hēbauuan̰ti garān tazišn* ud ān ī frauuaz *ī wārānīg*
>
> (b) *ud ān* ī *ahurānīš* ī *armēšt* ud *čāhīg ud abārīg* iz *āb ī anāmčištīg ud ān ī ahurahiiā* ī *šuhr ud ān ī huuapaŋ́hā mēšag huwidaragīh ašmā ā-mān* dād *kū-mān nam andar tan rawāg bawād*
>
> (c) *hudahagīh ars ud hušnāyišnagīh kū-mān xwēy az tan be āyād* ud *ān ī andar* har *dō axwān kāmag rōyn*[27]
>
> PY 67.7 (a) *ēdōn ašmā kē weh hēd ā-tān ohrmazd nām dād ī wehdahāg*
>
> (b) *ud kē-š ō ašmā dād pad awēšān ašmā yazom*
>
> (c) *u-m pad awēšān franāmād* ud *u-m pad awēšān* ā-t *niyāyišnēnād u-m pad awēšān abāmēnād*
>
> PY 67.8 (a) *āb* ān *ī ašmā ān ī azīš ašmā xayūg ud ān ī mātarə̄š ašmā āb ī andar hambawišnīh ī narān ud mādagān tōhm ud ān ī agəniiā̊ xōn ud ān ī driyōš dāyagānēnīdār āb* ī *andar pusyān*
>
> (b) *ud ān ī vīspō.pit ān guft āb ī pad urwarān ēwan ī urwar padiš* waxšēnēd ud *ān ī pahlom ud nēktar āb ī tantōhmag ī az urwar ēdōn ō ašmā kē weh hēd rād hom*
>
> (c) kē pad *dagrand bāzāyīh nayēd* andar *ān gēhān tan pad jud dahišnīh ud jud gōwišnīh* ān ī *mātarō.u.jītaiiō šīr*

The only significant difference is between Y 38.5c and Y 67.8c. The latter interrupts the flow of the Avestan text to include ritual instructions. These are: *darəgō.bāzāuš ∴ zōhr andak-ēw andar āb kunišn ∴ nāšū ∴ paitī ∴ zōhr abar āb nihišn ∴ viiādā̊ ∴ paitī ∴ abar barsom ∴ sə̄n̰dā̊ ∴ abar āb ∴ mātarō ∴ abar barsom ∴ jītaiiō ∴ abar āb.*

16.5.2   *xōn*

In PY 38.5a, *xōn* 'blood' glosses the hapax legomenon *agəniiā̊* 'O prize cows'.[28] It is conspicuous and maybe unexpected that a fluid such as blood, a pollutant in Zoroastrianism, is associated with a type of cow or bull that is regarded

---

[26] Text after Pt4. To facilitate comparison, I have underlined additions and different readings of PY 67, while text struck out denotes text which is missing in PY 67, but is present in PY 38. The Av. names frequently differ between the two chapters, but I have not marked these minor variations.

[27] ⟨MḤKŠYʾ⟩ Pt4.

[28] On *agəniiā̊*, see Hintze (2007a: 249ff.) with references.

as an outstanding exemplar of its species (Hintze 2007a: 250). Such an association, however, is not a unique case, as in PY 38.5 *azīš* 'milch cow' and *mātrāš* 'mother-cows' are similarly connected with *xayūg* 'saliva' and *āb ī andar hambawišnīh ī narān ud mādagān tōhm*, respectively.[29]

There is no doubt that bodily fluids such as urine, saliva, blood and semen are viewed as pollutants in Zoroastrianism:

> Dk 5.12.2[30] *ud abar pahikaftagīh ī har dō ēwēnag murdag ēk nasā ud ēk abārīg hixr čiyōn daštān ud šuhr ud xōn ud mešag ud xayūg ud abārīg ī az mardōm ud sag ud abārīg gyānwar ī rēman ud pid <ī> andar zīndagīh bahrīhā mīrēd*
>
> And on dealing with both types of dead matter: the corpse and other excrements such as menstruation, semen, blood, urine, saliva and others which (emanate) from people, dogs and other ritually filthy animals and from meat which is alive (but) partly dying.

In the above passage all bodily fluids mentioned in PY 38 are unambiguously considered to be a pollutant of the type *hixr*. The question arises as to why in the PYH these fluids are associated with waters with divine names?

Beside PY 38.5 (≈ PY 67.8), *xōn* only occurs once more in the PY, in a comment in PY 65.2:

> PY 65.2a[31] *kē harwispīn gušnān ō šuhr yōjdahrīh dahēd kū ka pāk*[32] *ud xōb nē abāg xōn ud rēm be āyēd dō*[33] *pad rāh ī ōy*
>
> Who (of) all the males will purify the semen? That is, so that[34] it comes on its way clean and good, not with blood and filth.

Here too, blood is considered as ritually polluted. It would, however, be wrong to associate the fluids mentioned in PY 38.3 and 5 with ritual uncleanliness. The mere fact that they are connected with divine entities such as the names of the waters suggests otherwise. The fluids in PY 38.5 have no ritual significance and are therefore not pollutants. Rather, as integral parts of various organisms and natural phenomena, these fluids form part of *Ohrmazd*'s creation. It is in this function that some of the highest pollutants can be associated with the divine. Although I am unable to retrace the development of the many waters from the *Avesta* through to these particular associations, this passage represents another network of correspondences being built in close proximity to the scripture. The doctrine

---

[29] The various editors of the Av. YH have extensively commented on the waters mentioned therein. For comprehensive overviews and discussions, see Hintze (2007a) with references.
[30] Text after Amouzgar and Tafazzoli (2000: 52–3).
[31] Text after Pt4.
[32] Followed by ומׄ in the margin.
[33] This number seems to be superfluous.
[34] *ka* 'when; if, since' is difficult here. One expects a second *kū*, which is reflected in my translation.

of the waters may be an old Zoroastrian dogma or a cultural borrowing of unknown age. But once associated with the scripture, its authority allowed it to spread to other priestly writings, as attested in the non-translation MP literature.

17. *PY 39*

17.1 PY 39.1

17.1.1 *ǰān*

The sequence of characters at the end of PY 39.1a which I have read as *ǰān* 'soul, ghost' allows a number of interpretations. Mills (1905b: 111) reads '*xayā*', an outdated transliteration for ⟨HYʾ⟩ *gyān/ǰān* 'soul, ghost'. Referring to the SktTr. *tam*, a dem. pronoun, he also considers the possibility of '*aš*'. Likewise, in PY 39.1b–c and 39.3c he prefers '*aš*'. However, he must have later changed his mind, as he translates '*xayā*' in PY 39.1a as 'by Him' rather than soul (Mills 1905a: 70). Dhabhar (1949: 173) has ࿘, while Malandra and Ichaporia (2010: 51) read *ā-š*. In spite of the ambiguities involved in the interpretation of the characters ࿘ and ࿘ or ࿘, there is compelling evidence here in support for the reading *ǰān*.

Nyberg (1964: 130) suggests that Iranian manuscripts write ࿘ for ⟨š⟩, while the Indian MSS have ࿘, which can also stand for ⟨g/d/y⟩ + ⟨h/ʾ⟩. Such distinction, however, is hardly observed in the manuscripts, at least not consistently. In this particular case, we find ࿘ (Pt4 F2 T6), ࿘ (Mf4 E7) and ࿘ (K5 J2 M1) in the manuscripts.[1] In PY 39.1b–c, Pt4 has ࿘ and ࿘, respectively, while F2 and T6 have in both cases ࿘. Thus far we can conclude that in PY 39.1 the MSS Pt4 F2 T6 make an attempt to distinguish between the first and the subsequent occurrences of this sequence of characters. In the same manner, Mf4 seems to differentiate between the two words by writing ࿘ ⟨ʾš⟩ in PY 39.1b, as opposed to ࿘ in PY 39.1a. In PY 39.1c, however, Mf4 reverts back to ࿘. Most importantly, in F2 T6 the scribes gloss ࿘ with جان 'soul, life', indicating that they read ࿘ as ⟨HYʾ⟩. By contrast, in

---

[1] R413 has ࿘.

PY 39.1b and c F2 has اوى and اورانِس, while T6 has او and آنِا. These pronouns suggest that the scribes of F2 and T6 assume, in agreement with Mf4, *ā-š* in PY 39.1b and c rather than *ǰān*. Considering this manuscript evidence, I have opted here for ⟨ḤYʾ⟩ *ǰān* 'soul, ghost' rather than *ā-š*. As variously discussed, *tan*, *ǰān* and *ruwān* often occur together (see Gignoux 1996). Therefore, it is hardly surprising that *ǰān* is mentioned in a list of the most important constituents of a living being.

While the outlined evidence is in my view unambiguous in the above case, I am aware of the limited scope of this investigation and hesitate to extend the result to the general palaeography of the manuscripts. Therefore, I wish to carefully express doubt about the accuracy of Nyberg's (1964: 130) observation that Iranian and Indian manuscripts write ⟨š⟩ differently. As shown above, the IrPY MSS Pt4 Mf4 F2 T6 have ᴗᴗ for *ā-š*. Contrary to Nyberg, K5 J2 M1 have in all three instances in PY 39.1 ᴗᴗ. These spellings can be interpreted in a number of ways. One could, for example, posit that the Indian MSS assumed *ǰān* in all three instances in PY 39.1. Various other passages that I have examined, however, show that the manuscripts are not consistent in the application of Nyberg's suggested rule. According to Nyberg, we would expect ᴗᴗᴗ in the MSS of the InPY. But K5 J2 M1 often prefer ᴗᴗᴗ *weh*.[2]

17.1.2 *amāgān*

We find the 1pl. possessive pronoun *amāgān* 'our' twice in the PYH, where it translates *ahmākāiš* in 37.3b and *ahmākə̄ṇg* in 39.1b.[3] The forms *ahmākāiš* and *ahmākə̄ṇg* are instr.pl. and acc.pl. of the possessive adj. *ahmāka-* 'our'. Reichelt (1903: 571) seems to have been the first scholar to discuss this pronoun, although he erroneously suggests that it occurs in PY 39.2 and that only the 1pl. of the pronoun is known in MP. Seemingly, he did not recognise the pronoun in PY 37.3b and missed the 1sg. form, *manīgān*, which is also attested.[4] These pronouns are rather rare and not widely attested in MP (Skjærvø 2010a: 208).

17.1.3 *ā-š dād*

A number of stanzas of the PYH offer a challenging interpretation of the Avestan original. PY 39.1 is one such instance. It is commonly assumed that in the Avestan version the sacrificers praise the souls of created beings and the fashioner of the cow. In the *Zand* of the stanza, however, the praise belongs

---

[2] See, for instance, PY 39.2 and 3.
[3] On *amāgān* in PY 40.3, see Section 18.2.2.
[4] On *manīgān*, see Section 18.1.4.

to the creator. PY 39.1a is unambiguous in this respect: *ēdar ēdōn yazom kē ān ī gōspandān ruwān ... dād* 'Here, in this way I worship (the one) who created the cattle's soul.' Nonetheless, the translators disambiguate the stanza furthermore by explicitly mentioning *ohrmazd* at the end of the line. PY 39.1b and c, however, are ambiguous as to who is being praised and worshipped. Thus, to remove any uncertainties, the words *ā-š dād* 'for he created (them)' are added to the end of both lines.

17.2 PY 39.2

17.2.1 PY 39.2

The MSS Pt4 Mf4 E7, K5 J2 M1 divide the stanza in three cola, as shown in Section 10.2. By contrast, the Pahlavi manuscripts F2 R413 T6 divide Y 39.2 into four cola:

(a) *daitikanąmcā aidiiūnąm hiiat̰ urunō yazamaidē*
(b) *aṣ̌āunąm āat̰ urunō yazamaidē*
(c) *kudō.zātanąmcīt̰ narąmcā nāirinąmcā*
(d) *yaēṣ̌ąm vahehīš daēnā̊ vanaiṇtī vā vəṇghən vā ⁺vaonarə vā*

The Sanskrit manuscripts S1 and KM7 follow Pt4's scheme as well, excluding influence from this family of MSS.[5]

Y 39.2 is repeated in Yt 13.154 (Narten 1986: 253).

17.2.2 *daitīkān-iz*

Here, *daitīkān-iz* corresponds to Av. *daitikanąmcā* 'wild animals'. Mills (1905b: 111) reads the beginning of PY 36.2a as '*daitīgān'ič ī asvārān*', translating it 'and to the Regulars (the infantry) and to the Cavalry, to whose souls I sacrifice'. Dhabhar (1949: 205), followed by Malandra and Ichaporia (2010: 51), correctly reads *daitīkān* 'wild animal, beast of prey'. One must agree with Malandra and Ichaporia (2010: 117) in assessing this word as 'simply a transliteration of the Av. word it glosses'. They go on to state that the 'SktGl *pāṅkticārī* "who walks in a row, foot-soldier" (see AirWb 678) suggests that the glossist had no idea what the word meant'. The peculiar agreement between Mills's translation and the SktY deserves a closer look.

The spelling of *daitīkān-iz* leaves room for various interpretations (see Figure 17.1). Particularly the handwriting in J2 would support a reading of the first part of the word, ꜩꜩꜩ, as *sidīg* 'third' or *stēy* 'erect'. Even an erroneous reading as *gētīg* would be possible. Therefore, other manuscripts introduce diacritic marks and transliterations in NP (F2 T6) to avoid confusion. Despite efforts to reduce ambiguity, *daitīkān-iz* was interpreted in light of the next word which translates *aidiiūnąm* 'not injuring', a gen.pl.m. of *aidiiu-*.[6] As the apparatus shows (Section 10.2), in K5 J2 M1 *aidiiūnąm* is rendered *ayārān* 'helpers'. The Iranian MSS, however, offer a number of different spellings which were interpreted as denoting 'horseman, rider'. With the difference of otiose strokes and a preceding *ezāfe*, Pt4 Mf4 and E7 have ꜩꜩꜩ.[7] NP

---

[5] The MSS S1 and KM7 have been indexed and published by Goldman (2013b,a).
[6] The acc.pl.m. *aidiiuš* of the same stem occurs in Y 40.3 where it is translated *hāzand* 'they will guide'.
[7] The context rules out a reading of ꜩꜩꜩ as *dēnār*, *dēwār* or *suxr*.

Figure 17.1 *daitīkān-iz*

glosses in Pt4 F2 T6 indicate that this word was read as سواران *sawārān* 'riders' or 'cavalry'. The younger MSS F2 R413 even have wrongly spelt forms of the correct MP word for rider, *aswār*, while T6 spells the word correctly as ܣܘܐܪ.

It is in this light that Pt4 F2 T6 gloss *daitīkān-iz* as پیادکان, پیاده‌روند and دیگاج respectively. F2 also has a marginal note defining پیادهٔ as: دیگاج پیاده یعنی پیادکان را. NP پیاده and پیاده‌روند do not just mean 'afoot' or 'pedestrian' but 'infantry'. The translation by Mills must have been influenced by the readings and interpretations found in the MSS. As Malandra and Ichaporia (2010) note, the military interpretation of this line was also adopted by the the SktY.

17.2.3 *wānīdār ... windišn ... weh mard*

In PY 39.2c we find three inflected forms of the verbal root *van* 'to prevail': *vanaiṇtī vā və̄nghən vā vaonarə vā* 'prevail, will prevail or have prevailed'.[8]

---

[8] On *vaonarə*, which I quote after Pt4, and the other forms, see Hintze (2007a: 270) and Hintze (2007a: 359), respectively.

17.2.3.1 *wānīdār*

The first form *vanaiṇtī*, a 3pl.in.d.act. from the present stem *vana-*, has been correctly recognised by the exegetes and translated as *wānīdār hēnd* 'they are conquerors' and glossed with *artēštār* 'warrior'.[9]

17.2.3.2 *windišn*

The 3pl.subj.act. *və̄nghən* is translated ᴴᵁᴶᴵᴵ *windišn* 'acquisition, earning' in Pt4 Mf4 T6 E7. In Pt4 Mf4 *windišn* is followed by superscript ᴴᵁᴶᴵᴵ, which has been incorporated into the main text in T6, while E7 only has *windišn*. F2 R413, K5 J2 M1 have ᴵᴴᵁᴶᴵ⁹ or possibly ᴵᴴᵁᴶᴵ⁹ᴵ. Relying on Dhabhar (1949: 173, fn. 8), Malandra and Ichaporia (2010: 51) remark that superscript ᴴᵁᴶᴵᴵ is missing in K5 and J2, and explain it in Mf4 by dittography. They suggest that ᴴᵁᴶᴵᴵ later got corrupted and was incorporated in other MSS such as KS through scribal error.[10] No doubt, the scribes of KS and T6 accepted the readings they found in manuscripts such as Pt4 or Mf4. However, Malandra and Ichaporia (2010) miss two points about the translation of *və̄nghən*. First, K5 J2 M1 do not just omit the word in superscript, but offer an erroneous spelling for *windišn*. Second, ᴴᵁᴶᴵᴵ is not just a corrupted form of *windišn*.

In PY 39.2c *windišn* 'acquisition, earning' is a curious translation for *və̄nghən* 'will prevail'. The erroneous spellings of this word and superscript ᴴᵁᴶᴵᴵ suggest that the scribes were uncertain about the translation. The first uncertainty concerns the spelling we find in F2 R413, K5 J2 M1. Dhabhar (1949: 173, fn. 8) suggests ᴵᴴᵁᴶᴵ⁹ᴵ as the spelling in K5 and J2.[11] This reading has the advantage that removing ⟨-k-⟩ from ᴵᴴᵁᴶᴵ⁹ᴵ results in *windišn*, but it also shows that the scribes were unaware of the correct reading. Secondly, F2 corrects ᴵᴴᵁᴶᴵ⁹ or ᴵᴴᵁᴶᴵ⁹ᴵ to *windišn*, again highlighting doubts in the spelling of the word. While the evidence seems to point to *windišn* as the intended translation, the superscript addition in Pt4 and Mf4 suggests that these manuscripts' scribes did not view *windišn* as a suitable translation either.[12] Therefore, they add a second word, ᴴᵁᴶᴵᴵ, which I propose to read *wanghān*, a transliteration of *və̄nghən*. Whether *windišn* was disputed as a correct translation, or whether the exegetes were unsure of its reading, they decided to add a transliteration of the original, perhaps to address a perceived shortcoming.

---

[9] MP *wānīdan*, *wān-* 'to conquer, overcome, destroy', Av. *van* and a number of other forms attested in other Old and MIr. languages are cognates, ultimately deriving from IE *$*$ṷen* 'to conquer, win'. See Cheung (2007: 417ff.) with references.

[10] On KS also known as T54, see Dhabhar (1949: 6).

[11] In line with Pt4 and Mf4 I have interpreted the first character as a separate ⟨W⟩ *ud*, suggesting ᴵᴴᵁᴶᴵ⁹ as a reading in F2 R413, K5 J2 M1.

[12] Both in Pt4 and Mf4 the superscript seems to be by the original hand.

17.2.3.3 *weh mard*

The third form derived from the root *van*, *vaonarə* 'they have prevailed', a 3pl.ind.act. from the perfect stem *vaon-*, must have been analysed as a compound containing a form of *vohu-* 'good' and *nar-* 'man', prompting a translation as *weh mard*, further explained by *āsrōn* 'priest'.

This curios translation was also noticed by Spiegel (1860: 60), who believes that a 'Huzvâresch' spelling of *vaonarə* as ﺍﻣﺮ must have been the reason for a reading as '*vohu-nare*'.

17.3 PY 39.3

17.3.1 āt̰ iθā 'ān ēdōn'

In the examined MSS *iθā āt̰ yazamaidē* is consistently translated as *ēdar ēdōn yazom* 'Here, I thus worship', while *āt̰ iθā yazamaidē* is rendered as *ān (ī) ēdōn yazom*.[13] K5 is the only manuscript to add a superscript *ēdar* 'here' above *ān ī*. M1, a copy of K5, incorporates this addition into its text. However, as the handwriting in K5 suggests, this is a secondary editorial intervention; possibly a later attempt to harmonise this stanza's translation with that of Y 37.1 and 39.1. Therefore, Bartholomae's (1904: 366) observation that *ēdar ēdōn* corresponds to both *iθā āt̰* (Y 37.1 and 39.1) and *āt̰ iθā* (Y 39.3) cannot be verified. The *Zand* avoids a mechanical translation and accounts for the inverted word order of Y 39.3 by rendering *āt̰ iθā yazamaidē* as *ān ēdōn yazom*.

17.3.2 *weh nar ān ī weh mādag*

In PY 39.3a *weh nar ān ī weh mādag* translates the acc.pl. *vaŋhūšcā īt̰ vaŋ^vhīšcā* 'both male and female', thus correctly rendering the gender of the Av. adjectives with *nar* 'male' and *mādag* 'female'. The pair *nar* and *mādag* often occur together and describe gender.[14] In this case the two terms refer to the bounteous immortals, as indicated by the gloss at the end of the line: *any amahraspandān* 'other *Amahraspandān*'.

In line with the translation paradigm of the *Zand*, according to which *spəṇta- aməša-* is not rendered *amahraspandān* (see Section 15.4.1), the following acc.pl. *spəṇtə̄ṇg aməšə̄ṇg* (Y 39.3b) is translated *kē abzōnīg hēnd ud amarg*. The gloss at the end of PY 39.3a is thus required to clarify the context of the stanza which is the praise of the *Amahraspandān* and not other male and female beings.

Y 39.3b–c are paraphrased in Y 4.4. The comment contained in the Pahlavi version of the passage reiterates that the *Amahraspandān* are immortal and that they ought not to be killed:

PY 4.4[15] (b) *amahraspandān huxwadāyān ī hudahāgān hamē zīndagān ī hamē sūdān ēk-ēw kū be nē mīrēnd ēk-ēw kē ōzad nē šāyēnd*

(c) *kē pad ān ī wahman mānēnd kē-šān mehmānīh ān gyāg kū wahman kē-iz wahman*

(b) The *Amahraspandān*, the good rulers, who are beneficent, the immortal ones, the advantageous ones; one is that they do not die, (and) one is that one cannot slay them.

---

[13] The MSS Pt4 Mf4 F2 R413 T6, J2 have *ān ēdōn*, but E7, K5 M1 read *ān ī ēdōn*.

[14] See, for instance, Bd 6e.4, 14.32 and 15.5–8. Although more frequently used to describe the gender of non-human beings, on occasion the pair is also used to describe the gender of people: Bd 35.42.

[15] Text after Pt4.

(c) who dwell on the side of *Wahman*, whose dwelling is in that place where *Wahman* is, who are also (like) *Wahman*.

The difference between the Av. passages is confined to the inflection of the adjectives *yauuaējī-* 'living forever' and *yauuaēsū-* 'thriving forever'. While Y 39.3b has an acc.pl., Y 4.4 prefers the ending for the dat.pl.: *yauuaējibiiō yauuaēsubiiō*. The *Zand* reflects this difference by translating *yauuaējibiiō yauuaēsubiiō* '*hamē zīndagān ī hamē sūdān*' rather than *hamē zīndag ud hamē sūd* in PY 39. Moreover, PY 4.4b and c contain comments missing in PY 39.3b and c, while *pad frārōnīh* is missing in PY 4.4c. Finally, in PY 39.3c *uitī* 'thus; equally' is translated *ēdōn* 'thus', it is left untranslated in PY 4.4c.[16]

---

[16] In all of its OAv. attestations, Y 38.4, 39.3 and Y 45.2, *uitī* is translated *ēdōn*.

17.4 PY 39.4

(P)Y 39.4 and 5 are repeated in (P)Y 13.5 and 6:

PY 13.5[17] (a) ēdōn čiyōn tō pad ān har dō [ast] ohrmazd pad ān har dō tis ī mēnōy ud gētīy menišn hē kū tis ī tō ōh menišn ud gōwišn hē kū tis ī tō ōh gōwišn ud dahišn hē[18] kū tan bē ō tō dahišn ud[19] warzišn[20] kū tis ī tō ōh warzišn ī weh pad hamāg kār[21] abāz

(b) ēdōn ō tō dahom xwad ud ēdōn čāšom ō kasān ud ēdōn tō pad āyišn [kunom] ka andar gēhān ōh āyom ud ōh šawom ā-t ōh yazom

(c) u-m ēdōn niyāyišnēnē nēkīh ī gētīy u-m ēdōn abāmēnē kū-m abām pad tō bawād ohrmazd
wičast bišāmrūdīg gōwišn

PY 13.6 (a) pad ān ī weh xwēš ud xwēš rawišnīh kū tō xwēš hom[22] ud pad ēd ī [abar] tō ēstom

(b) pad ān ī weh tarsagāhīh[23] ō tō b rasom kū tarsagāhīh[24] pad tis ī weh kunom

(c) pad ān ī weh sālārīh hordad ud amurdad pad ān ī weh bowandag menišnīh kū pad tis ī weh bowandag menišnīh[25] be bawom

The passages feature a number of expected variant readings and more significant differences within the same manuscript:

PY 39.4 (a) čiyōn tō pad ān ī har dō tis ī mēnōy ud gētīy ohrmazd menišn hē kū tis ī tō ōh menišn ud gōwišn hē kū tis ōh gōwišn ud dahišn hē ud warzišn hē ī kū weh warzom

(b) ēdōn ō tō dahom xwad ud ēdōn čāšom ō kasān kū be dahēd ud ēdōn tō pad āyišn ud šawišn ka andar gēhān ōh āyom ud ōh šawom ōh yazom

(c) u-m ēdōn niyāyišnēnē u-m ēdōn abāmēnē tō ohrmazd kū-m abām pad tō bawād wičast bišāmrūdīg gōwišn

PY 39.5 (a) pad weh xwēšīh ka tō xwēš hom xwēšrawišnīh hom ka pad xwēšīh ī ašmā ēstom

(b) pad ān ī weh tarsagāhīh ō tō be rasom

(c) pad ān ī weh sālārīh ka sālārīh pad frārōnīh kunom ud pad ān ī weh bowandag menišnīh ka tis bowandag menišnīhā kunom
yazišnīgīhā bišāmrūdīg gōwišn ∵ panj wičast sē gāh

---

[17] Text after Pt4.
[18] Superscript *hom* Pt4.
[19] ⟨YḤBWN-m⟩ in the margins.
[20] Subscript ⟨wlcm⟩ Pt4.
[21] Faint sec.m. addition in the margins.
[22] ܓܘܝܫܢ Pt4. *hom* subscript.
[23] ܛܪܣܓܐܗ Pt4.
[24] ܛܪܣܓܐܗ Pt4.
[25] ܡܢܫܢܝܗ Pt4.

17.5 PY 39.5

17.5.1 Recitation instructions

Recitation instructions that occur at the end of the chapters define the number of recitations prescribed for each chapter. These are in the format *yazišnīgīhā ēvāmrūdīg gōwišn*. The instructions for the recitation of the stanzas are in a different format, referring to the stanza (*wičast*): *wičast srišāmrūdīg gōwišn* (PY 35.4). While the stanza instructions differ in the number of the recitations, the chapter instructions seem to be standardised, as only one recitation is prescribed in most cases. However, in PY 35.9 and 39.5 some of the MSS disagree in the number of the suggested recitations. Ignoring some variant spellings, in PY 35.9 the MSS Pt4 F2 R413 T6 E7, J2 agree on *bišāmrūdīg* 'twice', while Mf4, followed by Dhabhar (1949), has *ēvāmrūdīg* 'once'. K5 M1 read ⟨⟩. In PY 39.5, Pt4 E7, K5 M1 attest variants of *bišāmrūdīg*, whereas Mf4, again followed by Dhabhar (1949), has *ēvāmrūdīg*. J2 reads ⟨⟩, while the instruction is missing in F2 R413 T6.

As the critical apparatus shows, the words *yazišnīgīhā* 'in the manner of worship' and the following numbers are subject to a wide range of variant spellings. In the above two cases, however, the differences are significant, even if attested in only one manuscript.

18. *PY 40*

18.1 PY 40.1

18.1.1 *mehīh*

In PY 40.1a *mehīh* 'greatness' translates *mazdąmcā*. According to Hintze (2007a: 348), here *mazdąmcā* is an acc.sg. of the feminine substantive *mazdā-* 'wisdom', a hapax legomenon.[1] Although both *mazdā-* f. 'wisdom' and *mazdā-* m. 'the wise one' form their acc.sg. as *mazdąm*, the translators do not confuse the forms here. But they seem to analyse *mazdąmcā* as a derivative from another OAv. hapax legomenon, namely *mazan-* ntr. 'greatness' which occurs in PY 37.2, translated *mehīh*. Elsewhere, cognates of OAv. *mazan-* such as YAv. *masan-* are translated *mehīh* as well: *mazibīš* in Y 32.11,[2] *masatā* in PY 54.1 and *masānascā* in PY 58.4.

18.1.2 *man*

The 1sg.pers.pron. ⟨L⟩ *man* 'I, me' in PY 40.1a does not translate an Av. pronoun and is only attested as a superscript addition in Pt4. F2 follows Pt4, but T6 and E7 have incorporated *man* into the main text. It is missing in Mf4 R413, K5 J2 M1. It stands at an awkward position within the clause, but could be translated 'When in those existences they thus bestow upon you, O *Ohrmazd*, greatness and completeness by means of my actions.' Although I have accepted the addition of *man* in Pt4, I have left the pronoun untranslated, as it is a later addition and at odds with the content of the line.

---

[1] For more on how *mazdā-* 'wisdom', here functioning as an appellative noun, differs from *mazdā-* 'the wise one' that forms part of the deity's name, see Hintze (2007a: 284–7).

[2] Av. *mazibīš* is an instr.pl. of *maz-* 'great'.

18.1.3 PY 40.1b

In the manuscripts, PY 40.1b, *rād hom ō ēd ī tō xrad pānagīh ō dēn ī tō az ān ka-m abar kū-m nēkīh az ān*, corresponds asymmetrically to *kərəšuuā rāitī tōi xrapaitī ahmat̰ hiiat̰ aibī*, as *kərəšuuā*, here translated *pad kardārīh*, belongs to the previous clause.[3] The main constituent parts of this line are *rād hom ō ēd ī tō xrad* and *az ān ka-m abar*, for they correspond to *rāitī tōi xrapaitī* and *ahmat̰ hiiat̰ aibī*, respectively. Therefore, I have interpreted *pānagīh ō dēn ī tō* as an extension of the preceding clause, *rād hom ō ēd ī tō xrad*, translating PY 40.1b 'I am generous towards this your wisdom (and offer) protection for your religion, for it is higher than me, that is, my goodness is from that.'

It is worth mentioning that *ahmat̰ hiiat̰ aibī* also occurs in Y 35.4, where it is likewise translated *az ān ka-m abar*.[4] In PY 35.4 the phrase is followed by *kū-m nēkīh aziš*, whereas in PY 40.1b we find *kū-m nēkīh az ān*.

18.1.4 *manīgān*

On *manīgān*, see Section 3.1.

---

[3] Av. *kərəšuuā* is a 2sg.ipt.mid. from the root aor. *car-/kərə-* of the root *kar* 'to do'.
[4] On the Avestan phrase, see Hintze (2007a: 77ff.) with references.

18.2 PY 40.3

18.2.1 *ān hērbed*

In PY 40.3a all manuscripts of the IrPY prefer the unmarked form *hērbed*, while the InPY reads *hērbedān*. As PY 40.3b begins with a subordinate clause featuring a verb in 3pl., *hāzānd*, it can be argued that *ān hērbedān* is the correct form: *ān hērbedān* (b) *ī ka-šān hāzānd* 'Those teacher-priests, (b) who shall guide them'. I have not emended the text, but my translation reflects the above view.

18.2.2 *amāgān*

Here, the manuscripts Mf4 F2 R413 T6, K5 J2 M1 have ⟨LNH⟩ *amā* 'we, us'. By contrast, Pt4 has ⟨LNH-^{n}⟩. Copying Pt4, E7 reads ⟨LNH-'n⟩. As **amāān* is not otherwise attested, I have emended the reading in Pt4 to account for the addition of the superscript ⟨-'n⟩. In this stanza, *amā* or *amāgān* translate Av. *ahmā* which is an instr. of the 1pl.pers.pron. *ahma-*, forming the first part of the compound *ahmā.rafənaŋhō* 'who are supported by us' (see Hintze 2007a: 297ff.).

18.3 PY 40.4

18.3.1 *īšt*

In PY 40.4c, *īšt* renders the acc.sg. *īštǝm* 'what is desired', a perf.pass.part. of the verbal root *iš* 'to seek, desire'.[5] As already noted by Dhabhar (1949: 194, 207), followed by Malandra and Ichaporia (2010: 141), in the PY *īšt* always translates *išta-* and is often glossed by *xwāstag*.[6] In PY 46.18b, for instance, we read: *kē ō man īšt kū-m xwāstag dahēd* '(The one) who (gives) *īšt* to me, that is, he gives me wealth.' The affinity of *īšt* with its Av. form *išta-* and the gloss *xwāstag* supports the above editors' proposed meaning as 'wish, wealth, property'. However, it is not clear what exactly *īšt* and *xwāstag* denote.

PY 44.10 and Ny 3.7 (= Yt 7.5) seem to suggest a connection between *īšt* and *bar*:

PY 44.10e *ā-š ēd tō īšt bar*[7] *kū ān mizd ī ō tō dahēnd ō-iz ōy dahēnd*

He (shall have) this your *īšt*, (namely) the yield, that is, that reward which they give to you, they also give it to him.

Likewise, Ny 3 prefers *bar* to *xwāstag*:

Ny 3.7[8] *āštīhōmand īštōmand kū bar ī ō gōspandān dahēd wizōyišnōmand kū kār ī dādestān sūdōmand kū bar ī āb ud urwar dahēd*

Full of peace, filled with wealth, that is, the yield that it gives to the cattle, investigative, that is, works of law, profitable, that is, it provides the yield of the waters and trees.[9]

As discussed in Section 15.1.6, *bar* 'yield' is one of the aspects associated with a legal object (*xwāstag*). Unfortunately, the above passages do not allow us to better determine the semantics associated with *xwāstag* and *bar*. In the wider MP literature *īšt* occurs at times in close proximity of *sūd* 'profit'.[10] The evidence seems to suggest that *xwāstag*, *bar* and *sūd*, which belong to the same semantic field, are used interchangeably without noticeably modifying the meaning.

---

[5] On *išta-*, see Hintze (2007a: 306) with references.

[6] The list of attestations given by Dhabhar and Malandra is not complete. Beside the PYH, *īšt* occurs in PY 32.9, 34.5, 44.10, 46.2, 46.18, 49.12, 51.2, 60.7, 65.11, 68.11, *Srōš Wāj Bun* 7, Ny 3.7 (= Yt 7.5) and Ny 5.6.

[7] ⟨blm⟩ Pt4.

[8] Text after Dhabhar (1923: 31).

[9] Dhabhar (1963: 56) provides a number of insightful text-critical comments on this passage. As he rightly observes, the *ō* preceding *gōspandān* is most likely superfluous. See *bar ī āb ud urwar dahēd* at the end of the passage. I have preserved and translated it here, as he preserves it in his edition of the text.

[10] See, for instance, Dk 3.286 and Dk 9.66. See also Ny 3.7 above.

In PY 40.4, all manuscripts of the present edition write *īšt* with an Av. long *ī*: ⟨ ⟩. On occasion, the final ⟨-t⟩ receives an otiose stroke. One such instance is found in Pt4 in PY 46.18: ⟨īšt'⟩. While the sequence ⟨-št-⟩ is identical both in Av. and Pahlavi scripts, the initial long *ī* identifies this word as a learned word from Avestan. Therefore, I have left *īšt* untranslated.

19. *PY 41*

19.1 PY 41.2

Mehendale (1996) criticises Narten's (1986: 47) translation of this stanza. In his view *nā vā nāirī vā* 'men and women' is used as a collective denoting humans who wish that *Ahura Mazdā* establishes a good rule over themselves (Mehendale 1996: 173). To counter Narten's translation of this passage, Mehendale adduces seven points, suggesting that *nā vā nāirī vā* cannot refer to a good ruler, be it a man or a woman. Mehendale (1996: 174) also disagrees with the translations provided by Humbach (1991) and Kellens and Pirart (1988). Although he does not discuss the *Zand*, Mehendale's observations deserve a brief mention, as they agree with the priestly interpretation of this stanza.

In contrast to Narten (1986: 264, fn. 46), who interprets *tū* as a particle and not as an enclitic pers. pronoun, Mehendale and the exegetes posit a 2sg.pers.pron. In PY 41.2, *tū* is rendered *tō*, most likely referring back to *Ohrmazd*: *ān ī ohrmazd tō*.[1] Like Mehendale (1996: 174), the exegetes realise that the 3sg.opt.mid. *xšaētā* 'may rule' disagrees with a 2sg.pers.pron. *tū*.[2] While Mehendale does not propose a viable solution, the *Zand* elegantly solves the problem by constructing a 3sg. causative denominative verb *pādixšāyēnēd*, preceded by an enclitic pronoun *ā-t*: 'he/she causes you, (O Ohrmazd), to rule'.

In Mehendale's translation *nā vā nāirī vā* seems to function as an apposition to the gen. 1pl.pers.pron. *nə̄* 'us', but the exegetes construct a

---

[1] In the present context it is very unlikely that *tō* refers to another entity than *Ohrmazd*. Also note that the Indian MSS read *huxwadāy* in place of *ohrmazd* of the Iranian MSS. While both translations are reasonable, most likely *huxwadāy* is the older translation.

[2] The verbal form *xšaētā* derives from the *a*-aorist stem *xša-* of the root *xša* 'to rule', 'to rule over' if it is governed by a gen. which is the case here (Hintze 2007a: 363).

subordinate relative clause introduced by *kē*, defining *amā* 'us' more closely as 'male (beings) and women'. Thus, both in Mehendale's translation and in the *Zand* the males and females refer to the speakers and not to a ruler. To make this point explicit, the *Zand* uses precise language here: *ō amā kē nar ud nārīg hēm ā-t pādixšāyēnēd* 'will make you rule over us, who are male (beings) and women'. It is noteworthy that in other passages of the PYH, the verb 'to be' is spelt ⟨HWH⟩ or ⟨HW⟩, denoting a 1sg. Although in contrast to other manuscripts J2 prefers the ending ⟨-ym⟩ to ⟨-m⟩ on occasion,[3] in PY 41.2 all MSS unanimously attest a 1pl.ind.act.: ⟨ḤWH-ym⟩ *hēm* 'we are'. In this way, the *Zand* excludes the possibility of alternative translations.

---

[3] See, for instance, PY 35.6, 36.1, 3 and 6 and 39.4 and 5.

19.2 PY 41.5

19.2.1 *hēnd*

In the manuscripts of the IrPY the verb *hēnd* (PY 41.5b) stands out as the only indicative form among four verbal forms in subjunctive: *abar rasānd ud hunsand hēnd ud padīrānd kū be padīrānd ud hunsandīhā ōh kunānd*.[4] In the MSS we find the following forms: ⟨⁺ḤWH-d⟩ Pt4 Mf4 E7, which I have emended to ⟨⁺ḤWH-d⟩, ⟨ḤWH-d⟩ F2 R413 T6 and ⟨ḤWH-ʾnd⟩ K5 J2 M1. Considering the chain of subjunctives in this line, we could argue that the reading of the InPY as *hānd* is the desired reading. However, in keeping with my editorial goals I have refrained from emending the verb, particularly as all MSS of the Iranian group agree on *hēnd*.

19.2.2 Recitation instructions

As evident from the instructions at the end of the stanzas, (P)Y 35.1, 35.7, 39.4, 41.3 and 41.5 are to be recited twice. The list of these stanzas agrees with the one enumerated in Wd 10.4.[5] Moreover, Wd 10.8 mentions (P)Y 35.4 as a stanza that is to be recited three times. Based on these and other correspondences, Hintze (2002: 33) points out in an important article that the present form of the *Yasna* must have been known to the composers of the *Wīdēwdād*.

---

[4] These verbs correspond in a rather obscure manner to *aogəmadaēcā usmahicā vīsāmadaēcā*.
[5] See also Andrés-Toledo (2009: 16).

Part IV

Epilogue

20. *Reflections on the Zand*

> These intentions, however, do not necessarily agree with what Zarathushtra wanted to express, the Pahlavi translation of the Gāthās being full of misinterpretations of grammatical forms and of erroneous etymologies of Gāthic words.
>
> (Humbach 1996: 260)

A decade ago, Stausberg (2008) observed that research on Zoroastrianism had to some extent become marginalised in the study of religions. These days, philology, its actors and critical editions seem to carry most of the blame for the unfavourable position that Old Iranian Studies have taken in the peripheries of the intellectual sphere. A colleague once went so far as to state, jokingly of course, that the term 'philologist' was often used as an insult in the USA. Be that as it may, such views are not limited to our small discipline. In an interview, Papst (2017: 14) reminds Wolfram Groddeck, one of the lead editors behind the critical edition of Robert Walser's work, that editorial projects are often criticised with the charge that 'a lot of public and private cultural funding is wasted here for something only a few can really benefit from'.[1] Groddeck's twofold reply holds true not only for research on Robert Walser but textual editions in general:

> Scholarly editions lay the basis for any future study of the texts. Walser is one of the greatest Swiss poets of the twentieth century, and the scholarly study of his work is an expression of appreciation in a society conscious of culture. In addition, historical-critical editions have a different relationship to time than, for example, scientific research. They safeguard our literary heritage and are an investment in the future.

---

[1] The interview, dated 26 February 2017, appeared in *Bücher am Sonntag*, a literary supplement to *NZZ am Sonntag* published by *Verlag der Neuen Zürcher Zeitung (NZZ)*.

Any text, ancient or modern, is the result and manifestation of a culture. Although not exclusively, many times texts are our only path to an engagement with the past. As such, critical editions, particularly of maginalised texts like the *Zand*, are our first stepping stones in an endeavour to renew an inquiry into the principles of the priestly reception of the *Avesta* in late antiquity, an approach that seems poised to extend our insights into Zoroastrian intellectual history. By according agency to the Zoroastrian scholiasts of late antiquity who composed and handed down the *Zand* as an expression of culture, I hope to have ventured a new approach to this corpus and challenged commonly held notions about Zoroastrian exegesis and its place in studies of Zoroastrianism.

20.1 WBW TRANSLATION

Spiegel (1860: 26–7) was perhaps the first scholar to state that the *Zand* represented a word-by-word translation that followed the word order of the original slavishly ('knechtisch treue'). Haug (1878: 338) too depicted the *Zand* as a 'slavishly literal translation, or even transliteration' of the original, leading generations of scholars to describe the Pahlavi versions of the *Avesta* in those exact terms.[2] The assumption of a WBW translation has had far-reaching consequences for the academic view of the *Zand*. Scholars have concluded that the rather rigid word order of MP, a result of its simplified morphology, does not permit the WBW translation to represent the complex syntactic relationships of the Av. original:

> Yet for all that, it is difficult enough to make appropriate use of the Pahlavi translation, its Middle Persian language lacking two important characteristics of Old Avestan, particularly of the poetic language of the Gāthās, first their highly differentiated inflexional system to substitute which Middle Persian Pahlavi has little means only, and secondly, in consequence, their free word order. (Humbach 1996: 259–60)

As such, the simplified morphology and the rigid word order of MP have been viewed as impediments to translating the Avestan in a WBW manner.[3] However, sweeping statements, such as made by Spiegel, Haug and other scholars up to recent times, only inadequately describe the MP versions of the *Avesta*.

The term WBW translation is strongly evocative of the linguistic glossing system or the WBW translations found in language primers. In fact, Bang (1890: 363) compares the *Zand* with Italian glosses to a Latin text offering

---

[2] See, for instance, West (1896–1904: 84), Taraf (1981), Dehghan (1982), Humbach (1996), Kreyenbroek (1996, 1999), Degener (2000), Ichaporia (2003), Cantera (2004) and Macuch (2009b).

[3] Already Spiegel (1860: 20ff.) pointed out that the simplified morphology of MP was a problem for the translations.

an example of the same. In such cases the translation is aligned with the original without much regard for literary style or comprehensibility of the translation. Such is not the case in the MP versions of the *Avesta*. As any attempt to align the *Zand* with the Avestan will show, the MP renderings do not represent a strict WBW alignment. It is true that the *Zand* follows the word order of the original, but its goal is not a highly accurate one-to-one correspondence between the source and target texts.

In Y 35.0b *vīspąm ašaonō stīm yazamaide mainiiəuuīmcā gaēθiiąmcā* is rendered as *harwisp ān ī ahlawān stī yazom kē mēnōy ud kē-iz gētīy*. A rigid WBW translation should have yielded a MP similar to the following: **harwisp ahlawān stī yazom mēnōy ud gētīy**. Instead, the translation deviates from the original in order to render a more comprehensible translation, while the word order of the original is still preserved. The syntagma *ān ī* and the relative pronoun *kē* deserve a closer look. A rigid WBW and still adequate translation of *ašaonō stīm* would have been *ahlawān stī*, which correctly expresses the possessive relationship between *ašaonō* and *stīm*. Instead, the translators opt for *ān ī ahlawān stī*, decreasing syntactic ambiguity on one hand and adding to the literary value of the passage on the other. The use of *kē* is peculiar too. The first relative pronoun, following the verb *yazom*, has no equivalent in the Avestan version. But *kē* is often used as a host for the enclitic adverb *-iz*, and thus *ud kē-iz* in the second part of the subordinate clause translates the Av. *-cā ... -cā*.[4] It is possible that the first *kē* was added to coordinate with the following *kē-iz*. Even if this was the case, this translation shows that the *Zand* can go beyond a mere WBW translation even if the deviations are as subtle as in the above example. Rather than blindly following the Av. original, the translator chooses to construct a subordinate clause and creates a meaningful MP translation.

In (P)Y 35.1c, *ān ī mard ō mard be abespārdār*, followed by *kirbag pad dād rāh*, correspond to *naēnaēstārō*. As argued in Section 13.2.5, the fact that the MP translation relates to the original in more than one way, favours the view that it represents an interpretive version rather than a WBW translation. The *Zand* of *naēnaēstārō* seems to be a literary or free translation with intact MP syntax.

Y 39.3b represents a similar case.[5] The four adjectives in acc.pl. that constitute Y 39.3b, *spəṇtə̄ṇg aməṣ̌ə̄ṇg yauuaējiiō yauuaēsuuō*, are again placed in a subordinate clause, *kē abzōnīg hēnd ud amarg ud hamē zīndag ud hamē sūd*, whereby the relative pronoun *kē* and the verb *hēnd* have no correspondence in the original. Here too, the conjunction *ud* has no Av. counterpart and seems to add to the literary value of the translation.

---

[4] On the various ways the *Zand* represents the enclitic coordinating conjunction *-cā*, see Section 13.1.4.
[5] For other observations on this passage, see Section 17.3.

A particularly illustrative example for the literary quality of the *Zand* is offered in PY 36.1:

(a) *ahiiā θβā āθrō vərəzə̄nā paouruiiē ⁺pairijasāmaidē mazdā ahurā*
(b) *θβā θβā mainiiū spə̄ništā yō ā axtiš*
(c) *ahmāi yə̄m axtōiiōi dåŋhē*

(a) *ēdōn ō ēd ī tō ātaxš pad warzišn fradom be rasom ohrmazd pad pahrēz ud šnāyēnīdārīh*
(b) *pad ēd ī tō gāhān pad ēd ī tō mēnōy ī abzōnīg čiyōn az dēn paydāg*
(c) *kē ō ōy xīndagīh kū pad abar ātaxš anāgīh kunēd ān-iz ō ōy xīndagīh dahēd kū ān-iz pad ōy anāgīh kunēd*

The adverb *ēdōn*, at the beginning of the stanza, is an addition in the *Zand* not linked to any words in the original. In the following *ahiiā θβā āθrō* 'ō ēd ī tō ātaxš', the gen.sg.m. *ahiiā* has correctly been translated *ēd ī*. In line with the *Zand*'s interpretation of the passage, the prepositional phrase *ō ēd ī tō ātaxš*, preceding the intransitive verb *rasīdan*, indicates that the fire is the goal which will be arrived at. But more importantly, by ending line (a) with *pad pahrēz ud šnāyēnīdārīh* 'with care and propitiation' the exegetes add their own view of the sacrificers' frame of mind. This addition does not translate an Av. phrase and is not introduced by *kū*, which often marks the start of a comment. It rather seems to be an integral part of the translation. Likewise, preceding the actual translation, in line (b) *pad ēd ī tō gāhān* modifies meaning without having been marked as a comment by a particle such as *kū*. Although line (b) ends with *yō ā axtiš*, its translation, '*kē ō ōy xīndagīh*', begins line (c), while line (b) ends with *čiyōn az dēn paydāg*. In contrast to a WBW translation of *yō ā axtiš ahmāi*, which should have been *kē xīndagīh ō ōy*, the *Zand* deviates from the word order of the stanza to yield, as it were, a *correct* MP clause: *kē ō ōy xīndagīh*. The exegetes do not seem to have translated the emphatic particle *ā*.

Like the above examples from the PYH, most stanzas of the PY challenge the notion of a rigid WBW translation. Yet, the *Zand* does follow the Av. word order. The consequences of this method can be severe in cases when a free and complex word order is employed in the Avestan, perhaps as a compositional technique. PY 35.4 is one example, where the original's free word order creates problems for the *Zand* (see Section 6.5). Similarly, in (P)Y 40.1c the rel.pron. *hiiat̰* precedes *mīždəm*: *hiiat̰ mīždəm ˟mauuaiθīm fradadāθā* 'the prize which you offer to someone like me'.[6] Accordingly, the MP relative pronoun *kē* precedes *mizd*: *kē mizd ō manīgān frāz dahē*. This construction, however, means 'which prize' rather than 'the prize which'.

---

[6] *hiiat̰* is an acc.sg.ntr. of the rel.pron. *ya-* 'who, which', and *mīždəm* an acc.sg. of *mīžda-* ntr. 'prize; reward; fee'.

Problematic translations are at times clarified by a following comment, but not in this case.

No doubt, overall the *Zand* constitutes a very literal translation. However, the adequacy of its translations are more often neglected than acknowledged. Some scholars tend to overly generalised statements about the *Zand*. Examining the translation technique of the Pahlavi versions of the *Avesta*, Cantera claims that as a result of the WBW paradigm no sentence in the *Zand* corresponds to the common syntax of MP:

> Dieser Übersetzungsstil beeinflußt die Syntax in grundlegender Weise. Fast kein Satz der PÜ entspricht der gewöhnlichen Syntax des Pahlavi, die wir in den Glossen und Kommentaren finden. (Cantera 2004: 241)

As evidence, he adduces *guft-aš ohrmazd ō spitāmān zardušt*, which translates the oft repeated clause *mraot̰ ahurō mazdå spitamāi zaraϑuštrāi* 'Ahura Mazdā spoke to Spitama Zaraϑuštra'. Cantera (2004: 242) views the attachment of the subject as an enclitic pronoun, -*aš*, to the verb, *guft-aš*, as highly unusual ('höchst ungewöhnlich') in MP. Although in a footnote he acknowledges the validity of such constructions in a NP dialect of Tehran, he goes on to suggest that the expected translation should be *ohrmazd bē ō zardušt guft*, a clause found in PRDd 4.1. Cantera cites several other examples of what he perceives to be ungrammatical constructions caused by the word order of the Avestan. He asserts that the presence of *guft-aš* in a MP text could be a reliable indication ('ein nahezu sicheres Indiz') for a translation from the *Avesta*. To demonstrate his point he quotes a passage from *Ayādgār ī Jāmāspīg* and offers a reconstruction of the presumably lost Av. source. Cantera's notion of grammaticality, however, only inadequately describes the above-mentioned MP clause. In fact, Skjærvø (2010a: 246) observes that contrary to MP's usual subject-object-verb word order, 'the verb is frequently raised, and, not infrequently, a subject, direct object, or another part of the sentence may be lowered to the position after the verb'. A number of sentences in the *Zand* as well as other MP texts agree with Skjærvø's observation. In PY 37.1a, for example, as a consequence of following the Av. word order the direct object comes to stand after the verb: *ēdar ēdōn yazom ohrmazd*. However, there is no basis on which we can disqualify PY 37.1a as ungrammatical or unusual. More importantly, Skjærvø (2010a: 247ff.) adds that if 'the verb is fronted, the agent can be enclitic to the verb', quoting passages from non-translation MP literature in support of his suggestion. Assessments such as Cantera's often neglect the complexities of primary sources in favour of a superimposed concept of grammaticality, which may not adequately describe the source material.[7] As Skjærvø (2010c) importantly observes:

---

[7] Cantera (2004) offers many valuable insights into the transmission of the *Zand*. Unfortunately, his otherwise unique work suffers from a number of inaccuracies in his translations and in the evaluation of

Paying attention to the text implies examining both the grammar, especially syntax and semantics, of the text and the manuscript readings (text criticism). It is a fact that we still do not have a comprehensive description of Pahlavi syntax, nor a reliable dictionary with text references.

Clearly, a literary translation of the *Avesta* was not one of the goals of the exegetes. To my mind, the *Zand* was conceived as a didactic tool from the start, and as a translation paradigm the literal rendering of the original was at the very core of the priestly translation project. As Bang (1890: 363–4) rightly observes, the MP renderings of the *Avesta* were thought of as an aid in the education of the Zoroastrian priesthood. This interpretation is corroborated by an often quoted passage, which presumably reflects an historical edict by *Xōsraw* I:

> ZWY 2.2–4[8] *ud ān anōšag*[9] *ruwān husraw*[10] *māhdādān ud *weh-šābuhr*[11] *dād-ohrmazd ī ādurbādagān dastwarān ud ādur farrōbāy ī a-drō ud ādurbād ādurmihr ud baxtāfrīd ō pēš xwāst* (3) *ud u-š paymān aziš xwāst kū ēn yasnīhā pad nihān ma dārēd bē pad paywand ī ašmā zand ma čāšēd* (4) *awēšān andar husraw paymān kard*

> And that immortal soul, Xōsraw ..., summoned ... of Māhdād and Weh-Šābuhr Dād-Ohrmazd,[12] the priests of *Ādurbādagān*, and the deceit-less Ādur Farrōbāy, and Ādurbād, Ādurmihr and Baxtāfrīd into his presence. (3) And he requested a pact of them: 'Do not keep these *Yasna*s secret, but do not teach the *Zand* to anyone except your offspring'. (4) They made a treaty with Xōsraw.

Regardless of the historical accuracy of the above paragraph, it reflects the notion of the *Zand* as being taught in priestly schools in connection with the

---

the primary sources. I have pointed out one such problem in my review of his work (see Zeini 2008), where I also briefly note that some of his important conclusions are based on very little, at times a single piece of evidence.

[8] The text has been edited by Cereti (1995: 80, 134). It has also been discussed by Kreyenbroek (1996: 228–9) and Cantera (2004: 161, 218) and with text-critical remarks by Secunda (2012: 322). The manuscripts have considerable differences in their readings, while Cereti's apparatus and Secunda's critical notes have some inaccuracies. Therefore, I reproduce the text of K20.

[9] K20 ⟨'nšk⟩.

[10] Here and in sentence 4, the final ⟨-b⟩ in ⟨hwslwb⟩ resembles an *ezāfe*. As has been pointed out by Secunda (2012: 322), we can assume that text is missing between *husraw* and *māhdādān*, which is a patronymic, but not that of *husraw*.

[11] Secunda (2012: 322, fn. 22) reads *weh-šāhpūr* in K20. Although from an orthographical point of view Cereti's reading as ⟨W W šhpwl⟩ is correct, *weh-šāhpūr* is the expected name (see Secunda 2012: 324–5).

[12] Kreyenbroek and Secunda assume two different priests by the names of Weh-Šābuhr and Dād-Ohrmazd. In fact, Secunda (2012: 232, fn. 32) points out a contradiction in the sources, as they refer to Weh-Šābuhr and Dād-Ohrmazd as Xōsraw I's *mowbedān mowbed*. However, if the name of the priest was Weh-Šābuhr Dād-Ohrmazd, both Weh-Šābuhr and Dād-Ohrmazd would have designated the same priest. The readings supplied by K20 as *Weh-Šābuhr Dād-Ohrmazd or by DH as Weh-Šābuhr ī Dād-Ohrmazd, both support my interpretation. On the priests mentioned in this passage, see Cantera (2004: 207–20) and Secunda (2012: 324–31).

Avesta.¹³ I would like to conclude this section with an important and nuanced analysis by Josephson:

> In summary the basic system of word for word equivalences between Avestan and Pahlavi was complemented by analysis of the context in which they occurred. The results of the analysis could override the word for word correspondences and lead to the usage of a different word than the usual. Finally there was the religious aspect in which the contemporary theological interpretation could also influence the choice of a word in the Pahlavi version. (Josephson 1999: 174–5)

20.2 SIMPLIFIED MORPHOLOGY

No doubt, the MP language has a simplified morphology compared to Avestan and other OIr. languages. In itself, however, this is not an impediment in translating from languages with a complex morphology. As variously and rightly observed, MP's simplified inflection is problematic when the *Zand* follows the Avestan original literally. In the translations of stanzas with complex syntactic relationships, MP's simplified inflection, its lack of congruence and the disturbed word order complicate the task of recognising syntactic relationships. At times, the *Zand* addresses such issues. In PY 36.1c, *kē ō ōy xīndagīh ... ān-iz ō ōy xīndagīh dahēd ...* would have been an ambiguous translation for *yā ā axtiš ahmāi yąm axtōiiōi dåŋhē* 'who indeed (is) harm for the one whom you consign to harm'. Thus, the literal part of the translation contains comments, marked by *kū*, which disambiguate the meaning: *kē ō ōy xīndagīh kū pad abar ātaxš anāgīh kunēd ān-iz ō ōy xīndagīh dahēd kū ān-iz pad ōy anāgīh kunēd*. Although the ambiguity of this line is not due to the Av. word order, the *Zand* does utilise comments and glosses to increase clarity and comprehensibility. Comments, however, are not consistently used, and a number of stanzas challenge the modern reader.

20.3 TRANSLATION TECHNIQUES

Since the early days of Iranian studies scholars have been divided in their assessment of the *Zand*. The initial rift, formalised and mostly referred to as a school dispute ('Schulenstreit'), so for example by Cantera (2004), was concerned with the utility of the *Zand* for a better understanding of Avestan texts. In the late twentieth century scholarship gradually shifted towards an assessment of the quality of its translations in general. As for the latter, a consensus does not seem in sight. While Humbach (1996) and Kreyenbroek

---

¹³ On the *Zand* in priestly schools, see Macuch (2009a: 264ff.). See also Spiegel (1860: 7), who thought that the purpose of the bilingual MSS of the *Avesta* was to serve the study of the Avestan text and not the performance of the rituals.

(1996) do not value the quality of the translations highly, Josephson is more careful in her appraisal of the *Zand*:

> Although we know little about when the translations were made, a comparison of the original and the translation shows that by the time this work was done in Middle Persian much knowledge of the exact meaning of words in Avestan had been lost and many of the resulting equivalences are inexact and erroneous. (Josephson 1999: 147)

More importantly, she recognises that the translators were methodological in applying traditional semantic analysis in the process of translating the *Avesta* (Josephson 1999: 177). In a later examination, Josephson (2003: 33) concludes that the Pahlavi version of the *Gāθās* retains the central themes of the original text, but observes that the lapse of time between original and translation has left its marks on the text. Her statements are in stark contrast to Shaked's:

> Most of the translations occurring in the Zand are perfectly correct, or at least as acceptable philologically as our own. [...] It is a work of interpretation, and it uses various techniques for reading the Gāthās in the light of the most important questions of Zoroastrian outlook and theology. This is an approach to scriptures employed in various civilizations. (Shaked 1996: 649–50)

To my mind, the question about the quality of the translations is not one most deserving an examination. We have no objective rules by which we can measure the quality and accuracy of the Pahlavi translations and face two important obstacles in the quest for an appraisal of the *Zand*. Firstly, centuries of academic research have not generated consensus on the meaning of the Avestan compositions. Scholars are divided as to how to explain Avestan morphology, syntax and semantics. Even if such agreements existed, every modern translation of the *Avesta* would still be a work of interpretation removed from the original by nearly three millennia and by two millennia from the *Zand*. These distant interpretations are rooted in very diverse cultural backgrounds, which complicate the task of a meaningful comparison. Secondly, we have yet to develop a solid understanding of the *Zand*, without which an assessment of the 'quality' of the translations cannot take place. A comparison of four translations of the Avestan version of Y 35.9 shall demonstrate my point:[14]

> In accordance with truth, good thought and good power, (we elect Thee), O Ahura, through these (words), with a praise above (all other) praises, (we elect Thee) with a statement (above all other) statements, (we elect Thee) with a worship (above all other) worships. (Humbach 1991: I 145)

---

[14] Some modern translations of other stanzas show greater disagreements. I have chosen this stanza for the comments made by West (2008).

On account of truth,
of good thought
and of good rule,
through these (verses), O Lord, praise now (follows on) from praise,
solemn utterance now from solemn utterance,
worship now from worship. (Hintze 2007a: 32)

(8) ... We make Thee both their [= these words'] hearer and their teacher, (9) in line with Rightness and Good Thought and Good Rule, be it with praises, Lord, upon praises or with speech upon speech or with worship upon worship. (West 2008: 131)

(8) ... We make Thee both their recipient and their teacher, (9) in accord with Right and Good Thought and Good Rule, be it with praises where praises are due or with utterances where utterance or with act of worship where acts of worship. (West 2010: 172)

While Humbach and Hintze analyse this stanza as a self-contained unit, West sets the syntactic as well as the semantic boundaries of the stanza differently. In a section entitled 'Interpolated vocatives', West (2008: 131) identifies *ahurā*, a voc.sg., as an intrusion in Y 35.9b, but still translates it. In his monograph, however, he omits the vocative in his translation (see West 2010: 172ff.).[15] I doubt that scholars of Iranian Studies will take West's proposition seriously, but this single example shows that a comparison of the MP version of this stanza (see Section 6.10) with the original is not a trivial task. We face uncertainties in our approach to both texts.

20.4 AUXILIARY SCIENCE

The underlying idea behind an edition of ancient texts seems to be that we can unlock their meaning if not their true meaning. Yet, most scholars of Zoroastrianism readily admit that the *Gāθās* are impenetrable, and that we may never fully grasp their ritual or religious function within an assumed *Gāθic* society. The task of an edition is infinitely more complex when two groups of texts are involved, one being a translation *cum* commentary separated from the original by nearly two millennia. Although the *Yasna Haptaŋhāiti* is not as linguistically dense as the *Gāθās*, a comparison of the original and its translation is not a trivial task. What binds a late antique translation to the original text whose function and meaning are largely contested? Do we turn to the *Zand* to understand how priests of the late antique era understood the original composition? If so, do we measure their interpretation by our own methods or do we step in as mere observers? If we

---

[15] West's (2008) proposed methodology for editing the *Gāθās* is reminiscent of Baunack's (1888) methods, and to my mind outdated.

cannot reach consensus on the ritual meaning of the Avetsan texts, how do we position our own reading of the *Zand*?

Scholars have variously recognised or rejected the value of the *Zand* for a better understanding of the *Avesta*.[16] The outcome of this debate was of paramount importance before philologists had developed a better understanding of the Avestan language.[17] However, the question of the *Zand*'s effectiveness as an auxiliary tool ('Hilfswissenschaft') for the study of Avestan was not limited to the last centuries. Klingenschmitt (1978: 104), for instance, recognises the *Zand*'s limited benefit for a better understanding of difficult Av. passages, while Humbach (1996) seems inclined to reject it.

The linguistic analysis of the *Zand* in comparison with the *Avesta* is bound to paint a negative picture of the Pahlavi versions. The application of the comparative method of historical linguistics will in most cases generate far more reliable or at least more acceptable linguistic results than can be expected of the traditional exegesis, which was not concerned with a linguistic analysis of the original.[18] The utility and value of the Pahlavi versions lie in their relevance for a better understanding of Zoroastrianism's historical development irrespective of the *Zand*'s accuracy in comparison with methods of modern linguistics. Recognising this value, Humbach (1996) and Kreyenbroek (1996) rightly advocate a paradigm shift in the study of the *Zand*. Bronkhorst (2011) advocates a similar shift that applies to studies of ancient cultures in general.[19]

20.5 TRANSMISSION

Scholars have long debated questions pertaining to the creation and transmission of the Zoroastrian scripture. The tradition's shift from an oral mode of transmission to literacy and written scripture has often been ascribed to religious contact and rivalries between Sasanian Zoroastrianism and other religious traditions of the time.[20] It is well-known that during late antiquity various religious cultures interacted with one another within a relatively small geographical confine. However, even if cultural exchange functioned as an agent of change, competition between religious elites does

---

[16] Spiegel (1860) was one of the early scholars who believed in the value of the *Zand* as an auxiliary science.

[17] For more on the debate between the *Traditionalist* and *Vedic* schools, see Section 2.1.

[18] Several lists of inflections compiled in the FiÖ reveal that the priests certainly engaged with linguistic matters pertaining to translation. For one example, see Section 15.3.2. It would, however, be wrong to expect them to use scientific comparative methods developed in the last century.

[19] I briefly summarise Bronkhorst's views towards the end of Chapter 2.

[20] See Klíma (1959: 16, 35), Bailey (1943: 80ff., 151) and Huyse (2008). Klíma (1959), for instance, views the translations as a necessary effort of the Sasanian Zoroastrians in refuting new religions as well as heretic movements during the sixth century.

not sufficiently explain the dynamics driving significant processes such as the creation of scripture and canon. In the case at hand, questions arise as to how received tradition is defined and how religious authority is ascribed to received tradition. Does exegesis at all relate to contemporary social or political issues? The discussions of the Arsacid and Sasanian archetypes have mainly been driven by philological and codicological arguments, contributing little to a deeper understanding of the social and historical context of the Zoroastrian tradition. The scholastic cross-cultural framework contributes to the discussions by focusing our attention on the dynamics at play between scripture, its exegesis (the *Zand*) and the wider Pahlavi literature. As Pollock (2006: xi) importantly remarks, the history and development of a sacred language and that of a vernacular are always intertwined and impossible to study in isolation.

Revisiting Geldner's (1886–96: xxxiv) stemma, Cantera and Vaan (2005: 39) tentatively modify the date for the *Zand*'s combination with the Av. *Yasna* in a single manuscript from 1110 CE to a date prior to 1020 CE, presumably to late tenth or early eleventh centuries.[21] To my knowledge, the latter proposition has not been challenged and remains valid until a new reading of Hōšang Sīyāwaxš's preface is put forward or new material is discovered.[22] With renewed access to many bilingual manuscripts, particularly late ones, our understanding of the texts' written transmission is currently developing. As discussed above, the nineteenth-century MSS of the family of the IrPY seem to have been subject to editorial modifications at the hands of the priests or the copying scribes (Section 1.4.2).

Scholars seem generally to agree that the *Zand* is based on a long tradition of exegesis.[23] The questions of date and mode of composition and transmission remain open and controversial. Despite arguments favouring an early date for the *Zand* (Skjærvø 1991, 1994; Cantera 2004), its various strata remain undated (Josephson 1999: 175). Recently, Cantera (2004: 220–31) has contributed much to the relative chronology of the *Zand* and its strata. See particularly Cantera (2004: 229–31), where he discusses one case of presumed stratification, suggesting that the PWd must have existed in written form before its final redaction. Following Bartholomae (1904: 1804), Cantera (2004: 230) suggests that in PWd 4.43 *ka wināh* for *hāmō.š iiaoϑna* is obviously wrong ('offensichtlich falsch') and a misreading of *ham-at wināh. Bartholomae's suggestion rests on the fact that ᛋ can be read as *ka* as

---

[21] For my discussion of Geldner's stemma, see Section 1.4.2.
[22] Although the above-mentioned stemma is not modified, Cantera (2014b) has now provided a new view of the Zoroastrian manuscript tradition.
[23] See Skjærvø (1994), Josephson (1999), Cantera (2004) and Vevaina (2007). Skjærvø (1994: 203–4 and fn. 10) offers in passing a brief but insightful analysis of the *Zand*.

well as *ham-at*. Since a comment in PWd 4.43 starts with *ka-šān*, Cantera proposes that the comment must be of a later date. In his view, the comment must have been based on an already existing written version of the *Zand*, as the comment resumes the earlier misreading of *ka* for *ham-at. We may agree with Cantera's assessment that *ka-šān* depends on *ka*. This, however, does not explain the situation sufficiently. Intriguing as Cantera's analysis is, it does not take into account that *ka* could have been the original translation. In the PYH, *ka* occurs several times without translating a corresponding word in the original. In PY 38.2a *ka pad abzōn* corresponds to *īžā̊*. In PY 39.4b it functions much like *kū* by introducing an additional clause that does not translate a clause in Avestan. See also PY 39.5 where four *ka* introduce comments and glosses. Likewise, in PY 41.3a *ka hu-framānīh* corresponds to *humāīm*, and in PY 41.5a *ka ō ēd ī tō* translates ϑβōi. Cantera does not qualify his statement as to why *ka* is obviously wrong, nor does he explain why *ham-at wināh* would be a better translation.[24] While I hesitate to propose any dates for the various stages involved in the *Zand*'s transmission, i.e. composition, oral transmission and commitment to writing, I would like to share some preliminary observations on the *Zand*'s compositional structure that may be relevant to the issue at hand.[25]

Shaked (1994: 118–19) views the written *Zand* as a post-Sasanian product, suggesting that 'only some considerable time after the Islamic conquest of Iran were the various *Zand* compilations written down'. In a criticism directed at Widengren, he maintains:

> The *Zand* that has reached us is thus the outcome not of a planned effort at editing and excluding certain materials, but of a well-intentioned activity of one or more groups of people in the ninth and tenth centuries, who sought to preserve what was in their opinion worthy of survival. (Shaked 1994: 118)

Rejecting Widengren's (1983) view of the *Zand* as having been edited at the time of *Xōsraw* I, in part to purge it of any Zurvanite material, Shaked (1994: 119) continues:

> I find this position unconvincing. I do not think it plausible that any *zand* existed in any written form during the Sasanian period, and it is not likely that the supposed anti-Zurvanite censorship of Khusrau could operate on oral transmission.

It is not my intention to discuss Widengren's position, which in turn is based on Wikander's (1946) work. However, I would like to point out that I am critical of Shaked's assessment of an oral tradition as being less receptive to conscious and deliberate editorial activities. A view similar to Shaked's

---

[24] It is unclear to me how he arrives at his own translation of *ham-at wināh* as 'deine gleichgesetzten Sünden' (Cantera 2004: 230).

[25] Cantera (2004: Ch. 3) discusses the past scholarship in great detail.

has been brought forward by Lance Cousins with regard to Buddhism and orality.²⁶ Cousins suggests that it is far more difficult to disseminate ideas and editorial changes in an oral setting, where individual bearers of the tradition need to be reached. Whether any type of exegesis can operate in an oral tradition is still a matter of debate and has in part been questioned by research carried out by Farmer et al. (2000). The working hypothesis of the authors is that the Eastern conquests of the Achaemenid Persian empire might have spread literacy to domains of the Vedic tradition, causing a counter reaction to literacy which resulted in the development of mnemonic techniques and the canonisation of the Vedas (Farmer et al. 2000: 68, fn. 55). If canonisation processes which require editorial interventions are possible within an oral setting, other types of editorial activities should also be possible in oral cultures. The canonisation of the *Avesta*, the arrangement of the *Yasna* as studied by Hintze (2002), the YAv. commentaries on the OAv. prayers, the composition and transmission of the *Zand* and the spread of its ideas to other exegetical literature such as the *Dēnkard* all seem to point towards the possibility of exegesis and editorial censorship in an oral setting.

Although the *Zand* has often been described as an oral composition, no attempts have been made to examine the texts in light of research on orality. Scholars have variously pointed out the importance accorded to memorisation in MP literature (see Bailey 1943: 158ff.). But the preference for memorisation does not negate the possibility of a parallel written transmission. The lack of early manuscripts is certainly important, but not definitive evidence for orality. If we agree that the *Zand* is the product of an oral culture, we have to ask how it was composed and memorised. Compositional techniques typical of oral-formulaic epic literature, for instance, have not been employed in the composition of the *Zand*.²⁷ Nor does the *Zand* make use of mnemonic devices.²⁸ It is difficult to memorise and transmit a text that does not adhere to the word order of the language it was composed in. Why complicate the task of memorisation by employing an unnatural word order that will always be in danger of sub-conscious correction by a native speaker? More importantly, why align the MP version with the word order of the source language in an oral setting where such parallelism is of little use and meaning to the reciter or the recipient?

I agree that the *Zand* is an oral composition with an initial period of oral transmission. Two features that support this view have been preserved in

---

²⁶ Cousins's idea has been discussed by McMahan (1998).
²⁷ On the use of formulas in oral epic traditions, see Lord (2000) and Ong (2007).
²⁸ The repetitive compositional structure of *māh hordād rōz frawardīn* might be an example of a mnemonic device and the result of the text's oral composition. But such devices are not widespread and certainly not evident in the *Zand*.

the manuscripts. Firstly, the division of individual stanzas into small units of meaning or cola, and secondly, the lack of visual marks differentiating between translation and commentary in the manuscripts. These two features are indicative of an oral background. Had the text been translated through writing, with the goal of a WBW translation, the translators would have aligned smaller units of text with the original – most likely at the level of words. I hypothesise that the use of writing would have led to an interlinear glossing of the Avestan, such as is the case in the NP translations found in more recent manuscripts. In these MSS, NP glosses and comments are positioned below the words they translate. Longer comments occur in the margins. But for the *Zand*, the translators chose small units of meaning which were followed by a MP version and sometimes a commentary.

The task of translating a text in an oral setting requires self-contained units of meaning that can be followed by a translation. If the source text is too long it becomes challenging for the translator as well as the recipient to relate the source and target texts. If the text to be translated is divided into very small units, such as the individual words, the lack of textual context complicates the task of translation and reception. Thus, smaller self-contained units of meaning are ideal for the translation. This would enable a meaningful reading or recitation of the texts, even if only within a school or scholastic tradition. In this approach a self-contained passage from the source text is followed by the translation in the target language. Interpretations of the passage can be added if necessary. A similar practice is common among Iranian clerics. The recitation of a section from the *Quran* is followed first by a literary translation and then by commentary, which usually relates the Quranic verse to the subject of the sermon. One might further hypothesise that the *Zand* was a literary or free translation of the *Avesta* which followed small units of meaning, the cola that we find in the manuscripts. Taking advantage of the new medium of transmission, namely paper, the free translations were aligned with the Av. source at the time the texts were committed to writing. This minimal parallelism between the two languages would make sense in a literate setting, but not in an oral recitation.

Texts adapt themselves to the medium of expression. Lines, paragraphs, punctuation and brackets are not inherent structural features of a text, but visual aids that came about with the advent of literacy. Such devices are difficult to express in an oral recitation or transmission. Therefore, oral compositions are less likely to mark divisions as known from printed texts.[29] Particles such as *kū*, *hād* or *ay*, which often precede comments,

---

[29] Larger divisions such as chapters are often pointed out. In the *Yasna*, the *yeṅhē hātąm* marks the end of a chapter and lives on as an oral device in the manuscripts. Smaller sections, however, are more difficult to highlight, as this undertaking would disrupt the recitation and memorisation.

form an integral part of the texts' language, but are never visually marked or set apart in the manuscripts. Additional words and comments that go beyond the original text, but are not introduced by particles, are likewise visually unmarked in the *Zand*. This is in stark contrast to the SktY where comments are often, though not consistently marked by a *daṇḍa* sign (|).[30] The unmarked text of the *Zand*, as preserved in the manuscripts, is indicative of the texts' oral composition and transmission.

The differences between the modes of composition are best exemplified by the extant manuscripts. While the Pahlavi translations of the *Avesta* follow the method described above, the NP glosses take a different approach. These interlinear glosses are aligned with the Avestan and MP texts at word level and seldom attempt to capture the meaning of the text in its larger context (see MSS F2 T6). Longer commentaries, which make sense of the passages, be it Avestan or MP, appear often in the margins of the manuscripts. The concept of two parallel lines with words aligned below each other is obviously impossible to replicate in an oral setting. Interlinear glossing is the product of writing and requires the two-dimensional medium of paper. As we have seen, the manuscripts do not present the MP versions of the *Avesta* in the form of interlinear glosses.

In line with the above observations, I hypothesise that the *Zand* initially represented a free or literary translation of the Avestan. A literary translation agreeing with the language's natural syntax is easier to memorise and transmit. At the time the Pahlavi versions were committed to writing the traditional division of the text into small units of meaning (cola) was retained, while the literary translations were broken up to correspond to the word order of the Avestan as much as possible. When these renderings produced ambiguous or unclear meaning, commentaries could be added, which are perhaps remnants of the older, oral *Zand*. If older or alternative commentaries existed, they could be incorporated in the written *Zand* as well. The *Zand* was subject to more editorial changes as the written tradition evolved and the manuscripts were copied. The extant Pahlavi translations are thus not a merely crystallised version of an oral composition, but constitute a new literary product which evolved over time and was subject to editorial revisions as late as the nineteenth century. The Pahlavi versions are thus positioned between a literary translation and a WBW alignment and perhaps a witness to the transition from orality to a literate tradition.

The causal relationship between 'media of expression' and their effect on 'modes of thought' in the composition of texts have variously been outlined (Ong 1965: 145).[31] Ong (1984: 1) differentiates between a 'primary orality' and

---

[30] I am grateful to my friend Leon Goldman for pointing out this feature of the SktY.
[31] For more references, see fn. 2 in the same paper. For other discussions, see Goody (1987) and Carr (2005).

a 'residual orality'. The former is defined as 'the pristine orality of cultures with no knowledge of writing' (Ong 1984: 1), and the latter as 'traces of oral culture' in literary products of a literate culture (Ong 1965: 146). I doubt that any ancient Iranian text contains any primary orality. The extant *Avesta*, for example, represents the fixed and crystallised version of orally composed texts, which would have qualified as primary orality at the time of their composition. However, I believe that the *Zand* is a fitting example of residual orality. It retains the divisions of the *Avesta* into small units of meaning and does not separate the constituent parts of the translation, be it the commentaries or individual words that go beyond the words of the *Avesta*.

20.6 CONCLUDING THOUGHTS

While we may agree with Shaked (1994: 118) that the extant *Zand* is the outcome 'of a well-intentioned activity of one or more groups of people in the ninth and tenth centuries, who sought to preserve what was in their opinion worthy of survival', the *Zand* as a whole is undeniably the result of millennia of priestly involvement with scripture. From a scholastic vantage point, scripture and its exegesis depend on one another, each informing the other's development. The exegetes' engagement with the *Avesta* certainly contributed to its present arrangement, determining the order of the texts, repetitions and cross-references. And at times exegesis became incorporated into the scripture (Y 19–21). The Pahlavi translations of the *Avesta* do not stand alone and are deeply intertwined with other MP texts in a meaningful way.[32]

However, previous scholarship has mostly attributed shortcomings and inadequacies to the *Zand*, thus contributing to the academic neglect of this corpus (see Chapter 2). Despite the many challenges the *Zand* poses to modern recipients, it is a treasure trove for investigations of late antique interpretations of the *Avesta*. Like any other interpretive tradition the *Zand* is by definition a reading of and a commentary on scripture. This defining feature, however, does not render the *Zand* an auxiliary science of Avestan studies. The linguistic analysis of the *Zand*, which has been the dominant approach in the field, has mostly focused on translation techniques employed in the various *Zand* texts, elucidating certain aspects of the translations,

---

[32] As it is stated in the *Bundahišn*, the text derives its knowledge from the *Zand* and the *dēn*, and the compilation frequently invokes both as the source of its knowledge. Zādspram's reliance on the PY in the ninth century for his elaboration on the *Ahunwar* prayer, as discussed by Gropp (1991), is another example of the close links between the MP literature and the *Zand*.

but ignoring the *Zand* as an exegetical text.[33] As Shaked (1996) rightly points out, the *Zand* is a work of interpretation, and as such requires a different perspective, or a paradigm shift as advocated by Humbach (1996) and Kreyenbroek (1996).

The comparatively small size of the MP corpus and its complex transmission are serious obstacles to the study of Zoroastrian exegesis. But it is due to precisely these hindrances that we must shift our focus from purely philological analyses of the texts to include new methodologies from the wider field of religious studies. In order to uncover and discuss the guiding principles of Zoroastrian exegesis, I have examined select passages of the *Zand* and MP literature in light of Cabezón's cross-cultural framework of decontextualised scholasticism (Chapter 3). This approach shifts our focus by assessing techniques of exegesis rather than ascribing linguistic inadequacies or intellectual decline to the *Zand*. No doubt the obscure and dense style of the *Zand* is in part responsible for the negative appraisals it has received. But textual contradictions, for example, may be more fruitfully viewed as the result of the proliferative character of scholastic traditions (Section 3.3). I have also applied the extension of Cabezón's scholastic category of *proliferativity* in my investigation of the fire's perception in Zoroastrianism (Chapter 4), to show how correlative structures, a feature shared by many religious traditions, emerged in Zoroastrianism. The exegesis of the *Avesta*, however, was not limited to the *Zand*, and is a characteristic shared by the wider MP literature as well. The numerological reflections upon the OAv. corpus, including the YH, in the Suppl.ŠnŠ (Chapter 5) and the commentaries in the *Dēnkard* (Section 4.3.6) are an example of this type of interpretive literature. Furthermore, the commentaries in the *Pursišnīhā* show that the PYH had textual authority beyond its ritual significance which made the text relevant to discussions of priestly, theological and legal questions (Sections 13.2.5, 13.9 and 15.1.7). Although it is nearly impossible to define the historical context of the *Zand* more closely, it is hoped that these examinations make a modest contribution towards a better understanding of the religious milieu from which these texts emanate.

I hope to have shown that the Pahlavi translations and commentaries should not be dismissed or marginalised, despite all opacity attributed to the *Zand*. When considered as interpretive religious literature, the *Zand* proves itself to be a rich source that deepens our understanding of Zoroastrianism in late antiquity. Indeed, the exegetes extended their authority beyond matters of theology and scripture to politics by defining, for instance, the rules of

---

[33] See, for example, Cantera (1999a, 2006) and Josephson (1997), who eliminates a number of MP comments from her edition of the *Hōm Yašt*.

good governance through interpretations of the sacred scriptures. The power and historical importance of the *Zand* in the political life of the Sasanian kings becomes evident when Xōsraw I allegedly gathers the most senior priests of the empire and orders:

> ZWY 2.3–4 *ud u-š paymān aziš xwāst kū ēn yasnīhā pad nihān ma dārēd bē pad paywand ī ašmā zand ma čāšēd* (4) *awēšān andar husraw paymān kard*
>
> (3) And he requested a pact of them: 'Do not keep these *Yasna*s secret, but do not teach the *Zand* to anyone except your offspring'. (4) They made a treaty with Xōsraw.

Appendices

A. *Transliteration and apparatus*

A.1 PY 5

A.1.1 PY 5.1

(a) LTMH ʾytwnʾ YDBHWN-m ʾwhrmzd MNW gwspndc ʾhlʾdyh 1
YḤBWN-t 2
(b) ʾP-š MYʾ YḤBWN-t W ʾwlwlc Y ŠPYL 3
(c) ʾP-š lwšnyh YḤBWN-t W¹ bwmc W² hlwsp ʾpʾtyh bwn W³ bl 4

1 ʾytwnʾ] Pt4 Mf4 R413 T6 E7, K5 M1
  ʾytwn F2
  ʾytwnʾʾ J2
1 MNW] Pt4 Mf4 F2 T6 E7, K5 M1
  MN R413
  MN• J2
1 gwspndc] Pt4 T6 E7 (p̄)
  gwspnd Mf4
  gwspnd W F2 R413
  gwsp̄nd YḤBWN-t Y K5
  gwspnd Y J2
  gwsp̄ndʾnᵈ YḤBWN-t Y M1
1 ʾhlʾdyh] Pt4 T6 E7, K5 M1
  ʾhlʾdyhc Mf4 F2 R413, J2
  ʾhlʾdyhc Y D
2 YḤBWN-t] Pt4 Mf4 E7
  YḤBWN-tʾc F2
  YḤBWN-t Y R413
  YḤBWN-tʾ T6, J2
  dʾtʾ K5 M1
3 MYʾ] Pt4 Mf4 F2 R413 E7, K5 J2 (torn after MYʾ) M1
  MYʾ-c T6
3 YḤBWN-t] Pt4 Mf4 E7
  YḤBWN-tʾ F2 R413
  dʾt YḤBWN-t T6
  dʾtʾ K5 M1

3 W] Pt4 Mf4 T6 E7
  deest F2 R413, K5 M1
3 ʾwlwlc Y] Pt4 E7, K5 M1
  ﺳﺪﯨﻊ Mf4
  ʾwlwlc F2 R413
  ﺳﺪﯨﻋﺎ T6
3 ŠPYL] Pt4 Mf4 F2 R413 E7, K5 J2 (ŠP•) M1
  ŠPYL W hlwstcʾt ʾpʾtyh Y bwn W bl T6
4 Line (c)] Pt4 Mf4 F2 R413 E7, K5 J2 M1
  deest T6
4 YḤBWN-t] Pt4 Mf4 E7
  YḤBWN-tʾ J2
  dʾtʾ F2 R413, K5 M1
4 W¹] Pt4 Mf4 E7
  deest F2 R413, K5 J2 M1
4 W²] Pt4 Mf4 F2 E7
  Y J2
  deest R413, K5 M1
4 hlwsp] Pt4 R413 (p̄)
  hlwspʾ Mf4 E7 (p̄)
  hlwspc Y J2
  hlwspc F2
  hlwspʾ K5 M1
4 W³] Pt4 Mf4 F2 R413, K5 M1
  deest E7, J2

---

1 J2: Missing entries for this MS are due to the many tears in the manuscript.

A.1.2 PY 5.2

(a) ʿLH MNW hwtʾyyh W msyh ptš ʾP-š hwpʾnkyh hcš
(b) ZK ʾytwnʿ MN yštʾlʾn Y BYN ZNH gyhʾn pṭʾ pyšlwbšnyh YDBḤWN-m pyšwpʾdyh
(c) MNW pṭʾ gwspndʾwmndyh KTLWN-d ʿLH-šʾn yštʾl

1 Line (a)] Pt4 Mf4 F2 R413 T6 E7, K5 M1
  illegible J2.
1 ʿLH] Pt4 Mf4 T6 E7, K5 M1
  ʿLH-šʾnʿ F2 R413
1 MNW] Pt4 Mf4 R413 T6 E7, K5 M1
  MNW F2
1 hwtʾyyh] Pt4 Mf4 F2 R413 E7, K5 M1
  hwtʾyh T6
1 ptš] Pt4 Mf4 F2 T6 E7, K5 M1
  ᵂptš R413
2 ZK] Pt4 Mf4 F2 R413 E7
  ZK Y T6
  ᵃᵏ⁻ᵘ K5 M1
2 ʾytwnʿ] Pt4 Mf4 T6 E7, K5 J2 M1
  ʾytwn F2 R413
2 yštʾlʾn] Pt4 Mf4 F2 R413
  yštʾlʾnʿ T6 E7, K5 J2 M1
2 Y] Pt4 Mf4, K5 J2 M1
  deest F2 R413 T6 E7
2 gyhʾn] Pt4 Mf4 F2
  gyhn gyhʾn R413

  gyhʾnʿ T6 E7, K5 J2 M1
2 YDBḤWN-m] Pt4 Mf4 T6 E7, K5 M1
  ycBḤWN-m F2 R413
3 pyšwpʾdyh] Pt4 Mf4 E7
  pṭʾ pyšwpʾdyh F2, K5 M1
  pṭʾ pyš pʾdyh R413
  pṭʾ pyšwʾdyh T6
  pṭʾ pyšpʾyh J2
4 pṭʾ] Pt4 Mf4 F2 R413 T6 E7, J2 M1
  pṭʾ K5
4 gwspndʾwmndyh] Pt4 Mf4 F2 T6 E7, K5 M1 J2
  gwspndʾn ~~mn~~ ʾwmndyh R413
4 KTLWN-d] Pt4 Mf4 E7, J2
  KTLWN-tʾᵐ F2
  KTLWN-ytʾ R413
  KTLWN-tʾ T6
  ᵃⁿᵈᵉᵍ K5 M1
4 ʿLH-šʾn] Pt4 Mf4, J2 M1
  LH-šʾnʿ F2
  ʿLH-šʾnʿ R413 T6 E7, K5

1 hwpʾnkyh : پاپانی‌نک gloss in Mf4 (subscr.)

Appendices 307

A.1.3 PY 5.3

(a) ZK ʾytwnʿ MNW hwtʾy ŠM W pṭʾ dʾnʾkyh dwšytʿ YKʿYMWN-yt ʾp̄zwnyk 1
YDḆḤWN-m 2
(b) ʿLH MNW LNH-kʾn tnʿ W yʾn zywšnʿ hcš YDḆḤWN-m 3
(c) ʿLH MNW ʾhlwbʾnʿ plwʾhl ZKL-ʾn W nʾlykʾn nywkyh ⁺hcš YDḆḤWN- 4
m 5

1 ʾytwnʿ] Pt4 Mf4 R413 T6 E7, K5 J2 M1
   ʾytwn F2
1 MNW] Pt4 Mf4 F2 T6 E7, K5 J2 M1
   deest R413
1 hwtʾy] Pt4 Mf4 F2 R413 E7, K5 J2 M1
   hwtʾ T6
1 W] Pt4 Mf4 E7, K5 J2 M1
   deest F2 R413 T6
1 dʾnʾkyh] Pt4 Mf4 F2 R413 T6, K5 M1
   dʾmʾkyh E7
1 dwšytʿ] Pt4 Mf4 T6, J2
   dwšyt F2 R413 E7, K5 M1
1 YKʿYMWN-yt] Pt4 Mf4 R413 E7, K5 M1
   YKʿYMW-yt F2
   YKʿYMWN-ytʿ T6, J2
1 p̄zwnyk] Pt4 Mf4 (superscr.) T6 E7
   p̄zwn ʸᵗʷᵐhcš F2
   p̄zwnyk pyš R413
   p̄zwnykyh K5 M1
2 YDḆḤWN-m] Pt4 F2 R413 T6 E7, K5 J2 M1
   ʸᴰᴮᴴʷᴺ⁻ᵐ Mf4
3 Line (b)] Pt4 Mf4 F2 R413 T6 E7, K5 J2 M1
   Av. & Zand in marg. T6
3 ʿLH] Z̶K̶ ̶ʾ̶y̶t̶w̶n̶ ʿLH Pt4
   ʿLH Mf4 F2 R413 T6 E7, K5 J2 M1
3 LNH-kʾn] Pt4 Mf4 F2 R413 E7, K5
   LNH-ʾnʿ T6
   LNH-kʾn J2 M1

3 W] Pt4 Mf4 T6 E7, K5 J2 M1
   deest F2 R413
3 yʾn] Pt4 Mf4 F2 R413 T6 E7
   yʾnʿ K5 J2 M1
3 zywšnʿ] Pt4 Mf4 F2 T6 E7, K5 J2 M1
   ⟨⟨⟩⟩ R413
3 YDḆḤWN-m] Pt4 Mf4 F2 T6 E7, K5 M1
   BRʾ YDḆḤWN-m R413
4 ʿLH] Pt4 Mf4 F2 T6 E7, K5 J2 M1
   ʿLH-šʾnʿ R413
4 ʾhlwbʾnʿ] Pt4 F2 R413 T6 E7, K5 (superscr.)
   M1 (-ʾn-)
   ʾhlwbʿ Mf4
   W ʾhlwbʾnʿ J2
4 plwʾhl] Pt4 Mf4 F2 R413 T6 E7, K5
   (superscr.) J2 M1
4 ZKL-ʾn] Pt4 Mf4, K5 M1
   ZKL-ʾnʿ F2 R413 T6 E7
4 W] Pt4 Mf4 T6, K5 M1
   deest F2 R413 E7
4 nʾlykʾn] Pt4 Mf4
   nʾylykʾnʿ F2 R413 E7, K5 M1
   nʾlykʾnʿ T6
4 ⁺hcš] ʿʷʿ Pt4 Mf4 E7
   hcš F2 R413 T6, K5 J2 M1
4–5 YDḆḤWN-m] Pt4 F2 R413 E7, K5 J2 M1
   ycwm Mf4 T6

A.1.4   PY 5.4

(a) ʾhlʾdyh ʾytwnʾ pʾhlwm YDBḤWN-m ʾšwhšt'
(b) Y nywk' p̄zwnyk ʾmlg
(c) Y lwšn tn' Y ʿLH MNW hlwst' p̄ʾtyh nywkyh hcš

1 ʾytwn'] Pt4 R413 T6 E7, K5 J2 M1
ʾytwn' Y Mf4
ʾytwn F2
1 YDBḤWN-m] Pt4 Mf4 F2 R413 T6, K5 J2 M1
ycyDBḤWN-m E7
1 ʾšwhšt'] Pt4 T6 E7, J2 M1
ʾšwhšt Mf4
سرحس F2
ʾYK ʾšwhšt' R413
ʾstw ʾšwhšt' K5
2 Y nywk'] Pt4 E7
Y nywk' Y Mf4
nywk F2 R413
ʾMT nywk T6
nywkyh Y K5 M1
nywk' J2
nywk Y D

2 p̄zwnyk] Pt4 R413 T6 E7, J2
ببالكي Mf4
بوكي F2
p̄zwnyk Y K5 M1
3 Y] Pt4 Mf4 E7, J2
deest F2 R413, K5 M1
MNW T6
3 lwšn] Pt4 Mf4 T6
lwšn' F2 R413 E7, K5 J2 M1
3 Y] Pt4 Mf4 F2 T6 E7, K5 J2 M1
deest R413
3 hlwst'] Pt4 Mf4 E7, K5 M1
hlwst F2 R413 T6
hlwsp̄' J2
3 p̄ʾtyh nywkyh] Pt4 Mf4 F2 R413 E7, K5 J2 M1
nywkyh p̄ʾtyh T6

A.1.5   PY 5.5

(a) ZK-c Y wyh mynšn' whwmn YDBḤWN-m W ZK-c Y wyh ⁺hwt'yyh 1
hštlwl 2
(b) W ZK-c Y wyh dyn' W ZK-c Y ŠPYL srd'lyh hwrdt 'mwrdt W ZK-c Y 3
wyh bwndk mynšnyh spndrmt' 4

1   ZK-c Y]   Pt4 Mf4, K5 M1
    ZK-c F2 R413, J2
    ZK Y c T6
    ZK E7
1   wyh mynšn']   Pt4 R413 T6, K5 M1
    wyhm'nšn' Mf4 (wyhmynšn' superscr. sec.m.)
    wyh mynšn F2
    ⟨⟨⟩⟩ E7
    wyhmynšn' Y J2
1   whwmn]   Pt4 F2 R413 T6
    whwmn' Mf4 E7, K5 J2 M1
1   W ZK-c]   Pt4 R413 T6 E7
    ZK-c Mf4 F2, K5 M1
1   Y]   Pt4 Mf4 T6
    deest F2 R413 E7, K5 M1
1   wyh]   wyh Pt4 E7
    ŠPYL Mf4 F2 R413 T6, K5 M1
1   ⁺hwt'yyh]   hwt'yh Pt4
    hwt'yyh Mf4 F2 R413 T6 E7, K5 J2 M1
3   W ZK-c Y]   Pt4 Mf4 T6
    ZK-c F2 R413 E7
    ZK-c Y K5 J2 M1
3   wyh dyn']   Pt4 T6 E7
    wyhdyn' Mf4
    ŠPYL dyn' F2 R413, K5 J2 M1

3   W ZK-c Y]   Pt4 Mf4 T6, J2
    ZK-c F2 R413
    W ZK-c E7
    ZK-c Y K5 M1
3   ŠPYL srd'lyh]   Pt4 Mf4 F2 R413 E7, K5 J2 M1
    wyh srt'lyh Y T6
3   hwrdt]   Pt4 Mf4 E7
    ⟨⟨⟩⟩ F2
    ⟨⟨⟩⟩ R413
    hwrdt' W T6
    hwrdt W K5 M1
3   'mwrdt]   Pt4 T6 E7, K5 M1
    ⟨⟨⟩⟩ Mf4 F2
    ⟨⟨⟩⟩ ⟨⟨⟩⟩ R413
    W 'mwrdt' J2
3   W ZK-c Y]   Pt4 Mf4 T6 E7, J2 M1
    ZK-c F2 R413
    W ZK Y-c Y K5
4   wyh]   Pt4 T6
    ŠPYL Mf4 F2 R413 E7, K5 J2 M1
4   mynšnyh]   Pt4 Mf4 F2 R413 T6 E7, K5 M1
    mynšnyh Y J2
4   spndrmt']   Pt4 T6 (p̄) E7 (p̄)
    spndrmt Mf4 F2 R413, K5 M1 (p̄)

A.1.6 PY 5.6

(a) MNW MN 'YT-'n 'ytwn' pt' ycšn' QDM ŠPYL 'YḴ ycšn' ZK ŠPYL Y 1
'whrmzd Y hwt'y l'd ʿBYDWN-yt 2
(b) 'whrmzd 'k's MN 'hl'dyh 'p̄'kyhc cyk'mc-HD ⁺cyk'mc-HD k'l W krpk 3
W mzd W p'td'šn' 'k's BRʾ YḤBWN-t 4
(c) hncmnyk'n ZKL-'n W NKḆ-'n YDBḤWN-m 'mhrspnd'n' 5

1 PY 5.6] Pt4 Mf4 E7, K5 J2 M1
   yeṅhe hātąm L'YŠH F2
   yeṅhe hātąm R413 T6
1 'YT-'n] Pt4 Mf4
   'st'n' E7
   'YT-'n' K5 J2 M1
1 QDM] Pt4 Mf4 E7
   QDM 'w' 'LH K5 M1
1 Y] Pt4 Mf4, K5 M1
   deest E7
   W J2
2 Y] Pt4 Mf4
   deest E7
   W K5 J2 M1
2 ʿBYDWN-yt] Pt4 E7
   ʿBYDWN-ȳt d Mf4
   ʿBYDWN-tȳ K5 M1
3 'p̄'kyhc] Pt4 Mf4 E7
   'p̄'kyh K5 J2 M1
3 cyk'mc-HD] Pt4 Mf4 E7, J2
   جعمىد K5 M1
3 ⁺cyk'mc-HD] جعمىد Pt4 Mf4
   cyk'mc-HD E7
   cyk'mc-HD L'WḤL atī cyk'mc-HD K5 M1

3 krpk] Pt4, K5 J2 M1
   krpk' Mf4 E7
4 W] Pt4 Mf4 F2 T6, K5 M1
   deest E7, J2
4 W] Pt4 Mf4
   deest E7, K5 M1
4 p'td'šn'] Pt4 Mf4 E7, J2
   p'td <lbr> p'td'šn' W K5
   p'td'šn' W M1
4 BRʾ YḤBWN-t] Pt4
   YḤBWN-t Mf4 E7
   YḤBWN-yt K5 J2 M1
5 hncmnyk'n] Pt4 Mf4
   hncmnyk'n' E7, J2
   ۺںٯسۻ K5 M1
5 ZKL-'n] Pt4 Mf4
   ZKL-'n' E7, K5 J2 M1
5 W] Pt4 Mf4 E7
   deest K5 J2 M1
5 NKḆ-'n] Pt4 Mf4, J2
   n'lyk'n' E7
   NKḆ-'n' K5 M1
5 'mhrspnd'n'] Pt4, J2
   'mhrspnd'n Mf4 E7 (p̄), K5 (p̄) M1 (p̄)

Appendices 311

A.2 PY 35

A.2.1 PY 35.0

yst' Y hpt h't' 1
pltwm h't' bwn 2
(a) 'whrmzd Y 'hlwb' Y 'hl'dyh lt' YDBḤWN-m MNW ltyh pt' pl'lwnyh 3
'mhrspnd'n Y hwhwt'y'n Y hwdh'k'n YDBḤWN-m 4
(b) hlwst' ZK Y 'hlwb'n sty ycwm MNW mynwd W MNW-c gytyȳ 5

1 **yst'**] Pt4 F2 E7
   yšt' Mf4 R413
   deest T6, K5 J2 M1
1 **Y**] Pt4 Mf4 F2 R413
   deest T6 E7, K5 J2 M1
1 **hpt**] Pt4 F2 R413
   hpt' Mf4 E7
   deest T6, K5 J2 M1
1 **h't'**] Pt4 E7
   h't' bwn Mf4 R413
   h't F2
   deest T6, K5 J2 M1
2 **h't'**] Pt4 Mf4 E7
   h't F2 R413
   deest T6, K5 J2 M1
2 **bwn**] Pt4 Mf4 R413 E7
   deest F2
   deest T6, K5 J2 M1
3 **Y**] Pt4 Mf4 R413, K5 J2 M1
   deest F2 T6 E7
3 **Y**] Pt4 Mf4 R413, K5 M1
   deest F2 T6 E7, J2
3 **lt'**] Pt4 Mf4 T6, K5 J2 M1
   lt F2 R413 E7
3 **YDBḤWN-m**] Pt4 F2 R413 T6 E7, K5 J2 M1
   ycm Mf4
3 **MNW ... pl'lwnyh**] Pt4 Mf4 F2 T6 E7, K5 M1
   pt' pl'lwnyh R413
   deest J2
4 **'mhrspnd'n**] Pt4 Mf4
   'mhrspnd'n' R413 E7, M1
   'mhrspnd'n' F2 T6, K5 J2 ('m•n')
4 **Y**] Pt4 Mf4 E7
   deest F2 R413 T6, K5 M1
   W J2
4 **hwhwt'y'n**] Pt4 Mf4 R413 E7
   ויהוהואטיאן F2

   ויהוהטיאן T6
   hwt'y'n' K5 M1
   hwhwt'y'n' J2
4 **Y**] Pt4 Mf4 E7
   deest F2 R413 T6, K5 M1
   W J2
4 **hwdh'k'n**] Pt4 Mf4
   hwdh'k'n' R413 T6 E7
   hwdhk'n' F2, K5 J2 M1
4 **YDBḤWN-m**] Pt4 Mf4 F2 T6 E7, K5 M1
   ycwm R413, J2
5 **hlwst'**] Pt4 F2 R413, K5 M1
   hlwsp' Mf4
   hlwst T6
   hlwst Y E7
   hlwsp'n' J2
5 **Y**] Pt4 Mf4 F2 E7, K5 J2 M1
   deest R413 T6
5 **'hlwb'n**] Pt4 Mf4, K5 J2 M1
   'hlwb'n' Y F2
   'hlwb'n' R413 T6 E7
5 **sty**] Pt4 Mf4 R413 T6 E7, K5 J2 M1
   gytyȳ F2
5 **ycwm**] Pt4 R413 T6, K5 M1
   ycm Mf4, J2
   YDBḤWN-m F2 E7
5 **MNW**] Pt4 Mf4 F2 R413 T6 E7, J2
   וזגי K5 M1
5 **mynwd**] Pt4 Mf4 F2 R413 T6 E7, J2
   mynwd'n K5 M1
5 **W**] Pt4 Mf4 E7, J2
   deest F2 R413 T6, K5 M1
5 **gytyȳ**] עטאי Pt4 R413 E7
   עטאי Mf4 F2 T6, J2
   ויטאעי K5
   וימאעי M1

---

3 **'whrmzd** : اورمزد gloss in Pt4 (subscr.)
3 **'hlwb** : اهو gloss in Pt4 (subscr.)

(c) pt̰' 'lcwk' Y 'w' ZK Y ŠPYL 'hl'dyh ⁺'p̄'dst' Y 'w' k'l W krpk' l'd W 'lcwk'   6
Y dyn' Y ŠPYL Y mẕdyst'n ⁺'p̄'dst' Y 'w' dyn' l'd   7

6 pt̰'] Pt4 Mf4 F2 R413 T6 E7, K5 M1
   illegible J2
6 'lcwk'] Pt4 Mf4 E7
   'lcwk' F2 R413 T6, K5 J2 M1
6 Y] Pt4 Mf4 E7, K5 M1
   deest F2 R413 T6, J2
6 Y] Pt4 Mf4 F2 R413 T6, K5 J2 M1
   deest E7
6 ⁺'p̄'dst'] 'p̄'st' Pt4 Mf4 F2 R413 T6 E7, J2
   'p̄'dst D
   'p̄'dst' K5 M1
6 Y] Pt4 Mf4 F2 R413 T6, K5 J2 M1
   deest E7
6 'w'] Pt4 Mf4 F2 R413 T6 E7, J2
   'L K5 M1
6 W] Pt4 Mf4 F2 R413 T6, K5 J2 M1
   deest E7
6 krpk'] Pt4 Mf4 T6 E7, K5 J2 M1
   krpk F2 R413
6 W] Pt4 Mf4 E7, K5 J2 M1
   deest F2 R413 T6

6 'lcwk'] Pt4 Mf4 E7, K5 J2 M1
   pt̰' 'lcwk' F2 (pt̰' superscr.) T6
   'lcwk R413
7 Y] Pt4 Mf4 F2 R413 T6 E7, K5 M1
   deest J2
7 Y] Pt4 Mf4 F2 R413 T6, J2
   deest E7, K5 M1
7 Y] Pt4 Mf4
   deest F2 R413 T6 E7, K5 J2 M1
7 mẕdyst'n] Pt4 Mf4
   mẕdyst'n' F2 R413, K5 J2 M1
   mẕdst'n' T6 E7
7 ⁺'p̄'dst'] 'p̄'st' Pt4 Mf4 F2 T6 E7, J2
   'p̄'dst R413
   'p̄'dst' K5 M1
7 Y] Pt4 Mf4 F2 T6, K5 M1
   deest R413 E7, J2
7 'w'] Pt4 Mf4 F2, J2
   deest R413 T6
   ZK E7
   'L K5 M1

A.2.2 PY 35.1

(a) hwmtʼn' hwhtʼn' hwwlštʼn' ʼMT LTMH dhšn' ʼP̱-š pt̲ʼ-c Y ZK Y ZK-ʼy   1
dhšn' ʼYḴ-š LTMH W TMH-c nywkyh hcš   2
(b) ZK Y wlcyt' ʽD KʽN W ⁺ZK-c Y wlcyhyt MN KʽN prʼc   3
(c) ⁺H̲WH-m QDM glptʼl ʼYḴ ʼw' NPŠH ʽB̲YDWN-mm ZK Y GBRʼ ʼw'   4
GBRʼ BRʼ ʼp̱spʼltʼl krpk' pt̲' dʼt lʼs cygwn ŠPYL ⁺H̲WH-m ʼYḴ cygwn   5
pʼhlwm ʼw' NPŠH ʽB̲YDWN-mm   6
wycdst' byšʼmlwtyk gwbšn'   7

1 hwmtʼn'] Pt4, K5 J2 M1 hwmtʼn Mf4 2 hwmtʼn' E7	3 wlcyhyt] Pt4 Mf4, K5 M1 wlcyhyt' E7, J2
1 hwhtʼn'] Pt4 E7, K5 M1 ⲓⲱⲉⲩⲓⲱ Mf4 W hwhtʼn' J2	4 ⁺H̲WH-m] ϭⲓⲣϭⲙ Pt4 Mf4 E7 H̲WH-m K5 J2 M1
1 hwwlštʼn'] Pt4 Mf4 E7, K5 M1 W hwwlštʼn' J2	4 glptʼl] Pt4 Mf4 E7, K5 M1 glptʼl H̲WH-m J2
1 ʼMT] Pt4 E7 MNW Mf4, K5 J2 (torn at N) M1	4 ʼw'] Pt4 Mf4, K5 J2 M1 ZK Y E7
1 LTMH] LTMH W TMH c Pt4 LTMH Mf4 E7 LTMH-c Y K5 M1 LTMH-c J2	4 ʽB̲YDWN-mm] Pt4 Mf4 ʽB̲YDWN-m E7 ʽB̲YDWN-m̱ K5 J2 M1
1 dhšn'] Pt4 Mf4 E7, J2 dhšn K5 M1	5 BRʼ] Pt4 E7, K5 J2 deest Mf4
1 pt̲ʼ-c Y] Pt4 pt̲ʼ-c Mf4 E7, K5 J2 M1	5 ʼp̱spʼltʼl] Pt4 Mf4 E7, J2 (preceded by ʼ•) ʼp̱spʼltʼl K5 M1
1 ZK] Pt4 Mf4, K5 J2 M1 deest E7	5 krpk'] Pt4 E7, J2 (krpʽkʼ) krpk' Y Mf4 W krpk' Y K5 M1
1 Y] Pt4, J2 deest Mf4 E7, K5 M1	5 dʼt] Pt4 Mf4 E7, K5 M1 dʼt' J2
2 dhšn'] Pt4 E7, K5 J2 M1 dhšn' h̵c̵š̵ Mf4	5 ⁺H̲WH-m] ϭⲓⲣϭⲙ Pt4 Mf4 E7 H̲WH-m K5 J2 M1
2 TMH-c] Pt4, K5 J2 M1 TMH Mf4 E7	6 ʼw'] Pt4 Mf4, J2 ZK E7 ʼw' Y K5 M1
3 wlcyt'] Pt4 Mf4, J2 wlcyt E7, K5 M1	6 ʽB̲YDWN-mm] Pt4 ʽB̲YDWN-m Mf4 E7 ʽB̲YDWN-m̱ K5 J2 M1
3 KʽN] Pt4 E7, K5 M1 ⲓⲓⲓⲋ Mf4	7 wycdst'] Pt4 E7 wycst Mf4 ⲓⲉⲱⲉⲱⲱ K5 wycst' J2 M1
3 W ⁺ZK-c] ⲉⲩϫⲓ Pt4 Mf4 W ZK-c E7 ZK-c K5 J2 M1	7 byšʼmlwtyk] Pt4 Mf4 E7 byšʼmwlwtyk K5 J2 M1
3 Y] Pt4 Mf4 E7, K5 M1 deest J2	

---

1 hwmtʼn' : *humatąm̊* ʽD LʽYŠH ⲣⲥⲥⲙ byšʼmlwtyk F2
humataŋąm ʽD wycst byšʼmlwtyk R413
humataŋąm ʽD T6

A.2.3   PY 35.2

(a) ʾwʾ ZNH ʾytwnʾ ʾDYNʾ kʾmkʾ YḤBWN-m ʾwhrmzd MNW ʾhlʾdyh nywkʾ   1
dynʾ   2
(b) ʾytwnʾ ZNH mynwmc W YMRRWN-mc W wlcwmc   3
(c) ʾYKʾ-m MN ʾYTʾ-ʾn ʾNŠWTʾ-ʾn ptʾ kwnšnʾ pʾhlwm ḤWH-t BYN KRʾ 2   4
ʾhwʾn ʾYK mzd YḤBWN-ʾnd   5

1 ʾwʾ] Pt4 Mf4 R413 T6 E7, K5 J2 M1
   ⟨⟩ F2
1 ZNH] Pt4 Mf4 F2 T6 E7, K5 J2 M1
   deest R413
1 ʾytwnʾ] Pt4 Mf4 T6 E7, K5 J2 M1
   ʾytwn F2 R413
1 ʾDYNʾ] Pt4 Mf4 T6 E7, K5 J2 M1
   ʾDYN F2 R413
1 kʾmkʾ] Pt4 Mf4 E7, K5 J2 M1
   kʾmk F2 R413 T6
1 ʾwhrmzd] Pt4 (superscr.) F2 (in marg.) T6 (in marg.) E7
   deest Mf4 R413, K5 J2 M1
1 nywkʾ] Pt4 Mf4
   nywk F2 T6 E7, K5 M1
   ⟨⟩ R413
   nywkʾ W J2
3 ʾytwnʾ] Pt4 Mf4 R413 T6 E7, K5 J2 M1
   ʾytwn F2
3 mynwmc W] Pt4
   mynmc W Mf4, J2
   ⟨⟩ F2
   mynmc R413, K5 M1
   ⟨⟩ T6
   MNDʾM-c mynwmc E7
3 YMRRWN-mc] Pt4 Mf4

   ⟨⟩ F2 R413 T6
   ⟨⟩ E7
   YMLLWN-mc K5 J2 M1
3 wlcwmc] Pt4 E7, J2 (-w- superscr.)
   wlcmc Mf4 R413 T6
   wlcwmcʾ F2
   wlcymc K5 M1
4 ʾYKʾ-m] ⟨⟩ Pt4 E7
   ʾYK-m Mf4 F2 (-m superscr.) T6, K5 J2 M1
   ʾYK R413
4 ʾYTʾ-ʾn] ⟨⟩ Pt4 Mf4
   ʾYT-ʾn F2 R413 T6, K5 J2 M1
   ⟨⟩ E7
4 ʾNŠWTʾ-ʾn] Pt4 Mf4
   ʾNŠWTʾ-ʾn F2 R413 T6 E7, K5 J2 M1
4 ḤWH-t] Pt4 Mf4, K5 M1
   ḤWH-tʾ J2
   ḤWH-d F2 R413
   ḤWH-dm T6
   ⟨⟩ E7
5 ʾhwʾn] Pt4 Mf4 F2 E7, J2
   ʾhwʾn R413 T6, K5 M1
5 YḤBWN-ʾnd] Pt4 Mf4, K5 J2 M1
   YḤBWN-yt F2 R413 T6
   YḤBWN-ʾnd ZK Y L YḤBWN-yt E7

A.2.4 PY 35.3

(a) ZK Y gwspnd'n dhšn' MY' W ZK Y ʿLH-š'n kwnšn' pʾhst' ʿLH-š'n   1
ʾNŠWT' Y BYN ẒNH gyhʾn' kʾl pʾhlwm plmʾdšn'   2
(b) P̱ʾ-š'n' lʾmšn'c W wʾstlc dhšn' gwspnd'n lʾmšn' W ʾp̱ybymyh   3
(c) MNW-c¹ ʿŠMHN-ʾk ʾYḴ-š hylptst'n krt' YKʿYMWN-yt' W MNW-c²   4

1 Y] Pt4 Mf4 F2 R413 E7, K5 J2 M1
  deest T6
1 gwspnd'n] Pt4 Mf4, J2
  gwspnd'n' F2 T6
  gwsp̄nd'n' R413 E7
  gwsp̄nd'n K5 M1
1 dhšn'] Pt4 Mf4 F2 T6 E7, K5 J2 M1
  dhšn R413
1 MY'] Pt4 Mf4 T6, J2
  MY' m F2
  MY' W w'stl R413
  W MY' W hwlšn' E7
  W MY' K5 M1
1 W ZK] Pt4 Mf4 R413 E7, J2
  ZK F2 T6, K5 M1
1 Y] Pt4 Mf4 F2 R413 T6 E7, K5 M1
  W J2
1 ʿLH-š'n] Pt4 Mf4 F2
  ʿLH-š'n' R413 T6 E7, K5 J2 M1
1 p'hst'] Pt4 Mf4 T6 E7, K5 M1
  ⲡⲉⲥⲛⲉⲗ R413
  ⲡⲉⲥⲥⲛⲉⲗ J2
  p'hst F2
1 ʿLH-š'n] Pt4 Mf4
  ʿLH-š'n' F2 R413 T6 E7, K5 J2 M1
2 ʾNŠWT'] Pt4 Mf4 R413 T6 E7
  mltwm F2
  ʾNŠWT'-'n' K5 J2 M1
2 Y] Pt4 Mf4 E7, K5 J2 M1
  deest F2 R413 T6
2 ẒNH] Pt4 Mf4 R413 T6 E7, K5 M1
  ش F2
  ẒNH J2
2 gyh'n'] Pt4 Mf4 F2 T6 E7, K5 M1
  gyh'n R413, J2
2 k'l] Pt4 Mf4 F2 E7
  k'l Y R413 T6, K5 J2 M1
2 plm'dšn'] Pt4 Mf4 F2 (ᵐ above -š-) R413 E7, K5 M1
  plm's̶n̶d̶ʸᵐ T6
  plm'dšn J2
3 P̱'-š'n'] Pt4 F2 R413 T6 E7, K5 M1
  ᵺ P̱'-š'n' Mf4
  P̱'-š'n J2

3 l'mšn'c] Pt4 T6 E7, K5 J2 M1
  l'mšnc Mf4 F2
  l'mšn'c Y R413
3 W] Pt4 F2 R413 T6 E7, J2
  deest Mf4, K5 M1
3 w'stlc] Pt4 Mf4 F2 (-ᵗˡᶜ) E7, K5 J2 M1
  w'stlc Y R413 T6
3 dhšn'] Pt4 Mf4 F2 R413 E7
  dhšn' MN T6
  dhšn' W K5 J2 M1
3 gwspnd'n] Pt4 Mf4 T6, J2
  MN gwspnd'n' F2
  gwsp̄nd'n' R413 E7
  gwsp̄nd'n K5 M1
  gwspnd'n' D
3 l'mšn' W] Pt4 Mf4 F2 R413, J2
  l'mšn' T6, K5 M1
  W l'mšn' W E7
3 p̱ybymyh] Pt4 Mf4 F2 R413 T6 E7, K5 M1
  p̱ybwymyh J2
4 ʿŠMHN-'k] Pt4 Mf4 R413 T6 E7, K5 J2 M1
  ʿŠMHN' k F2
4 ʾYḴ-š ... '-ʿŠMHN-'k] Pt4 Mf4 F2 T6 E7, K5 J2 M1
  deest R413
4 hylptst'n] Pt4 Mf4
  ᵗᵉ hylptst'n' F2
  hylptst'n' T6 E7, K5 (first -t- superscr.) M1
  hylpst'n' J2
4 krt'] Pt4 Mf4 T6, J2 (torn at kr-)
  krt F2, K5 M1
  ⲡⲉⲣⲟ E7
4 YKʿYMWN-yt'] Pt4 T6, J2
  YKʿYMWN-yt Mf4 E7, K5 M1
  YKʿYMWN'-yt F2
4 W] Pt4 Mf4 E7, K5 J2 M1
  deest F2 T6
4 MNW-c²] Pt4 F2 E7, K5 M1
  MNW Mf4, J2
  Q̶D̶M̶ ᴹᴺᵂ⁻ᶜ T6
4 '-ʿŠMHN-'k ... MNW-c³] Pt4 Mf4 F2 R413 T6 E7, J2
  deest K5 M1

ʾ-ʿŠMHN-ʾk ʾYḴ-š Lʾ krtʾ YKʿYMWN-ytʾ ʾš ʾytwnʾ kwnšnʾ ʾYḴ-š bym LʿYTʾ 5
W MNW-c³ ⁺pʾthšʾ W MNW-c⁴ ⁺ʾp̄ʾthšʾ 6

5 ʾ-ʿŠMHN-ʾk] Pt4 Mf4 E7, J2
  ʾPŠMHN-ʾk ʾ-ʿŠMHN-ʾk F2
  deest R413
  ʾ-ʿŠMHN-ytʾk T6
5 ʾYḴ-š] Pt4 Mf4 R413 T6, J2
  ʾYḴ-š hylptstʾnʾ F2 E7
5 krtʾ] Pt4 Mf4 T6 E7, J2
  krt F2 R413
5 YKʿYMWN-ytʾ] Pt4 T6, J2
  YKʿYMWN-yt Mf4 F2 R413 E7
5 ʾš] Pt4 Mf4 F2 R413 T6 E7
  ʾš J2 (in marg. sec.m.)
5 ʾytwnʾ] Pt4 Mf4 R413 T6 E7, J2
  ʾytwn F2
5 LʿYTʾ] Pt4 Mf4 T6 E7
  LʿYT F2 R413
  LʿY• J2

6 W MNW-c³] Pt4 Mf4 E7, J2 (W M•)
  MNW-c F2 R413 T6
6 ⁺pʾthšʾ] ᭫ᨠ᨟᨟ᨀ Pt4 Mf4 F2 T6 E7
  ᭫ᨠ᨟᨟ᨀ R413
  ŠLYTʾ-yh K5 M1
  ŠLYTʾ J2
6 W] Pt4 Mf4 F2 E7, J2
  deest R413 T6, K5 M1
6 MNW-c⁴] Pt4 Mf4 F2 R413 T6 E7
  MNW-c Y K5 J2 M1
6 ⁺ʾp̄ʾthšʾ] ᭫ᨠ᨟᨟ᨀ Pt4 Mf4 R413 T6
  ᭫ᨠ᨟᨟ᨀ F2
  ᭫ᨠ᨟᨟ᨀ E7
  ᭫ᨠ᨟᨟ᨀ K5 M1
  ʾp̄ʾthšʾ• J2
  ʾp̄ʾthšʾ D

A.2.5 PY 35.4

(a) ʿL pt̰ʾ ʿLH Y hwhwtʾytwm ʾDYN hwtʾyyh MN ZK ʾMT-m QDM ʾYḴ-m   1
nywkyh hcš   2
(b) YḤBWN-m BNPŠH W čʾẓšm ʾwʾ ʾYŠ-ʾn ʾYḴ BRʾ YḤBWN-yt W ZK-c   3
Y ʿḆYDWN-mm ʾYḴ dʾlšnʿ BRʾ ʿḆYDWN-mm   4
(c) ʾwʾ MNW ʾwhrmẓd W ʾšwhštʿc   5
wycdstʾ slyšʾmlwtyk gwbšn   6

1 ʿL pt̰ʾ] Pt4 Mf4
   ʿL-c pt̰ʾ E7
   deest K5 M1
   ʿL-c ʾwʾ J2
1 ʿLH Y] Pt4 Mf4 E7, J2
   ʿLH-c K5 M1
   ʿLH D
1 hwhwtʾytwm] Pt4 E7
   hwhwtʾktwm Mf4, K5 M1
   •hwtʾytwm J2
1 ʾDYN] Pt4 Mf4, K5 M1
   ʾDYN E7, J2
1 ZK] Pt4 Mf4 E7, K5 M1
   •K J2
1 ʾMT-m] Pt4 E7, J2
   MNW-m Mf4
   ʾMT-š K5 M1
1 ʾYḴ-m] Pt4 Mf4 E7, K5 M1
   ʾYḴ-š D
   ʾYḴ• J2
3 BNPŠH] Pt4 Mf4 E7, K5 M1
   BNPŠ• J2
3 W] Pt4 Mf4 E7, K5 M1
   • J2
3 čʾẓšm] Pt4 Mf4 E7, K5 M1
   čʾẓš• J2
3 ʾwʾ] Pt4 Mf4, K5 J2 M1
   ZK E7
3 ʾYŠ-ʾn] Pt4 Mf4
   ʾYŠ-ʾn E7, K5 J2 M1
3 YḤBWN-yt] Pt4 Mf4 E7, K5 J2 M1
   YḤBWN-ytʿ D
3 W ZK-c] Pt4 Mf4 E7, J2
   ZK-c K5 M1
4 Y] Pt4, K5 M1
   deest Mf4 E7, J2
4 ʿḆYDWN-mm] Pt4 Mf4, J2
   ʿḆYDWN-m E7, K5
   ʿḆYDWN-m̧ M1
4 ʿḆYDWN-mm] Pt4 Mf4, J2
   ʿḆYDWN-m E7, K5
   ʿḆYDWN-m̧ M1
5 W] Pt4 Mf4 E7, J2
   deest K5 M1
6 wycdstʾ] Pt4 E7
   wycstʾ Mf4, K5 J2
   wycst M1
6 slyšʾmlwtyk] Pt4 Mf4 E7, K5
   byšʾmwlwtyk J2
   slwšʾmwlwtyk M1
6 gwbšn] Pt4
   gwbšnʿ Mf4 E7, K5 M1
   deest J2

1 ʿL pt̰ʾ : huxšaϑrō.təmāi ʿD ašāicā.vahištā ﬦﬦ slyšmlwtyk
   gwbšnʿ F2
   huxšaϑrō.təmāi slyšʾmlwtyk gwbšnʿ R413
   huxšaiϑrō-tæəmāi T6

A.2.6 PY 35.5

(a) ʼytwnʼ ZK Y KRʼ 2 ZKL W nʼylyk ʼkʼs YḤWWN-d ʼškʼlkʼ

(b) ʼytwnʼ ZK ʼYTʼ wyhyh dynʼ W ZK-c ʼkʼsyhʼ YḤBWN-d ʼwʼ ʼYŠ-ʼn ʼYK BRʼ cʼšynd W wlcyndc ZK-ʼy prʼc ZK ʼwʼ ʻLH ZK-ʼy ʼkʼsynynd

(c) ʻLH-šʼnc Y ZK-ʼy hylpt ʼytwnʼ ʼYTʼ cygwn ZK wlcynd ʼYK ZK Y hʼwštʼ

1 ʼytwnʼ] Pt4 Mf4 R413 T6 E7, K5 M1
  ʼytwn F2
  ʼy• J2
1 ZK] Pt4 Mf4 F2 R413 T6 E7, K5 M1
  • J2
1 Y] Pt4 F2 R413, K5 M1
  deest Mf4 T6 E7
  • J2
1 KRʼ] Pt4 Mf4 F2 R413 T6 E7, K5 M1
  K• J2
1 ZKL] Pt4 Mf4 R413 E7, K5 J2 M1
  ZKL-ʼnʼ F2 (ʼnʼ sec.m.)
  Y ZKL̶-ʼnʼ T6 (ʼnʼ sec.m.)
1 W] Pt4 Mf4 F2 R413 T6 E7, K5
  deest J2 M1
1 nʼylyk] Pt4 Mf4 E7, K5 J2 M1
  nʼylykʼnʼ F2 R413 T6
1 YḤWWN-d] Pt4 Mf4 R413 T6 E7, K5 J2 M1
  YḤWWN-t⁻ᵈ F2
1 ʼškʼlkʼ] Pt4 E7
  ʼškʼlk Mf4 F2 T6, K5 J2 M1
  ⁺kʼškʼlk R413
2 ʼytwnʼ] Pt4 Mf4 R413 T6 E7, K5 M1
  ʼytwn F2
2 ZK] Pt4 Mf4 F2 R413 E7, K5 J2 M1
  ZK Y T6
2 ʼYTʼ] Pt4 Mf4 R413 T6 E7, K5 J2 M1
  ʼYT F2
2 wyhyh] Pt4 Mf4 T6, K5 J2 M1
  سوس F2
  سوس R413
  ױסוס ױסוי E7
2 dynʼ] Pt4 Mf4 F2 R413 T6 E7, K5 M1
  ױנ J2
2 W ZK-c] Pt4 Mf4 E7, J2
  ZK-c F2 R413, K5 (Z illegible) M1
  W ZK-c Y T6
2 ʼkʼsyhʼ] Pt4 Mf4 F2 T6 E7, K5 M1
  سوسوس R413
  ʼk•syhʼ J2
2 YḤBWN-d] Pt4 T6 E7, K5 J2 M1
  BYḤBWN-d Mf4
  YḤBWN F2 (-d sec.m.) R413
2 ʼYŠ-ʼn] Pt4, K5 M1
  ʼYŠ-ʼnʼ Mf4 F2 R413 T6 E7, J2 (ʼY•-ʼnʼ)
2 ʼYK] Pt4 Mf4 F2 R413 T6 E7, K5 M1
  •K J2
3 cʼšynd] Pt4 Mf4 R413 E7, K5 J2 M1
  cʼšʼⁿynd F2

3 سוسעו T6
3 W wlcyndc] Pt4 F2 R413 E7, J2
  ף ױאסⅡ Mf4
  W wlcyndc MNW-c T6
  עוסى סוייסى K5
  ױאסى M1
  סויאסى D
3 prʼc] Pt4 Mf4 F2 R413 E7, K5 M1
  ptʼ J2
3 ZK ʼwʼ] ZK ʼwʼ Pt4
  ʼwʼ Mf4 F2 R413 T6, J2
  ZK Y E7
  W ʼwʼ K5 M1
3 ʻLH] Pt4 Mf4 F2 R413 T6 E7, K5 M1
  ʻLH Y J2
3 ZK-ʼy] Pt4 Mf4 R413 T6 E7, K5 J2 M1
  deest F2
3 ʼkʼsynynd] Pt4 Mf4 E7
  סوس—سوسى F2
  سوسى R413 T6
  سوس — سوسى K5
  سوس• J2
  سوسى M1
4 ʻLH-šʼnc Y] Pt4 Mf4
  ʻLH-šʼnʼc F2 R413 T6
  ʻLH-šʼnc E7, K5 J2 M1
4 ZK-ʼy] Pt4 Mf4 F2 R413 T6 E7, K5 J2 M1
  ZK-̶y̶ ᴹᴺᵂ T6
4 hylpt] Pt4 Mf4 F2 R413 T6 (ʼyʼ-) E7, K5 M1
  hylptʼ J2
4 ʼytwnʼ] Pt4 Mf4 R413 T6 E7, K5 M1
  ʼytwn F2
4 ʼYTʼ] Pt4 Mf4 T6 E7, K5 J2 M1
  ʼYT F2 R413
4 cygwn] Pt4 Mf4 F2 R413 T6, K5 J2 M1
  cygwnʼ E7
4 ZK] Pt4 Mf4 F2 R413 T6
  ZK Y E7
  deest K5 J2 M1
4 wlcynd] Pt4 Mf4 F2 R413 T6 E7, J2
  ױאסⅡ K5 M1
4 ʼYK] Z̶K̶ ʼYK Pt4
  ʼYK Mf4 F2 R413 T6 E7, K5 M1
4 hʼwštʼ] Pt4 Mf4, K5 J2 M1
  hʼwštʼⁿʼ F2
  hʼwšt R413
  hʼwšt̶y̶hʼⁿʼ T6
  hʼwštʼyh E7
  hʼwwštʼ D

---

1 YḤWWN-d : ᴊᴊ gloss in R413 (subscr.).

ʾBYDWN-yt ʾš QDM ḴN ʿZLWN-yt¹ W ZK Y hʾwšt' MN ʾYŠ-ʾn QDM   5
ʿZLWN-yt²ʾš QDM Lʾ ʿZLWN-yt³   6

5   QDM ḴN] Pt4 Mf4 F2 R413 E7
    ʾL K5 M1
    QD• J2
5   ʿZLWN-yt¹] Pt4 Mf4 R413 E7
    ʿZLWN-yt K5 J2 M1
    ʿZLWN-ȳt' F2 T6
5   W ZK Y] Pt4 Mf4 E7, K5 J2 M1
    deest F2
    ZK R413
    ZK Y T6
5   hʾwšt'] Pt4, K5 J2 M1
    hʾwwšt' Mf4 E7
    deest F2
    hʾwšt R413
    hʾwštyhⁿ' T6
5   MN] Pt4 Mf4 R413 E7, K5 J2 M1
    deest F2
    MNW hylptstʾn' lʾd ʾBYDWN-yt MNW T6

5   ʾYŠ-ʾn] Pt4 Mf4
    deest F2
    ʾYŠ-ʾn' R413 T6 E7, K5 J2 M1
5   QDM] Pt4 Mf4 R413, K5 J2 M1
    deest F2 T6 E7
6   ʿZLWN-yt²] Pt4 Mf4 R413, K5 M1
    deest F2 T6 E7
    •L•t J2
    ʿZLWN-yt' D
6   ʾš] Pt4 Mf4 R413 E7, K5 J2 M1
    deest F2 T6
6   QDM] Pt4 Mf4 R413 T6 E7, K5 J2 M1
    deest F2
6   Lʾ] Pt4 Mf4 R413 T6 E7, K5 J2 M1
    deest F2
6   ʿZLWN-yt³] Pt4 Mf4 R413 T6 E7, K5 J2 M1
    deest F2
    ʿZLWN-yt' D

5   ʿZLWN-yt¹ : F2 ends here
5–6 ʾYŠ-ʾn ... ʿZLWN-yt³ : hylptstʾn' lʾd ʾBYDWN-yt MNW
        ʾYŠ-ʾn' QDM Lʾ ʿZLWN-yt T6

A.2.7 PY 35.6

(a) ZK Y 'whrmzd ycšn' W nyd'dšn' 'ytwn' MN ZK Y LKWM p'hlwm mynm
(b) W ZK-c Y gwspnd'n' k'l 'YK MN k'l Y gytyȳ p'hlyc' Y gwspnd'n' p'hlwm mynm
(c) 'ytwn' ZK Y LKWM wlcm dyn' W pr'cc 'k'synym 'w' 'YŠ-'n 'n 'nd cnd pt̲' twb'n hw'st'l ⁺ḤWH-m

1 'whrmzd] Pt4 Mf4 F2 T6 E7, K5 J2 M1
  deest R413
1 Y] Pt4 Mf4 R413 T6, K5 J2 M1
  deest F2 E7
1 mynm] Pt4 Mf4 F2 E7, K5 J2 M1
  سپم R413
  MNᴰ'M T6
2 W ZK-c] Pt4 Mf4 R413, J2
  ZK K5 M1
  ZK-c F2 T6 E7
2 Y] Pt4 Mf4 T6 E7, K5 M1
  deest F2 R413, J2
2 gwspnd'n'] Pt4 Mf4 F2 R413 (p̄) T6 E7 (p̄), J2
  gwspnd'n K5 M1
2 Y] Pt4 Mf4 F2 R413 T6 E7, J2
  deest K5 M1
2 gytyȳ]ـسم Pt4 Mf4 F2 E7, K5 J2
  سوم R413, M1
  wsp T6
2 p'hlyc'] Pt4 Mf4 E7, K5 J2 M1
  p'hlyc F2 R413 T6
2 Y] Pt4 Mf4 T6 E7, K5 J2 M1
  deest F2 R413
2 gwspnd'n'] Pt4 Mf4 F2 R413 E7 (p̄), K5 (p̄) J2 M1 (p̄)
  ~~gwspnd'n'~~ gwspnd'n' T6
3 mynm] Pt4 Mf4 F2 T6 E7, K5 J2 M1
  سپم R413
4 'ytwn'] Pt4 Mf4 F2 T6 E7, K5 J2 M1
  'ytwn R413
4 Y] Pt4 Mf4 F2 R413 T6, K5 J2 M1
  deest E7
4 wlcm] Pt4 Mf4 E7, K5 J2 M1
  wlcwm F2
  deest R413 T6
4 dyn'] Pt4 Mf4 F2 R413 E7, K5 J2 M1
  dyn' wlcᵐšn' T6
4 W pr'cc] Pt4 Mf4 F2 E7
  pr'c' K5 M1
  pr'cc R413 T6
  pr'c J2
4 'k'synym] Pt4 Mf4
  سوس رسم F2 (سوس subscr.)
  سوس R413
  سوس— T6
  'k'synm E7, K5 J2 M1
4 'w'] Pt4 Mf4 E7, K5 J2 M1
  'w' Y F2 R413 T6
4 'YŠ-'n] Pt4 Mf4
  'YŠ-'n' F2 R413 E7, K5 J2 M1
  ~~'YŠ-'n~~ 'YŠ-'n' T6
4 'n] Pt4 Mf4 R413 T6 E7, K5 M1
  'n' F2
  ZK Y J2
5 twb'n] Pt4 Mf4, K5 M1
  twb'n' F2 R413 T6 E7, J2
5 hw'st'l] Pt4 Mf4 F2 R413 T6 E7, K5 M1
  سرپسم J2
5 ⁺ḤWH-m] سرهم Pt4 Mf4 E7
  ḤWH-m F2 R413, K5 M1
  سرهم سدسپ T6
  ḤWH-ym J2

A.2.8 PY 35.7

(a) MNW pt̲ˈ ʾhlʾdyh ʾytwnˈ srdʾlyh ʾP̲-š pt̲ˈ ʾhlʾdyh wʾlwnyh ʾYK̲ dynˈ pt̲ˈ srdʾl 1
 W wʾlwn YHSNN-yt 2
(b) ktʾl MN ʾYTˈ-ʾn ʾNŠWTʾ-ʾn MNW zywšnʾwmndyh ʾytwnˈ cygwn gwptˈ 3
 pʾhlwm dhšnˈ pt̲ˈ KRʾ 2 ʾhwʾn 4
 wycdstˈ byšʾmlwtyk gwbšnˈ 5

1 ʾytwnˈ] Pt4 Mf4 T6 E7, K5 J2 M1
  ʾytwn F2 R413
1 srdʾlyh] Pt4 Mf4 F2 T6 E7, K5 J2 M1
  srtʾlyh R413
1 ʾP-š] Pt4 Mf4 R413, K5 J2 M1
  ʾP-š ʾYT F2
  ʾP-š ʾYT W̶N̶ T6 (⦀⧼⧽⧼)
  ⧼⧽ E7
1 pt̲ˈ] Pt4 Mf4 F2 R413 T6 (superscr.) E7, K5 J2 3
  M1
1 wʾlwnyh] Pt4 Mf4 F2 T6 E7, K5 J2 M1
  wʾlwn YHSNN-yt R413 (⧼⧽)
1 srdʾl] Pt4 Mf4 F2 T6 E7
  srdʾlyh R413, K5 J2 M1
2 W] Pt4 Mf4 R413 T6 E7
  deest F2
  Y K5 M1
  • J2
2 wʾlwn] Pt4 Mf4 R413 E7
  wʾlwnyh F2 (-yh) T6
  wʾlwnˈ K5 J2 M1
2 YHSNN-yt] Pt4 Mf4 R413 E7, K5 J2 M1
  YHSNN-ytˈ F2 T6, J2
3 ktʾl] Pt4 Mf4 F2 R413 T6 E7
  ktʾlc-HD K5 J2 M1
3 ʾYTˈ-ʾn] Pt4 Mf4
  ʾYT-ʾnˈ F2 R413 T6 E7, J2 M1
  ʾYTˈ-ʾnˈ K5
3 ʾNŠWTʾ-ʾn] Pt4 Mf4

ʾNŠWTʾ-ʾnˈ F2 R413 T6 E7, K5 M1
⧼⧽ J2
3 MNW] Pt4 Mf4 F2 R413 T6 E7, K5 M1
  deest J2
3 zywšnʾwmndyh] Pt4 Mf4, K5 J2 M1
  z̲w̲ zywšnˈ ʾwmn dyh F2
  zywšnˈ ʾwmndyh R413 E7
  zywšnˈ ʾwmnndyh T6
3 gwptˈ] Pt4 Mf4 T6 E7, J2
  gwpt F2 R413, K5 M1
4 dhšnˈ] Pt4 Mf4 F2 R413 T6 E7, J2
  dhšn K5 M1
4 pt̲ˈ] Pt4 F2 R413 T6 E7, K5 J2 M1
  ⧼⧽ Mf4
4 ʾhwʾn] Pt4 Mf4 F2 R413 E7, K5 J2 M1
  ʾhwʾnˈ T6
5 wycdstˈ] Pt4 Mf4, K5 M1
  wyst F2
  wycst R413
  deest T6 E7
  wycstˈ J2
5 byšʾmlwtyk] Pt4 Mf4 R413 E7, K5
  byšmlwtyk F2
  deest T6
  byšʾmwlwtyk J2 M1
5 gwbšnˈ] Pt4 Mf4 F2 R413 E7, K5 M1
  deest T6, J2
  gwbšn D

A.2.9 PY 35.8

(a) ZNH 'ytwn' shwn gwbšnyh 'whrmzd dyn' Y 'whrmzd pt̰' 'hl'dyh
mynyt'lyh Y ŠPYL pr'c YMRRWN-m pt̰' pl'lwn mynšnyh
(b) W LK 'DYN MN 'LH-š'n ptglšn' 'stšnyh W pr'c dhškyh YḤBWN-m
'YK MN 'mhrspnd'n MND'M Y LK wyš ptglm W pt̰' dhšk' BR' 'BYDWN-
mc

1 ZNH] Pt4 Mf4 F2 R413 T6 E7, K5 (ζ-) M1
   Y ZNH J2
1 'ytwn'] Pt4 Mf T6 E7, K5 J2 M1
   'ytwn F2 R413
1 shwn] Pt4 Mf4 F2 T6 E7
   deest R413
   ｍｍ K5 J2 M1
1 gwbšnyh] Pt4 Mf4 E7
   gwbšnyh Y F2 R413, J2
   gwbšnyh ⊥ T6
   gwbšn' Y K5 M1
1 Y] Pt4 Mf4 F2 R413 T6, K5 J2 M1
   deest E7
1 'whrmzd] Pt4 Mf4 F2 R413 T6 E7, K5 M1
   •mzd J2
2 Y] Pt4 Mf4 R413 T6, K5 J2 M1
   deest F2 E7
2 YMRRWN-m] Pt4 Mf4
   ｅｍｇ F2
   ｅｍｇ R413 T6 E7
   ｅｍｇ K5
   YMLLWN-m J2 M1
2 pl'lwn] Pt4 F2 R413 T6, K5 M1
   pl'lwn' Mf4 E7, J2
2 mynšnyh] Pt4 Mf4 E7, K5 J2 M1
   mynyt'l mynšnyk F2
   mynšnyk R413 T6
3 W LK] Pt4 Mf4 F2 T6 E7
   LK R413, K5 J2 M1
3 'DYN] Pt4 Mf4 F2 R413 T6
   'DYN' E7, K5 J2 M1
3 MN] Pt4 Mf4 T6 E7, J2
   MNW F2 R413

   MN Y K5 M1
3 'LH-š'n] Pt4 Mf4, J2
   'LH-š'n' F2 R413 T6 E7, K5 M1
3 ptglšn'] Pt4 Mf4 F2 T6 E7, K5 J2 M1
   ptgl R413
3 'stšnyh] Pt4 Mf4 F2 R413 E7, K5 J2 M1
   'sšnyh T6
3 W] Pt4 Mf4 F2 T6 E7, K5 J2 M1
   deest R413
3 pr'c] Pt4 Mf4 F2 R413 T6 E7
   pr'c W K5 M1
   [pr'c] J2
3 dhškyh] Pt4 Mf4 F2 R413 T6 E7, K5 M1
   dh[š]•yh J2
4 'mhrspnd'n] Pt4 Mf4, K5 (p̄) M1 (p̄)
   'mhrspnd'n' F2 R413 (p̄) T6 E7 (p̄), J2
4 MND'M Y] Pt4 Mf4 T6, M1
   deest F2 R413
   MND'M E7
   MNDM Y K5
   [MN]D'M Y J2
4 ptglm] Pt4 Mf4 F2 T6 E7, J2
   ｅｍｇ R413
   ptglym K5 M1
4 W] Pt4 Mf4 F2 E7, K5 J2 M1
   deest R413 T6
4 dhšk'] Pt4 F2
   dhšk Mf4 R413 T6 E7, K5 J2 M1
4-5 'BYDWN-mc] Pt4 Mf4 F2 R413
   'BYDWN-me T6
   'BYDWN-m E7
   'BYDWN-m̰ K5 J2 M1

A.2.10   PY 35.9

(a) MN ʾhlʾdyh ʾp̄ʾkyh MN ʾšwhšt' ⁺KḤDH W ZK-c Y wyh mynšn' whwmn 1
W ZK-c wyh hwtʾyyh ʾštlwl 2
(b) stʾdšn' Y LK ʾwhrmẓd hm MN stʾdšn'n QDM W MRYʾ Y LK ʾwhrmẓd 3
hm MN MRYʾ-'n QDM W ycšn' Y LK hm MN ycšn'n QDM 4
ycšnykyhʾ byšʾmlwtyk gwbšn' ∴ 9 wycdst' 3 gʾs 5

1 ʾhlʾdyh] Pt4 Mf4 F2 R413, K5 J2 M1
   ʾhldyh T6
   hc ʾhlʾdyh E7
1 ʾp̄ʾkyh] Pt4 Mf4 F2 R413 T6 K5 J2 M1
   ʾp̄ʾkyh ᵈʰˢᵏ BRʾ ḆYDWN-m E7
1 ʾšwhšt'] Pt4 Mf4 F2 T6, J2 M1
   [Aramaic script] R413
   ʾšwhšt E7, K5
1 ⁺KḤDH] [Aramaic script] Pt4 ([Aramaic script])
   KḤDH Mf4 R413 T6, K5 J2 M1
   KḤDHʾ F2 (m above ')
   [Aramaic script] E7
1 W] Pt4 Mf4 F2 R413 T6 E7, K5 M1
   deest J2
1 ZK-c Y] Pt4 Mf4 E7
   ZK-c R413 F2 T6, K5 J2 M1
1 wyh mynšn'] Pt4 R413 F2 T6 E7
   wyh mynšnyh Mf4
   wyhmynšn' Y K5 J2 M1
1 whwmn] Pt4 Mf4 F2 R413 T6 E7
   whwmn' K5 J2 M1
2 W] Pt4 Mf4 F2 T6 E7, K5 J2 M1
   deest R413
2 ZK-c] Pt4 Mf4 F2 R413 E7
   ZK-c Y T6, K5 J2 M1
2 wyh] Pt4 F2 E7
   ŠPYL Mf4 R413 T6, K5 J2 M1
2 hwtʾyyh] Pt4 Mf4 F2 E7, M1
   hwtʾkyh R413
   hwtʾyh T6, K5
   hwtʾyyh Y J2
2 ʾštlwl] Pt4 Mf4 F2 R413 T6, K5 J2 M1
   [Aramaic script] E7
3 Y] Pt4 Mf4 F2 R413 T6, K5 J2 M1
   deest E7
3 LK] Pt4 Mf4 F2 R413 T6 E7, K5 M1
   LK' J2
3 stʾdšn'n] Pt4 Mf4 R413 T6 E7
   stʾdšn' 'n' F2
   stʾdšn'n' K5 J2 M1
3 W] Pt4 Mf4 F2 R413 E7, K5 M1
   Wd T6
   Y J2

3 Y] Pt4 Mf4 F2 R413 T6, K5 J2 M1
   deest E7
3 LK] Pt4 Mf4 F2 R413 T6 E7, K5 J2 M1
   LK' J2
3 ʾwhrmẓd] Pt4 Mf4 F2 R413 T6 E7
   deest K5 J2 M1
4 MN] Pt4 Mf4 F2 R413 T6 E7, J2
   M K5
   deest M1
4 MRYʾ-'n] Pt4 Mf4 F2 E7, K5 J2 M1
   [Aramaic script] R413
   [Aramaic script] T6
4 W] Pt4 Mf4 F2 R413 T6, K5 J2 M1
   deest E7
4 Y] Pt4 Mf4 F2 R413 E7, K5 J2 M1
   deest T6
4 LK] Pt4 Mf4 F2 R413 T6 E7, K5 M1
   LK' J2
4 ycšn'n] Pt4 Mf4 R413 T6 E7
   ycšn' 'n' F2
   ycšn'n' K5 J2 M1
4 QDM] Pt4 Mf4 F2 R413 T6, K5 J2 M1
   QDM ○ BRʾ ḆYDWN-m E7
5 ycšnykyhʾ] Pt4 Mf4 E7
   ycšnyhʾ F2, J2
   ʾD gywʾk ycšnyhʾ F2 R413 T6
   ycš[n]yhʾ Y K5
   ycšn'yhʾ Y M1
5 byšʾmlwtyk] Pt4 E7
   ʾywʾmlwtyk Mf4
   byšmlwtyk F2 R413
   byšʾlwtyk T6
   [Aramaic script] K5 M1
   byšʾmwlwt[yk] J2
5 gwbšn'] Pt4 F2 R413 T6 E7, K5 J2 M1
   gwbšn Mf4
   • J2
5 9 ... gʾs] Pt4 Mf4 F2 R413 E7
   deest T6, K5 J2 M1
5 wycdst'] Pt4 E7
   wycdst Mf4
   [Aramaic script] F2
   [Aramaic script] R413

A.3 PY 36

A.3.1 PY 36.1

yst' dtykl h't'

(a) 'ytwn' 'w' ḤN' Y LK 'thš pt' wlcšn' pltwm BR' YḤMTWN-m 'whrmzd pt' p'hlyc' W šn'dynyt'lyh

(b) pt' ḤN' Y LK g's'n pt' ḤN' Y LK mynwd Y 'pzwnyk cygwn MN dyn' pyt'k

(c) MNW 'w' 'LH hyndkyh 'YḴ pt' QDM 'thš 'n'kyh ˙BYDWN-yt ZK-c 'w' 'LH hyndkyh YḤBWN-yt 'YḴ ZK-c pt' 'LH 'n'kyh ˙BYDWN-yt

1 yst'] Pt4 Mf4 E7
   yst F2
   ystp R413
   deest T6, K5 J2 M1
1 dtykl] Pt4 Mf4 F2 E7
   dtyklk R413
   deest T6, K5 J2 M1
1 h't'] Pt4 F2 E7
   h't' bwn Mf4
   h't bwn R413
   deest T6, K5 J2 M1
2 'w'] Pt4 Mf4 F2 R413 T6, K5 J2 M1
   ZK Y E7
2 ḤN'] Pt4 Mf4 F2 T6 E7, K5 J2 M1
   ܗܢ R413
2 Y] Pt4 Mf4 F2 R413 T6, J2
   deest E7, K5 M1
2 wlcšn'] Pt4 F2 R413 T6 E7, K5 J2 M1
   wlcšn' Y Mf4
2 YḤMTWN-m] Pt4 Mf4 F2 R413 T6 E7, K5 M1
   YḤMTWN-ym J2
3 pt'] Pt4 Mf4 F2 T6 E7, K5 J2 M1
   deest R413
3 p'hlyc'] Pt4 Mf4, J2 (p- illegible)
   p'hlyc F2 R413 T6 E7, K5 M1
3 W] Pt4 Mf4 F2 R413 E7, K5 J2 M1
   deest T6
3 šn'dynyt'lyh] Pt4 Mf4 F2 T6 E7, K5 J2 M1
   ܫܢܕܝܢܬܠܝܗ R413
4 ḤN'] Pt4 Mf4 F2 T6 E7, K5 J2 M1
   ܣܠܘ R413
4 Y] Pt4 Mf4, K5 M1
   deest F2 R413 T6 E7, J2
4 LK] Pt4 Mf4 F2 E7, K5 M1
   ܣܠܘ R413
   LK ~~mynwd 'pzwnyk~~ T6
   لو J2
4 g's'n] Pt4
   g's'n' Mf4 F2 E7, K5 J2 M1

ܛܣܘܣܢ R413 T6
4 Y] Pt4 Mf4 F2 R413 E7, K5 M1
   deest T6, J2
4 LK] Pt4 Mf4 F2 R413 T6 E7, K5 M1
   LK' J2
4 mynwd Y] Pt4 Mf4 F2, J2 (superscr.)
   ܪ عܡد R413
   mynwd T6 E7
   mynwd W K5 M1
4 MN] Pt4 Mf4 F2 E7, K5 J2 M1
   MNW R413
   MNW MN T6
6 'w'] Pt4 Mf4 F2 R413 T6 E7, K5 M1
   deest J2
6 'LH] Pt4 Mf4 F2 R413 T6 E7
   deest K5 M1
   'LH Y J2
6 hyndkyh] Pt4 Mf4 E7, K5 M1
   hynʿkyh YḤBWN-t F2 (YḤBWN-t in marg.)
   hyntkyh R413
   hyntkyh YḤBWN-yt' T6
6 QDM] Pt4 (QDM) F2 (QDM) T6 E7
   deest Mf4 R413, K5 J2 M1
6 ˙BYDWN-yt] Pt4 Mf4 F2 E7, K5 J2 M1
   ܐܣܘ R413 T6
7 'LH] Pt4 Mf4 F2 R413 T6 E7, J2
   'LH Y K5 M1
7 hyndkyh] Pt4 Mf4 F2 E7, K5 M1
   hyntkyh R413 T6
7 YḤBWN-yt] Pt4 Mf4 F2 R413 E7, K5 J2 M1
   YḤBWN-yt' T6
7 'YḴ ZK-c] Pt4 Mf4 F2 R413 T6 E7, K5 M1
   ZK-c Y J2
7 pt'] Pt4 Mf4 F2 R413 T6 E7, J2
   deest K5 M1
7 'LH] Pt4 F2 R413 T6 E7, J2
   ܗܢ Mf4, K5 M1
7 'n'kyh] Pt4 Mf4 F2 (-yh) R413 T6 E7, K5 ('n-) J2 M1

---

7 hyndkyh : آکوده بیمنی اوا کوبناه gloss in Mf4 (superscr.)
7 'n'kyh : اواک gloss in Mf4 (subscr.)

A.3.2 PY 36.2

(a) pt̰' ⁺'wlw'hmnyh 'w' 'LH GBR' pt̰' twb'n BR' YḤMTWN-yt 'thš Y   1
'whrmzd 'YK plyp 'BYDWN-yt   2
(b) pt̰' ⁺'wlw'hmnyh 'w' 'LH MNW-š ⁺'wlw'hmnyh hcš W pt̰' ⁺nyd'dšn'wmndyh 3
'w' 'LH Y ⁺nyd'dšn'wmnd GBR'   4
(c) pt̰' ZK Y ms k'l BR' YḤMTWN-yt pt̰' ps'ht' Y pt̰' tn' Y psyn'   5

1 ⁺'wlw'hmnyh] ‎‎ Pt4 Mf4
   'wlw'hmnyh F2 R413 T6 E7, K5 M1
   ‎‎ J2
1 'w'] Pt4 Mf4 R413 E7, K5 J2 M1
   ḤN'' F2
   ḤN' T6
1 twb'n] Pt4, M1
   twb'n' Mf4 F2 R413 T6 E7, K5 J2
1 YḤMTWN-yt] Pt4 Mf4 R413 E7, K5 M1
   YḤMTWN-ẹyt F2
   YḤMTWN-yt' T6, J2
1 'thš] Pt4 Mf4 R413 E7, M1
   p'thš F2
   pt̰' 'thš T6
   ‎‎ K5
   'hš J2
1 Y] Pt4 Mf4 F2 R413 E7, K5 J2 M1
   deest T6
2 'YK plyp 'BYDWN-yt] Pt4 (superscr. in red)
   deest Mf4 F2 R413 T6 E7, K5 J2
3 ⁺'wlw'hmnyh] ‎‎ Pt4 Mf4 T6
   ‎‎ ‎‎ F2
   'wlw'hmnyh R413 E7
   'wlw'hmnyh W K5 M1
   ‎‎ J2
3 ⁺'wlw'hmnyh] ‎‎ Pt4 Mf4 T6
   'wlw'hmnyh F2 R413 E7, K5 J2 M1
3 W] Pt4 Mf4 R413 F2, J2
   deest F2 T6, K5 M1
3 ⁺nyd'dšn'wmndyh] ‎‎ Pt4 (‎‎)

‎‎ Mf4 (‎‎)
   nyd'dšn' wmndyh F2
   nyd'dšn'wmndyh R413 E7, K5 J2 M1
   nyd'dšn' wmnndyh T6
4 'LH Y] Pt4
   'LH Mf4 F2 R413 T6 E7, K5 J2 M1
4 ⁺nyd'dšn'wmnd] ‎‎ Pt4 (‎‎)
   Mf4 (‎‎)
   nyd'dšn' wmnd F2
   nyd'dšn'wmnd R413 E7, K5 J2 M1
   MNW nyd'dšn' wmnd T6
   ‎‎ J2
5 Y] Pt4 Mf4 R413 E7, K5 J2 M1
   deest F2 T6
5 ms k'l] Pt4 Mf4 F2 R413 T6 E7
   msk'l K5 J2 M1
5 YḤMTWN-yt] Pt4 Mf4 F2 R413 E7, K5 M1
   YḤMTWN-yt' T6, J2
5 pt̰'] Pt4 Mf4 F2 R413 E7, K5 J2 M1
   pt̰' pt̰' T6
5 ps'ht'] Pt4 Mf4 R413 E7, K5 J2 M1
   ps'ht F2
   ‎‎ T6
5 Y] Pt4 Mf4 R413 E7, K5 M1
   deest F2 T6, J2
5 pt̰'] Pt4 F2 R413 T6 E7, K5 J2 M1
   deest Mf4
5 psyn'] Pt4 Mf4 F2 R413 E7, K5 J2 M1
   ‎‎ psyn' T6

___

5 ps'ht' : ‎‎ / ‎‎ gloss in Mf4 (in marg.)

A.3.3   PY 36.3

(a) ’tš pt̰’ ZK Y ’whrmzd ’k’s ’YT’’ pt̰’ dyn’ Y ’whrmzd W pt̰’ mynwdykyh 1
’k’s ’YT’’ ZK-š ’YT’’ ’MT-š pt̰’ wlhl’nyh BR’ YTYBWN-d 2
(b) ’pzwnyk ’YT’’ BNPŠH ‘D ’MT ‘LH Y LK ŠM cygwn Y w’zyšt’ 3
(c) ’w’ ’tš Y ’whrmzd Y LK pt̰’ ZK Y KR’ 2 BR’ YḤMTWN-m ’YK̰-š hyhl 4
Y mynwd W gytyy hcš L’WḤL YḤSNN-m 5

---

1 ZK] Pt4 Mf4 R413 T6 E7, K5 J2 M1
ܟܠ F2
1 ’YT’’] Pt4 Mf4 R413 T6 E7, K5 J2 M1
’YT F2
1 Y] Pt4 Mf4 F2 R413 T6, J2
deest E7, K5 M1
1 W] Pt4 Mf4, K5 J2 M1
deest F2 R413 T6 E7
1 mynwdykyh] Pt4 Mf4
mynwdyh F2 R413, K5 M1
ܡܝܢܘܝܗ T6
ܡܝܢܘܝܗ E7
mynw•yh J2
2 ’k’s] Pt4 Mf4 F2 R413 E7, K5 J2 M1
’k’k̰ s T6
2 ’YT’’] Pt4 Mf4 E7, K5 J2 M1
’YT F2 R413
’YT’’ ZK Y ’whrmzd ’k’s T6
2 ZK-š ’YT’’] Pt4 E7, J2 (superscr.) M1
ZK-š ’YT’’ Y Mf4 F2 R413 T6
ZK-š ’YT’’ BNPŠH ‘D K5
2 ’MT-š] Pt4 Mf4 F2 E7, K5 J2 M1
deest R413 T6
2 wlhl’nyh] Pt4 Mf4 R413 E7, K5 M1
ܐܪܣܟܣܢ F2
wlhl’nyh wl’hl’myh T6
p-1 wlhl’nyh J2
2 YTYBWN-d] Pt4 Mf4 R413 E7, K5 M1
YTYBWN-’nd T6
YHBWN-d J2
3 ’YT] Pt4 Mf4 T6 E7, K5 J2 M1
’YT F2 R413
3 BNPŠH] Pt4 Mf4 F2 R413 E7, K5 M1
NPŠH T6, J2

3 ’MT] Pt4 Mf4, K5 J2 M1
MNW F2 R413 T6 E7
3 ‘LH] Pt4 Mf4 F2 R413 T6 E7
ܠܘ K5 J2 M1
3 Y] Pt4 Mf4, K5 M1
deest F2 R413 T6 E7, J2
3 LK] Pt4 Mf4 F2 R413 T6 E7, K5 M1
LK’ J2
3 cygwn Y] Pt4 Mf4
cygwn F2 R413 T6 E7, K5 M1
cygwn W J2
3 w’zyšt’] Pt4 E7 (w’ sec.m.)
ܐܣܟܣܢ Mf4, K5 J2 M1
ܐܣܟܣܢ F2 T6
w’zyšt R413
4 Y] Pt4 Mf4 F2 R413 T6, K5 J2 M1
deest E7
4 Y] Pt4 Mf4 F2 R413 T6, K5 J2 M1
deest E7
4 LK] Pt4 Mf4 F2 R413 T6 E7
LK’ K5 J2 M1
4 Y] Pt4 T6, K5 J2 M1
deest Mf4 F2 R413 E7
4 YḤMTWN-m] Pt4 Mf4 F2 R413 T6 E7, K5 M1
YḤMTWN-ym J2
5 Y] Pt4 Mf4 F2 R413 T6 E7, K5 M1
W J2
5 gytyy] ܓܝܬܝ Pt4 R413, M1
ܓܝܬܝ Mf4 F2 T6 T6 E7, K5 J2 (•ȳ)
5 YḤSNN-m] Pt4 Mf4 F2 R413 T6 E7
YḤSNN-m̰ K5 M1
YḤMT YḤSNN-m J2

---

2 wlhl’nyh : ورحانه ‎یعنی آتش ورحان gloss in Mf4 (subscr.)
3 w’zyšt’ : نام آتش gloss in Mf4 (subscr.)

A.3.4 PY 36.4

(a) pt̠' ZK Y ŠPYL mynšn' 'w' LK ZK Y ŠPYL ⁺tlsk'syh 'w' LK   1
(b) pt̠' ZK Y ŠPYL plc'nkyh 'w' LK pt̠'-c kwnšn' W gwbšn' BR' YḤMTWN- 2
m   3

1 Y] Pt4 Mf4 F2 R413 T6, K5 J2 M1
   deest E7
1 ŠPYL] Pt4 Mf4 F2 R413 T6 E7, J2
   wyh K5 M1
1 LK] Pt4 E7
   LK pt̠' Mf4 F2 R413 T6, K5 M1
   LK' pt̠' J2
1 Y] Pt4 Mf4 T6, K5 M1
   deest F2 R413 E7, J2
1 ŠPYL] Pt4 Mf4 F2 R413 T6 E7, J2
   WŠPYL K5 M1
1 ⁺tlsk'syh] tlsk'yh Pt4 E7
   tls'yh Mf4
   ‏مـلـىـسـىـ‎ F2
   ‏مـلـىـوسـىـىـ‎ R413
   ‏مـلـىـوسـىـىـىـ‎ T6
   tlks's K5
   g̶w̶b̶š̶n̶' tlsk'yh J2 (tlsk's superscr.)

   tlsk'yh M1
1 LK] Pt4 Mf4 F2 R413 T6 E7, K5 M1
   LK' J2
2 Y] Pt4 Mf4 F2 R413 T6, K5 J2 M1
   deest E7
2 plc'nkyh] Pt4 Mf4 F2 R413 E7 T6, K5 M1
   pl'nkyh J2
2 'w'] Pt4 Mf4 F2 R413 T6, K5 J2 M1
   ZK Y E7
2 LK] Pt4 R413 T6 E7, K5 M1
   LK' Mf4, J2 (L[K]', ' on next line)
   LK-c F2
2 pt̠'-c] Pt4 Mf4 E7, K5 J2 M1
   pt̠' R413 F2 T6
2 kwnšn'] Pt4 Mf4 F2 T6 E7, K5 J2 M1
   kwnšn R413
2 gwbšn'] Pt4 Mf4 F2 R413 E7, K7 J2 M1
   g̶w̶ gwbšn' T6

A.3.5 PY 36.5

(a) ⁺nyd'dšnynyȳ 'P̱-m 'p̱'mynyȳ LK 'whrmẓd 'YK-m 'p̱'m pṯ' LK YḤWWN-'t

(b) pṯ' hlwst' hwmt' 'w' LK W pṯ' hlwst' ⁺hwht 'w' LK W pṯ' hlwst' hwwlšt' BR' YḤMTWN-m

1 ⁺nyd'dšnynyȳ] ⟨⟨⟩⟩ Pt4
   nyd'dšnynyȳ Mf4 T6, K5 J2 M1
   ⟨⟨⟩⟩ F2
   ⟨⟨⟩⟩ R413
   ⟨⟨⟩⟩ E7 (⟨⟩ superscr.)
1 'p̱'mynyȳ] Pt4 Mf4 T6 E7, K5 J2 M1
   'p̱'m F2
   'p̱'mc R413
1 'YK-m] Pt4 Mf4 R413 T6 E7, J2
   'YK F2, K5 M1
1 LK] Pt4 Mf4 F2 R413 T6 E7, K5 M1
   LK' J2
1–2 YḤWWN-'t] Pt4 Mf4 F2 R413 T6 E7, K5 M1
   YḤWWN-'t' J2
3 hlwst'] Pt4 Mf4 E7
   hlwsp' F2 R413 T6, K5 J2 M1
3 hwmt'] Pt4 Mf4 R413 T6 E7, K5 J2
   hwmt F2 (superscr. sec.m.)
   h⁎mt hwmt' M1

3 'w'] Pt4 F2 R413 T6 E7, K5 J2 M1
   deest Mf4
3 W] Pt4 Mf4 F2, K5 J2 M1
   deest R413 T6 E7
3 hlwst'] Pt4 Mf4 E7, K5 M1
   hlwsp' F2 R413 T6, J2
3 ⁺hwht] ⟨⟨⟩⟩ Pt4 Mf4, J2
   hwht' F2 R413 T6 E7, K5 M1
   hwht D
3 'w' LK] Pt4 Mf4 F2 R413 T6 E7
   deest K5 J2 M1
3 W] Pt4 Mf4 F2, K5 J2 M1
   deest R413 T6 E7
3 hlwst'] Pt4 Mf4 E7, K5 M1
   hlwsp' F2 R413 T6, J2
3 hwwlšt'] Pt4 Mf4 F2 E7, J2 M1
   hwlšt 'w' LK R413
   hwwlšt' 'w' LK T6, K5

1–2 YḤWWN-'t : ⟨⟩ gloss in R413 (subscr.)

A.3.6 PY 36.6

(a) nywk ʾn' HNʾ Y LK klp' ʾP̱-t ZK MN klpʾn nwykynšn' YḤBWN-m   1
  ʾwhrmzd ʾYḴ ḆYN gyhʾn ḴN YMRRWN-m ʾYḴ klp' HNʾ Y LK nywktl   2
(b) ẒNH lwbʾn 'w' ZK lwšnyh Y bʾlst' MN ZK Y pt̤' cšm pytʾk bʾlynynd   3
(c) TMH ʾYḴ hwlšyt' gwpt' ʾYḴ-m lwbʾn 'w' hwlšyt pʾdk YḤMTWN-ʾt   4

1 nywk ʾn'] Pt4 T6 E7
   nywk' Mf4
   nywk F2 R413, J2
   ࡯ࡲࡩ K5 M1
1 HNʾ] Pt4 Mf4 F2 R413 T6 E7
   HD K5 J2 M1
1 Y] Pt4 Mf4 R413 T6
   deest F2 E7, K5 J2 M1
1 LK] Pt4 Mf4 F2 R413 T6 E7, K5 M1
   LK' J2
1 klp'] Pt4 Mf4 E7, K5 M1
   klp F2 R413 T6, J2
1 ʾP̱-t ZK] Pt4 Mf4 R413 T6
   ʾP̱-t ʾn' F2 E7
   ʾP̱-t K5 J2 M1
1 klpʾn] Pt4 Mf4, J2
   klpʾn' F2 R413 T6 E7, K5 M1
1 nwykynšn'] Pt4 Mf4 F2 T6 E7
   nwykynšn R413 (-yn-)
   nwykšn' K5 J2 M1
2 gyhʾn] Pt4
   ࢣࢇ Mf4
   gyhʾn' F2 T6 E7, K5 J2 M1
   ࢣࢇ R413
2 YMRRWN-m] Pt4 Mf4
   ࢣ࢔ࢦ F2 R413 T6 E7
   YMLLWN-m K5 M1
   YMLLWN-ym J2
2 klp'] Pt4 Mf4 F2 E7, K5 M1
   ࢣ࢔ࢦ R413
   klp T6, J2
2 HNʾ] Pt4 Mf4 F2 R413 T6
   ẒNH E7
   HD K5 J2 M1
2 Y] Pt4 Mf4 R413 T6, K5 J2 M1
   deest F2 E7
2 LK] Pt4 Mf4 F2 R413 T6 E7, K5 M1
   ࢣ࢔ J2
2 nywktl] Pt4 Mf4 F2 E7, K5 M1
   nywtl R413
   nywktl ʾYT' T6

   tl J2
3 ẒNH] Pt4 Mf4 F2 R413 T6, K5 J2 M1
   HNʾ E7
3 lwbʾn] Pt4, K5 M1
   lwbʾn' Mf4 (ʾw-) F2 R413 T6 E7, J2
   lwwʾn' D
3 'w' ZK] Pt4 Mf4 F2 R413 T6, J2
   ZK 'w' E7
   'w' ZK Y K5 M1
3 lwšnyh] Pt4 Mf4 R413 T6 E7, K5 J2 M1
   lwšnyk F2
3 Y] Pt4 Mf4, K5 M1
   deest F2 R413 E7, J2
   ࢣ T6
3 bʾlst'] Pt4 Mf4 R413 T6 E7, K5 M1
   bʾlst F2
   ࢣ࢔࢘ J2
3 MN] Pt4 Mf4 E7, J2
   MNW F2 R413 T6
   ࢣ࢔ K5 M1
3 Y] Pt4 Mf4, K5 M1
   deest F2 R413 T6 E7
3 pt̤'] Pt4 F2 E7, K5 J2 M1
   pt̤'-c Mf4 T6
3 cšm] Pt4 Mf4 F2 R413 E7, K5 J2 M1
   ࢣmm T6
3 bʾlynynd] Pt4 Mf4 F2 R413 T6 E7
   bʾlynʾnd K5 J2 M1
4 ʾYḴ] Pt4 Mf4 F2 R413 T6 E7
   ʾYḴ ZK Y K5 J2 M1
4 hwlšyt'] Pt4 Mf4 T6 E7
   hwlšyt F2 R413, K5 M1
   ࢣ࢔࢘ J2
4 gwpt'] Pt4 Mf4 F2 T6
   gwpt R413 E7, K5 J2 M1
4 ʾYḴ-m ... YḤMTWN-ʾt] Pt4 (superscr.)
   deest Mf4, K5 J2 M1
   ʾYḴ-m lwbʾn' pt̤' hwlšyt pʾdk YḤMTWN-ʾt F2
     (in marg.) T6
   ʾYḴ-m lwbʾn' 'w' R413
   ʾYḴ-m lwbʾn' 'w' hwlšyt pʾdk YḤMTWN-ʾt E7

ycšnykyh' +'yw'mlwtyk gwbšn' ∵ 6 wycdst' 3 g's

5 ycšnykyh'] Pt4 Mf4 E7
'D L'YŠH ycšnyh' F2
'D ycšnykyh' R413
deest T6
ycšnnyh' K5 M1
ycšnyh' J2
5 +'yw'mlwtyk] سهرمدید Pt4 E7
'yw'mlwtyk Mf4
'ywš'mlwtyk F2 R413, K5
deest T6

•سهوسرم J2
'ywš'mwlwtyk M1
5 gwbšn'] Pt4 Mf4 E7, J2 M1
deest F2 R413 T6
gwbšn K5
5 6 ... g's] Pt4 Mf4 (-yc-) E7
wydst' F2
•wycst R413
wycdst T6
deest K5 J2 M1

Appendices 331

A.4 PY 37

A.4.1 PY 37.1

yst' ⁺stykl hʾtʾ 1
(a) LTMH ʾytwnʾ ycm ʾwhrm*z*d MNW gwspnd W ʾhlʾdyhc YḤBWN-t 2
(b) ʾP̱-š MYʾ-c YḤBWN-t W ʾwlwlc Y ŠPYL 3
(c) ʾP̱-š lwšnyh YḤBWN-t W¹ bwmc W² hlwstʾc ʾp̄ʾtyh bwn W bl 4

1 **yst'**] Pt4 Mf4 E7
   سرے R413
   yst F2 T6
   deest K5 J2 M1
1 **⁺stykl**] stygl Pt4 Mf4 R413 T6
   st ygl F2
   stykl E7
   deest K5 J2 M1
1 **hʾtʾ**] Pt4 T6 E7
   hʾtʾ bwn Mf4 R413 (hʾt)
   hʾt F2
   deest K5 J2 M1
2 ycm] Pt4 Mf4
   ycwm E7, K5 M1
   YDḄḤWN-m J2
2 gwspnd] Pt4 Mf4, J2
   gwsp̱nd E7, K5 M1
2 W] Pt4 Mf4 E7
   Y K5 J2 M1
2 ʾhlʾdyhc] Pt4 Mf4 E7, J2 (c subscr.)
   ʾhlʾdyhc Y K5 M1
2 YḤBWN-t] Pt4 Mf4, K5 M1
   YḤBWN-t o ʿD LʿYŠH BRʾ KRYTWN-m E7
   YḤBWN-tʾ J2
3 YḤBWN-t] Pt4 Mf4, J2
   dʾt K5 M1
3 W] Pt4 Mf4, K5 M1
   deest J2
3 Y] Pt4 Mf4
   deest K5 J2 M1
3 ŠPYL] Pt4 Mf4, K5 M1
   Š•L J2
4 W¹] Pt4 Mf4, J2
   deest K5 M1
4 W²] Pt4 Mf4
   deest K5 M1
   Y J2
4 hlwstʾc] Pt4
   hlwspʾc Mf4
   hlwsp̱ʾ K5 M1
   hlwsp̱ʾ Y J2
4 ʾp̄ʾtyh] Pt4 Mf4, K5 M1
   ʾp̄ʾtyh Y J2
4 bwn W bl] Pt4 Mf4, K5 M1
   bwn • bl J2

---

2 Y 37: F2 R413 T6 E7 abbreviate (see Section 15.1.1).
4 ʾp̄ʾtyh: نعمت gloss in Mf4 (subscr.).
4 bwn W bl: اززمین آآسان gloss in Mf4 (subscr.).

A.4.2 PY 37.2

(a) 'LH MNW hwt'yyh W msyh ptš ʾP-š hwp'nkyh hcš 1
(b) ZK ʾytwn' MN yšt'l'n Y BYN ZNH gyh'n pt̰' pyšlwbšnyh YDBḤWN-m 2
pt̰' ⁺pyš'wp'dyh 3
(c) MNW pt̰' gwspnd'wmndyh KTLWN-d 'LH-š'n yšt'l 4

1 'LH] Pt4 Mf4, K5 M1   2 pt̰'] Pt4, K5 J2 M1
•LH J2   p Mf4
2 yšt'l'n] Pt4 Mf4   2 YDBḤWN-m] Pt4 Mf4, J2
yšt'l'n' K5 J2 M1   ycm K5 M1
2 Y] Pt4 Mf4, J2   3 ⁺pyš'wp'dyh] pyš'wp'yh Pt4 Mf4
deest K5 M1   pyšp'dyh K5 J2 M1
2 gyh'n] Pt4 Mf4   4 gwspnd'wmndyh] Pt4 Mf4
gyh'n' K5 M1   gwsp̄nd'wmndyh K5 J2
•h'n' J2   gwsp̄ndyh M1

A.4.3 PY 37.3

(a) ZK ʼytwnˈ MNW hwtʼy ŠM W pṯˈ dʼnʼkyh dwšytˈ YKʻYMWN-yt 1
ʼp̄zwnykyh YḎBḤWN-m 2
(b) ʻLH MNW LNH-kʼn tnˈ W yʼn zywšnˈ hcš YḎBḤWN-m 3
(c) ʻLH MNW ʼhlwbʼn plwʼhl ZKL-ʼn W nʼylykʼn YḎBḤWN-m[1] hcš 4
YḎBḤWN-m 5

1 ZK] Pt4 Mf4, K5 M1
   ZK Y J2
1 ʼytwnˈ] Pt4 Mf4, K5 M1
   ʼytwnˈ W J2
1 W] Pt4 Mf4, J2
   deest K5 M1
1 dwšytˈ] Pt4 Mf4, J2
   dwšyt K5 M1
1 YKʻYMWN-yt] Pt4 Mf4, K5 M1
   YKʻYMWN-ytˈ J2 (YK- resembles p)
2 YḎBḤWN-m] Pt4 Mf4, K5 M1
   YḎB• J2

3 LNH-kʼn] Pt4 Mf4
   LNH-kʼnˈ K5 J2 M1
4 Line (c)] Pt4 in marg.
4 ʼhlwbʼn] Pt4 Mf4
   ʼhlwbˈʼn K5 M1
   W ʼhlwbʼnˈ J2
4 nʼylykʼn] Pt4 Mf4
   nʼylykʼn nywky K5
   nʼylykʼnˈ nywky J2 M1
4 YḎBḤWN-m[1]] Pt4 Mf4
   deest K5 J2 M1

A.4.4 PY 37.4

(a) ʾhlʾdyh ʾytwn' Y pʾhlwm YDBḤWN-m ʾšwhšt'
(b) Y nywk' Y ʾp̄zwnyk Y ʾmlg
(c) Y lwšn' tn' Y ʿLH Y MNW hlwst' ʾp̄ʾtyh nywkyh hcš

1 ʾhlʾdyh] Pt4 Mf4, M1
  ʾhlᐧ K5
  ʾšwhšt' ʾhlʾdyh J2
1 ʾytwn'] Pt4 Mf4, J2 M1
  superscr. K5
1 Y] Pt4 Mf4, J2 (faint)
  deest K5 M1
1 YDBḤWN-m] Pt4 Mf4
  ycm K5 J2 M1
1 ʾšwhšt'] Pt4 Mf4, K5 M1
  ʾšwhšt J2
2 Y] Pt4 Mf4

deest K5 J2 M1
2 nywk'] Pt4 Mf4
  nywk K5 J2 M1
2 Y] Pt4 Mf4, J2
  deest K5 M1
3 Y] Pt4 Mf4, J2
  deest K5 M1
3 Y] Pt4, K5 M1
  deest Mf4, J2
3 hlwst'] Pt4 Mf4, K5 M1
  hlwsp' J2

A.4.5   PY 37.5

(a) ZK-c Y wyh mynšn' whwmn ycwm W ZK-c Y wyh hwt'yyh hštlwl   1
(b) ZK-c Y ŠPYL dyn' W ZK-c Y ŠPYL srd'lyh hwrdt W 'mwrdt W ZK-c   2
Y ŠPYL dwysl bwndk mynšnyh spndrmt'   3
ycšnykyh' +'yw'mlwtyk gwbšn' ∵ 5 wycdst' LWTH iϑā i 3 g's   4

1 Y] Pt4 Mf4, K5 M1
   Y W J2
1 whwmn] Pt4 Mf4, K5 M1
   whwmn' J2
1 ycwm] Pt4
   YDBHWN-m Mf4, K5 J2
   ycm M1
1 wyh] Pt4 Mf4
   ŠPYL K5 J2 M1
2 ZK-c] Pt4, K5 M1
   W ZK-c Mf4, J2
2 dyn'] Pt4, K5 J2 M1
   dyn' ⊻ Mf4
2 srd'lyh] Pt4 Mf4, J2
   srd'lyh Y K5 M1
2 'mwrdt] Pt4 Mf4, K5 M1
   'm•dt' J2
3 Y] Pt4 Mf4, K5 M1
   deest J2
3 ŠPYL] Pt4 Mf4
   wyh K5 J2 M1
3 dwysl] Pt4 Mf4, J2 M1
   •] K5
3 bwndk] Pt4 Mf4, K5 M1
   bwndk bwndk J2
3 mynšnyh] Pt4 Mf4, J2

   mynšnyh Y K5 M1
3 spndrmt'] Pt4 Mf4, J2
   spndrmt K5
   spndrmt M1
4 ycšnykyh' ... gwbšn'] Pt4 Mf4 E7, K5 J2 M1
   deest R413
4 ycšnykyh'] Pt4 Mf4 E7
   ycšnyh' K5 J2 M1
4 +'yw'mlwtyk] ⟨script⟩ Pt4 E7
   'yw'mlwtyk Mf4
   ⟨script⟩ K5
   ⟨script⟩ J2
   ⟨script⟩ M1
4 gwbšn'] Pt4 Mf4 E7, M1
   gwbšn K5 J2
4 5 ... g's] Pt4 Mf4 F2 R413 T6 E7
   deest K5 J2 M1
4 5] Pt4 Mf4 F2 T6 E7
   wycst R413
4 wycdst'] Pt4 Mf4 E7
   wyst' F2
   6 R413
   wycst T6
4 iϑā i] Pt4 E7
   iϑā Mf4 F2 R413
   deest T6

A.5 PY 38

A.5.1 PY 38.1

yst' ch'lwm h't'
(a) ZNH zmyk LWTH NKB-'n 'ytwn' YDBḤWN-m
(b) MNW LNH bwlt'l MNW-c LK NKB 'whrmzd ʾYK LK NPŠH
(c) MN 'hl'dyh 'p'kyh MN 'šwhšt' KHDH pt' k'mk' 'LH-š'n YDBḤWN-m

1 yst'] Pt4 Mf4 R413 E7
مسي F2
deest T6, K5 J2 M1
1 ch'lwm] Pt4 Mf4 F2 R413 E7
deest T6, K5 J2 M1
1 h't'] Pt4 E7
h't' bwn Mf4
h't bwn F2 R413
deest T6, K5 J2 M1
2 LWTH] Pt4 Mf4 R413 T6 E7, K5 J2 M1
LW LWTH F2
2 NKB-'n] Pt4 Mf4, K5 J2 M1
NKB-'n' F2 R413 T6 E7
2 'ytwn'] Pt4 Mf4 T6 E7, K5 J2 M1
'ytwn F2 R413
2 YDBḤWN-m] Pt4 Mf4 F2 T6 E7, K5 J2 M1
ycwm R413
3 LNH] Pt4 Mf4 R413 T6 E7, K5 J2 M1
LNTH F2
LWTH E7
3 bwlt'l] Pt4 Mf4 R413 T6 E7, K5 J2 M1
bw'•lt'l F2
3 MNW-c] Pt4 Mf4 F2 R413 T6 E7, K5 M1
W MNW-c J2
3 LK] Pt4 Mf4 F2 R413 T6 E7, K5 M1
LK J2 (sec.m.)

3 NKB] Pt4 Mf4 F2 T6 E7, K5 J2 M1
B R413
3 'whrmzd] Pt4 F2 R413 T6 E7, K5 J2 M1
'whrmzd Mf4 (m sec.m.)
3 LK] Pt4 Mf4 F2 R413 T6 E7, K5 M1
LK' J2
3 NPŠH] Pt4 F2 R413 E7, K5 J2 M1
PŠH Mf4
NPŠH ḤWH-yỹ T6
4 MN] Pt4 Mf4 R413, K5 J2 M1
MNW F2 T6
MNW E7
4 'hl'dyh] Pt4 F2 R413 T6 E7, K5 J2 M1
بلسس Mf4
4 MN] Pt4 Mf4 F2 R413 T6 E7, J2
deest K5 M1
4 'šwhšt'] Pt4 Mf4 T6 E7, K5 J2 M1
'šwhšt F2 R413
4 KHDH] Pt4 F2 R413 T6, J2
KHDH' Mf4 E7, K5 M1
4 k'mk'] Pt4 Mf4 E7, J2
k'mk F2 R413 T6
k'mk Y K5 M1
4 'LH-š'n] Pt4 Mf4
'LH-š'n' F2 R413 T6 E7, K5 J2 M1

A.5.2 PY 38.2

(a) ʾMT pt̤ʾ ʾp̄zwnʾ ʾywcʾnd W pwrššnʾ bwndk mynšnyh ʾYK ZK MNDʿM   1
pwrsʾnd LKWM ʾp̄zwnʾ YḤWWN-ʾt W L bwndk mynšnyh YḤWWN-ʾt   2
(b) ZK Y ŠPYL ⁺tlskʾhyh pt̤ʾ ʿLH-šʾn ʾ-m YḤBWN-yt W ZK Y ŠPYL   3
hwʾdšnʾ hwʾstkʾ   4
(c) W ZK Y ŠPYL ʾp̄zwnʾ W ZK Y ŠPYL prʾc wʾp̄lykʾnyh W ZK Y pʾlnd   5
ycwm   6

1 ʾMT pt̤ʾ] Pt4 F2 R413 E7, K5 J2 M1
  deest Mf4
  MNW pt̤ʾ T6
1 ʾp̄zwnʾ] Pt4 Mf4 E7, J2
  ʾp̄zwnyk F2 R413 T6, K5 M1
  ʾp̄zwn D
1 ʾywcʾnd W] Pt4 Mf4 E7, J2
  ʾywcʾnd F2 R413 T6, M1
  ʾywcʾnd ʾwhrmzd K5
1 pwrššnʾ] Pt4 Mf4 (-šnʾ above illegible deletion) E7, K5 J2 M1
  pt̤ʾ ᵖʷʳššnʾ F2 T6 (no superscr.)
  וויסוּרו R413
1 bwndk] Pt4 Mf4 R413 T6 E7, K5 J2 M1
  bwnd F2
1 mynšnyh] Pt4 Mf4 F2 T6 E7, K5 J2 M1
  bmynšnyk R413
1 ZK] Pt4 Mf4 R413, K5 J2 M1
  ZK Y F2 T6 E7
1 MNDʿM] Pt4 Mf4 R413 T6 E7, K5 J2 M1
  MNDM F2
2 pwrsʾnd] Pt4 Mf4 E7
  pt̤ʾ ᵖʷʳššnʾd F2
  ויסוּרוּוֹאו R413
  ויסוּרוּוֹאו T6 (ויסוּרו superscr.)
  pwrsynd Y K5 M1
  pwrsynd J2
2 ʾp̄zwnʾ] Pt4 Mf4 E7
  ʾp̄zwn F2 R413
  ʾp̄zwnyk T6, K5 J2 M1
2 YḤWWN-ʾt] Pt4 Mf4 F2 R413 E7, K5 M1
  YḤWWN-ʾt' T6, J2
2 W ... YḤWWN-ʾt] Pt4 Mf4 F2 R413 T6 E7, K5 M1
  deest J2
2 W] Pt4 Mf4 F2 T6 E7, K5 M1
  W m R413
2 bwndk] Pt4 Mf4 R413 T6 E7, K5 M1
  bwnd F2
2 mynšnyh] Pt4 Mf4 R413 T6 E7, K5 M1
  mynšnyk F2
2 YḤWWN-ʾt] Pt4 Mf4 F2 R413 E7, K5 M1
  YḤWWN-ʾt' T6

3 Y ŠPYL] Pt4 Mf4 F2 E7, J2
  ŠPYL R413
  pt̤ʾ ŠPYL T6
  deest K5 M1
3 ⁺tlskʾhyh] مدروسى Pt4 Mf4 E7
  مدروسى F2 R413
  tlskʾs T6
  مدروسى K5 J2 M1
3 pt̤ʾ] Pt4 Mf4 E7, K5 J2 M1
  W pt̤ʾ F2 R413 T6
3 ʿLH-šʾn] Pt4, J2
  ʿLH-šʾnʾ Mf4 T6 E7, K5 M1
  ʿLH-šʾnʾ Y F2 R413
3 ʾ-m] Pt4 Mf4 F2 T6 E7, K5 J2 M1
  m R413
3 YḤBWN-yt] Pt4 Mf4 F2 R413 E7, K5 J2 M1
  YḤBWN-yt' T6
3 W ZK] Pt4 Mf4 F2 R413
  ZK T6 E7, K5 J2 M1
3 Y] Pt4 Mf4 F2 T6 E7, K5 M1
  deest R413, J2
4 hwʾstkʾ] Pt4 Mf4 E7
  W hwʾstk F2
  Y hwʾstk R413 T6
  hwʾstk K5 J2 M1
5 W ZK] Pt4
  ZK Mf4 F2 R413 T6 E7, K5 J2 M1
5 ʾp̄zwnʾ] Pt4 Mf4 R413 E7
  ʾp̄zwnyk F2 T6, J2
  W ʾp̄zwnyk K5 M1
5 W ZK] Pt4 Mf4 F2, K5 J2 M1
  ZK R413 T6 E7
5 wʾp̄lykʾnyh] Pt4 R413 T6 E7, K5 J2 M1
  wʾp̄lykʾnyh ·· Mf4
  ʾp̄lykʾnyh F2
5 W ZK] Pt4 Mf4 F2, J2
  ZK R413 T6 E7, K5 M1
5 Y] Pt4 Mf4 F2 E7
  Y ŠPYL R413, K5 J2 M1
  deest T6
6 ycwm] Pt4 R413 E7
  YDBḤWN-m Mf4 F2 T6, K5 J2 M1

1 ʾywcʾnd W : کوشش gloss in Pt4 (subscr.)
1 pwrššnʾ : پرسش gloss in Pt4 (subscr.)

A.5.3   PY 38.3

(a) MY⁾ ᵓytwn' YDBḤWN-m Y *maikiiṇt* pšng Y pt' ᵓwlwl QDM   1
YK'YMWN-yt mznydy W ZK-c Y *hēbuuaiṇti* ⁺glᵓn tcšn' ZK-c Y *frauuāzi* Y   2
wᵓlᵓnyk   3

(b) W ZK *ahurānīš* ᵓlmyšt' W cᵓhyk W ᵓp̄ᵓrykc MY⁾ Y ᵓnᵓmcštyk W ZK   4

1 Line (a)] Pt4 Mf4 T6 E7, K5 J2 M1
 in marg. sec.m. F2
 deest R413
1 ᵓytwn'] Pt4 Mf4 T6, K5 J2 M1
 ᵓytwn F2
 W ᵓytwn' E7
1 YDBḤWN-m Y] Pt4 Mf4
 YDBḤWN-m F2 T6 E7, K5 M1
 ycm J2
1 *maikiiṇt*] Pt4
 maikaiiṇt Mf4
 maikiiṇt-c F2
 maikaiiaṇt T6
 maikiiaṇt E7
 maēaiṇti K5 M1
 imaēaiṇt J2
 maēkaiṇti D
1 pšng] Pt4 Mf4
 illegible F2
 cšn' T6
 ycsn' E7
 pašṇa K5 J2 M1
1 Y] Pt4 Mf4 E7, K5 J2 M1
 deest F2 T6
1 pt'] Pt4 Mf4 F2 T6 E7, J2 M1
 • pt' m K5
2 YK'YMWN-yt] Pt4 Mf4 F2 E7, K5 M1
 YK'YMWN'-yt' T6
 ᵓytwn' YK'YMWN-yt' J2
2 mznydy] Pt4 Mf4 E7, J2
 MN mzn⁾ F2
 pt' mznydy T6
 • myznydy K5 M1
2 W ZK-c Y] Pt4 Mf4 F2, J2
 W ZK-c T6 E7
 ZK-c Y K5 M1
 deest D
2 *hēbuuaiṇti*] Pt4
 hōbauuaiṇti Mf4
 hē•aṇti F2
 hōbauuaṇti T6
 hēbauuaṇti E7
 haēbuuaṇt K5 M1

 hēbuuaṇti J2
2 ⁺glᵓn] ‎سلـ‎ Pt4 Mf4, J2
 MN glᵓn F2
 glᵓn' T6, K5 M1
 ‎سلـ‎ E7
2 tcšn'] Pt4 Mf4 F2 T6, K5 J2 M1
 twcšn' E7
2 ZK-c Y] Pt4 Mf4, K5 M1
 W ZK-c F2 T6
 ZK-c E7
 W ZK-c Y J2
2 *frauuāzi*] Pt4 Mf4 F2 E7, J2
 frauuaza T6 (in marg.)
 frauuaz K5 M1
 frauuāz D
2 Y] Pt4 Mf4 E7, K5 M1
 deest F2 T6, J2
3 wᵓlᵓnyk] Pt4 Mf4 F2 E7, K5 M1
 ‎سلـيـنو‎ T6 (in marg.)
 wᵓlᵓnyk' J2
4 W ZK] Pt4
 W ZK Y Mf4 F2, J2
 ZK Y F2 R413, K5 M1
 W ZK-c T6 E7
4 *ahurānīš*] Pt4 Mf4 R413, K5 J2 M1
 ahurānīš F2
 ahurānīš ahurahiiā T6
 ahurāinīš E7
 ahurāṇīš D
4 ᵓlmyšt'] Pt4 Mf4 T6 E7
 ᵓlmyšt F2 R413, K5 J2 M1
4 W] Pt4 F2 R413 E7, K5 J2 M1
 deest Mf4
4 ᵓp̄ᵓrykc] Pt4 Mf4 E7, K5 M1
 ᵓp̄ᵓryk F2 R413 T6, J2
4 MY⁾ Y] Pt4 Mf4
 MY⁾-c F2 R413 T6, J2
 MY⁾ E7, K5 M1
4 ᵓnᵓmcštyk] Pt4 Mf4 F2 R413 T6, K5 J2 M1
 ᵓnᵓmcyštyk E7
4–5 W ZK Y] Pt4 Mf4
 ZK Y F2 R413, K5 J2 M1
 ZK T6 E7

---

2 ⁺glᵓn : ‎س‎ gloss in Pt4 (subscr.)

Appendices 339

Y *ahurahiiā* Y šwsl W ZK Y *hauuapaŋhāi* myšk' hwwtlgyh LKWM ʾ-mʾn 5
YḤBWN-yt ʾYK-mʾn nm BYN tnʾ lwbʾk YḤWWN-ʾt 6
(c) hwdhkyh ʾls W ⁺hwšnʾyšnkyh ʾYK-mʾn hwyd MN tnʾ BRʾ YʾTWN- 7
ʾt W ZK Y BYN KRʾ 2 ʾhwʾn kʾmk' MḤŠYʾ 8

5 Y šwsl] Pt4 Mf4 E7
   šwsl F2 R413 T6, K5 J2 M1
5 W ZK Y] Pt4 Mf4 R413 T6 E7
   W ZK F2
   ZK Y K5 J2 M1
5 *hauuapaŋhāi*] Pt4 Mf4 E7, K5 M1
   huuapaŋhå F2 R413
   huuapaŋhā T6
   hauuapaŋhå J2
5 myšk'] Pt4 Mf4 E7
   myšk F2 T6, K5 J2 M1
   myšk ZK Y *huparə̄ϑβåscā vā* R413 T6 (W ZK Y)
5 hwwtlgyh] Pt4 Mf4 F2 E7, K5 J2 M1
   سا‍رسِ R413
   سااِرسِ T6
5 ʾ-mʾn] Pt4 Mf4 R413 T6 E7, K5 J2 M1
   ʾ-mʾnʾ F2
6 YḤBWN-yt] Pt4 Mf4 R413 E7, K5 M1
   YḤBWN-ytʾ F2 T6, J2
6 ʾYK-mʾn] Pt4 Mf4 E7
   ʾYK-mʾnʾ F2 R413 T6, K5 J2 M1
6 lwbʾk] Pt4 Mf4 F2 R413 T6 E7, K5 M1
   lwbʾkʾ J2
6 YḤWWN-ʾt] Pt4 Mf4 F2 R413 E7, K5 M1
   YḤWWN-ʾtʾ T6, J2
7 W] Pt4 Mf4 F2 R413 E7, K5 J2 M1
   deest T6

7 ⁺hwšnʾyšnkyh] سسسحسس Pt4 T6 E7
   hwšnʾyšnkyh Mf4 F2 (-wšnʾ-)
   سسسحسس R413
   hwšnʾysnkyh K5 M1
   hwʾ•nkyh J2
7 ʾYK-mʾn] Pt4 Mf4 F2, K5 J2 M1
   ʾYK-mʾnʾ R413 T6 E7
7 hwyd] Pt4 (سٮ aboveى) F2 (سٮ aboveى) R413, J2
   سسٮ Mf4
   سٮ ى T6 E7
   illegible K5
   سٮ M1
8 W ZK Y] Pt4 Mf4 E7
   ZK F2 T6, J2
   ZK Y R413, K5 M1
8 BYN] Pt4 Mf4 (superscr.) E7, K5 J2 M1
   deest F2 R413 T6
8 ʾhwʾn] Pt4 Mf4 F2 R413 E7
   سىسا T6
   ʾhwʾnʾ K5 J2 M1
8 kʾmk'] Pt4 Mf4 E7, J2
   kʾmk F2 R413 T6, K5 M1
8 MḤŠYʾ] Pt4 Mf4 T6 (Ḥ)
   سححسى F2 R413
   MḤŠYʾ YḤWWN-yt E7
   سححسى K5 J2 M1

5 myšk' : ‍ طخنرک subscr. gloss in Pt4 (رک also in marg.)
5 سسىىسى : سى glossed with خون, سسىكنى glossed with جارى Pt4
7 ʾls : سٮ gloss in Pt4 (in marg.)
7 ⁺hwšnʾyšnkyh : هوسايشن gloss in Pt4 (subscr.)
7 hwyd : هوش gloss in Pt4 (subscr.)

A.5.4 PY 38.4

(a) ʾytwnʾ LKWM MNW ŠPYL ⁺ḤWH-yt ʾ-tʾn ʾwhrmẓd ŠM YḤBWN-t Y wyhdhʾkʾ

(b) W MNW-š ʾwʾ LKWM YḤBWN-t pt̰ ʿLH-šʾn LKWM YDBḤWN-m

(c) ʾP̱-m pt̰ ʿLH-šʾn plnʾmʾt ʾP̱-m pt̰ ʿLH-šʾnʾ ⁺nydʾdšnynʾt ʾP̱-m pt̰ ʿLH-šʾn ʾp̄ʾmynʾt

---

1 ⁺ḤWH-yt] ⟨...⟩ Pt4 Mf4 E7
ḤWH-yt F2 R413, K5 J2 M1
ḤWH-ytʾ T6

1 ʾ-tʾn] Pt4 Mf4 E7
ʾ-tʾnʾ F2 R413 T6, K5 J2 M1

1–2 YḤBWN-t Y] Pt4 Mf4
YḤBWN-yt F2
YḤBWN-d R413 T6
YḤBWN-t E7, J2
dʾt K5 M1

2 wyhdhʾkʾ] Pt4
wyhdhʾk Mf4
⟨...⟩ F2 (⟨...⟩ subscr.), J2
⟨...⟩ R413
⟨...⟩ T6
⟨...⟩ E7
⟨...⟩ K5 M1

3 W MNW-š] Pt4 Mf4 E7, J2
MNW-š F2 R413, K5 M1
ŠPYL dtk MNW-š T6

3 ʾwʾ] Pt4 Mf4 F2 R413 T6, K5 J2 M1
ZK Y E7

3 YḤBWN-t] Pt4 Mf4, K5 J2 M1
YḤBWN-d F2 R413 T6

YḤBWN-yt E7

3 ʿLH-šʾn] Pt4 Mf4
ʿLH-šʾnʾ F2 R413 T6 E7, K5 J2 M1

3 YDBḤWN-m] Pt4 Mf4 T6
ycBšḤWN-m F2 (also faint ḤWN)
ycšnʾ R413, J2
ycwm E7, K5 M1

4 ʿLH-šʾn] Pt4 Mf4
ʿLH-šʾnʾ F2 R413 T6 E7, K5 J2 M1

4 plnʾmʾt] Pt4 Mf4 F2 T6 E7, K5 M1
plnʾnʾt R413
plnʾmʾtʾ J2

4 ʿLH-šʾnʾ] Pt4 F2 R413 T6 E7, K5 M1
ʿLH-šʾn Mf4, J2

4 ⁺nydʾdšnynʾt] ⟨...⟩ Pt4 E7
⟨...⟩ Mf4
nydʾdšnynʾt F2 R413, K5 M1
⟨...⟩ T6 (nydʾdšnynʾt)
nydʾdšnynʾtʾ J2

4 ʿLH-šʾn] Pt4 Mf4 R413
ʿLH-šʾnʾ F2 T6 E7, K5 J2 M1

5 ʾp̄ʾmynʾt] Pt4 Mf4 F2 R413 T6 (⟨...⟩ superscr.) E7, K5 M1
ʾp̄ʾmynʾtʾ J2

---

4 ⁺nydʾdšnynʾt : نايش كم gloss in Pt4 (subscr.)

A.5.5 PY 38.5

(a) MYʾ Y LKWM ZK Y *azīš* LKWM ⁺hʾdwk‵ W ZK Y *mātrəš* LKWM 1
MYʾ Y BYN ⁺hmbwšnyh Y ⁺ZKL-ʾn W NKḆ-ʾn twhm W ZK Y *agəniiå* hwn 2
W ZK Y dlgwš ⁺dʾykʾnynytʾl MYʾ BYN pwsdʾn 3

1 Line (a)] Pt4 Mf4 T6 E7, K5 J2
   ZK *azīš* ... *mātarəš* in marg. sec.m. F2
   deest R413
1 MYʾ Y] Pt4 E7
   MYʾ Mf4 (•Yʾ) F2 R413 T6, K5 M1
   M• J2
1 Y] Pt4 Mf4 E7, K5 J2 M1
   deest F2 T6
1 *azīš*] Pt4 Mf4 F2 T6 E7, K5 M1
   izīš J2
1 ⁺hʾdwk‵] ιومسد Pt4 Mf4 E7
   ZK MNW MN bwn ʾwlwl tcyt F2
   ιومسد ZK MNW MN bwn Y ʾwlwl tc• T6
   hʾdwk‵ K5 J2
   hʾdwk M1
1 W ZK] Pt4 Mf4 T6 E7, J2 M1
   ZK F2, K5
1 Y] Pt4 Mf4 E7, K5 J2 M1
   deest F2 T6
1 *mātrəš*] Pt4 Mf4 E7
   m•rəš F2
   mātarəš T6
   matrəš K5 J2 M1
1 LKWM] Pt4 Mf4 (LKW•) F2 T6 E7, K5 M1
   deest R413
   W LKWM J2
2 MYʾ Y] Pt4 Mf4 T6
   MYʾ F2 (inline and in marg.) R413 E7, K5 J2 M1
2 ⁺hmbwšnyh] سروسد Pt4 Mf4 E7
   hmbwšnyh F2 R413 T6, J2
   سروسد K5 M1
2 Y] Pt4 Mf4, K5 J2 M1
   deest F2 R413 T6 E7

2 ⁺ZKL-ʾn W NKḆ-ʾn] بدلسد اوبنبد Pt4 E7
   بدلسد اوىسد Mf4
   كوسد اوبـد F2 R413 T6, M1
   كوسد اوبسد K5
   بدلسد اوبـد J2
   ZKL-ʾn NKḆ-ʾnʾ D
2 twhm] Pt4 Mf4 E7
   twhmk F2 R413 T6, K5 J2 (tw•) M1
2 W ZK] Pt4 Mf4 R413 T6 E7, J2
   ZK F2, K5 M1
2 *agəniiå*] Pt4 Mf4 F2 E7, K5 J2 M1
   agəniiå R413
   againiiå T6
2 hwn] Pt4 Mf4 F2 R413
   hwnʾ T6, K5 J2 M1
   ZK hwn E7
3 W ZK] Pt4 F2, K5 M1
   ZK Mf4
   ZK ZK R413
   W ZK W ZK T6
   W E7
   W ZK W W ZK J2
3 Y] Pt4 Mf4 F2 R413 T6, K5 J2 M1
   deest E7
3 ⁺dʾykʾnynytʾl] سدىسروسد Pt4 Mf4 E7
   dʾykʾnynytʾ F2 (hwzynytʾl in mar.)
   dʾykʾnynytʾl R413, K5 J2 M1
   dʾykʾnznytʾl T6
3 MYʾ] Pt4 F2 R413 T6 E7, K5 J2 M1
   MYʾ Y Mf4
3 pwsdʾn] Pt4 Mf4
   pwsdʾnʾ F2 R413 T6 E7, K5 J2 M1

---

1 ⁺hʾdwk‵ : جو gloss in Pt4 (subscr.).
2 ⁺hmbwšnyh : خذن gloss in Pt4 (subscr.).
3 سدىسروسد : ; gloss to the first س in Pt4 (subscr.).

(b) W ZK Y *vīspō.pit* ZK gwpt' MY° Y pt̰' 'wlwl'n 'dwn' Y 'wlwl ptš whšyhyt 4
W ZK Y p'hlwm W nywktl MY° Y tntwhmk Y MN 'wlwl 'ytwn' 'w' LKWM 5
MNW ŠPYL ⁺ḤWH-yt l't' ⁺ḤWH-m 6
(c) MNW pt̰' dglnd b'c'yyh YḎLWN-yt ZK gyh'n' tn' pt̰' ywdt' dhšnyh W 7
ywdt' gwbšnyh *mātarō.jītaiiō* šyl 8

4 W ZK] Pt4 Mf4
   ZK F2 R413 T6, K5 J2 M1
   W ZK-c E7
4 Y] Pt4 Mf4 F2 R413 T6, K5 J2 M1
   deest E7
4 *vīspō.pit*] Pt4
   vīspōpit Mf4 E7, K5
   vīspō.paitiš F2 R413 T6
   vīspōpitīš J2
   vīspō.pait M1
4 ZK] Pt4 Mf4 E7, K5 M1
   ZK Y F2 R413 T6, J2
4 gwpt'] Pt4 Mf4 E7, J2
   gwpt F2 R413 T6, K5 M1
4 Y] Pt4 Mf4, K5 J2 M1
   deest F2 R413 T6 E7
4 'wlwl'n] Pt4 Mf4 F2 E7
   'wlwl R413, K5 J2 M1
   'wlwl'n' T6
4 'dwn'] Pt4, K5 M1
   ⟨⟩ Mf4
   deest F2 R413
   ⟨⟩ T6
   ⟨⟩ E7
   W 'dwn' J2
   'dwn D
4 Y 'wlwl] Pt4 Mf4 E7, K5 J2 M1
   deest F2 R413
   'wlwl T6
4 whšyhyt] Pt4 Mf4 E7, K5 M1
   whšyt F2 R413, J2
   whšyt' T6
5 W ZK] Pt4 Mf4 E7, K5 J2 M1
   ZK F2 R413 T6
5 W] Pt4 Mf4 F2 R413 E7, K5 J2 M1
   deest T6
5 tntwhmk] Pt4 Mf4, K5
   tntwhmk' F2
   tnthmk' R413, J2
   tn' twhmk' T6
   ⟨⟩ E7
   tnthmk M1

   tn' twhmk D
5 Y] Pt4 Mf4 F2 R413 T6, K5 J2 M1
   deest E7
5 MN] Pt4 Mf4 F2 R413 T6 E7, K5 J2 M1
   pt̰' MN Mf4
5 'ytwn'] Pt4 Mf4 R413 T6 E7, K5 J2 M1
   'ytwn F2
6 ⁺ḤWH-yt] ⟨⟩ Pt4 Mf4 E7
   ḤWH-yt F2 R413, K5 J2 M1
   ḤWH-yt' T6
6 l't'] Pt4 E7
   l't Mf4 F2 R413 T6, K5 J2 M1
6 ⁺ḤWH-m] ⟨⟩ Pt4 Mf4 E7
   ḤWH-m F2 R413 T6, K5 J2 M1
7 b'c'yyh] Pt4 Mf4 R413, K5 J2 M1
   b'c'yyh F2 (twb'n•yh in marg.)
   b'c'yyh twb'nyk T6
   b'c'yyh twb'nyh E7
7 ZK] Pt4 Mf4 E7, K5 M1
   BYN F2 R413 T6, J2
7 gyh'n'] Pt4 Mf4 F2 R413 T6 E7
   gyh'n K5 J2 M1
7 tn'] Pt4 Mf4 F2 T6, K5 J2 M1
   deest R413
   mltwm'n' tn' E7
7 ywdt'] Pt4 Mf4 T6 E7
   ywdt F2 R413, K5 J2 M1
7 W] Pt4 Mf4 F2 E7, K5 M1
   deest R413 T6, J2 (illegible, most likely missing)
8 ywdt'] Pt4
   ywdt Mf4 F2 R413 T6 E7, K5 J2 M1
8 gwbšnyh] Pt4 E7, J2
   deest Mf4 (space left blank)
   gwbšnyh ZK Y F2 R413 T6, K5 M1
8 *mātarō.jītaiiō*] Pt4 Mf4 R413 T6, K5 M1
   mātarō.zītaiiō F2
   mātarō.jītiiō E7
   ZK Y *mātarō.jītaiiō* J2
8 šyl] Pt4 F2 R413 T6 E7, K5 J2 M1
   deest Mf4

---

4 'dwn': ⟨⟩ gloss in Pt4 (subscr.)
7 YḎLWN-yt: ⟨⟩ gloss in Pt4 (subscr.)

ycšnykyh' ⁺'yw'mlwtyk gwbšn' ∴ 5 wycdst' 3 g's 9

9 ycšnykyh'] Pt4 Mf4 E7
  'D gyw'k cygwn npšt' F2 R413
  gyw'k cygwn npšt' T6
  ycšnyh' K5 (šn) J2 M1
9 ⁺'yw'mlwtyk] ܐܝܘܡܠܘܬܝܟ Pt4 E7
  ܐܝܘܡܠܘܬܝܟ Mf4
  ܐܝܘܡܠܘܬܝܟ F2
  deest R413 T6
  ܐܝܘܡܠܘܘ ܟ K5 M1

  ܐܝܘܡܠܘܘܓܟ J2
9 gwbšn'] Pt4 Mf4 F2 E7, M1
  deest R413 T6, K5 J2
9 5 ... g's] 5 wycdst' 3 g's Pt4 Mf4 R413 T6 E7
  deest F2, K5 J2 M1
9 wycdst'] Pt4 E7
  wycdst Mf4
  wsst R413
  wycst T6

A.6 PY 39

A.6.1 PY 39.1

yst' pncwm h't'
(a) LTMH 'ytwn' YDBḤWN-m MNW ZK Y gwspnd'n' lwb'n' tn' ḤY'
YḤBWN-t 'whrmzd
(b) W ZK Y LNH-k'n lwb'n' W pswyk'n-c MNW LNH zywšn hw'st'l
⁺ḤWH-d nywkyh 'š YḤBWN-t
(c) ʿLH-š'nc Y LK ZK Y 'ltyšt'l ʿLH-š'n MNW ⁺ḤWH-d w'stlywš 'š
YḤBWN-t

1 **yst'**] Pt4 Mf4 R413 E7
 deest F2 T6, K5 J2 M1
1 **pncwm**] Pt4 Mf4 R413 E7
 deest F2 T6, K5 J2 M1
1 **h't'**] Pt4 E7
 h't' bwn Mf4
 deest F2 T6, K5 J2 M1
 h't bwn R413
2 **YDBḤWN-m**] Pt4 Mf4 F2 T6 E7
 ycwm R413
 ycm K5 J2 M1
2 **Y**] Pt4 Mf4 F2 E7, K5 J2 M1
 deest R413 T6
2 **gwspnd'n'**] Pt4 T6, J2
 gwspd'n Mf4
 gwspnd'n' Y F2 R413 (p̄)
 gwspnd'n' E7
 gwspnd'n K5 M1
2 **lwb'n' tn'**] Pt4 Mf4 F2 T6 E7, J2
 lwb'k tn' R413
 tn'' lwb'n K5 M1
2 **ḤY'**] Pt4 Mf4 F2 T6 E7, K5 J2 M1
 ـسو R413
3 **YḤBWN-t**] Pt4 Mf4 F2 R413 E7, K5 J2 M1
 YḤBWN-yt T6
4 **W ZK Y**] Pt4 Mf4
 ZK Y F2 R413 T6 E7, J2 M1
 ZK K5
4 **LNH-k'n**] Pt4 Mf4 E7
 ڊسوݣ F2 (LNH-k'n in marg.)
 LNH R413
 LNH-k'n' T6, K5 J2 M1
4 **lwb'n'**] Pt4 Mf4 F2 R413 T6 E7, J2
 lwb'n K5 M1

4 **W pswyk'n-c**] Pt4 E7, J2
 pswyk'n-c Mf4, K5 M1
 W psywyg'n F2
 ولسوݣاݣس R413
 ولسوݣاݣس T6 (ولسوݣاݣس in marg.)
4 **zywšn**] Pt4 Mf4
 zywšn' F2 R413 T6 E7, K5 J2 M1
4 **hw'st'l**] Pt4 F2 R413 T6 E7, K5 J2 M1
 ـسوݣسد Mf4
5 **⁺ḤWH-d**] ـݣس Pt4 Mf4 F2 R413 T6 E7, K5
 J2 M1
 ḤWH-d D
5 **'š**] Pt4 F2 R413 T6 E7, K5 J2 M1
 ـشو Mf4
5 **YḤBWN-t**] Pt4 Mf4 F2 R413 E7, K5 J2 M1
 YḤBWN-t' T6
6 **ʿLH-š'nc**] Pt4 Mf4 F2 T6, J2
 ʿLH-š'n'c R413 E7, K5 M1
6 **Y**] Pt4 Mf4, K5 M1
 deest F2 R413 T6 E7, J2
6 **LK**] Pt4 Mf4 F2 R413 T6, K5 (superscr.) M1
 LK' E7, J2
6 **'ltyšt'l**] Pt4 Mf4 R413 T6 E7, K5 J2 M1
 ـݣltšt'l F2
6 **ʿLH-š'n**] Pt4 Mf4
 ʿLH-š'n' F2 R413 T6 E7, K5 J2 M1
6 **⁺ḤWH-d**] ـݣس Pt4 Mf4 (fourth ı superscr.)
 E7
 ـݣسدس F2
 ـݣس K5 M1
 ḤWH-d R413 T6, J2
7 **YḤBWN-t**] Pt4 Mf4 F2 R413 T6 E7, J2
 d't K5 M1
 d't' D

---

4 W pswyk'n-c: ـسو gloss in Pt4 (subscr.)

A.6.2 PY 39.2

(a) dytyk'nc Y ⁺hdyb'l'n MNW lwb'n ʾšʾn YDBḤWN-m   1
(b) ZK Y ʾhlwb'n lwb'n' 'ytwn' YDBḤWN-m ʾYḴ ⁺z'tk'nc ⁺ZKL-'n W   2
⁺n'ylyk'nc   3
(c) MNW ʿLH-šʾn ŠPYL dyn' ⁺ḤWH-d pt' 'ywkltkyh w'nyt'l ⁺ḤWH-d   4
'ltyšt'l W wndšn wngh'n ⁺ḤWH-d w'stlywš W ŠPYL GBRʾ ⁺ḤWH-d 'slwn   5

1 dytyk'nc] Pt4 Mf4 E7, K5 M1
  dytyk'n'c F2 R413 T6, J2
1 Y] Pt4 Mf4 E7, K5 M1
  deest F2 R413 T6, J2
1 ⁺hdyb'l'n] سنب ⸱ Pt4
  سنبب ⸱ Mf4
  سنببس F2
  سنببسر R413
  سنببسر T6
  سنببس E7
  hdyb'l'n K5 J2 M1
  hdyb'l'nc D
1 MNW] Pt4 Mf4 F2 T6 E7, K5 J2 (superscr.) M1
  MN R413
1 lwb'n] Pt4 Mf4, K5 M1
  lwb'n' F2 R413 T6 E7, J2
1 ʾšʾn] Pt4 Mf4, K5 J2 M1
  W ʾšʾn' F2
  ʾšʾn' R413 T6 E7
1 YDBḤWN-m] Pt4 Mf4 E7, J2
  ycm F2, K5 M1
  ycwm R413 T6
2 ʾhlwb'n] Pt4 Mf4, K5 M1
  ʾhlwb'n' F2 R413 T6 E7, J2
2 lwb'n'] Pt4 F2 R413 E7, K5 J2 M1
  lwb'n Mf4
  'ytwn' T6
2 'ytwn'] Pt4 Mf4 R413 E7, K5 J2 M1
  'ytwn F2
  lwb'n' T6
2 YDBḤWN-m] Pt4 Mf4 F2 T6 E7
  ycwm R413
  ycm K5 J2 M1
2 ⁺z'tk'nc] کسموبع Pt4 Mf4 E7
  z'tk'n'c F2 R413 T6
  z'tk'nc K5 J2 M1
2 ⁺ZKL-'n] بدس Pt4 Mf4 E7
  بدسااا F2 R413 (د → ڎ sec.m.) T6 (ڎ)
  بدطس K5 M1

2 W] Pt4 Mf4 F2 T6 E7
  deest R413, K5 J2 M1
3 ⁺n'ylyk'nc] n'yl'nc Pt4
  n'ylyk'nc Mf4
  n'ylyk'n'c F2 R413 T6, K5 J2 M1
  n'lyk'nc E7
4 ʿLH-šʾn] Pt4 F2, J2
  ʿLH-šʾn' Mf4 R413 T6 E7, K5 M1
4 ŠPYL dyn'] Pt4 Mf4 F2 R413 T6 E7, J2
  wyhdyn' K5 M1
4 ⁺ḤWH-d] دااىsد Pt4 Mf4 T6 E7
  ḤWH-d F2 R413, K5 J2 M1
4 w'nyt'l] Pt4 F2 R413 T6 E7
  W w'nyt'l Mf4, K5 J2 M1
4 ⁺ḤWH-d] دااىsد Pt4 Mf4 E7, K5 M1
  ḤWH-d F2 R413 T6, J2
5 'ltyšt'l] Pt4 Mf4 F2 R413 T6, K5 J2 M1
  'ltyšt'l'n E7
5 W] Pt4 Mf4 F2 R413, K5 J2 M1
  deest T6 E7
5 wndšn wngh'n] نسىععا معسا Pt4 Mf4
  بعد19 F2 (corr. to wndšn), K5 J2 M1
  بعد19 R413
  نسىععا نسىععا T6
  wndšn' E7
  نسىععا نسىععا D
5 ⁺ḤWH-d] دااىsد Pt4 Mf4 E7
  ḤWH-d F2 R413 T6, J2
  deest K5 M1
5 w'stlywš] Pt4 Mf4 R413 T6 E7, K5 J2 M1
  w'stlywkyh F2
5 W] Pt4 Mf4, K5 M1
  deest F2 R413 T6 E7, J2
5 ⁺ḤWH-d] دااىsد Pt4 Mf4 E7, K5
  ḤWH-d F2 (-d sec.m.) R413, J2 M1
  ḤWH-t T6
5 'slwn] Pt4 E7, K5 J2 M1
  'slwn' Mf4 R413 T6
  ⁺'slwn F2

1 dytyk'nc: بادكان gloss in Pt4 (in marg.)
1 ⁺hdyb'l'n: سوازان gloss in Pt4 (subscr.)

A.6.3   PY 39.3

(a) ZK 'ytwn' YDBḤWN-m ŠPYL ZKL ZK Y ŠPYL NKḄ ZK-'y 'mhrspnd'n
(b) MNW 'p̄zwnyk ⁺ḤWH-d W 'mlg W hm'y ⁺zyndk' W hm'y swt'
(c) MNW pṯ' whwmn KTLWN-d pṯ' pl'lwnyh W MNW-c 'ytwn' whwmn 'š YDBḤWN-m

1   ZK] Pt4 Mf4 F2 R413 T6, J2
    ZK Y E7
    ZK Y LTMH K5 (ᴸᵀᴹᴴ) M1
1   'ytwn'] Pt4 Mf4 T6 E7, K5 J2 M1
    'ytwn F2 R413
1   YDBḤWN-m] Pt4 Mf4 F2 T6 E7
    ycwm R413
    ycm K5 J2 M1
1   ZKL] Pt4 Mf4 F2 R413 T6 E7
    W ZKL• K5
    W ZKL-'y J2
    ZKL• M1
1   ZK Y] Pt4 Mf4 E7
    deest F2 R413 T6, K5 J2 M1
1   ŠPYL] Pt4 F2 E7, K5 M1
    Š• Mf4
    wyh R413
    W ŠPYL T6
    ŠPYL z J2
1   NKḄ] Pt4 Mf4 F2 R413 T6 E7, K5 M1
    NKᴺKB J2
1   ZK-'y] Pt4 Mf4 F2 (resembles ZK-yh) T6 E7, J2
    ZK-yh R413
    ZK Y K5 M1
1-2 'mhrspnd'n] Pt4 Mf4, J2 M1
    'mspnd'n F2 (faint addition of -hr- sec.m.)
    'mhrspnd'n' R413 T6
    'mhrspnd'n' E7
    'mhrspᵃnd'n K5
3   'p̄zwnyk] Pt4 Mf4 F2 R413 T6, K5 J2 M1
    ꜣⱴⱴⵉⵙⴻⴱ E7
3   ⁺ḤWH-d] ⴵⵉⴱ6⵰ Pt4 Mf4 F2 E7

    ḤWH-d R413 T6, K5 M1
    •6⵰ J2
3   W 'mlg W] Pt4 Mf4 T6 E7
    'mlg W F2
    'mlg R413, K5
    •lg W J2
    W 'mlg M1
3   hm'y] Pt4 Mf4 T6 E7, K5 J2 M1
    hm' F2
    hm'k R413
3   ⁺zyndk'] ⵉⴶⵡⵉⵙ Pt4 E7
    zyndk' Mf4, K5 J2 M1
    zyndk F2 R413 T6
3   hm'y] Pt4 Mf4 T6 E7, K5 J2 M1
    hm'k F2 R413
3   swt'] Pt4 Mf4 E7
    swtk F2 T6
    swt R413, K5 J2 M1
4   whwmn] Pt4 Mf4 F2 (w- sec.m.) R413 T6, K5 J2 M1
    whwmn' E7
4   pt'] Pt4 Mf4 F2 R413 E7, K5 J2 M1
    MNW ᵖᵗ' T6
4   pl'lwnyh] Pt4 Mf4 F2 R413 T6 E7, K5 J2 M1
    pl'lwnnyh D
4   'ytwn'] Pt4 Mf4 T6 E7, K5 J2 M1
    'ytwn F2 R413
4   whwmn] Pt4 Mf4 F2 (⁻ʰʷ⁻) R413 T6, K5 M1
    whwmn' E7, J2
    W 'NH D
5   YDBḤWN-m] Pt4 Mf4 E7, K5 J2 M1
    ycm F2
    ycwm R413 T6

A.6.4 PY 39.4

(a) cygwn LK pt̰ʾ ZK Y KRʾ 2 MNDʿM Y mynwd W gytyȳ ʾwhrmzd mynšnʾ 1
⁺ḤWH-yȳ ʾYḴ MNDʿM Y LK ḴN mynšnʾ W gwbšnʾ ⁺ḤWH-yȳ ʾYḴ 2
MNDʿM ḴN gwbšnʾ W dhšnʾ ⁺ḤWH-yȳ W wlcšnʾ ⁺ḤWH-yȳ Y ʾYḴ ŠPYL 3
wlcm 4
(b) ʾytwnʾ ʾwʾ LK YḤBWN-m BNPŠH W ʾytwnʾ cʾšm ʾwʾ ʾYŠ-ʾn ʾYḴ BRʾ 5
YḤBWN-yt W ʾytwnʾ LK pt̰ʾ YʾTWN-šnʾ W ʿZLWN-šnʾ ʾMT BYN gyhʾnʾ 6

1 LK] Pt4 Mf4 F2 R413 T6 E7, K5 M1
   LKʾ J2
1 Y] Pt4 F2 R413 T6 E7, K5 J2
   deest Mf4
   LK M1
1 2] Pt4 Mf4 F2 R413 T6 E7, K5 J2
   2 ʾwhrmzd pt̰ʾ ZK Y KRʾ 2 M1
1 MNDʿM] Pt4 Mf4 F2 R413 T6 E7, K5 J2 M1
   mynwg Mf4
1 Y] Pt4 Mf4 F2 R413 T6, K5 M1
   deest E7, J2
1 W] Pt4 Mf4 F2 T6 E7, K5 J2 M1
   deest R413
1 gytyȳ] Pt4 Mf4 R413 T6 E7, K5 J2 M1
   gyt̰ȳ F2
1 mynšnʾ] Pt4 Mf4 R413 T6 E7, K5 J2 M1
   mynšnʾ F2
   mynnšnʾ E7
2 ⁺ḤWH-yȳ] 𐭧𐭥𐭧𐭩 Pt4 Mf4 E7
   ḤWH-yȳ F2 R413, J2
   ḤWH-d T6
   ḤWH-ʾy K5 M1
2 LK] Pt4 Mf4 F2 R413 T6 E7, K5 M1
   LKʾ J2
2 W] Pt4 Mf1 F7
   deest F2 R413 T6, K5 J2 M1
2 ⁺ḤWH-yȳ] 𐭧𐭥𐭧𐭩 Pt4 Mf4 E7
   ḤWH-yȳ F2 R413, K5 J2
   ḤWH-d T6
   ḤWH-ʾy M1
2 ʾYḴ MNDʿM ḴN gwbšnʾ] Pt4 Mf4 F2 R413
   T6 E7, K5 ḤWH-ʾy
   deest J2
3 MNDʿM] Pt4 Mf4 E7, K5 M1
   MNDʿM Y LK F2 R413 T6
3 ḴN] Pt4 Mf4 F2 T6 E7, K5 M1
   ḴN Mf4
3 W dhšnʾ] Pt4 Mf4 E7 (superscr.), J2
   dhšnʾ F2 T6, K5 M1
   W dhšn R413
3 ⁺ḤWH-yȳ] 𐭧𐭥𐭧𐭩 Pt4 Mf4 E7
   ḤWH-yȳ F2 R413 T6, K5 J2 M1
3 W] Pt4 Mf4 R413 E7, K5 M1
   deest T6, J2
3 ⁺ḤWH-yȳ] 𐭧𐭥𐭧𐭩 Pt4 Mf4 E7
   ḤWH-yȳ F2 R413 T6, K5 J2 M1
3 Y] Pt4 Mf4, J2
   deest F2 R413 T6 E7, K5 M1

3 ʾYḴ] Pt4 (superscr.) F2 T6 E7
   deest Mf4 R413, K5 J2 M1
4 wlcm] Pt4 (superscr.) F2 T6 E7
   deest Mf4 R413, K5 J2 M1
5 ʾytwnʾ] Pt4 Mf4 R413 T6 E7, K5 J2 M1
   ʾytwn F2
5 ʾwʾ] ZK ʾwʾ Pt4
   ʾwʾ Mf4 F2 R413 T6, K5 M1
   ZK Y E7
   ḴN J2
5 LK] Pt4 Mf4 F2 R413 T6 E7, K5 M1
   LKʾ J2
5 YḤBWN-m] Pt4 Mf4 F2 R413 T6 E7, K5 M1
   pt̰ YḤBWN-m YʾTWN-šnʾ ʾMT BYN gyhʾnʾ ḴN
   J2
5 W] Pt4 Mf4 F2 E7, K5 J2 M1
   deest R413 T6
5 ʾytwnʾ] Pt4 Mf4 T6 E7, J2
   ʾytwn F2
   ʾytwn pt̰ʾ R413
   deest K5 M1
5 cʾšm] Pt4 Mf4 F2 R413 T6, J2
   W cʾšm E7, K5 M1
5 ʾwʾ] Pt4 Mf4 F2 R413 T6 E7, J2
   ḴN K5 M1
5 ʾYŠ-ʾn] Pt4 Mf4 F2 R413
   ʾYŠ-ʾn T6 E7, K5 J2 M1
6 YḤBWN-yt] Pt4 Mf4 F2 R413 E7
   YḤBWN-yt T6, J2
   deest K5 M1
6 W ʾytwnʾ] Pt4 Mf4 E7
   ʾytwn F2 R413
   ʾytwnʾ T6, K5 J2 M1
6 LK pt̰ʾ] Pt4 Mf4 E7, K5 M1
   pt̰ʾ LK F2 R413 T6
   LKʾ pt̰ʾ J2
6 W] Pt4 F2
   deest Mf4 R413 T6 E7, K5 J2 M1
6 ʿZLWN-šnʾ] Pt4 (superscr.) T6 E7
   deest Mf4 F2 R413, K5 J2 M1
6 ʾMT] Pt4 Mf4 F2 R413, K5 J2 M1
   MNW ʾMT T6
   MNW E7
6 gyhʾnʾ] Pt4 Mf4 F2
   ʾMT BYN gyhʾn F2
   gyhʾnʾ T6 E7, K5 J2 M1

KN Y'TWN-m W KN 'ZLWN-m KN YDBḤWN-m
(c) 'P̱-m 'ytwn' ⁺nyd'dšnynyȳ 'P̱-m 'ytwn' p̱'mynyȳ LK 'whrmzd 'YK-m 'p̱'m pṯ' LK YḤWWN-'t
wycst byš'mlwtyk gwbšn'

7 KN] Pt4 Mf4 F2 R413 E7, K5 J2 M1
  W KN T6
7 W] Pt4 Mf4 F2 R413 T6, K5 J2 M1
  deest E7
7 'ZLWN-m] Pt4 Mf4 F2 R413 T6 E7, K5 M1
  'ZLWN-ym J2
7 KN] ᴷᴺ Pt4
  deest Mf4 F2 R413 T6, K5 J2 M1
  'LH E7
7 YDBḤWN-m] Pt4 Mf4 E7, K5 J2 M1
  ycwm F2 R413
  ycBḤWN-m T6
8 'ytwn'] Pt4 Mf4 T6 E7, K5 J2 M1
  'ytwn F2 R413
8 ⁺nyd'dšnynyȳ] ⟨⟨⟨ Pt4 Mf4
  ⟨⟨⟨ F2 R413
  ⟨⟨⟨ T6
  ⟨⟨⟨ E7, K5 J2 M1
8 'P̱-m] Pt4 F2 R413 T6 E7, K5 J2 M1
  'P̱-t Mf4
8 'ytwn'] Pt4 Mf4 E7, K5 J2 M1
  'ytwn F2
  deest R413 T6
8 'p̱'mynyȳ] Pt4 Mf4 E7, K5 J2 M1

'p̱'mynyh F2 R413
'p̱'mynyhyȳ T6
8 LK] Pt4 Mf4 F2 R413 T6 E7, K5 M1
  LK' J2
9 pṯ'] Pt4 Mf4 F2 R413 E7, K5 J2 M1
  pṯ' 'p̱'m T6
9 LK] Pt4 Mf4 F2 R413 T6 E7, K5 M1
  LK' J2
9 YḤWWN-'t] Pt4 Mf4 R413 T6 E7, K5 M1
  YḤWWN-'tc F2
  YḤWWN-'t' J2
10 wycst] wycdst' Pt4 Mf4
  wḴycst' F2
  ⟨⟨⟨ R413
  deest T6
  wycdst E7
  wycst' K5 J2 M1
  wycst D
10 byš'mlwtyk] Pt4 Mf4 R413 E7
  byš'mwlwtyk F2, K5 (') J2 M1
  deest T6
10 gwbšn'] Pt4 Mf4 R413 E7, K5 J2 M1
  deest F2 T6

A.6.5   PY 39.5

(a) pt̠ʼ ŠPYL hwyšyh ʼMT LK hwyš ⁺ḤWH-m hwyšlwbšnyh ⁺ḤWH-m ʼMT   1
pt̠ʼ hwyšyh Y LKWM YKʽYMWN-m   2
(b) pt̠ʼ ZK Y ŠPYL ⁺tlskʼsyh ʼwʼ LK BRʼ YḤMTWN-m   3
(c) pt̠ʼ ZK Y ŠPYL srdʼlyh ʼMT srdʼlyh pt̠ʼ plʼlwnyh ʽBYDWN-yt W pt̠ʼ ZK   4
Y ŠPYL bwndk mynšnyh ʼMT MNDʽM bwndk mynšnyh ʽBYDWN-mm   5

1 pt̠ʼ] Pt4 F2 R413 T6 E7, K5 J2 M1
   deest Mf4
1 ŠPYL] Pt4 F2 R413 T6 E7, K5 J2 M1
   ⸗ ŠPYL Mf4
1 ʼMT] Pt4 Mf4 F2 R413 E7, K5 J2 M1
   MNW T6
1 LK] Pt4 Mf4 F2 R413 T6 E7
   LKʽ K5 J2 M1
1 ⁺ḤWH-m] ܚܘܚܡ Pt4 Mf4 E7
   ḤWH-m F2 R413 T6, K5 M1
   ḤWH-ym W J2
   ḤWH-m W **D**
1 ⁺ḤWH-m] ܚܘܚܡ Pt4 (superscr.) E7
   deest Mf4 F2 R413, K5 J2 M1
   ḤWH-m T6
1 ʼMT] Pt4 Mf4 F2 R413 T6, K5 J2 M1
   MNW E7
2 Y] Pt4 Mf4 F2 R413 T6, K5 J2 M1
   deest E7
2 LKWM] Pt4 Mf4 F2 R413 T6 E7
   LK K5 M1
   LKʽ J2
3 Line (b)] Pt4 Mf4 F2 R413 T6 E7, J2 M1
   in marg. K5
3 Y] Pt4 Mf4 F2 R413 T6, K5 J2 M1
   deest E7
3 ⁺tlskʼsyh] ܬܠܣܘܣܝܗ Pt4 E7, K5 M1
   ܬܠܣܝܣ Mf4
   ܬܠܣܝܣ F2
   ܬܠܣܝܣ R413
   ܬܠܣܘܣܝܗ T6
   ܬܠܣܘܣܝܗ J2 (-š)
3 LK] LK Pt4 Mf4 E7
   Y LK F2 R413 T6
   LKʽ K5 J2 M1
3 BRʼ] Pt4 Mf4 R413 T6 E7, K5 J2 M1
   ܒܪܝ F2
3 YḤMTWN-m] Pt4 Mf4 F2 R413 T6 E7
   YḤMTWN-ym K5 J2 M1

4 pt̠ʼ ZK Y] Pt4 Mf4 T6, K5 M1
   deest F2 R413
   pt̠ʼ ZK E7
   pt̠ʼ J2
4 ŠPYL] Pt4 Mf4 F2 R413 T6 E7, K5 M1
   deest J2
4 srdʼlyh] Pt4 Mf4 F2 R413 T6 E7, K5 J2
   srdʼls M1
4 srdʼlyh] Pt4 R413 T6 E7, K5 J2 M1
   ܢܣܠܣܝ Mf4
   srdʼlyh <lbr> yh F2
4 plʼlwnyh] Pt4 Mf4 F2 T6 E7
   plʼlwn Y R413
   ܦܠܣܠܘ K5 J2 M1
4 ʽBYDWN-yt] Pt4 Mf4 R413 E7
   ʽBYDWN-ᵐynd F2
   ʽBYDWN-m T6
   ʽBYDWN-m̠ K5 J2 M1
4 W pt̠ʼ] Pt4 Mf4
   pt̠ʼ F2 R413 T6 E7, J2
   W K5 M1
5 Y] Pt4 Mf4 F2 R413 T6, K5 J2 M1
   p E7
5 mynšnyh] Pt4 Mf4 E7, J2
   mynšnʼ F2, T6, K5 M1
   mynšn R413
5 ʼMT] Pt4 Mf4, K5 J2 M1
   MNW F2 E7
   ʼMT MNW R413 T6
5 MNDʽM] Pt4 Mf4 R413 E7
   MNDʽM Y <lbr> DʽM F2
   MNDʽM Y T6, K5 J2 M1
5 mynšnyh] Pt4 Mf4 E7
   mynšnʼ F2 R413 T6
   mynšnyʼ K5 J2 M1
5 ʽBYDWN-mm] Pt4 Mf4
   ʽBYDWN-m F2 R413 T6 E7
   ʽBYDWN-m̠ K5 J2 M1

ycšnykyh' byš'mlwtykgwbšn' ∴ 5 wycdst' 3 g's

6 ycšnykyh'] Pt4 Mf4 E7
   ycšn'yh' K5 M1
   ycšnyh' D
   deest F2 R413 T6
   ycycš' J2
6 byš'mlwtyk] Pt4 E7, K5
   'yw'mlwtyk Mf4
   deest F2 R413 T6
   byš'mwlwtyk M1
   ܐܠܝܣܘܢܐ J2

6 gwbšn'] Pt4 Mf4 E7, K5 M1
   deest F2 R413 T6, J2
6 5 ... g's] Pt4 Mf4 E7
   'D 6-wmd h't' bwn L'YŠH 5 wycst' 3 g's yst' F2
   'D R413
   deest K5 J2 M1
6 wycdst'] Pt4 Mf4
   wycst' F2 R413
   wycst T6
   wycdst' Y E7

A.7 PY 40

A.7.1 PY 40.1

yst' 6-wm h't' 1
(a) ’MT-t’n BYN ZK ’hw’n ’ytwn' QDM YḤBWN-’nd ’whrmẓd msyh 2
bwndkyh pt' krt'lyh L ’YK ZK MND‘M ‘BYDWN-d W YMRRWN-’nd 3
ZY-t’n msyh W bwndkyh pyt’ktl YḤWWN-’t 4
(b) I’t' ⁺ḤWH-m ’w' ḤN’ Y LK hlt' p’nkyh ’w' dyn' Y LK MN ZK ’MT-m 5
QDM ’YK-m nywkyh MN ZK 6

1 **yst'**] Pt4 Mf4 R413 E7
   yst T6
   deest K5 J2 M1
1 **6-wm**] Pt4 Mf4 R413 T6 E7
   deest K5 J2 M1
1 **h't'**] Pt4 E7
   h't' bwn Mf4
   h't' bwn R413 T6
   deest K5 J2 M1
2 **’MT-t’n**] Pt4 Mf4
   ’MT-t’n' F2 R413 T6, K5 J2 M1
   MNW-t’n' E7
2 **ZK**] Pt4 Mf4 E7, J2
   deest F2 R413 T6
   ZK Y K5 M1
2 **’hw’n**] Pt4 Mf4 F2 R413 E7
   ’hw’n' T6, K5 M1
   • J2
2 **’ytwn'**] Pt4 Mf4 R413 T6 E7, K5 J2 M1
   ’ytwn F2
2 **YḤBWN-’nd**] Pt4 Mf4 E7, K5 J2 M1
   YḤBWN-ynd F2
   BYḤBWN-ty R413
   YḤBWN-m T6
2 **msyh**] Pt4 Mf4 F2 R413 T6 E7, K5 J2 M1
   msyh W D
3 **bwndkyh**] Pt4 Mf4 F2 R413 T6 E7, K5
   بندہی J2
3 L] Pt4 F2 T6 (in line) E7 (in line)
   deest Mf4 R413, K5 J2 M1
3 **’YK**] Pt4 Mf4 F2 R413 T6 E7, K5 M1
   ’MT J2
3 **‘BYDWN-d**] Pt4 Mf4 E7
   ‘BYDWN-ᵐyt F2
   ‘BYDWN-yt R413
   ‘BYDWN-m T6
   ‘BYDWN-ynd K5 J2 M1
   ‘BYDWN-ty D
3 **W**] Pt4 Mf4 F2 R413 T6 E7, K5 M1
   deest J2
3 **YMRRWN-’nd**] Pt4 Mf4
   6-w F2
   6-w R413 E7
   6-w T6
   YMLLWN-’nd K5 M1
   YMLLWN-d J2
4 **ZY-t’n**] Pt4 Mf4 R413, K5 M1
   ZY-t’n' F2 T6 E7, J2
4 **W**] Pt4 Mf4 F2 R413 T6 J2, K5 M1
   deest E7
4 **bwndkyh**] Pt4 Mf4 F2 R413 T6 E7 J2
   bwndkyh ptš K5 M1
4 **YḤWWN-’t**] Pt4 Mf4 F2 R413, K5 M1
   YḤWWN-yt T6
   YḤWWN-’t' E7, J2
5 **I’t'**] Pt4 Mf4 E7
   I’t F2 R413 T6, K5 J2 M1
5 **⁺ḤWH-m**] 6-w Pt4 Mf4 E7
   ḤWH-m F2 R413 T6, K5 J2 M1
5 **’w' ḤN’ Y**] Pt4 Mf4 T6 E7, K5 J2 M1
   ’whrmẓd F2 (corr. to ’w' ḤN’)
   ’whrmẓd R413
5 **LK**] Pt4 Mf4 F2 R413 T6 E7, K5 M1
   LK' J2
5 **hlt'**] Pt4 Mf4 T6, K5 J2 M1
   hlt F2 R413
   I’t' E7
5 **dyn'**] Pt4 Mf4 T6 E7, K5 J2 M1
   dyn F2 R413
5 **Y**] Pt4 Mf4 F2 R413 T6, J2
   deest E7, K5 M1
5 **LK**] Pt4 Mf4 F2 R413 T6 E7
   LK K5
   LK' J2
   deest M1
6 **MN ZK**] Pt4 Mf4 F2 T6 E7, K5 J2 M1
   m̶z̶d̶ MN ZK R413

---
1 **yst' ...** : For the chapter heading in F2, see YH 39.5.
2 **YḤBWN-’nd** : سی gloss in Pt4 (in marg.).
2 **msyh** : سٚ gloss in K5 (superscr.).

(c) MNW mzd 'w' mnyk'n pr'c YḤBWN-yȳ ZK 'w' dynyk'n p̄'yt' YḤBWN-t' 'whrmzd

7 mzd] Pt4 Mf4 F2 R413 E7, K5 J2 M1
   ᶻᴷ mzd T6
7 'w'] Pt4 Mf4 F2 R413 T6, K5 J2 M1
   ZK Y E7
7 mnyk'n] Pt4 Mf4, K5 M1
   MN ZK 'n ᵐⁿʸᵏ'ⁿ F2
   mnyk'n' R413 T6, J2
   mn'yk'n' E7
7 YḤBWN-yȳ] Pt4 Mf4, K5 J2 M1
   YḤBWN-HDyȳ F2
   YḤBWN-HD R413
   YḤBWN-'ȳ T6
   YḤBWN-yt E7
7 ZK] Pt4 Mf4 F2 R413 T6 E7
   ZK Y K5 J2 M1
   deest D
7 'w'] Pt4 Mf4 F2 R413 T6, K5 J2 M1
   'w E7
7 dynyk'n] Pt4
   dyn'yk'n Mf4
   dynyk'n' F2 R413 T6 E7, K5 J2 M1
7 p̄'yt'] Pt4 Mf4 T6, K5 J2 M1
   p̄'yt F2 R413
   p'yt' E7
7–8 YḤBWN-t'] Pt4 Mf4, K5 J2 M1
   YḤBWN-d F2 R413 T6
   YḤBWN-tn' E7
   YḤBWN-t D

A.7.2   PY 40.2

(a) ZK Y ʿLḪ ZK ʾwˈ LNḤ YḤBWN-yȳ pṭˈ-c ZNḪ ʾhwʾn W pṭˈ-c mynwdʾn   1
(b) ʾYḴ ʾytwnˈ pṭˈ ZK ʾytwnˈ QDM YḤMTWN-ym   2
(c) ʾwˈ ḤNʾ Y LK hm-ʾḤ-kyh hmkrtʾlyh ʾhlʾdyhc hmʾy ʿD ʾwˈ wspˈ ʿD tnˈ Y   3
psynˈ   4

1 ʿLḪ] Pt4 F2 R413 T6 E7, J2   ZNḪ E7
   ʾwˈ Mf4, K5 M1   3 Y] Pt4 Mf4, K5 J2 M1
1 ZK] Pt4 Mf4, K5 J2 M1   deest F2 R413 T6 E7
   ZK Y F2 R413 T6   3 LK] Pt4 Mf4 F2 T6 E7, K5 J2 M1
   deest E7   deest R413
1 ʾwˈ] Pt4 E7, J2   3 hm-ʾḤ-kyh] Pt4 F2 T6, K5 J2 M1
   ʿLḪ Mf4, K5 M1   ٮحىوں Mf4
   deest F2   hmˈk hm-ʾḤ-kyh R413
   ʾw R413 T6   hm-ʾḤ-kyh W E7
1 YḤBWN-yȳ] Pt4 Mf4 F2 R413 T6, K5 J2 M1 3 hmkrtʾlyh] Pt4 Mf4 F2 R413 T6
   YḤBWN-yt E7   hmkrtʾl E7
1 ʾhwʾn] Pt4 Mf4 F2 T6   hmkrtʾlyh Y K5 J2 M1
   ʾhwʾn R413 E7, K5 J2 M1   3 ʾhlʾdyhc] Pt4 Mf4 F2 R413 T6 E7, J2
1 W pṭˈ-c] Pt4 Mf4   ʾhlʾdyh W K5 M1
   pṭˈ-c F2 R413 T6 E7, K5 J2 M1   3 ʾwˈ] Pt4 Mf4 E7, J2
1 mynwdʾn] Pt4 Mf4 F2, K5 M1   ʿLḪ F2 R413 T6
   mynwdʾnˈ R413 T6 E7, J2   اسٮ K5 M1
2 ʾytwnˈ] Pt4 Mf4 R413 T6 E7, K5 J2 M1 3 wspˈ] Pt4 Mf4 E7, K5 J2 M1
   ʾytwn F2   wsp F2 R413 T6 (وسپ)
2 ZK] Pt4 Mf4 F2 T6 E7   3 ʿD] Pt4 Mf4 E7, K5 J2 M1
   ZK Y R413, K5 J2 M1   ʿD ʿLḪ F2 T6
2 ʾytwnˈ] Pt4 Mf4 F2 R413 T6 E7, K5 J2 M1 ʿD ʿLḪ Y R413
   ʾytwn F2   3 Y] Pt4 Mf4 F2 R413, K5 J2
2 YḤMTWN-ym] Pt4 Mf4, K5 J2 M1   deest T6 E7, M1
   YḤMTWN-m F2 R413 T6 E7   4 psynˈ] Pt4 Mf4 R413 T6 E7, K5 J2 M1
3 ḤNʾ] Pt4 Mf4 F2 R413 (سٮلں) T6, K5 J2 M1 psnˈ F2

3 hm-ʾḤ-kyh : ڡٮعڡر gloss in K5 (in marg.)

A.7.3 PY 40.3

(a) YḤBWN-yẏ-m ʾytwnʿ ZK Y GBRʾ-ʾn ʾwhrmẓd hʾwštʾn Y GBRʾ-ʾn 1
hylptʾn ʾhlwbʿ Y ʾhlʾdyh kʾmkʿ ZK hylptʿ 2
(b) Y ʾMT-šʾn ⁺hʾcʾnd ʾm ʾwʿ ZK Y dgl YḤMTWN-šnʿ W ʾp̄zwnʿ tnʿ Y psynʿ 3
ptʿ ZK Y stpl ptʿ kʾl hm-ʾḤ-k YḤWWN-ʾnd 4
(c) ʾwʿ LNH ZK ⁺LNH-kʾn lʾmynytʾl YḤBWN-yẏ 5

1 YḤBWN-yẏ-m] ⟨gloss⟩ Pt4 E7
   ⟨gloss⟩ Mf4
   ⟨gloss⟩ F2
   YḤBWN-yẏ R413 T6
   ⟨gloss⟩ K5 (ؚ subscr., ؙ superscr.)
   ⟨gloss⟩ J2
   ⟨gloss⟩ M1
   ⟨gloss⟩ D
1 ʾytwnʿ] Pt4 Mf4 T6 E7, K5 J2 M1
   ʾytwn F2
   ⟨gloss⟩ R413
1 Y] Pt4 Mf4 R413 T6, K5 J2 M1
   deest F2 E7
1 GBRʾ-ʾn] Pt4 Mf4 F2, J2
   GBRʾ-ʾnʿ R413 T6 E7
   ⟨gloss⟩ K5 M1 (mltʾn in marg.)
1 hʾwštʾn] Pt4 Mf4 E7, J2
   hʾwštʾnʿ F2 R413 T6, K5 M1
1 Y] Pt4 E7, K5 J2 M1
   deest Mf4 F2 R413 T6
1 GBRʾ-ʾn] Pt4 Mf4 F2 E7
   GBRʾ-ʾnʿ R413 T6
   ⟨gloss⟩ K5 M1
   GBRʾ-ʾn Y J2
   GBRʾ-ʾnʿ Y D
2 hylptʾn] Pt4 Mf4 R413
   hylptʾnʿ F2 T6 E7
   hylptʾnʿ Y K5 M1
   hylptʾn Y J2
2 ʾhlwbʿ] Pt4 Mf4 F2 R413 T6 E7
   ʾhlwbʾn K5 J2 M1
   ʾhlwbʾnʿ D
2 Y] Pt4 Mf4, K5 J2 M1
   deest F2 R413 T6 E7
2 kʾmkʿ] Pt4 Mf4 E7, K5 J2 M1
   kʾmk F2 R413 T6
2 ZK] Pt4 Mf4 F2 E7, K5 J2 M1
   ZK Y R413 T6
2 hylptʿ] Pt4 Mf4 T6 E7
   hylptʿy F2
   hylpt R413
   hylptʾnʿ K5 J2 M1

3 Y ʾMT-šʾn] Pt4 Mf4 F2, J2
   ʾMT-šʾnʿ R413 T6, K5 M1
   Y ʾMT-šʾnʿ E7
3 ⁺hʾcʾnd] ⟨gloss⟩ Pt4 Mf4 R413 T6, J2
   ⟨gloss⟩ F2
   ⟨gloss⟩ E7, K5 M1
3 ʾm] Pt4 Mf4 T6 E7, K5 J2 M1
   deest F2 R413
3 ʾwʿ] Pt4 Mf4 (superscr.) F2 E7, K5 M1
   ؙ R413
   deest T6
   • J2
3 Y] Pt4 Mf4, K5 J2 M1
   deest F2 R413 T6
   ⟨gloss⟩ E7
3 YḤMTWN-šnʿ W] Pt4 Mf4 R413 E7
   YḤMTWN-šnʿ ptʿ F2 (ᵖᵗʾ) T6
   YḤMTWN-šnʿ K5 J2 M1
   YḤMTWN-šn D
3 ʾp̄zwnʿ tnʿ] Pt4 Mf4, K5 M1
   ʾp̄zwnyhtnʿ F2 (-ʸʰ-) E7
   ʾp̄zw tnʿ R413
   ʾp̄zwnyktnʿ T6
   ʾp̄zwnʿ tnʿ J2
3 Y] Pt4 Mf4 F2 R413, K5 J2 M1
   deest T6 E7
3 psynʿ] Pt4 Mf4 R413 T6 E7, K5 J2 M1
   ᵖˢʸⁿ F2 (also in marg.)
4 ZK Y] Pt4 F2 R413 T6 E7, J2
   ZK Mf4, K5 M1
4 hm-ʾḤ-k] Pt4 F2 R413 T6 E7, K5 J2 M1
   ⟨gloss⟩ Mf4
4 YḤWWN-ʾnd] Pt4 Mf4 F2 R413 E7, K5 J2 M1
   ⟨gloss⟩ T6
5 ZK] Pt4 Mf4 F2 R413 E7
   ZK Y T6, K5 J2 M1
5 ⁺LNH-kʾn] LNH-ʾn Pt4 (-ʾⁿ) E7
   LNH Mf4 F2 R413 T6, K5 J2 M1
5 lʾmynytʾl] Pt4 Mf4 F2 R413 E7, K5 J2 M1
   lʾmynytʾlʿ T6

---

1 GBRʾ-ʾn: ⟨gloss⟩ gloss in K5 (superscr.)
3 ⁺hʾcʾnd: ⟨gloss⟩ gloss in Pt4 (in marg., beg. cut off)
   ⟨gloss⟩ gloss in K5 (in marg.)

A.7.4 PY 40.4

(a) ʾytwn' NPŠH W ʾytwn' wʾlwn' ʾytwn' hm-ʾḤ-k ʾm ḤWH-t ʾYḴ-m 1
YḤBWN-ʾt 2
(b) ʾMT-šʾn hʾcʾnd ʾytwn' pṯ' ZK Y LKWM dyn' ʾytwn' ḤWH-t ʾwhrmẕd 3
ʾhlwb' W lʾst' ḤWH-t pṯ' īšt lʾt ḤWH-t pṯ' hwʾstk' ⁺hʾcʾnd 4
ycšnykyhʾ ʾywʾmlwtyk gwbšn' ∴ 4 wycdst' Y 3 gʾs 5

1 ʾytwn'] Pt4 Mf4 T6 E7, K5 J2 M1
  ʾytwn F2 R413
1 NPŠH] Pt4 Mf4 R413 E7, K5 J2 M1
  pṯ' NPŠH-yh F2 (faint -ṯ', NP- & -yh) T6
1 W ʾytwn'] Pt4 Mf4 E7, J2
  ʾytwn' F2 T6, K5
  ʾytwn R413
  deest M1
1 wʾlwn'] Pt4 Mf4 E7, K5 J2 M1
  wʾlwn R413
  pṯ' wʾlwnyh F2 (faint pṯ' & -yh) T6
1 ʾytwn'] Pt4 Mf4 F2 T6 E7, K5
  ʾytwn R413
  W ʾytwn' J2 M1
1 hm-ʾḤ-k] Pt4 F2 R413 E7, K5 J2 M1
  ࣭࣫ࢽ Mf4
  hm-ʾḤ-kyh T6
1 ʾm] Pt4 Mf4 F2 R413 T6 E7, J2 M1
  ʾm N̶P̶Š̶H̶ K5
1 ḤWH-t] Pt4 Mf4 E7, K5 J2 M1
  ḤWH-d F2 R413 T6
2 YḤBWN-ʾt] Pt4 Mf4 F2 E7, K5 J2 M1
  bʾt R413
  YḤWWN-yt' T6
3 ʾMT-šʾn] Pt4 Mf4, J2 M1
  ʾMT-šʾn' F2 R413 T6, K5
  ʾM-šʾn' E7
3 ʾytwn'] Pt4 Mf4 R413 T6 E7, K5 M1
  ʾytwn F2
  ʾytwn" J2
3 Y] Pt4 Mf4 F2 R413 T6, K5 J2 M1
  deest E7
3 LKWM dyn'] Pt4 (dyn') F2 (dyn' in marg.) T6 E7
  LKWM Mf4 R413, J2
  W LKWM K5 M1
3 ʾytwn'] Pt4 Mf4 R413 T6 E7
  ʾytwn F2
  ʾytwn' W K5 J2 M1
3 ḤWH-t] Pt4 Mf4, K5 J2 M1
  ḤWH-d F2 R413 T6

࣭࣠ࢽ E7
4 ʾhlwb'] Pt4 Mf4 F2 R413 E7, K5 M1
  ʾhlwbyh T6
  ʾhlwb" J2
4 W] Pt4 Mf4 E7, K5 J2 M1
  Y F2 R413
  deest T6
4 lʾst'] Pt4 Mf4 T6 E7, K5 J2 M1
  lʾst F2 R413
4 ḤWH-t] Pt4 Mf4 T6 E7, K5 J2 M1
  ḤWH-d F2
  deest R413
4 lʾt] l̶ʾ̶s̶t̶ lʾt' Pt4
  W lʾt' Mf4, K5 J2 M1
  lʾst F2
  deest R413
  lʾst' T6 E7
  lʾt D
4 ḤWH-t] Pt4 Mf4 E7, K5 J2 M1
  ḤWH-d F2 R413 T6
4 hwʾstk' ⁺hʾcʾnd] Pt4 (ࢽ࣫ࢽ) E7
  hwʾstk' Mf4, J2
  hwʾstk F2 R413 T6, K5 M1
5 ycšnykyhʾ] Pt4 Mf4 E7
  deest F2 T6
  ycšnyhʾ R413, K5 J2 (-yh-) M1
5 ʾywʾmlwtyk] Pt4 Mf4, K5
  deest F2 T6
  ࣭ࢽ࣭ࢽ R413
  ࣭ࢽ࣭ࢽ E7
  ࣭ࢽ࣭ࢽ J2 M1
5 gwbšn'] Pt4 Mf4 R413 E7, K5 J2 M1
  deest F2 T6
5 4 ... gʾs] Pt4 Mf4 R413 T6 E7
  ʾD LʾYŠH 6 wycst 3 gʾs F2
  deest K5 J2 M1
5 wycdst' Y] Pt4
  wycdst' Mf4 E7
  wycst R413
  wycdst T6

A.8 PY 41

A.8.1 PY 41.1

yst' hp̄twm h't'
(a) st'dšn' W ḤDWN-šn' W nyd'dšn' 'w' 'whrmzd W 'šwhšt'c
(b) YḤBWN-m BNPŠH W c'šm 'w' 'YŠ-'n W ZK-c nwykm pt̰' gwpt'

---

1 **yst'**] Pt4 Mf4 F2 R413 E7
   deest T6, K5 J2 M1
1 **hp̄twm**] Pt4 Mf4 R413 E7
   7-wm F2
   deest T6, K5 J2 M1
1 **h't'**] Pt4 E7
   h't' bwn Mf4 R413
   h't F2
   deest T6, K5 J2 M1
2 **st'dšn' W**] Pt4 Mf4 F2 E7, J2
   st'dšn' R413 T6, K5 M1
2 **ḤDWN-šn'**] Pt4 Mf4 F2 R413 T6, K5 J2 M1
   ḤDDW 'ḤDWN-šn' E7
2 **W**] Pt4 Mf4 F2 E7, K5 J2 M1
   deest R413 T6
2 **'w'**] Pt4 Mf4 T6 E7, K5 J2 M1
   Y F2 R413
2 **'whrmzd**] Pt4 Mf4 F2 R413 T6 E7, K5 J2 M1
   'whrmzdc D
2 **W**] Pt4 F2 R413 T6 E7, K5 J2 M1
   deest Mf4
2 **'šwhšt'c**] Pt4 Mf4 F2, J2
   'šwhštc R413 T6, K5 M1
   'šwhšt' E7
3 **BNPŠH**] Pt4 Mf4 F2 R413 T6 E7, J2
   NPŠH K5 M1
3 **W**] Pt4 Mf4 F2 R413 T6 E7
   deest K5 J2 M1
3 **'w'**] Pt4 Mf4 F2 R413 T6, K5 J2 M1
   ZK E7
3 **'YŠ-'n**] Pt4 Mf4 F2
   'YŠ-'n' R413 T6 E7, K5 J2 M1
3 **W ZK-c**] Pt4 Mf4 F2 T6 E7, J2
   ZK-c R413, K5 M1
3 **nwykm**] Pt4 Mf4 E7, J2
   ⟨nwykm⟩ F2 R413 T6
   ⟨nwykm⟩ K5 M1
3 **gwpt'**] Pt4 Mf4 T6 E7
   gwpt F2 R413, K5 J2 M1

A.8.2 PY 41.2

(a) ZK Y ŠPYL hwtʾyyh LK ʾwhrmẓd BRʾ ʾyʾp̄ynd hmʾy ʾD ʾwʿ wspʿ   1
(b) ZK Y ʾwhrmẓd LK ʾwʿ LNH MNW ZKL W nʾylyk ⁺ḤWH-ym ʾ-t   2
 pʾtʾhšʾyynyt   3
(c) B̲Y̲N̲ KRʾ 2 ʾhwʾn ʾYTʿ-ʾn hwdhʾktwm   4

1 Y] Pt4 F2 R413 T6, K5 J2 M1
   deest Mf4 E7
1 hwtʾyyh] Pt4 Mf4 F2 T6 E7
   hwtʾyyh Y R413, K5 J2 M1
1 LK] Pt4 Mf4 F2 R413 T6 E7, K5 M1
   LKʿ J2
1 BRʾ] Pt4 Mf4 F2 R413 T6, K5 J2 M1
   BRʾ BRʾ E7
1 ʾyʾp̄ynd] Pt4 Mf4 R413 E7
   ʾyʾp̄ndm F2
   ʾʾp̄ndm T6
   ʾyʾp̄ynyȳ K5 J2 M1
1 hmʾy] Pt4 Mf4 E7, J2 M1
   hmʾ F2
   hmʾk R413 T6
   hmʾy Y K5
1 ʾwʿ] Pt4 Mf4, J2
   ʾwʿ Y F2 R413 T6
   ZK Y E7
   ʿL K5 M1
1 wspʿ] Pt4 R413 T6 E7, K5 J2 M1
   wspʿʿ Mf4
   wsp F2
2 Y] Pt4 Mf4 F2 R413, K5 J2 M1
   deest T6 E7
2 ʾwhrmẓd] Pt4 Mf4 F2 R413 T6 E7
   hwhwtʾy K5 J2 M1
2 ʾwʿ] Pt4 Mf4 F2 R413 T6, K5 J2 M1

   ZK E7
2 MNW] Pt4 Mf4 E7, K5 J2 M1
   deest F2 R413 T6
2 nʾylyk] Pt4 R413 T6 E7, K5 J2 M1
   nʾylykʾn Mf4
   nʾyl F2
2 ⁺ḤWH-ym] ⟨gloss⟩ Pt4
   ⟨gloss⟩ Mf4
   ḤWH-ym F2 (ᴍ above -H-) R413 E7, K5 J2 M1
   H̶W̶H̶-y̶n̶ ḤWH-ym T6
3 pʾtʾhšʾyynyt] Pt4 E7
   pʾthš•yt Mf4
   pʾthšʾyynyt F2, J2
   p̶ʾ̶t̶p̶ʾ̶s̶ pʾthšʾyynyt R413
   pʾtʾhšʾyynytʿ T6
   pʾthšʾynyt K5 M1
4 ʾhwʾn] Pt4 Mf4 F2 R413 T6 E7, K5 M1
   ʾhwʾnʿ J2
4 ʾYTʿ-ʾn] Pt4 Mf4 E7
   ʾYT-ʾnʿ F2 T6, K5 M1
   ʾYT-ʾn R413
   ʾYTʿ-ʾnʿ J2
4 hwdhʾktwm] Pt4 Mf4 F2 R413 E7
   hwdhʾk̶ntwm T6
   ⟨gloss⟩ K5 M1
   hwdhktwm J2

---

2 ʾwhrmẓd : hwhwtʾyh gloss in F2 (in marg.)

A.8.3 PY 41.3

(a) ʾMT hwplmʾnyh Y LK ʾYḴ plmʾn Y LK YḆLWN-ʾnd W ʾp̄zwnʾ ʾYḴ 1
MNDʾM Y LK ʾp̄zʾdynd ʾP̱-t ycšnʾ MN ʾhlʾdyh ʾp̄ʾkyh YḤBWN-ʾnd ʾYḴ-t 2
MN ʾšwhšt̰ʾ KḤDH ḴN YḎBḤWN-ʾnd 3
(b) ʾytwnʾ MN LK LNH tnʾ W yʾn ḤWH-t ʾYḴ-mʾn *apagaiiehe* ʾL 4
YḤWWN-ʾt 5
(c) ḆYN KRʾ 2 ʾhwʾn ʾYTʾ-ʾn hwdhʾktwm ʿLH YḤBWN-yȳ 6

---

1 hwplmʾnyh] Pt4 Mf4 R413 T6 E7, J2 M1
  سواحسـو F2
  hwplʾnyh K5
1 Y] Pt4 Mf4 F2 R413 T6, K5 M1
  deest E7, J2
1 LK] Pt4 Mf4 F2 R413 T6 E7, K5 M1
  deest J2
1 ʾYḴ] Pt4 F2 R413 E7, K5 J2 M1
  ʾYḴ ptʾ Mf4
  YḆLWN-d ʾYḴ T6
1 plmʾn] Pt4 Mf4 F2 R413 E7
  plmʾnʾ T6, K5 J2 M1
1 Y LK] Pt4 Mf4 F2 R413 T6 E7, K5 M1
  deest J2
1 YḆLWN-ʾnd] Pt4 E7, J2 M1
  YḆLWN-ty Mf4, K5
  YḆLWN-ȳt^m F2
  YḆLWN-ȳt R413 T6
1 W] Pt4 Mf4 F2 E7, K5 J2
  deest R413 T6, M1
1 ʾp̄zwnʾ] Pt4 Mf4, J2
  ʾp̄zwn^yh F2
  ʾp̄zwn R413 E7
  ʾp̄zwnyk T6, K5 M1
2 Y] Pt4 F2 R413 T6 E7, K5 M1
  deest Mf4, J2
2 LK] Pt4 Mf4 F2 R413 T6 E7, K5 M1
  LKʾ J2
2 ʾp̄zʾdynd] Pt4 F2 R413 T6 E7, K5 J2 M1
  ʾp̄zʾdyndt Mf4
2 ycšnʾ] Pt4 Mf4 F2 R413 E7, K5 J2 M1
  ڛڛ ycšnʾ T6
2 ʾp̄ʾkyh] Pt4 Mf4 F2 T6, K5 J2 M1
  ʾp̄ʾk R413
  سوسـو E7
2 YḤBWN-ʾnd] Pt4 Mf4 F2 R413 E7, K5 J2 M1
  ـوسرڛـ F2
  YḤBWN-ynd T6
2 ʾYḴ-t] Pt4 Mf4, K5 J2 M1
  ʾ F2 T6
  ʾm R413
  ʾYḴ E7
3 MN] Pt4 Mf4 F2 T6 E7, K5 J2 M1

deest R413
3 ʾšwhšt̰ʾ] Pt4 Mf4 T6 E7, K5 J2 M1
  ʾšwhšt̰ F2 R413
3 YḎBḤWN-ʾnd] Pt4 Mf4 T6 E7
  yc ẏeBḤWN-ʾnd F2
  ycBḤWN-ʾnd R413
  ycʾnd K5 J2 M1
4 ʾytwnʾ] Pt4 Mf4 T6 E7, J2
  ʾytwn F2 R413
  ʾytwnʾ W K5 M1
4 W] Pt4 Mf4 F2 R413 E7, K5 M1
  deest T6
  Y W J2
4 yʾn] Pt4 Mf4 F2 R413 T6, K5 M1
  yʾnʾ E7, J2
4 ḤWH-t] Pt4 Mf4 E7
  ḤWH-d F2 R413 T6
  ḤWH-ʾt K5 M1
  ḤWH-ʾtʾ J2
4 ʾYḴ-mʾn] Pt4 Mf4, K5 M1
  ʾYḴ-m•ʾn F2
  ʾYḴ-mʾnʾ R413 T6 E7,'
4 *apagaiiehe*] Pt4 Mf4 F2 E7
  apagaiiahe R413
  apagaiiāhe T6
  apagiiehe K5 (§) M1
  apaga^iie hīie J2
5 YḤWWN-ʾt] Pt4 Mf4 F2 R413 E7, K5 J2 M1
  YḤWWN-ʾtʾ T6
6 2] Pt4 Mf4 F2 R413 T6 E7, K5 J2
  deest M1
6 ʾhwʾn] Pt4 Mf4 T6 E7, K5 M1
  ʾhwʾnʾ F2 R413, J2
6 ʾYTʾ-ʾn] Pt4 Mf4 E7
  سـاالسر F2
  سـاالسـر R413
  سر االالسـر T6
  ʾYTʾ-ʾnʾ K5 J2 M1
6 hwdhʾktwm] Pt4 Mf4 F2 R413 T6 E7
  hwdhktwm K5 J2 M1
6 ʿLH] Pt4 E7
  deest Mf4 F2 R413 T6, K5 J2 M1
6 YḤBWN-yȳ] Pt4 Mf4 R413 T6 E7, K5 J2 M1
  mYḤBWN-yȳ F2

---

6 ḆYN KRʾ 2 ʾhwʾn : اندر مردمان gloss in J2 (subscr.)

wycdst' byšʾmlwtyk gwbšn' 7

7 wycdst'] Pt4 Mf4 E7
  wycst' K5 M1
  wycst' F2
  deest R413 T6, J2
7 byšʾmlwtyk] Pt4 Mf4 E7
  yššʾmltyk F2

  byšʾmltyk R413
  deest T6, J2
  رسیدم K5
  byšʾmwlwtyk M1
7 gwbšn'] Pt4 Mf4 E7, K5 M1
  deest F2 R413 T6, J2

A.8.4   PY 41.4

(a) ⁺ʾlcʾnykynyȳm pt̰ʾ mzd pʾtdʾšn' ʾP-m zynʾhwndynyȳ ʾwhrmzd

(b) LK pt̰ʾ lʾmynytʾlyh pt̰ʾ² dgl YḤMTWN-šnyh pt̰ʾ tn' Y psyn' hwʾstʾl ⁺ḤWH-m pt̰ʾ ḤNʾ Y LK pt̰ʾ dyn' Y LK Wʾ ʾmʾwnd ⁺YḤWWN-ʾnd

(c) lʾmynytʾlyh LK ʾwʾ LNH pt̰ʾ dgl YḤMTWN-šnyh Y BYN ʾYTʾ-ʾn hwdhʾktwm ʾmʾn YḤBWN-yȳ

1   ⁺ʾlcʾnykynyȳm] ⟨lbr⟩ Pt4
    Mf4 E7, K5 J2 M1
    F2 R413 T6
    ʾlcʾnykynyȳm D
1   zynʾhwndynyȳ] Pt4 E7
    Mf4
    F2 R413 T6, K5 J2 M1
2   pt̰ʾ²] pt̰ʾ ḤN² Y Pt4
    pt̰ʾ Mf4 F2 R413 T6 E7, K5 J2
    deest M1
2   Y] Pt4 Mf4 F2 R413 T6, K5
    deest E7, J2 M1
2–3 hwʾstʾl ⁺ḤWH-m] Pt4 E7
    (in line)
    hwʾstʾl ḤWH-m F2 (ḤWH-m in marg.) T6
    hwʾstʾl Mf4 R413, K5 J2 M1
3   Y] Pt4 Mf4 F2 R413 T6, K5 J2 M1
    deest E7
3   LK] Pt4 Mf4 F2 R413 T6 E7, K5 M1
    LKʾ J2
3   pt̰ʾ] Pt4 Mf4 F2 R413 T6 E7, K5 M1
    pt̰ʾ J2 (sec.m.)
3   Y] Pt4 Mf4 F2 R413 T6, K5 J2 M1
    deest E7
3   LK] Pt4 Mf4 F2 R413 T6 E7, K5 M1
    LKʾ J2
3   W] Pt4 Mf4 F2, J2

    deest R413 T6 E7, K5 M1
3   ʾmʾwnd] ʾmʾwnd Pt4 Mf4 F2 R413 T6 E7, J2
    ʾmʾwndyh K5 M1
3   ⁺YḤWWN-ʾnd] YḤWWN-ʾnm Pt4
    YḤWWN-ʾnd Mf4 R413 E7, K5 J2 M1
    YḤWWN-ʾndm F2
    YḤWWN-ymd T6
4   lʾmynytʾlyh] Pt4 Mf4, K5 J2 M1
    lʾmynytʾl F2 R413 T6 E7
    lʾmynytʾlyh Y D
4   LK] LK Pt4 Mf4 F2 R413 T6 E7
    LKʾ K5 J2 M1
4   Y] Pt4 Mf4 F2 T6
    deest R413 E7
    Y W K5 M1
    W Y J2
4   BYN] Pt4 Mf4 E7
    yʾnʾ F2 R413 T6, K5 J2 M1
4   ʾYTʾ-ʾn] Pt4
    Mf4
    MN ʾYTʾ-ʾn' F2 R413 T6
    ʾYTʾ-ʾn K5 M1
    ʾYTʾ-ʾn' E7, J2
5   hwdhʾktwm] Pt4 Mf4 R413 T6 E7
    hwdhktwm F2, K5 J2 M1
5   ʾmʾn] Pt4 Mf4 F2, K5 J2 M1
    ʾmʾn' R413 T6 E7

A.8.5   PY 41.5

(a) ʾMT ʾwʾ ḤNʾ Y LK stʾdytʾlyh W mʾnslykyh ʾwhrmẓd   1
(b) QDM YḤMTWN-ʾnd W ⁺hwnsnd ⁺ḤWH-d W MKḆLWN-ty ʾYḴ BRʾ   2
ptglʾnd W ⁺hwnsndyhʾ ḴN ⁺ʿBYDWN-ʾnd   3
(c) ʾy mzd Y ʾwʾ mnykʾn prʾc YḤBWN-yȳ ZK Y ʾwʾ dynykʾn ʾp̄ʾytʾ YḤBWN-   4
tn ʾwhrmẓd   5
wycdstʾ byšʾmlwtyk gwbšnʾ   6

1 ʾMT] Pt4 Mf4 F2 R413 T6, K5 J2 M1
   MNW E7
1 ʾwʾ] Pt4 Mf4 F2 R413 T6, K5 J2 M1
   ZK E7
1 Y] Pt4 Mf4 F2 R413 E7, K5 J2 M1
   deest T6
1 LK] Pt4 Mf4 F2 R413 T6 E7, K5 M1
   LKʾ J2
1 W] Pt4 Mf4 F2 E7, K5 J2 M1
   deest R413 T6
1 mʾnslykyh] Pt4 Mf4 F2 T6, K5 J2 M1
   mʾnyklykyh R413
   mʾnslyklyh E7
2 W] Pt4 Mf4 F2 R413 T6 E7, J2
   deest K5 M1
2 ⁺hwnsnd] ܫܘܐܝܣ Pt4 E7
   ܫܘܐܝܣ Mf4
   hwnsnd F2 R413, K5 J2 M1
   hwlsnd T6
2 ⁺ḤWH-d] ܫܘܐܝܣ Pt4 Mf4 E7
   ḤWH-d F2 R413 T6
   ḤWH-ʾnd K5 J2 M1
2 MKḆLWN-ty] Pt4 Mf4 E7, K5 M1
   MKḆLWN-tym F2
   MKḆLWN-ȳt R413
   MKḆLWN-tȳd T6
   MKḆLWN-tȳʾnd J2
3 ptglʾnd] Pt4 Mf4 E7, K5 M1
   MKḆLWN-tyd F2
   MKḆLWN-tȳ R413
   MKḆLWN-ȳm T6
   MKḆLWN-ʾnd J2
3 W] Pt4 Mf4 F2 R413 E7, K5 J2 M1
   deest T6
3 ⁺hwnsndyhʾ] ܫܘܐܝܣܘܘ Pt4 Mf4 E7
   hwnsndyhʾ F2 R413 T6, K5 J2 M1
3 ḴN] Pt4 Mf4 F2 R413 E7, K5 J2 M1
   ʿLH E7
3 ⁺ʿBYDWN-ʾnd] ܫܘܐܝܫܘ Pt4 Mf4
   ʿBYDWN-tydm F2

ʿBYDWN-ty R413
ʿBYDWN-tȳd T6
ʿBYDWN-tȳʾnd K5 J2 M1
ʿBYDWN-ʾnd D
ܫܘܐܝܣ E7
4 Y] Pt4 Mf4
   deest F2 R413 T6 E7, K5 M1
   W J2
4 mnykʾn] Pt4 Mf4 E7
   mnykʾnʾ F2 R413 T6, K5 J2 M1
4 prʾc] Pt4 Mf4 R413 T6 E7, K5 M1
   prrʾc F2
   prʾc W J2
4 YḤBWN-yȳ] Pt4 Mf4 F2 R413 E7, K5 J2 M1
   deest T6
4 Y] Pt4 Mf4, K5 M1
   Y dynʾ F2 R413 T6, J2
   deest E7
4 ʾwʾ] Pt4 Mf4 F2 R413 T6, K5 M1
   ʾw E7
   W ʾwʾ J2
4 dynykʾn] Pt4 Mf4 E7
   dynykʾnʾ F2 R413 T6, K5 J2 M1
   dynʾykʾnʾ D
4 ʾp̄ʾytʾ] Pt4 Mf4 F2 E7, K5 J2
   ʾp̄ʾyt R413 T6 M1
4-5 YḤBWN-tn] Pt4 Mf4 E7, K5 J2 M1
   YḤBWN-t F2 R413
   YḤBWN-ʸt T6
6 wycdstʾ] Pt4 E7
   ܝܣܘܘܝ Mf4
   wycstʾ F2, K5 J2 M1
   deest R413 T6
6 byšʾmlwtyk] Pt4 Mf4 R413 E7
   ܝܫܘܗܣܘܝ F2, J2 M1
   deest T6
   ܝܫܘܗܣܘܝ K5
6 gwbšnʾ] Pt4 Mf4 R413 E7, K5 J2 M1
   deest F2 T6

A.8.6 PY 41.6

(a) ZK Y ⁺'LH ZK 'w' LNH YḤBWN-yȳ pt̰-c ZNH 'hw'n' pt̰-c mynwd'n   1
(b) 'YK 'ytwn' pt̰ ZK 'ytwn' QDM YḤMTWN-ym   2
(c) 'w' ḤN' Y LK srd'lyh W 'hl'dyhc hm'y 'D 'w' wsp'   3
yeṅhē hātąm ycšnykyh ⁺'yw'mlwtyk gwbšn' *humatanąm* byš'mlwtyk gwbšn' *yaθā*   4
ahū vairiiō ⁺cslwš'mlwtyk gwbšn' *ašəm vōhū* slyš'mlwtyk gwbšn' *yasnəm sūrəm*   5

1 ⁺'LH] ܫ Pt4
  ܫ ܪ̈ܝ Mf4
  'LH F2 R413 T6, J2
  deest E7
  ܐܫ K5 M1
1 ZK] Pt4 Mf4 F2 T6, K5 J2 M1
  ZK Y R413
  deest E7
1 mynwd'n] Pt4 Mf4, K5 M1
  mynwd'n' F2 R413 T6 E7, J2
2 'YK] Pt4 Mf4 R413 T6 E7, K5 M1
  ܥܝܒ ܢ F2, J2
2 'ytwn'] Pt4 Mf4 T6 E7, K5 J2 M1
  'ytwn F2 (superscr., sec.m.) R413
2 ZK] Pt4 Mf4 E7
  ZK Y F2 R413 T6, K5 J2 M1
2 'ytwn'] Pt4 Mf4 T6 E7, K5 J2 M1
  'ytwn F2 R413
3 'w'] Pt4 Mf4 F2 R413 T6 E7, K5 J2 M1
3 ḤN' Y] Pt4 Mf4, K5 M1
  ܣ F2 R413, J2
  ḤN' T6 E7
3 srd'lyh W] Pt4 Mf4 F2 R413 E7
  srd'lyh T6, K5 M1
  W srd'lyh W J2
3 'hl'dyhc] Pt4 Mf4 F2 R413 T6, K5 J2 M1
  'hl'dyh E7
3 hm'y] Pt4 Mf4 F2 E7, K5 J2 M1
  hm'k R413 T6
3 'w'] Pt4 Mf4 F2 T6 E7, K5 J2 M1
  tn' Y R413
3 wsp'] Pt4 Mf4 F2 E7, K5 J2 M1
  wsp R413 T6
4 *yeṅhē hātąm*] Pt4
  yeṅhe hātąm Mf4 F2 R413 T6 E7, K5
  yeṅhe hātąm J2 M1
4 ycšnykyh] Pt4
  ycšnykyh' Mf4 E7
  'D L'YŠH F2
  'D R413
  deest T6
  ycšnyh' K5 J2 M1

4 ⁺'yw'mlwtyk] ܐܦܠܡܘܛܝܩ Pt4 Mf4 F2 E7
  ܐܦܠܡܘܛܝܩ R413
  deest T6
  ܐܦܠܡܘܛܝܩ K5 M1
  ܐܦܠܡܘܛܝܩ J2
4 gwbšn'] Pt4 E7, K5 J2 M1
  gwbšn Mf4
  deest F2 T6
  gwbšnyh R413
4 *humatanąm*] Pt4 F2 R413 T6 E7, K5 M1
  hma humatanąm Mf4
  deest J2
4 byš'mlwtyk] Pt4 Mf4 F2 (in marg.) E7, K5
  2 b'l R413
  deest T6, J2
  byš'mwlwtyk M1
4 gwbšn'] Pt4 E7, K5 M1
  byt' Mf4
  deest F2 R413 T6, J2
5 ⁺cslwš'mlwtyk] ctlwš'mlwtyk Pt4 E7
  ܐܦܠܡܘܛܝܩ Mf4
  cyklwš'mlwtyk F2
  4 b'l R413
  deest T6
  ܐܦܠܡܘܛܝܩ K5
  cslwš'mwlwtyk J2 M1
5 gwbšn'] Pt4 Mf4 E7, K5 J2 M1
  deest F2 R413 T6
5 *vōhū*] Pt4 Mf4 F2 R413 T6 E7
  vohū K5 J2 M1
5 slyš'mlwtyk] Pt4 Mf4 F2 E7, K5
  3 R413
  deest T6
  slyš'mwlwtyk J2 M1 (-īk in Av.)
5 gwbšn'] Pt4 Mf4 F2 E7, J2 M1
  deest R413 T6, K5
5–6 *yasnəm … yazamaide*] Pt4 Mf4 F2 T6 E7, K5 J2 M1
  ašauuanəm ašahe ratūm deest R413
5 *sūrəm*] Pt4 Mf4 F2 R413 E7, K5 J2 M1
  sūirəm T6

---

4 ⁺'yw'mlwtyk: ܐܦܠܝܪܘ gloss in Pt4 (in marg.)

Appendices 363

haptaŋhāitīm ašauuanəm ašahe ratūm ẏaz. pt̰' yst' Y 'p̄z'l Y 7 h't' Y 'hlwb' Y 'hl'dyh   6
lt' YDḄḤWN-m *yeñhe hātąm* ycšnykyh' ⁺'yw'mlwtyk gwbšn' 6 wycdst' 3 g's ∴ ∴   7

6 *haptaŋhāitīm*] Pt4 Mf4 F2 R413 T6, K5 J2 M1
   haptaŋhātəm E7
6 *ašauuanəm*] Pt4 Mf4 F2 R413 T6 E7, K5 M1
   ašuuanəm J2
6 *ẏaz.*] Pt4
   ẏazamaide Mf4
   yaz. K5 (in marg., sec.m.: *yeñhe hātąm* 'D gyw'k) F2 R413 T6 E7
   deest J2
   ẏazamaide M1
6 yst' Y] Pt4 F2 T6, J2
   yšt' Y Mf4
   yst Y R413, K5 M1
   yst' E7
6 Y] Pt4 Mf4 F2 R413 T6, K5 J2 M1
   deest E7
6 7] Pt4 Mf4 E7, J2
   hp̄t F2 R413 T6, K5 M1
6 h't' Y] Pt4 Mf4 F2 R413 T6 E7, K5 J2 M1
6 Y] Pt4 Mf4 R413, K5 M1
   deest F2 T6 E7
   W J2
7 lt'] Pt4 Mf4 F2 T6 E7, K5 J2 M1
   lt R413
7 YDḄḤWN-m] Pt4 Mf4 F2 R413 T6 E7, K5 J2

ycm M1
7 *yeñhe hātąm*] Pt4 Mf4 F2 R413 T6 E7, M1
   deest K5 J2
7 ycšnykyh'] Pt4 E7
   ycšnykyh Mf4
   deest F2, K5 J2
   'D ycšnyh' R413
   ycšn' pt̰' h't'n LʿYŠH T6 (in marg.)
   ycšnyh' M1
7 ⁺'yw'mlwtyk gwbšn'] ܝܘܡܠܘܬܝܟ ܓܘܒܫܢ Pt4 F2
   'yw'mlwtyk gwbšn' Mf4
   ܝܘܡܠܘܬܝܟ ܓܘܒܫܢ R413
   deest T6, K5 J2
   ܝܘܡܠܘܬܝܟ ܓܘܒܫܢ E7
   ܝܘܡܠܘܬܝܟ ܓܘܒܫܢ M1
7 6 ... g's] Pt4 Mf4 F2 R413 T6 E7
   deest K5 J2 M1
7 wycdst'] Pt4 Mf4
   wycst' F2
   ܘܝܨܕܣܬ R413
   wycst T6
   wycdst' Y E7
7 g's] Pt4 Mf4 F2 R413 T6
   ܓܣ E7

B. Y 9.1

B.1 MIΘRŌ ZIIĀT̰ ZARAΘUŠTRƎM

The above clause is only attested in some of the *Avesta* manuscripts as part of (P)Y 9.1c.[1] As I point out in Section 3.3, I do not consider *miϑrō ziiāt̰ zaraϑuštrǝm* a fragment from a lost Av. text, but a newly composed Avestan sentence.

Spiegel (1861: 52) includes '*mithrô zayât̰ zarathustrem*' in his Sanskrit text, but is unable to translate it. Agreeing with Burnouf, Spiegel considers the possibility of this fragment being a quotation from an unknown Av. text, perhaps its beginning words. Observing that the clause does not occur in the Pahlavi section, Spiegel goes on to suggest that it corresponds to '*miϑrō upāit zarduš*t'.[2] Bartholomae (1904: 1659) prefers *zayāt̰* as well, suggesting it could be a preterite derived from *zan* 'to know'. To support this translation, he adduces a phrase from the *Zand*, *paydāg kū-š šnāxt*, proposing that it translates *zayāt̰*. Like Spiegel, Bartholomae seems to equate Av. *miϑrō ziiāt̰ zaraϑuštrǝm* with *miϑrō upāit zarduš*t, as it is the latter which is followed in the *Zand* by *paydāg kū-š šnāxt*. Based on Geldner's (1886–96: 39) apparatus, Kellens (2007: 46) translates *miϑrō.ziiāt̰ zaraϑuštrǝm* as 'Zaraθuštra loin de celui qui frustre Miθra'. Discussing Kellens's translation, Skjærvø (2009c: 706) too assumes a correspondence between the two clauses, stating that 'In the oldest manuscripts, however, the fragment is written in Pahlavi [*miϑrō upāit zarduš*t] and is part of the Pahlavi commentary, while the Avestan version [*miϑrō ziiāt̰ zaraϑuštrǝm*] is found in later manuscripts.'[3]

---

[1] For the distribution of the clause in the MSS, see Section B.1.1 and Figure B.1 for same examples.

[2] According to the custom of the time, Spiegel uses the Hebrew alphabet for the transliteration of Pahlavi. I have normalised his transliteration above.

[3] I have added the original text in brackets for clarity.

No doubt, *miϑrō upāit zardušt* is part of the *Zand* of Y 9.1c and is attested in all manuscripts. As Skjærvø (2009c: 706) correctly observes, in almost all manuscripts it is written as ⟨mtlwk hwp 'YT' zltwšt'⟩. A transcription as *mihr xūb ast zardušt* is tempting. The common spelling for *mihr*, however, is ⟨mtr'⟩, and the actual and contextual meaning of *mihr xūb ast zardušt* is unclear. An Avesticised form such as *mihrō* in line with Pahlavi spelling conventions is unlikely. Skjærvø's suggested reading as *miϑrō upāit zardušt* fits the context of the section best. I, however, fail to see how *upāit* corresponds to *ziiāt̰*. In my view, these two clauses constitute two different constructions that play a crucial role in the narrative of the meeting between Zardušt and *Hōm* (see Section 3.3). It is unclear why the exegetes chose the deity *Miϑra* in Y 9.1c to explain why Zaraϑuštra had to ask who was approaching him. However, as a meeting between Zaraϑuštra and *Miϑra* is not attested in the scripture, the exegetes had to contextualise *miϑrō upāit zardušt* 'Miϑra approached Zardušt'. To do so, they add that the deity, *Miϑra*, knew Zaraϑuštra (*miϑrō ziiāt̰ zaraϑuštrəm*).

This clause seems to be a later addition, generally appearing in the more recent manuscripts, particularly in the family of the Indian MSS. As the overview below illustrates, it made its way into older manuscripts in form of a marginal note (Pt4), and in some cases its position within the Pahlavi commentaries was not fixed (F2 R413 T6). The trilingual Sanskrit Yasna KM7 is the only manuscript that has a MP comment on *miϑrō ziiāt̰ zaraϑuštrəm* as *ēdōn paydāg kē ān tō be šnāxtēm kē tō zardušt hē* 'It is thus evident, that I recognised who you are, you who are Zardušt.'[4] Furthermore, in this MS, *ziiāt̰* is provided with a subscript gloss in NP ڪڔ 'recognised.'[5]

B.1.1 Distribution

The following overview highlights the distribution and attestation of this clause in the manuscripts accessible to me at the time of writing (March 2013). According to Geldner (1886–96: 39), *miϑrō ziiāt̰ zaraϑuštrəm* also appears in the manuscripts J3 J5 J6 J7, L3 L13 K11 and P6 to which I did not have access.

B.1.1.1 IrPY

In Pt4, *miϑrō ziiāt̰ zaraϑuštrəm* is written by a second hand in the margin. It is missing in Mf4 E7, but occurs in the revised IrPY F2 R413 T6.[6] F2 R413

---

[4] KM7 is a curious manuscript with a currently unknown history.
[5] The comments support the translation of *ziiāt̰* as 'knew', which is intended to reflect the exegetes' view of this word. The fact that KM7 treats *miϑrō ziiāt̰ zaraϑuštrəm* as an Avestan section in its own right and provides it with a Pahlavi and NP translation could indicate that this is a more recent MS.
[6] On these revised MSS, see Section 1.4.2.

append it to the end of the Av. section Y 9.1c, placing it before the start of Pahlavi Y 9.1c. By contrast, T6 positions it at the end of the Pahlavi Y 9.1c, putting it immediately before Y 9.1d.

B.1.1.2 InPY

Not cited in K5 J2 M1 T55b.

B.1.1.3 SktY

Occurs in S1 K6 T55a KM7. Like T6, the trilingual KM7 sets it at the end of the Pahlavi section PY 9.1c, treating *miϑrō ziiāt̰ zaraϑuštrəm* as an Av. clause in its own right, adding comments in MP, Sanskrit and NP.

B.1.1.4 IrYS

Missing in F3a ML15284.

B.1.1.5 InYS

Cited in B3 (in marg., sec.m.) L17 (in marg., sec.m.) Bh5 G97. Missing in Lb2 G26b (marks set, text missing).

B.1.1.6 IrWdS

Missing in Ave976 Ave977/978 Ave991 Ave1001 ML15283 ML16226 4055 RSPA230 YL1.

B.1.1.7 InWdS

Cited in G106 G112 B4 ML630 FIRES1. Missing in L1 B2 M2 T46 O2.

B.1.1.8 IrWrS

Missing in G18b G27 2101 2102 MZK2.

B.1.1.9 InWrS

Missing in K8.

Appendices

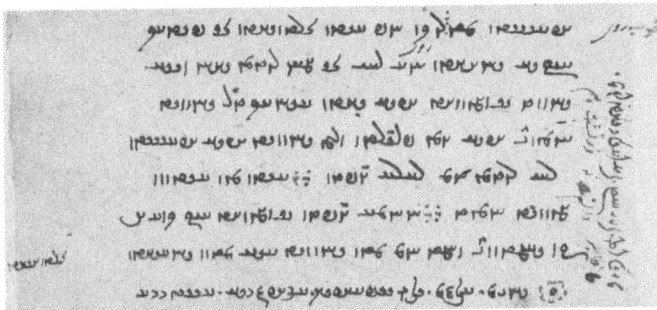

(a) Pt4

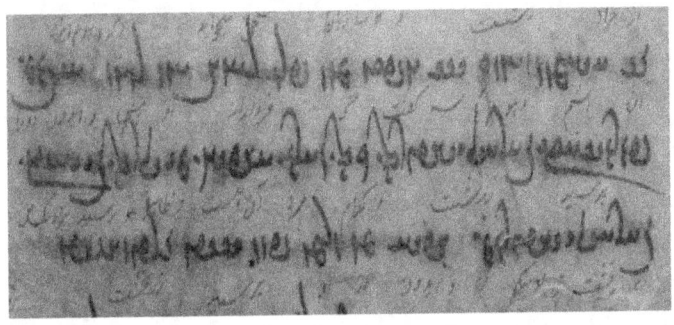

(b) F2

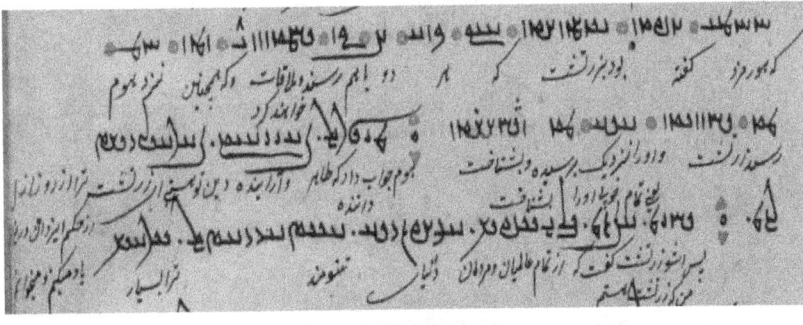

(c) T6

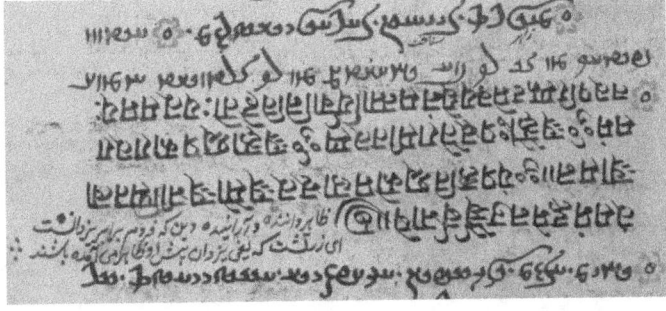

(d) KM7

Figure B.1 Y 9.1c

C. *Fire in the Older Avesta*

Y 31.3[1] *yąm dā mainiiū āθrācā ašācā cōiš rānōibiiā xšnūtəm
hiiat̰ uruuatəm ⁺cazdōŋhuuadəbiiō tat̰ nō mazdā vīduuanōi vaocā
hizuuā θβahiiā åŋhō yā juuantō vīspə̄ṇg vāuraiiā*

The satisfaction which you created with (your) spirit and assigned to both parties by means of the fire and *aša*;
that agreement which is for (your) followers. For us to know that, speak, O Wise one,
with the tongue of your mouth, by which I might retain all the living.

Y 31.19 *guštā yō mantā ašəm ⁺ahūm.biš vīduuå ahurā
ərəžuxδāi vacaŋhąm xšaiiamnō hizuuō vasō
θβā āθrā suxrā mazdā vaŋhāu vīdātā rąnaiiå*

The healer of the existence, the knowledgeable one who conceives *aša*, has listened, O Lord,
he who at will has command over (his) tongue for the straight utterance of words
at (the time of) the good distribution to both parties by means of your red fire, O Wise one.

Y 34.4 *at̰ tōi ātrəm ahurā aojōŋhuuaṇtəm ašā usəmahī
asīštīm əmauuaṇtəm stōi rapaṇtē ciθrā.auuaŋhəm
at̰ mazdā daibišiiaṇtē zastāištāiš dərəštā.aēnaŋhəm*

Thus, O Lord, we wish your strong fire, the swiftest (and) most powerful, to be a brilliant support to the supporting one in accordance with *aša*,
but, O Wise One, a visible harm to the hostile one by means of its hands.

---

[1] All text after Humbach (1991), translations are mine.

Y 43.4 *at̰ θβā mə̄nghāi   taxməmcā spəṇtəm mazdā*
hiiat̰ tā zastā   yā tū hafšī auuå
yå då ašīš   drəguuāitē ašāunaēcā
θβahiiā garəmā   āθrō ašā.aojaŋhō
hiiat̰ mōi vaŋhə̄uš   hazə̄ jimat̰ manaŋhō

Then, I shall realise that you are brave and bounteous, O Wise one,
because you sustain support by that hand by which
you hold the rewards which are for the truthful ones and the deceitful ones,
by the heat of your fire, strong through *aša*,
when the force of good thought shall come to me.

Y 43.9 *spəṇtəm at̰ θβā   mazdā ⁺mə̄nghī ahurā*
hiiat̰ mā vohū   pairī.jasat̰ manaŋhā
ahiiā fərasə̄m   kahmāi vīuuīduiiē vašī
at̰ ā θβahmāi   āθrē rātąm nəmaŋhō
ašahiiā mā   yauuat̰ isāi maniiāi

Then, I realise that you are bounteous, O Wise Lord,
when he approached me with good thought.
To that question, 'For whom do you wish to know', (I then reply:)
'For your fire. I will consider as much as I may be able the gift of reverence for *aša*.'

Y 46.7 *⁺kə̄mnā mazdā   mauuaitē pāiiūm ⁺dadå*
hiiat̰ mā drəguuå   dīdarəšatā ⁺aēnaŋhē
aniiə̄m θβahmāt̰   āθrascā manaŋhascā
yaiiå šiiaoθanāiš   ašəm θraoštā ahurā
tąm mōi dąstuuąm   daēnaiiāi frāuuaocā

Whom, O Wise One, have you appointed as a protector for one like me,
when the deceitful one looks to harm me?
(Whom), O Lord, other than your fire and thought,
through whose actions one nourishes *aša*?
Proclaim that message to my religious view.

Y 47.6 *tā då spəṇtā   mainiiū mazdā ahurā*
āθrā vaŋhāu   vīdāitīm rānōibiiā
ārmatōiš   dəbązaŋhā ašax́iiācā
hā zī pourūš   išəṇtō vāurāitē

By means of that bounteous spirit, O Wise Lord, (and) the fire you shall give the distribution at the good to both parties
in accordance with the solidity of right-mindedness and *aša*.
For, that shall retain the many who approach.

Y 51.9 *yąm xšnūtəm rānōibiiā dā̊   ə̄βā ā̆θrā suxrā mazdā*
aiiaŋhā xšustā aibī   ahuuāhū daxštəm dāuuōi
rāšaiieṅhē drəguuaṇtəm   sauuaiiō ašauuanəm

Which satisfaction you shall give to both parties by means of your glowing fire, O Wise One!

With the molten metal, a sign shall be given among the beings,
to cause harm to the deceitful ones (and) to revitalise the orderly ones.

D. *iϑā*

Herb 16.3 *hād ka-š yašt pad wināhgārīh nē kard estēd ud ka-z harw bār-ē iϑā āat̰ ẏazamaide ud ašəm vohū ē gōwēd rāy <nē> tuwān guftan ud nē gōwēd ā-z-iš drāyān-jōyišnīh kunišn ka harw 2 ēk-ē tuwān guftan iϑā āat̰ ẏazamaide gōwēd ayāb ašəm vohū gōwēd ka-š ašəm-*ē tuwān būd guftan ud nē gōwēd ēdōn wināhgār bawēd ciyōn ka-š hamāg tuwān būd guftan u-š ēk-iz nē guft* (Kotwal and Kreyenbroek 1992: 74)

Yes. If he has failed to perform the ritual in sin, and also each time when he might say the *iϑā āat̰ ẏazamaide* and *ašəm vohū*, (but) is unable to say it and does not say it, then, too, he is to be made guilty of chattering while eating. (And) when he is able to say one of the two, he can say the *iϑā āat̰ ẏazamaide* or the *ašəm vohū*. If he could have said one *ašəm vohū* and he does not say it, he is thus sinful, as he could have recited the whole (prayer), and did not say even one.

N 10.49 *ka-z-iš ranjagīhā ēn and az pāy gōwišn bīšāmrūd ud srīšāmrūd, ud šnūman wizārišnīh ud wāz-gīrišnīh ud iϑā āat̰ ẏazamaidē kardag-ē*

Even if it is troublesome, one should recite the following standing up: the passages to be recited twice, those to be recited three times, the recitation of the *šnūman(s)*, the taking of the *bāj*, and a section of *iϑā āat̰ ẏazamaidē*. (Kotwal and Kreyenbroek 1995: 74–7)

N 10.50 *pad iϑā harw tis-ē pad xwarišn mehmān be nigērišn pas ka nihuft estēd ā-š weh*

[A]t *iϑā* he should gaze at all the things which are amenable to consumption; afterwards it is better if they are covered. (Kotwal and Kreyenbroek 1995: 76–7)

N 10.56 *ēn 3 ud 4* ašəm vohū **anēraxt cāšt estēd zōt ka iϑā* ašəm vohū *gōwēd ā (*nē) šāyēd ka* ašəm *iϑā gōwēd ā nē šāyēd rāspīgān pēš ud pas*

These three and four *a.v.* are taught without dissension. If the *zōt* recites *iϑā* (followed by) *a.v.* it is not (?) permissible. If he recites *a.v.* (followed) by *iϑā* it is not permissible, (for) the *rāspīs'* (recitation becomes) mixed up. (Kotwal and Kreyenbroek 1995: 78–81)

PRDd 57 *zand ī iϑā āat̲[1] yazamaide ēdar ēdōn yazēm ohrmazd kē-š gōspand ud ahlāyīh-iz dād u-š āb-iz dād ud urwar-iz ī weh u-š rōšnīh-iz dād ud būm-iz ud harwisp ābādīh ahlāyīh ābādīh ī pahlom ast kū *hambār ēn weh kār ud kirbag ī pad frārōnīh nēk ast ēn kār ud kirbag nēk ōy kē az ān ōy nēkīh kadār-iz-ēw kū kadār-iz-ēw az nēkīh ī ōy nēkīh zand ī iϑā ud ašǝm vohū*

The explanation of *iϑā āat̲ yazamaide*: 'Here thus (*iϑā ēdōn*) we worship Ohrmazd who created beneficent animals, and also righteousness, and he created also water, and also good plants, and he created also light, and also earth, and all prosperity'. 'Righteousness is the best prosperity', *i.e.* this *store (is) good, good deeds (performed) with honesty; 'it is good', these good deeds, 'good is he from whom goodness comes to someone', *i.e.* goodness comes to someone from his goodness. The explanation of *iϑā* and *ašǝm vohū*. (Williams 1990: I 200–1)

ŠnŠ 3.35 *ka yašt kard ēstēd har bār-ēw drōn yašt pad šnūman ī ⟨srōš⟩ ul gōwišn ast kē iϑā ašǝm vohū gōwēd* (Tavadia 1930: 83)[2]

When worship is performed, each time the *drōn yašt* is to be spoken loudly at the dedication to *Srōš*. There is one who says *iϑā ašǝm vohū*.

ŠnŠ 5.2 *ud az hašt sālag tā pānzdah sālag mard ud zan agar-iz pad yašt kardan a-wināh bē-š iϑā u ašǝm vohū tuwān guftan ud nē gōwēd ā-š drāyān-jōyišnīh ōh bun ud ka-š yašt narm tuwān kardan ud iϑā ašǝm vohū gōwēd būd kē guft kū ēdōn bawēd čiyōn ka-š yašt nē kard ēstēd ud gstwplyt nē bawēd ud būd kē guft kū drāyān-jōyišnīh nē bawēd* (Tavadia 1930: 91–2)

And from eight year old to fifteen year old, man and woman, even if they are innocent at the (time of) worship, but can say *iϑā u ašǝm vohū* and they do not say it, then the sin of chattering while eating is thus on their account. And when he or she can perform the worship by heart and says *iϑā ašǝm vohū*, there was one who said, that in this way (it) is like when he or she did not perform a worship and (that it) is not ⟨gstwplyt⟩; and there was one who said, that (it) is not the sin of chattering while eating.

ŠnŠ 5.7 *karr ud gung ka-š ašem-ēw nē tuwān guftan ā-š drāyān-jōyišnīh nē kunēd ud ka-š ašǝm-ēw tuwān guft ā-š ašǝm ašǝm ašǝm sē bār bē gōwēd ud agar-iš iϑā ud ašemwohū tuwān guftan xūb ud ka-š iϑā tanīhā tuwān guftan ā-š kār nēst* (Tavadia 1930: 95)

When the deaf and dumb cannot say an *ašem* (prayer), then they do not commit the sin of chattering while eating. And if they can say an *ašǝm*, (and) then they say three times *ašǝm ašǝm ašǝm* and if they can say *iϑā* and *ašemwohū*, (that) is good. And if they can only say *iϑā*, then (that) is not valid.

Suppl.ŠnŠ 13.18 *iϑā āat̲ yazamaide 5 wačadast stāyišn ud spās az ōhrmazd pad dādan ī weh dahišnān* (Kotwal 1969: 7)

---

[1] Williams (1990: I 200) prefers *āat̲*, while four out of six MSS consulted by him read *āt̲* (see Williams 1990: I 267). Most likely, MS IO does not contain this passage (see Williams 1990: I 21), in which case MR would be the only MS to read *āat̲*.

[2] I have modernised the transcription of Tavadia's (1930) text. Translations are mine.

The *iϑā āaṯ yazamaide* has five strophes, (offering) praise and gratitude to *Ohrmazd* on account of creating the good creations.

Suppl.ŠnŠ 13.20 *iϑā 5 wačadast čeōn āniz ī pēš* (Kotwal 1969: 46–7)

iϑā has five strophes, like that one which was before.

Suppl.ŠnŠ 13.42 *ud ēwag hāt ī gāh-ē 4 gāh ē wačadast be iϑā ī haiϑyā narō čē x^vadāy ud dahibed hamē andar gēhān ēwag*

And (it is a) *Gāϑā* of one section, (having) 4 lines to each verse except *iϑā ī haiϑyā narō*, because there is always (only) one lord and sovereign in the world. (Kotwal 1969: 51)

Suppl.ŠnŠ 13.51 ... *be iϑā ī čē ān ēwag 5 *gāh wahištōīšt 9 wačadast harw wačadast-ē 4 gāh hammis pad 278 wačadast*

... *Vahištōīštī*, 9 verses, each verse (having) 4 lines, except *iϑā ī*, since that one (has) 5 lines – altogether 278 verses. (Kotwal 1969: 55)

PWd 16.7 *u-šān drōn pad šnūman srōš ul gōwišn ast ī kē iϑā ašǝm gōwēd* (L4:232r)

And the *drōn* is to be spoken loudly by them at the dedication to *Srōš*. There is one who says *iϑā ašǝm*.

ZWY 5.3 *kē andar ān ī škoft āwām /iϑā āṯ yazamaidē u ašǝm vohū/ bē gōwēd <ud> warm kard ēstēd ēdōn čiyōn andar xwadāyīh ī wištāsp šāh dwāzdah-hōmāst-ēw ī pad zōhr <yašt kard>*

He who, in those hard times, will say *iϑā āṯ yazamaidē* and *ašǝm wohū* <and> will have learned them by heart <will gain merit> as if during the rule of king *Wištāsp* <he had celebrated> a *dwāzdah-hōmāst* complete of offerings. (Cereti 1995: 140, 158–9)

E. *MSS Concordance*

	Mf4	R413	E7	K5
Y 5	104	106	132	41r
Y 35	407	519	127	175v
Y 36	412	526	137	179r
Y 37	415	532	142	180v
Y 38	417	532	142	182r
Y 39	420	537	148	183v
Y 40	423	541	153	185v
Y 41	425	545	156	186v
Y 42	428	550	162	188v

Bibliography

Alram, Michael, Maryse Blet-Lemarquand and Prods Oktor Skjærvø. 2007. Shapur, king of kings of Iranians and Non-Iranians. In Rika Gyselen (ed.), *Des Indo-Grecs aux Sassanides: Données pour l'histoire et la géographie historique* (Res Orientales XVII), 11–39. Bures-sur-Yvette: Groupe pour l'Étude de la Civilisation du Moyen-Orient.

Amouzgar, Jaleh and Ahmad Tafazzoli (eds). 2000. *Le cinquième livre du Dēnkard* (Studia Iranica 23). Paris: Association pour l'avancement des études Iraniennes.

Andreas, Friedrich Carl. 1904. Die Entstehung des Awesta-Alphabets und sein ursprünglicher Lautwert. In *Verhandlungen des XIII. internationalen Orientalisten-Kongresses. Hamburg September 1902*, 99–106. Leiden: E. J. Brill.

Andrés-Toledo, Miguel Ángel. 2009. *Vīdēvdād 10–12. Critical edition, translation and commentary of the Avestan and Pahlavi texts*: Universidad de Salamanca, dissertation.

Andrés-Toledo, Miguel Ángel (ed.). 2010. *The Avestan manuscript T6 (Pahlavi Yasna) of the First Dastur Meherji-rana Library in Navsarī* (Avestan Digital Archive Series 26).

Anklesaria, Behramgore Tehmurasp (ed.). 1918. *The Dastur Hoshang memorial volume*. Bombay: The Gatha Society.

Anklesaria, Behramgore Tehmurasp. 1964. *Vichitakiha-i Zatsparam: With text and translation. Part I*. Bombay: The Trustees of the Parsee Punchayet Funds and Properties.

Anklesaria, Ervad Tehmuras Dinshaw (ed.). 1913. *Dânâk-u Mainyô-i Khard: Pahlavi, Pazand and Sanskrit Texts*. Bombay: Fort Printing Press.

Anquetil-Duperron, Abraham Hyacinthe. 1771. *Zend-Avesta*. Paris: N.M. Tilliard.

Apple, James. 2009. *Stairway to Nirvāṇa: A study of the Twenty Saṃghas based on the works of Tsong Kha Pa*. Albany: State University of New York Press.

Asli, Behram. 1918. A glance at the Pahlavi Commentaries. In Anklesaria (1918), 111–15.

Azargushasb, Ardashir. 1971. *Atish Dar Iran-i Bastan*. Tehran: Chap-i Arya.

Bailey, Harold. 1943. *Zoroastrian problems in the ninth-century books*. Oxford: Clarendon Press.

Bakhos, Carol and Rahim Shayegan (eds). 2010. *The Talmud in its Iranian context* (Texts and Studies in Ancient Judaism 135). Tübingen: Mohr Siebeck.

Bang, Wilhelm. 1890. Ein Beitrag zur Würdigung der Pahlavi-Gāthās. *Zeitschrift der Deutschen Morgenländischen Gesellschaft* 44. 363–70.

Barr, Kaj. 1936. Remarks on the Pahlavi ligatures ൧ and ൨. *Bulletin of the School of Oriental Studies* 8(2/3). 391–403.

Bartholomae, Christian. 1904. *Altiranisches Wörterbuch*. Straßburg: Karl J. Trübner.

Bartholomae, Christian. 1905. *Die Gatha's des Awesta: Zarathushtra's Verspredigten*. Straßburg: Karl J. Trübner.

Bartholomae, Christian. 1906. *Zum altiranischen Wörterbuch*. Straßburg: Karl J. Trübner.

Bartholomae, Christian. 1917. *Zur Kenntnis der mitteliranischen Mundarten*. Heidelberg: Carl Winters Universitätsbuchhandlung.

Baunack, Theodor. 1888. Der Yasna haptaṅhāiti. In *Studien auf dem Gebiete der griechischen und der arischen Sprachen*, Erster Band, zweiter Teil, 327–461. Leipzig: Verlag von S. Hirzel.

Benveniste, Emile. 1970. Le terme iranien *mazdayasna*. *Bulletin of the School of Oriental and African Studies* 33(1). 5–9.

Bharucha, Ervad Sheriarji Dadabhai. 1906. *Collected Sanskrit writings of the Parsis: Old translations of Avestâ and Pahlavi-Pâzend books as well as other original compositions, with various readings and notes*, vol. I. Bombay: Trustees of the Parsee Punchayet Funds and Properties.

Bharucha, Ervad Sheriarji Dadabhai. 1910. *Collected Sanskrit writings of the Parsis: Old translations of Avestâ and Pahlavi-Pâzend books as well as other original compositions, with various readings and notes*, vol. II. Bombay: Trustees of the Parsee Punchayet Funds and Properties.

Blois, François de. 1990. The Middle-Persian inscription from Constantinople: Sasanian or Post-Sasanian? *Studia Iranica* 19. 209–18.

Bowker, John (ed.). 1997. *The Oxford dictionary of world religions*. Oxford: Oxford University Press.

Boyce, Mary. 1964. The use of relative particles in Western Middle Iranian. In *Indo-Iranica. Mélanges présentés à Georg Morgenstierne*, 28–47. Wiesbaden: Otto Harrassowitz.

Boyce, Mary. 1966. Ātaš-zōhr and Āb-zōhr. *Journal of the Royal Asiatic Society of Great Britain and Ireland* (3/4). 100–18.

Boyce, Mary. 1968a. Middle Persian literature. In Bertold Spuler (ed.), *Handbuch der Orientalistik. Literatur*, Abt. 1, Bd. 4, Abschn. 2, Lfg. 1, 32–66. Leiden: E. J. Brill.

Boyce, Mary. 1968b. On the sacred fires of the Zoroastrians. *Bulletin of the School of Oriental and African Studies, University of London* 31(1). 52–68.

Boyce, Mary. 1975. On the Zoroastrian temple cult of fire. *Journal of the American Oriental Society* 95(3). 454–65.

Boyce, Mary. 1977. *A Persian stronghold of Zoroastrianism* (Persian Studies Series 12). Oxford: Clarendon Press.

Boyce, Mary. 1986. Ardwahišt. In *Encyclopædia Iranica*, vol. II, fasc. 4, 389–90. New York: Columbia University.

Boyce, Mary. 1987. Ātaš. In *Encyclopædia Iranica*, vol. III, fasc. 1, 1–5. New York: Columbia University.

Boyce, Mary (ed.). 1990. *Textual sources for the study of Zoroastrianism*. Chicago: University of Chicago Press.

Boyce, Mary. 1992. *Zoroastrianism: Its antiquity and constant vigour*, Columbia Lectures on Iranian Studies. Costa Mesa: Mazda Publishers/Bibliotheca Persica.

Boyce, Mary. 1996. *A history of Zoroastrianism. The early period*, Handbuch der Orientalistik. Leiden: E. J. Brill.

Boyce, Mary. 1997a. The origins of Zoroastrian philosophy. In Carr and Mahalingam (1997), 4–20.

Boyce, Mary. 1997b. Zoroastrianism. In John R Hinnells (ed.), *A new handbook of living religions*, 236–61. Oxford: Blackwell.

Boyce, Mary. 2001. *Zoroastrians. Their religious beliefs and practices*, The Library of Religion Beliefs and Practices. London: Routledge.

Boyce, Mary. 2003. Haoma ii. The rituals. In *Encyclopædia Iranica*, vol. XI, 662–7. New York: Columbia University.

Boyce, Mary and Firoze Kotwal. 1971a. Zoroastrian "bāj" and "drōn"–I. *Bulletin of the School of Oriental and African Studies* 34(1). 56–73.

Boyce, Mary and Firoze Kotwal. 1971b. Zoroastrian "bāj" and "drōn"–II. *Bulletin of the School of Oriental and African Studies* 34(2). 298–313.

Brockhaus, Hermann. 1850. *Vendidad Sade. Die heiligen Schriften Zoroaster's: Yaçna, Vispered und Vendidad*. Leipzig: F. A. Brockhaus.

Bronkhorst, Johannes. 2008. Is there correlative thought in Indian philosophy? *Journal Asiatique* 296(1). 9–22.

Bronkhorst, Johannes. 2011. The invisible interpreter. *Asiatische Studien / Études Asiatiques* LXV(1). 35–43.

Brown, Peter. 1971. *The world of late antiquity*. London: Thames & Hudson.

Buyaner, David. 2014. On a Pahlavi metonymic figure and its Indo-European roots. *Estudios Iranios y Turanios* 1. 7–24.

Buyaner, David. 2016. *Penitential sections of the Xorde Avesta (patits). Philological edition with commentary and glossary* (Iranica 22). Wiesbaden: Harrassowitz Verlag.

Cabezón, José Ignacio. 1994. *Buddhism and language. A study of Indo-Tibetan scholasticism*. Albany: State University of New York Press.

Cabezón, José Ignacio (ed.). 1998. *Scholasticism: Cross-cultural and comparative perspectives*. Albany: State University of New York Press.

Callieri, Pierfrancesco. 2006. Water in the art and architecture of the Sasanians. In Antonio Panaino and Andrea Piras (eds), *Proceedings of the 5th Conference of the Societas Iranologica Europæa, held in Ravenna, 6–11 October 2003*, vol. I, 339–49. Milano: Mimesis.

Canepa, Matthew. 2009. *The two eyes of the earth: Art and ritual of kingship between Rome and Sasanian Iran* (The Transformation of the Classical Heritage 45). Berkeley: University of California Press.

Cantera, Alberto. 1998. *Estudios sobre la traducción Páhlavi del Avesta: Las versiones Avéstica y Páhlavi de los cuatro primeros capítulos de Videvdad*. Salamanca: Universidad de Salamanca, dissertation.

Cantera, Alberto. 1999a. Die Stellung der Sprache der Pahlavi-Übersetzung des Avesta innerhalb des Mittelpersischen. *Studia Iranica* 28(2). 173–204.

Cantera, Alberto. 1999b. Review of J. Josephson: *The Pahlavi translation technique as illustrated by Hōm Yašt*. Bulletin of the School of Oriental and African Studies 62(2). 364–6.

Cantera, Alberto. 2004. *Studien zur Pahlavi-Übersetzung des Avesta* (Iranica 7). Wiesbaden: Harrassowitz Verlag.

Cantera, Alberto. 2006. Die Pahlavi-Übersetzung altavestischer Texte in der Pahlavi-Übersetzung des Vīdēvdād. *Studia Iranica* 35(1). 35–68.

Cantera, Alberto. 2011. Breve tipología e historia de los manuscritos avésticos de la liturgia larga. *Aula Orientalis* 29. 199–243.

Cantera, Alberto. 2012. How many chapters does the "Yasna of the Seven Chapters" have? *Iranian Studies* 45(2). 217–27.

Cantera, Alberto. 2013. Talking with god: The Zoroastrian *ham.parsti* or intercalation ceremonies. *Journal Asiatique* 301(1). 85–138.

Cantera, Alberto. 2014a. Repetitions of the Ahuna Vairiia and animal sacrifice in the Zoroastrian long liturgy. *Estudios Iranios y Turanios* 1. 25–9.

Cantera, Alberto. 2014b. *Vers une édition de la liturgie longue zoroastrienne: Pensées et travaux préliminaires* (Studia Iranica Cahier 51). Paris: Association pour l'Avancement des Études Iraniennes.

Cantera, Alberto. 2015. The usage of the Frauuarāne in Zoroastrian rituals. *Estudios Iranios y Turanios* 2. 71–97.

Cantera, Alberto. 2016a. A substantial change in the approach to the Zoroastrian long liturgy. About J. Kellens's Études avestiques et mazdéennes. *Indo-Iranian Journal* 59. 139–85.

Cantera, Alberto. 2016b. Visparad Sāde. Arranged by A. Cantera mainly on the basis of the manuscript G18b. Date: 14/01/2016. Online publication: http://ada.usal.es/img/pdf/visperad.pdf. Accessed September 2017.

Cantera, Alberto and Miguel Ángel Andrés Toledo. 2008. The transmission of the Pahlavi Vīdēvdād in India after 1700 (I): Jamasp's visit from Iran and the rise of a new exegetical movement in Surat. *Journal of the Cama Oriental Institute* 68. 81–142.

Cantera, Alberto and Michiel de Vaan. 2005. Remarks on the colophon of the Avestan manuscripts Pt4 and Mf4. *Studia Iranica* 34(1). 31–42.

Carr, Brian and Indira Mahalingam (eds). 1997. *Companion encyclopedia of Asian philosophy*. London: Routledge.

Carr, David McLain. 2005. *Writing on the tablet of the heart: Origins of scripture and literature*. Oxford: Oxford University Press.

Cereti, Carlo. 1995. *The Zand ī Wahman Yasn. A Zoroastrian apocalypse* (Serie Orientale Roma LXXV). Rome: Istituto Italiano per il Medio ed Estremo Oriente.

Cereti, Carlo. 1998. Review of J. Josephson: *The Pahlavi translation technique as illustrated by Hōm Yašt*. Die Sprache 38. 219–23.

Cereti, Carlo and Farrokh Vajifdar (eds). 2003. *Ātaš-e dorun, the fire within* (Jamshid Soroush Soroushian Memorial Volume 2). United States: 1st Books Library.

Cheung, Johnny. 2007. *Etymological dictionary of the Iranian verb* (Leiden Indo-European Etymological Dictionary Series 2). Leiden: Brill.

Cheung, Johnny. 2009. Two notes on Bactrian. In Sundermann, et al. (2009), 51–58.

Choksy, Jamsheed. 1995. Drōn. In *Encyclopædia Iranica*, vol. VII, fasc. 5, Columbia University.

Circassia, Sarah and Mohammad Kangarani (eds). 2011. *The Avestan manuscript F2_415 (Iranian Pahlavi Yasna) of the First Dastur Meherji-rana Library of Navsarī* (Avestan Digital Archive Series 36).

Clooney, Francis Xavier. 1998. Scholasticism in encounter: Working through a Hindu example. In Cabezón (1998), 177–99.

Crosby, Kate. 2005. What does not get translated in Buddhist studies and the impact on teaching. In L. Long (ed.), *Translation and religion. Holy untranslatable?*, 41–53. Clevedon: Multilingual Matters Ltd.

Darmesteter, James. 1884. *The Zend-Avesta. Part II: The Sīrōzahs, Yasts and Nyāyis* (Sacred Books of the East XXIII). Oxford: Clarendon Press.

Darrow, William. 1988. Keeping the waters dry: The semiotics of fire and water in the Zoroastrian "Yasna". *Journal of the American Academy of Religion* 56(3). 417–42.

Daryaee, Touraj. 2008. *Sasanian Iran (224–651 CE): Portrait of a late antique empire*. Costa Mesa: Mazda Publishers.

Degener, Almuth. 1991. Neryosanghs Sanskrit-Übersetzung von Škand Gumānīk Vičār. In Emmerick and Weber (1991), 49–58.

Degener, Almuth. 2000. Review of J. Josephson: *The Pahlavi translation technique as illustrated by Hōm Yašt*. *Indo-Iranian Journal* 43(4). 403–6.

Dehghan, Keyvan. 1982. *Der Awesta-Text Srōš Yašt (Yasna 57). Mit Pahlavi- und Sanskritübersetzung* (Münchener Studien zur Sprachwissenschaft: Neue Folge 11). München: R. Kitzinger.

Desai, H. J. M. and H. N. Modi (eds). 1996. *K. R. Cama Oriental Institute, second international congress proceedings (5th to 8th January 1995)*. Bombay: K. R. Cama Oriental Institute.

Dhabhar, Bamanji Nusservanji. 1923. *Descriptive catalogue of all manuscripts in the First Dastur Meherji Rana Library, Navsari*. Bombay: Commercial Printing Press of the Tata Publicity Corporation.

Dhabhar, Bamanji Nusservanji. 1927. *Zand-i Khūrtak Avistāk* (Pahlavi Text Series 6). Bombay: Trustees of the Parsi Punchayet.

Dhabhar, Bamanji Nusservanji. 1949. *Pahlavi Yasna and Visperad. Edited with an introduction and a glossary of select terms* (Pahlavi Text Series 8). Bombay: Trustees of the Parsi Punchayet.

Dhabhar, Bamanji Nusservanji. 1963. *Translation of Zand-i Khūrtak Avistāk*. Bombay: The K. R. Cama Oriental Institute.

Dhalla, Maneckji Nusservanji. 1908. *The Nyaishes or Zoroastrian litanies: Avestan text with the Pahlavi, Sanskrit, Persian and Gujarati versions*. New York: Columbia University Press.

Dhalla, Maneckji Nusservanji. 1918. The Pahlavi text of the Ohrmazd Yasht. Edited from fifteen ancient MSS. In Anklesaria (1918), 378–91.

Dresden, M. J. (ed.). 1966. *Dēnkart. A Pahlavi text. Facsimile edition of the manuscript B of the K. R. Cama Oriental Institute Bombay*. Wiesbaden: Otto Harrassowitz.

Durkin-Meisterernst, Desmond. 2004. *Dictionary of Manichaean Middle Persian and Parthian texts* (Corpus Fontium Manichaeorum 3, 1). Turnhout: Brepols.

Ebbesen, Sten. 1982. Ancient scholastic logic as the source of medieval scholastic logic. In Kretzmann, Kenny, Pinborg and Stump (1982), 101–27.

Emmerick, Roland and Dieter Weber (eds). 1991. *Corolla Iranica: Papers in honour of Prof. Dr. David Neil MacKenzie on the occasion of his 65th birthday on April 8th, 1991*. Frankfurt: Peter Lang.

Emmerick, Ronald and Maria Macuch (eds). 2009. *The literature of pre-Islamic Iran* (A History of Persian Literature 17). London: I.B. Tauris.

Epp, Eldon. 1976. The eclectic method in New Testament textual criticism: Solution or symptom? *The Harvard Theological Review* 69(3/4). 211–57.

Farmer, Steve, John Henderson and Michael Witzel. 2000. Neurobiology, layered texts, and correlative cosmologies: A cross-cultural framework for premodern history. *Bulletin of the Museum of Far Eastern Antiquities* 72. 48–90.

Ferrer, Juan José (ed.). 2010. *The Avestan manuscript M1 (Pahlavi Yasna) of the Bayerische Staatsbibliotek aus München* (Avestan Digital Archive Series 21).

Ferrer, Juan José (ed.). 2012. *The Avestan manuscript J2_500 (Yasna Indian Pahlavi) of the Bodleian Library (University of Oxford)* (Avestan Digital Archive Series 28).

Fram, Edward. 2005. In the margins of the text. Changes in the page of Talmud. In Sharon Liberman Mintz and Gabriel M. Goldstein (eds), *Printing the Talmud: from Bomberg to Schottenstein*, 91–7. New York: Yeshiva University Museum.

Garzilli, Enrica (ed.). 1996. *Translating, translations, translators: From India to the West* (Harvard Oriental Series 1). Cambridge, MA: Harvard University Press.

Geiger, Wilhelm and Ernst Kuhn (eds). 1896–1904. *Grundriss der iranischen Philologie*, vol II. Strassburg: K. J. Trübner.

Geldner, Karl Friedrich. 1886-96. *Avesta. The sacred books of the Parsis*, vols I–III. Stuttgart: Kohlhammer.

Geldner, Karl Friedrich. 1896–1904. Awestalitteratur. In Geiger and Kuhn (1896–1904), 1–53.

Gershevitch, Ilya. 1967. *The Avestan hymn to Mithra* (Oriental Publications 4). Cambridge: Cambridge University Press.

Gershevitch, Ilya. 1993. Dissent and consensus on the Gāthas. In Farrokh Vajifdar (ed.), *Proceedings of the first gāthā colloquium, held in Croydon, England (5–7 November 1993) under the auspices of the world zoroastrian organisation*, 11–26. London: World Zoroastrian Organisation.

Gignoux, Philippe. 1984. Ahlaw. In *Encyclopædia Iranica*, online edition, http://www.iranicaonline.org/articles/ahlaw

Gignoux, Philippe. 1994. La doctrine du macrocosme-microcosme et ses origines gréco-gnostiques. In Petr Vavroušek (ed.), *Iranian and Indo-European studies. Memorial volume of Otakar Klíma*, 27–52. Prague: Enigma Corporation.

Gignoux, Philippe. 1996. The notion of soul (ruwān) in the Sasanian Mazdaeism. In Desai and Modi (1996), 23–35.

Gignoux, Philippe. 2004a. L'eau et le feu dans le zoroastrisme. In Gérard Capdeville (ed.), *L'eau et le feu dans les religions antiques: Actes du premier colloque international d'histoire des religions organisé par l'Ecole Doctorale Les Mondes de l'Antiquité, 18–20 mai 1995*, 269–82. Paris: De Boccard.

Gignoux, Philippe. 2004b. Microcosm and macrocosm. In *Encyclopædia Iranica*, online edition, http://www.iranicaonline.org/articles/microcosm-and-macrocosm

Gignoux, Philippe and Ahmad Tafazzoli. 1993. *Anthologie de Zādspram. Édition critique du texte Pehlevi* (Studia Iranica 13). Paris: Association pour l'avancement des études Iraniennes.

Goldman, Leon (ed.). 2013a. *The Avestan manuscript KM7-5-19222_682 (Sanskrit Yasna) of the Ketāb xāne-ye Melli (Tehran)* (Avestan Digital Archive Series 55).

Goldman, Leon (ed.). 2013b. *The Avestan manuscript S1_677 (Sanskrit Yasna) of the Columbia University Library* (Avestan Digital Archive Series 54).

Goldman, Leon. 2015. *Rašn Yašt* (Beiträge zur Iranistik 39). Wiesbaden: Reichert Verlag.

Goody, Jack. 1987. *The interface between the written and the oral*. Cambridge: Cambridge University Press.

Grassmann, Hermann. 1873. *Wörterbuch zum Rig-Veda*. Leipzig: F. A. Brockhaus.

Gropp, Gerd. 1991. Zādsprams Interpretation des Ahunavairyo-Gebetes. In Emmerick and Weber (1991), 79–89.

Gyselen, Rika (ed.). 1995. *Au carrefour des religions. Mélanges offerts à Philippe Gignoux* (Res Orientales VII). Bures-sur-Yvette: Groupe pour l'Étude de la Civilisation du Moyen-Orient.

Halbfass, Wilhelm. 1988. *India and Europe: An essay in understanding*. Albany: State University of New York Press.

Haug, Martin. 1862. *Essays on the sacred language, writings, and religion of the Parsees*. Bombay: printed at the 'Bombay Gazette' Press.

Haug, Martin. 1878. *Essays on the sacred language, writings, and religion of the Parsees*. London: Trübner & Co.

Henderson, John. 1991. *Scripture, canon, and commentary. A comparison of Confucian and Western exegesis*. Princeton: Princeton University Press.

Henderson, John. 1998. Neo-Confucian scholasticism. In Cabezón (1998), 159–75.

Henning, Walter Bruno. 1933. Das Verbum des Mittelpersischen der Turfanfragmente. *Zeitschrift für Indologie und Iranistik* 9. 158–253.

Henning, Walter Bruno. 1941. The disintegration of the Avestic studies. *Transactions of the Philological Society* 41(1). 40–56.

Henning, Walter Bruno. 1958. Mitteliranisch. In Bertold Spuler (ed.), *Handbuch der Orientalistik. Linguistik*, Abt. 1, Bd. 4, Abschn. 1, Lfg. 1, 20–130. Leiden: E. J. Brill.

Heston, Wilma Louise. 1976. *Selected problems in fifth to tenth century Iranian syntax*. Philadelphia: University of Pennsylvania, dissertation.

Hintze, Almut. 1994. *Der Zamyād-Yašt. Edition, Übersetzung, Kommentar* (Beiträge zur Iranistik 15). Wiesbaden: Reichert Verlag.

Hintze, Almut. 2000. *»Lohn« im Indoiranischen: Eine semantische Studie des Rigveda und Avesta* (Beiträge zur Iranistik 20). Wiesbaden: Reichert Verlag.

Hintze, Almut. 2002. On the literary structure of the older Avesta. *Bulletin of the School of Oriental and African Studies* 65(1). 31–51.

Hintze, Almut. 2004. On the ritual significance of the Yasna Haptaŋhāiti. In Stausberg (2004b), 291–316.

Hintze, Almut. 2007a. *A Zoroastrian liturgy. The worship in seven chapters* (Iranica 12). Wiesbaden: Harrassowitz Verlag.
Hintze, Almut. 2007b. The fire Wāzišt and the demon. In Macuch et al. 119–34.
Hintze, Almut. 2008. Treasures in heaven: A theme in comparative religion. In Shaul Shaked and Amnon Netzer (eds), *Irano-Judaica VI. Studies relating to Jewish contacts with Persian culture throughout the ages*, 9–36. Jerusalem: Ben-Zvi Institute.
Hintze, Almut. 2009a. Avestan literature. In Emmerick and Macuch (2009), ch. 1, 1–71.
Hintze, Almut. 2009b. Disseminating the Mazdayasnian religion. An edition of the Avestan Hērbedestān chapter 5. In Sundermann et al. (2009), 171–90.
Hintze, Almut. 2013a. Change and continuity in the Zoroastrian tradition. SOAS, London. Inaugural lecture 2012.
Hintze, Almut. 2013b. Perceptions of the Yasna Haptaŋhāiti. In Pirart (2013), 53–73.
Hoffmann, Karl. 1969. Zur Yasna-Überlieferung. *Münchener Studien zur Sprachwissenschaft* 26. 35–8.
Hoffmann, Karl. 1984. Zur Handschriftenüberlieferung der Gathas. *Münchener Studien zur Sprachwissenschaft* 43. 123–31.
Hoffmann, Karl and Bernhard Forssman. 1996. *Avestische Laut- und Flexionslehre* (Innsbrucker Beiträge zur Sprachwissenschaft 84). Innsbruck: Institut für Sprachwissenschaft der Universität Innsbruck.
Hoffmann, Karl and Johanna Narten. 1989. *Der Sasanidische Archetypus. Untersuchungen zu Schreibung und Lautgestalt des Avestischen*. Wiesbaden: Reichert Verlag.
Holdrege, Barbara. 2004. Dharma. In Sushil Mittal and Gene Thursby (eds), *The Hindu world*, ch. 10, 213–48. New York: Routledge.
Horn, Paul. 1893. *Grundriss der neupersischen Etymologie*. Strassburg: Verlag von Karl J. Trübner.
Hübschmann, Heinrich. 1872. Avestastudien. In *Sitzungsberichte der philosophisch-philologischen und historischen Classe der k.b. Akademie der Wissenschaften*, vol. 2, 639–710. München: Akademische Buchdruckerei von F. Straub.
Humbach, Helmut. 1959. *Die Gathas des Zarathustra*, vols I–II, Indogermanische Bibliothek. Heidelberg: Carl Winter Universitätsverlag.
Humbach, Helmut. 1973. Beobachtungen zu der Überlieferungsgeschichte des Awesta. *Münchener Studien zur Sprachwissenschaft* 31. 109–22.
Humbach, Helmut. 1991. *The Gāthās of Zarathushtra and the other old Avestan texts*, vols I–II. Heidelberg: Carl Winter Universitätsverlag.
Humbach, Helmut. 1996. The Gāthās and their Pahlavi translation. In Desai and Modi (1996), 259–65.
Humbach, Helmut. 2003. Neriosangh and his Sanskrit translations of Avesta texts. In Cereti and Vajifdar (2003), 199–212.
Humbach, Helmut and Josef Elfenbein. 1990. *Ērbedestān. An Avesta-Pahlavi Text*, Münchener Studien zur Sprachwissenschaft. München: R. Kitzinger.
Humbach, Helmut and Klaus Faiss. 2010. *Zarathushtra and his antagonists. A sociolinguistic study with English and German translations of his Gāthās*. Wiesbaden: Reichert Verlag.
Humbach, Helmut and Kaikhusroo Jamaspasa. 1969. *Vaeθā Nask: An apocryphal text on Zoroastrian problems*. Wiesbaden: Otto Harrassowitz.

Humbach, Helmut and Kaikhusroo Jamaspasa. 1971. *Pursišnīhā: A Zoroastrian catechism*, vols I–II. Wiesbaden: Otto Harrassowitz.
Humphries, Mark. 2017. Late antiquity and world history: Challenging conventional narratives and analyses. *Studies in Late Antiquity* 1(1). 8–37.
Hutter, Manfred. 2009. The impurity of the corpse (nasā) and the future body (tan ī pasēn): Death and afterlife in Zoroastrianism. In Tobias Nicklas, Friedrich Reiterer and Joseph Verheyden (eds), *The human body in death and resurrection* (Deuterocanonical and Cognate Literature Yearbook 2009), 13–26. Berlin: Walter de Gruyter.
Huyse, Philip. 1999a. *Die dreisprachige Inschrift Šāhuhrs I. an der Kaʿba-i Zardušt (ŠKZ)* (Corpus Inscriptionum Iranicarum part III, vol. I). London: School of Oriental and African Studies. Vols I and II.
Huyse, Philip. 1999b. Review of Panaino, A. (1999). *Abstracta Iranica* 17–19. 29.
Huyse, Philip. 2006. Die sasanidische Königstitulatur: eine Gegenüberstellung der Quellen. In Josef Wiesehöfer and Philip Huyse (eds), *Ērān ud Anērān: Studien zu den Beziehungen zwischen dem Sasanidenreich und der Mittelmeerwelt* (Oriens et Occidens 13), 181–201. Stuttgart: Franz Steiner Verlag.
Huyse, Philip. 2008. Late Sasanian society between orality and literacy. In Vesta Sarkhosh Curtis and Sarah Stewart (eds), *The Sasanian era* (The Idea of Iran 3), 140–55. London: I.B. Tauris.
Ichaporia, Pallan. 2003. The Gāthās in the Pahlavi tradition exemplified by Yasna 30. In Cereti and Vajifdar (2003), 213–20.
Insler, Stanley. 1975. *The Gāthās of Zarathustra* (Acta Iranica 8). Leiden: E. J. Brill.
Insler, Stanley. 1996. Avestan *vāz* and Vedic *vāh*. In Desai and Modi (1996), 151–66.
Jaafari-Dehaghi, Mahmoud. 1998. *Dādestān ī Dēnīg* (Studia Iranica 20). Paris: Association pour l'avancement des études Iraniennes.
Jackson, Abraham Valentine Williams. 1892. *An Avesta grammar in comparison with Sanskrit*. Stuttgart: W. Kohlhammer.
Jamasp-Asana, Jamaspji Dastur Minocheherji (ed.). 1897. *Pahlavi texts. Contained in the codex MK, copied in 1322 A.D. by the scribe Mehr-Âwân Kai-khûsrû*, vol. I. Bombay: Fort Printing Press.
Jamaspasa, Kaikhusroo. 1985. On the *Drōn* in Zoroastrianism. In Pierre Lecoq and Jacques Duchesne-Guillemin (eds), *Papers in honour of Professor Mary Boyce*, vol. I (Acta Iranica 24), 334–56. Leiden: Brill.
Jamaspasa, Kaikhusroo. 2003. Fire in Zoroastrianism. In Cereti and Vajifdar (2003), 247–63.
Jamaspasa, Kaikhusroo and Mahyar Nawabi (eds). 1976a. *Manuscript D90. Yasnā with its Pahlavi translation* (The Pahlavi Codices and Iranian Researches 19, 20). Shiraz: Asia Institute of Pahlavi University. Mf4 in Geldner's notation.
Jamaspasa, Kaikhusroo and Mahyar Nawabi (eds). 1976b. *Manuscript E7. Yasnā bā nīrang with its Pahlavi translation* (The Pahlavi Codices and Iranian Researches 12, 13). Shiraz: Asia Institute of Pahlavi University.
Jamaspasa, Kaikhusroo and Mahyar Nawabi (eds). 1976c. *Manuscript F35. Šāyest-nē-Šāyest (incomplete Pahl. text) Āfrīn-i Zartuxst, Čim-i Drōn* (The Pahlavi Codices and Iranian Researches 34). Shiraz: Asia Institute of Pahlavi University.

Jamaspasa, Kaikhusroo and Mahyar Nawabi (eds). 1976d. *Manuscript J1. Khorde Avesta with its Pahlavi translation* (The Pahlavi Codices and Iranian Researches 6). Shiraz: Asia Institute of Pahlavi University.

Jamaspasa, Kaikhusroo and Mahyar Nawabi (eds). 1976e. *Manuscript R413. Yasna. The entire Avesta text with its Pahlavi version* (The Pahlavi Codices and Iranian Researches 17, 18). Shiraz: Asia Institute of Pahlavi University.

Jamaspji, Hoshengji and Martin Haug (eds). 1867. *An old Zand-Pahlavi glossary.* London: Messrs. Trübner and Co.

Jamaspji Asa, Hoshangji and Martin Haug. 1872. *The book of Arda Viraf.* London: Messrs. Trübner and Co.

Jong, Albert de. 2005. Zoroastrian ideas about the time before Zarathustra. In Shaul Shaked (ed.), *Genesis and regeneration: Essays on conceptions of origins*, 192–209. Jerusalem: Israel Academy of Sciences and Humanities.

Josephson, Judith. 1997. *The Pahlavi translation technique as illustrated by Hōm Yašt* (Acta Universitatis Upsaliensis. Studia Iranica Upsaliensia 2). Uppsala: Uppsala Universitetsbibliotek.

Josephson, Judith. 1999. Semantics and the Pahlavi translators. In Folke Josephson (ed.), *Categorisation and interpretation. Indological and comparative studies from an international Indological meeting at the Department of Comparative Philology, Göteborg University. A volume dedicated to the memory of Gösta Liebert* (Meijerbergs Arkiv för Svensk Ordforskning 24), 147–78. Göteborg.

Josephson, Judith. 2003. Remarks on the Pahlavi version of the Gāthās. *Studia Iranica* 32(1). 7–34.

Kanga, Maneck Fardunji. 1975. A Pahlavi commentary on the Ašəm Vohu. *Bulletin of the Asia Institute* 2. 1–20.

Kanga, Maneck Fardunji. 1976. Pahlavi version of Gāθā Spənta Mainyu. *Bulletin of the Asia Institute of Pahlavi University* 1–4. 45–96.

Karanjia, Ramiyar Parvez. 2004. The Bāj-dhārnā (Drōn Yašt) and its place in Zoroastrian rituals. In Stausberg (2004b), 403–23.

Kellens, Jean. 1989. Avestique. In Schmitt (1989), ch. 2.1, 32–55.

Kellens, Jean. 1998. Considérations sur l'histoire de l'Avesta. *Journal Asiatique* 286(2). 451–519.

Kellens, Jean. 2000. *Essays on Zarathustra and Zoroastrianism.* Costa Mesa: Mazda Publishers. Trans. and ed. Prods Oktor Skjærvø.

Kellens, Jean. 2006. *La quatrième naissance de Zarathushtra.* Paris: Éditions du Seuil.

Kellens, Jean. 2007. *Le Hōm Stōm et la zone des déclarations. (Y 7.24–Y 15.4, avec les intercalations de Vr 3 à 6)* (Études avestiques et mazdéennes 2). Paris: De Boccard.

Kellens, Jean and Éric Pirart. 1988. *Les textes vieil-avestiques. Introduction, texte et traduction*, vol. I. Wiesbaden: Reichert Verlag.

Kellens, Jean and Éric Pirart. 1990. *Les textes vieil-avestiques. Répertoires grammaticaux et lexique*, vol. II. Wiesbaden: Reichert Verlag.

Kellens, Jean and Éric Pirart. 1991. *Les textes vieil-avestiques. Commentaire*, vol. III. Wiesbaden: Reichert Verlag.

Kenny, Anthony and Jan Pinborg. 1982. Medieval philosophical literature. In Kretzmann et al. (1982), 11–42.

Kiel, Yishai. 2016. *Sexuality in the Babylonian Talmud: Christian and Sasanian contexts in late antiquity*. New York: Cambridge University Press.
Klingenschmitt, Gert. 1968. *Frahang-i ōīm. Edition und Kommentar*. Erlangen, Nürnberg: Friedrich-Alexander-Universität, Inaugural-Dissertation.
Klingenschmitt, Gert. 1969. Die Pahlavī-Version des Avesta. In W. Voigt (ed.), *XVII. Deutscher Orientalistentag vom 21. bis 27. Juli 1968 in Würzburg. Vorträge*, 993–7. Wiesbaden: ZDMG, Supplementa I.
Klingenschmitt, Gert. 1971. Neue Avesta-Fragmente (FrA.). *Münchener Studien zur Sprachwissenschaft* 29. 111–74.
Klingenschmitt, Gert. 1972. Avestisch hōməmiiāsaitē und Pahlavī hmystk'n'. *Münchener Studien zur Sprachwissenschaft* 30. 93–109.
Klingenschmitt, Gert. 1978. Der Beitrag der Pahlavī-Literatur zur Interpretation des Avesta. *Münchener Studien zur Sprachwissenschaft* 37. 93–107.
Klingenschmitt, Gert. 2000. Mittelpersisch. In Bernhard Forssman and Robert Plath (eds), *Indoarisch, Iranisch und die Indogermanistik: Arbeitstagung der Indogermanischen Gesellschaft vom 2. bis 5. Oktober 1997 in Erlangen*, 191–230. Wiesbaden: Reichert Verlag.
Klíma, Otakar. 1959. Awesta – Die altpersischen Inschriften – Das mittelpersische Schrifttum. In Jan Rypka (ed.), *Iranische Literaturgeschichte* (Iranische Texte und Hilfsbücher 4), 1–67. Leipzig: Harrassowitz Verlag.
Knipe, David. 1972. One fire, three fires, five fires: Vedic symbols in transition. *History of Religions* 12(1). 28–41.
Kotwal, Firoze. 1969. *The supplementary texts to the Šāyest Nē-Šāyest* (Det Kongelige Danske Videnskabernes Selskab, Historisk-filosofiske Meddelelser 44, 2). København: Munksgaard.
Kotwal, Firoze and James Boyd. 1991. *A Persian offering. The Yasna: A Zoroastrian high liturgy* (Studia Iranica 8). Paris: Association pour l'avancement des études Iraniennes.
Kotwal, Firoze and Philip Kreyenbroek. 1992. *The Hērbedestān and Nērangestān. Vol. I: Hērbedestān* (Studia Iranica 10). Paris: Association pour l'avancement des études Iraniennes.
Kotwal, Firoze and Philip Kreyenbroek. 1995. *The Hērbedestān and Nērangestān. Vol. II: Nērangestān, Fragard 1* (Studia Iranica 16). Paris: Association pour l'avancement des études Iraniennes.
Kotwal, Firoze and Philip Kreyenbroek. 2003. *The Hērbedestān and Nērangestān. Vol. III: Nērangestān, Fragard 2* (Studia Iranica 30). Paris: Association pour l'avancement des études Iraniennes.
Kotwal, Firoze and Philip Kreyenbroek. 2009. *The Hērbedestān and Nērangestān. Vol. IV: Nērangestān, Fragard 3* (Studia Iranica 38). Paris: Association pour l'avancement des études Iraniennes.
Kretzmann, Norman, Anthony Kenny, Jan Pinborg and Eleonore Stump (eds). 1982. *The Cambridge history of later medieval philosophy: From the rediscovery of Aristotle to the disintegration of scholasticism 1100–1600*. Cambridge: Cambridge University Press.
Kreyenbroek, Philip. 1985. *Sraoša in the Zoroastrian tradition* (Orientalia Rheno-Traiectina 28). Leiden: E. J. Brill.

Kreyenbroek, Philip. 1987. The Zoroastrian priesthood after the fall of the Sasanian empire. In *Transition periods in Iranian history* (Studia Iranica 5), 151–66. Paris: Association pour l'avancement des études iraniennes. Actes du Symposium de Fribourg-en-Brisgau (22–24 Mai 1985).

Kreyenbroek, Philip. 1993. Cosmogony and cosmology i. In Zoroastrianism/Mazdaism. In *Encyclopædia Iranica*, vol. V/3, 303–7. New York: Bibliotheca Persica.

Kreyenbroek, Philip. 1996. The Zoroastrian tradition from an oralist's point of view. In Desai and Modi (1996), 221–37.

Kreyenbroek, Philip. 1999. Exegesis. In Zoroastrianism. In *Encyclopædia Iranica*, vol. IX/2, 113–16. New York: Bibliotheca Persica.

Kristeva, Julia. 1980. *Desire in Language: A Semiotic Approach to Literature and Art.* New York: Columbia University Press.

Kugel, James L. 1981. *The idea of Biblical poetry: Parallelism and its history.* New Haven: Yale University Press.

König, Götz. 2005. Zur Figur des „Wahrhaftigen Menschen" (*mard ī ahlaw*) in der zoroastrischen Literatur. *Zeitschrift der Deutschen Morgenländischen Gesellschaft* 155. 161–88.

König, Götz. 2010. Der Pahlavi-Text *Zand ī Fragard ī Juddēvdād*. In Maria Macuch, Dieter Weber and Desmond Durkin-Meisterernst (eds), *Ancient and Middle Iranian studies. Proceedings of the 6th European conference of Iranian studies, held in Vienna, 18–22 September 2007* (Iranica 19), 115–32. Wiesbaden: Harrassowitz Verlag.

König, Götz. 2015. Zur Frage 'ewiger' Feuer im Avesta und in der zoroastrischen Tradition. *Iran and the Caucasus* 19(1). 9–68.

König, Götz. 2018. *Studien zur Rationalitätsgeschichte im älteren Iran. Ein Beitrag zur Achsenzeitdiskussion* (Iranica 26). Wiesbaden: Harrassowitz Verlag.

Lommel, Herman. 1927. *Die Yäšt's des Awesta* (Quellen der Religionsgeschichte 15, Gruppe 6). Göttingen: Vandenhoeck & Ruprecht.

Lord, Albert B. 2000. *The singer of tales*, Harvard Studies in Comparative Literature. Cambridge, MA: Harvard University Press, second rev. edn.

MacKenzie, David Neil. 1967. Notes on the transcription of Pahlavi. *Bulletin of the School of Oriental and African Studies* 30(1). 17–29.

MacKenzie, David Neil. 1972. Review of Jamaspasa and Humbach: *Pursišnīhā: a Zoroastrian catechism*. *Bulletin of the School of Oriental and African Studies* 35(2). 372–5.

MacKenzie, David Neil. 1990. *A concise Pahlavi dictionary.* Oxford: Oxford University Press.

Macuch, Maria. 1993. *Rechtskasuistik und Gerichtspraxis zu Beginn des siebenten Jahrhunderts in Iran: Die Rechtssammlung des Farroḫmard i Wahrāmān* (Iranica 1). Wiesbaden: Harrassowitz Verlag.

Macuch, Maria. 2005. On Middle Persian legal terminology. In Carlo Cereti and Mauro Maggi (eds), *Middle Iranian lexicography: Proceedings of the conference held in Rome, 9–11 April 2001*, Orientalia Romana, 375–86. Rome: Istituto Italiano per l'Africa e l'Oriente.

Macuch, Maria. 2007. The Pahlavi model marriage contract in the light of Sasanian family law. In Macuch et al. (2007), 183–204.

Macuch, Maria. 2009a. Disseminating the Mazdayasnian religion. An edition of the Pahlavi Hērbedestān chapter 5. In Sundermann et al. 251–77.

Macuch, Maria. 2009b. Pahlavi literature. In Emmerick and Macuch (2009), ch. 3, 116–96.

Macuch, Maria. 2009c. The Hērbedestān as a legal source: A section on the inheritance of a convert to Zoroastrianism. In Carol Altman Bromberg, Nicholas Sims-Williams and Ursula Sims-Williams (eds), *Iranian and Zoroastrian Studies in Honor of Prods Oktor Skjærvø* (Bulletin of the Asia Institute 19), 91–102. Bloomfield Hills: Bulletin of the Asia Institute.

Macuch, Maria. 2015. Substance and fruit in the Sasanian law of property and the Babylonian Talmud. In Markham Geller (ed.), *The archaeology and material culture of the Babylonian Talmud* (IJS Studies in Judaica 16), 245–59. Brill.

Macuch, Maria, Mauro Maggi and Werner Sundermann (eds). 2007. *Iranian languages and texts from Iran and Turan. Ronald E. Emmerick memorial volume* (Iranica 13). Wiesbaden: Harrassowitz Verlag.

Madan, Dhanjishah Meherjibhai (ed.). 1911. *The complete text of the Pahlavi Dinkard*, vols I and II. Bombay: The Society for the Promotion of Researches into the Zoroastrian Religion.

Malandra, William. 1987. Review of Kreyenbroek: *Sraoša in the Zoroastrian Tradition*. *Journal of the American Oriental Society* 107(2). 369–70.

Malandra, William and Pallan Ichaporia. 2010. *The Pahlavi Yasna of the Gāthās and Yasna Haptaŋhāiti*. Ahura Publishers.

Marenbon, John. 2010. The emergence of medieval Latin philosophy. In Robert Pasnau and Christina van Dyke (eds), *The Cambridge history of medieval philosophy*, vol. 1, 26–38. Cambridge: Cambridge University Press.

Mayrhofer, Manfred. 1992–2001. *Etymologisches Wörterbuch des Altindoarischen* (Indogermanische Bibliothek 2. Reihe). Heidelberg: Carl Winter Universitätsverlag.

Mayrhofer, Manfred. 2005. Review of A. Cantera: *Studien Zur Pahlavi-Übersetzung des Avesta*. *Historische Sprachforschung* 118. 309–12.

Mazdapur, Katayun. 1999. *Dāstān-ī Garšāsb, Tahmuras va Jamšid, Golšāh va matnhāye digar: Barrasi-ī dastnevis-ī M.U. 29*. Tehran: Agah.

McGann, Jerome. 1992. *A critique of modern textual criticism*. Charlottesville, VA: University Press of Virginia.

McMahan, David. 1998. Orality, writing, and authority in South Asian Buddhism: Visionary literature and the struggle for legitimacy in the Mahayana. *History of Religions* 37(3). 249–74.

Mehendale, Madhukar Anant. 1996. On Yasna 41.2. In Desai and Modi (1996), 173–6.

Mills, Lawrence Heyworth. 1887. *The Zend-Avesta. Part III: The Yasna, Visparad, Âfrînagân, Gâhs, and miscellaneous fragments* (Sacred Books of the East XXXI). Oxford: Clarendon Press.

Mills, Lawrence Heyworth. 1892. *A study of the five Zarathushtrian (Zoroastrian) Gâthâs with text and translations: Commentary*. Leipzig: Brockhaus.

Mills, Lawrence Heyworth (ed.). 1893. *The ancient manuscript of the Yasna with its Pahlavi translation, generally quoted as J2*. Oxford: Clarendon Press.

Mills, Lawrence Heyworth. 1894. *A study of the five Zarathushtrian (Zoroastrian) Gâthâs with text and translations*. Leipzig: Brockhaus.

Mills, Lawrence Heyworth. 1900. Items from the Gāthic Pahlavi. *The American Journal of Philology* 21(3). 287–94.

Mills, Lawrence Heyworth. 1903. Pahlavi Yasna I. Edited with all the MSS. collated. *Zeitschrift der Deutschen Morgenländischen Gesellschaft* 57. 766–70.

Mills, Lawrence Heyworth. 1904. Pahlavi Yasna I, for the first time critically translated. *Journal of the Royal Asiatic Society* 57. 687–702.

Mills, Lawrence Heyworth. 1905a. The Pahlavi texts of the Yasna Haptanghaiti (Y. XXXV-XLI (XLII)), for the first time critically translated. *Journal of the Royal Asiatic Society of Great Britain and Ireland* 55–78.

Mills, Lawrence Heyworth. 1905b. The Pahlavi texts of the Yasna Haptaṅghāiti, Yasna XXXV-XLI (XLII) edited with all MSS. collated. *Zeitschrift der Deutschen Morgenländischen Gesellschaft* 59. 105–15.

Mills, Lawrence Heyworth. 1906. *The Pahlavi text of the first chapter of the Yasna*. Louvain: J.-B. Istas.

Mills, Lawrence Heyworth. 1910. *A study of Yasna I*. Leipzig: F. A. Brockhaus.

Mirfaxrāi, Mahšid. 2003. *Barresi ī hafthā*. Tehran: Frawahar.

Mokhtarian, Jason Sion. 2015. *Rabbis, sorcerers, kings, and priests: The culture of the Talmud in ancient Iran*. Oakland: University of California Press.

Monier-Williams, Monier. 1899. *A Sanskrit-English dictionary*. Oxford: Oxford University Press.

Morony, Michael G. 2008. Should Sasanian Iran be included in late antiquity. *e-Sasanika* 6.

Narten, Johanna. 1982. *Die Aməša Spəntas im Avesta*. Wiesbaden: Otto Harrassowitz.

Narten, Johanna. 1986. *Der Yasna Haptaŋhāiti*. Wiesbaden: Reichert Verlag.

Nawabi, Mahyar (ed.). 1978. *The Avesta codex K5. Containing the Yasna with its Pahlavi translation and commentary* (The Pahlavi Codices and Iranian Researches 43, 44, 56). Shiraz: Asia Institute of Pahlavi University.

Nicholson, Oliver (ed.). 2018. *The Oxford dictionary of late antiquity*. Oxford: Oxford University Press.

Nyberg, Henrik Samuel. 1964. *A manual of Pahlavi. Texts, alphabets, index, paradigms, notes and an introduction*, vol. 1. Wiesbaden: Otto Harrassowitz.

Nyberg, Henrik Samuel. 1974. *A manual of Pahlavi. Ideograms, glossary, abbreviations, index, grammatical survey*, vol. 2. Wiesbaden: Otto Harrassowitz.

Nünning, Ansgar (ed.). 2004. *Metzler Lexikon Literatur- und Kulturtheorie. Ansätze – Personen – Grundbegriffe*. Stuttgart: Verlag J. B. Metzler, 3rd edn.

Ong, Walter J. 1965. Oral residue in Tudor prose style. *Publications of the Modern Language Association of America* 80(3). 145–54.

Ong, Walter J. 1984. Orality, literacy, and medieval textualization. *New Literary History* 16(1). 1–12.

Ong, Walter J. 2007. *Orality and literacy: The technologizing of the word*. London: Routledge. Reprint of the 2002 edition.

Orian, Said. 1992. *Pahlavi texts: Transcription, transliteration.* Ed. Jamaspji Dastur Minocherji Jamasp-Asana. Tehran: National Library of Iran.

Pakzad, Fazlollah. 2005. *Bundahišn. Zoroastrische Kosmogonie und Kosmologie* (Ancient Iranian Studies Series 2). Tehran: Centre for the Great Islamic Encyclopaedia.

Panaino, Antonio. 1990. *Tištrya. Part I: The Avestan Hymn to Sirius* (Serie Orientale Roma LXVIII, 1). Rome: Istituto Italiano per il Medio ed Estremo Oriente.

Panaino, Antonio. 1993. Philologia avestica III. *Annali di Ca' Foscari* 32(3). 135–71.

Panaino, Antonio. 1995a. *Tištrya. Part II: The Iranian myth of the star Sirius* (Serie Orientale Roma LXVIII, 2). Rome: Istituto Italiano per il Medio ed Estremo Oriente.

Panaino, Antonio. 1995b. Uranographia Iranica I. The three heavens in the Zoroastrian tradition and the Mesopotamian background. In Gyselen (1995), 205–25.

Panaino, Antonio. 2002. *The lists of names of Ahura Mazdā (Yašt I) and Vayu (Yašt XV)* (Serie Orientale Roma 94). Rome: Istituto Italiano per l'Africa e l'Oriente.

Panaino, Antonio. 2003. Once again upon the Middle Persian *māzdēsn. In Siamak Adhami (ed.), *Paitimāna. Essays in Iranian, Indian, and Indo-European studies in honor of Hanns-Peter Schmidt*, 320–25. Costa Mesa: Mazda Publishers. Vols I and II.

Panaino, Antonio. 2004. Aspects of the interiorization of the sacrifice in the Zoroastrian tradition. In Stausberg (2004b), 233–52.

Papst, Manfred. 2017. «Walsers Wortschatz toppt sogar Goethe». Manfred Papst spricht mit dem Germanisten Wolfram Groddeck über die Editionsarbeit an Robert Walsers Texten. *Bücher am Sonntag* 2. 12–14. Verlag der Neuen Zürcher Zeitung.

Pieper, Josef. 1978. *Scholastik: Gestalten und Probleme der mittelalterlichen Philosophie.* München: Deutscher Taschenbuch Verlag.

Pirart, Éric. 2006. *L'Aphrodite Iranienne. Études de la déesse Ārti, traduction annotée et édition critique des textes avestiques la concernant.* Paris: Harmattan.

Pirart, Éric. 2013. Autour de l'*Abar-vārag ī Hapt-bāt Yasn*. In Pirart (2013), 159–75.

Pirart, Éric (ed.). 2013. *Le sort des Gâthâs et autres études Iraniennes in memoriam Jacques Duchesne-Guillemin* (Acta Iranica 54). Leuven: Peeters.

Pollock, Sheldon. 2006. *The language of the gods in the world of men: Sanskrit, culture, and power in premodern India.* Berkeley: University of California Press.

Punegar, Khodabax Edalji. 1943. Interpretation of Yasna Hā 38.5. In *Papers on Zoroastrian and Iranian subjects. Dinshah Irani memorial volume*, 87–90. Bombay: The Dinshah J. Irani Memorial Fund Committee.

Ragozin, Zénaïde A. 1889. *Media, Babylon and Persia, including a study of the Zend-Avesta or religion of Zoroaster, from the fall of Nineveh to the Persian War.* London: T. Fisher Unwin.

Reichelt, Hans. 1903. Das Pronomen im Mittelpersischen. *Zeitschrift der Deutschen Morgenländischen Gesellschaft* 57. 570–5.

Rezania, Kianoosh. 2010. *Die zoroastrische Zeitvorstellung. Eine Untersuchung über Zeit- und Ewigkeitskonzepte und die Frage des Zurvanismus* (Göttinger Orientforschungen, III. Reihe: Iranica. Neue Folge 7). Wiesbaden: Harrassowitz Verlag.

Rezania, Kianoosh. 2015. Einige Anmerkungen zur sasanidisch-zoroastrischen Religionspraxis im Spiegel der interreligiösen Dialoge der Christen und Zoroastrier. In Claudia Rammelt, Cornelia Schlarb and Egbert Schlarb (eds), *Begegnungen in Vergangenheit und Gegenwart: Beiträge dialogischer Existenz* (Theologie 112), 172–80. Münster: LIT Verlag.

Rix, Helmut and Martin Kümmel. 2001. *Lexikon der indogermanischen Verben: Die Wurzeln und ihre Primärstammbildungen.* Wiesbaden: Reichert Verlag, 2nd edn.

Salemann, C. 1895–1901. Mittelpersisch. In Wilhelm Geiger and Ernst Kuhn (eds), *Grundriss der iranischen Philologie*, vol. I, 1, 249–332. Strassburg: K. J. Trübner.

Sanjana, Darab Dastur Peshotan. 1916. *The Dînkard. Book VIII, contents of the Avesta Nasks, part I*, vol. XV. London: Kegan Paul, Trench, Trübner & Co.

Sanjana, Peshotan Dastur Behramjee. 1897. *The Dinkard*, vol. VIII. Bombay: Duftur Ashkara Oil Engine Press.

Schlerath, Bernfried. 1986. Die Problematik von Metaphern in the Gathas. *Studien zur Indologie und Iranistik* 11/12. 192–201.

Schmidt, Hanns-Peter. 1985. *Form and meaning of Yasna 33* (American Oriental Society Essay no. 10). New Haven, CT: American Oriental Society. With contributions by Wolfgang Lentz and Stanley Insler.

Schmitt, Rüdiger (ed.). 1989. *Compendium linguarum iranicarum.* Wiesbaden: Reichert Verlag.

Schmitt, Rüdiger. 2000. *Die iranischen Sprachen in Geschichte und Gegenwart.* Wiesbaden: Reichert Verlag.

Schmitz, Thomas A. 2007. *Modern literary theory and ancient texts: An introduction.* Oxford: Blackwell.

Schwartz, Martin. 2003. Women in the old Avesta: Social position and textual composition. *Bulletin of the Asia Institute* 17. 1–8.

Secunda, Shai. 2009. Talmudic text and Iranian context: On the development of two Talmudic narratives. *AJS Review* 33(1). 45–69.

Secunda, Shai. 2012. On the age of the Zoroastrian sages of the Zand. *Iranica Antiqua* 47. 317–49.

Secunda, Shai. 2013. *The Iranian Talmud: Reading the Bavli in its Sasanian context.* Philadelphia: University of Pennsylvania Press.

Shahmardan, Rashid. 1967. *Parastishgah-i Zartushtiyan.* Bombay: Sazman-i Javanan-i Zartushti-i Bamba'i.

Shaked, Shaul. 1971. The notions *mēnōg* and *gētīg* in the Pahlavi texts and their relation to eschatology. *Acta Orientalia* 33. 59–107.

Shaked, Shaul. 1979. *The Wisdom of the Sasanian Sages (Denkard VI). By Aturpāt-i Ēmētān* (Persian Heritage Series 34). Boulder: Westview Press.

Shaked, Shaul. 1994. *Dualism in Transformation: Varieties of Religion in Sasanian Iran* (Jordan Lectures in Comparative Religion XVI). London: School of Oriental and African Studies.

Shaked, Shaul. 1995. *From Zoroastrian Iran to Islam: Studies in religious history and intercultural contacts*, Variorum Collected Studies Series. Aldershot: Variorum.

Shaked, Shaul. 1996. The traditional commentary on the Avesta (Zand): Translation, interpretation, distortion? In *La Persia e l'Asia Centrale. Da Alessandro al X Secolo*.

Atti del Convegno Internazionale (Rome, 9–12 Novembre 1994) (Atti dei Convegni Lincei 127), 641–56. Rome: Accademia Nazionale dei Lincei.
Shaked, Shaul. 1998. Eschatology i. In Zoroastrianism and Zoroastrian influence. In *Encyclopædia Iranica*, vol. VIII, fasc. 6, 565–9. New York: Bibliotheca Persica.
Shaked, Shaul. 2003. Scripture and exegesis in Zoroastrianism. In Margalit Finkelberg and Guy Stroumsa (eds), *Homer, the Bible, and beyond: Literary and religious canons in the ancient world* (Jerusalem Studies in Religion and Culture 2), 63–74. Leiden: Brill.
Shaked, Shaul. 2004. The Yasna ritual in Pahlavi literature. In Stausberg (2004b), 333–44.
Shaki, Mansour. 1994. Dēn. In *Encyclopædia Iranica, online edition*, vol. VII, fasc. 3, 279–81. New York: Columbia University.
Sims-Williams, Nicholas. 1981. Notes on Manichaean Middle Persian morphology. *Studia Iranica* 10(2). 165–76.
Sims-Williams, Nicholas. 1998. The Iranian languages. In Giacalone Ramat and Paolo Ramat (eds), *The Indo-European languages*, 125–53. London: Routledge.
Sims-Williams, Nicholas. 2007. *Bactrian documents from Northern Afghanistan II: Letters and Buddhist texts* (Studies in the Khalili Collection 3). London: Nour Foundation in association with Azimuth Editions.
Skjærvø, Prods Oktor. 1983. *The Sassanian inscription of Paikuli: Commentary*, vol. 3.2. Wiesbaden: Reichert Verlag.
Skjærvø, Prods Oktor. 1986. Verbs in Parthian and Middle Persian inscriptions. In Rüdiger Schmitt and Prods Oktor Skjærvø (eds), *Studia Grammatica Iranica: Festschrift für Helmut Humbach*, 425–39. München: R. Kitzinger.
Skjærvø, Prods Oktor. 1991. Review of Hoffmann and Narten: *Der Sasanidische Archetypus*. *Kratylos* 36. 104–9.
Skjærvø, Prods Oktor. 1994. Hymnic composition in the Avesta. *Die Sprache* 36(2). 199–243.
Skjærvø, Prods Oktor. 1995a. Iranian elements in Manicheism: A comparative contrastive approach. Irano-Manichaica I. In Gyselen (1995), 263–84.
Skjærvø, Prods Oktor. 1995b. The Avesta as source for the early history of the Iranians. In George Erdosy (ed.), *The Indo-Aryans of ancient South Asia: Language, material culture and ethnicity* (Indian Philology and South Asian Studies 1), ch. 6, 155–76. Berlin: Walter de Gruyter.
Skjærvø, Prods Oktor. 2003. Truth and deception in ancient Iran. In Cereti and Vajifdar (2003), 383–434.
Skjærvø, Prods Oktor. 2005. The Achaemenids and the *Avesta*. In Vesta Sarkhosh Curtis and Sarah Stewart (eds), *Birth of the Persian empire* (The Idea of Iran 1), 52–84. London: I.B. Tauris.
Skjærvø, Prods Oktor. 2005–6. The importance of orality for the study of old Iranian literature and myth. *Nāme-ye Irān-e Bāstān* 5(1&2). 9–31.
Skjærvø, Prods Oktor. 2008a. Review of A. Cantera: *Studien zur Pahlavi-Übersetzung des Avesta*. *Kratylos* 53. 1–20.
Skjærvø, Prods Oktor. 2008b. *Translations of the Avesta*. Unpublished.
Skjærvø, Prods Oktor. 2009a. *Introduction to Pahlavi*. Unpublished.

Skjærvø, Prods Oktor. 2009b. OL' news: ODs and ends. In Sundermann, Hintze and Blois (2009), 479–95.
Skjærvø, Prods Oktor. 2009c Review of J. Kellens: *Le Hōm Stōm et la zone des déclarations*. *Orientalistische Literaturzeitung* 104(6). 703–8.
Skjærvø, Prods Oktor. 2010a. Middle West Iranian. In Windfuhr (2010), 196–278.
Skjærvø, Prods Oktor. 2010b. Old Iranian. In Windfuhr (2010), 43–195.
Skjærvø, Prods Oktor. 2010c. On the terminology and style of the Pahlavi scholastic literature. In Bakhos and Shayegan (2010), 178–205.
Skjærvø, Prods Oktor. 2010d. *The Pahlavi Yasna*. Unpublished.
Sohn, Peter. 1996. *Die Medizin des Zādsparam: Anatomie, Physiologie und Psychologie in den Wizīdagīhā ī Zādsparam, einer zoroastrisch-mittelpersischen Anthologie aus dem frühislamischen Iran des neunten Jahrhunderts* (Iranica 3). Wiesbaden: Harrassowitz Verlag.
Spiegel, Friedrich von. 1856. *Einleitung in die traditionellen Schriften der Parsen. Erster Theil: Huzvâresch-Grammatik*. Wien: Verlag von Wilhelm Engelmann.
Spiegel, Friedrich von. 1858. *Avesta. Die heiligen Schriften der Parsen. Im Grundtexte sammt der Huzvâresch-Übersetzung*. Wien: Kais. Kön. Hof- und Staatsdruckerei.
Spiegel, Friedrich von. 1859. *Avesta. Die heiligen Schriften der Parsen. Aus dem Grundtexte übersetzt, mit steter Rücksicht auf die Tradition. Vispered und Yaçna*, vol. II. Leipzig: Wilhelm Engelmann.
Spiegel, Friedrich von. 1860. *Einleitung in die traditionellen Schriften der Parsen. Zweiter Theil: Die traditionelle Literatur*. Wien: Verlag von Wilhelm Engelmann.
Spiegel, Friedrich von. 1861. *Neriosengh's Sanskrit-Uebersetzung des Yaçna*. Leipzig: Wilhelm Engelmann.
Spiegel, Friedrich von. 1868. *Commentar über das Avesta. Vispered, Yaçna und Khorda-Avesta*, vol. II. Leipzig: Wilhelm Engelmann.
Spiegel, Friedrich von. 1882. Zur Textkritik des Awestâ. *ZDMG* 36. 586–619.
Stausberg, Michael. 1998. *Faszination Zarathushtra: Zoroaster und die europäische Religionsgeschichte der frühen Neuzeit*, Religionsgeschichtliche Versuche und Vorarbeiten. Berlin: Walter de Gruyter.
Stausberg, Michael. 2002. *Die Religion Zarathushtras. Geschichte – Gegenwart – Rituale*, vols 1 and 2. Stuttgart: W. Kohlhammer.
Stausberg, Michael. 2004a. *Die Religion Zarathushtras. Geschichte – Gegenwart – Rituale*, vol. 3. Stuttgart: W. Kohlhammer.
Stausberg, Michael (ed.). 2004b. *Zoroastrian rituals in context* (Studies in the History of Religions 102). Leiden: Brill.
Stausberg, Michael. 2008. On the state and prospects of the study of Zoroastrianism. *Numen* 55. 561–600.
Stroumsa, Guy 2002. Thomas Hyde and the birth of Zoroastrian studies. *Jerusalem Studies in Arabic and Islam* 26. 216–230.
Stroumsa, Guy. 2012. *Das Ende des Opferkults: Die religiösen Mutationen der Spätantike*. Berlin: Verlag der Weltreligionen, 2nd edn.
Sundermann, Werner. 1987. Review of Kreyenbroek: *Sraoša in the Zoroastrian tradition*. *Indo-Iranian Journal* 30(4). 287–91.
Sundermann, Werner. 1989. Mittelpersisch. In Schmitt (1989), ch. 3.1.2, 138–64.

Sundermann, Werner, Almut Hintze and François de Blois (eds). 2009. *Exegisti monumenta. Festschrift in honour of Nicholas Sims-Williams* (Iranica 17). Wiesbaden: Harrassowitz Verlag.

Swennen, Philippe. 2016. Le Yasna Haptaŋhāiti entre deux existences. In Céline Redard (ed.), *Des contrées avestiques à Mahabad, via Bisotun. Études offertes en hommage à Pierre Lecoq* (Civilisations du Proche-Orient. Série 3, Religions et Culture 2), 143–53. Neuchâtel: Recherches et Publication.

Tafazzoli, Ahmad. 1997. *Tarikh-i adabiyat-i Iran pish az Islam*. Tehran: Intisharat-i sukhan.

Taraf, Zahra. 1981. *Der Awesta-Text Niyāyiš. Mit Pahlavi- und Sanskritübersetzung* (Münchener Studien zur Sprachwissenschaft: Neue Folge 10). München: R. Kitzinger.

Tavadia, Jehangir C. 1930. *Sāyast-Nē-Sāyast: A Pahlavi text on religious customs* (Alt- und Neu-Indische Studien 3). Hamburg: Friederichsen, De Gruyter.

Tavadia, Jehangir C. 1956. *Die Mittelpersische Sprache und Literatur der Zarathustrier* (Iranische Texte und Hilfsbücher 2). Leipzig: Harrassowitz Verlag.

Tedesco, Paul. 1923. *a*-Stämme und *aya*-Stämme im Iranischen. *Zeitschrift für Indologie und Iranistik* 2. 281–315.

Tremblay, Xavier. 2009. Les prépalatales indo-européennes devant dentale en iranien. In Éric Pirart and Xavier Tremblay (eds), *Zarathushtra entre l'Inde et l'Iran. Études indo-iraniennes et indo-européennes offertes à Jean Kellens à l'occasion de son 65e anniversaire* (Beiträge zur Iranistik 30), 327–59. Wiesbaden: Reichert Verlag.

Unvala, Jamshedji Maneckji. 1924. *Neryosangh's Sanskrit version of the Hōm Yašt (Yasn IX–XI) with the original Avesta and its Pahlavi version*. Vienna: Adolf Holzhausen.

Utas, Bo. 1976. Verbs and preverbs in the Ayyātkār ī Zarērān. *Acta Orientalia* 37. 75–110.

Utas, Bo. 1984. Verbal ideograms in the Frahang ī Pahlavīk. In Wojciech Skalmowski and Alois van Tongerloo (eds), *Middle Iranian studies* (Orientalia Lovaniensia Analecta 16), 57–67. Leuven: Uitgeverij Peeters. Proceedings of the International Symposium Organized by the Katholieke Universiteit Leuven from the 17 to 20 May 1982.

Vaan, Michiel de. 2003. *The Avestan vowels* (Leiden Studies in Indo-European 12). Amsterdam: Rodopi.

Vaan, Michiel de. 2007. Review of A. Cantera: *Studien Zur Pahlavi-Übersetzung des Avesta*. *Indo-Iranian Journal* 50(1). 67–71.

Vahman, Fereydun. 1986. *Ardā Wirāz Nāmag. The Iranian 'Divina Commedia'*. London: Curzon Press.

Vevaina, Yuhan Sohrab-Dinshaw. 2007. *Studies in Zoroastrian exegesis and hermeneutics with a critical edition of the Sūdgar Nask of Dēnkard Book 9*. Cambridge, MA: Harvard University, dissertation.

Vevaina, Yuhan Sohrab-Dinshaw. 2010a. "Enumerating the Dēn": Textual taxonomies, cosmological deixis, and numerological speculations in Zoroastrianism. *History of Religions* 50(2). 111–43.

Vevaina, Yuhan Sohrab-Dinshaw. 2010b. Relentless allusion. Intertextuality and the reading of Zoroastrian interpretive literature. In Bakhos and Shayegan (2010), 206–32.

Vevaina, Yuhan Sohrab-Dinshaw. 2010c. Sūdgar Nask and Warštmānsar Nask. In *Encyclopædia Iranica*, online edition, http://www.iranicaonline.org/articles/sudgar-nask-and-warstmansr-nask

Vevaina, Yuhan Sohrab-Dinshaw. 2012. Scripture versus contemporary (interpretive) needs: Towards a mapping of the hermeneutic contours of Zoroastrianism. In Shai Secunda and Steven Fine (eds), *Shoshannat Yaakov*, 465–85. Leiden: Brill.

Wackernagel, Jakob. 1930–57. *Altindische Grammatik*, vols I–III. Göttingen: Vandenhoeck & Ruprecht.

Watkins, Calvert. 1995. *How to kill a dragon. Aspects of Indo-European poetics*. Oxford: Oxford University Press.

Weber, Dieter. 2007. Pahlavi morphology. In Alan S. Kaye (ed.), *Morphologies of Asia and Africa*, 941–73. Winona Lake, Indiana: Eisenbrauns.

Weber, Dieter. 2009. A Pahlavi letter from Egypt re-visited (P. 44). In Sundermann et al. (2009), 537–50.

Wesendonk, O. G. von. 1931. *Die religionsgeschichtliche Bedeutung des Yasna Haptaŋhāiti*. Köln-Bonn: L. Röhrscheid.

Wesendonk, O. G. von. 1933. *Das Weltbild der Iranier*. München: Verlag Ernst Reinhardt.

West, Edward William. 1880. *Pahlavi texts. Part I: The Bundahis, Bahman Yast, and Shâyast lâ-Shâyast* (Sacred Books of the East V). Oxford: Clarendon Press.

West, Edward William. 1882. *Pahlavi texts. Part II: The Dādistān-ī Dīnik and the epistles of Mānūškihar* (Sacred Books of the East XVIII). Oxford: Clarendon Press.

West, Edward William. 1896–1904. Pahlavi literature. In Geiger and Kuhn (1896–1904), 75–129.

West, Edward William. 1897. *Pahlavi texts. Part V: Marvels of Zoroastrianism* (Sacred Books of the East XLVII). Oxford: Clarendon Press.

West, Martin Litchfield. 2007. *Indo-European poetry and myth*. Oxford: Oxford University Press.

West, Martin Litchfield. 2008. On editing the Gāthās. *Iran* 46. 121–34.

West, Martin Litchfield. 2010. *The hymns of Zoroaster. A new translation of the most ancient sacred texts of Iran*. London: I.B. Tauris.

West, Martin Litchfield. 2011. *Old Avestan syntax and stylistics. With an edition of the texts* (Abhandlungen der Akademie der Wissenschaften zu Göttingen Neue Folge, Band 13). Berlin: De Gruyter.

Westergaard, Nils Ludwig. 1852–54. *Zendavesta or the religious books of the Zoroastrians*, vol. 1. Copenhagen: Printed by Berling Brothers.

Widengren, Geo. 1983. Leitende Ideen und Quellen der iranischen Apokalyptik. In David Hellholm (ed.), *Apocalypticism in the Mediterranean World and the Near East*, 77–162. Tübingen: J. C. B. Mohr (Paul Siebeck).

Wikander, Stig. 1946. *Feuerpriester in Kleinasien und Iran*. Lund: C.W.K. Gleerup.

Williams, Alan. 1990. *The Pahlavi Rivāyat accompanying the Dādestān ī Dēnīg* (Historisk-filosofiske Meddelelser 60: 1–2), vols I–II. Copenhagen: The Royal Danish Academy of Sciences and Letters.

Williams, Alan. 1997. Later Zoroastrianism. In Carr and Mahalingam (1997), 21–41.

Windfuhr, Gernot (ed.). 2010. *The Iranian languages*, Routledge Language Family Series. London: Routledge.

Wolff, Fritz. 1910. *Avesta: Die heiligen Bücher der Parsen*. Leipzig: Trübner.

Zaehner, R. C. 1975. *The teachings of the Magi. A compendium of Zoroastrian beliefs*. London: Sheldon Press.

Zeini, Arash. 2008. Review of Cantera, Alberto: *Studien zur Pahlavi-Übersetzung des Avesta. Bibliotheca Orientalis* 65(5–6). 785–90.

Zeini, Arash (ed.). 2012. *The Avestan manuscript Pt4_400 (Iranian Pahlavi Yasna) of the Bodleian Library* (Avestan Digital Archive Series 39).

Zeini, Arash. 2015. Preliminary observations on word order correspondence in the Zand. *DABIR* 1(1). 31–5.

Zeini, Arash. 2018. The king in the mirror of the Zand: Secrecy in Sasanian Iran. In Touraj Daryaee (ed.), *Sasanian Iran in the context of late anitquity: The Bahari lecture series at the University of Oxford* (Ancient Iran Series VI), 149–62. Irvine: UCI Jordan Center for Persian Studies.

Zeini, Arash. Forthcoming. Ritual and ritual text in the Zoroastrian tradition: The extent of *Yasna* 41. *Journal of the Royal Asiatic Society*.

Index of passages quoted

Ardā Wirāz nāmag
7, 9	106
14.9	234
42	206

Bundahišn
1.53	234
1a.3	90
4.21	196
11b.1	254
14.14	241
18.1	81, 82, 84
26.100	50

Čīdag handarz ī pōryōtkēšān 48, 237

Dādestān ī Dēnīg
39.12	51

Dēnkard
3.123.44	234
3.364.1	51
4.19, 4.22	56
4.25	55
5.1	57, 97
5.12.2	261
6.27	103
6.283	58
6.C26	45

6.D9	48
7.8.50	117, 120
8.1.5	58
8.1.6	57
8.1.7–8	59
8.20.63	99
9.11.1, 9.12.1, 9.12.3	86
9.12.5	88
9.35.1	99, 100, 108
9.35.3	195
9.35.10–14	87
9.40.7	195
9.40.12	78
9.43.7	107
9.57.1	192
9.57.12–15	87
9.57.18	215
9.57.28	238

Frahang ī ōīm

69–72	245
222	198

Hērbedestān

16.3	371

Mādayān ī Hazār Dādestān

105.10	240

Mēnōy ī Xrad

0.39	180
1.42–3, 1.46–7	176
6.1–12	105
14.16–21	237

Nērangestān

10.49–50, 10.56	371
83.1–3	229

Niyāyišn

1.5	213
3.7	277
4.2	253

Pahlavi Rivāyat accompanying the Dādestān ī Dēnīg

3.2	50
18d1	82
18d2	84
18d14	78
18d20	89
18d21	78
23.13	106
57	372

Patit ī Pašēmānīh

1.1.2	237

Pursišnīhā

18	191
19	202
53	239

Supplementary texts to the Šāyest nē Šāyest

13.16	14, 104
13.17	104
13.18	109, 372–3
13.19	110
13.20	111, 373
13.21	111
13.22	115
13.42, 13.51	373

Srōš Yašt Sar Šab

20	177

Šāyest nē Šāyest

3.35, 5.2, 5.7	372

Škand Gumānīg Wizār

1.11	96

(Pahlavi) Wisperad

16.1	94

Wizīdagīhā ī Zādspram

3.17	84
3.77	83, 84
29.3	85
30.31	85

(Pahlavi) Wīdēwdād

7.52	228
11.6	195
16.7	373

(Pahlavi) Yasna

0.2	73
0.5	236
0.15	179
3.3	233
4.4	270
7.24	46
8.1	177
9.1	52
10.20	196
12.8	112
12.9	236
13.5–6	272
17.11	73, 79, 81, 82, 84
20.3	180
28.0	76
28.1	116
28.7	47
28.8	47, 119, 177
31.3	67, 77, 368
31.19	68, 77, 368
33.1	222
33.10	177
34.3	238
34.4	65, 77, 368
34.5	68
35.2	101
35.5	198
35.6	101, 199
35.8	102
35.9	292–3

(Pahlavi) Yasna – (Continued)

36.1	288
36.3	117
36.5	111
36.6	105, 213
38.4	258
39.2	266
39.3	16
39.4	111
40.1	46
40.2	119
40.3	113
41.5	46
41.6	119
43.4	77, 369
43.9	79, 369
44.10	277
45.2	178
45.3	222
46.7	68, 79, 369
46.11	119
47.1	178
47.2	177
47.4	223
47.6	66, 68, 77, 369
49.8	114, 120
51.9	67, 77, 370
53.1	120
53.4	120
53.5	224
53.6	223, 224
58.7	206
58.8	213
65.2	261
67.6–8	260
68.20	104
68.23	213
71.25	195

(Pahlavi) Yašt

1.15	177
17.60	230

Zand ī Wahman Yasn

2.2–4	290
2.3–4	302
5.3	373

EU representative:
Easy Access System Europe
Mustamäe tee 50, 10621 Tallinn, Estonia
Gpsr.requests@easproject.com

www.ingramcontent.com/pod-product-compliance
Lightning Source LLC
Chambersburg PA
CBHW052054300426
44117CB00013B/2117